Tragedy and Athenian Religion

Greek Studies: Interdisciplinary Approaches
Series Editor: Gregory Nagy, Harvard University
Assistant Editor: Timothy Power, Harvard University

On the front cover: A calendar frieze representing the Athenian months, reused in the Byzantine Church of the Little Metropolis in Athens. The cross is superimposed, obliterating Taurus of the Zodiac. The choice of this frieze for books in *Greek Studies: Interdisciplinary Approaches* reflects this series' emphasis on the blending of the diverse heritages—Near Eastern, Classical, and Christian—in the Greek tradition. Drawing by Laurie Kain Hart, based on a photograph. Recent titles in the series are:

Nothing Is As It Seems: The Tragedy of the Implicit in Euripides' Hippolytus
    by Hanna M. Roisman
Lyric Quotation in Plato
    by Marian Demos
Exile and the Poetics of Loss in Greek Tradition
    by Nancy Sultan
The Classical Moment: Views from Seven Literatures
    Edited by Gail Holst-Warhaft and David R. McCann
Nine Essays on Homer
    Edited by Miriam Carlisle and Olga Levaniouk
Allegory and the Tragic Chorus in Sophocles' Oedipus at Colonus
    by Roger Travis
Dionysism and Comedy
    by Xavier Riu
Contextualizing Classics: Ideology, Performance, Dialogue
    Edited by Thomas M. Falkner, Nancy Felson, and David Konstan
The Pity of Achilles: Oral Style and the Unity of the Iliad
    by Jinyo Kim
Between Magic and Religion: Interdisciplinary Studies in Ancient Mediterranean Religion and Society
    Edited by Sulochana Asirvatham, Corinne Ondine Pache, and John Waltrous
Iambic Ideas: Essays on a Poetic Tradition from Archaic Greece to the Late Roman Empire
    Edited by Antonio Aloni, Alessandro Barchiesi, and Alberto Cavarzere
The Ritual Lament in Greek Tradition, Second Edition
    by Margaret Alexiou
    revised by Dimitrios Yatromanolakis and Panagiotis Roilos
Homeric Variations on a Lament by Briseis
    by Casey Dué
Imagining Illegitimacy in Classical Greek Literature
    by Mary Ebbott
The Usable Past: Greek Metahistories
    Edited by K. S. Brown and Yannis Hamilakis
Tragedy and Athenian Religion
    by Christiane Sourvinou-Inwood

Tragedy and Athenian Religion

Christiane Sourvinou-Inwood

LEXINGTON BOOKS
Lanham • Boulder • New York • Oxford

LEXINGTON BOOKS

Published in the United States of America
by Lexington Books
An imprint of The Rowman & Littlefield Publishing Group
4501 Forbes Boulevard, Suite 200, Lanham, Maryland 2070

PO Box 317
Oxford
OX2 9RU, UK

Copyright © 2003 by Lexington Books

All rights reserved. No part of this publication may be reproduced, stored in a retrieval system, or transmitted in any form or by any means, electronic, mechanical, photocopying, recording, or otherwise, without the prior permission of the publisher.

British Library Cataloguing in Publication Information Available

Library of Congress Cataloging-in-Publication Data

Sourvinou-Inwood, Christiane.
    Tragedy and Athenian religion / Christiane Sourvinou-Inwood.
       p. cm. – (Greek studies)
    Includes bibliographical references and index.
    ISBN 0-7391-0399-7 (alk. paper) – ISBN 0-7391-0400-4 (pbk. : alk. paper)
    1. Greek drama (Tragedy)—History and criticism. 2. Religious drama, Greek—History and criticism. 3. Religion and literature—Greece—Athens. 4. Athens (Greece)—Religion. I. Title. II. Series.

PA3136 .S68 2002
882'.0109—dc21
                                                                                    2002034906

Printed in the United States of America

∞™ The paper used in this publication meets the minimum requirements of American National Standard for Information Sciences—Permanence of Paper for Printed Library Materials, ANSI/NISO Z39.48–1992.

for Mike

Contents

List of Photographs	xi
Foreword	xiii
On the Jackson Lectures	xv
Preface	xvii

Part I. Tragedy, Audiences, and Religion 1

1. Tragedy and Religion: Shifting Perspectives and Ancient Filters 1

2. Setting Out the Distances: Religion, Audiences, and the World of Tragedy 15
   i. Filters and Distances 15
   ii. Tragic Settings and Shifting Distances 15
   iii. Zooming and Distancing in Action: Euripides' *Erechtheus* and *Iphigeneia in Tauris* 25
   iv. Performances outside Athens: Aeschylus' *Aitnaiai* and Euripides' *Archelaos* 40
   v. Preferred Setting and Religious Exploration; Universality and Its Construction 45
   vi. Ritual Context, Tragic Performance and Permeability 50

Part II. The Ritual Context 67

1. The Great Dionysia: A Reconstruction 67
   i. Reconstruction and Methodology 67
   ii. The Festival: *Xenismos* of Dionysos, *Komos*, Procession, Sacrifices, and Performances 69
     a) Literary, Epigraphical, and Comparative Evidence 69
     b) Iconographical Evidence 82
     c) A Set of Conclusions 89
     d) Topographical Evidence and Further Comparative Evidence; Pindar, Dithyramb fr. 75 89
     e) Another Set of Conclusions 98
     f) The Reconstruction of the City Dionysia: A Summary 99

Contents

    iii. Changes and Developments: The Early History of the
        Great Dionysia   100
        a) Changes and Beginnings: The Polis Dimension   100
        b) A Process of *Bricolage*: City Dionysia, Anthesteria, and
           Other Festivals   104
        c) Reconstructing the Early Festival   106
        d) The Early City Dionysia and Its Developments:
           A Summary   118
    Appendix: Lenaia and Lenaion   120

2. [Re]constructing the Beginnings   141
    i. *Tragodoi* and the Emergence of Tragedy   141
        a) *Tragodoi* and *Tragos* Sacrifice   141
        b) Singing at the Sacrifice   145
        c) From Sacrificial Hymns to Prototragedy: Mythological
           Content and Problematization   149
        d) From Sacrificial Hymns to Prototragedy: Some
           Reconstructions   154
        e) From Sacrificial Hymns to Prototragedy: Some
           Possible Scenarios   157
        f) Ritual and *Skene*   160
        g) Further Reconstructions: The Question of *Mimesis*   162
        h) "Thespis" and Another Poet   168
        i) Fissions and Enlargements; The Satyr Play   170
        j) Epilogue   172
    ii. *Komos* and Comedy   172
    iii. Men and Women at the Dionysia   177

3. The Great Dionysia and the "Ritual Matrix" of Tragedy   197

Part III. Religion and the Fifth-Century Tragedians   201

1. "Starting" with Aeschylus   201
    i. Introduction and Methodological Problems   201
    ii. *Suppliants*   203
    iii. *Persai*   220
    iv. *Septem*   227
    v. *Oresteia*   231
    vi. The *Skene* in the *Oresteia*   246
    vii. Conclusions: Aeschylean Tragedy and Religion   250

2. From Phrynichos to Euripides: The Tragic Choruses   265

3. Euripidean Tragedy and Religious Exploration 291
   i. Euripidean Tragedy and Religion; Problematik, Methodology
      and Euripides' Reception 291
      (1) Introduction, Problematik, Some Methodological Remarks 291
      (2) The Reception of Euripides: "Atheism" and Aristophanes 294
      (3) Modern Criticism and Ancient Audiences 297
   ii. The Tragedies: Part One 301
      (1) *Iphigeneia in Tauris* 301
      (2) *Medea* 308
      (3) *Suppliants* 310
   iii. The Religious Dimension: Some Remarks 316
   iv. The Tragedies: Part Two 317
      (1) *Alcestis* 317
      (2) *Herakleidai* 322
      (3) *Hippolytos* 326
      (4) *Andromache* 332
      (5) *Hecabe* 339
      (6) *Electra* 345
      (7) *Troades* 350
      (8) *Heracles* 361
      (9) *Phoenissai* 377
      (10) *Orestes* 386
      (11) *Ion, Helen, Bacchae, Iphigeneia at Aulis* 402
   v. Conclusions: Differences, Patterns, and Meanings 403
   Appendix 1: Other Views on *Orestes*: a Brief Critique 410
   Appendix 2: Euripidean Endings: Strategies of Closure and Ancient
      Audiences 414

4. Walking among Mortals? Modalities of Divine Appearance
   in Aeschylus, Sophocles, and Euripides 459
   i. Divine Appearances in Tragedy and in Lived Religion 459
   ii. Aeschylus 462
   iii. Euripides 469
   iv. Sophocles 482
   v. Modalities of Divine Appearance: Shifts, Constants, and Meanings 489

Part IV. A Summary of the Central Conclusion 513

Bibliography 519

Index Locorum 543

About the Author 547

List of Photographs

PHOTOGRAPH 1: Neck amphora (Oxford 1965.126)

PHOTOGRAPH 2: Neck amphora (Oxford 1965.126)

PHOTOGRAPH 3: Neck amphora (Oxford 1965.126)

PHOTOGRAPH 4: Neck amphora (Oxford 1965.126)

PHOTOGRAPH 5: Neck amphora (Oxford 1965.126)

PHOTOGRAPH 6: Cup (Oxford G.262 [V.516])

PHOTOGRAPH 7: Janiform head kantharos (Ferrara, Museo Nazionale di Spina 9410 [T 256 B VP])

PHOTOGRAPH 8: Janiform head kantharos (Ferrara, Museo Nazionale di Spina 9410 [T 256 B VP])

PHOTOGRAPH 9: Janiform head kantharos (London 786)

PHOTOGRAPH 10: Janiform head kantharos (London 786)

Greek Studies: Interdisciplinary Approaches
Foreword by Gregory Nagy, General Editor

Building on the foundations of scholarship within the disciplines of philology, philosophy, history, and archaeology, this series spans the continuum of Greek traditions extending from the second millennium B.C.E. to the present, not just the Archaic and Classical periods. The aim is to enhance perspectives by applying various disciplines to problems that have in the past been treated as the exclusive concern of a single given discipline. Besides the crossing-over of the older disciplines, as in the case of historical and literary studies, the series encourages the application of such newer ones as linguistics, sociology, anthropology, and comparative literature. It also encourages encounters with current trends in methodology, especially in the realm of literary theory.

Tragedy and Athenian Religion, by Christiane Sourvinou-Inwood, was originally presented as the Carl Newell Jackson lectures at Harvard University (spring 1994). It now appears as a book of major proportions in impact as well as amplitude. Sourvinou-Inwood examines tragedy as a central mode of public self-expression for the polis of fifth-century Athens. The Athenian tragic perspective, which is here painstakingly reconstructed on the basis of all available evidence, is fundamentally religious. As the author observes, "Tragedy was perceived by the fifth-century audiences not as a discrete unit, a purely theatrical experience, simply framed by ritual, but as a ritual performance; and that the deities and other religious elements in the tragedies were not insulated from the audience's religious realities, but were perceived to be, to a greater or lesser extent, somehow close to those realities, part of those realities, in ways that need to be defined."

The definitions of this book rely on a vast array of literary and archaeological evidence, yielding important new readings of Aeschylus, Sophocles, and Euripides. Of special interest is Sourvinou-Inwood's revisionist assessment of Euripides: she sees him as a serious religious thinker, not as the glib and conflicted ironist or atheist who emerges as a typical creation of twentieth-century scholarship.

On the Jackson Lectures

The Department of the Classics at Harvard is delighted that Christiane Sourvinou-Inwood's memorable Jackson Lectures of 1994 are now appearing in the series *Greek Studies: Interdisciplinary Approaches*. On behalf of the Department I am happy to recall the memory of those lectures, and there can be no better way of doing so than by quoting the introduction given by my colleague, Richard Tarrant:

"Our lecturer is Christiane Sourvinou-Inwood, Senior Research Fellow at University College, Oxford, and the topic of the lectures is 'Greek Tragedy and Athenian Religion: A Discourse of Exploration'.

"Before introducing our lecturer I should like to say a few words about the Jackson Lectures and the man who made them possible. This lecture series is the result of an extraordinary act of generosity, and it is only proper that we, its beneficiaries, should periodically give thanks for what we have received.

"Carl Newell Jackson was born in 1875 and graduated from Harvard College in 1898. He remained at Harvard for graduate study, and obtained his Ph.D. in what now seems the astonishingly short time of three years. His dissertation was a study of the role of horses in Greek religion (or, in its Latin dress, *Quas partes equi habebant in religionibus Graecorum?*). In 1905 Jackson joined the faculty of the Department as an Instructor; he rose to become Eliot Professor of Greek Literature, a chair from which he retired in 1943. Jackson published very little, but his teaching and force of personality exerted a profound influence on generations of Harvard classicists; in a memoir of Jackson John Finley described him as a man of 'Promethean largeness, [which] showed itself in the heavy lines of his face, in his measured and deliberate speech, in his raw-boned figure and somewhat awkward gestures, and in the general ruggedness of his mind and appearance'—a description which is borne out, at least in externals, by the remarkable photograph of Jackson that hangs in Smyth library. Yet this imposing figure was also a shy and modest man. He never married, and it may be that his beloved Harvard and Radcliffe came to occupy the place of a family in his affections. On his death in 1946 it was learned that he had left the entire income of his estate to the Department of the Classics, an act of devotion as commendable as it is uncommon.

"The Samuel and Sarah Morrill Jackson Fund—named for Jackson's parents—became available to the Department in 1955, and a lecture series was established in 1957. The first Jackson lecturers delivered one or two lectures each, which were subsequently published in *Harvard Studies in Classical Philology*. They included J. B. Ward-Perkins, Sir Ronald Syme, Bernard Knox, Werner Jaeger, Russell Meiggs, and James

Notopoulos. In 1964 it was decided to expand the lectureship into a biennial series of four lectures. The first series in the new format was delivered by Sir Roger Mynors in 1966; subsequent Jackson lecturers have been Arnaldo Momigliano, Sir Denys Page, Jacqueline de Romilly, Peter Brown, Eugene Vanderpool, E. J. Kenney, Walter Burkert, Machteld Mellink, Fergus Millar, Anna Morpurgo Davies, and Peter Dronke.

"To this distinguished list we are now pleased to add the name of Christiane Sourvinou-Inwood, one of the most original and exciting scholars now working in the area of Greek literary and cultural studies. No one with an interest in the Greeks will be unfamiliar with her work, but few will perhaps be aware of its full range, which extends from Minoan glyptic rings to the choral odes of the Antigone, from female initiation rituals to scenes of erotic pursuit on Greek vases. The subtitle of her lectures, 'a discourse of exploration', well describes one of the leading characteristics of her scholarship, her effort to understand Greek myth, religion, art, and literature in the rich complexity of their interrelations. Several of her articles bear titles such as 'myth and history' or 'myths in images', and the important collection of her essays published by Oxford in 1991 is significantly called *'Reading' Greek Culture: texts and images, rituals and myths.* Her Jackson Lectures bring together two of her long-standing interests, in Athenian religion and in Greek tragedy, and so with great pleasure and anticipation I present Christiane Sourvinou-Inwood."

Richard F. Thomas
Chair, Department of the Classics
Harvard University

Preface

Though I have been working on the relationship between tragedy and Athenian religion for many years, this book would not have been written if the Department of the Classics of Harvard University had not done me the great honor of inviting me to give the Carl Newell Jackson Lectures. I am enormously grateful to them; for the honor and also for the warmth, hospitality, and friendship they so lavishly offered, and for the exciting discussions and problem raising after the lectures. But their generosity went further: they most kindly provided a subvention to help with the production of a book that turned out to be very much longer than was expected. They have my gratitude. My very special gratitude is owed to Professor Greg Nagy, whose help and support during the completion and publication of this book has been truly invaluable.

I have benefited very significantly from discussions with many colleagues and friends over the many years of this book's preparation and it seems invidious to single out a few; so I will limit myself to those who have been, in one way or another, a continuous presence: my former colleagues Dr. C. B. R. Pelling and Dr. Peter Wilson and also Dr. Ian Rutherford, who had been at Harvard when I gave the lectures, and subsequently became my colleague at Reading; Professor Pat Easterling; and above all, Professor Robert Parker, whose learned interaction and friendship were a constant inspiration.

Short versions of a few parts of the book formed the basis of lectures given in London and Oxford, including the Gaisford Lecture, which was delivered in Oxford in May 1998.

For the photographs I am indebted to Mr. Michael Vickers of the Ashmolean Museum, Oxford, to Dr. Dyfri Williams of the British Museum, to Dottoressa Fede-Berti of the Museo Archeologico Nazionale di Spina in Ferrara, and Dr. M. Marini Calvani, Soprintendente, Soprintendenza Archeologica of Emilia Romagna.

Finally, I would like to express my warmest thanks to Timothy Power, who has prepared the manuscript for publication with great sensitivity, helpfulness, and learning.

I. Tragedy, Audiences, and Religion

I.1. Tragedy and Religion: Shifting Perspectives and Ancient Filters

This book is about many things, but above all it is about the relationship between tragedy and religion.[1] One of its important aims is to change the nature of the perceptual filters through which Greek tragedy is made sense of by modern readers, to change them in complex ways that will restore the religious dimension, which, I will be arguing, the tragedies had had in the eyes of the fifth-century audiences, for whom, I will also be arguing, tragedies were, among other things, a discourse of religious exploration, part of the religious discourse of the polis.

I am arguing that for the fifth-century audiences tragedy was not a "purely theatrical" experience, which had included gods and other religious elements as theatrical devices. The notion of such elements as simple theatrical devices includes a spectrum of possibilities, and different scholars have taken different positions along this spectrum. At one end would be, for example, the perception of deities *ex machina* as empty rhetorical gestures of closure. At the other end would be the perception that the tragic gods were serious gods in the world of the tragedy, but were located only within the tragedy, insulated from the world of the audience and its religious realities. In theory, tragedy could have involved religious exploration even if it had been a purely theatrical experience, in which religious elements were no more than theatrical devices. But what I am arguing is something different: that tragedy was perceived by the fifth-century audiences not as a discrete unit, a purely theatrical experience, simply framed by ritual, but as a ritual performance; and that the deities and other religious elements in the tragedies were not insulated from the audience's religious realities, but were perceived to be, to a greater or lesser extent, somehow close to those realities, part of those realities, in ways that need to be defined.

I will be building up this case in a variety of ways, and in different layers in the different chapters. Thus, for example, I discuss cult foundations and aetiologies at one level in chapter I.2, and then return to them in a fuller and more detailed way in chapters III.3 and III.4, engaging with, and attempting to show the fallacy of, views that perceive aetiologies to be other than religiously serious and religiously charged, in the context of the in-depth investigation of Euripidean tragedies. Thus also the lightness of this introductory chapter, that only skims the surface of issues that will be considered in increasing depth throughout the book.

I will be keeping the different strands of the argument separate and independent, to avoid cross contamination from fallacious assumptions and unconscious adjustment to make the different parts of the evidence fit, and also in order to be able to cross-check the results of the different lines of enquiry. For if the results of independently conducted sets of investigation, mostly deploying different sets of evidence, converge, this would offer significant validation for these results.

If my central thesis is right, one of its many implications would be that the fashionable notion that tragedy challenges the polis discourse by which it is framed[2] would be based on a misunderstanding of what the polis discourse is: on my reading tragedy is part of the polis discourse, and this polis discourse is much more complex than is often assumed.

The notion that we must replace the perception of Greek tragedy as in some ways comparable to, and so to be to some extent understood in terms of, our notion of theater needs to be defended against an obvious objection: that this perception of tragedy as comparable to what we understand by theater has the most authoritative ancient authority on its side.[3]

If no Greek tragedy had survived and our sole source of information on the genre had been Aristotle's *Poetics* we would have had a rather idiosyncratic idea of what fifth-century tragedy had been like, and we would have certainly believed that religion had only had a very small and marginal place in it. The perception of tragedy underlying the *Poetics* was shaped by rigidly rationalizing perceptual filters and structured through the conceptual schemata Aristotle set out to construct, schemata which reflected his own preoccupations and assumptions. It is methodologically dubious to use the perceptions of a rationalizing thinker, who was not even a participant in the culture, since he did not live in the fifth century and he was not Athenian, as evidence for those of the audience of fifth-century Athenians.

The distorting selectivity of Aristotle's presentation of tragedy has been acknowledged and stressed in recent years.[4] Nevertheless, modern perceptions of tragedy have been influenced by Aristotle's *Poetics*, if only in strengthening the conceptual bias towards what we perceive as "the rational" which reflected modern conceptual hierarchies. Of course, in this respect also things have changed in recent years, and the place of religion in tragedy is no longer underplayed. However, the Aristotelian mind cast and the marginalization of religion in tragedy have not disappeared, and they can take many forms. I shall mention

Chapter 1: Tragedy and Religion

one moderate view of Aristotelian inspiration as an illustration, in order to bring into sharper focus the parameters of the debate. While acknowledging that tragedy has a theological content, Heath claims that the fact that tragedies were performed in the course of a religious festival is not related to what religious content they may have: "[T]he theological content derives, not from the requirements of a religious occasion, but from the nature of the material on which the tragic plots are based. The world of Greek heroic legend is a world in which the gods are everywhere at work; the narrative of events in which they are at work must of necessity have some theological structure, for if one is going to tell a story about gods, they must be gods of some particular kind, standing in a certain relation to the world and other characters, and so forth." The alternative he perceives is simple and expressed in intentionalist terms as involving "a concern with theological reflection in its own right, a desire to explore problems in religious thought or to commend answers to those problems." He believes that "the assumption of such specifically intellectual interests will be superfluous."[5]

To begin with the last, the notion that the exploration of religious problems is a purely intellectual exercise, motivated by purely intellectual interests, is a culturally determined perception which takes no account of the nature of Greek religion. I will return to this. Further, the religious content of tragedy is not limited to what may be classified as "theology." Easterling has recently discussed the important place of ritual in tragedy and I shall be discussing this and other aspects of the religious discourse articulated in tragedy throughout this book. Most importantly, because it illustrates the tendency to privilege rationalizing perceptions which are mistaken for neutral readings, the notion that the presence of religion is the simple result of the fact that tragedies are set in the world of Greek legend is implicitly circular; for it is based on two a priori (and culturally determined) assumptions. First, that the primary element was the narrative and the religious elements were secondary; given tragedy's ritual context, this assumption is even a priori less likely than a hypothesis that involves a religious content as a basic component. And second, that the fact that tragedies were set in this legendary world in which the gods were everywhere was a prior and natural phenomenon that needs no explanation and was unrelated to the performances' religious context. Besides the a priori implausibility of this assumption, the fact that a short experiment with contemporary settings by Phrynichos and Aeschylus did take place is one indication that the settings were not a necessary, but a *preferred* choice. I shall be returning to this in chapter I.2. Besides, as we shall see in chapter

III.4, the gods were not everywhere to the same extent in the heroic age represented in the different tragedies by the different tragedians. Again, it was a matter of choices.

Aristotelian ideas have not disappeared, but at the overt level, things have changed in recent years: it has become more or less generally accepted that religion is important for the understanding of tragedy. Thus, for example, the articulation of rituals in tragedy, and of tragedy through rituals, has been studied,[6] the character of the dramatic performances as part of a religious festival is now stressed[7] and Dionysiac aspects of tragedy have been discussed.[8] But the argument in this book goes much further. It articulates the thesis that Greek tragedy was, among other things, but very importantly, also a discourse of religious exploration, that it was one important locus where the religious discourse of the Athenian polis was explored and elaborated in the fifth century; and that this religious exploration is intimately connected with the ritual context in which tragedies were performed, and within which tragedy had been generated.

If this set of arguments is wrong, it will not convince, but will not corrupt the discourse. But if it is right, the ways in which the fifth-century audience made sense of the tragedies would by necessity be different from the ways "we" do; therefore, unless we reconstruct these assumptions, and try to make sense of the tragedies through filters shaped by them, we will inevitably be reading into the tragedies our own constructs, centering our readings on our own (shifting and changing, because culturally determined) assumptions and preoccupations. It is, then, methodologically more neutral to explore the possibility that the religious elements in tragedy were significant, and that this was connected with the ritual context of tragedy, than to assume that this was not the case; for if the latter assumption is wrong, the reading and interpretative discourse would be corrupted. I therefore suggest that the investigation of these possibilities is a methodological necessity, however many the problems our radically limited evidence may create.

One of the conclusions of my investigation into the ritual context of tragedy in part II is that religious exploration was one of the main characteristics of tragedy from the very beginning, indeed, one of the factors that led to the emergence, first of prototragedy, and then early tragedy. This conclusion converges with the conclusions of the wholly independent sets of analyses in part III, the readings of many fifth-century tragedies that conclude that most tragedies articulated, among other things, a discourse of religious exploration. If these conclusions are right, and their convergence suggests that they probably are, we may conclude that though tragedy changed significantly, though

Chapter 1: Tragedy and Religion

various changes and major developments—as well as experimentations—took place, and tragedy came to encompass a variety of wide problematizations, it did not, in the fifth century, lose its role as a locus of religious exploration, which had been a major factor in the generation of tragedy.

The reading of the tragedies in part III is conducted as far as possible through the reconstructed perceptual filters of the fifth-century Athenian audience.[9] Of course, this audience was not homogeneous; but all fifth-century Athenians' assumptions were determined by certain parameters which were radically different from ours. To use a very crude example to illustrate this: an interpretation of the end of Euripides' *Medea* that is open to a modern audience but was not open to an ancient one is to take the chariot of the Sun to be a disguised helicopter with Medea taking advantage of Jason's distraught state to make a fool of him. We *can* reconstruct these parameters of the ancient assumptions to a considerable extent, and this give us the parameters for the reconstruction of the ancient audience's perceptual filters.[10]

I should explain one omission. I have taken account, and discussed aspects, of Sophoclean tragedies, especially in my discussions pertaining to developments in fifth-century tragedy and similarities and differences between tragedians in chapters III.2 and III.4. But restrictions of space have forced me not to include readings of Sophoclean tragedies.[11] The notion that Sophoclean tragedies have a significant religious content would not, I believe, be controversial. I have offered elsewhere[12] detailed readings of one Sophoclean tragedy, and I hope to have shown, first, the complexity of its discourse, and especially its religious discourse, which, I argued, has been misunderstood, and second, the relevance of its religious dimension to the religious discourse of the Athenian polis.

Before I present the positive part of my argument, I should clear the air by saying something about a recent thesis that, if correct, would present insurmountable difficulties to the perception of tragedy as, among other things, a locus of religion presented here. Mikalson has recently put forward the thesis that the gods of Greek tragedy were not real gods, but artificial literary constructs not perceived by the Athenians to be representations of the divinities they worshiped in cult.[13] I argue elsewhere that this thesis can be shown to be mistaken,[14] to be a culturally determined construct that distorts the ancient realities through a failure to try to reconstruct the process of meaning creation by the ancient audience, starting with a reconstruction of the perceptual filters that shaped their perceptions and were themselves shaped by the society's cultural assumptions. I will not repeat that argument here, but I hope that the various tragic readings I will be setting out will illustrate unambiguously the fallacy of that thesis by showing that, and how, the fifth-century Athenian audiences perceived such divinities as representations of the "real" divinities of cult, and also, and most importantly, that these tragedies articulated and explored things that were felt to be problematic or disquieting in the lived religion of the audience.[15]

The case against the approach which interprets religious elements in tragedy, and especially Euripidean divinities, as simple theatrical devices, above all gestures of closure, will be presented throughout this book, especially in chapters III.3 and III.4. Here I will only consider one small part of this case, the part which is directly relevant to the effect of Aristotelian, and generally, *pensée claire*, statements on modern perceptions of fifth-century tragedy. The notion that Euripidean divinities on the *mechane* are simply theatrical devices reflects modern ideological hierarchies. Insofar as this view has ancient authority, it is based on three passages, one by Aristotle, one by Plato, and one from a writer of Middle Comedy. I will now argue that these passages in fact do not support the idea that these deities are no more than theatrical devices, "empty" closure devices.

In Plato *Cratylos* 425d Socrates says that when the tragic poets are at a loss they take refuge in using the *mechane* and raise up gods. A comparable point is made by the comic poet of Middle Comedy Antiphanes; in fr. 189.13-17 Kassel-Austin PCG 2, in the context of a comparison between the art of the tragedian and of the comic poet, he says that when the tragedians are at a loss about what to say and have entirely given up on the plays, they lift the *mechane*, and that is sufficient for the spectators, while there is no such way out for the comic poets. *Cratylos* is a later dialogue, but there is really no way of being certain which formulation is the earliest. So let me first make a point relevant to both, because it is independent of genre. The validity of these comments for the assessment of Euripidean tragedy is dubious. Whatever their exact date, both passages were written at least several years after the death of Euripides and the heyday of tragedy. It is possible that by then perceptions may have changed; it is possible, for example, that epiphanies of gods had lost their charge through overuse by lesser tragedians.[16] But the main point is that neither passage suggests that this way of looking at gods in epiphany in tragedy represents the perceptions of tragedy's audiences.

To start with Antiphanes, what he says is a paratragic joke. Paratragedy deconstructs tragedy for laughs—in a variety of ways, by laying bare its conventions, mocking its high-flown language through imitation and incongruous usage, and so on.[17] It does not set out popular perceptions of tragedy. In this case the tragic modality '*deus ex*

Chapter 1: Tragedy and Religion

machina solves problems in the world of tragedy and brings the events, and so the tragedy to conclusion' has been inverted to *'deus ex machina* used as an easy solution to compositional problems, the problems of a tragedian who does not know how to bring the tragedy to conclusion'. Here, as in other instances, paratragedy depends on a shift of focus from the tragedy in performance and the audience to the poet and the process of composition. When it shifts back to the tragedy in performance and the audience we are told that the spectators are satisfied. In other words, the spectators do not see it in the terms in which the comic poet has just described it. Tragedy, unlike comedy, is not a metatheatrical genre. This is what makes choral self-referentiality and other ritual permeabilities, which will be discussed in chapter I.2, especially striking. One of the ways in which paratragic comedy mocks tragedy is by re-presenting aspects of it from a metatheatrical perspective. But this is not the perspective from which its audiences viewed tragedy.

The Platonic passage says, "unless you want, as when the tragic poets are at a loss they take refuge in using the *mechane* and raise up gods, that we should get off this way, by saying that it was the gods that established the first names."[18] It does not, therefore, imply that these deities were perceived as simple devices by the audience; this is Plato's interpretation of the motivation of the tragedians' choices—or, at least, of some tragedians' choices. Socrates expresses the view that bringing in the gods as a solution is a device, of which the best example is tragedians bringing in deities *ex machina* when at a loss. Plato was an intellectual thinker looking at tragedy critically from the outside—indeed he may well have deployed a notion first developed in comedy, because in a way the two viewpoints share this critical outsideness.

In these circumstances, it is clear that these passages do not indicate that the ancient audiences perceived deities *ex machina* as compositional devices. On the contrary, the Antiphanes passage suggests that they did not.

Another ancient passage that speaks of deities *ex machina* is Aristotle, *Poetics* 1454a39-b8.[19] After he has stated that the characters should speak or act according to necessity or probability, Aristotle says, "Consequently, it is evident that the unravelling of the plot must arise out of the plot itself, and not, as in *Medea*, be brought about *ex machina (apo mechanes)*. But the *mechane* should be used for events external to the drama, events that happened before, which it is not possible for a human being to know, or events that will take place later, which need to be reported or announced (in the sense of 'foretold'). For we ascribe to the gods the power to see everything. But nothing within the action should be irrational, or if not, the irrational should be situated outside the tragedy, as in Sophocles' *Oidipous*." It is abundantly clear that what is at issue here is the plausibility of the plot. On Aristotle's view, what is wrong with epiphanies is that they make the plot (what Aristotle considers to be) less plausible, less mimetic—though the *mimesis* he considers desirable is one that can best be described as "idealized naturalism." The context confirms that what is at issue here is the notion of plausibility in comparison with real life, *mimesis* in the sense of "idealized naturalism"; indeed the sentence following the passage cited above is *epei de mimesis estin e tragodia beltion . . . dei mimeisthai tous agathous eikonographous; kai gar ekeinoi apodidontes ten idian morphen homoious poiountes kallious graphousin*. It is for this reason, to achieve this type of *mimesis*, that the supernatural must be excluded from the action, though he allows the gods to be brought in *apo mechanes* in circumscribed circumstances: to speak of events external to the drama, since this affects the mimetic character of the drama itself only minimally, and he accepts that it may be necessary to bring in previous events, or mention events that will happen; the gods are appropriate for this, since in real life "we" ascribe to the gods the power to see everything—in other words this use of the gods is, in a limited way, mimetic of the audience's realities.

The minimum we may deduce from these formulations in this context is that Aristotle understood the audience to have perceived the tragic characters' perceptions of, and relationships to, the deities who appeared *apo mechanes* in the tragedies as equivalent to the audience's perceptions of, and relationships to, the deities in their lived reality—which was as serious divine beings, able, among other things, to see everything. This means that in the eyes of the ancient audience the *apo mechanes* deities were not for the tragic characters empty or ironic gestures of closure, or indeed literary creations of any kind, but seriously perceived deities issuing serious orders, guidance, prophecies.

So what are the implications of this? The fact that in the eyes of the audience the *apo mechanes* deities were for the tragic characters seriously perceived deities issuing serious orders indicates that the audience would have perceived them as serious deities offering serious solutions; given the centrality of *mimesis*, they would have perceived them as representations of their own divinities. Thus, I suggest, Aristotle's choice of formulation in itself suggests that the assumptions that had helped determine the parameters of selection shaping his choices had included the perception that the audience, even in his time, had perceived those deities as mimetic representations of their

Chapter 1: Tragedy and Religion

own divinities. We shall see in chapters I.2, III.3, and III.4 that there are many, very much stronger, separate, and independent arguments that lead to the same conclusion.

I am not, of course, arguing that tragedies are simply discourses of religious exploration, or doubting that many other important problems are also explored, or that tragedies involve emotional experiences. But I am arguing that one of the reasons why the exploration of so many human problems is closely intertwined with religion is (besides the Greek perceptions of the cosmos, in which the mortals' interactions with the divine were of crucial importance for, and affected the course of, human lives, behavior, and relationships) because the matrix which shaped these other developments and problematizations was a matrix of religious exploration.

I suggest that this is also the reason why tragedy did not explore political or other contemporary issues directly, why any exploration of such moment-specific questions always takes place at a distance.[20] We see tragedy as a genre involving universality: "[T]he function of tragedy in its social and historical context is not to comment directly on the times, but to raise to universality and touch with emotion the experience of the dramatist and his fellow-citizens, to interpret in myth and drama their deepest concerns as human beings."[21] But it is not self-evident why this should be so; why this particular genre should have come to be, and to remain, "universal" in this way, especially since in the fifth century dramatic performances at the City Dionysia were part of a polis event that was one of the loci of the Athenian polis discourse,[22] and since comedy was not universal but very particular and moment-specific.

I will return to this question of universality in chapter I.2. Here I will only say that my interpretations can account for the "universality" of tragedy, which can be made sense of in the context of the ways in which the relationships between the world of the tragedy and the world of the audience operated, partly shaped by the parameters of determination generated by the context in which tragedy emerged, as reconstructed here, but most importantly by the fact that these parameters corresponded to the assumptions about what was perceived to be fulfilling what came to be perceived as the function of tragedy.

This need to make sense of aspects of tragedy that are often taken for granted as self-evident is only one of the reasons why it is important not to neglect the question of the origins of tragedy, in the sense of the ritual context and circumstances in which tragedy was generated, not simply to assume that it is irrelevant to our understanding of fifth-century tragedy.

The problem of the origins of tragedy has fallen out of fashion with most scholars, but there are strong reasons why this problem should be reexamined. Besides the fact that it is interesting in its own right, and that it may help us answer, for example, questions about fifth-century perceptions about the nature of tragedy in relation to its settings, or questions pertaining to the differences between tragedy and comedy, it will also provide some sort of control for the readings proposed here. It may be objected that a tentatively reconstructed festival context would not necesarily tell us anything about fifth-century tragedy, since drastic changes may well have altered things so significantly that the attempt to relate the two may be doomed to be culturally determined delusion. However, if the results of the independently conducted arguments, the reconstruction and the readings, both point in the same direction, if, as we shall see is the case here, the thesis based on the readings of fifth-century tragedies, that tragedy was very importantly also a discourse of religious exploration, coincides with the independently derived conclusion that tragedy in a way began as a discourse of religious exploration, that the potential for such exploration generated in one particular ritual context was one important factor in a complex process that led eventually to the generation of tragedy, this offers, I submit, some confirmation for the validity of both sets of analyses.

A further reason for attempting to investigate the origins of tragedy is because if we do not try to investigate this question systematically, and through a carefully constructed methodology, the vacuum is not usually left blank, but becomes implicitly and insidiously filled by assumptions derived from earlier, less methodologically aware, investigations. For though, by necessity, much cannot but remain speculative because evidence is extremely scarce and fragmentary, a careful methodology can maximize rigor, as I will be arguing in section II.1.i.

The notion that the origins and early history of tragedy has no relevance to the ways in which we understand fifth-century tragedy in general, and early Aeschylean tragedy in particular, is an a priori assumption which, if invalid, will vitiate the investigation. For since the assumptions of each generation shape the perceptions and expectations of the next, it is not legitimate simply to assume that our understanding of tragedy in the 470s cannot be improved by an attempt to understand what happened in the previous fifty years. The neutral approach is to consider whether the origins of tragedy can throw light on our understanding of historical tragedy by investigating these origins entirely independently from the process of reconstruction of the meanings of the historical tragedies. And this is what I will be doing. I

Chapter 1: Tragedy and Religion

will be approaching the question of the origin of tragedy from a different angle from that from which it is usually approached, not from the literary historical side, but from the ritual side, starting with the reconstruction of the ritual context of the Dionysia in which tragedy was generated.

The central conclusion of my investigation into the ritual context of tragedy in part II is that tragedy was generated in the context of a rite of *xenismos* of Dionysos that was part of the City Dionysia; what had begun as a choral performance accompanying the *xenismos* sacrifice eventually developed new forms, so that it became what we may call "prototragedy," a new genre that involved the exploration of religious matters. On my argument, the ritual performance and the exploration had begun by focussing on the festival myth of the City Dionysia, which involved a world that was both other, in that it was part of the heroic past, and also part of the world of the present, in that it involved the introduction of the cult of Dionysos, which was most importantly part of the Athenian present, as were the relationships between the god and the Athenians set up in that heroic past. Subsequently, these explorations encompassed other Dionysiac myths that were perceived to be comparable to the festival myth, and to have invited the generation of comparable explorations. Eventually, these explorations widened their scope to take in other, non-Dionysiac, religious matters. I will be arguing that the fact that the festival myth, and the other, related, Dionysiac myths had, as I will try to show, strongly invited exploration, indeed exploration of a type that would have implicated also wider questions pertaining to religion in general, was one of the factors that led to generation of new forms that eventually led to the emergence of tragedy.

If my reconstruction is convincing, it would follow that the main parameters of determination of the tragic genre had been set in place in this ritual context and continued to affect the subsequent developments of tragedy, above all in the relationships between the world of the audience and the world of the tragedy, which will be discussed in detail in chapter I.2. The fact that (on this reconstruction) the parameters of determination generated by the ritual context did not change radically as tragedy developed, and remained in place in fifth-century tragedy, suggests that they had corresponded to tragedy's perceived nature, to what was perceived to be fulfilling the needs of what came to be perceived as the function of tragedy. This, I submit, would, in its turn, suggest that exploration, above all, in the early stages, religious exploration, was indeed a central aspect of tragedy.

The nature of Greek religion, which had no revelation, or dogma, or canonical body of beliefs, no scriptural texts[23] and no professional divinely anointed priesthood claiming a special knowledge or authority, invited religious exploration, invited the creation of a locus of exploration of religious problems. Perhaps this need became sharper in times of crisis, or even in other circumstances conducive to cognitive insecurity. The changing circumstances in the course of the early history of tragedy, the rearticulation of the polis through the Kleisthenic reforms, the Persian threat and then the victory over this powerful enemy, are likely to have generated cognitive fluidity and unstable conceptual horizons, which would have made explorations, religious explorations and explorations of the human position in the cosmos, highly desirable.[24]

Of course all this did not come out of nothing; earlier poetry, starting with Homer and Hesiod de facto "explored" aspects of religion, insofar as they set out particular articulations of, above all, the world of the gods and the gods' relationships to mortals. Since Greek religion did not have sacred texts with special authority, it was the poets who above all set out theology and mythology, but their versions were not authoritative; poets were inspired by the Muses, but the Muses also lied.[25] However, religious exploration in tragedy is different in nature, as well as being more extensive and deeper and darker. Tragedy, I will be arguing in this book, focussed on problematization; on my interpretation, this was an in-built part of the genre, and the nature of the genre, its mimetic nature and the double perspective of both distance and relevance to the world of the audience, as well as its institutional ritual framework, some important aspects of which I will try to set out, made tragedy the privileged locus for religious exploration. This included also explorations of the darker side of the cosmos, which the Greek collective representations acknowledged, and, through such explorations, tried to make sense of the cosmos, tried to show that the world in which they lived was not the anomic, chaotic result of an anomic, chaotic universe.

Notes

1. The bibliography on most of the topics discussed in this book is enormous. I have therefore drastically limited both references and engagement with the literature to discussions that are interesting and/or directly relevant to my argument and (all things

Chapter 1: Tragedy and Religion 13

being equal, which they often are not) to the most recent discussions, which include bibliographical references to earlier ones.

2. Cf. e.g. Goldhill 1990, 114, 124, 127-9 (cf. also 114-29). Goldhill discusses tragedy and comedy together; this, I believe, is not legitimate. It is a priori the least methodologically neutral approach; and I will be arguing that the Athenians perceived the two through radically different perceptual filters.

3. On approaches to, and perceptions and different aspects of, performance, cf. Carlson 1996.

4. Cf. Taplin 1995, 94-6 on Aristotle's underprivileging of the visual dimension of tragedy; Gould 1996, 217 and Goldhill 1996, 244 on the chorus; and especially Hall 1996a, 295-309 (esp. p. 296 on religion), who argues that Aristotle had excised the polis from tragedy.

5. Heath 1987, 48 (and 48-64).

6. Cf. esp. Easterling 1988, 87-109; Zeitlin 1965, 463-508; Vidal-Naquet 1972, 133-58; cf. also Friedrich 1996, 269-70 on whose position I comment below in chapter I.2 n. 125. Jouanna 1992, 406-34 restates the position that the presence of rituals in the surviving tragedies has nothing to do with the cultic origin of tragedy, a position I hope to build a case against in the course of this book.

7. Cf. esp. Goldhill 1990, 97-129.

8. Cf. a short survey of such approaches in Henrichs 1994/5, 57-8 (with bibl. in 91-2 nn. 5-7); and cf. also his own contribution in that paper (Henrichs 1994/5, 56-111) and elsewhere, esp. Henrichs, 1984, 205-40; Henrichs 1993, 13-43; to which add Des Bouvrie 1993, 79-112; Friedrich 1996, 257-83; Seaford 1996, 284-94. Cf. also Bierl 1989, 43-58 (as well as Bierl 1991, which is cited by Henrichs); Zeitlin 1993, 147-82; Vernant 1986, 17-24. Seaford 1994 investigates the relationship between tragedy and Dionysiac cult, but in a very different way from the ways in which I am doing so in this book. Cf. a brief and very perceptive review by Segal: Segal 1995, 651-7.

9. I have set out the arguments on which these statements and this methodology are based elsewhere: Sourvinou-Inwood 1989a, 134-6 cf. 134-48 passim; Sourvinou-Inwood 1991, 3-23; Sourvinou-Inwood 1995, 1-9.

10. The reception and responses of the fifth-century audiences is a different matter, of less central concern to us here; they were, of course, potentially (and undoubtedly often actually) varied (cf. Sourvinou-Inwood 1997b, 257-8; Pelling 1997b, 220-1). But there is a fundamental distinction (which is sometimes blurred) between such responses on the one hand, and the basic parameters affecting their perception on the other.

11. I hope to do so in a separate study.

12. In Sourvinou-Inwood 1989a; Sourvinou-Inwood 1989b; Sourvinou-Inwood 1987-1988; Sourvinou-Inwood 1990c.

13. Mikalson 1991.

14. Sourvinou-Inwood 1997a, 161-86.

15. One of Mikalson's arguments in favor of his thesis is that (see e.g. Mikalson 1991, 18-9, cf. 25-6) unlike real people (by which in fact he means people in the orators and certain other types of discourses), who only attributed good things to the gods, characters in tragedy ascribed their misfortunes to the gods. Parker (Parker 1997, 143-60) has discussed this "discrepancy" between the more positive presentation of the gods in oratory and comedy and the darker one in tragedy and argued wholly persuasively that it is not a discrepancy resulting from the fact that one was "real" and the other "literary," but that what we see is sets of differences resulting from the different contexts which involve different constraints and requirements, generating different characteristics in the genres. He concludes (p. 159) that it is wrong to disregard the "corrective to civic optimism that tragedy provides." And that "Tragedy expresses some part of what it was like to believe in Greek gods no less than prose texts do."

16. It will certainly become clear in section III.4.iii that the epiphanies in the pseudo-Euripidean fourth-century *Rhesos* are different from those in fifth-century tragedies.

17. On paratragedy see Rau 1967.

18. On Plato's views on tragedy see most recently Nightingale 1992, 137-9, 121 n.1 with bibl.

19. Which, I believe, has, implicitly or explicitly, influenced modern perceptions of such deities, especially of deities whose actions change the course of the plot.

20. See on this most recently Pelling 1997b, 216-7. Bowie 1997, 39-62 argues that in a few tragedies "particular historical events are made homologous with mythical stories in such a way that the action of the dramas provides various models for viewing the events" (61).

21. Macleod 1982, 131; cf. also 144, and 124-44 passim.

22. See part III below.

23. No "sectarian" sacred texts; the Orphics did, of course, have sacred books (see esp. West 1983).

24. I do not mean by this that tragedy's nature as spectacle was not crucially important for its continuing development and popularity, but that circumstances may have facilitated its development in a particular direction, so that religious exploration remained an important aspect. But it is possible that this may have happened in any case given the "needs" created by the nature of Greek religion.

25. Hesiod *Theogony* 23-34.

I.2. Setting Out the Distances: Religion, Audiences, and the World of Tragedy

I.2.i. *Filters and distances*

Since my aim is to reconstruct, as far as possible, the ways in which the ancient audiences made sense of the tragedies, it is necessary to reconstruct, as far as possible, those audiences' perceptual filters, or, at the very least, the important parameters determining the assumptions which shaped those filters. A set of parameters determining the audience's assumptions, and their reception of tragedy, that is of fundamental importance pertains to their perceptions of the relationship between their world and that of the tragedies. I shall attempt to reconstruct those perceptions.

It may be argued that, since any attempt to reconstruct such perceptions depends on our reading of the tragedies, the argument is circular; that since our own culturally determined judgment is inevitably deployed in assessing the relationship between the world of the audience and that of the tragedies this attempt to reconstruct the ancient perceptual filters cannot but be another version of a culturally determined reading. I will try to show that this is incorrect; that it is possible to set the parameters determining the perception of the relationship between the world of the audience and that of the tragedies step by step, deploying as much as possible evidence that does not depend on the reading of the tragedies, in a way that does not depend on culturally determined assumptions and perceptions of what is "reasonable."

I.2.ii. *Tragic Settings and Shifting Distances*

Starting at the most basic level, the overt relationship, there are three different types of relationships between the world of the play and the world of the audience in Greek tragedy.[1] First, the relationship that obtains when the setting of the tragedy is the heroic age, which is the usual, the preferred choice setting in Greek tragedy. We know from a variety of sources that the relationship between fifth-century Athens and the heroic age was perceived by the fifth-century Athenians as being governed by two intertwined perspectives. On the one hand the world of the play was other, distanced in time from the present, a time when men could have direct contact with, and sometimes were descended from, gods, and when the most prominent and important of them became the heroes of present-day cult. On the other hand it was part of the present; for the heroic age was a crucial part of the fifth-century Athenians' past in which took place very many important things that shaped the world of "today" in fifth-century Athens: for example, Athens was synoecized by Theseus, Eleusis became part of the Athenian polis after the war in which Erechtheus was killed and the cult of Poseidon Erechtheus was instituted, Iphigeneia founded the cult of Artemis Brauronia, and so she receives cult in the present. Consequently, this double perspective provided the most basic parameters of determination for the perception of the relationship between the world of the audience and that of the play in tragedies with the preferred choice of setting, the heroic age. On the one hand the world of the tragedy was distanced and other; on the other it was also part of their own world.

The second type of relationship between the world of the tragedy and that of the audience is the relationship that is marked as transgressive, that is, in Phrynichos' *Capture of Miletos*. The characteristics of the transgressive choice are that the world of the play is basically the same as the world of the audience. According to Herodotos,[2] when Phrynichos' *Capture of Miletos* was produced, shortly after the event,[3] dealing with events that took place in 494, the audience burst into tears and the Athenians fined Phrynichos a thousand drachmas for reminding them of *oikeia kaka*, and forbade that this play should ever be staged again.[4] *Oikeia kaka* can be taken to refer to the misfortunes of their kin the Milesians, and also to their own misfortunes; Rosenbloom has recently argued[5] that both meanings were involved and that the Athenians' own misfortunes referred to the threat of the Persian might and the audience's fear that the capture of Miletos mirrored their own future fate. This is probably right; but in any case, it is clear that the absence of distance or at least of sufficient distance between the world of the play and the world of the audience was inappropriate.

The third type of relationship between the world of the audience and that of the play is the one that obtains when the setting is contemporary but the relationship is not marked as transgressive. This type of relationship is one with which Phrynichos and Aeschylus experimented; though it is not marked as transgressive it nevertheless represented a limited experiment that was abandoned. Let us consider how this relationship differs from the transgressive choice.

In Aeschylus' *Persai*, first, the articulations pertaining to the audience were positive, and all the negative things were distanced to the enemy other; second, the play did involve a double perspective, but of a different type than that of the preferred choice setting tragedies. In the *Persai* the distanced world is geographically and culturally dis-

Chapter 2: Setting Out the Distances

tanced;[6] it is not distanced in time nor is it distanced in the nature of the interaction between the divine and human worlds; but it is also part of the audience's world, in that it is its enemy other, whose real-life defeat by the audience is central to the tragedy. Phrynichos' *Phoinissai*—and, if it was not the same play, but part of the same trilogy, his *Persai*[7]—was probably produced at 476;[8] its subject was, as in Aeschylus' *Persai*, the battle of Salamis. We are told that the opening scene of the *Phoinissai* was set in Persia and showed a servant setting seats for the Persian nobles. Thus this play had the same type of double perspective as Aeschylus' *Persai*.

Besides the tragedies that we can ascribe to one of these three categories, there are a few tragedies we know very little about which require some discussion.[9] First, we hear that Pratinas spoke of Thaletas the Cretan freeing Sparta from plague.[10] We therefore need to consider what category of setting was involved here, and how it related to the three main categories we have distinguished above. Thaletas the Cretan was one of the "great wandering healers of the archaic age" and he (and Bacis and Abaris) were "shadowy and legendary figures."[11] In fact, I have argued elsewhere, in an entirely different context, that even Epimenides, who was more historically anchored, had been mythologized in complex ways by the fifth century in Athens.[12] So, despite the apparent historicity of the subject matter, in Athenian eyes the setting would have been perceived to have been distanced into a chronological, and to a lesser extent geographical, other in ways that made it comparable (though of course not identical) to the setting in the heroic age which, it must be remembered, was perceived by the Athenians (and the Greeks in general) as no less part of their historical past than the age of Solon.

Second, fragments of a tragedy involving Gyges have survived on papyrus.[13] The date of this tragedy is not certain; some consider it to be contemporary of Aeschylean tragedy, others date it to the Hellenistic period.[14] If it was an early fifth-century tragedy, its setting was doubly other, geographical and chronological. Early seventh-century Lydia and Gyges were remote, and to all intents and purposes mythological, in the sense of mythologized, so the setting was, in terms of distancing, comparable to that in Pratinas' tragedy that referred to Thaletas, only more distanced, in the Oriental "other."

Third, the hydria fragments Corinth T 1144 represent an Oriental king on a pyre, with attendants in distress and an *aulos* player.[15] Beazley argued that it represents a lost tragedy, with an Oriental, probably Persian, subject.[16] Kroisos is considered to be the obvious candidate,[17] and Page connected this image with the tragedy involving Gyges just mentioned.[18] If the image on the Corinth hydria fragments does indeed reflect a Kroisos tragedy it would be one in which Kroisos on the pyre was part of the performance; for this is what is suggested by the presence of the *aulos* player; that the image represents a performance; that it is an actual, extremely rare, representation of a performance, not, as is normally the case, of the myth influenced by the performance, or even of elements of the performance. If there was such a Kroisos tragedy the point of the pyre would have been his past hubris and his new understanding of the precariousness of human life and fortune. Whether or not this hypothetical tragedy had any connection with the *Gyges*, which was concerned with events over a century earlier, remains an open question,[19] especially since, we saw, the Gyges tragedy may have been of post-fifth-century date. If there had been a Kroisos tragedy the distance between the world of the audience and the world of the tragedy would have been greater than in Aeschylus' *Persai* and Phrynichos' *Phoinissai*—and, if it was not the same play, but part of the same trilogy, his *Persai*, but lesser than in the Gyges tragedy.[20]

According to Aristotle,[21] Agathon's *Anthos* or *Antheus*[22] did not involve any known incident or name, only made-up, fictitious ones. But this does not necessarily entail that the tragedy was not set in the heroic past; on the contrary, the context suggests that it was. For Aristotle first says,[23] in the context of discussing the ways in which poetry attaches names to characters, that tragedies still keep to real names, and then mentions that in some tragedies only one or two names are known and the other are made up. There can be no doubt that what is meant here by "real" names and "known" names (which are oppposed to made-up names) is names of known mythological characters; and therefore also that the made-up characters were made-up mythological characters. It is here as part of this comment, following the statement that in some tragedies only one or two names are known and the others are made up, that Aristotle says that in some, as in Agathon's *Anthos/-eus*, all names are made up. In this context there can be little doubt that the made-up characters were made-up mythological characters. This, I suggest, is confirmed by what follows; for Aristotle continues with the comment that it is not necessary to stick at all costs to the *paradedomenoi muthoi*, which are the usual subject of tragedy, but the poet should make up *muthoi* rather than verses; then, in the next sentence, he sanctions the use of real events, if they are appropriate, for making tragic plots. In these circumstances, I suggest that there can be very little doubt that Agathon's *Anthos* or *Antheus* was set in the mythological past.[24]

Chapter 2: Setting Out the Distances

Finally,[25] very little can be said about the fragment *TrGF* ii Adespota F 685 other than it may be a fragment from a tragedy with a setting comparable to that of Aeschylus' *Persai*.[26]

None of these distances, then, in these elusive (to us) tragedies is comparable to the transgressive distance in Phrynichos' *Capture of Miletos*.

Consequently, we can see that a whole gamut of distances was explored and tried at a certain point in the development of tragedy. At one end of the spectrum of these choices what was became crystallized as the canonical setting, the world of the heroic past, which continued to provide the common setting in the tragedies of this experimental period also;[27] at the other end was what defined the limits by defining what was transgressive, the transgressive, reduced, distance in Phrynichos' *Capture of Miletos*. In between these two poles other possibilities had been explored, choices that were eventually abandoned: first, in an (it would seem) small number of tragedies the setting was of the type illustrated by Aeschylus' *Persai*; second, a small number of tragedies were set in the non-heroic but remote and shadowy past, exemplified by the the tragedy in which Pratinas referred to Thaletas, and by the Gyges tragedy, if it is indeed of early fifth-century date; third, a few, such as the hypothetical Kroisos tragedy, seem to have been set at a distance about halfway between these two.

It is therefore even more significant than it may first appear that after all these explorations, it was the setting in the heroic past, the setting that had already been the most common setting in early tragedy,[28] that became crystallized as the canonical choice.

Why, then, was the preferred choice preferred, and what, if anything, does this tell us about the significance and function of the heroic setting, and thus about Greek tragedy in general? In order to attempt to answer this question we need to consider the characteristics of the preferred choice, and the ways in which these differ from those of the rejected choice and the transgressive choice. As we saw, the characteristics of the transgressive choice are that the world of the play is basically the same as the world of the audience; the absence of distance, or at least of sufficient distance, between the world of the play and the world of the audience was considered inappropriate. Clearly, it is the nature of the otherness of the world of the tragedy and the (interconnected) place of the world of the tragedy in the world of the present, that differ in the different non-transgressive settings. Therefore, it is the nature of the otherness of the world of the tragedy and the place of the world of the tragedy in the world of the present of the heroic age that made it the preferred choice of setting. It is there, then, that we must locate the reasons why it became the preferred setting. In the preferred choice the world of the tragedy was a very significant part of the audience's present, and its otherness and the fact that it is such a significant part of the present were intertwined. One clear way in which sometimes the world of the tragedy was a very significant part of the present, and a way in which the preferred setting is differentiated from the other settings, is that often one or more of the characters in the tragedy are cult recipients in the world of the present. This fact is connected with, is one aspect of, the most important general characteristic of the otherness of the preferred choice setting, and the most important way in which the world of the audience is differentiated and distanced from the heroic age: the fact that in the heroic age men and gods walked together and communicated directly and many of the heroes of tragedy were the children or descendants of gods and founded institutions, above all ritual institutions, which are part of the audience's present. The fact that those aspects of the otherness of the heroic age are consistently activated (albeit in different modalities, the details of which will be discussed in chapters III.1, III.3 and especially III.4) shows that this was not an incidental characteristic of the tragedies' preferred settings, but a very important and significant one.[29] This is what was distinctive about the heroic setting, and it is correlative with the fact that the preferred choice became the preferred setting in fifth-century tragedies.

In the world of the audience's present, the foundation of cults and ritual institutions by various heroic figures was one of the most important things that took place in the heroic past which shaped the world of today. Tragedies often represent such foundations, most importantly on the instructions of a deity. In order to assess the significance of this phenomenon we need to consider what cult foundations by heroes meant, if anything, in the religious discourse of the polis, and the religious perceptions of the audience which were shaped by the religious discourse of the polis.

Greek religion included a perception (not usually foregrounded in religious practice and discourse, but nevertheless shaping the parameters of practice—for example in religious innovation), a perception that traditional beliefs were also ultimately uncertain, that they were one particular set of representations of, and responses to, a divine world, which was ultimately unknowable, and that human knowledge about the divine and about the right way of behaving towards it was limited and circumscribed. This perception is correlative with the fact that, as has been already mentioned in chapter I.1, Greek religion had no divinely revealed knowledge, no scriptures, and no professional divinely anointed priesthood. This was one trend in the perception of the religious discourse of the polis; another, and more dominant, observable in

Chapter 2: Setting Out the Distances

classical Athens, was to consider that the religious system of the polis was validated through tradition. First, because those cults were believed to have been founded by heroic figures that had lived in the heroic past in which men had a closer connection with the divine and were often themselves descended from gods. Then, because those particular cults and relationships to the divine had been shown to be efficacious in the past by the fact that the gods saved the polis and brought prosperity to the present-day citizens' ancestors. Thus, Lysias states,[30] "So then our ancestors, by performing the sacrifices prescribed on the *kyrbeis*, handed over to us the greatest and happiest of all Greek cities, so that it is fit for us to perform the same sacrifices as they did, if for no other reason, because of the good fortune that resulted from those ritual acts." The context is forensically loaded; but the rhetorical strategy of the speaker, who is attacking Nikomachos, who codified the Athenian sacred calendar between 403 and 399 B.C., operated within the parameters of collective assumptions, since otherwise it would have been ineffective. Thus, it was especially in times of crisis, of which this was one for Athens, that communities asked themselves more openly what god they may have offended or neglected, and generally favored the possibility of innovation—in the constant and complex tension between tradition and innovation that characterized Greek religion.[31]

The anchoring of cults in the heroic past was articulated through myths attributing their foundation to heroic figures, and was acted out in cult, as when such cult founders were worshiped next to the divinity. Thus, at Brauron Iphigeneia was worshiped next to Artemis. I shall return to this cult to consider how Euripides' *Iphigeneia in Tauris* presented its foundation. Here I want to say that, since tragedy often dramatized the foundation of cults by heroes at the instigation of divinities, represented as interacting with mortals, it inevitably became, de facto, an important locus for this anchoring which was an important aspect of Greek religious discourse.

The fact that something that happens a lot in the tragedies, aetiologies in general and the foundation of ritual institutions in particular, first, was the product of the distinctive nature of the setting which became the preferred choice of setting, and second, was important in the world of the audience, suggests that its representation in tragedy was significant, that it was significant in the world of the audience, and not simply a theatrical device. We will find that many independent arguments will lead us to the same direction throughout this book.

The closeness of the relationship between mortals and gods in the heroic age, and the fact that the heroes of the tragedies were cult recipients in the world of today, made it possible to give some authority to the explorations and to what one may provisionally call "answers"—though I shall be discussing the nature of this authority and of those "answers" in detail in chapters III.3 and III.4.

This distanced the world of the play from that of the audience.[32] "Answers" and cult foundations are mostly part of the tragedies' closure. But the question of distancing is important for the tragedies as a whole. Too great a distance between the world of the tragedy and the world of the audience would have created the potential for a perception that the world of the tragedy was very different in nature from that of the audience, and that therefore what happened there was not directly relevant to the audience's world—except insofar as it pertained to a past that affected the present; that is, it would have created the potential for a perception that the emotions and misfortunes of the heroes could not be related to the experiences of the audience. If that potential had been realized, the possibilities of tragic explorations of all kinds would have been severely limited. For example, the choice to illustrate the darkness of a world which Greek religion does not pretend is unambiguously good with unambiguously good divinities, through exploring the experiences and deep emotions of distress of those caught up in its dark side, would not have been possible. In reality, we know that the heroes of tragedy were also felt to be in some ways like the audience, because we know enough about the ancient reception of tragedy to know that this is how the ancient audiences perceived them. For example, the assumptions about reception underlying Aristotle's explanatory construct pertaining to *phobos*, fear, in *Poetics* includes the perception that the tragic heroes were felt to be in some way also "like" the audience. For first he says that tragedy, through pity and fear, achieves *katharsis* of these emotions[33] and then[34] he states that fear is aroused by the misfortunes of someone like ourselves.

How, then, did this otherness and sameness operate? I have argued with reference to Sophocles' *Antigone* that the relationship between the world of the audience and that of the tragedy was not constant and inert, but was manipulated in the course of each tragedy through textual devices that operated in interaction with the assumptions which the audience shared with the tragedian: "distancing devices," which had the effect of distancing the action from the world of the fifth-century Athenian polis, differentiating the two; and "zooming devices," which had the effect of bringing the world of the play nearer, pushing the audience into relating their experiences and assumptions directly to the play.[35] The distancing devices allowed the "other" nature of the heroic world to be stressed, a stress which itself allowed a variety of things, such as the closeness to the gods that gave authority to, for example, the foundation of a cult; or the exploration of some-

Chapter 2: Setting Out the Distances

thing perceived to be disturbing, like the polis getting an aspect of its religious discourse wrong—which is what, I argued, happens in Sophocles' *Antigone*—at a safe symbolic distance from the audience's world. The zooming devices brought the world of the play nearer the world of the audience, and thus stressed the relevance of the explorations of the play for the world of the audience. I will illustrate the operation of these devices later on in this chapter, and set out that operation in more detail in part III. One particular set of such devices form what one may call the "distanced setting," in which the otherness of the heroic age is activated, and gods walk among men—as opposed to "zoomed setting," from which the gods are absent and far away. For the heroic nature of the heroic age is not constantly present; it is activated in particular circumstances for particular purposes, for example, to allow a certain authority to the explorations and the "answers." Thus, the gods are absent from Aeschylus' *Agamemnon* and *Choephoroi*, in which access to the divine is not radically different from that in the world of the audience; but in the last play of the trilogy, the *Eumenides*, the heroic nature of the age when men walked with gods is activated and some "answers," however complex and ambiguous, are given. Of course, there is always prophecy, and in tragedy all prophecies as true, but in the world of the play the characters do not know this, and, as in the world of the audience, they worry that human greed or fallibility may have produced a wrong oracle. This is comparable to what happens at the end of Sophocles' *Trachiniae*, where, in my view, in the world of the play the characters are ignorant of Heracles' future apotheosis, which is not signalled, and the hero only knows his terrible suffering, while the audience, while empathizing with the suffering (qua suffering, not, of course its precise form) inevitably put that suffering in a different perspective. For their ritual knowledge of Heracles as a recipient of divine and heroic cult was too deeply rooted not to have come into play to provide a knowledge of the future that is not available to the characters and thus to place Heracles' suffering in a cosmic context that does not diminish it, but in some ways deconstructs it.

In these circumstances, the double perspective in the relationship between the world of the audience and the world of the play, generated when the setting is in the heroic age because of the nature of that age and its relationship to the present, was clearly fundamental in allowing tragedy both to explore problems and issues at a distance, and to relate them directly to the audiences' experiences, with the distances manipulated through distancing and zooming devices. The fact that the heroic age became the preferred, indeed the exclusive, choice of setting shows that this was the setting best suited to the requirements of tragedy, which coincides with this conclusion that this double distance was very important, and suggests that the things for which this particular double distance was crucial, among which religious exploration is central, were also very important. This is confirmed by the fact that first, the second type of setting, in the enemy land, though not transgressive, came to be perceived as an evolutionary dead end, which suggests that in some ways it did not fulfil what were perceived to be the requirements of a tragic setting; and second, and most importantly, whatever may have happened in Phrynichos' *Phoinissai*, certainly Aeschylus' *Persai* show that the second type of setting and distancing (geographical distancing, which is a manifestation of, and a metaphor for, cultural distancing) came under the strong influence of, and was shaped by, that of the first type, the preferred choice; for in the world of the play, which is alien to that of the audience, Dareios is comparable to the figures of the Greek heroic age—though he belonged to the immediate past—and also partly comparable to the gods in that heroic age,[36] with Xerxes a poor version of the Greek heroes who were children of the gods.

The double perspective was very important in Greek tragedy; but it could operate also in non-heroic age settings. It was the nature of the otherness of the heroic age and its place in the present that was unique, and which was clearly perceived as desirable to the extent that it eliminated all alternatives.

Geographical setting is one aspect of the relationship between the world of the tragedy and the world of the audience. The fact that the setting of the events is so often in tragedy not Athens has been used as an argument against the ritual origin of tragedy.[37] But such views are based on a misunderstanding. For in Athenian perceptions the non-Athenian Greeks were part of a conceptual map—of which Athens was, of course, the center—which was a Panhellenic configuration of Greek religion, in which what happens in one place is relevant to others—and this map includes non-Greek places of relevance to Greeks. Thus, the myth of Pentheus explored in Euripides' *Bacchai*—like that of Lykourgos in Aeschylus' *Edonoi* and the fourth stasimon of Sophocles' *Antigone*[38]—tells a story of resistance to Dionysos that is directly relevant to Athenian cult, for, as we shall see in chapters II.1-2, it is similar to the myth of the festival of the City Dionysia which was the ritual context of tragedy. But Pentheus' was a more savage version than the Athenian myth.

This greater savagery of things located elsewhere is not limited to this myth. It is often the case that the more negative things and versions are explored at a greater distance from Athens while at the same time their relevance to the audience's experience is activated through

Chapter 2: Setting Out the Distances 25

a series of zooming devices at the appropriate places.[39] This is what, I argued, took place, for example, in Sophocles' *Antigone*—with the zooming devices including echoes of the Athenian ephebic oath.[40] The barbarian other has a place in this map precisely as barbarian other, which is both other and thus contrasted with the self, but also in some ways like the self, and thus offers ways of speaking about the self, as we shall see shortly in the discussion of aspects of *Iphigeneia in Tauris*. This discussion will illustrate the ways in which geographical distancing, in this case to the barbarian other, is one parameter in the manipulation of distancing that allows the exploration of problematic notions at a symbolic distance. But first we will consider the exploration of—among other things—the same problem, that of human sacrifice, in a tragedy set at the very center of Athens, Euripides' *Erechtheus*.[41]

The consideration of these two tragedies will bring out the ways in which human sacrifice was explored, and illustrate briefly the type of religious exploration that, as I will be arguing in chapter III.3, was articulated in Euripidean tragedies.

The reason why I begin my tragic readings with Euripides' *Erechtheus*, a fragmentary tragedy, is because it can illuminate very strikingly one important aspect of the processes of meaning creation by the ancient audiences that I have been discussing here. Some of the statements made in this section imply that the zooming of the world of the tragedy to the world of the audience includes, in significant places, the penetration of the world of the audience by the world of the tragedy. In theory, zooming devices can operate without penetrating the world of the audience, simply in terms of similarity, or closeness, to the world of the audience. And indeed many zooming devices in Greek tragedies do operate in this way. However, in significant places, above all pertaining to religion, the world of the tragedy does penetrate the world of the audience; and what happens in the world of the tragedy is perceived also as part of the world of the audience. The case limit in certainty and strength of penetration is Euripides' *Erechtheus*.

I.2.iii. *Zooming and Distancing in Action: Euripides'* Erechtheus *and* Iphigeneia in Tauris

The action in Euripides' *Erechtheus* takes place in Athens while Erechtheus was king and the Eleusinians with an army of Thracians led by the Thracian Eumolpos, son of Poseidon, were threatening Athens. Eumolpos wanted to replace Athena with his father Poseidon as the poliad divinity of Athens, though Poseidon had been the loser in the contest. This threat is clearly the context of fragment 41:

*ololyzet', o gynaikes, hos elthei thea
chrysen echousa Gorgon' epikouros polei.*

Raise the *ololyge*, the shrill cry, women, so that the
goddess may come to help the polis, wearing
the golden aegis with the Gorgon.[42]

My translation unpacks, and makes explicit, the metonymic reference to the aegis. For the Athenians would have understood the expression "golden aegis with the Gorgon" through their assumptions that included the statue of Athena Parthenos by Pheidias, in the Parthenon, which had a golden aegis with an ivory head of Gorgon. There can be little doubt that these verses would have evoked the goddess Athena, who was the poliad divinity protecting Athens in real life; the persona of Athena protecting the polis was a strong theme in Athenian ideology and was embodied in the statue of Athena Parthenos by Pheidias, in the Parthenon,[43] which is directly evoked by the description of Athena wearing a golden aegis with a *gorgoneion*, as that statue did, its *gorgoneion* being made of ivory. The metonymic reference to the aegis would have reinforced the notion of Athena's protective action, for in myth the aegis powerfully protected from attack.[44] Only a few years before the play's production (which probably took place at the end of the 420s B.C. or soon after)[45] the audience would have themselves invoked Athena's help when the Spartans were annually invading Attica first under Archidamos, then under Kleomenes, and then under Agis.[46] The fact that both function and iconography of Athena in the tragedy coincided with those of the goddess in Athenian cult as represented especially in her most magnificent statue in the polis, would have constituted a nexus of zooming devices, zooming the world of the tragedy very closely to that of the audience whose past that tragedy was enacting. The strength of the zooming would have been further reinforced by the fact that the situation of the invocation almost certainly evoked similar situations of invocation of the goddess in comparable circumstances in real life in the audience's immediate past.

To continue with the action, the Delphic oracle told Erechtheus that he would be victorious if he sacrificed his eldest daughter to Persephone. In fragment 50 Erechtheus' wife Praxithea, the girl's mother, gives her reasons for consenting to the sacrifice.[47] Her speech expresses the patriotic feelings of the funeral orations and articulates the notion that the loss of one life and the grief this causes is less important than the prevention of the destruction of the city, and that the individual should be sacrificed to save the many. Praxithea also values the honor her daughter will get by sacrificing herself to save the city. A very

Chapter 2: Setting Out the Distances 27

important point here is the notion she expresses at lines 22-35, that if she had had sons she would have sent them to fight for their country, however fearful she may have been for their safety, and that sacrificing a girl to save the city is no different; it is in fact better, because of the individual glory involved. This deconstructs the savagery of human sacrifice by presenting it as the same as the acceptable and ideologically glorified death of young men in war. But the latter is not itself presented as an unproblematic concept here; it is not only the question of human sacrifice, a religious problem, that is explored, but also the very notion of individual deaths for the sake of the collectivity, dying for one's polis—a question of fundamental importance to a polis at war.

For besides the voice that glorifies death in war, we hear another. The less dominant voice expresses the notion that not all mothers share such values; the feelings of the mothers who do not share Praxithea's priorities and would rather have their sons cowards and alive than faithful to their honor, are negatively framed, since it is Praxithea who articulates them and colors them with her disapproval. Praxithea's coloring and evaluation are wholly positive in the tragedy. The fact that she becomes priestess of Athena Polias on Athena's orders is a manifestation, and confirmation, of this positive coloring.

However, the fact that these feelings *were* articulated sets out, if in a subdued tone, the, or at least especially overtly, felt by the mothers, to whom such feelings, which were negative in the ideology of the polis, symbolically drift. Through their drifting to the women, the personal grief and tragic loss involved in the death of men, especially young men, in war, which official ideology glorified—a grief and loss which many in the audience would have experienced in the recent past—are acknowledged, but made less threatening to this ideology, which is necessary for the polis' survival. And, of course, the dominant voice is further reinforced by the fact that the woman who is actually asked to sacrifice her child does not show such womanly weakness, for, in the play's dominant discourse, reflecting the official ideology, even women, if they are good women, will accept the ideology of the polis. It is, as Praxithea makes clear, a matter of self-preservation.[48]

Ideologically stronger than self-preservation, and not only in the official polis ideology, is the notion, articulated at 14-5, that the very reason we beget children is in order to defend the altars of th other side of heroism and self-sacrifice, the individual grief, especially e gods and our country. This theme returns strongly at 44-9, where the desire to preserve the old *thesmia* handed down by one's ancestors, and especially to ensure that the cult of the Athenian polis is not changed, that Athena is not replaced by Poseidon as the poliad divinity, is set at the very center of Praxithea's desire to save the city. This gives the notion of dying for one's country a religious core, which corresponds to the deeply felt perception that religion was at the center of the Athenian politeia.[49] Praxithea's lamentations later on in the play do not indicate changed priorities; they articulate the human cost of such priorities.

To move the action on, Erechtheus sacrificed his daughter, and two more daughters sacrificed themselves of their own volition because of an oath they had taken with their sister. As a result, the enemy was defeated and Eumolpos killed by Erechtheus. However, Erechtheus was himself killed by Poseidon. We take up the story at fragment 65 line 55,[50] where, after a messenger speech which announced the result of the battle and the death of both Eumolpos and Erechtheus, after Praxithea's bitter lamentations, and while Poseidon, enraged at the defeat and death of his son, sends an earthquake and Athens trembles, Athena appears. She first berates Poseidon and then turns to Praxithea; she gives her instructions to bury her daughters and informs her that their *psychai* did not go to Hades, but that she, Athena, installed their *pneuma* in the ether (71-2: *psychai men oun tond' ou bebas' Haiden para, eis d' aither' auton pneum' ego [k]atoikisa*), and she made them into the goddesses Hyakinthides, whose cult she is now instituting, giving specific instructions about the sacrifices and other rites that should in future be performed in their honor.[51]

A very important thing here is the fact that the expression *psychai men oun tond' ou bebas' Haiden para, eis d' aither' auton pneum' ego [k]atoikisa* resembles closely, and thus would have recalled for the Athenian audience, the public epitaph for the men who died in the battle of Poteidaia:[52] *aither men psychas hypedechsato so[mata de chthon]*. This would have zoomed the world of the tragedy to the world of the audience, and presented the Hyakinthides as the models for the heroization of the Athenian war dead,[53] confirming the association between the sacrifice of a virgin and the death of men in war, which is also enshrined in the cult which associates Aglauros, another virgin, who in one version sacrificed her life to save the city, with the ephebes, who swear the ephebic oath in her sanctuary and in her name before that of any other god or hero.[54]

Then Athena goes on to institute the cult of Poseidon Erechtheus; what she says is that Erechtheus will take the name of his killer and be invoked in cult as Poseidon. This is one interpretation of the cult title Poseidon Erechtheus. Athena orders that a sanctuary be built for this cult in the middle of the city. Obviously, the cult itself would have zoomed the world of tragedy to the world of the audience, a zooming made stronger by the fact that at that very moment a sanctu-

Chapter 2: Setting Out the Distances

ary to Poseidon Erechtheus was being built in the middle of the city, as Athena was instructing the Athenians of the heroic age in which Erechtheus had died to do: the Erechtheion, which housed, besides minor cults and sacred spots, the cults of Poseidon Erechtheus and of Athena Polias. The latter was the most important cult of the Athenian polis; it honored the goddess issuing the instructions in the world of the play, who mentions this very cult, her own, in her next words, when she makes Praxithea the first priestess of this cult, thus instituting this cult in the form in which it is practiced today, in fifth-century Athens. This, of course, zooms the world of tragedy to the present and anchors the present cult securely in the heroic world and in Athena's will.

Thus, in this play, the double perspective allowed the exploration at a distance first, of the problematic notion of human sacrifice (a problem in the religious discourse of the present, in the sense of what it may be saying about the polis' gods); and second, of the notion of dying for one's country, with regard to which it articulates the other voice that stresses the human tragedy of war, and almost questions its value, an articulation which had drifted to the women, and the less good women at that, which had been distanced to the heroic age and negatively framed, but nevertheless articulated.

The double perspective also allowed the presentation of the symbolic anchoring of the most important Athenian cult, of Athena Polias, and of its associated cult of Poseidon Erechtheus; the fact that, we saw, the world of tragedy was zoomed to the world of the audience allowed the latter's cult to be symbolically reinforced through the representation of their foundation in the heroic age when men walked with, were born of, and were killed by gods, on the orders of Athena herself.

For the fact that here the world of the tragedy penetrated the world of the audience is very difficult to doubt. This tragedy was portraying events that (in the audience's perceptions) had happened in their own past, very near the place in which they had happened, and it is showing them shaping the present as it is now, so that what happened on stage was de facto part of the audience's present. Through dense zooming, the tragedy had identified the goddess Athena of the tragedy with the goddess worshiped by the audience, above all in the poliadic cult; so that when "the goddess" appeared on stage, "she" would have been perceived as a representation of the real goddess Athena, comparable to a representation of a deity in sacred drama, especially as she is presented as shaping the poliadic cult in its present form by appointing its first priestess, and ordering the foundation of, among others, another cult with which the poliadic cult is closely associated in the present. This closure would have evoked, and thus been perceived as partly comparable to, reenactments of cult foundations in sacred drama.

Erechtheus is the case limit. But *Iphigeneia in Tauris* is not very different in this respect, despite the differences in the setting, as will become clear in the course of its discussion.

Euripides explored the question of human sacrifice many times, in many tragedies.[55] Here I will consider the ways in which the question of human sacrifice is explored in *Iphigeneia in Tauris*, in a tragedy located at the other extreme of distancing from the *Erechtheus*: it takes place in a barbarian land. At the overt level of presentation it is on the one hand the barbarian and on the other the generally Greek (those who sacrificed Iphigeneia) that are at the center of the theme's exploration. But at another level things are more complex. Before considering this tragedy it is necessary to try to reconstruct some of the assumptions that had shaped the audience's filters by considering their assumptions concerning human sacrifice. First, it must be stressed again that the Greeks never practiced human sacrifice; the notion that they did is a product of the historicist intepretation of myths.[56] In ancient Greek eyes human sacrifice was an exceptionally practiced rite of the heroic past.

Let us consider the schemata shaping myths of human sacrifice. I call "schemata" one particular configuration of assumptions:[57] particular models of organizing experience which structure myths, collective representations and texts (such as "patricide," which structures all myth involving patricide) and are themselves structured by, and so express, the society's realities, perceptions, and ideologies. One of the schemata shaping the myth of human sacrifice is "animal substitution,"[58] the notion that the sacrifice of an animal to the divinity is instead of the sacrifice of a human being. A divine claim to human life is settled without loss of human life. This is expressed most vividly in the myths in which the human sacrifice does not take place and the girl (it is always a girl in such cases) is replaced by an animal.[59] But in several myths the girl did die.

Another schema that shaped myths of human sacrifice was the symbolic equivalence between an unmarried girl and an animal, expressing the notion of the wildness, the metaphorical animality of the parthenos, which corresponds to the Greek perception that girls are wild and need to be tamed and acculturated.[60]

The fact that these myths were shaped by schemata that reflected perceptions that formed part of the Athenians' conceptual universe, and that therefore, they expressed, among other things, the notion that normally mankind pays a cheap price for divine favor, killing animals, the creatures below them, to propitiate those above them

Chapter 2: Setting Out the Distances

without loss of human life, does not mean that human sacrifice was unproblematic. What tragedy does is to tease out, and stress, the problematic side by setting on stage, and sometimes focussing on, the victim. In this way it problematizes human sacrifice, and through that ultimately, the nature of the gods who demand it. But this does not entail condemnation or rejection of the gods or criticism of polis religion. After all, the Greek perceptions of the cosmos acknowledged that the world was hard and the human condition precarious. And in a religion without a devil, the same gods have a dark and dangerous as well as a benevolent side. But they are not, I will be arguing throughout this book,[61] arbitrarily cruel; Greek tragedy presents this hard and dangerous world as an ordered world, not one of cosmic *anomie* that creates despair. To the dark sides that are explored there are complex "resolutions" in the tragedies that do not wash away the pain, but make sense of it.

One "resolution" of the problem of the human sacrifice that does take place is that presented in Euripides' *Erechtheus*: an exceptional price is demanded by a divinity to save a community in exceptional circumstances, and the girl giving her life to save the community is explicitly compared to the death of the young men who die fighting for their country, presented as a patriotic choice for the sake of the community, comparable to young men giving their life in war to save the city, the regular male contribution to the city in war matched by an exceptional female contribution.[62] Both types of death express devotion to duty and to the polis,[63] which must be valued above oneself, and are used as moral paradigms for appropriate behavior for all.[64]

In *Iphigeneia in Tauris*,[65] the exploration is pushed further, beyond the salvation of the sacrificial victim: the focus is on a victim who survived, and who now has to perform the same human sacrifice rite herself on others, in a barbarian land where human sacrifice is relatively common—and the victims are Greeks. So the exploration takes place at a distance, but, as we shall see, this distance is unstable.

Central for determining the nature of this exploration is the question of how the Artemis of the tragedy would have been perceived by the Athenian audience. Would she have been perceived as a wholly different Artemis from the Artemis they worshiped, a literary creation of little relevance to their religious reality? I have already argued elsewhere that Artemis in this tragedy (in which she does not appear in person) was perceived as a representation of the goddess Artemis worshiped in Athens, with a special emphasis on her cult and persona as Brauronia and Tauropolos.[66] This last fact is very important for our purposes of investigating the distances between the world of the audience and the world of the tragedy. So I will consider the presentation of the goddess and her cult in the tragedy, focussing on the relationships of distance or proximity between the world of the tragedy and the world of the audience and the ways in which these affect the exploration of human sacrifice.

Artemis and her cult are first mentioned in this tragedy in connection with the human sacrifice, by Iphigeneia, in the Prologue, in line 9, when she speaks of her own sacrifice at Aulis. The fact that it is Iphigeneia herself, alive, who speaks of her sacrifice frames it in a less savage light. Anyway, the emphasis of her words is on her father's actions (8-9): *esphaxen Helenes hounek'* . . . *pater / Artemidi*. The fact that Helen and Menelaos were the reason for her sacrifice is explained by reference to the vow that Agamemnon had made to sacrifice to Artemis the fairest thing born in the year in which Iphigeneia was born; hence, Kalchas told Agamemnon, he had to sacrifice Iphigeneia to Artemis now, otherwise Artemis would continue to send adverse winds and they would not be able to sail to Troy. She then mentions how Artemis saved her by replacing her with a hind. So Iphigeneia makes clear from the start that Artemis did not simply demand the sacrifice of Iphigeneia, in which case it could be argued that Agamemnon and the Greeks had a religious duty to obey; she simply prevented the Greeks from sailing to Troy. Agamemnon and the Greeks had a perfectly good choice open to them, abandon the expedition and not sacrifice Iphigeneia. This emphasis on the human agents of the sacrifice, and the fact that they had a choice, recurs throughout the play.

The sacrifice of Iphigeneia was part of her Panhellenic myth; but it was also part of of the Attic cultic myth of the sanctuary of Artemis at Brauron, where Iphigeneia shared in the cult.[67] This Athenian dimension is brought to the fore and stressed through the fact that the expression used to refer to Artemis, to Agamemnon's vow to Artemis, in 21, *phosphoro thysein thea*, refers to Agamemnon's vow. For this relates the goddess of the play directly to the Attic cult of Artemis, especially the Brauronian cult (and also the closely related Mounichian cult), where the torch-bearing Artemis was a common iconographical representation.[68] In this way the Artemis spoken of in the prologue was zoomed to the Artemis of Athenian cultic reality; the Athenian audience would have perceived this Artemis to whom Iphigeneia was sacrificed as a representation of the goddess Artemis worshiped in Athens with the emphasis on her aspect as Brauronia. Since the audience's assumptions included the ritual knowledge that Iphigeneia received a heroic cult at Brauron,[69] the evocation of Artemis Brauronia would have strengthened the awareness that ultimately Iphigeneia was saved and received her just reward, which, in its turn, would have put her sacrifice and present suffering in a wider perspective. But since all these evocations were very light, this wider perspective would have been at this point only very lightly sketched as one element in the audience's reception.

Subsequently, the world of the play is strongly distanced from the world of the audience, and this distancing provides the frame for the presentation of the Taurian cult of Artemis. In 30ff Iphigeneia mentions that Artemis saved her and took her to the land of the Taurians, which is strongly distanced from the Greek world through the formulation *hou ges anassei barbaroisi barbaros Thoas*. Artemis made Iphigeneia the priestess of her cult in this barbaric land where unspeakable sacrifices were offered to her. If lines 38-9 are genuine,[70] the audience would already hear, here, of the custom to sacrifice to Artemis any Greek who came to its shores. If, as is more likely, they are not, the distancing would have been somewhat less dramatic, but still radical. For Iphigeneia's comment at 36-7, "the festival only the name of which is fair, but as for the rest I stay silent, for I fear the goddess," sets out the distancing between this ritual practice and Greek perceptions before any more specific reference to the practice. In this context, even without the activation of the audience's mythological knowledge about the barbaric practices in the Tauric cult of Artemis, the perception that *arrheta sphagia* referred to human sacrifice would have been formulated.

In this way the Tauric Artemis is distanced from the Greek cult of Artemis. The goddess is the same as the Greek Artemis, the same person whom the audience had first perceived as the Attic Artemis; but this goddess is perceived, and worshiped, differently, savagely, by the Taurians. The savage Artemis is an aspect of the goddess' cultic persona among the Taurians at a double distance from the audience's own world, in the heroic part and in another, savage, land. However, subsequently the distance between the Taurians and the Greeks of the heroic past is destabilized: for the references to Iphigeneia's sacrifice at 338-9 and especially, in Iphigeneia's own mouth, at 357-77, closed the distance. The emphasis on this latter passage is, again, on the human agents of her sacrifice, especially Helen, Menelaos and, above all, her father Agamemnon. The repeated mention of Helen would have evoked for the audience the knowledge that Artemis did not simply demand the sacrifice of Iphigeneia, in which case it could be argued that it was a religious duty to obey it. She simply prevented the Greeks from sailing to Troy. Agamemnon and the Greeks had the choice to abandon the expedition and not sacrifice Iphigeneia. This existence of a choice is brought to the fore by Iphigeneia's mention of her supplication of her father not to sacrifice her at lines 362ff.

Almost immediately after this, in 380-91, a new notion is articulated, which on the surface reopens the distance between Greek and barbarian, in that at the overt level it refers to the barbarians' religious discourse and its relationship to the divine world; in fact, this distance is deceptive.

This is a complex speech. Iphigeneia begins by reproaching Artemis because on the one hand she considers polluted, and keeps away from her altars, anyone who has bloodstained hands[71] or had touched a corpse or a woman who has just given birth, and on the other she rejoices in human sacrifices. But then Iphigeneia moves on to speculate that the human sacrifices offered to Artemis by the Taurians was not something that Artemis really wanted, but what the Taurians who were *anthropoktonoi* thought she wanted because they attributed their own inclinations to her.[72] She concludes with an explanation of her belief which is at the same time a more general statement of confidence, "For I do not think that any of the gods is *kakos*." This attempt to make sense of what appear objectionable practices from the viewpoint of a relatively enlightened worshiper, and the solution which consists in the view that people project their own cultural norms onto the gods, though not new in Greek thought, had a deep resonance in a religion which acknowledged the ultimate unknowability of the divine world.

Here, as elsewhere, the exploration of the problem takes place at a distance, in the world of the barbaric other that has been contrasted to the self. But the distance is unstable, transparently deceptive, as is made virtually explicit through the fact that Iphigeneia intertwines this speculation that the Taurians attributed their own inclinations to Artemis with the expression of disbelief that the gods would have eaten a child's flesh at the banquet offered them by Tantalos. Such expression of disbelief about the cannibalism of the gods in the myth of Tantalos is not new; it is comparable to Pindar's discourse on Tantalos,[73] in which he refers to the story of Tantalos' cannibalistic crime but professes to refrain from ascribing cannibalism to the gods.[74] To an audience familiar with Pindar's discourse, Iphigeneia's words would have evoked that discourse, and this would have inevitably brought to the fore the notion that there were Greek myths that ascribed savage traits to the gods. Nevertheless, this speculation that human sacrifice was not desired by Artemis, but reflected the barbarity of the Taurians, frames the subsequent references to, and preparations for, the impending human sacrifice; and this distances the goddess Artemis from this particular cult, albeit without eliminating the connection, especially since the audience may have found Iphigeneia's speculation convincing, but had no way of knowing whether it was right.

Chapter 2: Setting Out the Distances

The distancing is strengthened, but the unknowability of the will of the goddess is at the same time stressed, by the coryphaeus' address to Artemis at 463-6:[75] "Mistress, if these rites performed by this polis are to your liking, receive the sacrifices which the law in our country [i.e., Greece] proclaims unholy." Arguably, however, this distancing is deconstructed by the entrance of Iphigeneia, whose very presence in Tauris was the result of the fact that her father and the other Greeks had offered her as a human sacrifice.

Iphigeneia speaks to Orestes of her sacrifice first at 563-6, while he is still ignorant of her identity. In this exchange Artemis and the human sacrifice are not mentioned explicitly (though, of course, they were inevitably evoked): *sphageises thygatros*, "the father who killed her," "she died for the sake of an evil woman." So here the goddess' role is strongly underplayed, almost elided, and it is the human action that is the focus. Then, at 783-6, she explains to Pylades, so that he can explain it to her brother—for she is still not aware of Orestes' identity—what happened to her and how she came to be still alive. She says that Artemis saved her, replacing her with a hind, into which her father plunged the knife thinking it was Iphigeneia, and brought her to dwell in the land of the Taurians. Once again, the guilt is focussed on the father, and the goddess appears as Iphigeneia's savior. But Iphineneia's salvation has not meant her return to an unproblematic life, but to a life in a strange land among barbarians in which she is obliged to perform human sacrifices.[76] So her life was saved, but Iphigeneia is suffering, as is stressed by her message to Orestes, at 774-6, in which she was asking him to take her back to Argos before she died, to take her away from the barbarian land and from the sacrifices in which she has to kill strangers.

Nevertheless, this suffering does not alter the fact that Artemis saved her life, and Iphigeneia returns to this at 1082-8, where she invokes Artemis as the goddess who saved her from her father's killing hand and asks her to save her again together with Orestes and Pylades. So here even more strongly and explicitly than before she puts the responsibility for the human sacrifice entirely onto Agamemnon who took the decision to do it; the fact that it had been Artemis who had requested it is elided, and Artemis is credited only with Iphigeneia's salvation; all the guilt has drifted to the father and all the credit for the salvation to the goddess. As we saw, this is how Iphigeneia apportions the blame for her sacrifice also elsewhere in the play, though not in as strikingly expressed and contrastive a manner as here. As we saw, the mentality behind this perception is that Agamemnon had had a choice: to abandon the expedition or sacrifice his daughter; and he chose to sacrifice his daughter. In this way the savagery which the myths associated with the cult of Artemis in Greece in the mythological past is played down.

In the ode that follows almost immediately afterwards, the second stasimon,[77] in the first strophe, at 1097-1105, the chorus zooms Artemis to her Greek cultic persona with their expression of longing for an Artemis firmly placed in the Delian cultic context.[78] This brings the world of the tragedy very near the world of the audience. Then a distancing from the world of the audience and from the Greek cult of Artemis is effected at 1112-6, where the chorus, in singing about the fact that they were sold into captivity in the land of the Taurians, refer to Artemis' Taurian cult as having altars on which it is not sheep that are sacrificed (*bomous ou t' melothytas*).[79] The very expression brings up strongly the contrast between Greek cult, in which Artemis' altars received sacrifices of sheep, and the Taurian cult in which her altars do not receive sacrifice of sheep but of human beings. In this way the savagery has again been made to drift to the barbarian other.

The exploration of the relationship between savage practices distanced from the present and the cultic practices of the present reaches a climax in a divine speech. At 1435 Athena appears and addresses first Thoas and then Orestes and Iphigeneia.[80] At 1449-67 she orders Orestes to take the statue to Athens, to set it up and found a sanctuary at Halai where Artemis shall be worshiped as Tauropolos; and at her festival, as a compensation for Orestes' slaughter, the sword shall be held to a man's throat and blood spilled for form's sake so that the goddess receives her due honors.[81] Iphigeneia is to become the *kleidouchos* (key-holding) priestess of Artemis Brauronia, and she will die and be buried in the sanctuary and receive the dedication of the clothes of women who died in childbirth. In Greek religious terms this means that Iphigeneia will be heroized and receive cult; this in turn implies that Iphigeneia was to be the founder of this cult of Artemis Brauronia, according to the schema "heroic figure founds a cult"—a fact that was in any case known to the Athenian audience as ritual knowledge pertaining to the important cult of Artemis Brauronia.[82]

This, then, is a very strong zooming of the world of the tragedy to the world of the audience, a penetration of the world of the audience. What at the beginning of the play had been evoked (I argued) through the zooming of Artemis to her persona of Artemis Brauronia is now set out explicitly. The culmination of the events of the tragedy was the foundation of these two cults and rites; and conversely, it is as a result of what happened in this tragedy that the cult of Artemis Tauropolos at Halai Araphenides and the cult of Artemis Brauronia at Brauron were founded. The slant of this speech is very reassuring. It establishes a distance between the savage Taurian cult of Artemis on the one hand and the Attic cult of Artemis on the other, and also the superiority of the latter. The rite of blood spilling in the cult of Artemis Tauropolos is presented as a milder form of the human sacrifice which in another time and place had been thought to have been appropriate for Artemis; so the cult itself is presented as an acculturated version of the Tauric cult, ordered by Athena.

At the overt level this tragedy problematized the savage religious practices of the Taurians and established their distances from the Greek ones. These barbarians, instead of respecting strangers, sacrificed them to Artemis. This is contrasted to Greek practices and attitudes in the tragedy. However, this overt problematization, through the character of Iphigeneia, and in the ways we saw, was intertwined with, and explored also, the problem of human sacrifice in Greek religion, the fact that human sacrifice crops up in the myths which are closely connected with present-day cults.

Even in Athena's speech, there are elements that may have disturbed a little the reassuring image. The cult of Artemis Tauropolos is presented as having certain links with the Taurian cult of Artemis. Its statue had been brought from there, it had originally been the statue of that cult, which had received human sacrifices; and now it was honored with a rite that was more civilized than the barbarian practices of human sacrifice to which it is explicitly contrasted—and also than the earlier exceptional Greek practice of human sacrifice which in this context is implicitly evoked. But this very rite, or rather, Athena's formulation of her instructions to establish it, may have deconstructed somewhat the reassuring slant that permeates the conclusion of the play. For it complicates one question that arises throughout the tragedy. If Artemis did not really want the human blood, as her salvation of Iphigeneia may indicate, why does she want the Taurians to perform human sacrifice? The tragedy does give a tentative answer, Iphigeneia's answer: Artemis does not desire human sacrifices; it is the Taurians who think she does, attributing their savagery to the goddess. However, this is only one opinion, and the audience has no way of knowing whether it is right. And also this opinion still would not "explain" everything. For if Artemis does not desire human blood, why does Athena say that there should be a rite of spilling some blood as a compensation for Orestes' slaughter, so that the goddess receives her due honors? Would this not evoke the possibility that Artemis wanted the Taurians to sacrifice human beings? Or would the Athenian audience have understood this to mean only that in this way she would be compensated for the fact that victims destined to her had not in fact been sacrificed to her?

Artemis certainly saved Iphigeneia, and from this it is possible to conclude that she did not really want human blood. And this can be said to be the dominant voice in the tragedy, constructed in a variety of ways, as we saw, such as Iphigeneia's putting the emphasis on the guilt of Agamemnon who had had a choice. But this is not the only voice; there is another voice, constructed by the ancient audience who made sense of the tragedy through perceptual filters shaped by their religious assumptions. For these included the knowledge that the gods have asked for human sacrifices in other circumstances. People still had a choice, but when it was necessary to perform a human sacrifice to save the city, in the eyes of the ancient Athenians the choice was virtually nonexistent. However, the compulsion involved in such cases is itself deconstructed through the fact that in such cases human sacrifice can be seen as not very different from the sacrifice of the young men's lives at war to save the city (and indeed, at least a segment of Athenians may have felt, for less life-important reasons and causes). This is the position set out in Euripides' *Erechtheus*, as we saw above.[83]

The fact that the *Iphigeneia in Tauris* shows Athena instituting a cult that was a mild transformation of human sacrifice creates the notion that those savage practices really were remote and located in the geographical and chronological other; it is these mild versions that have the sanction of the poliadic goddess, on whose orders they were instituted. So the explorations in this tragedy conclude with the presentations of the present day Athenian cult and perceptions of Artemis as a superior version of those in the barbarian other and also in certain respects of those in the heroic past. Nevertheless, in these perceptions is articulated the notion that the Attic cult of Artemis Tauropolos includes aspects that are not unrelated to savage rites, in myth negatively distanced into the other, rites which express the dark side of Artemis in particular and Greek divinities in general.

For it is crucially important to remember that Greek religion acknowledged the dark side of the cosmos, and the dark side of the Greek gods reflected this perception. Because the Tauric cult and the persona of Artemis implicated in it are intimately connected with the goddess' Attic cult, both in the assumptions of the audience and through the strong activations and zoomings of the play, they allow certain dark aspects of Athenian cult to be articulated, problematized, and explored at a safe symbolic distance. The distance between the Tauric Artemis and the Greek one allows the exploration of the savagery to take place at a safe distance, while the instability of that distance makes the exploration directly relevant to both Attic and Panhellenic religion. In addition, the negative facet of the exploration is deconstructed through the fact that the Athenian cult, the foundation of which is

Chapter 2: Setting Out the Distances   39

ordered by Athena, is presented as more civilized than the earlier Greek, as well as the barbarian, practices. The darkness does not disappear; but it does, ultimately, become somewhat "acculturated"; it is certainly presented as not only distanced but also largely superseded, and thus less threatening.

This complex interplay of zooming and distancing, and the emphasis placed by Iphigeneia on human guilt, of Agamemnon especially, protects the exploration of the problem of the cruelty of the human sacrifice in the mythological past from dwelling on the darkness of the divinities who demand it. Another element that also functions in the same way is the exceptionality of the fate of the victims, which may be taken as "compensation" for the suffering. Iphigeneia, who survived but suffered, will found the Brauronian cult and be its first priestess, she will become a priestess in a civilized Artemis cult in Greece, at the center of Greece from the viewpoint of tragedy and its audience, and after her death she will receive heroic cult. This does not neutralize her suffering, but it puts it in perspective; correlative with her exceptional suffering is her exceptional fate and her exceptional relationship to the goddess. Other sacrificed girls were also heroized or deified.[84] In *Erechtheus* the mother of the sacrificed girl will become a priestess and the girl and her sisters, who had killed themselves, will be deified.

So this is one "resolution" of the problem of sacrifice: the victims' exceptional suffering goes together with an exceptional proximity to the divinity and/or an exceptional fate after death. This does not neutralize the suffering. But it makes sense of the world and of the gods. And it also makes this suffering less threatening to the ordinary people in the audience who do not have exceptional proximity to the gods.

In *Iphigeneia in Tauris*, then, problems pertaining to the cult of Artemis, above all human sacrifice—which is not restricted to this goddess' cult—were explored at a safe symbolic distance, and then made relevant to the audience's immediate cultic reality, through a series of zooming and distancing devices. So this tragedy explores in very complex ways a problem, human sacrifice, pertaining to the mythological past of present-day cults, and by doing so also explores the nature of the gods, who are the gods worshiped in the present. Then, it anchors symbolically, it gives authority to, present-day cults, by presenting them as having being founded on the instructions of the polis' poliadic deity. It is Athena rather than Artemis herself who orders the foundation of these cults because in this way Athena, the poliad divinity of Athens, is shown as sanctioning, and participating in, the foundation of the two cults. And this is a representation of a strong anchoring of these cults in the mythical past, which, we saw, was of importance in Greek religious perceptions.

I.2.iv. Performances outside Athens: Aeschylus' Aitnaiai and Euripides' Archelaos

I will now consider another major question pertaining to the relationship between the world of the tragedy and the world of the audience. How do tragedies written by Athenian tragedians to be performed outside Athens fit into this picture I have been drawing here?[85] I would suggest that they fit unproblematically. The mythicoritual web that tragedy deployed and explored was both Panhellenic and local. In tragedies written to be performed outside Athens this web was viewed, and structured, from a different conceptual center (albeit the structuring eyes were still Athenian), that of the place of intended performance, which also brought into play that place's local myths. The modality of operation appears to be the same.

Thus, for example, we know enough about Aeschylus' *Aitnaiai*[86] to know that the story is relevant to the cultic history of its place of production: it is set in Aitna and other places in Sicily (the scene of the action switches around);[87] the chorus consisted of women of Aitna; and it deals with the birth of the twin gods Palici, who were worshiped in the area and who were the sons of a nymph called Thaleia or Aitna. Zeus had sex with her; afterwards, afraid of Hera's anger, she prayed to be swallowed up by the earth; her prayers were answered but when she was due to give birth the earth opened up again and twin boys emerged, who became the gods Palici. Because it was relevant to the area's past, this tragic articulation was relevant to its present.

That the performance of this tragedy was not perceived as a discrete event insulated from real life may perhaps be confirmed by the fact that the *Life of Aeschylus* gives expression to the idea that this performance and the Aitnaians' real life were not sealed off from each other; the *Life* crystallizes a relationship between the two in the form of an omen:[88] "[H]aving come to Sicily when Hieron was founding the city of Aitna, Aeschylus produced *Aitnaiai* as an omen of a good life for those who came to settle in the polis." Since we know so little about the play, we can only speculate as to the ways in which the representation of events in the cultic history of the area in the heroic age, which had shaped things so that they are as they are now, would be considered a good omen in Greek mentality. A benign re-presentation of the foundation of the cult of the Palici may have been seen as, among other things, a sort of renewal of the bond between the gods and the men in the area, at the critical point of Aitna's foundation as a succes-

Chapter 2: Setting Out the Distances

sor to Katane, whose previous inhabitants Hieron had removed and replaced with new settlers; there may have been possible explorations about matters felt to be important: for example, the religious status of the refoundation of a city and the removal of its inhabitants to replace them with newcomers; and/or the presentation of a promise for the future, inherent in the representation of relationships in the past. One of the places the action of the tragedy moved to was Syracuse. Hieron's refoundation of Catania under the name Aitna may have been given a mythological paradigm, become symbolically "anchored," through the articulation of a similar relationship in the heroic past which provided the roots of the present.

In these circumstances, I submit that what we know about this play suggests that there the same permeability between, and the same double perspective in the relationship of, the world of the tragedy and the world of the audience as that we have seen in the Athenian tragedies produced to be performed in Athens that we considered in this chapter. I would venture to suggest that if we possessed the text of the tragedy we would have found comparable zoomings and distancings.

Euripides wrote *Archelaos* for production in Macedonia, sometime in 408/7, thereby pleasing his host, the Macedonian king Archelaos.[89] We do not know where exactly the play was produced. Pella is by far the least likely candidate.[90] Of the other two, Aigai and Dion, Aigai (modern Vergina) would appear to have the strongest claim. First, Aigai was still the capital of the Macedonian kingdom; and second, the play ended with an oracle on the foundation of Aigai. This last fact has led some scholars to opt for Aigai as the likely place for *Archelaos* to be performed. Harder opts for Dion instead, but the argument on which she based this choice is not persuasive. It consists of two parts: on the one hand, the notion of an ancient festival at Aigai is not secure, while on the other, at Dion we hear of Archelaos founding the dramatic festival Olympia in honor of Zeus and the Muses "probably meant in imitation of similar Greek festivals and part of Archelaos' attempts at Hellenization. So the idea that a play celebrating Archelaos' Greek descendance was produced at these Olympia is rather attractive."[91]

Recent finds from the archaic and early classical period at Aigai and elsewhere have shown that the rather simplistic concept of fifth-century Hellenization needs radical redefinition. The remains of the Vergina theater are to be dated in the fourth century.[92] But I wonder whether further research may not reveal an earlier phase, in which wood had played an even more important role than in the present theater.[93] For, given especially Archelaos' interest in the theater, it is perhaps less likely that theatrical performances only began to take place at Aigai after the capital had moved to Pella—which may have been late in Archelaos' reign.

Euripides' *Archelaos* articulates the myth that connected the audience, through its king, who was the tragedy's patron, to the Panhellenic mythological web, the myth according to which the Macedonian kings were descended from Heracles. In terms of Greek mythological mentality, kings define kingdoms—unless otherwise stated. Thus the articulation of the notion that the Macedonian royal house was descended from Heracles gave the Macedonians a place in the mythological map of the Greek heroic age; it did not simply involve the glorification of Archelaos, as rationalizing modern readings have tended to assume.[94]

According to Macedonian foundation myths, the Macedonian royal house was descended from an exiled Argive, a descendant of Temenos, who was a descendant of Heracles. In Herodotos this founder is a descendant of Temenos called Perdikkas.[95] In Euripides' *Archelaos* he is a son of Temenos called Archelaos. Some of the myths about the "early history" of Macedonia involve a Delphic oracle connecting the foundation of Aigai with goats (*aiges*).[96] Apollo is the most suitable deity to command the foundation of Aigai because he is the deity whose oracles guided Greek colonization,[97] and who came to be perceived in the Greek representations as the guide par excellence for city foundations. It is a culturally determined misunderstanding to see such stories in terms of crude political propaganda; the deployment of such a myth says something about perceived relationships at the time when the myth is deployed. This aspect of myth, as constructed history with a direct relevance to the present, may, but need not, include an element based on actual past historical events.[98] Such myths articulate what was perceived to have been the past that shaped the present. Thus, not only Thucydides mentions as a fact[99] that the ancestors of the Macedonian king were Temenidai from Argos, but also elsewhere[100] he states that Perdikkas' political decisions about alliances in the present were influenced by the fact of his Argive descent. The opposition "myth vs. history" is not relevant to Greek mentality. "History" was not perceived to be more true and more valid that the "mythological history" which constructed images of the heroic past articulating, among other things, perceptions of one's identity, relationships to others and place in the world—in terms of local relationships, in the Panhellenic map, with regard to the non-Hellenic world and above all, in terms of relationships to the gods and heroes that were implicated in this mythological history and are part of the present, as shapers of the past (including through the foundation of cults), and recipients of cult.

Chapter 2: Setting Out the Distances

The story articulated in *Archelaos* is that Archelaos, son of Temenos, was exiled from Argos by his brothers; he went to king Kisseus of Thrace who was at war and promised Archelaos his kingdom and his daughter if Archelaos helped him against his enemies. Archelaos defeated these enemies, but Kisseus reneged and plotted to kill Archelaos. However, the latter, alerted by a slave of the king about Kisseus' plotting, killed Kisseus instead. He then fled to Macedonia, led by a goat, according to a command of Apollo (who probably appeared as a *deus ex machina*)[101] and founded the city of Aigai, named after the goat.

Thus, this tragedy involved the same zooming and the same modality of legitimating institutions for the Macedonians and especially the court and the other inhabitants of Aigai—wherever it may have been performed; the zooming would have been especially striking if in fact *Archelaos* was performed at Aigai.

It is possible, I submit, to detect also other zoomings to the audience's reality, cultic reality, even in the not very considerable fragments of the tragedy that survive. It is especially significant for the manipulation of the distances that there was a zooming to the audience's reality, cultic reality, towards the beginning, in fr. 2A lines 19-22 where Archelaos, who speaks the Prologue, after the sweep of Panhellenic myth involved in his recital of his family history and before he has revealed who he is, tells the audience that his father Temenos, who was childless, went to consult the oracle of Dodona about having children, and there the cult servant of Dione told him that Zeus will give him a son, whom he must call Archelaos. To an Athenian audience it would seem strange that Temenos should have gone to Dodona from Argos, rather than to the much nearer and more famous Delphic oracle, the oracle which other Euripidean characters consulted about their childlessness.[102] But for the Macedonian audience the Dodona oracle would have been the more familiar choice because of its (relative) geographical proximity and the fact that it belonged to the same cultural milieu. Thus the mention of the Dodona oracle and of Dione, Zeus' *paredros* at Dodona, would have zoomed the world of the play to this particular audience's world.

Furthermore, I would like to suggest that there may be another possible zooming to the cultic reality of the court of Archelaos and the Macedonians, and the inhabitants of Aigai in particular. In Euripides' *Hippolytos* there are six mentions of *eukleia* or *euklees*, and this is considered to be an especially dense pattern of appearance of this concept, a fact which, it is argued, has a special significance, contributing to the creation of certain meanings in the tragedy.[103] As for the other extant tragedies by Euripides, there are six mentions of *eukleia* or *euklees* in *Heracles* also, five mentions in *Alcestis*, three each in *Iphigeneia at Aulis*, *Phoinissai*, and *Medea*, two each in *Heraklidai*, *Helen*, and *Andromache*, and one each in *Ion*, *Suppliants*, and *Orestes*.[104] Only 109 more or less complete and intelligible verses survive of the *Archelaos*, and among these there are four mentions of *eukleia* or *euklees*, three of which express variations on the notion that one must work hard to gain *eukleia*, while the fourth speaks of *euklea phatin*.[105] This importance of *eukleia* in this version of the Macedonian foundation myth can be seen as correlative with the fact that in this version—unlike that in Herodotos 8.137-9—victory in war is a crucial part of the story of the Temenid founder of the Macedonian dynasty.

The fact that there was so much stress on *eukleia* and the attainment of *eukleia* at an early part of the tragedy, combined with the fact that this concept was especially relevant to the central character Archelaos, who had been exiled from his native city and needed to win *eukleia*, and who had in fact won it (but the treacherous king planned death for him, instead of the reward he had promised, which would have acknowledged this *eukleia*), may lead us to expect that Archelaos' attainment of *eukleia* would be stressed and celebrated at the end of the play. The established Greek modality for stressing and celebrating the attainment of *eukleia* after military victory is through the foundation of a cult of *Eukleia*. Thus the Athenians built a temple to *Eukleia* as a thanksoffering after the victory at Marathon.[106] It is far from implausible, then, that the foundation of a cult of *Eukleia* at Aigai was mentioned in Apollo's speech that commands the foundation of Aigai.

This is, of course, speculation. But is it a coincidence the cult of *Eukleia* was a most important cult at Aigai, located at about eighty meters distance from the theater, to the north,[107] the direction toward which the theater opened up, and, according to the excavator, probably connected to the theater through a road starting at the theater's west side?[108] In its present form, the shrine of Eukleia at Vergina dates from the end of the third century B.C., but tests have shown that it had been built on earlier remains;[109] the date of the beginning of the cult is unclear, but that the cult of *Eukleia* at Aigai predated the present shrine was in any case clear from the fact that two statue bases bear the dedicatory inscription "Eurydice daughter of Sirra, to Eukleia,"[110] and one of the bases has been associated with a statue of about 340 B.C. which puts the identification of the dedicator with Philip's mother Eurydice beyond doubt.[111]

If the hypothesis of a reference to the foundation of a cult of *Eukleia* is right, it would have zoomed the tragedy very strongly to the audience's cultic reality, especially if the play had been performed at Ai-

Chapter 2: Setting Out the Distances

gai, with the shrine in the immediate vicinity of the theater. But even if no such cult foundation had been predicted in the tragedy, a lot had been made in that tragedy in connection with Archelaos, the founder of the dynasty and of the city, of a concept correlative with a deity whose cult was important to the royal house and to Aigai; so, even if the play had not spoken of the foundation of the cult of *Eukleia* at Aigai, the audience would have constructed the connection with the cult, and thus zoomed it to its own cultic reality.

Whether or not this is right, I suggest that it is clear that this tragedy that had been written for the Macedonians would have, like those written for Athens—the context in which the modality had been initially developed—articulated a story that was relevant to the audience's present, which was shaped by the past represented in the tragedy, and in certain places zoomed the world of the play to the audience's reality, especially its cultic reality.[112] Here too, the relationship of the world of the audience to that of the tragedy was governed by a double perspective: it was both other and part of the audience's past in the heroic age and by virtue of that of its present. In the course of the play the distance between the two was manipulated through zooming devices and—presumably also—distancing devices.

I.2.v. *Preferred Setting and Religious Exploration; Universality and its Construction*

If this analysis is correct, the fact that tragedy would have been operating through the same modality when outside Athens supports the validity and importance of this modality I am suggesting.

In part II I will be arguing that this double perspective governing the distances between the world of the audience and the world of the tragedy in fifth-century tragedy had first been set in place in the ritual context in which tragedy was generated. In particular, that the particular version of that double perspective that was to become the preferred option of setting, the setting in the heroic age, had originated in the ritual context in which "prototragedy" had developed. That preferred option involved a setting removed from the present, but which was also part of the present in varying degrees of closeness (depending, for example, on whether the setting is Athens or somewhere else), since important aspects of the present, such as cults, were perceived as having originated in the heroic age. On the one hand that world was distanced, other, a different sort of world in which men walked with gods, shaped today's world, and eventually could become cult recipients; on the other hand, they were an important part of the audience's world, of the audience's present, precisely because they were cult recipients, they had shaped the world of the present.

The fact that this setting became the preferred option, and that a form of double perspective was not abandoned in the successful experimentations with other settings, suggests first, that this double perspective was of fundamental importance in the perceived nature of tragedy, and second, that the particular version involved in the preferred option answered the perceived "needs" of the genre better than any other. I will be arguing in chapter II.2 that religious exploration was one of the important factors that led to the generation of prototragedy and the development of tragedy. In this chapter we saw that this type of complex and shifting distancing allowed religious exploration, exploration of areas in Greek religion which could have been perceived as potentially or actually problematic. For the double perspective of the heroic setting, and the shifting of the distances through the use of zooming and distancing devices, allowed the exploration of problems to take place at a distance, so that the explorations were not symbolically threatening to the audience, but at the same time it allowed them to be relevant to the audience's realities. There is, then, a close relationship between religious explorations, and the other explorations that (on my reconstruction) were modelled on it, and the double perspective and the complex type of distancing governing the relationships between the world of the audience and the world of the tragedies.

The notion that distancing and religious exploration were closely related may gain some support from the following consideration. Religious exploration in tragedy involves, among other things, an exploration of the darker side of the gods. This side is articulated, in order to be explored, and in one way or another "made sense of."[113] I mentioned in chapter I.1 that there is a perceived "discrepancy" between the more positive presentation of the gods in oratory and comedy and the darker one in tragedy, and that Parker has persuasively argued that the differences result from the different contexts which involve different constraints and requirements, generating different characteristics in the genres.[114] I would suggest that the differences in distancing are of fundamental importance as far as the differences between tragedy and comedy are concerned. Comedy takes place in the here and now, and presents itself as part of the world of the audience; and comedy has an optimistic presentation of the positive side of the gods' perceived behavior towards mortals.[115] Even though, we shall see,[116] the gods of comedy were perceived as comic constructs, rather than representations of the gods, their relationship with the city of Athens in the present was presented in optimistic terms. I would argue that the correlation

Chapter 2: Setting Out the Distances 47

between on the one hand the stress on the positive in the gods and the elision of distance between the world of the play and that of the audience, and on the other the exploration of darkness and the shifting distances governed by the double perspective between the world of the play and that of the audience in tragedy is significant. If this is right it would suggest that the darkness in religion can only be articulated, and explored, at a distance, which may perhaps give a little support to the view that the setting of tragedy, and its double perspective, was closely related to the fact that (on my thesis) tragedy began as a locus of religious exploration and developed into a locus of exploration both of religious issues, and of issues such as the place of man in the cosmos and related concepts such as free will, fate, social relationships, and so on, all of which were, in Greek perceptions, closely intertwined with religion.[117]

Let me now return to the question of the universality of tragedy which I broached in chapter I.1. A question may arise, as to whether the universality of Greek tragedy can be reconciled with my thesis that an important aspect of tragedy in fifth-century eyes was that it was a locus of religious exploration, since such exploration would inevitably have been culture specific, relevant only to Greek religion. Clearly, some aspects pertaining to Greek religion and the problems involved in it, such as the problem of the limits, if any, to free will, and its relationship to the notion of preordained fate, are "universal" in the sense that they arise in a variety of religious and cosmological systems, and though some religious systems give more definite answers than others, the problematization has resonances for all. Thus, modern readers reading tragedies through perceptual filters shaped by entirely different assumptions can relate to these resonances, while underplaying, for example, the role of the Delphic oracle, implicitly treating it as though it were simply a textual device. But there are other religious matters that are specifically focussed on Greek religion. The question of human sacrifice, for example, involves, we saw, the problematization of the dark side of the gods. Again, read through modern assumptions, this can be interpreted as "criticism" of the gods; and the issues that have wider resonances, such as death in war, duty to one's community or family, or the sacrifice of one for the good of the many, can be placed at the center of a modern reading.

I will illustrate the way universality is constructed by modern readers, through the underplaying of some aspects of the tragedies, the stressing of others, and the structuring of the interpretations through preconceived assumptions, at the expense of the religious explorations that tragedy involved in ancient eyes, by summarizing what, I have argued elsewhere, has happened in the case of Sophocles' *Antigone*.[118]

Modern commentators have read this tragedy through the perceptual model of the individual obeying her conscience in opposing the state in the interests of a just cause, a reading very different from those of the ancient audience who, unlike modern ones, did not privilege individual rights and freedom and suspicion of the state but, on the contrary, shared assumptions in which the interests of the polis were paramount. This (and other elements) made Kreon a true representative of the polis in the opening scene. Modern commentators also underestimated the complexity of the issue of burial and of Kreon's error, when perceived through ancient eyes. For what Kreon did wrong was not that he denied burial to Polyneikes, but that he left his corpse exposed on the plain, neither throwing it out of the frontiers, so that others could bury it, nor handing it over symbolically to the nether gods by disposing of it, for example by throwing it into the pit, as the Athenians did in certain circumstances. So he kept in the upper world something that belonged to the nether gods, and so offended all the gods and disturbed the cosmic order.

Those two culturally determined readings (among many others, but these two crucially) led to a misunderstanding of what, on my reading, was a central issue in the tragedy for the fifth-century Athenians: the problematization of the limits of, the dangers of errors being committed by, the religious discourse of the polis, a problem explored at a distance, through (as well as zooming devices that made it relevant to the present) distancing devices that made at crucial points Kreon tyrannical, and the Thebes of the play distanced from the Athens of the audience.

This suggests that when Greek tragedies are read as floating texts, divorced from their audience and context of production, and so by default through the perceptual filters of other cultures, they yield simplified and distorted versions of the meanings which they had in the eyes of the fifth-century audience, meanings from which the religious explorations have been written out. I believe that the fact that religious exploration was a very culture-specific aspect of tragedy is one of the reasons why the role of religion in Greek tragedy has been underplayed by modern readers.

Of course, this is not to deny all universality to Greek tragedy. On the contrary; the fact that such universality can be constructed out of these culture-specific dramas is because the ways in which they deal with such problems makes them partly transcend their culture-specific matrix. I would suggest that this universality is correlative with the fact that, on my reconstruction, all problematizing in tragedy arose out of, and was modelled on, religious problematization which involved major human issues. Religious problematization partly involved ques-

Chapter 2: Setting Out the Distances

tions, or aspects of questions, that transcend the culture specific, and partly it was culture specific (in the sense of involving issues particular to Greek religion, not to the particular circumstances of the tragedy's production at a particular moment in the fifth century, though these circumstances may have generated interest in the issues). For example, the limits to the polis discourse and the ultimate unknowability of the divine will is culture specific to this religion which had no revelation, or dogma, or canonical body of beliefs, no scriptural texts, and no professional divinely anointed priesthood claiming a special knowledge or authority.

These religious explorations took place at a distance, and they set the parameters for all other explorations, for example of issues pertaining to human relationships, which also therefore took place at a distance, in a heroic past that was in significant ways other than the present. Thus, everything was handled in a more generic, non-moment-specific way, an idiom which facilitated the construction of universality as defined here.[119] These parameters were so firmly in place, that when experimentations with other settings took place these included the double perspective of a world distanced, but also part of the world of the audience; what seems to have been an experimentation with a setting that did not was deemed to be transgressive.

To sum up some of the main points. In the audience's assumptions the relationship between the world of the audience and the world of the tragedy in the preferred option in which the setting was the heroic age was governed by a double perspective. On the one hand it was distanced, other, a different sort of world in which men walked with gods, shaped today's world, and eventually became cult recipients in the world of the present; on the other hand, they were an important part of the audience's world, of the audience's present precisely because they were cult recipients, they had shaped the world of the present, and so on. It was these assumptions, shared by the audience, that set the parameters of the way in which they made sense of each tragedy in performance. The tragedy itself manipulated the distance between the world of the audience and the world of the tragedy, through the deployment of zooming devices and distancing devices, so that the distance shifted throughout the play. Sometimes the distance was increased, the otherness of the world of the play stressed; this on the one hand allowed unpleasant things to be explored at a safe symbolic distance, without threatening the audience's world, and on the other allowed, for example, the representation, and thus the symbolic strengthening, of the foundation of institutions, above all cults, that were important in the present.

This notion assumes that, as I am arguing throughout this book, the performance and content of tragedies were not insulated from their religious framing; it was not a discrete unit, a purely theatrical experience, simply framed by ritual, which included gods simply as theatrical devices, but was itself perceived as a ritual occcasion to which ritual mentality pertained.[120] In the next section I offer a further argument in favor of this view.

I.2.vi. *Ritual Context, Tragic Performance and Permeability*

I will now set out an argument pertaining to the audience's perceptions of the relationship between the world of the audience and the world of tragedy as we can reconstruct them first on the basis of external evidence, and then, independently, on the basis of the internal evidence of the tragedies. The perceptions that concern us pertain to the identity of the chorus, the chorus' relationship qua chorus to the here and now. I will argue that in the eyes of the fifth-century audiences the tragic chorus was not only perceived as a group of people in the world of the play, in the present's past, but was also as a chorus, a group of male citizens acting as ritual performers, in the here and now, a chorus to Dionysos in the world of the present.

As many scholars have noted,[121] first, the terminology used by the Athenians to speak of tragedy places the chorus at the center, defines tragedy through the chorus; and second, the chorus remained central in the organization of the production. *Tragodoi* continues to be used to denote tragic performances in, for example, Aristophanes, Lysias, and Plato. Clearly, this does not mean that the chorus was perceived to be dramatically more important, especially given its decreasing role within tragedy. Consequently, this centrality may perhaps be reflecting the tragic chorus' importance in the wider context of the festival of Dionysos. Such an explanation in terms of the chorus' ritual importance would coincide with the ritual importance of choruses in Greek festivals in general. But were tragic choruses really also perceived as choruses in honor of Dionysos in the here and now? I believe that they were.

That the members of tragic as well as dithyrambic choruses had to be citizens,[122] and thus that they were, like other choruses, singing as representatives of the polis—while actors and poets could be foreigners—is one pointer in the direction of the perception of the tragic choruses as also ritual choruses in the here and now.[123] As Easterling has stressed,[124] in tragedy the chorus is never simply a group of bystanders or witnesses reacting and commenting; they are also a *choros* ready to perform lyrics patterned on ritual song and dance and accompanied by

Chapter 2: Setting Out the Distances

appropriate music, for example, a paean giving thanks for victory, as in the parodos of *Antigone*.[125] I would take this even further and suggest that, for example in the particular case of the parodos of *Antigone*, as the chorus processed in, singing a cult song the usual mode of performance of which was processional, it would have been very difficult for the audience not to perceive this hymn as being sung also in the real world of the here and now.[126] Then, there are choral passages in which references to *choroi* amount to choral self-referentiality,[127] in which choruses "draw attention to their ritual role as collective performers of the choral dance-song in the orchestra."[128]

In my view, such self-referentiality could not but have activated for the audience the chorus' identity as chorus in the present performing in honor of Dionysos.[129] The mask, while locating the chorus in the other world of the heroic past,[130] at the same time draws attention to the fact that the *choreutai* are not in fact "other," that their otherness is constructed, and located above all in the mask, while they are also, underneath the mask, a chorus of male Athenians in the present.

Another argument for the view that the identity of the chorus as a chorus in the here and now, though subordinated, was not wholly neutralized, is provided by Plato *Laws* 800C-801A. Plato expresses his disapproval of the fact that, as he puts it, after a public sacrifice many choruses, standing not far from the altars, pour blasphemies over the sacrifices by singing mournful songs and racking the souls of the listeners and making them cry. There can be no doubt that tragic choruses are the main choruses involved here; for it is tragedy and rhapsodic performances[131] that Plato elsewhere accuses of producing such effects on the listeners.[132] We need to reconstruct the common assumptions underlying Plato's idiosyncratic polarization,[133] the shared assumptions that have to be taken for granted for Plato's articulation to work. The most important of these emerges clearly: the fact that this idiosyncratic polarization was possible indicates that in the Athenian assumptions the tragic chorus was also perceived as a chorus in the present; for unless that was the case such a polarization would not make sense.

Even more strikingly, the Platonic image entails that it *could* be presented as being the case that the world of the present could be penetrated by the world of the tragedy, that the mourning songs *could* be presented as constituting blasphemy within the ritual performed in the here and now. This coincides with Easterling's observation that the fact that the world of the audience was permeable by that of the tragedy, that the latter was not insulated, is shown by the concern for *euphemia* in the tragedies, as illustrated, for example, by the fact that "in *Eumenides* when the Furies threaten to blight and poison the land, Athena always has a well-omened reply."[134] This is surely correlative with the fact that on the one hand the performance is part of a ritual occasion in the present, and on the other what happens in the world of the play is also part of the world of the audience, since it happened in its heroic past, in which were laid the foundations of the polis' relationships with the divine world.

Another argument in favor of the view that the chorus was also perceived as a chorus in the present may be provided by the floating tailpieces addressing Nike and requesting a prize in Euripides' *Orestes*, *Iphigeneia in Tauris*, and *Phoinissai*, especially if they were Euripidean.[135]

If tragic choruses were indeed also perceived, albeit not as dominantly, as choruses for Dionysos in the present, it follows that in the fifth century tragic performances were not perceived as ritual only in the sense that they were part of the festival of Dionysos and were framed by ritual; the tragedies themselves were shot through by ritual, not only insofar as ritual acts were important in the action in the other world enacted by the tragedy, but also, most importantly, it was shot through by ritual performed in the present; so tragedy itself could not have been perceived as other than fundamentally religious.

I must make clear that, on my argument, there can be little doubt that for the audience the perception that what happened in the orchestra and the skene took place in the other world of the tragedy was dominant. But I am arguing that this was not the only perception, and that there was, at certain points, both a less dominant perception of the chorus as a chorus also in the here and now, and also of a certain permeability between the two worlds. A question that is intertwined with this is what may be called the precise status of this mimetic performance, its relationship of similarities to, and differences from, mimetic performances of a "straightforward" ritual kind, so-called sacred dramas in which divinities were impersonated by priestly personnel. In order to try even to begin to answer this question it is necessary to investigate first the ritual context in which tragedy was generated. I will set out this investigation in part II, and will return to this question in part III.

The investigation of the ritual context in which tragedy emerged is also necessary for another reason. It might be objected to the remarks made above that comedy should make us cautious about concluding that the identity of the tragic chorus as a chorus for Dionysos in the here and now can be considered an argument in favor of a ritual nature of tragedy that would go together with the notion that tragedy can be seen as a religious discourse. Comedy's metatheatricality, the fact that the identity of the comic chorus as a chorus in a festival of Di-

Chapter 2: Setting Out the Distances

onysos in the here and now is stressed, especially in the parabasis, and that comedy can refer to itself as the *patrioi teletai tou Dionysou*,[136] does not entail that representations of the gods in comedy were accurate reflections of the real gods of lived religion. On the contrary, it is precisely this metatheatricality that allows them to be perceived as comic constructs, which can thus be irreverently depicted,[137] in the same way that the presentation on stage of what purports to be the Thesmophoria in Aristophanes' *Thesmophoriazousai* is possible because the play's strong metatheatricality foregrounds its character as a comic construct—not a representation of the festival. So how can we be sure that something comparable is not operating in tragedy?

Obviously, one answer is that our readings show that the gods in tragedy, when perceived through the audience's religious assumptions, were indeed constructed as representations of the real gods of cult. However, we need to test those readings for cultural determination; and we also need to explain why a different situation should pertain in comedy, if we are to be able to use the ritual nature of the tragedies as an argument in favor of the view that tragedy was also seen as a religious discourse. In order to achieve both these aims it is necessary to investigate the ritual contexts in which comedy and especially tragedy were generated.

This is one of the several reasons why, as we saw in the last chapter, it is important not to neglect the question of the origins of tragedy, and attempt to explore the ritual context in which tragedy was generated.

Notes

1. That we know of.
2. Herodotos 6.21.
3. On the date cf. the discussion in Rosenbloom 1993, 170-2.
4. Cf. also *TrGF* i 3 T 10f, T 14.
5. Rosenbloom 1993, 159-96 with earlier bibliography.
6. Calame 1995, 113 describes this as Aeschylus substituting a geographical and actorial distance for the temporal distance of myth by focussing the action not on the Athenians but on the Persians.
7. On Phrynichos: Lloyd-Jones 1990, 230-7. On Phrynichos' *Phoinissai* probably being different from, but probably part of the same trilogy as, his *Dikaioi* (*The Just Ones*), or *Persai* or *Synthokoi* (*The Counsellors*) [*TrGF* i 3 F 4a], see Lloyd-Jones 1990, 233-4. Bowie 1997, 39-42 (who surveys briefly "historical tragedies" in the sense of tragedies referring specifically to particular recent events—a category that is therefore much broader than mine, since it is

concerned with references rather than the setting of the play) believes that it cannot be excluded that the subject of this tragedy may have been mythological rather than historical.

8. Cf. Hall 1989, 64 and n. 27.

9. I will not include post-fifth-century tragedies (such as, for example, Theodektas *TrGF* i 72 F 3b or *TrGF* ii Adespota F 733), since I believe that tragedy in the fourth century became a different thing from tragedy in the fifth century, which (and its antecedents) is my concern here.

10. *TrGF* i 4 F 9.

11. Parker 1983, 209.

12. Sourvinou-Inwood 1997b, 155-9.

13. *TrGF* Adespota (vol. ii) F 664 (*Gyges*?) with bibliography and views on possible date.

14. Cf. *TrGF* Adespota F 664. Hall 1989, 65 calls it "post-fifth-century" (cf. op. cit. n. 67 for a discussion of the date).

15. ARV 571. 74; Add 261; to which add Taplin 1993, 7 pl. 7.119A; cf. *TrGF* Adespota (vol. ii) F 5e.

16. Beazley 1955, 319.

17. Cf. Hall 1989, 65.

18. Page 1962, 47-9.

19. Page 1962, 49 argued that the fall of Kroisos would have been the retribution for the actions of Kandaules and the Queen in the *Gyges*; this may well be right, but it may also be a culturally determined judgment, influenced by Herodotos 1. 13.

20. Hall 1989, 65 considers both Gyges' story and Kroisos' story to be indistinguishable from myth for the Athenians of the mid-fifth century. I am inclined to think that there were certain distinctions in the perceptions of distances, as I am trying to outline here.

21. Aristotle *Poetics* 1451b19-26.

22. *TrGF* i 39 F 2a.

23. Without going into his whole complex argument about poetry and history, which would take us too far afield from our concerns.

24. *TrGF* i 39 F 2a. In Parthen. 14 Antheus, a youth from Halikarnassos, was sent as hostage to Phobios, a Neleid who ruled Miletos.

25. I cannot see any reason for imagining that the fragment *TrGF* Adespota F 646 came from a fifth-century tragedy with a historical subject.

26. Cf. *TrGF* ad loc. It refers to the Lydians in fr. 1 and has in fr. 3.1 *o genos Persǫn* and in 3.3 *basilea emon*; this suggests that someone is probably looking back to the Lydians from a Persian perspective. On this fragment see now also Hall 1996b, 8.

27. Thus, even in the case of Phrynichos it would seem that in the majority of his tragedies the setting was that of the heroic age, to judge by the fact that of the ten of his tragedies we know about seven were set in the mythological past (*Aigyptioi, Aktaion, Alkestis, Antaios* or *Libyes, Danaides, Pleuroniai, Tantalos*).

Chapter 2: Setting Out the Distances

28. Insofar as we are able to judge from the fragmentary information available to us this would appear beyond doubt.

29. Cf. a comparable perception in Easterling 1997b, 167-8 who rightly says that aetiologies in drama function as a device for making the audience aware of more than one plane of reality since what is laid down is already part of the audience's history and present. She also rightly notes that such patterns are established with great solemnity, and are not to be seen as antiquarian oddities or signs of passing playfulness.

30. Lysias 30, *Against Nikomachos*, 18.

31. Which I have discussed in Sourvinou-Inwood 1990a, 303-4.

32. To a varying degree, as I am arguing in chapter III.4.

33. Aristotle *Poetics* 1449 b 28.

34. In *Poetics* 1453 a 7.

35. Sourvinou-Inwood 1989a, 134-48.

36. On the ancient audience's complex perceptions of Dareios' ghost see below chapter III.1, the discussion of *Persai*.

37. Cf. e.g. Else 1965, 63.

38. See on this myth Sourvinou-Inwood 1989b, 141-65; West 1983, 63-71.

39. Cf. Zeitlin 1990, 130-67 [=Zeitlin 1986, 101-41]; Easterling 1989, 13-14; Zeitlin 1993, 147-82; cf. also Sourvinou-Inwood 1989a, 134-48 passim.

40. Sourvinou-Inwood 1989a, 144.

41. Cf. bibliography on *Erechtheus* and a short survey of discussions in Collard, Cropp, and Lee 1995, 147-55. I will not engage with the view that Euripides "undercuts" the play's religious values; I am considering this type of approach to Euripides in chapter III.3 below; as for *Erechtheus*, I suggest that this position collapses when an attempt is made to reconstruct the audience's perceptual filters and make sense of the play through them, as is selectively illustrated here—even before account is taken of the ancient reception as illustrated by Lykourgos, *Leocr*. 100-101 (cf. also Collard, Cropp, and Lee 1995, 154-5).

42. Fragment 41 Austin 1968 (fr. 351 in Collard, Cropp, and Lee 1995). Cf. also, on *Erechtheus*: Austin 1967, 11-67. The translation is my own.

43. Cf. e.g. the discussion in Stewart 1990, 157-8.

44. Cf. e.g. Homer *Il*. 21.400-1.

45. Cf. Collard, Cropp, and Lee 1995, 155 with bibliography; cf. also Austin 1967, 17.

46. Cf. Thuc. iii. 2, 26, 89 (cf. also Hornblower 1991, ad loc. [pp. 381, 409, 497]); iv.2, 6.

47. Fr. 50 Austin = Collard, Cropp, and Lee 1995, fr. 360.

48. For Loraux 1990, 46-7, 57-66 the tragedies are articulating the mothers' grief, which civic discourse fears and tries to suppress, while Praxithea had other priorities and is not a tragic mother (p. 63). But, I am arguing, the situation is more complex than that. Everyone, including mothers, partook, to a greater or lesser extent, of a whole spectrum of attitudes, including that of the polis ideology about death to save the city. If a polis leader delivering an *epitaphios* stands at the most civic, grief-denying, polis-privileging spectrum of attitudes, the figure of the mother stands at the other end; but this does not entail that

mothers did not share in the polis ideology, or that the notion of private grief is truly denied in the polis discourse—as opposed to marginalized in certain contexts, while in others it is expressed through the figure of the mothers, to whom this concept of private grief has drifted. I have discussed a comparable drift to women of the fear of death in fifth-century Athenian polis ideology in Sourvinou-Inwood 1995, 344-6. Praxithea is very much a tragic mother, only one that represents attitudes at a different end of the spectrum from most other tragic mothers. This is correlative with the fact that in the figure of Praxithea we have both a mother and someone who will become a first priestess, a paradigmatic figure of a priestess.

49. I discussed this in Sourvinou-Inwood 1990a, 304-5.

50. Collard, Cropp, and Lee 1995, 370K.

51. In the Hyakinthides cf. Kearns 1989, 59-63; 201-2; Larson 1995, 20, 101-6 passim.

52. Hansen 1983, 10, line 5.

53. On the heroization and immortality of the Athenian war dead and the epitaph for the men who died in the battle of Poteidaia, cf. Sourvinou-Inwood 1995, 194, 202 (cf. also op. cit. on the extension of such immortality to ordinary dead people in the fourth century).

54. On Aglauros and her connection with ephebes: Kearns 1990, 330-1, 338; Kearns 1989, 139-40, 24-7; Larson 1995, 39-41.

55. See below chapter III.3.

56. With the help of a few interpretations of a few Bronze Age archaeological data which I consider perverse, because inspired by the desire to match archaeologically such historicist interpretations of myths.

57. I have discussed this notion of schemata in Sourvinou-Inwood 1991, 247, 246-61 passim; Sourvinou-Inwood 1989a, 136-7, 145.

58. On human sacrifice see esp. Henrichs 1981, 195-235; Hughes 1991; Bonnechere 1994; Kearns 1990, 323-44; Burkert 1983, 58-67.

59. These myths have, of course, a variety of other meanings also, but these are not relevant to our concerns here. I have discussed some of those meanings with reference to Iphigeneia in Sourvinou-Inwood 1990b, 52-8; and in more detail in a book in preparation (*Women, Religion and Tragedy*).

60. Cf. op. cit. (previous note).

61. Cf. also my brief discussion in Sourvinou-Inwood 1997a, 184-6.

62. In other human sacrifices in Euripides the patriotic ideology of dying for one's polis has been modified into a self-sacrificing choice to die for one's group, be it narrower than the polis, as in the case of Heracles' daughter who dies to save her family in *Heracleidai* or wider, Panhellenic, as in *IA*, where Iphigeneia is replaced by an animal. In the transformation of the "virgin sacrifice to save the city" schema in Euripides' *Phoinissai*, (on which see Mastronarde 1994, 392-3; Larson 1995, 107-9) Menoikeus, in explaining why he cannot but choose to sacrifice himself to save the city, compares his choice to the choices made by the

Chapter 2: Setting Out the Distances 57

young men who were fighting to save the city without shrinking from death (999-1005). I discuss Menoikeus and *Phoinissai* in chapter III.3 below.

63. Cf. also below and bibliography in n. 83 on the patriotic ideology associated with human sacrifice.

64. Before moving on to consider the case of *Iphigeneia in Tauris*, the setting of which is the mirror image of that of *Erechtheus*, a barbarian land as opposed to the very center of Athens, it is perhaps necessary to say something briefly about one version of Iphigeneia's sacrifice in a tragedy which appears "unresolved," in the sense that she dies, and her sacrifice is a savage butchery inflicted upon her by her father. However, though most scholars think that she was meant to have died in Aeschylus' *Agamemnon*, I have argued elsewhere (in a book in preparation, *Women, Religion and Tragedy*) that this is wrong, that this is a culturally determined reading; that the tragedy left it open whether or not she did; though the characters in the play think she has died; for this was necessary to the plot which had Klytemestra presenting her murder of Agamemnon as revenge for their daughter's sacrifice. But that the audience, making sense of the tragedy through religious assumptions in which Iphigeneia had survived and become priestess of Artemis at Brauron, a fact which, I am arguing, was evoked by the description of the sacrifice in Aeschylus' *Agamemnon*, would have understood her to have survived. The same is true, in my view, of Pindar's allusion to the sacrifice in *Pythian* 11.17-25: Klytemestra certainly believed that Iphigeneia had died, but that would have been the case even if in reality Artemis had replaced the girl with an *eidolon*. It is clear that in *Iphigeneia in Tauris* Iphigeneia was believed by the Greeks to have died when she was sacrificed (cf. lines 563-6, 770-2, 783-6).

65. Which I will discuss in greater detail in chapter III.3.

66. In Sourvinou-Inwood 1997a, 171-5, in the context of a wider argument (op. cit. 161-86) setting out the many reasons why it is wrong to doubt that the gods in tragedy were perceived by the audience as the same gods as those they worshiped.

67. Cf. Kearns 1989, 27-33; Lloyd-Jones 1983, 91-6, 174; Brulé 1987, 179-222; Kontis 1967, 160-4; Sourvinou-Inwood 1990b, 52-4.

68. For the torch-bearing Artemis, the iconographical representation of Artemis with the epithet Phosphoros, is one of the most frequently encountered types among the votives, especially votive reliefs, found in the Brauron sanctuary (see e.g. Kahil 1983, 233), which shows that this persona of Artemis was important in the Brauronian cult as it was in the goddess' Mounichian sanctuary, which was intimately associated with that of Brauron (on Phosphoros at Brauron see Kahil 1979, 77-8; at Mounichia: Palaiokrassa 1991, 36-8, 52-3, 91, 95).

69. In the heroon of Iphigeneia at Brauron, associated with a cave identified as her grave, cult appears to have begun at c. 700 (see Themelis 1971, 24-6). Since she was believed to have been buried there, and the successive structures associated with a cave would fit the configuration of a heroon associated with a grave, doubting the identification constitutes special pleading.

70. Cf. on this Platnauer 1938, 63-4 ad loc. and esp. Diggle 1994, 28-33 who excises 38-9 and reads *heortes* . . . *katarchomai*, "I consecrate the festival . . . while the infamous sacrifices are the care of others inside the temple" (p. 31).

71. On the meaning of *hapsetai phonou* see also Platnauer 1938, ad 382.

72. This passage is discussed by Wolff 1992, 309-12, who sees it as Iphigeneia's "effort to regenerate the goddess Artemis," which is "incomplete and compromised" (312). What I am suggesting is that the fifth-century audience, making sense of this passage through perceptual filters shaped by their particular religious and cultural assumptions, would see it as an exploration that may well be right.

73. Pindar, *Ol*. 1. 23ff.

74. Cf. on this Nagy 1986, 83-8; Sourvinou-Inwood 1986, 44-5.

75. For the text see Platnauer 1938 ad 466.

76. That Iphigeneia had already practiced human sacrifice is clear; cf. e.g. lines 38, 347; 621-2.

77. Lines 1089ff.

78. Cf. Platnauer 1938, 152-3 on the various references.

79. On the text cf. Platnauer 1938, ad 1116.

80. This part of the play has been recently discussed by Wolff 1992, 312-24, 330-1 (with extensive bibliography).

81. Cf. also on this rite and associated perceptions Graf 1979, 33-41; Lloyd-Jones 1983, 96-7, 89-100; Hughes 1991, 81. On the cult of Artemis at Halai Araphenides cf. also Bonnechere 1994, 48-52. I return to some of the questions that have been raised in connection with Athena's speech in chapter III.3 and its appendix. There I will be discussing the theory that the real-life cults of Artemis at Halai and Brauron differed significantly from the ways in which they are presented in *IT*, and I will also be considering in detail the theory that aetiologies and gods in epiphany can be seen simply as closure devices, in the context of the overall consideration of Euripidean tragedies, since some of the arguments depend on evidence that will be reconstructed in the course of that discussion.

82. Cf. previous note.

83. The patriotic ideology associated with human sacrifice is discussed in Loraux 1985, 76-82; Bonnechere 1994, 261-9; Larson 1995, 103-6; Wilkins 1990, 177-94. Bonnechere 1994, 260-72 has an interesting discussion on human sacrifice in Euripides. But he thinks (261) that Euripides manipulated old myths to galvanize the young around the ideology of glorious death for one's country, and (270-1) presented a failure of the polis ideals, a situation of decadence in which only the self-sacrificing victims stand above the rest, because his main intention was to revive the spirit that had made Athens great thirty years before. There are many objections to this approach. I will mention three main problems. It is hardly revolutionary, these days, to doubt the value of the search for the author's intentions; two of the most obvious reasons for this position are, first, the fact that the author's intentions are beyond our grasp, never more so than in the case of the ancient tragedians; and second, that this approach is reductionist in assuming conscious decisions at every

Chapter 2: Setting Out the Distances

level. That is why it is advisable to focus on the audience; their assumptions, shared by the tragedian and his contemporaries, shaped their perceptual filters and so the parameters of determination governing the creation of meaning by the tragedian and the construction of meaning, the reading, by the audience. Second, such a monosemic reading inevitably forces a series of complex plays into a reductive matrix centered on a particular version of patriotic ideology. These readings are a priori, and so inevitably culturally determined, since they are not based on an attempt to reconstruct the process of meaning creation in each tragedy through filters shaped by the ancient assumptions. Hence the overprivileging of the "political" and the underprivileging of the religious. For such readings are implicitly based on the assumption that religion does not matter; that the ancient audience was not concerned about the question of human sacrifice, and will therefore see everything from the viewpoint of the polis ideology—the revitalization of which is conceived here as the object of the exercise. Space prevents me from going through all the relevant tragedies and demonstrating this. I will therefore only say that such a reading cannot make sense of the problematization of human sacrifice in *Iphigeneia in Tauris*, which is of crucial importance in this tragedy. Nor can it make sense of the ways in which polis ideology is deployed in *Erechtheus*, where the ideology of good death at war is partly a given and partly is itself explored in the complex ways suggested above. Insofar as it is a given, it helps explore human sacrifice: through the comparison of human sacrifice of a virgin to the glorious death of the war dead, what would appear to be the cruelty of the gods is deconstructed. Similarly, things that Bonnechere sees as elements suggestive of a recession or destabilization of the religious dimension are, I would suggest, when seen through filters shaped by ancient Greek assumptions, the opposite. Distrust of prophets is a manifestation of a common Greek attitude: the notion that the human agents in prophecy are flawed is what protected prophecy from invalidation in Greek mentality. The god always spoke true, but the human intermediary was sometimes flawed, either corrupt or inadequate, and that is why people could never know if a given prophecy was a true prophecy. In tragedy prophecies always come true; but that is part of the assumptions of the audience, it is knowledge in the world of the audience; in the world of the tragedy the characters do not know that is so; they are in exactly the same position as ordinary people are in everyday life.

   84. Cf. e.g. Kearns 1989, 57-63; Larson 1995, 8, 40-1, 101-6. In some versions of her myth Iphigeneia becomes immortal; for example, in the pseudo-Hesiodic Catalogue of Women fr. 23 a.15-26, she becomes Artemis *einodia*.
   85. On such plays see especially Easterling 1994, 73-80.
   86. On Aeschylus' *Aitn(ai)ai*: TrGF iii T 1.33-4; TrGF iii pp. 126-30 (F6-F11), Cf. also Taplin 1977, 416-8.
   87. Cf. the hypothesis in P.Oxy. 2257; TrGF iii pp. 126-7.
   88. TrGF iii T 1.33-4.
   89. Cf. testimonium 1 in Harder 1985, 145. Harder 1985, 125 n.1 has rightly argued against an automatic scepticism throwing doubt on a firmly established tradition without

any evidence to the contrary. (If my analyses are convincing, they will provide further arguments in support of the tradition.) On the date see Harder 1985, 125-6.

90. See Harder 1985, 126.

91. Harder 1985, 127.

92. On the Vergina theater see Andronikos 1984, 46-9; its exact date is difficult to determine (see *Egnatia* 1 [1989] 346-7).

93. Even in this theater only the first row of seats was made of stone.

94. That this genealogy was not just simply an elevation of Archelaos but was relevant to the Macedonians in general was also suggested by Harder 1985, 130.

95. Herodotos 8.137-9.

96. Harder 1985, 135-6; Parke and Wormell 1956, 1.63-4. In a different version the oracle is given to Karanos, son of Poeanthes, when he left Argos to find a colony in Macedonia (cf. Parke and Wormell 1956, 1.63-4; 2.92-3). The schema of an animal serving as some sort of guide is a well-established Greek mythological foundation schema; cf. also on this type of oracle Harder 1985, 174-5 (her commentary on test. 7.13-4) with bibliography; on oracles directing the foundation of cities under the direction of animal guides; see also Bowie 1993a, 154-6.

97. Malkin 1987, 17-91.

98. Another instance of a genealogical myth articulating the relationship between the Macedonians and the Greeks south of Olympos is the mytheme in the *Catalogue of Women* fr. 7 M-W, according to which a daughter of Deukalion, Thyia, had two sons from Zeus, Magnes and Macedon. The myths about Deukalion's descendants articulate the relationships between those who perceived themselves as Greeks. Greeks are, of course, placed at the center in this myth; and the genealogies express the perception that all Greek ethnic groups, the speakers of different Greek dialects, had a common descent, as well as a shared language. But the Macedonians and the Magnetes were marginal and inferior because they were descended from Deukalion's daughter, rather than his son Hellen, the eponymous hero of the Greek nation.

99. Thucydides 2.99.3; cf. Hornblower 1991, 375 ad loc.

100. Thucydides 5.80.2

101. Cf. Harder 1985, 174 ad testimonium 7.13.

102. Cf. e.g. Aigeus in *Medea* 667-9; Kreousa and Xouthos in *Ion* 64-7; *Phoenissae* 13-6.

103. Braund 1980, 184-5. (There is also one *dysklees* and one *aklees*.)

104. Cf. *Concordance* 254-5 s.v.

105. Fr. 237=11A Harder: 1.2: *euklees aner*; fr. 238=12A: *eukleian*; fr. 240=14A *euklees*; fr. 242=16A : *euklea . . . phatin*.

106. Paus. 1.14.5. On Eukleia cf. also Nilsson 1967, 493-4.

107. Andronikos 1984, 49.

108. Andronikos 1984, 46

109. *Ergon* 1987, 58; *ArchRep* 1988-9, 80. On the shrine of Eukleia cf. also Andronikos 1984, 49-51; *Egnatia* 2 (1990) 363-5; *Egnatia* 3 (1991-2) 238-42. The shrine may have been part of the Agora of Aigai (cf. *Egnatia* 2 [1990] 364; *Egnatia* 3 [1991-2] 241).
110. Cf. esp. *Ergon* 1990, 83-4 and figs. 116-8; cf. *ArchRep* 1982-3, 44; *ArchRep* 1983-4, 47 fig. 82.
111. Cf. *Ergon* 1990, 83-4.
112. Even if one adopts for the sake of the argument the most negative and culturally restrictive hypothesis, that only the royal family partook of Greek culture and the others did not share (which is becoming increasingly difficult to sustain for the fifth century), it was still valid for the royals—so, on that hypothesis the "audience" would have shrunk to the patron; but even for the alleged others, the world of the play would have been zoomed to the foundation of their town, and to a cult known to them, even if on this hypothesis they did not share in it.
113. We saw above how Artemis' association with human sacrifice and the practice of human sacrifice in myths in general was "resolved" in two tragedies. I will be considering other cases of "making sense" of comparable darkness in part III.
114. Parker 1997, 143-60.
115. Cf. Parker 1997, 143 and passim.
116. Cf. below this chapter, and esp. section II.2.ii.
117. Griffith 1995, 62-129, in an otherwise interesting article, has given a "political" interpretation of the persistance of the heroic setting, virtually writing off its religious significance with reference to the present. The following quotation illustrates the flavor of his approach (p. 116): "Given that tragedy reached its acme under the new democratic system of which the Athenians were so proud, the persistence throughout the fifth and fourth centuries of these elite oriented tragic plots is indeed quite remarkable." He sees tragic performances as on the one hand the elite's way of dramatizing their own continuing role of leadership, risk, and self-sacrifice, disguising it behind the royal figures from the past, and on the other the demos licensing their elites to stage out-of-control tyrants and doomed royal houses whose anonymous community recovers (cf. pp. 123-4). I cannot here discuss this interpretation in detail and unpick an argument that, even on its own terms, presents serious problems. For example, to give an illustration of this, his implicit claim that his interpretation is supported by the statement (p. 116), "Conspicuously lacking is any story involving the replacement of ancestral aristocratic-monarchical rule with a democratic sharing or alternation of power," relies on the underplaying of the construct of Theseus as a democratic king, and the complex ways in which this construct was deployed so that Theseus functioned as a locus of self-definition for the whole polis. Easterling 1997, 24 has already pointed out that the heroes had paradigmatic relationships with everyone, not simply the elites, and also that the place of the heroes in Athenian fifth-century religious life and art affected the way in which the past was perceived and the heroes made sense of in tragedy. I would go further and say that the type of schematic thinking required by Griffith's interpretation (royal families in the heroic past in some way corresponding to the

elites in the present) is not, in my view, compatible with what we know of the modalities of operation of the Greek mythological mentality, which centered on the specific and concrete, on an individual, or a family, or a whole community, a polis, not on a concept like "elite." What is compatible with that mentality is the connection of particular mythological heroes with certain families; and here this theory presents further problems. For we do not find the focus on such relationships that we would expect if the interpretation were correct, least of all do we find attempts at connecting the heroes of the past with Athenian elite families of the present. For example, let us take Ajax, whom Griffith mentions, and who is the most important Trojan hero connected with Athens (on Ajax in Attica cf. Kearns 1989, 81-2; 141-2; Kron 1976, 171-6; Shapiro 1981, 173-5). His descendants were alleged to have migrated to and settled in Athens (Sourvinou-Inwood 1974, 217-8; Humphreys 1990, 247). He was claimed as an ancestor by the Philaids, the genos of which Kimon was a member, through Philaios (on the Philaids see Herodotos vi. 35; Hellanikos FGrH 4F22; Pherekydes FGrH 3F2; Davies 1971, 294-312; cf. also 10-2), and by the Salaminioi, through Eurysakes (on the Salaminioi see Ferguson 1938, 1-74; Sourvinou-Inwood 1974, 217-8; Humphreys 1990, 243-48). If it is true that Ajax in tragedy would have been perceived not (as I believe was the case) as a Homeric hero in myth and a tribal hero in cult, but as a representative of the elite, where are the very many tragedies centering on Ajax that ought to have been produced during Kimon's heyday by the logic of the argument under discussion? And if tragedy had indeed been a locus for the elites to articulate their power in a heroic guise, given the modalities of operation of Greek mythology, given that Theseus was the major Athenian hero at that time, would we not have expected tragedy to have connected him to major families, and stressed, and played with, such a connection? Indeed, if it is right, as Barron persuasively proposed (Barron 1980, 2-3 and n. 30), that Pherekydes had suggested, in the context of Kimonian propaganda, that Ajax was the son of Theseus and Eriboia/Periboia/Phereboia, on Griffith's theory, tragedy ought to have stressed and celebrated this version in which Theseus was Kimon's ancestor. But tragedy did not operate in this way. Besides all these problems, Griffith's interpretation does not account for the stability of the double perspective (as described above) even when tragedy experimented with other settings; nor does it account for the fact that the distance between the world of the audience and world of play is not static in the tragedies, but shifts in ways that appear meaningful to the exploration of major problems, as is illustrated, for example, in the pattern of the relationship between distancing and darkness in religion. I hope that my arguments about the reasons behind these choices of setting are more persuasive.

118. Sourvinou-Inwood 1989a, 134-48; Sourvinou-Inwood 1989b, 141-65; cf. also Sourvinou-Inwood 1987-1988, 19-35.

119. Cf. Easterling 1997, 21-37 for the ways in which tragedians constructed this heroic setting. Cf. Easterling 1997, 25 for the notion of "heroic vagueness" which, she argues, makes it possible for plays to be understood as offering something for everyone in the audience, and that the fact "that political, legal and social issues are dealt with in language

Chapter 2: Setting Out the Distances 63

carefully integrated into the heroic setting enables problematic questions to be addressed without overt divisiveness and thus to be open from the start to different interpretations." If this absence of divisiveness is right, I would see it as another result of the fact that, on my interpretation, the parameters were set by a nonpartisan, non-moment-specific, matrix of religious exploration.

120. This is one of the arguments against Goldhill's (Goldhill 1990, esp. 126-9) complex version of what one may call implicit insulation between ritual and plays seen as separate and different—though on this view interacting through their very juxtaposition to create complex meanings. Goldhill has argued that tragic and comic performances set up a complex dialectic between the proclamation of social norms, situated in the pre-performance rituals, and their possibilities of transgression situated in the plays, tragic and comic. For Goldhill, "Tragedy and comedy do not simply reverse the norms of society but inculcate a questioning of the very basis of those norms.... If ritual is designed to leave the structural position of society legitimized, the tragic texts seem designed to leave an audience with a question (as often as not about the legitimation of social positions)" (127-8). I will be arguing in this book that this perception is culturally determined. In chapter II.2 I will be arguing that tragedy and comedy were generated in different cultic contexts, and these different contexts created very different parameters of determination for the creation, development, and reception of the genres, which therefore must not be assumed to be comparable. In chapter III.1 I will be arguing that if we compare an independent reading of the tragedies with the ritual matrix out of which (I will have argued in chapter II.2) tragedy had developed, we are led to conclude that this ritual matrix had shaped the articulation of the earliest surviving Aeschylean tragedies, and that we can to some extent map the development from this to "mature" tragedy, a development which involved a manifold expansion of, and developments out of, the ritual matrix, not its abandonment. In the readings of Euripidean tragedies in chapters III.3 and III.4 I will be arguing that what is at issue is exploration, in a religion in which unknowability is fundamental, not questioning in the sense of challenging.

121. Cf. e.g. Burkert 1990, 15 and 31 n.11; Winkler 1990, 42; Wilson and Taplin 1993, 170. Cf. also *DFA* 84 for some of the terminology. For a few among the vast number of examples see Lys. 19.29; Lys. 21.1; Plato *Rep.* 395B.

122. E.g. Plutarch *Phokion* 30; cf. MacDowell 1989, 69-77; cf. also Csapo and Slater 1995, 351.

123. Some of the questions and problems raised by Gould 1996 and Goldhill 1996 concerning the "authority" of the chorus will be discussed in chapter III.2, after the attempted reconstruction of the ritual context of the generation of tragedy, and of the role and composition of the chorus in that context, has been set out.

124. Easterling 1988, 88-9. Cf. also Calame 1994/5, 147-8.

125. Rutherford 1994/5, 126-7 discusses the paeanic aspect of the parodos of *Antigone* and its complex relationship to Pindar's Paean 9, in a paper which is an excellent discussion of the complex ways in which paeans are deployed in tragedy, Rutherford 1994/5,

112-35. He remarks (p. 127), "The parodos of the *Antigone* can itself be thought of as a paean, although this would be a celebratory victory paean, contrasting with the fearful and apotropaic song of Pindar." On Pindar's Paeans see Rutherford forthcoming.

126. Scholars who do not focus on the ways in which the audience made sense of tragedies through perceptual filters shaped by assumptions we need to reconstruct have taken a different view. For example, Bremer 1981, 212-3 acknowledges that "It cannot be fortuitous that especially in the parodos of tragedy and the parabasis of comedy the chorus sings songs to one god or a group of gods, in perfect hymnic style," but thinks that the poet has made the cultic convention serve a non-cultic purpose; he thinks that these hymns are not cultic because they are integrated in the theatrical performance. The position taken by Furley 1995, 29-46 seems to me less clear-cut; on the one hand (Furley 1995, 37) he speaks of dramatists including faithful copies of hieratic poetry when a scene called for them, on the other he makes other statements that seem to me to leave open the question of whether, or at least not entirely to exclude the possibility that, these would have been perceived by the audience as in some ways also hymns in the here and now. Angeli Bernardini 1991, 94 took a view similar to that of Bremer, in acknowledging that some tragic choral songs are very closely connected to ritual hymnal poetry, but again speaking of hymnic forms which tragedy derived from the ritual experiences of the community, which presumably implies that they had themselves no ritual character. I am arguing that the situation is much more complicated: precisely because the chorus was perceived to be a chorus in the here and now as well as in the world of the play, the hymns they sang had the same double identity, with the aspect pertaining to the world of the play generally dominant.

127. Cf. on this Wilson and Taplin 1993, 170-4; and esp. Henrichs 1994/5, 56-111, a most insightful, subtle, and rich discussion of such choral self-referentiality and the very complex ways in which such choral self-referentiality, and the language of ritual performance, are deployed in Greek tragedy.

128. Henrichs 1994/5, 58.

129. Especially given the Dionysiac connections of the choruses who comment on their own performance (Henrichs 1994/5, 60 and passim): in Sophocles such choruses are assigned explicit Dionysiac identities and in Euripides choral self-referentiality is more prominently connected with Dionysos than with any other deity; choral self-referentiality is extremely rare in the surviving Aeschylean tragedies. I do not believe that there is any other self-referentiality in Greek tragedy other than choral self-referentiality. Other candidates are not convincing, but it is beyond my scope to discuss this here.

130. Which is why it is considered as one of the distance-creating elements in the performance (see e.g. Calame 1994/5, 148).

131. In Plato's view, rhapsodic performances belonged together with tragedies, for he considered Homer to be a sort of first tragedian and teacher and guide of tragedians. Homer the first of tragedians: Plato *Republic* 607A; the first teacher and guide of tragedi-

Chapter 2: Setting Out the Distances 65

ans: 595C, 598D, 607A ; Homer a tragedian: 605D ; cf. also on this motif Halliwell 1988, ad 595 C1; cf. also Halliwell 1988, ad 602 B10.

132. Cf. e.g. Plato *Republic* 605D; *Philebus* 48A. It may be argued that the fact that Plato puts Homer and the tragedians together argues against the ritual nature of tragedy; however, the fact that this putting them together also involved the virtual elision of the fundamental *formal* differences between Homeric epics and tragedy, and also involved a very idiosyncratic concept of *mimesis* (cf. e.g. Halliwell 1988, ad 602 B10) shows that the elisions, marginalizations, and polarizations that sustain this classification are extreme, and would have been perceived by his contemporaries who shared his assumptions as such, so that there was no disjunction between his presentation and their experience, but a perception of polarized manipulations in the service of bringing out a particular relationship perceived by him as central, from his own ideologically loaded perceptual perspective.

133. I am not concerned with Plato's own views and his hostility to tragedy. It is the common assumptions that underlie the articulation of these views that I am trying to tease out and reconstruct. To place this in some sort of perspective let me give a short crude summary of Plato's relevant position in the *Republic*. For Plato religion is good, but in the present forms of religion perceptions of gods are articulated in poetry which provide bad moral exempla. Poets must be forced to follow certain rules about how to represent gods and heroes. In addition, tragedy (and Homer) stir up emotions in a way that is bad, so poetry and religious practice should not include things that are bad, stir up emotions, and are like blasphemy to the gods. It is, obviously, beyond my scope to discuss the major questions involved here. I will only say something very briefly about the ways in which this relates to my presentation of tragedy as articulating, exploring, and "resolving" complex religious matters. In my view, Plato, on the implicit assumption that complexities escape popular perceptions and that people need simple, clear moral exempla, applied to Greek myths perceptual filters that are simplistic and rationalizing, in the service of creating good moral influences and eliminating bad ones (cf. e.g. 377d-383c, 390C, 391A-B). The application of these simplistic and rationalizing filters reduced the complex ambivalences of Greek religion reflected in mythology, which is exquisitely articulated and explored above all in tragedy, in which the complex reality and the suffering are acknowledged, but are made sense of, are shown as part of an ordered cosmos which does not annihilate suffering but puts it in perspective and keeps anomic terror at bay, to logical schemata of "good moral exempla" and "bad moral exempla."

134. Easterling 1988, 109. Friedrich 1996, 269-70 unpersuasively criticizes Easterling for this position. The only concrete objection he brings against Easterling's position (as opposed to a general odor of incredulity) is his notion that it "flies in the face of the general tenor of her argument which emphasizes the 'metaphorical status' of the rituals in Greek tragedy and their being part of the dramatic (that is artistic) fiction." This criticism, then, relies on the a priori assumption that such a metaphorical status in the world of the play excludes any permeability to the world of the audience. There is nothing to support this a priori notion, which reduces the complexity of the Greek tragic discourse, and what has been

said about the double persona of the chorus is an objection against it. In addition, Friedrich's position implicitly assumes a static relationship between the world of the tragedy and the world of the audience, and ignores the particular context in which the permeability brought out by Easterling takes place: this is Athens, and anything that happened in Athens in the heroic past is directly relevant to the Athens of today; and this, in the eyes of the fifth-century Athenians, would have zoomed the world of the tragedy to the world of the audience, and made the latter permeable to the former.

135. And in some manuscripts of *Hippolytos*, after the play's own tailpiece (cf. Barrett 1964, 417-8 ad 1462-6). Barrett 1964, 417-8 ad 1462-6 is suspicious of Euripidean tailpieces, especially recurrent tailpieces, which he considers to be actors' interpolations; but cf. also Willink 1986, 360 ad 1691-3. I have argued (Sourvinou-Inwood 1997c, 260-1) that in the *Medea* the epilogue, far from being inapposite, was, in fact, very significant. McDermott 1989, 111-2 and Kovacs 1993, 65-7 also consider the *Medea* epilogue significant. I discuss these epilogues in detail in the appendix to chapter III.3. But even if the particular floating tailpieces that concern us here (which are of a very special type) were actors' interpolations, they would still testify to perceptions in which the chorus was also perceived as a chorus in the present. The argument put forward by Mastronarde concerning these tailpieces in *Phoinissai, Orestes,* and *Iphigeneia in Tauris* (Mastronarde 1994, 645 ad 1764-6), "The break of illusion is foreign to tragedy, so one may suspect that this tailpiece reflects a post-classical practice"—he suggests that they may even have been added by scribes against their authenticity in performance—is, from our perspective here, circular; for if it is correct that the tragic chorus was also perceived as a chorus in the present (the notion of "break of illusion" is too crude a concept for the complex situation that the tragic performance involved) this argument would be invalid; this part of the chorus' persona would have been zoomed at the end of the tragedy. I shall return to the question of epilogues and other closures in ch. III.3 and its appendix.

136. In Aristophanes *Frogs* 368.

137. Cf. on these questions below chapter II.2.ii.

II. The Ritual Context

II.1. The Great Dionysia: A Reconstruction

II.1.i. Reconstruction and Methodology

In this chapter I will reconsider the ritual context in which tragedy was generated, the festival of the City Dionysia,[1] in detail, and in a historical perspective. I will begin with a brief description of the main elements of the festival as we know them from the classical period onwards. The fact that the evidence is fragmentary, and the different fragments come from different periods, and many from late sources, entails the possibility that the ritual nexus may have changed in the course of time, and that either the surviving evidence relates only to the later versions, or that its different fragments refer to different periods; that what we have is an amalgam containing elements that had not belonged together in ritual reality.

In this investigation also, it is methodologically advisable to pursue independently the different lines of enquiry that pertain to different sets of evidence. This procedure avoids cross-contamination from fallacious assumptions and unconscious adjustments to make the different parts of the evidence fit, and also permits some cross-checks: if the results of the independent lines converge, this provides some validation. It is important to stress that not taking account of some of the evidence because its nature and relevance to the festival under investigation cannot be proved, or are problematic, is not a methodologically rigorous procedure; it is not "healthy scepticism." For if that evidence that was left out had in fact been relevant to the festival, if it had reflected one or more facets of that festival, its omission would lead to distortion, to a faulty reconstruction of a truncated version of what had been the ancient festival. And this leads to the faulty understanding of even those parts of the festival that had been correctly reconstructed. For all elements acquire meaning in context; for example, the ritual abandonment of normality and dissolution enacted in a particular festival, as in so-called "New Year festivals,"[2] acquires its full meanings in the context of, and in relation to, the ritual new beginnings enacted in that particular festival. Consequently, the methodologically neutral, and so rigorous, strategy for the attempted reconstruction of an ancient festival involves the consideration of even problematic fragmentary data that may be relevant, through the strategy of the independent study of the different lines of investigation that pertain to different sets of evidence.

In this chapter I will attempt to determine some of the changes that took place in the festival between its beginnings and the time when it becomes more visible. Given that we know that some changes did take place in the course of the centuries of the festival's history, and especially in the period around 500, not least the introduction of the tribally organized *agones*, as well as the movement of the performances from the Agora to the theater, we are not entitled to assume that the overall shape of the ritual had remained unchanged. Nor is it more rigorous to refrain from attempting to reconstruct these changes and developments because of the extremely fragmentary state of the evidence; for refraining from making a systematic attempt means that the default mode is the implicit assumption that things were basically the same—or as much the same as makes no difference to any significant extent or purpose. This, however, though it appears superficially rigorous, because it takes the guise of "we cannot know" and "the evidence does not allow us to determine," is ultimately far more flawed methodologically than a systematic attempt to reconstruct possible developments using as rigorous a methodology as possible, and revealing all the steps in the argument so that they can be assessed appropriately, including perhaps eventually in the light of new evidence.

One important strategy that can help us block, as far as possible, the effect of "commonsense" culturally determined judgments based on culturally determined assumptions from affecting our reading of the evidence and attempted reconstruction of the festival is to try to compare the reconstructed rites to other Greek rituals, to determine whether there are close parallels, which would indicate that the reconstructed rites fit Greek ritual logic and ritual schemata. If they do fit, this gives some support to the reconstructions. For besides the shared ritual logic that can be seen to structure Greek rituals, the festivals of different cities were not impermeable to influence from festivals of other cities, above all, influence from Panhellenic festivals celebrated in the major Panhellenic sanctuaries. Thus, in Athens the reorganized Panathenaia at c. 566 acquired competitions open to all Greeks, on the model of the recently founded Pythian, Nemean, and Isthmian Panhellenic Games, the very foundation of which, in quick succession, testifies to this phenomenon of interaction and influence which, we shall see, is relevant to our investigation.

Finally, I have to answer the objection that may be raised that one should not try to speculate when the evidence is so scanty. My answer is that speculation that has, first, tried to keep the different parts of the argument separate, to avoid contamination from implicit circularity and, as much as possible, from the intrusion of modern culturally determined assumptions of plausibility, and second, exposed all its parts explicitly, and is thus wholly open to scrutiny, is methodologically preferable to the generation of a vacuum that is implicitly structured by assumptions derived from less open, and less methodologically aware older speculations.

II.1.ii. *The Festival:* Xenismos *of Dionysos,* Komos, *Procession, Sacrifices and Performances*

a) *Literary, Epigraphical, and Comparative Evidence*

The main elements of the City Dionysia were a procession, *pompe*, sent by the archon who was the magistrate responsible for the festival,[3] competitions, and something called a *komos*. The *komos* is mentioned as a part of the festival in Demosthenes 21. 10; *komoi to Dionyso*, in the plural, in *IG* II² 2318 refers to the whole festival.[4]

There were two sets of competitions, dithyrambic and dramatic; the latter involved three tragedians presenting three tragedies and a satyr play each, and after 487/6 also the production of comedies, normally five. It is an important fact that the statue of Dionysos was present in the theater during the performances.[5] There were two dithyrambic competitions: one between ten choruses of boys, each representing one of the ten Athenian tribes, the other between ten choruses of men, similarly representing each of the tribes. Just before the festival proper started, a preliminary rite took place: the statue of Dionysos Eleuthereus was removed from its sanctuary underneath the Acropolis and taken to a shrine a little outside the center of Athens, in the Academy;[6] eventually it was ceremonially escorted back to the theater in the sanctuary of Dionysos Eleuthereus, by ephebes at nighttime.[7] An interesting question is why the statue was taken to the theater, and not to the temple, or perhaps the space just outside the temple, where it needed to be the next day to receive the procession and sacrifices.[8] The process of the statue's transport to the sanctuary is referred to as the *eisagoge apo tes escharas*, an expression normally understood to refer to the transfer of the statue from the shrine at the Academy to the theater. I have argued,[9] and will be arguing in a wider context below, that this view is mistaken, and that the *eschara* referred to was the *eschara* in the Agora, near the Altar of the Twelve Gods, where the statue was brought to from the Academy prior to its transfer to the sanctuary. There is nothing to support the notion that the *eschara* referred to stood at the shrine at the Academy—other than (inevitably culturally determined) inference—while we shall see, a series of arguments support the thesis that it was the *eschara* near the Altar of the Twelve Gods. At least some ritual activity took place in connection with the stay of Dionysos' statue at the *eschara*: a sacrifice was performed,[10] and hymns were sung to *ep' escharas* Dionysos.[11]

The procession of the Dionysia culminated in the sanctuary of Dionysos Eleuthereus, but we do not know where it started, or what its route was, though, we shall see below, it is possible to reconstruct its main points of reference. We do know that in the classical period its route was elaborate, it was not a short straightforward procession. For Xenophon mentions,[12] in a context in which he is speaking of processions, which, he argues, ought to include a ride around all the shrines in the Agora, that at the Dionysia (which in the context can only mean the Dionysia procession), the dances of choruses gratified in addition (to Dionysos) the Twelve Gods and other gods.

Masks were not worn in the procession of the Dionysia. The notion that they had been is based on a misreading of two texts.[13] First, Demosthenes 19.287. Demosthenes says of Epikrates, referred to here by a nickname, Kyrebion, *hos en tais pompais aneu tou prosopou komazei*. We have Aeschines' reply to this accusation,[14] which makes clear what Demosthenes meant: Aeschines asks who ever saw Epikrates behave in an indecent manner, "either by day, as you say, at the Dionysia procession, or by night?" This makes clear that Demosthenes' meaning was that Epikrates had behaved at the Dionysia procession as though he were at a *komos*, as though this had been the *komos* of the Dionysia, rather than its procession, which involved a certain solemnity; he behaved as though he were in a *komos*, in which people fooled around, wearing masks, without the mask that characterizes the *komos*. As we shall see, there is some other evidence that suggests that at least some people wore masks at the *komos*, masks of drunken men. An implication of Aeschines' formulation is probably that at the Dionysia the *komos* took place at night. I shall return to this. The second text adduced in support of the notion that masks were worn at the Dionysia procession is Plutarch, *Moralia* 527D. But this passage does not say that masks were worn at the procession of the City Dionysia; what it says is that in the old days the *patrios ton Dionysion heorte* was simple and homely, while now there are gold vessels, rich clothes and carriages and masks. Plutarch says this happened at the Dionysia, not at the procession; therefore, since there is reason to believe that masks were worn at the *komos*, it makes perfect sense to understand the masks referred to as being the masks worn at the *komos*, especially since the carriages mentioned in this passage almost certainly were part of the *komos*; for according to Plato,[15] in Athens the Di-

Chapter 1: The Great Dionysia

onysia provide an excuse for *komazein meta methes*, sometimes in carriages.[16]

The Dionysia procession involved a *kanephoros parthenos* who carried a *kanoun* with *aparchai*.[17] Among the sacrificial animals escorted by the procession and subsequently sacrificed, sometimes in large numbers[18] was at least one bull (the ephebes led a bull in the procession and sacrificed it in the sanctuary)[19] and cattle. Bloodless offerings, such as loaves and wineskins, were also carried. A ritually important part of the procession involved the carrying of phalloi. Metics, resident foreigners, as well as citizens took part in this procession. The metics wore purple garments and carried *skaphai*, small tubs or basins; citizens wore whatever they liked and carried wineskins. As we will see, women also participated in the procession. The *choregoi*, the men who financed the dramatic and dithyrambic choruses, processed wearing magnificent clothes and golden crowns. There was, then, a differentiation between the different elements that made up the polis, an articulation of the polis into its constituent parts. Athenian colonists also took part in the procession of the Great Dionysia; they were sometimes required to send a phallos to the Dionysia and a cow and a panoply to the Panathenaia, and sometimes a cow and a phallos to the Dionysia and a cow and a panoply to the Panathenaia.[20] The Athenian Allies were also given a role in both festivals. The Allies' tribute was brought to Athens at the Dionysia and displayed in the theater,[21] while at the Great Panathenaia they were required to bring a cow and a panoply like colonists.[22]

People also were displayed in the theater as part of Athenian ideological construction: the orphan sons of the war dead who had been raised at the polis' expense and had come of age were paraded in the full armor given them by the polis before the performances.[23] Also before the performances, the honors given to citizens and foreigners for great services to the polis were proclaimed.[24] This was also an act of positive self-presentation and part of the ideological construction of Athenian democracy.

Thus, in the fifth century the Dionysia had become a locus for the polis' self-definition. This may appear to be simply motivated by pragmatic considerations, that is, to be the result of the fact that the theater offered the appropriate stage for the display of tribute as well as of the orphans and the Athenian honors list and for the announcement of honors. But we cannot assume that this is not simply a culturally determined judgment; we should not assume that there may not have been reasons connected with the ritual which led to the polis articulating itself at the Dionysia. The other festival in which the Athenian polis articulated itself, and which was similarly a locus for the polis' self-definition, was the Panathenaia. As in the Dionysia, so also in the Panathenaia, the procession articulated, and was articulated by, the whole Athenian polis as one unit.[25] The polis articulated in the City Dionysia and the Panathenaia was an open system, that included foreign residents and colonists—in a hierarchically inferior position. It is due to this character of the Dionysia as a locus for the articulation of the whole polis, which generated particular ideologies of self-definition at particular times, that before the performances the orphan sons of the war dead raised at the polis' expense were paraded in the full armor given them by the polis, and that the honors given to citizens and foreigners were proclaimed.

Because the City Dionysia and the Panathenaia were loci for articulating symbolically the polis as an open system, they became loci for the articulation of the wider system, the new configurations, of the Athenian Empire: for this was one of the results achieved by the fact that the Allies' tribute was brought to Athens at the Dionysia and displayed in the theater, while at the Great Panathenaia the Athenian allies were required to bring a cow and a panoply like colonists. The fact that at the festival the polis articulated itself symbolically in this way as an open system, is perhaps more easily intelligible in the Panathenaia, the major whole polis festival of the poliadic deity, than in the Dionysia. So why did this also take place at the Dionysia? What aspect of the Dionysia shaped this character, and how, if at all, is this connected to the festival's ritual?

The answer to this will become clear when we have considered what this festival was about. When compared to the Anthesteria, the festival perceived to have been the oldest Athenian festival of Dionysos, *ta archaiotera Dionysia*,[26] which included many and varied rites, and had several aetiological myths connected with it, the Great Dionysia appears to be a simple (in the sense of noncomplex, though lavish) festival with one simple myth.

According to the festival myth of the City Dionysia,[27] Pegasos of Eleutherai brought Dionysos' statue to Athens, but the Athenians did not receive the god with honor. Dionysos was enraged and struck the male sexual organs with an incurable disease. They consulted the oracle who told them to bring in the god with every honor; they manufactured phalloi, both privately and publicly, and with these they honored the god, commemorating their misfortune. This is a particular version of the "resistance" mythological schema associated with the introduction of the cult of Dionysos in Greek mythology. There are many myths, with different human protagonists, that say that when the cult of Dionysos first arrived in a place it was badly received, as in the case

Chapter 1: The Great Dionysia

of Athens—or, in some versions, the king resisted its introduction of the cult of Dionysos and was severely punished for this.

How does the festival myth relate to the ritual? Clearly, the removal of the statue to the Academy and its ceremonial return means that the festival celebrated the arrival of the statue, and so of the cult, of Dionysos. That is, this festival belongs to the important category of Greek festivals that celebrated the deity's advent.[28] The Athenians reenacted their reception of the god with honor, and this was especially marked by the carrying of the phalloi in the procession. A procession is a common rite in Greek festivals; each procession acquired its particular meanings in the context of the whole festival, as well as through its particular forms. In the Dionysia procession the phallophoria is directly connected with, and reenacts, the first phallophoria in the festival myth of the City Dionysia, when the Athenians first received the god and established his cult. The procession would have been perceived as both a procession in the present and as a reenactment of the first procession that had established the cult. As for the *komos*, the identity of which is problematic, as we shall see below, it was also directly connected with the reception of Dionysos. There was also a direct connection between the dramatic and dithyrambic competitions and the ritual that celebrated the reception of the cult of Dionysos: the fact that the statue of Dionysos was present in the theater during the performances shows that a strong dimension in the perception of the festival was that the dramatic and dithyrambic competitions were entertainment for Dionysos. The offering of entertainment to Dionysos is very appropriate in a ritual involving the reception of the god, in which he was honored and propitiated, and his cult introduced after the initial offense against him.

Thus, the festival myth does indeed reflect the core aspect of the festival of the Great Dionysia as perceived by the participants, and this core aspect was the reception and welcoming and entertainment of the god; in other words a rite of *xenismos*.

That the focus of the festival of the Great Dionysia was the celebration of the introduction of the cult of Dionysos through a ritual of reception and entertainment of the god is confirmed by the fact that Plutarch *Demetrios* 12 also points us strongly in the same direction; for it tells us that someone had proposed that the polis should receive Demetrios Poliorcetes every time he came *tois Demetros kai Dionysou xenismois*, with the same [rites of] guest entertainment[s] as those offered to Demeter and Dionysos. The context makes clear that what is at issue here is "entertainment on the god's arrival."

The first reason for concluding that the rites of entertainment offered to Dionysos referred to here were part of the City Dionysia is that of all Dionysiac festivals in Athens it was the City Dionysia that was *focussed* on the reception of Dionysos. In addition, it was to the City Dionysia that the Athenians attached festival days in honor of Demetrios, adding them to the festival and giving to the City Dionysia the double name Demetria and Dionysia;[29] and this points in the same direction, an association between Demetrios, *xenismoi* for Dionysos and the City Dionysia.

The two deities mentioned by Plutarch in connection with a ritual *xenismos*, Dionysos and Demeter, share an aspect of their persona that makes special sense of such a *xenismos*: they both arrived from outside and brought important agricultural gifts to Athens.[30] According to Apollodoros iii.14.7, Demeter and Dionysos came to Attica at the same time, the time of king Pandion; Demeter was received by Keleos and Dionysos by Ikarios.[31] Pandion's name was probably derived from that of the festival Pandia.[32] This was a festival of Zeus, but it was intimately connected with the City Dionysia, since the assembly in which the conduct of, and any offenses committed during, the Dionysia were discussed took place on the day following the Pandia.[33] The coincidence between on the one hand the festival's intimate relationship to the Dionysia, and on the other the myth according to which Pandion was king in Athens when Dionysos arrived in Attica and was received by Ikarios, suggests that it was probably some role that Pandion had played in that visit, or the events that followed, that may have motivated his involvement in a festival connected with the Dionysia, and that the Pandia involved a reference to Dionysos' arrival in Attica. If so, this would indicate that myths pertaining to the arrival of Dionysos himself in Attica had been attracted into the orbit of the City Dionysia, and ritually connected with the installation of his cult, so that the god's visit and the arrival of his statue and foundation of his cult, were woven into one festive system focussed on the City Dionysia. This would be the ritual correlative of the myth that connects the two in Pausanias 1.2.5: the Delphic oracle helped Pegasos introduce the cult of Dionysos by recalling that Dionysos had visited Ikarios. If this is right, it would provide a little further confirmation for the importance of Dionysos' *xenismoi* in the City Dionysia. The notion that the god's visit and the arrival of his statue and foundation of his cult were woven into one festive system focussed on the City Dionysia may find some confirmation in the oracle pertaining to this festival cited in Demosthenes,[34] which reflects the belief that the cult of Dionysos was introduced in Athens during the reign of Pandion. The other Athenian king associated with a reception of Dionysos was Amphictyon, who learnt from Dionysos how to mix wine.[35] Pausanias mentions clay statues representing Amphictyon entertaining with a feast

Chapter 1: The Great Dionysia

other gods and Dionysos;[36] Pegasos is also represented, and it is here that Pausanias mentions that Pegasos had been helped by the Delphic oracle, which had recalled that Dionysos had visited Ikarios.

A final argument for the thesis that a rite of *xenismos* of Dionysos had an important place in the City Dionysia is provided by the fact that what appears to have been the most important festival of Dionysos in Callatis, celebrated in the spring month Lykeos, was clearly influenced by the Athenian City Dionysia, since during its celebration, at the theater, honors were proclaimed and crowns awarded to people who had benefited the polis. The name of this festival was *ta xenika Dionysia*, the Dionysia in which takes place a *xenismos* of Dionysos.[37]

Is there any evidence about the forms of Dionysos' reception? For the general ritual schema, let us look at other Athenian ritual receptions. The cases of Iakchos (in the course of the Eleusinian Mysteries) and Asklepios (at the Epidauria), in which the procession escorting the god ended in a ritual reception, *hypodoche*, show that the ritual schema of such a reception of a god involved choruses singing hymns and dancing.[38] In both cases the procession escorting the god ended in a *hypodoche*, followed (immediately or eventually) by a *pannychis*.[39] If there was a ritual reception (*hypodoche*) of Dionysos, the rite of the *xenismos* of Dionysos would follow after, and in a way be a continuation of, this reception. A *xenismos* ritual in Greek religion involved the entertament of a god or hero,[40] the offering of a meal to the god; this meal sometimes, though not always, involved sacrifice and sacrificial meat.[41] The meal was either offered in the god's sanctuary, by the god's statue, or the god's statue was moved somewhere else for the entertainment; in either case a couch and a table was set out next to the statue. The actual meal was in fact shared by the worshippers. The gods were believed to be present in the city when their *theoxenia/xenismos* was being celebrated.[42] *Theoxenia/xenismos* could also be attached to, or could form the centerpiece, of a festival with animal sacrifice.[43] Jameson considers the cult of Asklepios to be an example of such a combination of *xenismos* and other rites, including sacrifices and a *pannychis*.[44] At the Epidauria, besides these rites there was, we saw, also a ritual reception.

I will not base my attempted reconstruction of the rites of the Dionysia on the a priori presupposition that they were the same as these comparable rites in other Athenian festivals. I will try to reconstruct them on the basis of the data that are, or may be, relevant to those particular rites; if then there is a match between the reconstructed rites and the ritual schema pertaining to such rites as it emerges from other Athenian festivals, this would provide some confirmation for the validity of these reconstructions.

As we saw, according to Plutarch *Demetrios* 12, someone had proposed that the polis should receive Demetrios Poliorcetes every time he came with the same rites of guest entertainments as those offered to Demeter and Dionysos. We hear something that may be informative about the reception part of the *xenismos* offered him by the Athenians from other sources, which describe the ways in which the Athenians had disgraced themselves by treating Demetrios as a god and give details of the form of this impious behavior. Most importantly, the contemporary orator, historian, and statesman Demochares, who was an opponent of Demetrios, and who may have been a significant source for Plutarch's *Demetrios*, says that the Athenians received Demetrios on his return from Leukas and Corcyra not only with offerings of incense and crown and libations, but also "processional choruses (*prosodiakoi choroi*) and *ithyphalloi* with dancing and singing met him."[45] *Ithyphallos* means "erect phallos" and is both the name of an ode and dance performed in Dionysiac ritual, and of the performer of such a song and dance. The mention of *ithyphallos* gives support to the hypothesis arising from Plutarch's information, that this reception is based on Dionysiac ritual,[46] that it was probably modelled on the *xenismos* of Dionysos, and that therefore the ritual reception of Dionysos had involved processional choruses and *ithyphalloi*. The fact that *prosodiakoi choroi* were involved confirms that this reception was modelled on the reception of a deity, since *prosodia* were the hymns sung as the choruses approached the god (in procession towards the god),[47] which normally meant the altar or the temple[48]—while in this reception of Dionysos it was the god's statue; the *ithyphalloi* confirm that this deity was Dionysos.

Douris of Samos, another contemporary historian and politician (also probably used as a source by Plutarch for *Demetrios*), cites this *ithyphallos* sung to Demetrios.[49] It is not a comic song, but a serious (if impious) hymn, inappropriately addressed to a mortal, on his arrival. The song compares Demetrios' arrival to that of Demeter, who has come to celebrate the Mysteries at the same time as Demetrios arrived. So here also we see echoes of the notion reported in Plutarch of the polis receiving Demetrios *tois Demetros kai Dionysou xenismois*. Since this was an *ithyphallos*, it was probably modelled on the type of hymn that was sung to Dionysos on his arrival.

The fact that processional choruses and *ithyphalloi* had met Demetrios suggests that these actions had been modelled on the ritual acts that normally took place at Dionysos' *reception*, rather than the Dionysia *pompe*. That Dionysos should have been received with processional hymns fits the notion of receiving the god with honor; that *ithyphalloi* songs should have been included, performed by *ithyphal-*

loi performers, fits the context of the reception as given in the myth. The disease of the male organs the Athenians suffered from as a result of Dionysos' wrath, which was then cured through the reception of Dionysos and the introduction of his cult, including the rite of phallos-bearing, is believed to have been a permanent erection.[50] Another possibility is the opposite, the total inability to have an erection. In either case not only *phallophorein*, but also *ithyphalloi*, erect phallos songs, sung by men with erect phalloi, have a direct relevance to the reception of Dionysos at the City Dionysia. If the disease had been a permanent erection, which is perhaps most likely, if hymns called *ithyphalloi* had been performed at the reception of Dionysos by *ithyphalloi* men, the latter would have been men enacting the disease of the male organs the Athenians suffered from, of which they were then cured through the reception of Dionysos and the introduction of his cult, signalled by the rite of *xenismos*; so that after that, in the procession to the sanctuary, they were cured, and they held up artificial phalloi in commemoration of their earlier disease.

The time before the reception of Dionysos represents ritually the time before present normality was established (in myth as perceived history), an abnormality that included the men's permanent erection, which made them into *ithyphalloi*. Consequently, in the perception of the first reception of Dionysos *ithyphalloi* men would have been among those meeting Dionysos singing *ithyphalloi* songs.[51] And in the ritual reception of Dionysos at the Dionysia, which reenacted that first reception, *ithyphalloi* men were among those meeting Dionysos, singing *ithyphalloi*. If, as is less likely, the disease had involved a total inability to have an erection, the *ithyphalloi* would have been enacting the desirable state of affairs which it was hoped would be achieved through the reception of Dionysos.

In any case, though the argument connecting Demochares' and Douris' information about Demetrios' reception with the reception of Dionysos at the great Dionysia, and so also the conclusion that *ithyphalloi* and processional choruses were part of a reception of Dionysos at the Great Dionysia, may not be strong in itself, due to lack of evidence, the fact that erect phalloi are of central relevance to this reception of Dionysos at the Great Dionysia, together with the fact that processional choruses also fit the context, and that this reconstructed rite would fit the ritual schema of *hypodoche*, offers independent support for this interpretation. This context of the reception of Dionysos at the Dionysia not only would explain the use of *ithyphalloi* at the reception of Demetrios, but would also account for the solemnity of the *ithyphallos* song, which may appear *para prosdokian*, not only because of our culturally determined expectations, but also because of the perceived ancient association between *phallika* and comedy: according to Aristotle,[52] comedy developed from the *phallika*, the phallic songs, which were still in use in many cities in his time.

In another Dionysiac ritual context in which *ithyphalloi* performers were involved there was less solemnity. Semos of Delos speaks of *ithyphalloi* performers performing in the orchestra of the theater.[53] According to Semos the *ithyphalloi* wore masks of drunken men; they recited towards the audience: "Give way, give way, make room for the god! For the god wants to walk through your midst upright (*orthos*) and bursting." After that Semos describes the *phallophoroi*, who were not masked, and wore a bonnet of tufted thyme and holly with a wreath of ivy and violets over it, entering the theater marching in step and reciting a hymn to Dionysos, after which they jeered at whoever they chose.

The recitation of the *ithyphalloi* is clearly associated with a movement of the god, which means of the statue of the god. This would make sense if the ritual context involved the bringing of the god's statue into the theater. It is clear that the *ithyphalloi* speak as the statue of Dionysos is about to be brought in the theater; this is a ritual entrance. When did it take place? The context of the movement of the statue, in combination with the *ithyphalloi* and *phallophoroi*, indicate the City Dionysia. The jeering is an element that occurs also in other festivals of Dionysos—and not only Dionysos. We do not know that Semos is speaking of Athens. But the following reasons suggest that this information was relevant to the Athenian Dionysia. First, that *ithyphalloi* performed in the theater, in the orchestra, in Athens is indicated by Hyperides fragment 52. So, even if Semos is not speaking of Athens, the Hyperides fragment suggests that something similar had involved the *ithyphalloi* in Athens. Second, in most cities the festival of the Dionysia was heavily influenced by the Athenian City Dionysia, so that even if Semos had been speaking of Delos, the rite was likely to be based on Athenian practice, especially since Athenian influence on Delos was very strong.[54]

So, when in the Dionysia would this rite have taken place? There are, I believe, two possibilities. First, the statue of Dionysos may have been moved from the sanctuary to the theater ritually in the company of *ithyphalloi* and *phallophoroi* every day before the performances.[55] Or, second, and in my view more likely, this rite was part of the *eisagoge apo tes escharas*, which brought the statue to the theater from the *eschara*, escorted by ephebes. I shall return to this. First it is necessary to return to the question of the *komos*.

The *komos* was an important part of the Dionysia, but we do not know exactly what it was. It is mentioned, we saw, as part of the festi-

Chapter 1: The Great Dionysia

val in Demosthenes 21.10. *Komoi to Dionyso*, in the plural, in *IG* II² 2318 refers to the whole festival. Various interpretations have been proposed for the meaning of *komoi* and *komos* at the Dionysia, but none is, I believe, without difficulties.[56] So, what do we know about the *komos*? Of course, the word's meanings themselves provide important information, but I shall consider those meanings after I have reviewed what else we know about the *komos* at the Dionysia.

First, we saw that Demosthenes 19.287, taken together with Aeschines 2.151, suggests that masks were worn at the *komos*. Second, the same two passages may indicate that the *komos* took place at night. Third, that drunkenness was common;[57] fourth, that these drunken people were sometimes in carriages.[58] The fact that the *komos* involved drunkenness, taken together with the fact that the *ithyphalloi* wore masks of drunken men suggests the possibility that the *ithyphalloi* may have been connected to the *komos*. This would also fit the fact that the *ithyphalloi* wore wreaths.[59] If this is right, and if the above reconstruction is correct, the *komos*, through the *ithyphalloi*, would be connected with the reception of Dionysos, and the *ithyphalloi* would have been one group of people that were masked at the *komos*.

Let us now consider the meanings of the word *komos* and also the fact that *Komoi to Dionyso* could be used to refer to the whole festival. One piece of information relevant to the last question is that there is one example of a comparable usage of the plural: Euripides in *Helen* 1469 refers to *komoi (komois) Hyakinthou*. Now the meanings of the word *komos*. Ghiron-Bistagne sees three types of activity referred to as *komos*: symposion, a type of procession (often a drunken procession), and choral singing and dancing.[60] That *komos* can denote "song of celebration" is clear.[61] The first two meanings are closely intertwined; sometimes *komos* seems focussed on the notion of symposion with revelries;[62] sometimes it seems to be distinguished from the symposion, though closely associated with it.[63] But in both cases the *komos* is very closely associated with drinking and drunkenness. The drinking and drunkenness fit what we know about the *komos* at the Athenian Dionysia, but where did people do their drinking? And how was this related to the reception of Dionysos?

Let us consider a piece of evidence relevant to the Dionysia which, in my view, has not been placed in its proper perspective. A very late source, Philostratos,[64] tells us that whenever the Dionysia came round and the statue of Dionysos *katioi eis Akademian*, Herodes Atticus would furnish wine at the Kerameikos to both citizens and foreigners *katakeimenous epi stibadon kittou*. The formulation suggests that he is reporting a benefaction during a part of the festival that he refers to elliptically because he assumes it to be well known; he is not describing something unknown. The *stibades kittou*, beds of leaves of ivy, fits an established ritual schema for ritual dining at a sanctuary during a festival, reclining on beds of leaves of the relevant deity's sacred plant and wearing wreaths of the same plant. This is, for example, what happened at the Samian Heraion, where at the festival of the Tonaia the worshippers wore crowns of *lygos* and reclined on *stibades* of *lygos*, Hera's sacred plant at that sanctuary.[65] Since crowns of ivy were certainly worn in the course of the Dionysia[66] the pattern is the same here.[67] Thus, the ritual schema that underlies this use of the god's sacred plant suggests that Philostratos is reflecting benefaction at a correctly reported ritual which took place either at, or in connection with, a sanctuary.[68]

The fact that this ritual took place when the statue went to the Academy means that it took place in the part of the festival that preceded the establishment of the new order which started with, and was signalled by, the reception of Dionysos, in a period of abnormality and reversal; for this period preceding the cult's foundation, like that before any foundation, was in Greek mentality a period of abnormality, symbolically associated with disorder and reversed world. This set of meanings coincides precisely with the fact that in Greek religious mentality dining while reclining on *stibades* has connotations of dissolution of normality.[69] Among the festivals in which this ritual took place, the ritual dining on *stibades* of *lygos* at the Samian Tonaia is, I believe, the closest to the ritual dining on *stibades* of ivy at the Dionysia. For, like the City Dionysia, this was also a festival celebrating the deity's advent.[70] According to Menodotos of Samos *FGrH* 541 F 1, in commemoration of an attempted theft that failed, every year the statue was carried to the shore, where it was purified, offerings of barley cakes placed by it and then returned to its pedestal. Thus, in both festivals dining on *stibades* of the ritually appropriate plant wreathed with wreaths of the same plant goes together with a statue's movement, departure and return, a reenactment of a similar movement in the festival myth; also with dissolution of normality. This convergence, and more generally, the fit between Greek ritual logic and what Philostratos describes confirms that this rite was indeed a part of the Dionysia and not "a late perversion of a festival which had lost its meaning."[71]

That lying on *stibades* was a not insignificant part of the cult of Dionysos is confirmed by other evidence. First, the Alexandrian festival Lagynophoria, established by Ptolemy, who founded all kinds of festivals and sacrifices, especially ones connected with Dionysos, was undoubtedly based on established cultic modalities. First, because this is

Chapter 1: The Great Dionysia

how new cults are constructed; and second, because in this festival we can identify at least one element which originated in an Athenian festival of Dionysos, the Anthesteria. For at the Lagynophoria, people dined reclining on *stibades*, and each drunk from a flagon (*lagynos*) he himself had brought,[72] as happens with the wine drank from individual jugs (*choes*) in the Choes at the Anthesteria in Athens.[73] But at the Anthesteria in Athens, people drank in a competition while seated. So here we have a conflation of elements from different festivals. In fact, since a *thallophoros* seems to have been associated with this festival, and since in Athens *thallophoroi* were part of the Panathenaia, the conflated festival had clearly been constructed from elements from more than one deity's cult and festivals. So this cannot prove that the element "dining and drinking reclining on *stibades*" had been part of the City Dionysia, but in this context I suggest that the presumption should be that it belonged to a major Athenian festival of Dionysos; and the Dionysia is the only festival for which there is any evidence for such a rite, evidence which fits perfectly the ritual logic of the festival.

That dining and drinking reclining on *stibades* was part of an important festival of Dionysos is also suggested by the fact that *stibas* is the name of a ritual banquet in Dionysiac thiasoi, both in Athens and elsewhere.[74] For example, in Istria[75] *stibas* is the feast accompanied by a banquet involving a thiasos of Dionysiac *hymnodoi*. Since of all Athenian festivals of Dionysos it was the City Dionysia that influenced the cults of other cities most, this, I suggest, offers a little support for the view that this was the festival from which the association with *stibades* originated. In Athens, the most important festival of the thiasos of the Iobakkchoi is called *Stibas*.[76] This thiasos festival may offer further support for the conclusions reached here. For the most likely interpretation of this inscription is that *Stibas* was the name, or the *Stibas* was part, of the festive complex through which the Iobakkchoi marked the celebration of the City Dionysia.[77] If this is right, it would provide further confirmation for the argument set out here.

In these circumstances, I submit that different strands of evidence, some more compelling in themselves than others, converge to indicate that ritual dining on *stibades*, beds of ivy, had taken place at the City Dionysia, before the procession. Because the arguments are independent this convergence strongly validates this conclusion.

b) *Iconographical Evidence*

Further, independent confirmation for the thesis that ritual dining on *stibades*, beds of leaves of ivy took place at the City Dionysia from an early period is offered, I will now argue, by a series of images on vases.

Reading ancient images on vases is not a simple matter. Athenian images were not attempts to reproduce reality, or, in mythological images, imagined reality. They are complex constructs, with complex meanings. Reading them in ways that are as close as possible to the ways in which the ancient viewers made sense of them requires a systematic attempt: first, to reconstruct the ancient assumptions shared by the vase painter and his contemporary viewers, and then, to shape perceptual filters out of those assumptions, abandoning direct, intuitive, "commonsense" readings that are inevitably based on modern presuppositions, which are deployed by default in the absence of a systematic attempt to block them, and replace them with the cultural assumptions that are reflected in, and shaped, the vase painters' selections, and the contemporary viewers' reading of this image.[78] The problem is compounded here by the fact that the aim is to reconstruct the ritual reality reflected in the images; so special caution is needed to avoid circularity.

The images that concern us represent males reclining on the ground, instead of on a *kline*, in a Dionysiac context, often wearing a ivy wreath. They include representations, first, of Dionysos reclining on the ground, second, of a satyr, with or without a Maenad, reclining on the ground, and third, of youths or men reclining on the ground.[79] There are also images involving the schema "reclining on the ground" in which the context is not Dionysiac;[80] but in Attic iconography this schema is very closely associated with Dionysos and the Dionysiac sphere. Many of the images involving men have close Dionysiac associations, as, we shall see, do many of the vases which these images decorate.

The iconographical schema "reclining on the ground against a cushion in a religious context" is deployed on non-Attic vases to represent worshippers reclining on *stibades* in the course of ritual dining and drinking in sanctuaries in which such a rite took place. This is the schema through which is represented the ritual dining on *stibades* of *lygos*, beds of willow leaves, at the sanctuary of Hera at Samos in the context of the Tonaia,[81] on some of the representations of which the sanctuary location (and so also the ritual nature of the symposion) are signified through an altar. The schema is found also on Laconian pottery representing ritual dining during a Laconian festival,[82] almost certainly the Hyakinthia,[83] during which such ritual dining on *stibades* took place.[84] Reading ancient images in ways as much as possible through the eyes of the ancient viewers who had shared the vase painter's assumptions requires, we saw, the need to abandon direct, intuitive, "commonsense" readings. Thus, these non-Attic vases show that the fact that the beds of leaves are not represented in the pictures, and that the figures are shown leaning on cushions,[85] does not constitute an argument against the interpretation that the Attic images represent figures reclining on beds of ivy leaves in a ritual symposion—as perhaps modern culturally determined expectations might lead people to expect. Clearly, in the conventional idiom of Greek iconography the fact that the reclining shown was not "couch" but "on the ground" conveyed to the ancient viewer (in combination with signs that indicated that this was not a simple picnic) the relevant ritual dining, in Athens in a Dionysiac context[86] on *stibades* of ivy leaves, at Samos *stibades* of *lygos*, and so on.[87] Many of the Athenian images involving reclining on the ground represent the ritually significant plant in another form, in the ivy wreaths worn by Dionysos and the symposiasts, satyrs[88] or human.[89]

The images of men reclining on the ground in a Dionysiac context must be made sense of also in terms of the fact that Dionysos himself is shown reclining on the ground, sometimes with a reclining satyr.[90] The representation of the god through the same iconographical schema as his human worshippers is an established modality in Attic iconography: the deity is represented performing an activity that men perform in that deity's cultic domain or sphere of power; for example, Apollo is shown sitting on a tripod, as the Pythia did when prophecying; Eros is shown chasing a woman.[91] Dionysos is also shown elsewhere through this modality: for example, he is represented tearing an animal in a frenzy, like his mythological worshippers.[92] Dionysos reclining on the ground, then, represents the god in a ritual activity, ritual dining and drinking reclining on the ground, which was performed by his worshippers.

Satyrs are also often shown reclining on the ground,[93] with or without a Maenad. In Attic iconography human activities are often less commonly shown than (what is perceived as) their mythological paradigms or, as in this case, counterparts. One of the semantic facets of satyrs is that they are a particular type of refraction of certain aspects of the human male, wilder aspects, which are especially relevant in the context of abnormality and dissolution in which the ritual dining on *stibades* at the City Dionysia, would, on my reconstruction, belong. This would make the satyrs reclining on the ground especially appropriate mythological refractions of Athenian men dining on *stibades* at the City Dionysia. Insofar as they are also mythological companions of Dionysos, and are shown together with the god in this context, they also serve as symbolic mediators between god and worshippers; they bring the god symbolically nearer to the human sphere.

Consequently, we may conclude that one of the dimensions of signification of these images is as reflections and refractions of a ritual of Dionysos, in which ritual dining took place on *stibades* of ivy, with the symposiasts wearing ivy wreaths. Already at this stage of the investigation of the images, the fact that, on this interpretation, the images seem to offer a pictorial articulation reflecting a rite which we know took place at the Dionysia in a late period provides some confirmation for the thesis that this rite was an early and significant part of the City Dionysia.[94] But in fact, these images offer further support for this interpretation, as we shall see in a moment.

A transformation of the schema discussed here shows Dionysos reclining on the ground under a vine.[95] This schema also has a correlative image located in the human world.[96] That this schema may not have lost all connection with the Dionysia may be suggested by the black-figure phallus cup (cup with a foot in the form of a penis and testicles) Oxford AM 1974.344,[97] on the tondo of which men are shown dining under vines, two wearing ivy wreaths and two turbans evocative of Ionia, while on the outside satyr heads are represented between apotropaic eyes. The phallus cup is an extremely rare shape.[98] Though the phallus was associated with Dionysos in general, it is clear from the festival myth and the *phallophorein* that it has a special connection with, and importance at, the City Dionysia. So this vase may have been perceived as especially connected with the City Dionysia (indeed, for all we know may have been produced for the celebration of that festival); the dining while reclining on the ground underneath vines would have been a construct, refracting the ritual dining on *stibades* at this festival in a more indirect way, stressing the Dionysiac and the wine drinking through the vines, and so creating a new schema, in which the Dionysiac symposion, refracting the ritual dining on *stibades* of the Dionysia, is located in a vineyard.

Dionysos (who, of course, is also shown reclining on a couch at the symposion) is the main god shown reclining on the ground in Attic iconography; Heracles is the most frequent other,[99] with some examples of Hermes. Heracles, like Dionysos, is also frequently shown at the banquet on a *kline*. Both Heracles and Hermes scenes of this type are heavily influenced by the Dionysiac images,[100] and sometimes Dionysos is shown reclining together with the other god.[101] The schema of Dionysos reclining on the ground, like that of Heracles reclining on the ground, should not be interpreted in isolation of their images in which they are shown reclining on a couch. With regard to reclining

Chapter 1: The Great Dionysia

banqueting gods and heroes in general, in reliefs as well as in vase paintings, recent research has shown that one of the meanings they have is that they reflect a *theoxenia*, an ideal or actual *xenismos* for a god or hero.[102] With regard to Heracles and Dionysos in Attic vase painting in particular, Verbanck-Pierard,[103] in studying the iconography of the reclining Heracles at the banquet, suggested that the reason why this schema was especially designed for Heracles and Dionysos was perhaps because their religious personalities share many common traits. Since the ritual offering of a meal to the god who is treated as a guest, a *theoxenia*, is especially connected to Heracles, she suggests that one of the things that this representational schema in both its forms, on the *kline* and on the ground, may be reflecting is a *theoxenia* of Heracles. This interpretation has been accepted by Jameson.[104]

The interpretation that one of the meanings of the reclining god is that it reflects a cultic *xenismos* would fit Dionysos since, we saw, on my reading, a *xenismos* of Dionysos was central to the City Dionysia. But of course the interpretation of our schema simply in terms of this *xenismos* would not explain why the god was shown reclining on the ground rather than on a couch.[105] Nor would it explain the fact that satyrs and men are also shown reclining on the ground. So another factor was also involved here. This "missing" factor corresponds to, and is thus provided by, my earlier conclusion, based on comparisons of images within this small corpus, and between them and other comparable Attic and non-Attic schemata, that one of the dimensions of signification of these images is that they reflected and refracted a ritual of Dionysos, a festival, in which ritual dining took place on *stibades* of ivy, with the diners wearing ivy wreaths. In these circumstances, we may conclude that this schema was shaped through the interaction of two schemata, Dionysos at the banquet reflecting a rite of *xenismos* of Dionysos, and "reclining on the ground wearing wreaths of the ritually significant plant," reflecting a rite of ritual dining on *stibades* of ivy. This would indicate that these images reflect and refract a ritual nexus in which these two rites were closely connected. On my reconstruction of the City Dionysia, these two rites were indeed closely associated; and the convergence of two independent arguments offers, I submit, some confirmation of the validity of the two sets of analyses.

In addition, the dates of the images fit the notion that they reflect a City Dionysia festival that began some time in the 530s. For the images of Dionysos represented alone reclining on a *kline* or on the ground appear for the first time in the last quarter of the sixth century,[106] not too many years after the festival's foundation, perhaps at a time when the early changes and developments I will try to reconstruct later in this chapter drew attention to, or increased the popularity of, this festival.

A few images support the conclusions reached above, by confirming a connection between the schema "reclining on the ground in a Dionysiac context" and the *xenismos* of Dionysos at the City Dionysia. First, a set of images on a plastic kantharos, the janiform head kantharos Ferrara, Museo Nazionale di Spina, 9410 (T 256 B VP),[107] which is in the shape of a head of Dionysos on one side, a head of satyr on the other, a vase wholly given to Dionysiac imagery and cult. On the side above Dionysos' head the god is represented again, reclining on the ground against a cushion and holding out a kantharos in his right hand and a vine in his left. A pointed amphora is leaning against his feet. On the other side is shown the sacrifice of a *tragos*, a billy goat, the moment at which the animal's carcass is being dismembered. Given the context of which the scene is part, there is no doubt that this is a sacrifice to Dionysos.[108]

This set of images, then, connects Dionysos reclining on the ground with the sacrifice of a *tragos* to Dionysos. If the interpretation of the schema constructed above is right, this set of images would reflect a connection between ritual dining on *stibades* of ivy and the *xenismos* of Dionysos involving the sacrifice of a *tragos*. As we shall see in II.2.i below, there are also other reasons for associating the sacrifice of a *tragos* with the City Dionysia, indeed for ascribing this sacrifice to the *xenismos* of Dionysos in that festival. So this set of images appears to refract a reality that would correspond exactly to my reconstruction of the festival. For if we accept that it was this ritual nexus, ritual dining on *stibades* of ivy associated with the *xenismos* of Dionysos involving the sacrifice of a *tragos*, that was refracted in these images, and so shaped the selections that constructed them, we can make sense of these images in terms of established Greek iconographical modalities and relationships as well as in terms of Greek mentality.

On one side Dionysos is shown in a ritual activity, ritual dining and drinking while reclining on the ground, which was performed by his worshippers, and which also evoked his *xenismos*, which was connected with the ritual dining; on the other side there is an image of the sacrifice that provided the central part of the *xenismos* meal; the animal is being turned into meat, to be offered to the god. In another register, on one side we see the god, on the other a mythological worshipper, especially appropriate in this context of dissolution, represented by the shape of the head, and a human worshipper, involved in the the sacrifice of an animal to the god, and so also the worship of the god at the expense of an animal. I submit that this correspondence between the ritual reality which, on these readings, is refracted in these im-

Chapter 1: The Great Dionysia 87

ages, and the reconstruction of the ritual I am proposing offers support for my reconstruction.

This is confirmed by the fact that the association between the *tragos* and Dionysos reclining on the ground, and more generally, between the *tragos* and a Dionysiac symposion involving reclining on the ground, occurs repeatedly. For example, on side A of the cup Copenhagen Ny Carlsberg inv. 2700[109] Dionysos is reclining on the ground against a rock, wearing an ivy wreath, a billy goat on either side.[110] The same schema of Dionysos reclining on the ground wearing an ivy wreath, a billy goat on either side is also found on other vases; on the oinochoe Munich Antikensammlung 1806[111] Dionysos appears to be interacting with the *tragos* on the right. Other images associate a *tragos* with a symposion of human males reclining on the ground.[112] This combination is sometimes said to be decorative, a decorative combination of separate motifs.[113] However, the definite association between Dionysos and the *tragos*,[114] the fact that Dionysos himself is shown reclining on the ground in the company of one or more *tragoi*, as well as the fact that in some images the *tragos* is interwoven into the image of the symposion on the ground, shows that there was a perceived association between the two. The notion of a decorative combination without semantic implications cannot be sustained; selections were shaped by cultural assumptions, and since the definite association between Dionysos and the *tragos* was part of those assumptions, it is meaningless to think that the *tragos* would have been perceived as unrelated to the Dionysiac scene. This suggests that these assumptions had included a perception of an association between the Dionysiac symposion lying on the ground and the *tragos*.

Another image shows an association between Dionysos reclining on the ground and sacrifice, sacrifice in the divine world; a kantharos in Boston[115] shows on side A Dionysos reclining on the ground against a cushion, holding a big branch from which grow both vine leaves and ivy. On his left a satyr holds a pointed amphora wreathed with ivy; on his right a satyr holds a wineskin. The satyrs are wreathed with ivy. A skin *aulos*-case is also depicted. On the other side of the vase there is a mythological sacrificial scene: Dionysos and Maenads by an altar, the god pouring a libation from a kantharos, a *kanoun* on the ground and one Maenad stretching her hands over the altar, perhaps strewing a handful of groats as part of the sacrificial ritual.

The Ferrara vase discussed in detail above was a plastic kantharos, a head vase, a janiform head kantharos. Dionysiac scenes involving reclining on the ground scenes are also shown on other vases of this type. Thus, for example, another janiform head kantharos has a satyr's head on one side and a woman's head on the other.[116] The image over the satyr's head shows a satyr playing the *aulos* with a Maenad holding a drinking cup; both are reclining on the ground against cushions. The image over the woman's head shows Dionysos reclining on the ground against a cushion holding a vine in one hand, while gesticulating with the other towards a wineskin crowned with a garland of ivy. There are more images of figures reclining on the ground on such vases.[117] The kantharos is, of course, the par excellence Dionysiac vase; but the series of plastic kantharoi in particular, and also other shapes of plastic vases, which also have scenes of a Dionysiac symposion reclining on the ground,[118] have a very pronounced Dionysiac content and, it is argued by Lissarague,[119] tend to represent various types of otherness, such as women, blacks, satyrs, grotesques, "other" than the central Athenian male identity. If this is right, the frequency of reclining on the ground scenes on such vases may perhaps suggest that this context of otherness was somehow suitable for, and so attracted, these Dionysiac images. The notion that they fitted a context of otherness would lend a little independent support to my hypothesis, that these images reflect the ritual dining on *stibades*, the *komos*, which belonged to the period of dissolution and abnormality before the reception of Dionysos.

In these circumstances, I suggest that some of these images reflect and refract a ritual nexus in the cult of Dionysos that involved a *xenismos* that included the sacrifice of a *tragos*, and a ritual symposion reclining on *stibades* of ivy wearing wreaths of ivy.[120] In real life, Dionysos was deemed to be dining on the *kline* (together with certain Athenians) at the *xenismos* rite after the sacrifice of the *tragos*, which had been preceded by the ritual dining on the ground on *stibades* of ivy. The images reflected, refracted, and combined elements from the two ritual dining rites in different ways, to articulate different perceptions pertaining to Dionysos and the Dionysiac sphere.

I have tried to read these images as much as possible through ancient eyes, deploying meanings established for the relevant iconographical elements in other images, and reconstructing those of the relevant iconographical schemata through comparisons, and on the basis of established modalities of representation in Attic iconography. I have not produced ad hoc readings to fit my reconstruction of the festival. Therefore, I submit, the fact that the two converge provides confirmation for my reconstruction of the ritual dining and drinking on *stibades* of ivy at the City Dionysia, and its association with the *xenismos* of the god; and indicates that the ritual dining on *stibades* had taken place already in the sixth and early fifth centuries.

Chapter 1: The Great Dionysia   89

c) *A Set of Conclusions*

In these circumstances, I suggest that there is little doubt that no later than the last quarter of the sixth century a ritual involving a symposion in which men were lying on beds of ivy took place in connection with the statue of Dionysos' movement to the shrine at the Academy. Since there is a very important element of the festival, the *komos*, the identity of which it has not been possible to pin down, and the name of which would aptly describe this reconstructed ritual, I suggest that it was this ritual dining and drinking on beds of leaves of ivy that was referred to as the *komos*—or at least part of it, since the *komos* also involved drunken people in the streets afterwards. Drunkenness (and perhaps masks for at least some people) characterized the *komos*. We found good reasons for thinking that drunkenness and masks, drunkenness expressed through masks, was involved in the reception of Dionysos, and perhaps also in the transfer of the statue into the theater, the *eisagoge apo tes escharas*, in the figure of the *ithyphalloi*. We found reasons to think that the statue was met by processional choruses and *ithyphalloi*. We can see a direct connection between the ritual dining on *stibades/komos* and the *ithyphalloi*: not only were the latter (symbolically) drunken men, as the men at the *komos* were, but they were also erect-phallos ones, which is what the original Athenians in mythological time would have been at that stage in the myth, while waiting to receive Dionysos. Consequently, I suggest that the latter part of the *komos* involved the reception of the statue of Dionysos, with processional choruses and *ithyphalloi*, which marked the first stage in the reestablishment of order, or rather, of the new order which includes the cult of Dionysos, and of normality, following the period of abnormality and dissolution marked by the movement of the statue to the shrine at the Academy.

d) *Topographical Evidence and Further Comparative Evidence; Pindar Dithyramb fr. 75*

Before I go on, for reasons that will become apparent, I need to consider the location of this ritual reception, and more generally questions of topography and spatial relationships pertaining to this whole ritual nexus.

First, where did the ritual dining on *stibades* take place? We can exclude the shrine at the Academy as a possible location, since Philostratos distinguishes the two, on the one hand when the statue *katioi eis Akademian*, on the other the ritual dining *en Kerameiko*. But does *en Kerameiko* really mean at the Kerameikos as we understand it in the classical period? Given that, after the archaic city wall was abolished, and the boundaries of the Inner Kerameikos ceased to be well defined, the northern lower part of the Agora also came to be called Kerameikos, and given that Philostratos calls the Odeion of Agrippa, which was, very roughly, towards the center of the N-S axis of the Agora, "the theatre in the Kerameikos called the Agrippeion,"[121] the indication *en Kerameiko* could have been referring to any space from the northern part of the Agora onwards, including the area to the NW of the Agora, where, at least by Pausanias' time, Dionysos had a space sacred to him, somewhere to the NW of the northwestern part of the Agora along the road from the Academy to the Agora, which he did not have in the classical period.

Pausanias 1.2.5 mentions a *temenos* to Dionysos in a stoa; the building that was Dionysos' shrine was certainly dedicated to this use after the fifth century, for in the fifth century it had been the house of Poulytion in which the profanation of the Mysteries had taken place. After the sanctuary of Dionysos, Pausanias continues, there is a building in which there are clay statues representing Amphictyon entertaining with a feast other gods and Dionysos; Pegasos of Eleutherai is also represented. As we saw, Pausanias adds that Pegasos had been helped by the Delphic oracle, which had recalled that Dionysos had visited Ikarios. The following reasons lead us to conclude that the group of statues represented Amphictyon's reception of Dionysos in the presence of the other gods:[122] the proximity to the sanctuary of Dionysos; the presence of Pegasos in Amphictyon's represented entertainment of the gods; and the myth[123] that Amphictyon had learnt from Dionysos to mix wine, which allowed people to "tame" (as it were) their wine drinking, retain control and remain upright—a myth clearly connected with this sanctuary of Dionysos, since it contained a representation of Akratos (Unmixed) described by Pausanias as an attendant demon of Dionysos. This is part of the mythological nexus of Dionysos' reception in Athens, a companion myth to that of the cult's introduction by Pegasos, that articulates the notion of taming, bringing under control the aspects of the Dionysiac nexus that had seemed threatening. Clearly, then, this Dionysiac nexus relates to the persona of the god as Dionysos Eleuthereus, his reception at Athens and the festival of the City Dionysia. This is hardly surprising, since this sanctuary is on the road from the Academy to the center of Athens, indeed at the edge of the center.[124] Thus, the hypothesis suggested above that the *komos* ritual dining was connected with the reception of Dionysos would fit this sanctuary's location and mythological associations.

But, we saw, this sanctuary was not there in the classical period. So even if in the second century A.D. the ritual dining had taken place in

Chapter 1: The Great Dionysia

this sanctuary of Dionysos to the NW of the Agora this could not have been the case in the classical period. So what happened in the classical period?

There is one structure, also on the way to and from the Academy, on the northwestern corner of the Agora, which, I will now argue, can be connected with this ritual nexus of the arrival of the statue of Dionysos from the Academy. So let us now leave the question of the location of the ritual dining for the moment and consider another important question of topography relevant to the ritual movement of the statue, and in particular to the *eisagoge apo tes escharas*: the identity and location of the *eschara* where the statue of Dionysos had stood before being taken to the theater. Before we consider this, we must look at the ritual movements that took place in connection with the Dionysia in a historical perspective.

The dramatic performances had not taken place in the theater from the beginning. According to the lexicographers they were transferred to the Theater of Dionysos from the Agora in the 70th Olympiad (499/6).[125] The construction of the first theater in the sanctuary of Dionysos Eleuthereus can be dated by archaeological evidence, pottery in the earliest layer of the fill beneath the seats, as not much later than c. 500.[126] This convergence of the archaeologically based date of the beginning of the theater with the date given for the same event in the notice in Suda confirms, I suggest, the validity of the latter. Since we know that the statue of Dionysos was present during the dramatic performances in the classical period and later, and that this entertainment of the god was intimately connected with the nature of the festival as a celebration of the first introduction of the cult of Dionysos in Athens, the ritual grammar of the festival entails that the statue would have been present also when the performances had taken place in the Agora. If that is right, where was it located?

One structure in the Agora which we know had something to do with the Dionysia was the Altar of the Twelve Gods, since, we saw, Xenophon mentions, in a context in which he is speaking of processions, that at the Dionysia, which in the context can only mean the Dionysia procession, the dances of choruses gratified in addition (to Dionysos) the Twelve Gods and other gods. The formulation may suggest a special emphasis on the Altar of the Twelve Gods, which may indicate that, whatever the significance of the choruses dancing at various shrines may have been, other than simply honoring the gods,[127] it would have been stronger in the case of the Altar of the Twelve Gods.

If, as, we shall see below, is almost certain, the dithyramb by Pindar to which fragment 75 S-M belongs, was performed at the Dionysia, rather than the Anthesteria,[128] it would confirm the importance of the

Altar of the Twelve Gods at the Dionysia. For the Altar in the Agora referred to could only have been the Altar of the Twelve Gods: only two altars in Athens could possibly have been called *asteos omphalon thyoenta*, the *hestia* at the prytaneion and the Altar of the Twelve Gods; and of the two only the altar of the Twelve Gods fits the overall description and context. The choruses' dances at the Altar of the Twelve Gods and at other shrines during the procession was, among other things, a physical expression of the cult of Dionysos' arrival and incorporation in the pantheon of the city; of the relationship of this cult to that of the other, already established gods—especially since the Twelve Gods would have been perceived as also a metaphor for the polis' pantheon.

The Altar of the Twelve Gods is in the immediate proximity of the area in which the performances would have taken place.[129] More significantly, in front of the Altar of the Twelve Gods, in the immediate proximity of the area in which the performances would have taken place, between the Altar of the Twelve Gods and the performance area, at the time when the dramatic performances would have been taking place in the Agora, in the closing years of the sixth century, a new structure was built, a ground altar of the type that would have been referred to by the Greeks as an *eschara*. The function of this *eschara* has never been established. It had been suggested that it was the shrine of Aiakos, the Aiakeion, but that proposed identification has now been shown to be fallacious by Stroud who has conclusively shown that the Aiakeion was in another part of the Agora.[130]

Let us set the parameters for the reconstruction of the function of this *eschara*.[131] First, it was sited in a very prominent location, near the entrance to the Agora on the NW, very close to the Altar of the Twelve Gods. Second, it had the same orientation, and similar material and workmanship, as the Altar of the Twelve Gods, from which it was separated by a narrow passage.[132] Their relationship suggests that the *eschara* was sited in relation to the Twelve Gods;[133] the close proximity especially suggests that they were part of one cultic complex. Third, it was of substantial size and of substantial construction, which, together with its location, has led scholars to conclude that it had served a cult of some civic importance.[134] It consisted of a rectangle floored with field stones enclosed by a poros curb of 1.76 x 3.77 meters which rose at each end. Then, shortly after it was constructed it was surrounded by a pavement, wider on the west side, and the whole was enclosed by a wall with an entrance in the form of a recessed porch on the east side and probably a doorway on the west. Finally, it went out of use "probably" in the Hellenistic period, and then was overlaid by an exedra facing north.

My suggestion is that the *eisagoge apo tes escharas* does not refer to the bringing of the statue to the theater from the temple at the Academy, but from this *eschara* in the Agora, which was its first stop in the center of Athens. This would make sense of the expression *apo tes escharas*, which is surely a very odd way of referring to the bringing of a statue from the Academy. In addition, since it is unlikely that the term *eschara* was used loosely in this context, it is puzzling why the Academy shrine should have an *eschara* altar since, to my knowledge, there is nothing in the cult of Dionysos Eleuthereus to account for it. It is true that such distinctions in altar types and the terms used for them are less than straightforward, and mostly beyond our reconstruction, but the fact that the altars in the sanctuary of Dionysos Eleuthereus are not of the *eschara* type adds, I submit, some strength to this argument. More importantly, on this hypothesis, the statue of Dionysos would be located exactly where we would expect it to be during the performances.

In terms of function and ritual logic the *eschara* in the Agora fits much better than a hypothetical *eschara* in the Academy shrine. If the Academy shrine had indeed stood symbolically for Eleutherai, the place the statue had come from, as is often assumed, it would certainly have been inappropriate as a locus of the statue's and cult's reception in Athens. Even if it had not, whatever its precise symbolic meaning may have been, it was neither at the center, where the central reception of the cult was clearly located—given the location of both the sanctuary of Dionysos Eleuthereus and of the main part of the festival of Dionysia—nor extraurban, in which case it could have been standing symbolically for the statue's first reception on unequivocally Attic soil.

The hypothesis that the statue of Dionysos had stood by the *eschara* in the Agora, after it was brought back from the Academy, can be supported by further arguments. As we saw, shortly after its construction the *eschara* acquired a pavement and an enclosing wall. It may be a complete coincidence, and it cannot count as serious evidence, though it may add a little to the cumulative weight of the evidence all of which points, I submit, to the same direction, but the hypothesis proposed here would account for this change: around, or a few years after, 500, the performances were transferred to the sanctuary of Dionysos, where the first theater was constructed. Thus, Dionysos' statue would no longer have watched the performances standing by the *eschara*, and it would have been no longer necessary to have a free view line to the performance space; certainly, the *eschara* would no longer have had an intimate cultic relationship with the area to its south. This would account for the fact that it acquired an enclosure, and that the east-west axis, which was important for sacrifice, was emphasized.

The hypothesis that the statue of Dionysos had stood by the *eschara* in the Agora for a time during the City Dionysia would also explain the puzzling fact that the *eisagoge apo tes escharas* took the statue to the theater, not to the temple, despite the fact that its first active role would have been not in the theater, but in the sanctuary, at the culmination of the *pompe*. On my hypothesis, it was taken to the theater because the theater was the locus of the second activity with which the statue had been involved at the *eschara*, the functions of which as a ritual locus were now split between two spaces, the *eschara* in the Agora and the theater, with a ritual movement, the *eisagoge apo tes escharas*, connecting the two.

Finally, is it a coincidence that the *eisagoge apo tes escharas* disappears from later texts,[135] and that some time during the Hellenistic period the *eschara* in the Agora was abandoned,[136] while at least by Pausanias' time Dionysos had a space sacred to him somewhere to the NW of the northwestern part of the Agora (in which was located the *eschara*), along the road from the Academy to the Agora, which he did not have in the classical period, and which, we found reasons for thinking, may have been associated with the reception of Dionysos and the ritual dining on *stibades*? It is surely possible that the three facts were correlative; and that this ritual dining on *stibades* had taken place in the sanctuary of Dionysos to the NW of the Agora after the *eschara* fell into disuse, while earlier it had taken place in the Agora in association with the *eschara*, where the statue of Dionysos was brought as the first stop at the center of Athens, and where some reception ritual, sacrifices, and singing hymns, had taken place.

What evidence there is gives us very good reasons for thinking, first, that there was a strong connection between the area to the NW of the northwestern corner of the Agora and Dionysos' reception in Athens and the City Dionysia;[137] then, that at least some of it was the result of a later expansion and development, and that there was ritual activity associated with that area, connected with the movement of the statue to and from the Academy. My suggestion that that ritual had earlier been associated with the *eschara* by the Altar of the Twelve Gods is undoubtedly based on insufficient evidence, but it would fit the ritual and topographical structure of the ritual. The space associated with Dionysos in the later period was on the road from the Academy to, and on the edge of, the center of the polis, and it was associated with Dionysos' reception. Since those parts of Dionysos' reception ritual that can be located took place at the very center, it is possible to see this space as an extension of that center, with the cultic focus having moved further to the NW, for reasons we shall consider in the next section.

Chapter 1: The Great Dionysia

Finally, this reconstruction can be confirmed when we go back to the consideration with which we started this section. Since dramatic performances had taken place in Agora before they were moved to the theater in the sanctuary, and since the statue of Dionysos would have been present at those performances,[138] it follows that at least at that stage in the history of the festival the movement of the statue was not simply from the Academy to the sanctuary. At that stage at least it had to have been taken from the Academy to the Agora and then from the Agora to the sanctuary.

Why the statue of Dionysos should have been brought at the *eschara* to be received will become clear in the next section when we consider the changes and developments of the festival in the course of the sixth century. And this will add further support to the view that the *eisagoge apo tes escharas* does not refer to the bringing of the statue to the theater from the temple at the Academy—the default hypothesis for which there is no evidence; but to the movement from the *eschara* in the Agora, which was its first stop in the center of Athens.

Now we need to return to the Altar of the Twelve Gods to explore further its ritual relationship with the Dionysia and with the *eschara*. On my reconstruction, the *eschara*, which was closely associated with the Altar of the Twelve Gods, was the locus of a rite of *xenismos* of Dionysos.

The notion of the Twelve Gods (representing the pantheon of a city) being involved in a rite of *xenismos* in which they are guests, rather than recipients of sacrifice, is not unparallelled in Greek religion. In a decree for the festival of Zeus Sosipolis at Magnesia on the Meander[139] the temporary structure in which the *theoxenia* takes place, the tholos, was pitched in the Agora, near the Altar of the Twelve Gods.[140] That is in the same place as, on my interpretation, the *xenismos* of Dionysos would have taken place. In the Magnesian festival images of the Twelve Gods were carried in the procession. This involvement in the procession is a different, but in some ways not totally unrelated, involvement from that in the Dionysia procession in Athens, in the course of which choruses honored the Twelve Gods at their altar. The Twelve Gods involved in this rite of Theoxenia are guests at the feast, rather than receiving sacrificial victims and a meal themselves.[141] This, then, gives us a parallel for the reconstructed association between *xenismos* and the altar of the Twelve gods, as well as for the attested ritual connection of the Altar of the Twelve Gods with the City Dionysia. Incidentally, I submit, the fact that the reconstruction of spaces and movements proposed on other grounds here would place the *xenismos* adjacently to the Altar of the Twelve Gods, in exactly the same position as another *xenismos* rite whose location we know, offers support for this reconstruction.

The same situation involving other gods, and the Twelve Gods in particular, obtains at the Delphic Theoxenia, in which Apollo was the god receiving the *xenismos*. The paean by Philodamos of Scarphea, written to be performed at the Theoxenia, and inscribed in the sanctuary in 340/39 B.C., speaks (lines 109-12) of performing this poem to the sacred family of the gods at the Theoxenia. In addition, Apollo's mother Leto was also involved: the person who presented the largest spring onion to Leto won the award of a portion of the meat from the table.[142]

It would appear, then, that, according to Greek ritual mentality, when rites of *xenismos* were performed for an Olympian god, all the twelve Olympian gods were believed to have visited as well, as guests, rather than recipients of the *xenismos*, and were acknowledged in various ways. This would give us a context for, and explain why, the Altar of the Twelve Gods was especially acknowledged in the course of the procession, and why the Twelve Gods had a special significance in this festival.

This brings us to Pindar's dithyramb in praise of Athens to which fragment 75 S-M belongs. I submit that it is likely that this dithyramb was performed at the rite of *xenismos* at the *eschara* in the Agora, in the City Dionysia, that this is the dithyramb sung by a chorus approaching the altar during the sacrifice,[143] since this dithyramb is processional.[144]

Δεῦτ' ἐν χορόν, Ὀλύμπιοι,
ἐπί τε κλυτὰν πέμπετε χάριν, θεοί,
πολύβατον οἵ τ' ἄστεος ὀμφαλὸν θυόεντ'
ἐν ταῖς ἱεραῖς Ἀθάναις
οἰχνεῖτε πανδαίδαλόν τ' εὐκλέ' ἀγοράν·
ἰοδέτων λάχετε στεφάνων τᾶν τ' ἐαρι-
  δρόπων ἀοιδᾶν,
Διόθεν τέ με σὺν ἀγλαΐᾳ
ἴδετε πορευθέντ' ἀοιδᾶν δεύτερον
ἐπὶ τὸν κισσοδέταν θεόν,
τὸν Βρόμιον, τὸν Ἐριβόαν τε βροτοὶ καλέομεν,
γόνον ὑπάτων μὲν πατέρων μελπόμεν⟨οι⟩
γυναικῶν τε Καδμεϊᾶν {Σεμέλην}.
ἐναργέα τ' ἔμ' ὥτε μάντιν οὐ λανθάνει.
φοινικοεάνων ὁπότ' οἰχθέντος Ὡρᾶν θαλάμου
εὔοδμον ἐπάγοισιν ἔαρ φυτὰ νεκτάρεα.
τότε βάλλεται, τότ' ἐπ' ἀμβρόταν χθόν' ἐραταί
ἴων φόβαι, ῥόδα τε κόμαισι μείγνυται,
ἀχεῖ τ' ὀμφαὶ μελέων σὺν αὐλοῖς,
οἰχνεῖ τε Σεμέλαν ἑλικάμπυκα χοροί.

Chapter 1: The Great Dionysia

That the context for this dithyramb was the City Dionysia is indicated by a series of arguments,[145] which I will briefly list here. First,[146] it is not true that the fact that the time of the year spoken of in the dithyramb was early spring indicates the Anthesteria; for the Athenians early spring is associated above all with the City Dionysia.[147] Second, the City Dionysia is indicated by the fact that the Altar of the Twelve Gods is involved, which only came into play in the City Dionysia among Dionysos' festivals; but of course, this is an agument *ex silentio*, and this is its weakness. However, a third consideration indicates very strongly not simply the City Dionysia, but also the particular rite of *xenismos* in that festival: the importance of the Twelve Gods themselves in the poem. For their appearance can be made sense of, because it can be seen as reflecting, the importance of the Twelve Gods in this, as in other rituals of *xenismos* for an Olympian deity. It is, I believe, only this interpretation that can answer the question, as formulated recently by van der Weiden, "why Pindar introduced the Olympians into this Dionysiac hymn."[148]

In addition, the formulations in lines 7-10 (*epi ton kissodetan theon*) suggest that he is presenting himself as singing in the presence of Dionysos, which suggests the *xenismos* ritual in which the god was present, represented by his statue.[149] My interpretation is the only one that makes sense of the fact that the destination of the chorus was a statue of Dionysos,[150] but at the same time, the Altar of the Twelve Gods was in the immediate vicinity, since Pindar (line 8) invites the Twelve Gods to look upon him. If, as is likely, the reference to a rite in honor of Semele indicates a rite for Semele directly connected with the context of the dithyramb's performance, it would fit the rite of *xenismos* in which she would be involved, as Leto was at the Delphic Theoxenia. The fact that immediately after the City Dionysia, on 16 Elaphebolion, the deme of Erchia sacrificed a goat to Semele and also a goat to Dionysos, two sacrifices performed on the same altar,[151] may perhaps be taken as confirmation that Semele also had had a place in the City Dionysia, and that the deme ritual reflected this.[152]

Finally, another element that points, I believe, in the same direction is the wreaths. The fact that the other Olympians receive *iodeton stephanon*, wreaths bound with violets,[153] while Dionysos is wreathed with ivy, again fits the context of the rite of *xenismos* at the City Dionysia. For this combination of ivy and violets corresponds to, and may perhaps be reflecting, the wreaths of violets and ivy worn by the *phallophoroi* when they appear with the *ithyphalloi* in the theater, in a context which, I suggested, was the context of this *xenismos* at the Dionysia. Since the two arguments are independent, their convergence offers some support for the validity of both.

In these circumstances, I suggest that there is a strong case in favor of the view that this dithyramb was performed during the *xenismos* sacrifice at the City Dionysia.[154] On my reconstruction this had taken place at the *eschara* in the Agora. In Pindar's dithyramb the Olympian gods are going to the Altar of the Twelve Gods, with which the *eschara* formed one cultic complex. So, once again, there is a convergence in the results of the two independent arguments; and this, I submit, offers confirmation for both analyses.

e) *Another Set of Conclusions*

On this reconstruction of the festival, then, after the reception of the statue by the Athenians the statue would have been installed at the *eschara*, and the rites at the *eschara*, the singing of hymns and sacrificing would have taken place. The notion that the statue at the *eschara* was an important locus for hymns, which fits the rite of reception, also fits Alkiphron's formulation *kai ton ep' escharas hymnesai kat' etos Dionyson*.[155] The fact that what we know of the rites at the *eschara*, hymns and sacrifices in the presence of the god's statue, fit the main elements of the ritual schema of *xenismos* may add a little support to this reading of the evidence and reconstruction.

We have, we saw, some evidence to suggest that the *komos* had taken place at night. The fact that symposia and ordinary post-symposia *komoi* took place in the evening and at night may point in the same direction. In addition, a passage in Plutarch suggests an association between nighttime and public *komoi* in honor of Dionysos.[156] In the *eisagoge apo tes escharas* the statue was escorted in a torchlight procession,[157] and so at night. It is possible then, that this was also part of the same ritual nexus that began with the *komos*, ritual dining on *stibades*, then the statue arrived in the Agora and was received by revellers, with hymns, including processional choruses and the *ithyphalloi*, who, with drunken men's masks and erect phalloi, represented all the Athenian men before normality was restored by the reception of Dionysos and the establishment of his cult.

The statue was installed at the *eschara*, hymns were sung and sacrifices performed, and then the statue was taken to the theater by the ephebes, and others, undoubtedly those who participated in its reception, and who may have preceded it in a *komos*, so that they watched the entrance of the statue in the theater, announced by the *ithyphalloi*, and preceded by the jeering *phallophoroi*—whose ritual jeering would fit the occasion as reconstructed here.[158]

In this reconstruction, then, there is a connection between drunkenness, the *komos*, and the movement of the statue from the *eschara* in

Chapter 1: The Great Dionysia

the Agora to the theater. I suggest that this fits a sliver of evidence about a rite we hear about, and that this may be not without significance. Athenaeus 10.428E refers to Dionysos in a state of drunkenness being led on a wagon (*agousi epi tes hamaxes*) through the middle of the Agora. Dionysos in a state of drunkenness means the statue of the god, symbolically drunk, and this would fit perfectly the context reconstructed here.[159] Athenaeus does not say anything about occasion or place, but the formulation suggests a well-known rite that needs no explanation; this would best fit an Athenian rite that influenced other cities, as, we know, was the case with the City Dionysia; most importantly, the movement through the middle of the Agora fits the reconstruction proposed here. Such a reconstruction of the *komos* and associated rites may make it easier to understand why, as we saw, *komoi to Dionyso*, in the plural, in *IG* II² 2318 refers to the whole festival by metonymy: because the *komos* was such a ritually crucial part of the festival.

f) *The Reconstruction of the City Dionysia: A Summary*

To sum up. On the reconstruction constructed in this chapter, from the early fifth century onwards the Great Dionysia consisted of the following rites. First the statue of Dionysos was removed from the sanctuary and taken to the shrine in the Academy; while it was there, in the evening, a ritual dining on *stibades* of ivy took place in the northwestern part of the Agora; it included some masked figures and was, with its immediate aftermath involving the reception of the statue of Dionysos, called *komos*; the statue was received by processional choruses and *ithyphalloi*, and it was taken to the *eschara* by the Altar of the Twelve Gods, where hymns were sung and a sacrifice was offered. Then the statue was ceremonially taken to the theater by the ephebes, accompanied also by revellers, and its entrance in the theater was preceded, and introduced, by *ithyphalloi* and *phallophoroi*. The procession to the sanctuary took place the next day, on 10th Elaphebolion, and culminated in sacrifices. In the following days took place the dramatic and dithyrambic competitions.[160]

The pre-procession part of the ritual as reconstructed here, then, contains the same elements that we found in the ritual schemata of other *hypodoche* and *xenismos* rituals, with the addition of further elements, which correspond to the particularities of the cult and festival complex that make this a complex nexus: *hypodoche* of Dionysos, with hymns; *xenismos* with hymns and sacrifices; and a sort of *pannychis* following, consisting of a continuation of the *komos*, the *eisagoge apo tes escharas*, and the reception of the statue in the theater. I suggest that this fit between reconstruction and known ritual schema offers some support to this reconstruction.

In order to make sense of these ritual elements, and also to try to reconstruct the context in which tragedy was generated, it is necessary to attempt to reconstruct something of the history of the festival, some of the ways in which it had changed in the sixth and perhaps very early fifth century. This I will try to do in the next section. I submit that the reconstruction of the Dionysia proposed here will gain further support from those analyses in the next section, where the reasons for some of the elements and locations of the rites will become clear.

II.1.iii. *Changes and Developments: The Early History of the Great Dionysia*

a) *Changes and Beginnings: The Polis Dimension*

I will now try to determine some of the changes that the festival underwent in the period before the time when it becomes more visible in the form in which I have reconstructed it above.

We have already seen that one change that had taken place was that at about, or just after, 500 B.C. the dramatic and dithyrambic performances had moved from the Agora to the theater. Some other changes can also be detected. The fact that the dithyrambic competitions had a tribal articulation reflecting the Kleisthenic subdivisions shows that they had been reorganized in the context of the Kleisthenic reforms. The theatrical competitions had a whole-polis articulation, in that both the selection of the poets and of the *choregoi* by the archon is personal, and not by polis subdivision; the archon appointed three *choregoi* for tragedy from all the Athenians;[161] so it is the whole polis that constitutes the selection unit; only the selection of the judges involved a tribal articulation.[162] This is comparable to the situation in the Panathenaia, where some of the competitions were organized by tribes.[163] That in festivals of this type more activities could become subsequently articulated through new polis subdivisions, thus strengthening symbolically a new polis articulation, can be seen also in the Panathenaia, the Athenian whole-polis festival par excellence, in which, first, it was the demarchs that mustered the procession, and second, the meat of the sacrificial victims was distributed deme by deme, among the participants sent by each deme.[164] At the other end of the spectrum, the Panathenaia had a Panhellenic facet; for the musical, rhapsodic, and athletic games were Panhellenic.[165] Similarly, in the City Dionysia a non-Athenian poet could be given a chorus and the *aulos* player could also be a foreigner.

Chapter 1: The Great Dionysia

The pattern of the City Dionysia and of the Panathenaia is both comparable to, but also different from, that of the Thargelia, which, like the City Dionysia, was under the control of the archon.[166] It is comparable, in that the Thargelia also had dithyrambic *agones* arranged by tribes juxtaposed to a ritual nexus that was otherwise articulated. It is different, in that that ritual nexus was twofold, one part involving articulation by polis subdivisions other than tribes, namely, phratries, while the other focussed on an expulsion that purified the community. Since there can be no doubt that the Panathenaia were founded at the latest in the second quarter of the sixth century, and the Thargelia is generally believed to be early, these comparisons suggest that in the case of the City Dionysia also, an older festival with a whole-polis focus had been reorganized to include, at the edges of the core ritual, an articulation through the new polis subdivisions.

It is usually assumed that the City Dionysia arose from, and celebrated, a real life annexation of a cult of Dionysos from Eleutherai when the latter became part of Athens. But there are problems with this view, which was recently reformulated by Connor.[167] Connor thinks that the pattern of the City Dionysia was appropriate for a festival of integration following the annexation of Eleutherai, that could easily grow into a celebration of Athenian freedom and might; he compares this hypothetical annexation and ensuing ritual to those of Eleusis. I have argued elsewhere that the Eleusinian cult was not annexed, but had been part of Athenian polis religion from the beginning of that polis.[168] Nevertheless, that ritual does express the integration of this outlying part of the polis and its intimate relationship with the center in spatial movements. But the ritual grammar of the Eleusinian ritual and of similar cults involving symbolic integration with the center is radically different from that of the City Dionysia. For a fundamental element in the ritual articulation of such integrations is a procession from the center towards the "outlying" sanctuary, as is the case with Eleusis, Brauron, the Argive Heraion and so on. Though we do not know the route of the Dionysia procession, we do know that it did not go to Eleutherai. Eleutherai is, of course, a long way from Athens, but it is not all that much farther than Brauron. Even the movement of the statue to and from the shrine at the Academy, which on the annexation theories should be a kind of symbolic representation of Eleutherai, is not ritually prominent. If the Dionysia were an integration/annexation festival, the movement of the statue from the Academy to the sanctuary would have been a central part of the festival. Far from fitting the integration procession schemata the Dionysia ritual is radically different from them. Indeed, we may wonder why the statue was not taken to Eleutherai in the preliminary part of the ritual, and why Eleutherai was not important in that ritual.

The focus of the festival is in the center of the city. It is not the process of the bringing of the cult, or its place of origin, that are focussed on, but the god's arrival and his reception. The focus of myth is not the introduction of the cult of Dionysos Eleuthereus from Eleutherai to Athens; the myth is about the first introduction of the cult of Dionysos in Athens—which, it says, came from Eleutherai—and it is this introduction of the cult of Dionysos in general that the City Dionysia celebrates. Of course, this festival was not perceived to have been the oldest Dionysos festival; it was the Anthesteria that was considered *ta archaiotera Dionysia*.[169] But, irrespective of when exactly the myth was generated, the festival celebrates the installation of the cult of Dionysos in Athens, and the title and cult of Dionysos Eleuthereus honors specifically the occasion and the persona of the god that was manifested in this particular myth, the arrival of his cult in the shape of the statue brought by Pegasos and the particular version of the resistance myth associated with this event.

The story that the statue and cult came to Athens from Eleutherai belongs to the same category of myths as that told by Euripides in *IT* 1450-7, the myth that the statue of Artemis Tauropolos was brought to Athens from the Taurid by Orestes and Iphigeneia, discussed in chapters I.2 and III.3. Such myths distance, and thus underplay and almost elide, the human origins of cult statues and ultimately of the cults. Other myths involve a stronger modality of distancing: some cult statues, for example the olive wood statue of Athena Polias in Athens,[170] were said to have fallen from the sky.

The mythicoritual schema involving the introduction of a cult from a locality that possessed an especially important version of that cult can be seen in Athenian cult practice; the cult of Asklepios was introduced in the last quarter of the fifth century from Epidaurus, and this origin was reflected in the cult, not least in the name of one of the god's festivals, the Epidauria. What of Eleutherai? It was Thebes that was the god's birthplace, and it was from Thebes that a statue of Dionysos Lysios was taken to Sikyon by the Theban Phanes at the command of the Pythia.[171] But there does seem to have been a connection between Dionysos and Eleutherai as well. There is a problematic reference to a *patrios thysia* by Thebans at Eleutherai that may be reflecting a perceived connection between the cult of Dionysos at Thebes and Eleutherai.[172] Then there is a myth that Eleutherai was founded by Dionysos.[173] If this last was early, it would mean that the myth of the bringing of his cult from Eleutherai to Athens would almost be claiming an indirect foundation of the cult by Dionysos himself. It is

Chapter 1: The Great Dionysia

conceivable that the similarity between the name "Eleutherai" and the notion of "liberation" brought about by Dionysos in a variety of ways, a notion which is also expressed in Dionysos' title Lysios,[174] may have created a perceived special connection between the god and Eleutherai. I am not denying the possibility that Eleutherai being "in the news" as far as the Athenians were concerned, for whatever reason, and for however long or short a time, may also have been a factor in shaping the myth. But I think it is clear that the festival of the City Dionysia must not be interpreted as an annexation ritual and its origins must not be tied with the history of Eleutherai.

Recently, Connor challenged the established view that a Peisistratid City Dionysia was reorganized during the Kleisthenic reforms, and that this is why the victors' lists would appear to begin at 502/1, because they tell us about this reorganization, and cannot be assumed to be reflecting the beginning of the festival.[175] He argued that the City Dionysia was created at the end of the sixth century, in the context of the Kleisthenic reforms, possibly around 506. He also argued that the first form of this festival had involved a *komos*, a ritualized revel which may have included dithyrambic choruses, and that soon thereafter tragic and then comic performances were added to it until its fully developed classical form was achieved. On his view the plays of Thespis and several other early Attic tragedians were performed in the Rural Dionysia and only later were tragic performances held at the city festival.

This thesis is based on the down dating of the annexation of Eleutherai, which, we saw, is not relevant to the foundation of the City Dionysia. In addition, there are two further objections against it. First, the juxtaposition of an agonistic segment articulated partly through the Kleisthenic tribes, and a more centrally religious segment, which is closely comparable to that of the Panathenaia, but to some extent also to the Thargelia, suggests that, as in those cases, the articulation into Kleisthenic tribes of the agonistic segment was superimposed onto an earlier nexus that had been otherwise articulated; and that therefore the City Dionysia was earlier than the Kleisthenic reforms and was reorganized during those reforms. Then, there is another objection to Connor's hypothesis of the primacy of the dithyramb at the City Dionysia in the late sixth century. This argument focusses on the physical realities of early theaters, about which we now know that they did not have a circular orchestra; the earliest orchestras were irregular, vaguely and irregularly rectangular.[176] This suggests that the orchestras of the earliest theaters were shaped by spatial movements that were not circular; they were not shaped by the needs of the dithyrambs as *kyklioi choroi* involving dancing around the altar,[177] but by those of dramatic performances such as those of known tragedy.

Consequently, it is clear that the festival was pre-Kleisthenic in date. This fits with the accepted dating of the sanctuary of Dionysos Eleuthereus; this sanctuary began some time in the second half of the sixth century,[178] but only the fragmentary pediment which almost certainly comes from this temple suggests a more precise date, in the 530s.[179] But it cannot be excluded that the cult may have predated the temple by a little; a temporary structure is not unlikely to have been erected between the foundation of the cult and the completion of the temple. So perhaps a date some time in the earlier half of the third quarter of the sixth century is more likely to be nearer reality. The Marmor Parium[180] gives us a date between 540 and 520[181] for Thespis first presenting a drama in the city, the prize being a billy goat, a *tragos*. Suda places the date of Thespis' first presentation of a tragedy in the 530s (536-32).[182] We cannot assume that this evidence is necessarily trustworthy; West has argued against the reliability of the attested early dates pertaining to the early history of tragedy, and suggested that, as far as Thespis is concerned, we can do no more than acquiesce in the ancient belief that his activity began under Peisistratos.[183] But the rough coincidence of the different types of evidence may suggest that these sources may contain some genuine information that something to do with the City Dionysia and tragedy did begin somewhere around that time.

b) *A Process of Bricolage: City Dionysia, Anthesteria, and Other Festivals*

New festivals are not created out of nothing; they are constructed with raw material pertaining to the relevant cult, which is redeployed, modified, and generates new mythicoritual elements—shaped by the parameters of determination constituted by the parameters of the religious mentality pertaining to the cult. Among the ritual elements that went into the making of the City Dionysia some came from the Rural Dionysia, as the commmon element of the *phallophoria* shows.[184] We saw above that a comparison of the City Dionysia with the Anthesteria, *ta archaiotera Dionysia*, showed that in comparison with the complex Anthesteria the Dionysia was a ritually simple festival celebrating the establishment of the cult of Dionysos and centered on the reception, entertainment, and honoring of the god.

The Anthesteria also involved an arrival of Dionysos, both in ritual and in myth.[185] A ritual enactment of the arrival of Dionysos in a ship mounted on wheels almost certainly took place at the Anthesteria.[186]

Chapter 1: The Great Dionysia

The festival's connection with the arrival of Dionysos is also manifested in the myth which is the *aition* of one of the rites of the festival, the Aiora,[187] the swinging ritual which commemorated the suicide of Erigone,[188] who had hanged herself when she found the body of her father Ikarios in a well.[189] Dionysos had visited Ikarios, in Ikaria in Attica, and Ikarios had received the god hospitably; Dionysos gave him the gift of wine; Ikarios invited guests and offered them this wine; but when they started feeling its effects they thought they had been bewitched and killed Ikarios. This myth, then, also involves hostility to Dionysos and things Dionysiac, like the festival myth of the City Dionysia.

A central strand in the complex nexus of the Anthesteria is the theme "dissolution and new beginnings." One of the manifestations of this, at the most mundane level, is the opening of the jars of new wine, that took place at the Pithoigia. Homologous to this at a symbolically more important level is the gift of wine brought by Dionysos to Ikarios, and eventually (after a dark interval) to Athens as a whole. In that respect, the arrival of Dionysos is also, marks also, a new beginning.

The City Dionysia focussed on the installation of the cult of Dionysos in Athens, and honored specifically the occasion and the persona of the god that was manifested in the myth associated with the introduction of his statue and cult. As we saw, myths pertaining to the arrival of Dionysos himself in Attica had been attracted into the nexus of the City Dionysia and ritually connected with the installation of his cult, so that the god's visit, and the arrival of his statue and foundation of his cult, were woven into one festive system focussed on the City Dionysia. In some ways, then, the mythicoritual nexus of the City Dionysia continues and extends one of the nexuses that make up the Anthesteria; the arrival of Dionysos' statue and cult extends the narrative of resistance to the god, through the schema "resistance to Dionysos," which is common in Greek mythology, in combination with the schema "statue/cult brought to a place from elsewhere" I mentioned above.

Ikarios' guests/murderers had drunk unmixed wine; another arrival and reception of Dionysos involved a more controlled use of wine: another Athenian king associated with a reception of Dionysos, Amphictyon, learnt from Dionysos how to mix wine.[190] We note the tendency to multiply the arrivals of Dionysos in Attica.[191] According to another myth, Dionysos was received and given hospitality by Semachos and his daughter or daughters.[192] So we have multiplications along different axes: arrival of Dionysos himself—of his cult; arrival of Dionysos in different places, different local traditions in different demes; Dionysos arrives to bring the gift of wine—then to teach the mixing of wine. This multiplication fits the character of Dionysos as the par excellence arriving deity.[193] It may also indicate a special mythopoeic focus on myths involving Dionysos' arrivals, in circumstances that will be explored in II.2.i below.

To return to the relationship between the City Dionysia and the Anthesteria. One of the ways in which the later and simpler Dionysia may be seen is as an extension of one of the nexuses that make up the Anthesteria, a modified version of the nexus "arrival of Dionysos," in the form "arrival of Dionysos' cult," which is the focus of the City Dionysia. But, precisely because it is focussed solely on the establishment of the cult, which leads to a happy ending, the emphasis in the Dionysia is on the joyous and positive; there is dissolution here also, when the statue is moved, enacting the time of illness and abnormality; but then the statue is received with honor, and the cult's establishment is reenacted, and manifested, in the procession.

It is possible to see a direct relationship between the Dionysia and the Anthesteria; it is possible that ritual stuff from the latter had been taken over and adapted, and then had generated new ritual stuff, acccording to established schemata and cult mentality, and in interaction also with stuff from the Rural Dionysia and possibly an element or so from the Lenaia.[194]

Perhaps another element that went into the making of the Dionysia was the fact that in the Delphic month Theoxenios, which is the equivalent of Elaphebolion, the Theoxenia were celebrated at Delphi, a festival of *xenismos* of, above all, Apollo, but also involving other deities, including Dionysos.[195] This festival was widely known, because it was in some ways a Panhellenic festival.[196] Thus, it is plausible that, under Delphic influence, the schema "*xenismos* of a god in Elaphebolion" also came into play, and helped shape the selections that led to the creation of the festival of the City Dionysia—in interaction with the significant schemata we discussed above, such as resistance to Dionysos. It is possible that, when a festival centered on a *xenismos* was being shaped, the knowledge of what happened at the Delphic *xenismos* festival may have affected selections and developments.

c) *Reconstructing the Early Festival*

Whatever the exact circumstances of the generation of the City Dionysia, there can be little doubt that the core of the festival was the reception and honoring of the statue of Dionysos and celebration of the establishment of his cult. Therefore, the elements in the later form of the festival that would definitely have been part of its early form are:

Chapter 1: The Great Dionysia

the movement of the statue outside the center and back into the center of the city, the ritual dining on *stibades* and the reception and *xenismos* of Dionysos, the procession. We do not know whether competitions were an early element. The fact that the Dionysia competitions changed after the Kleisthenic reforms shows that they were not static. It is not legitimate to assume that they had been part of the festival from the beginning. Given their idiosyncratic nature, the fact that competitions were one of the main elements in (normally major) Greek festivals may explain why eventually dramatic and dithyrambic performances took this format, were cast through this schema; it does not necessarily entail that these competitions were part of it from the beginning.[197]

Let us now turn to the procession and try to reconstruct its route, which will also help us understand other aspects of the festival. To do this we should focus on spatial relationships. The one symbolically significant, symbolically charged, route leading to, and out of, the sanctuary and Theater of Dionysos is the Tripodes, the Street of the Tripods, along which choregic victory monuments were erected. According to Pausanias, the Street of the Tripods started at the prytaneion;[198] it connected the prytaneion with the Theater of Dionysos. It may have continued beyond the prytaneion and joined the Panathenaic way, but if so it changed name, it was not the Tripodes.[199] The fact that victory monuments were set up along it leads us to expect that the Tripodes may have had a symbolic significance pertaining not only to the procession but also to the performances. I will now set out the arguments which lead me to conclude that at an early stage in the history of the festival the statue of Dionysos was received and entertained at the prytaneion, that the prytaneion in the Old Agora was the starting point of the Dionysia procession, and that before the New Agora had been developed into the main civic center of the polis, the procession had gone directly from the prytaneion to the sanctuary of Dionysos.

Firstly, the prytaneion was, among other things, the symbolic center of each polis with, among other things, important religious functions.[200] In Athens the prytaneion was also the headquarters of the archon who had control and responsibility for this festival and sent out the procession.[201] Secondly, and most significantly, the prytaneion is where honored foreign guests, as well as honored citizens, were dined and entertained by the polis; it was thus an apt locus for the reception of a god whose cult arrived from the outside and had first been spurned, but is now received with great honor. Thirdly, the Athenian prytaneion was certainly a locus in which gods were entertained. It is certain that the Athenians entertained the Dioskouroi to a meal, called *aris-*

ton at the prytaneion.[202] So we are certain that in at least one case in Athens the rite of *xenismos/theoxenia* took place in the prytaneion.[203] This shows that the prytaneion was perceived to be a ritually appropriate place for such a rite. It is also possible that the god Apollo may have been given the right to dine at the prytaneion at public expense.[204] Finally, processions from the prytaneion to a shrine are a known modality of procession in Greece in general[205] and Athens in particular. In Athens, the procession for the goddess Bendis, whose cult was introduced in Athens some time before 429/8, started *apo tes hestias tes ek tou prytaneiou* and ended in the shrine at the Peiraeus.[206] So in Athens this ritual schema fits the festival of a new god. Dionysos was not a new god in terms of real cultic history, but in myth his persona as incoming god is at the center of the City Dionysia; therefore, the ritual schema deployed to celebrate his reception at this festival would be the schema which in Athenian ritual articulated the introduction of the cult of a new god. For the real new gods' rituals would have been modelled on what was perceived as the reception of a new god ritual in festivals such as the Dionysia.

Thus, different lines of argument lead us to the conclusion that the prytaneion, situated in the Old Agora, which, we now know, was in a different place from the excavated one, on the east of the Acropolis,[207] was an important locus in the City Dionysia; and that it was at the prytaneion that the rite of *xenismos* of Dionysos had taken place, and that the procession of the City Dionysia (which was centered on the god's reception as an honored divine guest), a procession which articulated the notion of the whole polis participating in the foundation of, and honoring, the cult of Dionysos, had gone from the prytaneion to the sanctuary of Dionysos.

I will attempt to reconstruct the nature of the rites that had taken place during the *xenismos* of Dionysos at the prytaneion below, where I will explore the ways in which, out of the choral singing at this *xenismos*, eventually, a kind of prototragedy emerged. Here I will only point out that the fact that the statue of Dionysos was present in the theater during the dramatic performances and watched the performances in the classical period (and later)[208] would fit the view that what became tragedy was a ritual performed for, and in front of, the statue of Dionysos Eleuthereus during a ritual of *xenismos* at the prytaneion, where the polis had received and entertained the god. There would then have followed a procession to the sanctuary, probably escorting the statue, and thus reenacting the cult's installation, in commemoration of which, and the events preceding it, the myth tells us, this procession took place.

Chapter 1: The Great Dionysia

However, we saw earlier in this chapter that in the classical period the procession did not go from the prytaneion to the sanctuary of Dionysos, at least not by a straight route. For, we saw, in Xenophon's time the Dionysia procession visited the Altar of the Twelve Gods in the "New" Agora.[209] Does this, then, invalidate the hypothesis of a procession from the prytaneion to the sanctuary of Dionysos? The Altar of the Twelve Gods was dedicated by Peisistratos, son of Hippias,[210] who was probably archon in 522/1.[211] If it is right that, as argued above, the City Dionysia festival had been instituted earlier, somewhere around the 530s, the Dionysia procession would have predated the foundation of the Altar of the Twelve Gods, and therefore the visiting of this altar by the Dionysia procession would have been a subsequent development. Since we know that some changes did take place in the course of the centuries of the festival's history, the assumption that the overall shape had remained unchanged must not be privileged.

The Altar of the Twelve Gods in the New Agora was in some ways equivalent to the prytaneion, in terms of meaning and function; for it came to be considered the center of Athens, since it was the central point from which distances were measured.[212] Also, the Altar of the Twelve Gods was, like the *hestia* at the prytaneion above all other *hestiai*, a locus for foreign suppliants.[213] Thus, this altar became another center of the polis, the importance of which grew as the New Agora developed into a major religious and civic center. For, from the end of the sixth century onwards, the New Agora became increasingly important, and an annex of the prytaneion came to be instituted there, the *prytanikon*, the earliest form of which appears to be dateable to the end of the sixth century.[214]

Consequently, first, different arguments converge to indicate a stage in which the prytaneion was the locus of the *xenismos* and the starting point of the procession; and second, there is a homology between the prytaneion with its *hestia* on the one hand and the nucleus Altar of the Twelve Gods and *eschara* on the other. I suggest that the interpretation of this state of affairs that is consistent both with Greek ritual logic and with the relationship between prytaneion and New Agora as can be seen in other evidence, is that there had been an early version of the festival in which the statue had been taken from the Academy to the prytaneion for a rite of *xenismos*, and then, in circumstances that I will now consider, the function of the prytaneion came to be devolved (at least partially) to the Altar of the Twelve Gods, which was the new, or at least the alternative to the prytaneion, center of the polis. It is possible that the *eschara* which is closely related to it may have been in a way duplicating the *hestia* at the prytaneion—perhaps complementing some functions of that *hestia* in a way comparable to that in which the *prytanikon* became the annex of prytaneion in the New Agora. At Kos there was a *hestia*, a hearth altar to Hestia, in the Agora, clearly not in a building.[215]

I will now consider the sacrifice that took place during the *xenismos* of Dionysos. As we shall see, a series of arguments lead to the conclusion that the animal that had been sacrificed at the *xenismos* of Dionysos at the City Dionysia had been a *tragos*.

The *tragos* was very closely associated with Dionysos in Athens.[216] It would seem that a *tragos* was sacrificed to Dionysos in at least some Athenian demes,[217] as it was in other places in the Greek world.[218] Most importantly, the Athenian calendar frieze of the Little Metropolis in Athens connects the *tragos* sacrifice with the City Dionysia: the month Elaphebolion, in which this festival took place, is represented by a comic actor leading a *tragos*.[219] In myth the *tragos* was associated with Dionysos' *xenismos*: a *tragos* is associated with the Ikarios story in Eratosthenes' *Erigone*, in which we have the earliest surviving mention of the Ikarios myth in the literary evidence, based probably on a story Eratosthenes found in one or more Atthidographers.[220] One of the fragments[221] mentions a *tragos* in an interesting context: *Ikarioi*, (which is a locative)[222] *tothi prota peri tragon orchesanto*. This clearly refers to the sacrifice of a *tragos*. It is likely that this is the same animal which had gnawed Ikarios' vine shoots.[223] Consequently, here we have the sacrifice of a *tragos* to entertain Dionysos, in a mythological *xenismos* of Dionysos. This constitutes one argument in favor of the view that the ritual *xenismos* of the god, which, we saw, was cultically associated with the mythological one, also involved the *tragos* as the sacrificial animal. It could be argued that this is late evidence, and cannot be shown to be relevant to the early period with which we are concerned. However, as we shall now see, the evidence of Athenian images on vases show that this association of the *tragos* with the arrival and *xenismos* of Dionysos was early, already established in the third quarter of the sixth century, and also that the mythological sacrifice was correlative with a cultic one.

A *tragos* is closely connected with Dionysos in very many images.[224] None is known to me from before the third quarter of the sixth century, while such images associating Dionysos with a *tragos* become very common in the last quarter of the sixth century and the beginning of the fifth. This pattern would be consistent with the hypothesis put forward here, in which there is a connection between the *tragos* and the City Dionysia, founded in the third quarter of the sixth century, which exploded in importance, especially in its *xenismos* part, and was radically expanded and restructured, in the last quarter of the sixth century and the beginning of the fifth. For in that case the popularity of the

Chapter 2: Setting Out the Distances

between on the one hand the stress on the positive in the gods and the elision of distance between the world of the play and that of the audience, and on the other the exploration of darkness and the shifting distances governed by the double perspective between the world of the play and that of the audience in tragedy is significant. If this is right it would suggest that the darkness in religion can only be articulated, and explored, at a distance, which may perhaps give a little support to the view that the setting of tragedy, and its double perspective, was closely related to the fact that (on my thesis) tragedy began as a locus of religious exploration and developed into a locus of exploration both of religious issues, and of issues such as the place of man in the cosmos and related concepts such as free will, fate, social relationships, and so on, all of which were, in Greek perceptions, closely intertwined with religion.[117]

Let me now return to the question of the universality of tragedy which I broached in chapter I.1. A question may arise, as to whether the universality of Greek tragedy can be reconciled with my thesis that an important aspect of tragedy in fifth-century eyes was that it was a locus of religious exploration, since such exploration would inevitably have been culture specific, relevant only to Greek religion. Clearly, some aspects pertaining to Greek religion and the problems involved in it, such as the problem of the limits, if any, to free will, and its relationship to the notion of preordained fate, are "universal" in the sense that they arise in a variety of religious and cosmological systems, and though some religious systems give more definite answers than others, the problematization has resonances for all. Thus, modern readers reading tragedies through perceptual filters shaped by entirely different assumptions can relate to these resonances, while underplaying, for example, the role of the Delphic oracle, implicitly treating it as though it were simply a textual device. But there are other religious matters that are specifically focussed on Greek religion. The question of human sacrifice, for example, involves, we saw, the problematization of the dark side of the gods. Again, read through modern assumptions, this can be interpreted as "criticism" of the gods; and the issues that have wider resonances, such as death in war, duty to one's community or family, or the sacrifice of one for the good of the many, can be placed at the center of a modern reading.

I will illustrate the way universality is constructed by modern readers, through the underplaying of some aspects of the tragedies, the stressing of others, and the structuring of the interpretations through preconceived assumptions, at the expense of the religious explorations that tragedy involved in ancient eyes, by summarizing what, I have argued elsewhere, has happened in the case of Sophocles' *Antigone*.[118]

Modern commentators have read this tragedy through the perceptual model of the individual obeying her conscience in opposing the state in the interests of a just cause, a reading very different from those of the ancient audience who, unlike modern ones, did not privilege individual rights and freedom and suspicion of the state but, on the contrary, shared assumptions in which the interests of the polis were paramount. This (and other elements) made Kreon a true representative of the polis in the opening scene. Modern commentators also underestimated the complexity of the issue of burial and of Kreon's error, when perceived through ancient eyes. For what Kreon did wrong was not that he denied burial to Polyneikes, but that he left his corpse exposed on the plain, neither throwing it out of the frontiers, so that others could bury it, nor handing it over symbolically to the nether gods by disposing of it, for example by throwing it into the pit, as the Athenians did in certain circumstances. So he kept in the upper world something that belonged to the nether gods, and so offended all the gods and disturbed the cosmic order.

Those two culturally determined readings (among many others, but these two crucially) led to a misunderstanding of what, on my reading, was a central issue in the tragedy for the fifth-century Athenians: the problematization of the limits of, the dangers of errors being committed by, the religious discourse of the polis, a problem explored at a distance, through (as well as zooming devices that made it relevant to the present) distancing devices that made at crucial points Kreon tyrannical, and the Thebes of the play distanced from the Athens of the audience.

This suggests that when Greek tragedies are read as floating texts, divorced from their audience and context of production, and so by default through the perceptual filters of other cultures, they yield simplified and distorted versions of the meanings which they had in the eyes of the fifth-century audience, meanings from which the religious explorations have been written out. I believe that the fact that religious exploration was a very culture-specific aspect of tragedy is one of the reasons why the role of religion in Greek tragedy has been underplayed by modern readers.

Of course, this is not to deny all universality to Greek tragedy. On the contrary; the fact that such universality can be constructed out of these culture-specific dramas is because the ways in which they deal with such problems makes them partly transcend their culture-specific matrix. I would suggest that this universality is correlative with the fact that, on my reconstruction, all problematizing in tragedy arose out of, and was modelled on, religious problemátization which involved major human issues. Religious problematization partly involved ques-

Chapter 2: Setting Out the Distances

tions, or aspects of questions, that transcend the culture specific, and partly it was culture specific (in the sense of involving issues particular to Greek religion, not to the particular circumstances of the tragedy's production at a particular moment in the fifth century, though these circumstances may have generated interest in the issues). For example, the limits to the polis discourse and the ultimate unknowability of the divine will is culture specific to this religion which had no revelation, or dogma, or canonical body of beliefs, no scriptural texts, and no professional divinely anointed priesthood claiming a special knowledge or authority.

These religious explorations took place at a distance, and they set the parameters for all other explorations, for example of issues pertaining to human relationships, which also therefore took place at a distance, in a heroic past that was in significant ways other than the present. Thus, everything was handled in a more generic, non-moment-specific way, an idiom which facilitated the construction of universality as defined here.[119] These parameters were so firmly in place, that when experimentations with other settings took place these included the double perspective of a world distanced, but also part of the world of the audience; what seems to have been an experimentation with a setting that did not was deemed to be transgressive.

To sum up some of the main points. In the audience's assumptions the relationship between the world of the audience and the world of the tragedy in the preferred option in which the setting was the heroic age was governed by a double perspective. On the one hand it was distanced, other, a different sort of world in which men walked with gods, shaped today's world, and eventually became cult recipients in the world of the present; on the other hand, they were an important part of the audience's world, of the audience's present precisely because they were cult recipients, they had shaped the world of the present, and so on. It was these assumptions, shared by the audience, that set the parameters of the way in which they made sense of each tragedy in performance. The tragedy itself manipulated the distance between the world of the audience and the world of the tragedy, through the deployment of zooming devices and distancing devices, so that the distance shifted throughout the play. Sometimes the distance was increased, the otherness of the world of the play stressed; this on the one hand allowed unpleasant things to be explored at a safe symbolic distance, without threatening the audience's world, and on the other allowed, for example, the representation, and thus the symbolic strengthening, of the foundation of institutions, above all cults, that were important in the present.

This notion assumes that, as I am arguing throughout this book, the performance and content of tragedies were not insulated from their religious framing; it was not a discrete unit, a purely theatrical experience, simply framed by ritual, which included gods simply as theatrical devices, but was itself perceived as a ritual occcasion to which ritual mentality pertained.[120] In the next section I offer a further argument in favor of this view.

I.2.vi. *Ritual Context, Tragic Performance and Permeability*

I will now set out an argument pertaining to the audience's perceptions of the relationship between the world of the audience and the world of tragedy as we can reconstruct them first on the basis of external evidence, and then, independently, on the basis of the internal evidence of the tragedies. The perceptions that concern us pertain to the identity of the chorus, the chorus' relationship qua chorus to the here and now. I will argue that in the eyes of the fifth-century audiences the tragic chorus was not only perceived as a group of people in the world of the play, in the present's past, but was also as a chorus, a group of male citizens acting as ritual performers, in the here and now, a chorus to Dionysos in the world of the present.

As many scholars have noted,[121] first, the terminology used by the Athenians to speak of tragedy places the chorus at the center, defines tragedy through the chorus; and second, the chorus remained central in the organization of the production. *Tragodoi* continues to be used to denote tragic performances in, for example, Aristophanes, Lysias, and Plato. Clearly, this does not mean that the chorus was perceived to be dramatically more important, especially given its decreasing role within tragedy. Consequently, this centrality may perhaps be reflecting the tragic chorus' importance in the wider context of the festival of Dionysos. Such an explanation in terms of the chorus' ritual importance would coincide with the ritual importance of choruses in Greek festivals in general. But were tragic choruses really also perceived as choruses in honor of Dionysos in the here and now? I believe that they were.

That the members of tragic as well as dithyrambic choruses had to be citizens,[122] and thus that they were, like other choruses, singing as representatives of the polis—while actors and poets could be foreigners—is one pointer in the direction of the perception of the tragic choruses as also ritual choruses in the here and now.[123] As Easterling has stressed,[124] in tragedy the chorus is never simply a group of bystanders or witnesses reacting and commenting; they are also a *choros* ready to perform lyrics patterned on ritual song and dance and accompanied by

Chapter 2: Setting Out the Distances

appropriate music, for example, a paean giving thanks for victory, as in the parodos of *Antigone*.[125] I would take this even further and suggest that, for example in the particular case of the parodos of *Antigone*, as the chorus processed in, singing a cult song the usual mode of performance of which was processional, it would have been very difficult for the audience not to perceive this hymn as being sung also in the real world of the here and now.[126] Then, there are choral passages in which references to *choroi* amount to choral self-referentiality,[127] in which choruses "draw attention to their ritual role as collective performers of the choral dance-song in the orchestra."[128]

In my view, such self-referentiality could not but have activated for the audience the chorus' identity as chorus in the present performing in honor of Dionysos.[129] The mask, while locating the chorus in the other world of the heroic past,[130] at the same time draws attention to the fact that the *choreutai* are not in fact "other," that their otherness is constructed, and located above all in the mask, while they are also, underneath the mask, a chorus of male Athenians in the present.

Another argument for the view that the identity of the chorus as a chorus in the here and now, though subordinated, was not wholly neutralized, is provided by Plato *Laws* 800C-801A. Plato expresses his disapproval of the fact that, as he puts it, after a public sacrifice many choruses, standing not far from the altars, pour blasphemies over the sacrifices by singing mournful songs and racking the souls of the listeners and making them cry. There can be no doubt that tragic choruses are the main choruses involved here; for it is tragedy and rhapsodic performances[131] that Plato elsewhere accuses of producing such effects on the listeners.[132] We need to reconstruct the common assumptions underlying Plato's idiosyncratic polarization,[133] the shared assumptions that have to be taken for granted for Plato's articulation to work. The most important of these emerges clearly: the fact that this idiosyncratic polarization was possible indicates that in the Athenian assumptions the tragic chorus was also perceived as a chorus in the present; for unless that was the case such a polarization would not make sense.

Even more strikingly, the Platonic image entails that it *could* be presented as being the case that the world of the present could be penetrated by the world of the tragedy, that the mourning songs *could* be presented as constituting blasphemy within the ritual performed in the here and now. This coincides with Easterling's observation that the fact that the world of the audience was permeable by that of the tragedy, that the latter was not insulated, is shown by the concern for *euphemia* in the tragedies, as illustrated, for example, by the fact that "in *Eumenides* when the Furies threaten to blight and poison the land, Athena always has a well-omened reply."[134] This is surely correlative with the fact that on the one hand the performance is part of a ritual occasion in the present, and on the other what happens in the world of the play is also part of the world of the audience, since it happened in its heroic past, in which were laid the foundations of the polis' relationships with the divine world.

Another argument in favor of the view that the chorus was also perceived as a chorus in the present may be provided by the floating tailpieces addressing Nike and requesting a prize in Euripides' *Orestes*, *Iphigeneia in Tauris*, and *Phoinissai*, especially if they were Euripidean.[135]

If tragic choruses were indeed also perceived, albeit not as dominantly, as choruses for Dionysos in the present, it follows that in the fifth century tragic performances were not perceived as ritual only in the sense that they were part of the festival of Dionysos and were framed by ritual; the tragedies themselves were shot through by ritual, not only insofar as ritual acts were important in the action in the other world enacted by the tragedy, but also, most importantly, it was shot through by ritual performed in the present; so tragedy itself could not have been perceived as other than fundamentally religious.

I must make clear that, on my argument, there can be little doubt that for the audience the perception that what happened in the orchestra and the skene took place in the other world of the tragedy was dominant. But I am arguing that this was not the only perception, and that there was, at certain points, both a less dominant perception of the chorus as a chorus also in the here and now, and also of a certain permeability between the two worlds. A question that is intertwined with this is what may be called the precise status of this mimetic performance, its relationship of similarities to, and differences from, mimetic performances of a "straightforward" ritual kind, so-called sacred dramas in which divinities were impersonated by priestly personnel. In order to try even to begin to answer this question it is necessary to investigate first the ritual context in which tragedy was generated. I will set out this investigation in part II, and will return to this question in part III.

The investigation of the ritual context in which tragedy emerged is also necessary for another reason. It might be objected to the remarks made above that comedy should make us cautious about concluding that the identity of the tragic chorus as a chorus for Dionysos in the here and now can be considered an argument in favor of a ritual nature of tragedy that would go together with the notion that tragedy can be seen as a religious discourse. Comedy's metatheatricality, the fact that the identity of the comic chorus as a chorus in a festival of Dionysos in the here and now is stressed, especially in the parabasis, and that comedy can refer to itself as the *patrioi teletai tou Dionysou*,[136] does not entail that representations of the gods in comedy were accurate reflections of the real gods of lived religion. On the contrary, it is precisely this metatheatricality that allows them to be perceived as comic constructs, which can thus be irreverently depicted,[137] in the same way that the presentation on stage of what purports to be the Thesmophoria in Aristophanes' *Thesmophoriazousai* is possible because the play's strong metatheatricality foregrounds its character as a comic construct—not a representation of the festival. So how can we be sure that something comparable is not operating in tragedy?

Obviously, one answer is that our readings show that the gods in tragedy, when perceived through the audience's religious assumptions, were indeed constructed as representations of the real gods of cult. However, we need to test those readings for cultural determination; and we also need to explain why a different situation should pertain in comedy, if we are to be able to use the ritual nature of the tragedies as an argument in favor of the view that tragedy was also seen as a religious discourse. In order to achieve both these aims it is necessary to investigate the ritual contexts in which comedy and especially tragedy were generated.

This is one of the several reasons why, as we saw in the last chapter, it is important not to neglect the question of the origins of tragedy, and attempt to explore the ritual context in which tragedy was generated.

Notes

1. That we know of.
2. Herodotos 6.21.
3. On the date cf. the discussion in Rosenbloom 1993, 170-2.
4. Cf. also *TrGF* i 3 T 10f, T 14.
5. Rosenbloom 1993, 159-96 with earlier bibliography.
6. Calame 1995, 113 describes this as Aeschylus substituting a geographical and actorial distance for the temporal distance of myth by focussing the action not on the Athenians but on the Persians.
7. On Phrynichos: Lloyd-Jones 1990, 230-7. On Phrynichos' *Phoinissai* probably being different from, but probably part of the same trilogy as, his *Dikaioi* (*The Just Ones*), or *Persai* or *Synthokoi* (*The Counsellors*) [*TrGF* i 3 F 4a], see Lloyd-Jones 1990, 233-4. Bowie 1997, 39-42 (who surveys briefly "historical tragedies" in the sense of tragedies referring specifically to particular recent events—a category that is therefore much broader than mine, since it is

concerned with references rather than the setting of the play) believes that it cannot be excluded that the subject of this tragedy may have been mythological rather than historical.

8. Cf. Hall 1989, 64 and n. 27.

9. I will not include post-fifth-century tragedies (such as, for example, Theodektas *TrGF* i 72 F 3b or *TrGF* ii Adespota F 733), since I believe that tragedy in the fourth century became a different thing from tragedy in the fifth century, which (and its antecedents) is my concern here.

10. *TrGF* i 4 F 9.

11. Parker 1983, 209.

12. Sourvinou-Inwood 1997b, 155-9.

13. *TrGF* Adespota (vol. ii) F 664 (*Gyges*?) with bibliography and views on possible date.

14. Cf. *TrGF* Adespota F 664. Hall 1989, 65 calls it "post-fifth-century" (cf. op. cit. n. 67 for a discussion of the date).

15. ARV 571. 74; Add 261; to which add Taplin 1993, 7 pl. 7.119A; cf. *TrGF* Adespota (vol. ii) F 5e.

16. Beazley 1955, 319.

17. Cf. Hall 1989, 65.

18. Page 1962, 47-9.

19. Page 1962, 49 argued that the fall of Kroisos would have been the retribution for the actions of Kandaules and the Queen in the *Gyges*; this may well be right, but it may also be a culturally determined judgment, influenced by Herodotos 1. 13.

20. Hall 1989, 65 considers both Gyges' story and Kroisos' story to be indistinguishable from myth for the Athenians of the mid-fifth century. I am inclined to think that there were certain distinctions in the perceptions of distances, as I am trying to outline here.

21. Aristotle *Poetics* 1451b19-26.

22. *TrGF* i 39 F 2a.

23. Without going into his whole complex argument about poetry and history, which would take us too far afield from our concerns.

24. *TrGF* i 39 F 2a. In Parthen. 14 Antheus, a youth from Halikarnassos, was sent as hostage to Phobios, a Neleid who ruled Miletos.

25. I cannot see any reason for imagining that the fragment *TrGF* Adespota F 646 came from a fifth-century tragedy with a historical subject.

26. Cf. *TrGF* ad loc. It refers to the Lydians in fr. 1 and has in fr. 3.1 *o genos Persǫn* and in 3.3 *basilea emon*; this suggests that someone is probably looking back to the Lydians from a Persian perspective. On this fragment see now also Hall 1996b, 8.

27. Thus, even in the case of Phrynichos it would seem that in the majority of his tragedies the setting was that of the heroic age, to judge by the fact that of the ten of his tragedies we know about seven were set in the mythological past (*Aigyptioi, Aktaion, Alkestis, Antaios* or *Libyes, Danaides, Pleuroniai, Tantalos*).

28. Insofar as we are able to judge from the fragmentary information available to us this would appear beyond doubt.

29. Cf. a comparable perception in Easterling 1997b, 167-8 who rightly says that aetiologies in drama function as a device for making the audience aware of more than one plane of reality since what is laid down is already part of the audience's history and present. She also rightly notes that such patterns are established with great solemnity, and are not to be seen as antiquarian oddities or signs of passing playfulness.

30. Lysias 30, *Against Nikomachos*, 18.

31. Which I have discussed in Sourvinou-Inwood 1990a, 303-4.

32. To a varying degree, as I am arguing in chapter III.4.

33. Aristotle *Poetics* 1449 b 28.

34. In *Poetics* 1453 a 7.

35. Sourvinou-Inwood 1989a, 134-48.

36. On the ancient audience's complex perceptions of Dareios' ghost see below chapter III.1, the discussion of *Persai*.

37. Cf. e.g. Else 1965, 63.

38. See on this myth Sourvinou-Inwood 1989b, 141-65; West 1983, 63-71.

39. Cf. Zeitlin 1990, 130-67 [=Zeitlin 1986, 101-41]; Easterling 1989, 13-14; Zeitlin 1993, 147-82; cf. also Sourvinou-Inwood 1989a, 134-48 passim.

40. Sourvinou-Inwood 1989a, 144.

41. Cf. bibliography on *Erechtheus* and a short survey of discussions in Collard, Cropp, and Lee 1995, 147-55. I will not engage with the view that Euripides "undercuts" the play's religious values; I am considering this type of approach to Euripides in chapter III.3 below; as for *Erechtheus*, I suggest that this position collapses when an attempt is made to reconstruct the audience's perceptual filters and make sense of the play through them, as is selectively illustrated here—even before account is taken of the ancient reception as illustrated by Lykourgos, *Leocr*. 100-101 (cf. also Collard, Cropp, and Lee 1995, 154-5).

42. Fragment 41 Austin 1968 (fr. 351 in Collard, Cropp, and Lee 1995). Cf. also, on *Erechtheus*: Austin 1967, 11-67. The translation is my own.

43. Cf. e.g. the discussion in Stewart 1990, 157-8.

44. Cf. e.g. Homer *Il*. 21.400-1.

45. Cf. Collard, Cropp, and Lee 1995, 155 with bibliography; cf. also Austin 1967, 17.

46. Cf. Thuc. iii. 2, 26, 89 (cf. also Hornblower 1991, ad loc. [pp. 381, 409, 497]); iv.2, 6.

47. Fr. 50 Austin = Collard, Cropp, and Lee 1995, fr. 360.

48. For Loraux 1990, 46-7, 57-66 the tragedies are articulating the mothers' grief, which civic discourse fears and tries to suppress, while Praxithea had other priorities and is not a tragic mother (p. 63). But, I am arguing, the situation is more complex than that. Everyone, including mothers, partook, to a greater or lesser extent, of a whole spectrum of attitudes, including that of the polis ideology about death to save the city. If a polis leader delivering an *epitaphios* stands at the most civic, grief-denying, polis-privileging spectrum of attitudes, the figure of the mother stands at the other end; but this does not entail that

mothers did not share in the polis ideology, or that the notion of private grief is truly denied in the polis discourse—as opposed to marginalized in certain contexts, while in others it is expressed through the figure of the mothers, to whom this concept of private grief has drifted. I have discussed a comparable drift to women of the fear of death in fifth-century Athenian polis ideology in Sourvinou-Inwood 1995, 344-6. Praxithea is very much a tragic mother, only one that represents attitudes at a different end of the spectrum from most other tragic mothers. This is correlative with the fact that in the figure of Praxithea we have both a mother and someone who will become a first priestess, a paradigmatic figure of a priestess.

49. I discussed this in Sourvinou-Inwood 1990a, 304-5.

50. Collard, Cropp, and Lee 1995, 370K.

51. In the Hyakinthides cf. Kearns 1989, 59-63; 201-2; Larson 1995, 20, 101-6 passim.

52. Hansen 1983, 10, line 5.

53. On the heroization and immortality of the Athenian war dead and the epitaph for the men who died in the battle of Poteidaia, cf. Sourvinou-Inwood 1995, 194, 202 (cf. also op. cit. on the extension of such immortality to ordinary dead people in the fourth century).

54. On Aglauros and her connection with ephebes: Kearns 1990, 330-1, 338; Kearns 1989, 139-40, 24-7; Larson 1995, 39-41.

55. See below chapter III.3.

56. With the help of a few interpretations of a few Bronze Age archaeological data which I consider perverse, because inspired by the desire to match archaeologically such historicist interpretations of myths.

57. I have discussed this notion of schemata in Sourvinou-Inwood 1991, 247, 246-61 passim; Sourvinou-Inwood 1989a, 136-7, 145.

58. On human sacrifice see esp. Henrichs 1981, 195-235; Hughes 1991; Bonnechere 1994; Kearns 1990, 323-44; Burkert 1983, 58-67.

59. These myths have, of course, a variety of other meanings also, but these are not relevant to our concerns here. I have discussed some of those meanings with reference to Iphigeneia in Sourvinou-Inwood 1990b, 52-8; and in more detail in a book in preparation (*Women, Religion and Tragedy*).

60. Cf. op. cit. (previous note).

61. Cf. also my brief discussion in Sourvinou-Inwood 1997a, 184-6.

62. In other human sacrifices in Euripides the patriotic ideology of dying for one's polis has been modified into a self-sacrificing choice to die for one's group, be it narrower than the polis, as in the case of Heracles' daughter who dies to save her family in *Heracleidai* or wider, Panhellenic, as in *IA*, where Iphigeneia is replaced by an animal. In the transformation of the "virgin sacrifice to save the city" schema in Euripides' *Phoinissai*, (on which see Mastronarde 1994, 392-3; Larson 1995, 107-9) Menoikeus, in explaining why he cannot but choose to sacrifice himself to save the city, compares his choice to the choices made by the

Chapter 2: Setting Out the Distances

young men who were fighting to save the city without shrinking from death (999-1005). I discuss Menoikeus and *Phoinissai* in chapter III.3 below.

63. Cf. also below and bibliography in n. 83 on the patriotic ideology associated with human sacrifice.

64. Before moving on to consider the case of *Iphigeneia in Tauris*, the setting of which is the mirror image of that of *Erechtheus*, a barbarian land as opposed to the very center of Athens, it is perhaps necessary to say something briefly about one version of Iphigeneia's sacrifice in a tragedy which appears "unresolved," in the sense that she dies, and her sacrifice is a savage butchery inflicted upon her by her father. However, though most scholars think that she was meant to have died in Aeschylus' *Agamemnon*, I have argued elsewhere (in a book in preparation, *Women, Religion and Tragedy*) that this is wrong, that this is a culturally determined reading; that the tragedy left it open whether or not she did; though the characters in the play think she has died; for this was necessary to the plot which had Klytemestra presenting her murder of Agamemnon as revenge for their daughter's sacrifice. But that the audience, making sense of the tragedy through religious assumptions in which Iphigeneia had survived and become priestess of Artemis at Brauron, a fact which, I am arguing, was evoked by the description of the sacrifice in Aeschylus' *Agamemnon*, would have understood her to have survived. The same is true, in my view, of Pindar's allusion to the sacrifice in *Pythian* 11.17-25: Klytemestra certainly believed that Iphigeneia had died, but that would have been the case even if in reality Artemis had replaced the girl with an *eidolon*. It is clear that in *Iphigeneia in Tauris* Iphigeneia was believed by the Greeks to have died when she was sacrificed (cf. lines 563-6, 770-2, 783-6).

65. Which I will discuss in greater detail in chapter III.3.

66. In Sourvinou-Inwood 1997a, 171-5, in the context of a wider argument (op. cit. 161-86) setting out the many reasons why it is wrong to doubt that the gods in tragedy were perceived by the audience as the same gods as those they worshiped.

67. Cf. Kearns 1989, 27-33; Lloyd-Jones 1983, 91-6, 174; Brulé 1987, 179-222; Kontis 1967, 160-4; Sourvinou-Inwood 1990b, 52-4.

68. For the torch-bearing Artemis, the iconographical representation of Artemis with the epithet Phosphoros, is one of the most frequently encountered types among the votives, especially votive reliefs, found in the Brauron sanctuary (see e.g. Kahil 1983, 233), which shows that this persona of Artemis was important in the Brauronian cult as it was in the goddess' Mounichian sanctuary, which was intimately associated with that of Brauron (on Phosphoros at Brauron see Kahil 1979, 77-8; at Mounichia: Palaiokrassa 1991, 36-8, 52-3, 91, 95).

69. In the heroon of Iphigeneia at Brauron, associated with a cave identified as her grave, cult appears to have begun at c. 700 (see Themelis 1971, 24-6). Since she was believed to have been buried there, and the successive structures associated with a cave would fit the configuration of a heroon associated with a grave, doubting the identification constitutes special pleading.

70. Cf. on this Platnauer 1938, 63-4 ad loc. and esp. Diggle 1994, 28-33 who excises 38-9 and reads *heortes . . . katarchomai*, "I consecrate the festival . . . while the infamous sacrifices are the care of others inside the temple" (p. 31).

71. On the meaning of *hapsetai phonou* see also Platnauer 1938, ad 382.

72. This passage is discussed by Wolff 1992, 309-12, who sees it as Iphigeneia's "effort to regenerate the goddess Artemis," which is "incomplete and compromised" (312). What I am suggesting is that the fifth-century audience, making sense of this passage through perceptual filters shaped by their particular religious and cultural assumptions, would see it as an exploration that may well be right.

73. Pindar, *Ol.* 1. 23ff.

74. Cf. on this Nagy 1986, 83-8; Sourvinou-Inwood 1986, 44-5.

75. For the text see Platnauer 1938 ad 466.

76. That Iphigeneia had already practiced human sacrifice is clear; cf. e.g. lines 38, 347; 621-2.

77. Lines 1089ff.

78. Cf. Platnauer 1938, 152-3 on the various references.

79. On the text cf. Platnauer 1938, ad 1116.

80. This part of the play has been recently discussed by Wolff 1992, 312-24, 330-1 (with extensive bibliography).

81. Cf. also on this rite and associated perceptions Graf 1979, 33-41; Lloyd-Jones 1983, 96-7, 89-100; Hughes 1991, 81. On the cult of Artemis at Halai Araphenides cf. also Bonnechere 1994, 48-52. I return to some of the questions that have been raised in connection with Athena's speech in chapter III.3 and its appendix. There I will be discussing the theory that the real-life cults of Artemis at Halai and Brauron differed significantly from the ways in which they are presented in *IT*, and I will also be considering in detail the theory that aetiologies and gods in epiphany can be seen simply as closure devices, in the context of the overall consideration of Euripidean tragedies, since some of the arguments depend on evidence that will be reconstructed in the course of that discussion.

82. Cf. previous note.

83. The patriotic ideology associated with human sacrifice is discussed in Loraux 1985, 76-82; Bonnechere 1994, 261-9; Larson 1995, 103-6; Wilkins 1990, 177-94. Bonnechere 1994, 260-72 has an interesting discussion on human sacrifice in Euripides. But he thinks (261) that Euripides manipulated old myths to galvanize the young around the ideology of glorious death for one's country, and (270-1) presented a failure of the polis ideals, a situation of decadence in which only the self-sacrificing victims stand above the rest, because his main intention was to revive the spirit that had made Athens great thirty years before. There are many objections to this approach. I will mention three main problems. It is hardly revolutionary, these days, to doubt the value of the search for the author's intentions; two of the most obvious reasons for this position are, first, the fact that the author's intentions are beyond our grasp, never more so than in the case of the ancient tragedians; and second, that this approach is reductionist in assuming conscious decisions at every

Chapter 2: Setting Out the Distances 59

level. That is why it is advisable to focus on the audience; their assumptions, shared by the tragedian and his contemporaries, shaped their perceptual filters and so the parameters of determination governing the creation of meaning by the tragedian and the construction of meaning, the reading, by the audience. Second, such a monosemic reading inevitably forces a series of complex plays into a reductive matrix centered on a particular version of patriotic ideology. These readings are a priori, and so inevitably culturally determined, since they are not based on an attempt to reconstruct the process of meaning creation in each tragedy through filters shaped by the ancient assumptions. Hence the overprivileging of the "political" and the underprivileging of the religious. For such readings are implicitly based on the assumption that religion does not matter; that the ancient audience was not concerned about the question of human sacrifice, and will therefore see everything from the viewpoint of the polis ideology—the revitalization of which is conceived here as the object of the exercise. Space prevents me from going through all the relevant tragedies and demonstrating this. I will therefore only say that such a reading cannot make sense of the problematization of human sacrifice in *Iphigeneia in Tauris*, which is of crucial importance in this tragedy. Nor can it make sense of the ways in which polis ideology is deployed in *Erechtheus*, where the ideology of good death at war is partly a given and partly is itself explored in the complex ways suggested above. Insofar as it is a given, it helps explore human sacrifice: through the comparison of human sacrifice of a virgin to the glorious death of the war dead, what would appear to be the cruelty of the gods is deconstructed. Similarly, things that Bonnechere sees as elements suggestive of a recession or destabilization of the religious dimension are, I would suggest, when seen through filters shaped by ancient Greek assumptions, the opposite. Distrust of prophets is a manifestation of a common Greek attitude: the notion that the human agents in prophecy are flawed is what protected prophecy from invalidation in Greek mentality. The god always spoke true, but the human intermediary was sometimes flawed, either corrupt or inadequate, and that is why people could never know if a given prophecy was a true prophecy. In tragedy prophecies always come true; but that is part of the assumptions of the audience, it is knowledge in the world of the audience; in the world of the tragedy the characters do not know that is so; they are in exactly the same position as ordinary people are in everyday life.

    84. Cf. e.g. Kearns 1989, 57-63; Larson 1995, 8, 40-1, 101-6. In some versions of her myth Iphigeneia becomes immortal; for example, in the pseudo-Hesiodic Catalogue of Women fr. 23 a.15-26, she becomes Artemis *einodia*.

    85. On such plays see especially Easterling 1994, 73-80.

    86. On Aeschylus' *Aitn(ai)ai*: *TrGF* iii T 1.33-4; *TrGF* iii pp. 126-30 (F6-F11), Cf. also Taplin 1977, 416-8.

    87. Cf. the hypothesis in P.Oxy. 2257; *TrGF* iii pp. 126-7.

    88. *TrGF* iii T 1.33-4.

    89. Cf. testimonium 1 in Harder 1985, 145. Harder 1985, 125 n.1 has rightly argued against an automatic scepticism throwing doubt on a firmly established tradition without

any evidence to the contrary. (If my analyses are convincing, they will provide further arguments in support of the tradition.) On the date see Harder 1985, 125-6.

90. See Harder 1985, 126.

91. Harder 1985, 127.

92. On the Vergina theater see Andronikos 1984, 46-9; its exact date is difficult to determine (see *Egnatia* 1 [1989] 346-7).

93. Even in this theater only the first row of seats was made of stone.

94. That this genealogy was not just simply an elevation of Archelaos but was relevant to the Macedonians in general was also suggested by Harder 1985, 130.

95. Herodotos 8.137-9.

96. Harder 1985, 135-6; Parke and Wormell 1956, 1.63-4. In a different version the oracle is given to Karanos, son of Poeanthes, when he left Argos to find a colony in Macedonia (cf. Parke and Wormell 1956, 1.63-4; 2.92-3). The schema of an animal serving as some sort of guide is a well-established Greek mythological foundation schema; cf. also on this type of oracle Harder 1985, 174-5 (her commentary on test. 7.13-4) with bibliography; on oracles directing the foundation of cities under the direction of animal guides; see also Bowie 1993a, 154-6.

97. Malkin 1987, 17-91.

98. Another instance of a genealogical myth articulating the relationship between the Macedonians and the Greeks south of Olympos is the mytheme in the *Catalogue of Women* fr. 7 M-W, according to which a daughter of Deukalion, Thyia, had two sons from Zeus, Magnes and Macedon. The myths about Deukalion's descendants articulate the relationships between those who perceived themselves as Greeks. Greeks are, of course, placed at the center in this myth; and the genealogies express the perception that all Greek ethnic groups, the speakers of different Greek dialects, had a common descent, as well as a shared language. But the Macedonians and the Magnetes were marginal and inferior because they were descended from Deukalion's daughter, rather than his son Hellen, the eponymous hero of the Greek nation.

99. Thucydides 2.99.3; cf. Hornblower 1991, 375 ad loc.

100. Thucydides 5.80.2

101. Cf. Harder 1985, 174 ad testimonium 7.13.

102. Cf. e.g. Aigeus in *Medea* 667-9; Kreousa and Xouthos in *Ion* 64-7; *Phoenissae* 13-6.

103. Braund 1980, 184-5. (There is also one *dysklees* and one *aklees*.)

104. Cf. *Concordance* 254-5 s.v.

105. Fr. 237=11A Harder: 1.2: *euklees aner*; fr. 238=12A: *eukleian*; fr. 240=14A *euklees*; fr. 242=16A : *euklea ... phatin*.

106. Paus. 1.14.5. On Eukleia cf. also Nilsson 1967, 493-4.

107. Andronikos 1984, 49.

108. Andronikos 1984, 46

Chapter 2: Setting Out the Distances 61

109. *Ergon* 1987, 58; *ArchRep* 1988-9, 80. On the shrine of Eukleia cf. also Andronikos 1984, 49-51; *Egnatia* 2 (1990) 363-5; *Egnatia* 3 (1991-2) 238-42. The shrine may have been part of the Agora of Aigai (cf. *Egnatia* 2 [1990] 364; *Egnatia* 3 [1991-2] 241).

110. Cf. esp. *Ergon* 1990, 83-4 and figs. 116-8; cf. *ArchRep* 1982-3, 44; *ArchRep* 1983-4, 47 fig. 82.

111. Cf. *Ergon* 1990, 83-4.

112. Even if one adopts for the sake of the argument the most negative and culturally restrictive hypothesis, that only the royal family partook of Greek culture and the others did not share (which is becoming increasingly difficult to sustain for the fifth century), it was still valid for the royals—so, on that hypothesis the "audience" would have shrunk to the patron; but even for the alleged others, the world of the play would have been zoomed to the foundation of their town, and to a cult known to them, even if on this hypothesis they did not share in it.

113. We saw above how Artemis' association with human sacrifice and the practice of human sacrifice in myths in general was "resolved" in two tragedies. I will be considering other cases of "making sense" of comparable darkness in part III.

114. Parker 1997, 143-60.

115. Cf. Parker 1997, 143 and passim.

116. Cf. below this chapter, and esp. section II.2.ii.

117. Griffith 1995, 62-129, in an otherwise interesting article, has given a "political" interpretation of the persistance of the heroic setting, virtually writing off its religious significance with reference to the present. The following quotation illustrates the flavor of his approach (p. 116): "Given that tragedy reached its acme under the new democratic system of which the Athenians were so proud, the persistence throughout the fifth and fourth centuries of these elite oriented tragic plots is indeed quite remarkable." He sees tragic performances as on the one hand the elite's way of dramatizing their own continuing role of leadership, risk, and self-sacrifice, disguising it behind the royal figures from the past, and on the other the demos licensing their elites to stage out-of-control tyrants and doomed royal houses whose anonymous community recovers (cf. pp. 123-4). I cannot here discuss this interpretation in detail and unpick an argument that, even on its own terms, presents serious problems. For example, to give an illustration of this, his implicit claim that his interpretation is supported by the statement (p. 116), "Conspicuously lacking is any story involving the replacement of ancestral aristocratic-monarchical rule with a democratic sharing or alternation of power," relies on the underplaying of the construct of Theseus as a democratic king, and the complex ways in which this construct was deployed so that Theseus functioned as a locus of self-definition for the whole polis. Easterling 1997, 24 has already pointed out that the heroes had paradigmatic relationships with everyone, not simply the elites, and also that the place of the heroes in Athenian fifth-century religious life and art affected the way in which the past was perceived and the heroes made sense of in tragedy. I would go further and say that the type of schematic thinking required by Griffith's interpretation (royal families in the heroic past in some way corresponding to the

elites in the present) is not, in my view, compatible with what we know of the modalities of operation of the Greek mythological mentality, which centered on the specific and concrete, on an individual, or a family, or a whole community, a polis, not on a concept like "elite." What is compatible with that mentality is the connection of particular mythological heroes with certain families; and here this theory presents further problems. For we do not find the focus on such relationships that we would expect if the interpretation were correct, least of all do we find attempts at connecting the heroes of the past with Athenian elite families of the present. For example, let us take Ajax, whom Griffith mentions, and who is the most important Trojan hero connected with Athens (on Ajax in Attica cf. Kearns 1989, 81-2; 141-2; Kron 1976, 171-6; Shapiro 1981, 173-5). His descendants were alleged to have migrated to and settled in Athens (Sourvinou-Inwood 1974, 217-8; Humphreys 1990, 247). He was claimed as an ancestor by the Philaids, the genos of which Kimon was a member, through Philaios (on the Philaids see Herodotos vi. 35; Hellanikos FGrH 4F22; Pherekydes FGrH 3F2; Davies 1971, 294-312; cf. also 10-2), and by the Salaminioi, through Eurysakes (on the Salaminioi see Ferguson 1938, 1-74; Sourvinou-Inwood 1974, 217-8; Humphreys 1990, 243-48). If it is true that Ajax in tragedy would have been perceived not (as I believe was the case) as a Homeric hero in myth and a tribal hero in cult, but as a representative of the elite, where are the very many tragedies centering on Ajax that ought to have been produced during Kimon's heyday by the logic of the argument under discussion? And if tragedy had indeed been a locus for the elites to articulate their power in a heroic guise, given the modalities of operation of Greek mythology, given that Theseus was the major Athenian hero at that time, would we not have expected tragedy to have connected him to major families, and stressed, and played with, such a connection? Indeed, if it is right, as Barron persuasively proposed (Barron 1980, 2-3 and n. 30), that Pherekydes had suggested, in the context of Kimonian propaganda, that Ajax was the son of Theseus and Eriboia/Periboia/Phereboia, on Griffith's theory, tragedy ought to have stressed and celebrated this version in which Theseus was Kimon's ancestor. But tragedy did not operate in this way. Besides all these problems, Griffith's interpretation does not account for the stability of the double perspective (as described above) even when tragedy experimented with other settings; nor does it account for the fact that the distance between the world of the audience and world of play is not static in the tragedies, but shifts in ways that appear meaningful to the exploration of major problems, as is illustrated, for example, in the pattern of the relationship between distancing and darkness in religion. I hope that my arguments about the reasons behind these choices of setting are more persuasive.

118. Sourvinou-Inwood 1989a, 134-48; Sourvinou-Inwood 1989b, 141-65; cf. also Sourvinou-Inwood 1987-1988, 19-35.

119. Cf. Easterling 1997, 21-37 for the ways in which tragedians constructed this heroic setting. Cf. Easterling 1997, 25 for the notion of "heroic vagueness" which, she argues, makes it possible for plays to be understood as offering something for everyone in the audience, and that the fact "that political, legal and social issues are dealt with in language

Chapter 2: Setting Out the Distances

carefully integrated into the heroic setting enables problematic questions to be addressed without overt divisiveness and thus to be open from the start to different interpretations." If this absence of divisiveness is right, I would see it as another result of the fact that, on my interpretation, the parameters were set by a nonpartisan, non-moment-specific, matrix of religious exploration.

120. This is one of the arguments against Goldhill's (Goldhill 1990, esp. 126-9) complex version of what one may call implicit insulation between ritual and plays seen as separate and different—though on this view interacting through their very juxtaposition to create complex meanings. Goldhill has argued that tragic and comic performances set up a complex dialectic between the proclamation of social norms, situated in the pre-performance rituals, and their possibilities of transgression situated in the plays, tragic and comic. For Goldhill, "Tragedy and comedy do not simply reverse the norms of society but inculcate a questioning of the very basis of those norms. . . . If ritual is designed to leave the structural position of society legitimized, the tragic texts seem designed to leave an audience with a question (as often as not about the legitimation of social positions)" (127-8). I will be arguing in this book that this perception is culturally determined. In chapter II.2 I will be arguing that tragedy and comedy were generated in different cultic contexts, and these different contexts created very different parameters of determination for the creation, development, and reception of the genres, which therefore must not be assumed to be comparable. In chapter III.1 I will be arguing that if we compare an independent reading of the tragedies with the ritual matrix out of which (I will have argued in chapter II.2) tragedy had developed, we are led to conclude that this ritual matrix had shaped the articulation of the earliest surviving Aeschylean tragedies, and that we can to some extent map the development from this to "mature" tragedy, a development which involved a manifold expansion of, and developments out of, the ritual matrix, not its abandonment. In the readings of Euripidean tragedies in chapters III.3 and III.4 I will be arguing that what is at issue is exploration, in a religion in which unknowability is fundamental, not questioning in the sense of challenging.

121. Cf. e.g. Burkert 1990, 15 and 31 n.11; Winkler 1990, 42; Wilson and Taplin 1993, 170. Cf. also *DFA* 84 for some of the terminology. For a few among the vast number of examples see Lys. 19.29; Lys. 21.1; Plato *Rep.* 395B.

122. E.g. Plutarch *Phokion* 30; cf. MacDowell 1989, 69-77; cf. also Csapo and Slater 1995, 351.

123. Some of the questions and problems raised by Gould 1996 and Goldhill 1996 concerning the "authority" of the chorus will be discussed in chapter III.2, after the attempted reconstruction of the ritual context of the generation of tragedy, and of the role and composition of the chorus in that context, has been set out.

124. Easterling 1988, 88-9. Cf. also Calame 1994/5, 147-8.

125. Rutherford 1994/5, 126-7 discusses the paeanic aspect of the parodos of *Antigone* and its complex relationship to Pindar's Paean 9, in a paper which is an excellent discussion of the complex ways in which paeans are deployed in tragedy, Rutherford 1994/5,

112-35. He remarks (p. 127), "The parodos of the *Antigone* can itself be thought of as a paean, although this would be a celebratory victory paean, contrasting with the fearful and apotropaic song of Pindar." On Pindar's Paeans see Rutherford forthcoming.

126. Scholars who do not focus on the ways in which the audience made sense of tragedies through perceptual filters shaped by assumptions we need to reconstruct have taken a different view. For example, Bremer 1981, 212-3 acknowledges that "It cannot be fortuitous that especially in the parodos of tragedy and the parabasis of comedy the chorus sings songs to one god or a group of gods, in perfect hymnic style," but thinks that the poet has made the cultic convention serve a non-cultic purpose; he thinks that these hymns are not cultic because they are integrated in the theatrical performance. The position taken by Furley 1995, 29-46 seems to me less clear-cut; on the one hand (Furley 1995, 37) he speaks of dramatists including faithful copies of hieratic poetry when a scene called for them, on the other he makes other statements that seem to me to leave open the question of whether, or at least not entirely to exclude the possibility that, these would have been perceived by the audience as in some ways also hymns in the here and now. Angeli Bernardini 1991, 94 took a view similar to that of Bremer, in acknowledging that some tragic choral songs are very closely connected to ritual hymnal poetry, but again speaking of hymnic forms which tragedy derived from the ritual experiences of the community, which presumably implies that they had themselves no ritual character. I am arguing that the situation is much more complicated: precisely because the chorus was perceived to be a chorus in the here and now as well as in the world of the play, the hymns they sang had the same double identity, with the aspect pertaining to the world of the play generally dominant.

127. Cf. on this Wilson and Taplin 1993, 170-4; and esp. Henrichs 1994/5, 56-111, a most insightful, subtle, and rich discussion of such choral self-referentiality and the very complex ways in which such choral self-referentiality, and the language of ritual performance, are deployed in Greek tragedy.

128. Henrichs 1994/5, 58.

129. Especially given the Dionysiac connections of the choruses who comment on their own performance (Henrichs 1994/5, 60 and passim): in Sophocles such choruses are assigned explicit Dionysiac identities and in Euripides choral self-referentiality is more prominently connected with Dionysos than with any other deity; choral self-referentiality is extremely rare in the surviving Aeschylean tragedies. I do not believe that there is any other self-referentiality in Greek tragedy other than choral self-referentiality. Other candidates are not convincing, but it is beyond my scope to discuss this here.

130. Which is why it is considered as one of the distance-creating elements in the performance (see e.g. Calame 1994/5, 148).

131. In Plato's view, rhapsodic performances belonged together with tragedies, for he considered Homer to be a sort of first tragedian and teacher and guide of tragedians. Homer the first of tragedians: Plato *Republic* 607A; the first teacher and guide of tragedi-

Chapter 2: Setting Out the Distances 65

ans: 595C, 598D, 607A ; Homer a tragedian: 605D ; cf. also on this motif Halliwell 1988, ad 595 C1; cf. also Halliwell 1988, ad 602 B10.

132. Cf. e.g. Plato *Republic* 605D; *Philebus* 48A. It may be argued that the fact that Plato puts Homer and the tragedians together argues against the ritual nature of tragedy; however, the fact that this putting them together also involved the virtual elision of the fundamental *formal* differences between Homeric epics and tragedy, and also involved a very idiosyncratic concept of *mimesis* (cf. e.g. Halliwell 1988, ad 602 B10) shows that the elisions, marginalizations, and polarizations that sustain this classification are extreme, and would have been perceived by his contemporaries who shared his assumptions as such, so that there was no disjunction between his presentation and their experience, but a perception of polarized manipulations in the service of bringing out a particular relationship perceived by him as central, from his own ideologically loaded perceptual perspective.

133. I am not concerned with Plato's own views and his hostility to tragedy. It is the common assumptions that underlie the articulation of these views that I am trying to tease out and reconstruct. To place this in some sort of perspective let me give a short crude summary of Plato's relevant position in the *Republic*. For Plato religion is good, but in the present forms of religion perceptions of gods are articulated in poetry which provide bad moral exempla. Poets must be forced to follow certain rules about how to represent gods and heroes. In addition, tragedy (and Homer) stir up emotions in a way that is bad, so poetry and religious practice should not include things that are bad, stir up emotions, and are like blasphemy to the gods. It is, obviously, beyond my scope to discuss the major questions involved here. I will only say something very briefly about the ways in which this relates to my presentation of tragedy as articulating, exploring, and "resolving" complex religious matters. In my view, Plato, on the implicit assumption that complexities escape popular perceptions and that people need simple, clear moral exempla, applied to Greek myths perceptual filters that are simplistic and rationalizing, in the service of creating good moral influences and eliminating bad ones (cf. e.g. 377d-383c, 390C, 391A-B). The application of these simplistic and rationalizing filters reduced the complex ambivalences of Greek religion reflected in mythology, which is exquisitely articulated and explored above all in tragedy, in which the complex reality and the suffering are acknowledged, but are made sense of, are shown as part of an ordered cosmos which does not annihilate suffering but puts it in perspective and keeps anomic terror at bay, to logical schemata of "good moral exempla" and "bad moral exempla."

134. Easterling 1988, 109. Friedrich 1996, 269-70 unpersuasively criticizes Easterling for this position. The only concrete objection he brings against Easterling's position (as opposed to a general odor of incredulity) is his notion that it "flies in the face of the general tenor of her argument which emphasizes the 'metaphorical status' of the rituals in Greek tragedy and their being part of the dramatic (that is artistic) fiction." This criticism, then, relies on the a priori assumption that such a metaphorical status in the world of the play excludes any permeability to the world of the audience. There is nothing to support this a priori notion, which reduces the complexity of the Greek tragic discourse, and what has been

said about the double persona of the chorus is an objection against it. In addition, Friedrich's position implicitly assumes a static relationship between the world of the tragedy and the world of the audience, and ignores the particular context in which the permeability brought out by Easterling takes place: this is Athens, and anything that happened in Athens in the heroic past is directly relevant to the Athens of today; and this, in the eyes of the fifth-century Athenians, would have zoomed the world of the tragedy to the world of the audience, and made the latter permeable to the former.

135. And in some manuscripts of *Hippolytos*, after the play's own tailpiece (cf. Barrett 1964, 417-8 ad 1462-6). Barrett 1964, 417-8 ad 1462-6 is suspicious of Euripidean tailpieces, especially recurrent tailpieces, which he considers to be actors' interpolations; but cf. also Willink 1986, 360 ad 1691-3. I have argued (Sourvinou-Inwood 1997c, 260-1) that in the *Medea* the epilogue, far from being inapposite, was, in fact, very significant. McDermott 1989, 111-2 and Kovacs 1993, 65-7 also consider the *Medea* epilogue significant. I discuss these epilogues in detail in the appendix to chapter III.3. But even if the particular floating tailpieces that concern us here (which are of a very special type) were actors' interpolations, they would still testify to perceptions in which the chorus was also perceived as a chorus in the present. The argument put forward by Mastronarde concerning these tailpieces in *Phoinissai, Orestes,* and *Iphigeneia in Tauris* (Mastronarde 1994, 645 ad 1764-6), "The break of illusion is foreign to tragedy, so one may suspect that this tailpiece reflects a post-classical practice"—he suggests that they may even have been added by scribes against their authenticity in performance—is, from our perspective here, circular; for if it is correct that the tragic chorus was also perceived as a chorus in the present (the notion of "break of illusion" is too crude a concept for the complex situation that the tragic performance involved) this argument would be invalid; this part of the chorus' persona would have been zoomed at the end of the tragedy. I shall return to the question of epilogues and other closures in ch. III.3 and its appendix.

136. In Aristophanes *Frogs* 368.

137. Cf. on these questions below chapter II.2.ii.

II. The Ritual Context

II.1. The Great Dionysia: A Reconstruction

II.1.i. *Reconstruction and Methodology*

In this chapter I will reconsider the ritual context in which tragedy was generated, the festival of the City Dionysia,[1] in detail, and in a historical perspective. I will begin with a brief description of the main elements of the festival as we know them from the classical period onwards. The fact that the evidence is fragmentary, and the different fragments come from different periods, and many from late sources, entails the possibility that the ritual nexus may have changed in the course of time, and that either the surviving evidence relates only to the later versions, or that its different fragments refer to different periods; that what we have is an amalgam containing elements that had not belonged together in ritual reality.

In this investigation also, it is methodologically advisable to pursue independently the different lines of enquiry that pertain to different sets of evidence. This procedure avoids cross-contamination from fallacious assumptions and unconscious adjustments to make the different parts of the evidence fit, and also permits some cross-checks: if the results of the independent lines converge, this provides some validation. It is important to stress that not taking account of some of the evidence because its nature and relevance to the festival under investigation cannot be proved, or are problematic, is not a methodologically rigorous procedure; it is not "healthy scepticism." For if that evidence that was left out had in fact been relevant to the festival, if it had reflected one or more facets of that festival, its omission would lead to distortion, to a faulty reconstruction of a truncated version of what had been the ancient festival. And this leads to the faulty understanding of even those parts of the festival that had been correctly reconstructed. For all elements acquire meaning in context; for example, the ritual abandonment of normality and dissolution enacted in a particular festival, as in so-called "New Year festivals,"[2] acquires its full meanings in the context of, and in relation to, the ritual new beginnings enacted in that particular festival. Consequently, the methodologically neutral, and so rigorous, strategy for the attempted reconstruction of an ancient festival involves the consideration of even problematic fragmentary data that may be relevant, through the strategy of the independent study of the different lines of investigation that pertain to different sets of evidence.

In this chapter I will attempt to determine some of the changes that took place in the festival between its beginnings and the time when it becomes more visible. Given that we know that some changes did take place in the course of the centuries of the festival's history, and especially in the period around 500, not least the introduction of the tribally organized *agones*, as well as the movement of the performances from the Agora to the theater, we are not entitled to assume that the overall shape of the ritual had remained unchanged. Nor is it more rigorous to refrain from attempting to reconstruct these changes and developments because of the extremely fragmentary state of the evidence; for refraining from making a systematic attempt means that the default mode is the implicit assumption that things were basically the same—or as much the same as makes no difference to any significant extent or purpose. This, however, though it appears superficially rigorous, because it takes the guise of "we cannot know" and "the evidence does not allow us to determine," is ultimately far more flawed methodologically than a systematic attempt to reconstruct possible developments using as rigorous a methodology as possible, and revealing all the steps in the argument so that they can be assessed appropriately, including perhaps eventually in the light of new evidence.

One important strategy that can help us block, as far as possible, the effect of "commonsense" culturally determined judgments based on culturally determined assumptions from affecting our reading of the evidence and attempted reconstruction of the festival is to try to compare the reconstructed rites to other Greek rituals, to determine whether there are close parallels, which would indicate that the reconstructed rites fit Greek ritual logic and ritual schemata. If they do fit, this gives some support to the reconstructions. For besides the shared ritual logic that can be seen to structure Greek rituals, the festivals of different cities were not impermeable to influence from festivals of other cities, above all, influence from Panhellenic festivals celebrated in the major Panhellenic sanctuaries. Thus, in Athens the reorganized Panathenaia at c. 566 acquired competitions open to all Greeks, on the model of the recently founded Pythian, Nemean, and Isthmian Panhellenic Games, the very foundation of which, in quick succession, testifies to this phenomenon of interaction and influence which, we shall see, is relevant to our investigation.

Finally, I have to answer the objection that may be raised that one should not try to speculate when the evidence is so scanty. My answer is that speculation that has, first, tried to keep the different parts of the argument separate, to avoid contamination from implicit circularity and, as much as possible, from the intrusion of modern culturally determined assumptions of plausibility, and second, exposed all its parts explicitly, and is thus wholly open to scrutiny, is methodologically preferable to the generation of a vacuum that is implicitly structured by assumptions derived from less open, and less methodologically aware older speculations.

II.1.ii. *The Festival:* Xenismos *of Dionysos*, Komos, *Procession, Sacrifices and Performances*

a) *Literary, Epigraphical, and Comparative Evidence*

The main elements of the City Dionysia were a procession, *pompe*, sent by the archon who was the magistrate responsible for the festival,[3] competitions, and something called a *komos*. The *komos* is mentioned as a part of the festival in Demosthenes 21. 10; *komoi to Dionyso*, in the plural, in *IG* II² 2318 refers to the whole festival.[4]

There were two sets of competitions, dithyrambic and dramatic; the latter involved three tragedians presenting three tragedies and a satyr play each, and after 487/6 also the production of comedies, normally five. It is an important fact that the statue of Dionysos was present in the theater during the performances.[5] There were two dithyrambic competitions: one between ten choruses of boys, each representing one of the ten Athenian tribes, the other between ten choruses of men, similarly representing each of the tribes. Just before the festival proper started, a preliminary rite took place: the statue of Dionysos Eleuthereus was removed from its sanctuary underneath the Acropolis and taken to a shrine a little outside the center of Athens, in the Academy;[6] eventually it was ceremonially escorted back to the theater in the sanctuary of Dionysos Eleuthereus, by ephebes at nighttime.[7] An interesting question is why the statue was taken to the theater, and not to the temple, or perhaps the space just outside the temple, where it needed to be the next day to receive the procession and sacrifices.[8] The process of the statue's transport to the sanctuary is referred to as the *eisagoge apo tes escharas*, an expression normally understood to refer to the transfer of the statue from the shrine at the Academy to the theater. I have argued,[9] and will be arguing in a wider context below, that this view is mistaken, and that the *eschara* referred to was the *eschara* in the Agora, near the Altar of the Twelve Gods, where the statue was brought to from the Academy prior to its transfer to the sanctuary. There is nothing to support the notion that the *eschara* referred to stood at the shrine at the Academy—other than (inevitably culturally determined) inference—while we shall see, a series of arguments support the thesis that it was the *eschara* near the Altar of the Twelve Gods. At least some ritual activity took place in connection with the stay of Dionysos' statue at the *eschara*: a sacrifice was performed,[10] and hymns were sung to *ep' escharas* Dionysos.[11]

The procession of the Dionysia culminated in the sanctuary of Dionysos Eleuthereus, but we do not know where it started, or what its route was, though, we shall see below, it is possible to reconstruct its main points of reference. We do know that in the classical period its route was elaborate, it was not a short straightforward procession. For Xenophon mentions,[12] in a context in which he is speaking of processions, which, he argues, ought to include a ride around all the shrines in the Agora, that at the Dionysia (which in the context can only mean the Dionysia procession), the dances of choruses gratified in addition (to Dionysos) the Twelve Gods and other gods.

Masks were not worn in the procession of the Dionysia. The notion that they had been is based on a misreading of two texts.[13] First, Demosthenes 19.287. Demosthenes says of Epikrates, referred to here by a nickname, Kyrebion, *hos en tais pompais aneu tou prosopou komazei*. We have Aeschines' reply to this accusation,[14] which makes clear what Demosthenes meant: Aeschines asks who ever saw Epikrates behave in an indecent manner, "either by day, as you say, at the Dionysia procession, or by night?" This makes clear that Demosthenes' meaning was that Epikrates had behaved at the Dionysia procession as though he were at a *komos*, as though this had been the *komos* of the Dionysia, rather than its procession, which involved a certain solemnity; he behaved as though he were in a *komos*, in which people fooled around, wearing masks, without the mask that characterizes the *komos*. As we shall see, there is some other evidence that suggests that at least some people wore masks at the *komos*, masks of drunken men. An implication of Aeschines' formulation is probably that at the Dionysia the *komos* took place at night. I shall return to this. The second text adduced in support of the notion that masks were worn at the Dionysia procession is Plutarch, *Moralia* 527D. But this passage does not say that masks were worn at the procession of the City Dionysia; what it says is that in the old days the *patrios ton Dionysion heorte* was simple and homely, while now there are gold vessels, rich clothes and carriages and masks. Plutarch says this happened at the Dionysia, not at the procession; therefore, since there is reason to believe that masks were worn at the *komos*, it makes perfect sense to understand the masks referred to as being the masks worn at the *komos*, especially since the carriages mentioned in this passage almost certainly were part of the *komos*; for according to Plato,[15] in Athens the Di-

Chapter 1: The Great Dionysia

onysia provide an excuse for *komazein meta methes*, sometimes in carriages.[16]

The Dionysia procession involved a *kanephoros parthenos* who carried a *kanoun* with *aparchai*.[17] Among the sacrificial animals escorted by the procession and subsequently sacrificed, sometimes in large numbers[18] was at least one bull (the ephebes led a bull in the procession and sacrificed it in the sanctuary)[19] and cattle. Bloodless offerings, such as loaves and wineskins, were also carried. A ritually important part of the procession involved the carrying of phalloi. Metics, resident foreigners, as well as citizens took part in this procession. The metics wore purple garments and carried *skaphai*, small tubs or basins; citizens wore whatever they liked and carried wineskins. As we will see, women also participated in the procession. The *choregoi*, the men who financed the dramatic and dithyrambic choruses, processed wearing magnificent clothes and golden crowns. There was, then, a differentiation between the different elements that made up the polis, an articulation of the polis into its constituent parts. Athenian colonists also took part in the procession of the Great Dionysia; they were sometimes required to send a phallos to the Dionysia and a cow and a panoply to the Panathenaia, and sometimes a cow and a phallos to the Dionysia and a cow and a panoply to the Panathenaia.[20] The Athenian Allies were also given a role in both festivals. The Allies' tribute was brought to Athens at the Dionysia and displayed in the theater,[21] while at the Great Panathenaia they were required to bring a cow and a panoply like colonists.[22]

People also were displayed in the theater as part of Athenian ideological construction: the orphan sons of the war dead who had been raised at the polis' expense and had come of age were paraded in the full armor given them by the polis before the performances.[23] Also before the performances, the honors given to citizens and foreigners for great services to the polis were proclaimed.[24] This was also an act of positive self-presentation and part of the ideological construction of Athenian democracy.

Thus, in the fifth century the Dionysia had become a locus for the polis' self-definition. This may appear to be simply motivated by pragmatic considerations, that is, to be the result of the fact that the theater offered the appropriate stage for the display of tribute as well as of the orphans and the Athenian honors list and for the announcement of honors. But we cannot assume that this is not simply a culturally determined judgment; we should not assume that there may not have been reasons connected with the ritual which led to the polis articulating itself at the Dionysia. The other festival in which the Athenian polis articulated itself, and which was similarly a locus for the polis' self-definition, was the Panathenaia. As in the Dionysia, so also in the Panathenaia, the procession articulated, and was articulated by, the whole Athenian polis as one unit.[25] The polis articulated in the City Dionysia and the Panathenaia was an open system, that included foreign residents and colonists—in a hierarchically inferior position. It is due to this character of the Dionysia as a locus for the articulation of the whole polis, which generated particular ideologies of self-definition at particular times, that before the performances the orphan sons of the war dead raised at the polis' expense were paraded in the full armor given them by the polis, and that the honors given to citizens and foreigners were proclaimed.

Because the City Dionysia and the Panathenaia were loci for articulating symbolically the polis as an open system, they became loci for the articulation of the wider system, the new configurations, of the Athenian Empire: for this was one of the results achieved by the fact that the Allies' tribute was brought to Athens at the Dionysia and displayed in the theater, while at the Great Panathenaia the Athenian allies were required to bring a cow and a panoply like colonists. The fact that at the festival the polis articulated itself symbolically in this way as an open system, is perhaps more easily intelligible in the Panathenaia, the major whole polis festival of the poliadic deity, than in the Dionysia. So why did this also take place at the Dionysia? What aspect of the Dionysia shaped this character, and how, if at all, is this connected to the festival's ritual?

The answer to this will become clear when we have considered what this festival was about. When compared to the Anthesteria, the festival perceived to have been the oldest Athenian festival of Dionysos, *ta archaiotera Dionysia*,[26] which included many and varied rites, and had several aetiological myths connected with it, the Great Dionysia appears to be a simple (in the sense of noncomplex, though lavish) festival with one simple myth.

According to the festival myth of the City Dionysia,[27] Pegasos of Eleutherai brought Dionysos' statue to Athens, but the Athenians did not receive the god with honor. Dionysos was enraged and struck the male sexual organs with an incurable disease. They consulted the oracle who told them to bring in the god with every honor; they manufactured phalloi, both privately and publicly, and with these they honored the god, commemorating their misfortune. This is a particular version of the "resistance" mythological schema associated with the introduction of the cult of Dionysos in Greek mythology. There are many myths, with different human protagonists, that say that when the cult of Dionysos first arrived in a place it was badly received, as in the case

Chapter 1: The Great Dionysia

of Athens—or, in some versions, the king resisted its introduction of the cult of Dionysos and was severely punished for this.

How does the festival myth relate to the ritual? Clearly, the removal of the statue to the Academy and its ceremonial return means that the festival celebrated the arrival of the statue, and so of the cult, of Dionysos. That is, this festival belongs to the important category of Greek festivals that celebrated the deity's advent.[28] The Athenians reenacted their reception of the god with honor, and this was especially marked by the carrying of the phalloi in the procession. A procession is a common rite in Greek festivals; each procession acquired its particular meanings in the context of the whole festival, as well as through its particular forms. In the Dionysia procession the phallophoria is directly connected with, and reenacts, the first phallophoria in the festival myth of the City Dionysia, when the Athenians first received the god and established his cult. The procession would have been perceived as both a procession in the present and as a reenactment of the first procession that had established the cult. As for the *komos*, the identity of which is problematic, as we shall see below, it was also directly connected with the reception of Dionysos. There was also a direct connection between the dramatic and dithyrambic competitions and the ritual that celebrated the reception of the cult of Dionysos: the fact that the statue of Dionysos was present in the theater during the performances shows that a strong dimension in the perception of the festival was that the dramatic and dithyrambic competitions were entertainment for Dionysos. The offering of entertainment to Dionysos is very appropriate in a ritual involving the reception of the god, in which he was honored and propitiated, and his cult introduced after the initial offense against him.

Thus, the festival myth does indeed reflect the core aspect of the festival of the Great Dionysia as perceived by the participants, and this core aspect was the reception and welcoming and entertainment of the god; in other words a rite of *xenismos*.

That the focus of the festival of the Great Dionysia was the celebration of the introduction of the cult of Dionysos through a ritual of reception and entertainment of the god is confirmed by the fact that Plutarch *Demetrios* 12 also points us strongly in the same direction; for it tells us that someone had proposed that the polis should receive Demetrios Poliorcetes every time he came *tois Demetros kai Dionysou xenismois*, with the same [rites of] guest entertainment[s] as those offered to Demeter and Dionysos. The context makes clear that what is at issue here is "entertainment on the god's arrival."

The first reason for concluding that the rites of entertainment offered to Dionysos referred to here were part of the City Dionysia is that of all Dionysiac festivals in Athens it was the City Dionysia that was *focussed* on the reception of Dionysos. In addition, it was to the City Dionysia that the Athenians attached festival days in honor of Demetrios, adding them to the festival and giving to the City Dionysia the double name Demetria and Dionysia;[29] and this points in the same direction, an association between Demetrios, *xenismoi* for Dionysos and the City Dionysia.

The two deities mentioned by Plutarch in connection with a ritual *xenismos*, Dionysos and Demeter, share an aspect of their persona that makes special sense of such a *xenismos*: they both arrived from outside and brought important agricultural gifts to Athens.[30] According to Apollodoros iii.14.7, Demeter and Dionysos came to Attica at the same time, the time of king Pandion; Demeter was received by Keleos and Dionysos by Ikarios.[31] Pandion's name was probably derived from that of the festival Pandia.[32] This was a festival of Zeus, but it was intimately connected with the City Dionysia, since the assembly in which the conduct of, and any offenses committed during, the Dionysia were discussed took place on the day following the Pandia.[33] The coincidence between on the one hand the festival's intimate relationship to the Dionysia, and on the other the myth according to which Pandion was king in Athens when Dionysos arrived in Attica and was received by Ikarios, suggests that it was probably some role that Pandion had played in that visit, or the events that followed, that may have motivated his involvement in a festival connected with the Dionysia, and that the Pandia involved a reference to Dionysos' arrival in Attica. If so, this would indicate that myths pertaining to the arrival of Dionysos himself in Attica had been attracted into the orbit of the City Dionysia, and ritually connected with the installation of his cult, so that the god's visit and the arrival of his statue and foundation of his cult, were woven into one festive system focussed on the City Dionysia. This would be the ritual correlative of the myth that connects the two in Pausanias 1.2.5: the Delphic oracle helped Pegasos introduce the cult of Dionysos by recalling that Dionysos had visited Ikarios. If this is right, it would provide a little further confirmation for the importance of Dionysos' *xenismoi* in the City Dionysia. The notion that the god's visit and the arrival of his statue and foundation of his cult were woven into one festive system focussed on the City Dionysia may find some confirmation in the oracle pertaining to this festival cited in Demosthenes,[34] which reflects the belief that the cult of Dionysos was introduced in Athens during the reign of Pandion. The other Athenian king associated with a reception of Dionysos was Amphictyon, who learnt from Dionysos how to mix wine.[35] Pausanias mentions clay statues representing Amphictyon entertaining with a feast

Chapter 1: The Great Dionysia

other gods and Dionysos;[36] Pegasos is also represented, and it is here that Pausanias mentions that Pegasos had been helped by the Delphic oracle, which had recalled that Dionysos had visited Ikarios.

A final argument for the thesis that a rite of *xenismos* of Dionysos had an important place in the City Dionysia is provided by the fact that what appears to have been the most important festival of Dionysos in Callatis, celebrated in the spring month Lykeos, was clearly influenced by the Athenian City Dionysia, since during its celebration, at the theater, honors were proclaimed and crowns awarded to people who had benefited the polis. The name of this festival was *ta xenika Dionysia*, the Dionysia in which takes place a *xenismos* of Dionysos.[37]

Is there any evidence about the forms of Dionysos' reception? For the general ritual schema, let us look at other Athenian ritual receptions. The cases of Iakchos (in the course of the Eleusinian Mysteries) and Asklepios (at the Epidauria), in which the procession escorting the god ended in a ritual reception, *hypodoche*, show that the ritual schema of such a reception of a god involved choruses singing hymns and dancing.[38] In both cases the procession escorting the god ended in a *hypodoche*, followed (immediately or eventually) by a *pannychis*.[39] If there was a ritual reception (*hypodoche*) of Dionysos, the rite of the *xenismos* of Dionysos would follow after, and in a way be a continuation of, this reception. A *xenismos* ritual in Greek religion involved the entertainment of a god or hero,[40] the offering of a meal to the god; this meal sometimes, though not always, involved sacrifice and sacrificial meat.[41] The meal was either offered in the god's sanctuary, by the god's statue, or the god's statue was moved somewhere else for the entertainment; in either case a couch and a table was set out next to the statue. The actual meal was in fact shared by the worshippers. The gods were believed to be present in the city when their *theoxenia/xenismos* was being celebrated.[42] *Theoxenia/xenismos* could also be attached to, or could form the centerpiece, of a festival with animal sacrifice.[43] Jameson considers the cult of Asklepios to be an example of such a combination of *xenismos* and other rites, including sacrifices and a *pannychis*.[44] At the Epidauria, besides these rites there was, we saw, also a ritual reception.

I will not base my attempted reconstruction of the rites of the Dionysia on the a priori presupposition that they were the same as these comparable rites in other Athenian festivals. I will try to reconstruct them on the basis of the data that are, or may be, relevant to those particular rites; if then there is a match between the reconstructed rites and the ritual schema pertaining to such rites as it emerges from other Athenian festivals, this would provide some confirmation for the validity of these reconstructions.

As we saw, according to Plutarch *Demetrios* 12, someone had proposed that the polis should receive Demetrios Poliorcetes every time he came with the same rites of guest entertainments as those offered to Demeter and Dionysos. We hear something that may be informative about the reception part of the *xenismos* offered him by the Athenians from other sources, which describe the ways in which the Athenians had disgraced themselves by treating Demetrios as a god and give details of the form of this impious behavior. Most importantly, the contemporary orator, historian, and statesman Demochares, who was an opponent of Demetrios, and who may have been a significant source for Plutarch's *Demetrios*, says that the Athenians received Demetrios on his return from Leukas and Corcyra not only with offerings of incense and crown and libations, but also "processional choruses (*prosodiakoi choroi*) and *ithyphalloi* with dancing and singing met him."[45] *Ithyphallos* means "erect phallos" and is both the name of an ode and dance performed in Dionysiac ritual, and of the performer of such a song and dance. The mention of *ithyphallos* gives support to the hypothesis arising from Plutarch's information, that this reception is based on Dionysiac ritual,[46] that it was probably modelled on the *xenismos* of Dionysos, and that therefore the ritual reception of Dionysos had involved processional choruses and *ithyphalloi*. The fact that *prosodiakoi choroi* were involved confirms that this reception was modelled on the reception of a deity, since *prosodia* were the hymns sung as the choruses approached the god (in procession towards the god),[47] which normally meant the altar or the temple[48]—while in this reception of Dionysos it was the god's statue; the *ithyphalloi* confirm that this deity was Dionysos.

Douris of Samos, another contemporary historian and politician (also probably used as a source by Plutarch for *Demetrios*), cites this *ithyphallos* sung to Demetrios.[49] It is not a comic song, but a serious (if impious) hymn, inappropriately addressed to a mortal, on his arrival. The song compares Demetrios' arrival to that of Demeter, who has come to celebrate the Mysteries at the same time as Demetrios arrived. So here also we see echoes of the notion reported in Plutarch of the polis receiving Demetrios *tois Demetros kai Dionysou xenismois*. Since this was an *ithyphallos*, it was probably modelled on the type of hymn that was sung to Dionysos on his arrival.

The fact that processional choruses and *ithyphalloi* had met Demetrios suggests that these actions had been modelled on the ritual acts that normally took place at Dionysos' *reception*, rather than the Dionysia *pompe*. That Dionysos should have been received with processional hymns fits the notion of receiving the god with honor; that *ithyphalloi* songs should have been included, performed by *ithyphal-*

Chapter 1: The Great Dionysia

loi performers, fits the context of the reception as given in the myth. The disease of the male organs the Athenians suffered from as a result of Dionysos' wrath, which was then cured through the reception of Dionysos and the introduction of his cult, including the rite of phallosbearing, is believed to have been a permanent erection.[50] Another possibility is the opposite, the total inability to have an erection. In either case not only *phallophorein*, but also *ithyphalloi*, erect phallos songs, sung by men with erect phalloi, have a direct relevance to the reception of Dionysos at the City Dionysia. If the disease had been a permanent erection, which is perhaps most likely, if hymns called *ithyphalloi* had been performed at the reception of Dionysos by *ithyphalloi* men, the latter would have been men enacting the disease of the male organs the Athenians suffered from, of which they were then cured through the reception of Dionysos and the introduction of his cult, signalled by the rite of *xenismos*; so that after that, in the procession to the sanctuary, they were cured, and they held up artificial phalloi in commemoration of their earlier disease.

The time before the reception of Dionysos represents ritually the time before present normality was established (in myth as perceived history), an abnormality that included the men's permanent erection, which made them into *ithyphalloi*. Consequently, in the perception of the first reception of Dionysos *ithyphalloi* men would have been among those meeting Dionysos singing *ithyphalloi* songs.[51] And in the ritual reception of Dionysos at the Dionysia, which reenacted that first reception, *ithyphalloi* men were among those meeting Dionysos, singing *ithyphalloi*. If, as is less likely, the disease had involved a total inability to have an erection, the *ithyphalloi* would have been enacting the desirable state of affairs which it was hoped would be achieved through the reception of Dionysos.

In any case, though the argument connecting Demochares' and Douris' information about Demetrios' reception with the reception of Dionysos at the great Dionysia, and so also the conclusion that *ithyphalloi* and processional choruses were part of a reception of Dionysos at the Great Dionysia, may not be strong in itself, due to lack of evidence, the fact that erect phalloi are of central relevance to this reception of Dionysos at the Great Dionysia, together with the fact that processional choruses also fit the context, and that this reconstructed rite would fit the ritual schema of *hypodoche*, offers independent support for this interpretation. This context of the reception of Dionysos at the Dionysia not only would explain the use of *ithyphalloi* at the reception of Demetrios, but would also account for the solemnity of the *ithyphallos* song, which may appear *para prosdokian*, not only because of our culturally determined expectations, but also because of the perceived ancient association between *phallika* and comedy: according to Aristotle,[52] comedy developed from the *phallika*, the phallic songs, which were still in use in many cities in his time.

In another Dionysiac ritual context in which *ithyphalloi* performers were involved there was less solemnity. Semos of Delos speaks of *ithyphalloi* performers performing in the orchestra of the theater.[53] According to Semos the *ithyphalloi* wore masks of drunken men; they recited towards the audience: "Give way, give way, make room for the god! For the god wants to walk through your midst upright (*orthos*) and bursting." After that Semos describes the *phallophoroi*, who were not masked, and wore a bonnet of tufted thyme and holly with a wreath of ivy and violets over it, entering the theater marching in step and reciting a hymn to Dionysos, after which they jeered at whoever they chose.

The recitation of the *ithyphalloi* is clearly associated with a movement of the god, which means of the statue of the god. This would make sense if the ritual context involved the bringing of the god's statue into the theater. It is clear that the *ithyphalloi* speak as the statue of Dionysos is about to be brought in the theater; this is a ritual entrance. When did it take place? The context of the movement of the statue, in combination with the *ithyphalloi* and *phallophoroi*, indicate the City Dionysia. The jeering is an element that occurs also in other festivals of Dionysos—and not only Dionysos. We do not know that Semos is speaking of Athens. But the following reasons suggest that this information was relevant to the Athenian Dionysia. First, that *ithyphalloi* performed in the theater, in the orchestra, in Athens is indicated by Hyperides fragment 52. So, even if Semos is not speaking of Athens, the Hyperides fragment suggests that something similar had involved the *ithyphalloi* in Athens. Second, in most cities the festival of the Dionysia was heavily influenced by the Athenian City Dionysia, so that even if Semos had been speaking of Delos, the rite was likely to be based on Athenian practice, especially since Athenian influence on Delos was very strong.[54]

So, when in the Dionysia would this rite have taken place? There are, I believe, two possibilities. First, the statue of Dionysos may have been moved from the sanctuary to the theater ritually in the company of *ithyphalloi* and *phallophoroi* every day before the performances.[55] Or, second, and in my view more likely, this rite was part of the *eisagoge apo tes escharas*, which brought the statue to the theater from the *eschara*, escorted by ephebes. I shall return to this. First it is necessary to return to the question of the *komos*.

The *komos* was an important part of the Dionysia, but we do not know exactly what it was. It is mentioned, we saw, as part of the festi-

Chapter 2: [Re]constructing the Beginnings 143

structions at the Theater of Dionysos, there is no archaeological evidence to show whether or not there had been an altar in the orchestra of the Theater of Dionysos, and if so, where exactly, and what form it had. The two earliest surviving altars situated in the orchestra of a theater were off-center, and off-center in different ways, which suggests that their exact position was not significant.[14]

One piece of lexicographical evidence[15] speaks of the *thymele* as an altar in the orchestra,[16] which it describes as "an altar of Dionysos, a square-built structure empty in the middle." In my view, this description fits only one type of structure, an altar of the *eschara* type, a hearth altar, with a stone sheathing.[17] So, if this information has any value and validity for late archaic and classical Athens, it would indicate that there was a hearth altar in the orchestra. According to Pollux,[18] the *thymele* was in the orchestra of the theater, and it was either some sort of podium (*bema*) or an altar. Like other Greek theatrical terms, *thymele* as a theatrical term was used erratically in later times.[19] It came to indicate also 'orchestra' and 'stage', two meanings which were derived from the earlier and primary meaning 'altar in the orchestra'.[20] According to one ancient view,[21] the *thymele* in the theater takes its name from the table on which the sacrificial victims were cut up; and it was a table on which they stood in the fields and sang before tragedy "had acquired and ancient form." The latter meaning given for *thymele* almost coincides with the meaning of *eleos* given by Pollux,[22] according to whom *eleos* was an ancient table on which, before Thespis' time, someone climbed and answered the chorus—in other words played the role of the *hypokrites*. Both definitions involved early tragic performers standing on a table.[23]

The sources, then, associate four different semantic fields with the word *thymele*:[24] (1) an *eschara*-type altar; (2) a table for cutting sacrificial victims; (3) a table on which stood personnel involved in the earliest tragic performance; and (4) a speaker's platform. (1) corresponds to the main semantic field of *thymele*. (3) roughly corresponds to the semantic field of another word associated with the same context of early tragic performances, *eleos*; this semantic field (almost) shared between the two words fits the main semantic field of *eleos*, kitchen table; and this main semantic field of *eleos* makes it not unrelated to (2). On the other hand, (3) and (4) are related, and one of them can be seen as derivative from the other. (1), a particular type of altar, is semantically connected with (2), table connected with sacrifice. Insofar as choral performances are associated with sacrifice, (2) and (3) are also somehow connected. The connection can be seen as having been generated more specifically in the context of early tragedy born out of choral singing at a sacrifice: the table on which the sacrificial victims were cut could also have functioned, or could have been imagined to have functioned, as the table on which someone stood to address the chorus, a sort of platform. We can make sense of all this on the basis of the perception (whether genuine historical memory or simply later speculation) that in tragedy's earliest forms the *hypokrites* had stood on the table on which the sacrificial victims were cut up to address the chorus.

Whatever else this may indicate, it certainly, and incontrovertibly, shows that in the ancient perceptions there was a close connection between the beginnings of tragedy and sacrifice. In sacrificial practice, of course, the altar is a distinct structure from the table on which the sacrificial victims were cut up—or indeed any other table connected with sacrifice. So a comparison between this ritual reality and the definitions we have seen shows that concepts associated with two distinct structures have been conflated into one nexus and ascribed to the *thymele*.[25]

It is possible to speculate on the type of scenario that can explain this state of affairs. A not impossible scenario of this type would be as follows. At the beginning there was sacrificial practice involving a hearth altar and table on which the sacrificial victims were cut up. Eventually, either the *hypokrites* stood on the *eleos* to address the chorus, or at some point it came to be believed that he had done so—and this also came to be projected backwards, to past performances in the fields. What happened after that can best be explained by the hypothesis that it had actually happened, that at an early stage the *hypokrites* had stood on the *eleos* to address the chorus. For in that case we may speculate that when prototragedy developed, and became separated from its sacrificial context, the table for cutting the sacrificial victims disappeared from the immediate vicinity of the performances, and so the meanings of both drifted to *thymele*, which continued to be spatially associated with theatrical performances.

Such a scenario would fit excellently with my reconstruction. On this reconstruction, the dramatic performances had originally taken place by the *hestia* in the prytaneion, then by the *eschara* in the Agora, both *eschara*-type altars. If the information that there was a hearth altar in the orchestra in the theater has any validity for late archaic and classical Athens, this would coincide with the hypothesis proposed here. For if there was such an altar in the orchestra of the Theater of Dionysos, it would offer support to my reconstruction, which places a hearth altar, first the *hestia* in the prytaneion, and then the *eschara* in the Agora, at the center of the ritual in the context of which tragedy was generated. Furthermore, the word *thymele* would be an appropriate term for it, not the same as the *hestia* in the prytaneion or the *es-*

Chapter 2: [Re]constructing the Beginnings 145

chara in the Agora, but a word primarily associated with this same *type* of altar.

All this would imply that, though writers like Pollux were themselves uncertain about the meanings of *thymele*,[26] it is not impossible that some genuine information may have been (in however distorted a manner) reflected in these lexicographical sources. In any case, it is difficult to doubt what primarily concerns us here: that the evidence relating to *thymele* and *eleos*, such as it is, strongly supports the view that in the ancient perceptions there was a close connection between the beginnings of tragedy and sacrifice. And this offers some confirmation for the notion that tragedy began in the context of singing at the sacrifice of a *tragos*.[27]

b) *Singing at the Sacrifice*

The evidence of the name *tragodoi* would lead us to think that singing in connection with the sacrifice of a *tragos* had been at the center of the thing out of which tragedy was generated. As we saw when considering *xenismos* rituals, the schema "sacrifice, singing and dancing" would not have been out of place in the *xenismos* of Dionysos. That hymns were an important part of *xenismos* rituals is illustrated by the Delphic Theoxenia, and by some of the paeans that had been sung at this festival, including Pindar's Paean 6,[28] and the fact that we hear that the Athenian Kleochares had composed a prosodion, a paean and a "hymn" which were sung by a chorus of boys at the sacrifice of the Theoxenia, and which the Delphic authorities had decided would be performed annually.[29]

Kleochares' composition illustrates the fact that in Greek ritual practice there was more than one type of song sung in connection with the performance of sacrifice.[30] The first type is processional songs, sung as the sacrificial procession moved towards the altar. As we saw in II.1.ii.a, there is a term for such songs, *prosodia*, though the usage of the term is complicated.[31] The second type of song sung in connection with sacrifice is sung at the altar. Proklos[32] calls this the *kyrios hymnos*, the hymn proper,[33] sung *hestoton*, and he claims that it is sung to the kithara—while the prosodion was accompanied by the *aulos*. Proklos' information about the music is unlikely to be wholly right, or at least it cannot be reflecting normal archaic and classical ritual practice. For the images tell a diffferent story. These images do not normally represent the chorus, but they do represent musical instruments.[34] The kithara, the most common string instrument in such scenes, is shown less commonly than the *aulos* in sacrificial processions, and is hardly ever used in such processions without accompanying *aulos*, while the *aulos* is often on its own.[35] More importantly, the music at the sacrificial scenes at the altar is almost exclusively provided by the *aulos*; when a string player appears he is usually Apollo.[36]

Singing by the altar was obviously a very important ritual modality in Greek religion. In some terminological systems the hymn performed at or around an altar was called a *parabomion*.[37] There is some lexicographical evidence which suggests that the basic articulation of songs sung in connection with sacrifice into processional songs and songs sung at the altar reflects common ritual practice. In the Etymologicum Magnum s.v. *prosodion, mele,* and *hymnoi* are classified into three types: those called *prosodia*, those called *hyporchemata*, and those called *stasima; prosodia* are those sung as the victims were brought to the altar; *hyporchemata* those sung dancing and running in a circular movement around the altar while the sacrificial victims were burning, and *stasima* those sung while they were resting after they had run around the altar. This is, of course, very different from the system we find in Plato *Ion* 534C in which *hyporchema* is a genre equivalent to, and distinguished from, dithyramb, *enkomion, epos,* and *iambos*. But the accuracy of the terminology and its relationship with that of the choral genres is not important here. What seems clear is that the basic articulation of songs sung in connection with sacrifice into processional songs and songs sung at the altar seems constant in the sources concerned with such matters, and since what other evidence there is on this seems to fit this picture, we may conclude that this articulation reflects common ritual practice.

Consequently, in at least some sacrifices accompanied by several hymns, those hymns would have had a basically bipartite articulation: a processional hymn, sung as the sacrificial procession moved towards the altar, and one or more songs sung dancing by the altar. The latter category is sometimes perceived as consisting of two parts, one sung when going in a circular movement around the altar and one dancing in place.

The *stasima* of this classification correspond to Proklos' "main hymn" which was sung *hestoton*. It is now accepted that *hestoton* does not mean immobile, but is used in contrast to "in procession," that is, it means dancing in place.[38] According to Angeli Bernardini the relationship between the *prosodion* and the hymn sung *hestoton* is similar to that between tragedy's parodos and stasima.[39] For the latter does not consist in the stasima involving no movement, but in a difference in the movement; where the parodos involves a march and entrance, the stasima involve a choral performance with a measured dance, without accelerated and mimetic movements, involving stylized stances and rhythmical movements, and with long pauses.[40]

Chapter 2: [Re]constructing the Beginnings

As we saw, the Athenian Kleochares had composed a *prosodion*, a paean, and "a hymn" which were sung by a chorus of boys at the sacrifice of the Delphic Theoxenia. The *prosodion* was sung at the procession to the altar. The hymn referred to simply as "hymn" would be Proklos' main hymn, sung *hestoton*. If the order of hymns in the inscription reflected their order of performance, then the paean would have been sung at the altar. The usual mode of performance of cult paeans was processional.[41] Some at least of these paeans performed the function of *prosodia* in a sacrificial procession. Another common mode of performance of cult paeans was circular motion around an altar.[42] If the order in the inscription reflects performance, Kleochares' paean would have been sung in the latter manner. But if the order in the inscription did not reflect the order in performance, then the paean would have been sung before the *prosodion*, as seems to have been the case in two other instances of hymns associated with the Delphic Theoxenia. Rutherford has shown that at least at some stage in antiquity, Pindar's Paean 6 was perceived to have consisted of two parts, a paean and a *prosodion*.[43] Even if that division was late, and did not in fact reflect a "split" performance, this may reflect a perception of a bipartite division, first a paean and then a prosodion, in the performance of hymns at the Delphic Theoxenia. In any case, an articulation of this type seems to be reflected in the Hellenistic paean by Limenios, which the title of the poem refers to as a "paean and *prosodion*."[44] Of course, the fact that in certain cases a paean seems to have been sung before the *prosodion* does not mean that another paean may not also have been sung at the altar; it is simply that the nature of our evidence is such that we do not have access to such information, except in exceptional circumstances, and only when one poet had composed more than one of these hymns.

Whatever the precise details, it would appear that in the *xenismos* ritual at the Delphic Theoxenia there was an articulated performance of hymns that included a *prosodion* and at least one hymn sung at the altar. If the latter bipartite articulation we find in this *xenismos* at the Delphic Theoxenia had also structured the hymns sung at the *xenismos* of Dionysos in Athens, we would have a *prosodion* and a hymn or hymns sung while the chorus was dancing in place. If the tripartite articulation of hymns that may have been reflected in the composition of the Athenian Kleochares at the Delphic Theoxenia had also structured the hymns sung at the *xenismos* of Dionysos in Athens, we would have a *prosodion*, a hymn sung in a circular motion around the altar, and a hymn or hymns sung while the chorus was dancing in place. In either case, it is not unlikely that the hymns were dithyrambs, since the dithyramb was the hymn most closely associated with Dionysos.[45]

If so, there would have been a marching dithyramb as a *prosodion*; perhaps a dithyramb, the par excellence *kyklios choros*, sung as the chorus danced around the altar; and finally a dithyramb or other hymn sung as one or more *stasima*, sung *hestoton*.

If a dithyramb had been sung as the chorus danced around the altar Eratosthenes' *tothi prota peri tragon orchesanto* would not have been an invention, but a projection to the mythological past, to the paradigm, of present practice, that undoubtedly continued as part of the ritual of the *xenismos* of Dionysos at the City Dionysia, singing dithyrambs while dancing around the altar on which a *tragos* was sacrificed to Dionysos. Indeed, even if there had been no separate hymn to be performed in the performance context which the Etymologicum Magnum s.v. *prosodion* ascribes to the *hyporchema*, dancing and running in a circular movement around the altar while the sacrificial victims were burning, hymn singing such as could be reflected in Eratosthenes' formulation would in any case have taken place while the chorus was moving around the altar, when the sacrificial procession arrived, and moved in a circular movement around the altar; the chorus would have presumably in that case still been singing a *prosodion*.

The nexus of choral songs just reconstructed for the *xenismos* sacrifice at the early City Dionysia bears a striking resemblance to the articulation of choral songs in tragedy, its basic skeleton of parodos and stasima. This suggests that this schema articulating the tragic choral odes may reflect the ritual schema of songs that had been part of the sacrificial ritual during the rite of *xenismos* of Dionysos; that the latter had produced the template of what was to be one basic schema articulating tragedy, the parodos and stasima, which would be reflecting a processional hymn, sung as the sacrificial procession moved towards the altar, and songs sung dancing by the altar.

As to how this may have happened I shall try to offer some tentative suggestions, or rather, suggest some of the parameters of the process, in a moment. Here I want to make clear that I imagine the process out of which prototragedy emerged as one of duplication, rather than simple splitting; so that, on this hypothesis, when prototragedy emerged, and became separated from sacrifice, hymns continued to be performed at the sacrifice at the *xenismos* of Dionysos. We saw in II.1.ii.d that there are good reasons for thinking that the dithyramb by Pindar to which belongs fragment 75 had been performed at the *xenismos* of Dionysos at the *eschara* in the Agora. The reconstruction offered here would give us the context in which this had happened: at the sacrifice of the *xenismos*, in the function of a *prosodion*, since this dithyramb is processional; this would fit the content of the poem and its relationship to the Altar of the Twelve Gods.

Chapter 2: [Re]constructing the Beginnings

But is there any reason for thinking that such songs were sung at the *tragos* sacrifice at the sixth-century (pre-Kleisthenic) City Dionysia? Obviously, the very fact with which we started, the implication of an intimate connection with sacrifice inherent in the name *tragodoi* is one reason; the fact that the ritual schema of choral songs that, on this hypothesis, had been part of the sacrificial ritual during the rite of *xenismos* of Dionysos corresponds to the schema articulating choral odes in tragedy may also be considered an argument in favor of this hypothesis.[46] For since the starting point of the hypothesis had not been the attempt to explain the tragic schema, but the intimate relationship between choral song and *tragos* sacrifice indicated by the name, this relationship of correspondence is independent, and not part of a circular argument.

Furthermore, we saw, *xenismos* rituals involve hymns, and we found one example, at the Delphic Theoxenia (a festival of Panhellenic nature, and so of a radiance likely to have exerted influence in similar rituals elsewhere), that would appear to have involved such an articulated series of hymns. Obviously, it would fit the nature of this *xenismos* to have included several hymns; for hymns honor and praise the divinity and the ritual occasion requires this very strongly, as it is one of propitiation and reception and honor.

c) *From Sacrificial Hymns to Prototragedy: Mythological Content and Problematization*

If this reconstruction is not inaccurate, where does *mimesis* come in, how did we get from these songs sung in connection with the sacrifice of a *tragos* to the introduction of the *hypokrites* and eventually to tragedy? And why did tragedy develop out of this particular ritual performance out of all others? What were the factors that were conducive to this development?

Such developments do not, of course, have a single cause, they result from complex interactions, which also involve different established ritual and schemata coming into play, since rituals develop through the bricolage modality. I will try to reconstruct the parameters which governed this transformation, in which out of a set of hymns accompanying sacrifice were generated the new forms that eventually became prototragedy.[47] Whatever the forms of pre- and prototragedy, I submit that the ritual context in which tragedy was generated had set certain parameters for its generation and development which we can reconstruct.

The first aspect of the question that needs to be considered is the content of the hymns.[48] Hymns such as dithyrambs and paeans have in general a propitiatory character.[49] As the context of this particular ritual is one of special propitiation, after an offense, we would certainly expect the festival myth to be a prominent subject in the hymns, and perhaps also we might expect other myths about analogous situations to have come into play at least sometimes.[50] Pindar's Paean 6, for another *xenismos* rite, the Delphic Theoxenia, involves complex mythological explorations, involving two parts, a Delphian paean part, in which the myth that was the aition of the festival and its background were narrated, and an Aeginetan part performed as a *prosodion*, perhaps by the same, perhaps by another chorus as the paean part, and which had a more complex and distanced relationship with the festival myth.[51] Therefore, the mythological component of the hymns, almost certainly dithyrambs, sung at this *xenismos* of Dionysos, out of which, on this thesis, prototragedy was born, was clearly a crucial element. If this interpretation is right, it was in some way conducive to the generation of tragedy. We therefore need to consider whether we can make sense of such a state of affairs in the ritual context reconstructed here; whether there are parameters determining the content of these hymns in this ritual context that seem conducive to developments that eventually generated prototragedy.

First, at the general level, we can set certain parameters on the basis of common characteristics between archaic choral lyric and choral songs in tragedy. The similarities between archaic choral lyric and choral songs in tragedy are many and varied; the relationship is generally acknowledged, as it was by the ancient Greeks, to be one of continuity (with changes).[52] Consequently, we are entitled to assume that they were shared by the choral songs out of which tragedy was generated, and take them into account in attempting to reconstruct the parameters that governed the generation of tragedy.

Like tragic choral songs, religious choral lyric had, among other things, an educational role; through both the *gnome* and the mythological paradigm the poet celebrated virtues and concepts pertaining to the deity to whom the song is dedicated.[53] And this is what, I will now be arguing, happened in the case of the City Dionysia. The festival myth gave the opportunity for hymns to explore crucial aspects of Dionysos, which led to the formulation of appropriate types of behavior, and which then also led to the exploration of other comparable myths, which had comparable paradigmatic functions, and this led to wider explorations and formulations of appropriate behavior towards the gods, in ways that I will now set out.

The ritual center of the festival is, we saw, the welcoming of Dionysos and the establishment of his cult. The myth of the festival involved first resistance to, and then the welcoming of, the god. Resis-

Chapter 2: [Re]constructing the Beginnings

tance to Dionysos' first arrival was an important part of the god's persona. Here the resistance schema shapes also the myth of the introduction of his cult.

The other Attic myth of resistance to Dionysos, which involves an actual visit by the god, gives one reason why things Dionysiac were (in myth) received with hostility. As we saw in II.1.iii, Dionysos was received by Ikarios, to whom he gave the gift of wine, which Ikarios offered to guests, who thought they had been bewitched and killed him.[54] This myth expresses the notion of loss of control of the self, parallel to the disturbance of order in society created by Dionysos' cult in the myths of Pentheus and Lykourgos. For the myths of resistance to Dionysos and his cult do not reflect historical reality; they articulate ritual tensions and symbolic oppositions, a contrast between divine madness and human order.[55] The myth of Ikarios expresses the notion of loss of control of the self brought about by Dionysos' gift, and the same notion is also expressed in another myth involving the first arrival of wine in Athens. According to this myth,[56] the Aetolians brought wine to Athens, wishing to share the god's friendship with the Athenians; but the Athenians, being unaccustomed to wine, drank it in such a way that they fell over and were lying on the ground; when their relatives saw them they assumed that they were dead, that they had been poisoned by those who had given them the wine, and they killed the Aetolians. They were then struck by barrenness as a punishment, and the oracle told them to bring *choai* to the Aetolians and celebrate a festival called Choes.[57]

This notion of loss of control of the self brought about by Dionysos' gift expressed in these two myths about the first arrival of wine in Athens, was also articulated in another Athenian myth, which involved the arrival and reception of Dionysos in Athens, but this time it is combined with the notion of control of the potential loss of control. According to this myth,[58] Amphiktyon learnt from Dionysos the mixing of wine, so that people could drink and remain *orthoi*, upright, in other words retain control of themselves. And for this reason Amphiktyon founded an altar of Dionysos Orthos.

Another version of the schema "failure to understand that the apparently inappropriate, the too disrespectful, and disorderly, should be accepted as part of Dionysos' cult leads to punishment through a disease of the sexual organs" is located in Paros. The Mnesiepes inscription at the heroon of Archilochos tells us that the Parians had punished Archilochos for having improvised a composition in honor of Dionysos, probably a dithyramb, and taught it, a composition which they judged to be "too iambic"; the Delphic oracle told them that in order to stop the disease they must honor Archilochos.[59]

In the context of the myth of the rejection of the cult of Dionysos brought by Pegasos leading to a disease of the male sexual organs, the disease, whatever its nature, clearly involved the disfunction of the male sexual organs because of the offense to Dionysos; and the recovery of their health and potency was thanks to the institution of his cult. So the upright phalloi carried aloft in the procession of the Dionysia were a representation of Dionysos' disturbing power and the need to surrender control to him by honoring him appropriately. If the disease had been one of continuous erection, the upright phalloi carried aloft would have been a commemoration of their past misfortune in the most immediate sense. But at the same time they would have been perceived as a visual articulation of the desired state of affairs, in moderation, which it was hoped the worship of Dionysos would ensure, normal potency. For the disease sent by Dionysos can be seen as, among other things, a polarization of men's sexual precariousness, a polarized image of the notion that men do not have conscious control over the potency and movements of their sexual organs. But if they embrace Dionysos, the god who patrols loss of control, who invites men to abandon conscious control by drinking wine, by engaging in, or accepting, orgiastic ritual practices, they will have his protection, and all will go well. In this context, the controversy as to whether the title of Dionysos Orthos had sexual connotations is rather meaningless. Since *orthos* can be used for the phallos held upright at a phallophoria for Dionysos,[60] Dionysos Orthos could not but evoke this dimension of the god's power and ritual. In addition, in the recitation in the theater which, on the reconstruction set out in II.1.ii, preceded the entrance of the god's statue in the theater, the *ithyphalloi* described Dionysos as being *orthos esphydomenos*; and this, said by the erect-phallos men would undoubtedly have been understood to have a sexual meaning.[61]

The fact that Dionysos Orthos is connected both with the righting of this disorder, making men's phalloi properly *orthoi* again, and with teaching how to avoid total loss of control through wine drinking, so that men can drink and retain control and remain *orthoi*, suggests that the epithet Orthos may have characterized Dionysos in his persona as teacher of controlling the loss of control, and as deity righting the negative aspects of loss of control, making things *ortha* again. Once one accepts Dionysos the god will ensure that one does not suffer catastrophic loss of control. But if one refuses to surrender control by accepting him disaster will follow.

I suggest that it is this myth of rejection of the cult of Dionysos, and its consequences, and possibly also other myths of such resistance, that were the subject matter of the performances at the center of the early City Dionysia. In those myths men's control over themselves and their

Chapter 2: [Re]constructing the Beginnings 153

world is under threat, and their logic tells them that to save them they must oppose the forces of disorder and the threat of loss of control associated with Dionysos. But, as Lykourgos, Pentheus, and others found out, that perception was mistaken. It turned out that only by surrendering control and embracing disorder in the service of Dionysos can men ultimately maintain order and avoid catastrophic loss of control. This is a paradox, and paradox characterizes religion and the world of the gods which is unknowable to men. The cult of Dionysos articulates this paradox: by placing oneself in disorder under the protection of Dionysos, by surrendering control, literally or symbolically, to the state of *entheos mania* in the context of his ritual, one is protected from the dangers of anomic disorder that, these myths say, can be sent by the god in whose domain disorder and loss of control lies, who, in a way, patrols the limits of human rationality.

The resisters' false understanding pertains to the crucial problem of the limits of human understanding concerning the divine world and religion, and the limits of, and fear of getting wrong, the socially established religious discourse. Such myths, then, articulate the tension between perceived reality and order as established in human society, and a deeper unknowable reality that lies beyond the limits of human rationality.[62] This is why these myths were especially conducive to religious exploration. Some of the tensions, problems, and human limits articulated in these myths of resistance to Dionysos were explored by the three major tragedians, and some of these explorations are accessible to us, by Euripides in *Bacchae*, by Sophocles in the fourth stasimon of *Antigone*, and, to a much lesser extent, by Aeschylus in *Edonoi*.

I am arguing that tragedy was, among other things, very importantly a discourse of religious exploration. I suggest that it is these fundamental questions inherent in the myths at the center of the ritual performances of the early City Dionysia, and the explorations they generated, that were crucially conducive to the generation of tragedy. Above all other Greek myths, I suggest, the myths of resistance to Dionysos exemplify, and articulate, the ultimate unknowability of the divine world that traverses Greek religion, and then, above all others, invite exploration. Thus, I suggest, the pre- and prototragic articulations pertaining to the myths of resistance to Dionysos created a dynamic matrix of exploration of other aspects of the divine that appear difficult to fathom, and of the proper way of relating to the gods, and of man's place in the cosmos, and ultimately of aspects of the human order that are grounded in the divine order, so that tragedy expanded its explorations, and developed its forms, in a variety of directions.

The explorations in the early performances, that, on this reconstruction, had centered on the festival myth, would have been generated as a result of the polis' attempt to articulate its relationship to the god. The polis conducting the ritual was directly implicated in the resistance myth; insofar as there was continuity between mythical Athens and the "present-day" Athens conducting the ritual, among other things, because the present-day religious system was set in place in the former's age, the present participants were atoning for the past mistake in the guilt of which they share, though in their own religious system Dionysos has an honored place. This involved a double perspective: on the one hand the present ritual was a reenactment of that past incident, and on the other it was a present day festival that resulted from that incident, and which protected the polis by gaining Dionysos' benevolence, through, among other acts of worship, the reenactment of that incident and its rectification.

I hope to have shown in chapter I.2 that this double perspective remained fundamental in tragedy; tragedy was a ritual performance in honor of the god in the present, and also enacted an "other" world, which in the preferred option of historical tragedy was both other and a part of the world of the audience because it involved their own, Athenian or more widely Greek, heroic past, in which their religious practices were anchored—as had been the case in the ritual in which, on this hypothesis, tragedy was generated.

d) *From Sacrificial Hymns to Prototragedy: Some Reconstructions*

I will now consider the development of the forms. If the different hymns that made up the set of sacrificial songs had been connected, this may have been conducive to complex thematic explorations of the type postulated above. The case of Kleochares at the *xenismos* festival that was the Delphic Theoxenia shows that sometimes the same poet composed a whole nexus of hymns for one *xenismos* festival sacrifice;[63] we do not know that these were connected in content, but they may well have been. Pindar's *Paean* 6 perhaps also shows the same poet composing more than one hymn for the same occasion, and also an articulated relationship between the two hymns.[64]

That what we may call prototragedy began with a form consisting of a chorus and the *hypokrites* cannot be doubted. The question is how the genre involved developed from choral narrative to prototragedy if it is correct that prototragedy developed out of the hymns sung at the *xenismos* of Dionysos. The form of the dithyramb was narrative; it was not mimetic and dramatic.[65] It is methodologically dangerous, and thus wrong, simply to assume that the origins of tragedy must lay in a mimetic genre, whether in a postulated early version of dialogue-mimetic

Chapter 2: [Re]constructing the Beginnings 155

forms of dithyramb, or anything else. In fact in this case, as we shall see, what evidence there is points in the opposite direction.

There is every reason to think the *hypokrites* spoke *in propria persona* to an unmasked chorus. The first argument in favor of this view derives from the ritual context as reconstructed above. For, we saw, the chorus was singing hymns to Dionysos on behalf, and as representatives, of the community; they were above all a chorus in the present performing a ritual; through this performance they were also reenacting the original *xenismos* when the cult was first established, and so reenacting the actions of that original mythological chorus, as were all the participants in the ritual reenacting the actions of the mythological participants at the foundation of the cult. This suggests that the earliest *tragodoi* would not have been masked; they were an ordinary chorus with this double perspective shared by the other participants in which the "present" dimension was dominant.

In addition, the fact that, for a considerable period in the early history of tragedy,[66] the poet himself acted as a *hypokrites*, especially when taken together with the fact that it took so long to introduce the second *hypokrites*,[67] places the *hypokrites* in the tradition of the poet-leader of the chorus in archaic lyric. This would suggest that in the earliest stages of prototragedy the *hypokrites* had spoken *in propria persona*, and that the masking and *mimesis* were a subsequent development.

This view, that in the earliest stages of prototragedy the *hypokrites* had *spoken in propria persona*, is also supported by the testimonia, which is evidence totally independent of the hypothesis of the ritual origin. First, the testimonia tell us that it had been Thespis who had introduced the use of masks,[68] eventually, after he had experimented with increasingly stronger ways of "hiding" his face in the performance, beginning with the mild form of rubbing white lead (used as a pigment to whiten the skin) on it.[69] This suggests the perception that masks developed in the course of a progressively stronger veiling of the identity of the performers, and thus distancing them from the here and now—rather than being determined by the desire to give them a new identity. For, of course, masks were used in Greece long before the emergence of tragedy, and this would have been widely known. What these stories are talking about is the increasingly strong distancing of the performers from their identities in the ritual here and now, and corresponding strengthening of the "other" dimension of the double perspective.

All this would suggest that the Greeks believed that at the very beginning of prototragedy, represented by the figure of Thespis, there was no concealment of the face, and no elision of the *hypokrites'* own identity. This may also be supported by the story that Solon had berated Thespis for telling lies during a performance in front of so many people; for though of no historical validity and clearly invented, the story reflects a perception that the *hypokrites*, to begin with, spoke *in propria persona*.[70] For this first-person narrative by the poet *hypokrites* could make much better sense of the notion of telling lies.

These different bits of evidence, then, converge to suggest that, according to the ancient perceptions, the *hypokrites* had at first spoken *in propria persona*—for what those perceptions are worth. But they are certainly worth more than our own culturally determined judgments, which are shaped by perceptual filters far further removed from the sixth-century realities and perceptions than those reflected in the testimonia. So, what evidence there is suggests that, to begin with, the *hypokrites* spoke *in propria persona*. There is absolutely no evidence to suggest otherwise, only inference based on preconceived ideas. For it is not methodologically legitimate to believe that there should be a presumption in favor of the view that the earliest *tragodoi* were masked. The notion that the chorus was masked from the beginning is simply an assumption, accepted as fact because it seems to "make sense," and because, these days especially, there is felt to be a special connection between masks and Dionysos. But Dionysos has many faces and must not be forced into one simple mould.

Let us now compare the structure of choral lyric with those of prototragedy consisting of a chorus and the *hypokrites*. Whether or not in the earliest stages of prototragedy the *hypokrites* had spoken *in propria persona*, but especially if he did, when we compare the dithyramb and other religious choral lyric forms with prototragedy we find an analogy between them, in that both, in different ways, involve on the one hand the poet's voice and on the other the choral voice. This is an especially close analogy if we compare these religious choral lyric forms to the schema "chorus-*hypokrites* speaking *in propria persona*." For example, in paeans and dithyrambs,[71] including Pindar Paean 6, sung at the Delphic Theoxenia, and Pindar Dithyramb fr. 75.7-9, sung at the City Dionysia, there is a partly comparable schema: the choral song includes segments in which a "bardic I" utters and foregrounds itself.[72] The implication of this is that the poet's voice as a separate voice is there as a potential already in the lyric genre; an embryonic matrix for the separation was already there. But, of course, there is a major difference, besides the fact that prototragedy involved a dialogue, while the bardic I flowed in and out of the choral voice: the other major difference is that the *hypokrites*, and also the chorus in response to him, did not sing, but recited. Consequently, other schemata would have come into play and helped create the selections that led to the generation of prototragedy, if it is correct that the latter emerged out of a nexus of hymns sung at the *xenismos* of Dionysos.

First, another connection with choral lyric that, I will now argue, also supports the view that the *hypokrites* had spoken *in propria persona*—as does the very relationship we have just considered between religious choral poetry and a form of prototragedy in which a *hypokrites* spoke *in propria persona*. If it is correct that, as I suggested above, there was an increasing complexity in the religious explorations in the hymns, and this was a major factor in the development of prototragedy, such complexity would have created the need for more complex forms to handle them. One form that can fulfill such a need is the "*hypokrites* as instructor speaking to the chorus" schema. The model of an instructor and the audience he instructs is implicit in the perception of the poet in choral lyric; what the "*hypokrites* as instructor of the chorus" schema does is to have the chorus, which is a segment of the polis representing the polis in singing for the god, also represent the entire audience in being directly addressed and "instructed" by the *hypokrites*.

Given the subject matter, it is not impossible that the model of the religious expounder, the *exegetes*, may also have come into play.[73] This, again, would entail a *hypokrites* speaking *in propria persona*, as a poet-instructor. This would fit perfectly with, and thus could be said to find some validation in, the name *hypokrites*, expounder, interpreter, as well as "answerer," which characterizes the poet as performer in this new genre.[74] This would also fit the hypothesis that the mythological content of the myths had led to explorations that made the content of the hymns more complex, and this development generated more complex forms. If this is right, while before the chorus' only role was to act on behalf of the community singing hymns to the god as instructed by the poet, hymns which included "instruction" in the form of *gnomai*, it came to acquire an additional role, ask questions on behalf of the community, so that the poet could expound to them, and through them to the community. Insofar as this was also done on the instructions of the poet, so that it was a pretend exchange, it can be argued that this schema already contained the seeds of *mimesis* in an embryonic form.

e) *From Sacrificial Hymns to Prototragedy: Some Possible Scenarios*

Before considering how prototragedy became a mimetic genre I need to investigate some more basic lines of development. If the songs out of which tragedy arose had been sung at the sacrifice of a *tragos* at the *hestia* inside the prytaneion, obviously at some point two things happened: they became separated from the sacrifice, and the performance moved somewhere else, perhaps outside the prytaneion to begin with,[75] perhaps straightaway to the New Agora. The two developments may have been interrelated, and they cannot be separated from the emergence of tragedy. If it is true that at a very early stage the *hypokrites* had stood on the table on which the sacrificial victims were cut to address the chorus, it is more likely than not that the role of the *hypokrites* developed before the hymnal nexus became separated from the sacrificial ritual, inside the prytaneion. If that information does not reflect historical reality the role of the *hypokrites* may have developed as a result of the separation.

Let us compare the nexus "*prosodion*, sacrifice, interwoven with stasima" to the tragic schema reflected in Aeschylus' *Suppliants* and *Persians*, "parodos, epeisodia separating stasima," which is one of the forms of early tragedy, and which in tragedy with one *hypokrites* would have taken the form "parodos, *hypokrites*-chorus exchanges separating stasima." There is clearly a correspondence between the structural position of sacrifice and that of the *hypokrites*-chorus exchanges. This is correlative with the fact that, if it is right that prototragedy developed out of this nexus of sacrificial hymns, it would follow that the *hypokrites* and the *hypokrites*-chorus exchanges took the place previously occupied by the rite of sacrifice.

One way of making sense of such a change would be to suggest, for example, that the hymns sung at the sacrifice became interesting enough, perhaps thematically related enough to each other, and perhaps also with more interesting content, exploring the possibilities of the festival myth as proposed above, so that their performance might have become somewhat obtrusive in the sacrifice, which, in any case, may have come to be perceived to be too restrictive a context for what these performances were becoming. So it may have come to be seen as both possible and desirable that the songs should be separated from the actual performance of the sacrifice, and moved outside, to make their performance accessible to a very much larger audience, and thus turn this segment of a previously restricted ritual to a spectacle with wide participation. Since, on my hypothesis, the sacrifice had articulated the hymns into one nexus, their disjunction from the sacrifice would have generated the space for another articulating agent, which would, at the same time, perform the function of linking the hymnal nexus now performed outside with the sacrifice and the *xenismos* inside which had generated it; in a way framing, by articulating verbally the context from which the hymns were now disjointed.

On the other hand, it is possible that the *hypokrites* may have emerged before the separation of the nexus of hymns from the sacrifice.

Chapter 2: [Re]constructing the Beginnings

If that is what had happened, the *hypokrites*-chorus exchanges would have to have been situated after the killing of the animal, since it is after the killing, when the victims were burning, that the second segment of the chorus' operation (the *prosodion* being the first) was located in the normal nexus of hymns associated with sacrifice, the type of hymn which on one terminology was called *hyporchema*. The placing of the *hypokrites* after the meat had been placed on the fire would also fit the notion of his standing on the table on which the sacrificial victim had been cut: an element (the table) which ceased to be active in one role was deployed in another. At that point there would normally have been a long gap between hymns, between the *prosodion* and the rest, taken up by the rites at the altar and the killing and its immediate aftermath; if the hymns had become thematically connected, the gap would have created the space for a connecting link, a space which, I am suggesting, may have been taken up by the poet and leader of the chorus.

Whether the *hypokrites* emerged before the separation of the hymnal nexus from the sacrifice, or as a result of this separation, the sacrificial ritual and the place of the hymns in it meant that the fact that the prayer was uttered by the priest before the killing, and in between the *prosodion* and what we may for convenience's sake call *hyporchema*, established the formal schema "hymn-recitation-hymns." I suggest that the prayer recited during the sacrifice would have offered a formal schema "sung hymns separated by some form of spoken or recitative speech," which may have helped shaped the parameters of selection that helped develop the forms of the hymnal nexus, thus generating what we might call prototragedy. It may have done so in interaction with another schema; for the schema "sung hymns separated by some form of spoken or recitative speech" may also have brought into play the schema "recitative prayers as prooimia," such as the Homeric Hymns, and thus also perhaps the model of the rhapsode. Else had considered the bard's or prologue's prelude to be the most plausible source for the invention of the prologue by Thespis.[76]

If the *hypokrites* had emerged as a result of the disjunction of the chorus' performance from the sacrifice, another factor may also have shaped the parameters of selection that shaped the form of the new performance. The disjunction of the chorus' performance from the sacrifice threw that performance into greater prominence and relative autonomy, and thus increased the importance of the person responsible for giving form to the performance of the chorus, the chorus leader, who was, at least symbolically, even when not actually, the poet, and whom Nagy has described as the ritual substitute for a cult-receiving mythological figure, the divine models of choral lyric, Apollo and the

Muses.[77] According to Lonsdale,[78] the dithyrambic poet was perceived by the Greeks as a representative and ritual substitute of Dionysos. On the hypothesis put forward here, the role that the poet as *hypokrites* came to play as a result of the interactive process that generated proto-tragedy could be said to have been in some ways, and almost, that of the ritual substitute for the priest. And of course the priest sometimes acts as the ritual substitute of, impersonates, the god.

Whatever the precise circumstances in which emerged the *hypokrites*, and the new form of *hypokrites*-chorus exchanges, a poetic function involving expounding and interpretation in sixth-century Athens would have evoked the tradition and schema "Solonian iambic and trochaic poems" which, as argued by Else and Herington, functioned as models for tragedy's basic recitative meters.[79]

f) *Ritual and* Skene

Let us return to the ritual. When the *xenismos* rite moved to the Agora, focussed on the *eschara* by the Altar of the Twelve Gods, if, as seems likely, it followed the same basic lines of operation as the *xenismos* rite by the Altar of the Twelve Gods in Magnesia,[80] a temporary structure would have been erected for the couches and the actual ritual dining. In Magnesia this temporary structure was referred to as *tholos*. The word *tholos* in this inscription is used as a synonym for the usual *skene*,[81] the common name for structures set up for ritual dining in sanctuaries.[82] *Skenai* were also erected in Sparta for a type of ritual dining which has some elements similar to those of this part of the City Dionysia as reconstructed here: the ritual dining called *kopis*, a type of festival meal,[83] for which, according to Athenaeus[84] the Lacedaimonians erected *skenai* near the god's temple, and in them they placed *stibades* of brushwood, on which they placed rugs, and on them they reclined and dined; only goats are sacrificed at the *kopis*.[85] As was the case at the ritual dining on *stibades* of ivy at the Athenian City Dionysia, so in the *kopides*, foreigners, *xenoi*, as well as citizens were entertained.[86] The ritual elements were differently arranged in the *kopis* from the way they were, on my reconstruction, at the City Dionysia, where the ritual dining was not in *skenai*, but, as at Magnesia, only one *skene* would have been erected in connection wth the *xenismos*, the sacrifice at which, we saw, involved restricted dining. But, of course, it is often through the remodelling and restructuring of established ritual elements that new ritual schemata, and so new rituals and new festivals, are created, through bricolage. The fact that, on my reconstruction, the *xenismos* rite had originally taken place at the prytaneion, and then moved to this nexus Altar of the Twelve Gods, *eschara*,

Chapter 2: [Re]constructing the Beginnings 161

which was in some ways a doublet of the prytaneion and its *eschara*, makes it more likely that a *skene* would have been erected for the ritual dining at the *xenismos*, reproducing the indoor space of the prytaneion and marking off this particular ritual dining as restricted.

This *skene* for the ritual dining at the *xenismos* of Dionysos at the City Dionysia would have been set up next to the statue of Dionysos that stood at the *eschara*. This nexus, "Altar of the Twelve Gods, *eschara*, statue of Dionysos and *skene*" was to the immediate north of the area in which the orchestra, the place of performances, has been placed.[87] Whatever the exact position of the *skene* with reference to the *eschara*—which would depend on where exactly the statue had stood—it would seem that this *skene* would have provided some kind of background to the performances. If it is right that early proto-tragedy had first moved from inside to the outside of the prytaneion when it became separated from the sacrifice, the position of the *skene* with reference to the performance area would have been, like its function, the same as that of the prytaneion in the earlier period. This may suggest that, as is likely to have been the case with the prytaneion, there may have been some movement of the performers, or perhaps only of the poet/*hypokrites* from the *skene* to the performance area outside. As the only appropriate covered space it may also have served as a dressing room. The *skene*, then, would have been one of the elements to be transferred to the Theater of Dionysos when the performances were moved from the Agora to the theater in the sanctuary of Dionysos Eleuthereus, in this new spatial context taking the changed form of a rectangular wooden structure to fit the new spatial needs, but still remaining a temporary structure throughout the fifth century. This fact is far from self-explanatory, and may suggest that the *skene*'s temporary, wooden nature was part of the assumptions associated with it.[88] In the next chapter we shall see some reasons that may have strengthened the tendency to preserve its temporary nature; the interpretation offered here would make sense of the basic initial conception of the *skene* as a temporary wooden structure, instead of a permanent building.

The fact that this reconstruction of the early history of the *skene* is based entirely on the consideration of established ritual elements, and of structures and the spatial relationships between them, means that the fact that this reconstruction corresponds to, and can make sense of, the name and function of the *skene* in the theater,[89] the name and origin of which, in my view, has never been satisfactorily explained, may be considered to provide some confirmation for the validity of this reconstruction.

g) *Further Reconstructions: The Question of* Mimesis

On my reconstruction, then, the basic schema structuring prototragic performances after their separation from the sacrificial rite was "linking part spoken by the *hypokrites*, parodos, exchanges between *hypokrites* and chorus separating stasima"; this would be reflected in the early tragic schema "prologue, parodos, epeisodia separating stasima." *Septem* is structured by a form of this basic schema. The form in Aeschylus' *Suppliants* and *Persians*, which begins with the parodos, was a transformation of this schema, closest to, and reflecting, the earliest prototragic forms, when they had still been integrated in the sacrificial rite, if such had existed before the separation from the sacrifice; if not, it would be reflecting the hymnal nexus that preceded the earliest prototragic forms; in either case, earliest prototragic or pre-prototragic, the performance had begun with the *prosodion*. In this context of development and change it is likely that prototragedy and early tragedy had experimented with more than one form.

Because of the scarcity and nature of the evidence I can only offer this reconstruction as a possible scenario that can make sense of all our scarce data while also fitting the known modalities of Greek religion. But there is also a piece of evidence that I tried to exclude from my thinking in this attempted reconstruction, in order to allow it to exercise some minimal control, which may be seen as providing a little, albeit inevitably limited, confirmation. The basic structure emerging from this reconstruction, the choral hymns developing into choral songs with a prologue and other recitative parts, coincides precisely with a statement of Aristotle cited by Themistios,[90] according to which, to begin with, the chorus came in and sang to the gods, and then Thespis invented prologue and *rhesis*.[91] His statement in *Poetics* that tragedy developed *apo ton exarchonton ton dithyrambon*[92] can be seen, then, as an interpretation of this core perception, an interpretation in which he takes the *hypokrites* to have emerged in connection with a particular genre of hymns, dithyrambs.[93] This need not necessarily imply that he intended to convey the idea that no external elements were imported; for this statement may, but need not, imply that the recitative had been a transformation of a sung solo—which does not appear very likely. If *exarchontes* is taken in the sense of *didaskontes*,[94] then there is no necessary implication that Aristotle could not have meant the poet in his role as *hypokrites* reciting.[95]

If the poet as *hypokrites* had expounded in the way suggested above, the chorus would have taken on both the role of the people of the past, who did not know what is right, and those of the present, who do know what was right as far as receiving the cult of Dionysos is concerned, but

Chapter 2: [Re]constructing the Beginnings

who need to be reminded, not simply of this incident, but also of the complexities and unfathomability of the will of the gods that it exemplifies, the paradoxes, and the fact that some things are beyond human rationality, and what one should do in the face of all that. So, if the reconstruction of the ritual offered here is right, the early chorus out of whose hymns prototragedy developed consisted of Athenians of the present who were acting in the present and at the same time reenacting the past, in a way impersonating the Athenians of the past—as were the other participants in the ritual. Insofar as it was a reenactment of past acts, it had the seeds of *mimesis* in it. Then, eventually, the reenactment facet became dominant for the performers. If it is right that to begin with the poet had acted as *hypokrites in propria persona*, something happened that pulled the chorus and him towards *mimesis* and the introduction of the mask.[96] Masks go with *mimesis*.[97] Masks and *mimesis* involve stressing the "other" dimension in the double perspective in which the performers were located. The mask privileges the perspective of the past, and involves the hiding of the identity of the performers as ritual performers in the present. So the introduction of the mask marked a shift from privileging the "ritual act in the present" aspect of the performance, to privileging the perspective of the past, the aspect "reenactment of the original performance of the event, the first reception and *xenismos* of Dionysos," a distancing from the present. But the ritual context ensured that the aspect of "ritual in the present" did not disappear but remained important.

I will now try to make some of the ideas set out above more concrete, by giving an example of how I envisage early prototragedy, in which the *hypokrites* appeared and spoke *in propria persona*.

Prologue
HYPOKRITES: When Pegasos of Eleutherai brought the statue of the god to Athens our ancestors did not receive it with honor. The king said, "We will not worship the son of Semele who. . . ."

Parodos
CHORUS: Oh Bromie etc. We hymn you, son of Zeus, ivy-wreathed god, Dionysos, etc.

Rhesis
HYPOKRITES: And then the god said, "I will punish them etc. And he sent disease to the male sexual organs. . . ."

First Stasimon
CHORUS: Lord Dionysos have pity on us and protects us etc.

Rhesis
HYPOKRITES: And they could do nothing to heal it; they went to the oracle and the god told them to receive the god with honor. . . . And so

we today. . . .
Second Stasimon
CHORUS: Lord Dionysos, who etc. We sing your glory etc. When you had once visited Ikarios you gave us the gift of wine. But . . . and they killed him. . . .
Dialogue
HYPOKRITES: For men are foolish and do not understand the gift of the god.
CHORUS: The will of the gods is hidden.
HYPOKRITES: Things to do with the gods are difficult to know. So men must respect [whatever *gnome* would have been considered appropriate here].
Exodos[98]

Alternative versions of the second stasimon could involve similar stories from other places; for example:

CHORUS: But I hymn you, ivy-wreathed god, Dionysos, who punished king Pentheus when you visited Thebes etc.

It is, I suggest, through these narratives that the expansion to comparable themes located in different places and involving non-Athenians took place, above all to Thebes and Pentheus, a closely comparable myth, and a location symbolically and geographically close—especially when compared to Lykourgos' Thrace.[99] This, on my reconstruction, was the first step towards the enlargement of themes described above that helped create tragedy. In fact, I suggest that it is because of this prototragic matrix of development that Thebes established itself in Athenian tragedy as the most important "other" place, in which some negative things are explored;[100] because it was the first place other than Athens in which prototragic explorations were located, a place which was relevant to Athens, but less directly relevant, in that it involved a past that was less directly part of the Athenians' present than the events involving Pegasos or Ikarios. From the explorations in the choral narratives eventually one of these stories became the center of the performance.

It is possible that it is in this context that the performance shifted into *mimesis*; that in the context of a narrative about another place, the chorus' hymns and utterances were recontextualized, came to appear to be emanating from the collectivity implicated in the narrative; so that (in the double perspective in which the choral performers were located) the distance between the "chorus in the present" perspective and the "other" perspective increased, and as a result the emphasis

Chapter 2: [Re]constructing the Beginnings 165

shifted, the "other" dimension was stressed more, and eventually, in symbiosis with a parallel shift in the persona of the *hypokrites*, the performance developed into full *mimesis* with masks. Perhaps this expansion of themes that led the chorus of Athenians to sing of, and eventually impersonate, the Thebans in the time of Pentheus was the first step in the development that led from the collectivity of Athenians that were the chorus reenacting, as on my hypothesis they had done initially, the ritual actions of the collectivity of Athenians of the past, which were directly relevant to their present, to their representing mimetically other collectivities. In both cases, though, obviously, less strongly in the second than in the first, they also remained a chorus singing in honor of Dionysos in the present. When prototragedy became mimetic and the chorus came to represent other collectivities, the impersonating part of their persona became dominant in the performance; but their identity as a chorus for Dionysos in the present was marginalized, not destroyed; it was activated by the ritual framework in which the performance took place.

When, just after 500, the performances were moved from the Agora to the theater in the sanctuary of Dionysos Eleuthereus, these performances, the entertainment of Dionysos, became detached from the *xenismos* spatially and temporally, and took place over several days after the procession. This changed things. The rite of *xenismos* of Dionysos had a double identity, as an enactment of the past, the first introduction of the cult, and as a celebration in the present. This double identity section ended with the procession and the sacrifices in which it culminated, which were themselves both a reenactment of the establishment of the cult of Dionysos and a cultic act in the present. In the form in which we know the festival, with the performances following the procession, the ritual and symbolic time in which the performances took place changed; they were now in the present. In this context, the "reenactment of the first installation of the cult" aspect of the performances and of the chorus' persona would have peeled off. But by that time, this "not chorus in the present" facet of the chorus' identity had evolved into the (dominant) mimetic facet of the chorus' identity, having helped establish, in the context of the overall ritual framework, the double identity of the chorus in a fully mimetic performance. Hence, we saw in chapter I.2, in the perceptions of the ancient audience the tragic choruses were both choruses in the world of the play, Theban elders or whatever, and a chorus for Dionysos in the present, at the City Dionysia.

I will now set out the ways in which, on my reconstruction, the shift in the persona of the *hypokrites* took place in symbiosis with the shift concerning the chorus, so that eventually the whole performance became transformed into a mimetic performance with masks. As we saw, there were seeds of *mimesis* in the early prototragic performances in which the *hypokrites* was speaking *in propria persona*, among them the direct speech that would have been contained in his narrative. I suggest that the *hypokrites'* shift into *mimesis* took place through the development of those seeds, in the circumstances described above, in interaction with, and under the influence of, the following (interacting) perceptions and ritual schemata which had formed the parameters of determination governing this shift. First, the series of perceptions we discussed above. One, the general perception of the poet/chorus leader/*hypokrites* as a representative, or even ritual substitute, of the god; two, the role of *hypokrites* as a kind of ritual substitute of a priest; and three, the comparability of the *hypokrites* to the *exegetes*. And second, a set of established ritual schemata, which we will now consider. One, the ritual schema of mimetic representations in which priestly personnel impersonated deities, in mimetic ritual performances such as that at the Eleusinian Mysteries, in which the priestess of Demeter and Kore appears to have impersonated Kore, and perhaps the *hierophantis* of Demeter had impersonated Demeter.[101]

According to Plutarch,[102] the festival of the Septerion at Delphi,[103] was a *mimema*[104] of the god's battle with the Python and its aftermath—when Apollo went to Tempe to be purified, and there he cut some laurel, crowned himself with it, and brought some back to Delphi. At this festival a temporary structure was erected, which Plutarch calls *kalias*,[105] which can mean 'hut' or 'shrine', and Strabo calls *skene*.[106] According to Plutarch,[107] it represented (was a *mimema* of) a palace, not the dragon's lair, and it was burnt down in the course of the ritual. The Septerion was a complex enneateric festival, which was ultimately connected with the Panhellenic *agones*, in that this burning of the hut is the beginning of a ritual that continues with a *theoria* of boys to Tempe, from where they bring the laurel that will be used for the laurel wreaths of the victors at the Pythian Games. The details and problems do not concern us. What is interesting is the ritual reenactment, which also involved a temporary structure being a *mimema* of something else.

This ritual schema "a temporary, 'hut', structure involved in ritual reenactment and *mimesis*," would not appear to be very different from that which, on my reconstruction, had involved the *skene* in the Agora, out of which came the *hypokrites*. If the schema seen in the Delphic ritual had been an established ritual schema, it may have helped the *skene* in the Agora attract *mimesis*, so that the *skene* could have come to be perceived as standing for a palace, or whatever, in symbiosis with the attraction of *mimesis* by the *hypokrites* and the chorus.

Chapter 2: [Re]constructing the Beginnings

In some ways comparable to the Athenian rite is another mimetic ritual enacted at another Delphic festival, the festival Charila, in which a cult which had been founded to expiate for a past offense involved a mimetic reenactment of the events which had led to the foundation of the rite, with someone impersonating the king who had committed the offense.[108]

One Athenian cult, the Eleusinian Mysteries, involved the coexistence of revelation by one male religious official (the hierophant in the Telesterion) with a mimetic representation in which priestly personnel impersonated deities. If it is correct that at the very beginning the *hypokrites* was in some ways also revealing and expounding, albeit in a very different manner from the hierophant, this complex ritual schema in which "revealing/expounding" and "impersonation of deities" had coexisted may have formed one of the models, one of the parameters shaping developments, bringing into play options and possibilities that facilitated the shift to *mimesis*. The Eleusinian schema would have been an even closer model for the *hypokrites* if, as is likely—though we have no evidence to that effect—the main male role in the "sacred drama," that of Hades in the abduction of Kore,[109] had been played by the main male religious official of the cult, the hierophant. For in that case there would have been a combination of the roles of expounder and impersonator of a god into one male figure, and this may have functioned as a model for the shift of the *hypokrites* from expounder and pseudo-impersonator (through the use of direct speech) to impersonator and *hypokrites* in the sense in which we understand it in tragedy.

In any case, whether or not the reconstruction according to which the *hypokrites* had initially spoken *in propria persona* is right, whenever it was that prototragedy had taken mimetic forms,[110] the ritual schema of mimetic representations in which priestly personnel impersonated deities would inevitably have come into play. For as a mimetic performance in a ritual context it could not but have come to be seen also in terms of these other ritual performances involving *mimesis*, mimetic prototragedy inevitably would also have been seen through the filters created by the knowledge of such performances.

This, I submit, would have invested the *hypokrites* with some of the connotations associated with priests impersonating gods in ritual mimetic performances; and this, in its turn, would have reinforced further the aspects of the perceptions associated with the chorus leader (who was, at least symbolically, even when not actually, the poet) that connected him with religious personnel. Perhaps the fact that the number of *hypokritai* did not increase beyond three[111] to match the numbers of parts in the tragedies, but, once it had reached a number that allowed multipart performances, it remained fixed, may also point in the same direction: the notion of a fixed number of performers, as was the case in "sacred drama" when this number and allocation of parts was determined in relation to the priestly personnel involved in the cult. If this is right, it would confirm that in the ancient perceptions, at least while tragedy was still developing its basic forms in the second quarter of the fifth century, these performances were seen through filters, and were invested with connotations, at least partly comparable to those associated with "sacred drama" rituals, such as that of the Eleusinian Mysteries.

h) "Thespis" and Another Poet

We have identified certain factors which, in interaction with each other, and with various ritual and poetic schemata, eventually led to the generation of prototragedy in Athens at this particular time. Important among those factors were the festival myth and the nature of the cult and the nature of the ritual of *xenismos*, and also, implicit in the discussion above, the fact that the circumstances encouraged the development of spectacle,[112] and so encouraged further developments in the emerging genre. What I have not yet discussed is the question of individual creativity.

Let us, then, consider Thespis. Even if the testimonia reflect elements of historical reality, we cannot be certain that these elements may not have been perceived through the assumptions of later periods, and thus recast to fit those assumptions. For example, it is possible that all, or most of, the agonistic elements that are projected to the earliest period in most sources[113] had in fact been introduced during the Kleisthenic reform of the festival. As we saw, we cannot exclude the possibility that at some point there may have been an agonistic element involving the *tragodoi*. But as the *xenismos* was, to begin with, a restricted participation ritual, it is more likely that this agonistic element, if it had existed, had been simply a matter of preselection for the honorific role of poet-chorus leader, which involved the *time* of a share of the meat, rather than an actual competition in performance. As for tragic poets, there is very little (at most, if we so place them, the names of Choirilos and Pratinas) to bridge the many years' gap which according to the testimonia's chronology separate Thespis' given date in the 530s[114] from the historical figures of early tragedy such as Phrynichos.[115] So, the date of Thespis is unlikely to be of any value as evidence for the date of the invention of tragedy.[116] But what about the very existence of Thespis?

Chapter 2: [Re]constructing the Beginnings 169

The fact that Thespis from Ikaria bears a paradigmatic name for a poet/singer, 'filled with the words of god, inspired', and is said to come from the place par excellence associated with Dionysos in the Attic countryside, raises the possibility that he may have been a later construct, generated to reflect the notion that tragedy had an inventor—a characteristically Greek approach to innovation. Whether or not Thespis had been a historical figure, the big step towards the creation of tragedy on the reconstruction proposed here is surely to be located in the composition of the dithyrambs sung at the sacrifice; in the composition of hymns interesting enough, perhaps interconnected enough, and perhaps also exploring the possibilities of the festival myth as proposed above, for it to have generated new forms, and to have come to be seen as possible and desirable that the songs should be separated from the performance of the sacrifice and moved outside to make it accessible to a very much larger audience. Thus, an exceptional dithyramb poet would be a factor that would have facilitated developments of the kind that led to the emergence of prototragedy. Such a development would become more intelligible, and thus also its reconstruction more plausible, if we postulate the agency of a great choral poet.

As it happens, we know that there *was* a great choral poet operating in Athens at about the relevant time, a poet who was famous for precisely the choral genre that is generally assumed to have been involved in the beginning of tragedy, and which certainly had an important part in the City Dionysia, the dithyramb, a poet who we are told had been involved in innovations pertaining to the City Dionysia and dithyrambs, and had taken an interest in at least some things religious, oracles: Lasos of Hermione, who, until his fame began to decline in the second century B.C., had a reputation as a very major poetic and musical figure.[117] One tradition credits him with the introduction of dithyrambic competitions,[118] while another[119] goes as far as crediting him, obviously incorrectly, with the very invention of the dithyramb.[120]

On this hypothesis, that Lasos had played an important role in the shaping of the things that went into the making of Greek tragedy, the Doric elements, the Doric words and forms, in the tragic choruses would be the direct result of this important role played by Lasos, and not simply of the general influence of the choral lyric tradition of the Peloponnesians and Western Greeks. If the testimonia about his involvement concerning the dithyramb and the Dionysia reflect historical reality, there are various possible ways of interpreting this, especially if we believe that the agonistic element is due to the structuring of later perceptions, in which the dithyramb at the Dionysia was associated with competition. It may involve confusion, and it may be reflecting the state of affairs hypothetized here, Lasos' transforming the dithyrambs sung at the sacrifice of the *tragos* into the coherent and interesting hymnal nexus proposed here. Or, another possibility, it may have involved his being active in the process through which the nexus of sacrificial hymns turned into a prototragic performance that eventually expanded in spheres other than that of Dionysos. This process would have also involved the redithyrambization of the nexus of hymns sung at the sacrifice of a *tragos*; for when, on this hypothesis, this nexus, which had began to develop along prototragic lines, became separated from the sacrifice, a new set of dithyrambs would have taken its place, and it may have been Lasos who had been most active in shaping the directions of these compositions.

i) *Fissions and Enlargements; The Satyr Play*

If this is (approximately) right, a further fission involving the dithyramb would have taken place in the context of the Kleisthenic reforms: the nexus of tragedy performed separately from the sacrifice, and a set of dithyrambs performed during the sacrifice would have engendered a series of *agones*: the tragic performance would have become a set of *agones* involving three tragedians, the dithyrambs at the sacrifice would have continued to be performed, but would also have engendered the dithyrambic *agones* as we know them, articulated through, and articulating, the new tribal subdivisions of the Athenian polis. Alternatively, it is possible that the introduction of *agones* may have predated the Kleisthenic reforms, and that in the context of those reforms, these *agones* were restructured through the new polis subdivisions—and as a result also enlarged.[121]

I suppose that for this reconstruction of the emergence of tragedy to be sustainable, it is necessary for it to be able to account for satyr drama; that is, show that it is possible to explain the emergence of satyr drama, and its relationship to tragedy, in the framework of the reconstruction of the emergence of tragedy proposed here. This is what I will very briefly try to do; for it is beyond my scope to investigate properly this question.[122] Until some point in the fourth century,[123] each tragedian had to produce a satyr play together with his three tragedies. This shows that tragedy and satyr play were connected. It is not impossible to see the connection as one of subordination, but Easterling prefers the notion of culmination of each tragedian's competitive entry.[124] It is beyond my scope here to discuss the nature of satyr drama, and the ways in which it is different from tragedy.[125] What matters for my present purposes is what most basically defines satyr

Chapter 2: [Re]constructing the Beginnings 171

drama: its chorus of satyrs. For this—among many other complex things—gives satyr drama a more overtly, more visibly, Dionysiac coloring than tragedy.[126] The notion that satyr drama developed to compensate for the deficiency in things Dionysiac after tragedy moved to non-Dionysiac subjects is also expressed in an ancient tradition,[127] to which I will return. This perception may seem simplistic, in the sense that it may appear to present a crude image of what would have been a complex relationship between tragedies and satyr play in peformance, but it does not follow from this that the notion of satyr play beginning as an emphatically Dionysiac offshoot of tragedy is wrong.

My reconstruction can account for precisely such a development, satyr drama emerging as an offshoot of prototragedy to which drifted overtly Dionysiac forms, to enhance the visibly Dionysiac dimension of the performances, after prototragedy had embraced themes and explorations beyond the Dionysiac sphere, so that eventually the latter came to occupy a very small part of prototragic and tragic themes. The notion of satyr drama as an offshoot of tragedy is expressed in one of the two ancient traditions about the origins of satyr drama.[128] One of these traditions sees satyr drama as a later addition to tragedy.[129] According to the other,[130] tragedy developed out of a short plot to a form involving a greater canvas, and the grotesque diction of the earlier satyric form was discarded, so that at length tragedy assumed a dignified form. Seaford tried to reconcile the two, through a tradition ascribed to the Peripatetic Chamaileon,[131] that in earlier times they had written about Dionysos, and that is why the genre was called Satyrika, but then tragedy developed, and the stories moved away from Dionysos, there were complaints that it had nothing to do with Dionysos, hence the proverb *ouden pros ton Dionyson*. And for this reason satyr drama was introduced.

It seems to me that the important thing is that ultimately all these traditions take satyr drama as we know it to be an addition to, an offshoot of, tragedy; the difference is that one strand of traditions includes the speculation that early tragedy had been like what satyr drama is now. This is a logical speculation of a learned kind, modelled on the developmental model that structures most Greek thought and mythopoea, that higher forms develop out of lower forms. As such I do not believe that it has any particular evidential value. The same is true for the interpretation of the proverb that coincides with my reconstruction of the circumstances of the emergence of satyr drama. But there is one difference. The latter testifies to a fact: the fact that in Greek perceptions it was credible that a desire to reinforce the Dionysiac dimension of the performances could have been felt when tragedy developed in the directions suggested above.

j) *Epilogue*

This reconstruction of the generation of tragedy is, inevitably, speculative because of the extreme scarcity of the evidence and the ambiguous status of so much of what it available. However, I would claim that the reconstruction is based, as much as possible, on avoidance of the major methodological pitfalls of cultural determination through the series of strategies described in II.1.i above. At the very least, the construction of this one possible reconstruction has been systematic, all the moves have been laid bare, the difficulties set out, and an attempt made to face, rather than elide them; because the whole operation is out in the open it can be assessed accordingly. This is my minimum claim. My maximum claim is that, in my opinion, it makes sense of all the available evidence in terms of Greek perceptions and mentality.

II.2.ii. Komos *and Comedy*

This section does not involve a systematic attempt to investigate the origins of comedy;[132] only an attempt to set out the parameters that governed the creation of Attic comedy,[133] and the ways in which these differed from the parameters that had governed the generation of tragedy—as both sets of parameters emerge from my reconstructions of the City Dionysia.

I suggested that the *komos* at the Dionysia consisted of ritual dining on beds of ivy leaves, and of its aftermath, which involved among other things, drunken men in masks participating in the reception of Dionysos. On this reconstruction, the ritual dining and drinking on beds of ivy leaves had taken place in the part of the festival that had preceded the establishment of the new order which started with, and was signalled by, the reception of Dionysos at the prytaneion. This period that preceded the cult's foundation, like that before any foundation, and like that in comparable festivals celebrating the deity's advent, such as the Tonaia in Samos,[134] was, in Greek mentality a period of abnormality, symbolically associated with disorder and reversed world, as was, we saw, the ritual dining on *stibades*.

If this is right, since *komodoi* means 'singers in the *komos*' we would expect the chorus of *komodoi* to have started life singing at the ritual dining on *stibades* of ivy before the statue arrived. If this ritual dining and drinking reclining on *stibades* is indeed part of the *komos*, and the chorus of *komodoi* started life singing at this ritual revel in a period of abnormality, dissolution, and reversal, their performance would have been suited to the nature of the occasion; it would have involved activities, and have attracted preexisting Dionysiac rites, of an appro-

Chapter 2: [Re]constructing the Beginnings 173

priate nature, such as burlesque and masked dances, jeering, mockery, and ritual obscenity. So it is likely to have also attracted performances of animal choruses like those reflected on sixth-century images.[135] On this hypothesis, from this type of performance "protocomedy" and then comedy arose, a genre involving one structured whole (even if that structure is diffuse), instead of a series of disparate performed elements, and was eventually—in 486—incorporated in the agonistic part of the festival; as Aristotle tells us, before that comedy was performed on a voluntary basis.[136]

We may get an idea of what these performances at the *komos* would have been like in terms of spatial arrangements from two images on the janiform head kantharos London 786,[137] dating from around the time when comedy became incorporated in the official festival program. One image shows satyrs "performing" in front of Dionysos, who is shown reclining on the ground. In the other a satyr with a lyre is striking a pose in front of Dionysos and of another man shown reclining on the ground. This image, then, involves the mythological prototypes of the "wild men" who took part in the *komos*. This iconographical schema gives us an idea of the intimacy between spectators and performers, the latter moving among the former, that would have encouraged and facilitated the type of jeering exchanges between them that, on my reconstruction, became transformed into the comparable metatheatrical elements of comedy.

If we imagine a mixture of such elements, of exchanges involving obscenity and jeering, interspersed with animal or other choruses of men,[138] this would give us a schema which would not be radically different from the basic structural schema of Old Comedy as we know it.[139] We can locate one bout of jeering in the theater, thanks to the Semos passage discussed above:[140] the *phallophoroi* operated as a chorus of men who recited and also jeered whomever they picked on. On the reconstruction set out here, this bout of jeering in the theater had taken place in the concluding part of the *komos*—after the festival had undergone some changes resulting from the transfer of the performances from the *eschara* in the Agora to the theater; before that this part of the ritual did not exist. As we saw, at least one segment of the performers involved in the mini-reception of the statue in the theater, the *ithyphalloi*, had connections both with the reception of the statue of Dionysos, and with the part of the *komos* that had involved ritual dining and drinking reclining on *stibades* of ivy. It is possible to see the mini-reception in the theater as including ritual elements that were transformations of elements that had previously been part of the *komos*. If so, these *komos* elements would have developed in two different directions: on the one hand, the main direction, into comedy, on the other, some went to form part of the reception of the statue in the theater.

The jeering in the theater had been done by the *phallophoroi*. As we saw, the Greeks associated comedy with the *phallika*; according to Aristotle,[141] comedy developed from the *exarchontes* of the *phallika*, the phallic songs, which were still in use in many cities in his time. That the *phallika* are to be understood as involving *phallophorein* can be demonstrated in at least one instance: according to Philomnestos, in sixth-century Rhodes a comic writer presented comedies as an *exarchon* among *phallophoroi*.[142] Phallos-wearing or phallos-bearing was probably the norm in everything that would be perceived as belonging to the category *ta phallika*. Thus, the reconstruction according to which the *phallophoroi* were jeering at the theater at the mini-reception of the statue of Dionysos, and the hypothesis that this was one transformation of original performances at the *komos*, would involve a connection between *phallophoroi* and comedy which coincides with an ancient perception about the origins of comedy.

The literary form of the ritual jeering and obscenities in the cults of Dionysos and Demeter is iambic poetry, involving monologues and songs that included attacks on people or types of people, and obscenity.[143] In terms of poetic genre Aristotle connected comedy with iambic poetry.[144] That iambic poetry provided inspiration for the development of comedy is also a modern perception,[145] and it is undoubtedly correct.

According to Athenaeus, the performers whom the Sikyonians call *phallophoroi*, others call *autokabdaloi* (which means improvisers);[146] according to Semos of Delos[147] the *autokabdaloi* recited standing (*staden eperainon rheseis*) and wearing wreaths of ivy; later they, and their poetry, were called *iamboi*. Given the Greek assumptions about the relationship between *iamboi* and comedy, what is being argued here is that there had been a development from the *autokabdaloi*, improvisers reciting standing, and wearing ivy wreaths, to *iamboi*, and from those to comedy. The notion that they recited standing and wearing ivy wreaths places them close to the *komos* at the Dionysia as reconstructed here: wreaths of ivy were (on this reconstruction) worn by the participants in this *komos*, and the use of the expression *staden*, 'in a standing position', makes sense if the context of their recitation that Semos had in mind was in front of reclining people, as on the the janiform head kantharos London 786 vase illustrated in photographs 9 and 10. Semos may have based this statement on information about developments that had been available to him, or he may have been inferring such developments on the basis of knowledge he possessed about the individual types of performances and performers. Indeed, the "*autokabdaloi* to *iamboi*" development (to which would

Chapter 2: [Re]constructing the Beginnings 175

have been added—by Semos, and not included in the citation by Athenaeus because it was too obvious, or supplemented mentally by Semos' readers—"and from *iamboi* to comedy") may be simply reflecting what had become established belief, that comedy developed out of *iamboi*. But whatever his exact knowledge and the extent of his guessing, what is important for us is that Semos is describing the *autokabdaloi*, whom he sees as predecessors of comedy, in a way that makes them coincide with one type of the original performers at the *komos* as reconstructed here.

The *phallophoroi* had jeered at the theater,[148] and on my reconstruction they would also have jeered at the *komos*. By contrast to the *ithyphalloi* they were not masked, and they did not have an erect phallos; they simply carried a phallos. So, while the *ithyphalloi*, drunken men with erect phalloi, were correlative with, and representatives of, the Athenian men struck by the sexual disease sent by Dionysos before the introduction of his cult, the *phallophoroi* represented the men of the present, with no mask, carrying a phallos, in commemoration of the past misfortune, but not with an erect phallos. This would fit the notion that *phallophoroi* and *autokabdaloi* were not far apart; the latter would seem to be closer to the participants of the *komos* as reconstructed here, to the reclining men, who were wearing ivy wreaths, like the *autokabdaloi*, while the *phallophoroi* wore a bonnet of thyme and chervil and over it a wreath of violets and ivy. We are told about the *autokabdaloi* that they recited *staden* and about the *phallophoroi* that they jeered *staden*; the *autokabdaloi* also must have been perceived as performing jeering and similar activities, since they are presented as the predecessors of iambic poetry who improvised their recitations. So *autokabdaloi* and *phallophoroi* are closely related in their roles. It is impossible to reconstruct what the historical relationship between these two types of performers had been, and attempt to determine whether there had ever been performers called *autokabdaloi* in Athens, or whether that role had devolved on the *phallophoroi*. There are many possibilities. Let me put forward one. The term *autokabdaloi* may have been equivalent to the performing persona that went into the creation of, and developed into, comedy, disappearing from the ritual at the Dionysia, so that the *autokabdaloi* were remembered as the precursors of comedy; while the term *phallophoroi*, involving an activity with a close attachment to the Dionysiac procession, may have been attached to the performing persona implicated in the reception in the theater and remained associated with the ritual sphere.

After discussing the *autokabdaloi*, in the next sentence Semos, as cited by Athenaeus,[149] speaks of the role of the *ithyphalloi* in what I have argued was the mini-reception of Dionysos in the theater at the completion of the *eisagoge apo tes escharas*.[150] The *ithyphalloi*, drunken men with erect phalloi singing the sort of song Semos tells us they did, are clearly performers in a genre that would come under the category of *phallika*.[151] It would appear then, that *autokabdaloi*, *phallophoroi*, and *ithyphalloi* were perceived to have had something to do with the origins of comedy. All this would, I submit, to some extent coincide with the reconstruction offered here, according to which comedy began in the context of the *komos*, the first part of which had consisted of people reclining on beds of ivy leaves wearing wreaths of ivy leaves, and entertained by performers, some of them masked choruses, some of them jeering, which slides into reciting rheseis of an iambic kind; and that one set of performers, the *ithyphalloi*, had a fixed ritual role, as representations of the Athenian men struck by the disease of the sexual organs sent by Dionysos before the introduction of his cult. The *phallophoroi* represented the men of the present.

When the performances were transferred to the theater, elements from them became attached to the mini-reception of Dionysos at the theater—while there was a main development at the *komos*, a cohering of those elements of comic performance at the *komos* into "protocomedy" and then comedy, which, a few years after the performances had been transferred to the theater, became part of the official festival program of the City Dionysia. It is possible, then,[152] that the *autokabdaloi/phallophoroi* may have contributed to the creation of both comic actors and chorus in the parabasis, in terms of what they did and said; and that the *ithyphalloi* may have contributed to the creation of the comic actors in terms of costume: the *ithyphalloi* would have had erect phalloi: the comic actors had long dangling phalloi, which are not normally erect;[153] some comic actors did have erect phalloi, such as the two on the Getty Birds vase.[154] The third element that would have gone into the making of comedy would have been masked choruses.[155] But this is speculation. Let us now return to the main lines of the reconstruction.

If this reconstruction is correct, while tragedy arose in the context of the establishment of order that began with the *xenismos* of Dionysos, and was completed with the processions and sacrifices that followed it, comedy emerged in the context of ritual dissolution, abnormality, and reversals. The different ritual contexts of the two genres account, I suggest, for some of their differences. It is beyond my scope to discuss these. I will only say something very briefly about the radically different ways in which the gods are presented in the two genres.

Chapter 2: [Re]constructing the Beginnings 177

I have been arguing that in tragedy the gods were perceived by the Greeks to be representations, almost impersonations, of the real gods; and that the gods in tragedy are not only not mocked, but also not, ultimately, "criticized"; polis religion is not "challenged." The world is problematized in tragedy, and the human condition, and so religious issues, are explored, and the darkness of the cosmos acknowledged. In comedy the gods are mocked, in the sense of made fun of—most strikingly for a ritual in honor of Dionysos, Dionysos in Aristophanes' *Frogs*. Clearly, there is something in Greek religion that makes it possible to make fun of a god without insulting him, at least in certain contexts. For, in my view, the context is fundamentally important, and there are two factors pertaining to comedy that account for the permissibility of the mockery of the gods. First, the metatheatricality of comedy entails that the gods in comedy were perceived as comic constructs, rather than representations of the real gods; their identity as comic constructs was constantly foregrounded through the metatheatricality of the genre. Second, the reason why they were mocked may be the result of comedy having been generated in a ritual context of an abnormal reversed world with the parameters of the reversed world continuing to affect the genre and its development even when it became removed from the *komos* context.

This does not mean that this was a carnival world, insulated from the real world of the polis, in which anything went; on the contrary, I agree with Henderson that the comical political discourse was part of the polis discourse.[156] But I suggest that, as far as the *religious* aspect is concerned, the parameters of reversed world continued to operate, because these were the ritual parameters which had operated in the ritual context, and once it became separated from the ritual context the ritual parameters would have remained more or less set, reinforced by the well-established and common model of ritual contexts of reversal and dissolution, above all the *komos* at the City Dionysia, of which comic performances would have been seen as an offshoot, to the extent of allowing the incorporation of "mockery towards the gods" in comedy.

II.2.iii. *Men and Women at the Dionysia*

In my view, there can be no doubt that respectable Athenian women took part in the City Dionysia[157] and (a point still considered controversial) that they were present in the theatrical performances. There is ample evidence indicating the women's presence in the theater; not all pieces of this evidence are totally conclusive on their own, but the fact that they all independently point in the same direction, the women's presence, entails that there is a very strong case in favor of the view that women were part of the audience in the dramatic performances. This conclusion is strengthened by the fact that there is no unambiguous and clear evidence suggesting that women were excluded from the theater; only modern scholars' preconceptions, inferences, based on certain preconceived hypotheses (culturally determined perceptions, for example, about how we would expect the Athenian polis to be presenting itself), and certain doubtful readings of a few comic passages.

I will first consider the evidence for the participation of women in the festival of the City Dionysia. The following evidence shows that women took part in the procession, both as spectators and as active participants. First, a fragment of Menander makes clear that in his time at least women took part, at least as spectators.[158] Then, the female gender was symbolically present among the active participants in the procession in the figure of the *kanephoros*, the daughter of a noble family who carried the sacrificial basket,[159] a *parthenos* of marriageable age, performing an office symbolically associated with beauty and marriageability.[160] Finally, according to Demetrios of Phaleron,[161] metics were obliged by law to carry *skaphai* and metics' daughters to carry *hydreia* and *skiadeia en tais pompais*. This expression would suggest that the City Dionysia procession was one of those in which this happened, since it was the second most important *pompe* after the Panathenaia, a hypothesis which gains very strong support from the fact that the metics certainly carried *skaphai* in the *pompe* of the Dionysia.[162] Consequently, it would appear that metics' daughters and generally metic women took an active part in the Dionysia procession. If this is right, the participation of girls from noble families as *kanephoroi* on the one hand, and of metic women on the other, indicates the participation of women in the middle of the spectrum between the two, ordinary Athenian respectable citizen women.

But did respectable Athenian women participate in all parts of the festival? There is one part of the festival from which I believe they were probably excluded. I think that it is highly unlikely that respectable Athenian women had taken part in the *komos*. For it involved (at the very least symbolically) drunken males, dining in a modality which is symbolically correlative with dissolution, in the abnormal time which symbolically stood for the time when the Athenian men's sexual organs were struck by the disease sent by Dionysos. The latter consideration would have also made the *komos* a primarily male concern—as well as the sort of ritual occasion that is unlikely to have involved mixing with respectable women.

Chapter 2: [Re]constructing the Beginnings 179

But whatever may have happened at the *komos*, for our purposes what is most important is what had happened at the *xenismos*, since, on my reconstruction, it is as part of the rite of *xenismos* that proto-tragedy emerged. It is because propitiating Dionysos was, above all, a male concern, and because it was the men who, apparently, above all, had to atone—since it is they who had been punished—that the chorus singing at the *xenismos* was a chorus of men. The chorus was singing hymns to Dionysos on behalf, and as representatives, of the community, as, for example, choruses of *parthenoi*, or of *paides*, did in other festivals; though of course the fact that they were males emphasized most strongly the segment most at fault and most affected. But the whole polis was symbolically involved in the *xenismos* of the god and the establishment of his cult. Given that there was generally restricted participation in rites of *xenismos*, it is not likely that many women would have been present, and so also it is not likely that many women would have been present at the performances out of which proto-tragedy emerged, while these were part of the sacrificial ritual, which, on my reconstruction, had taken place at the prytaneion at the earliest stage of the festivals' history. However, one or two women may even then have been present, as I will now argue.

First, I must make clear that the notion that women were allowed in the prytaneion in Greece is mistaken. Athenaeus tells us[163] that at Naukratis no woman was allowed to enter the prytaneion except the flute girl.[164] But this does not imply that the exclusion of women from the prytaneion was common custom. On the contrary, one thing it proves is that such exclusion of women from the prytaneion could not be a universal Greek custom, otherwise there would have been no point in Athenaeus mentioning this prohibition. In addition, we know of at least some cases in which women entered, and had an active role in, the prytaneion. The Pythia was involved in a ritual at the Delphi prytaneion.[165] In fact we know that in some cities, including Athens, women played certain ritual roles in the prytaneion. Plutarch says that in Greece, in contrast to Rome, whenever there was *pyr asbeston*, unquenched, eternal fire, as at Delphi and Athens, it was tended not by virgins, but by women past the age of marriage.[166] That this eternal flame was at the prytaneion in Athens is clear from other sources.[167] At Ephesos in the Roman period there were women prytaneis who lived in the prytaneion.[168] Since the ritual logic governing gender exclusion is much less likely to have changed than the titles of offices, or the number of political offices open to women, this, I suggest, provides further support against the notion that women would have been excluded from the prytaneion. Other functions in the cult of Hestia could also involve women: at Ephesos a husband and wife couple had served Hestia for a year.[169]

As for Hestia's priesthoods, the gender of the priest differs from one city to another; it can be either male or female.[170] With regard to Athens, we know that there had been female personnel tending the fire, but we cannot be certain that Hestia had a priestess for her cult at the prytaneion. However, there was a priestess of Hestia on the Acropolis.[171] This suggests that if a priesthood had been involved in her cult at the prytaneion besides the women tending the fire, that priesthood would have been held by a woman. If Hestia had had a priestess for her cult in the prytaneion, it is extemely unlikely that this priestess would have been excluded from the *xenismos*. It is also in any case likely that the priestess of Athena Polias would have been present in a rite of reception of an incoming god, since as the priestess of the poliadic deity, she was representing the city's major deity who was, in a way, the hostess of the other gods. This role of the priestess of Athena may be illustrated in another periodical ritual arrival: during the Eleusinian Mysteries, the *hiera* of the cult were brought from Eleusis to the Eleusinion in Athens, accompanied by the priests and priestesses of the Eleusinian cult; when they arrived, the *phaidyntes*, a minor Eleusinian official, went to the Acropolis and notified the priestess of Athena Polias of their arrival.[172] The notion that the priestess of Athena Polias would have been present at this rite of *xenismos*, and taken part in the ritual dining, is reinforced by the fact that in this, as in other *xenismos* rituals, deities other than the main one whose festival it is were believed to have taken part; above all, we saw, the Twelve Gods. The Twelve Gods, the Dodekatheon, besides being the most important gods, the family of the Olympian Gods,[173] can also be seen as standing metonymically for a city's pantheon. Besides Dionysos, who was the primary recipient of the *xenismos*, another deity stands out among the Twelve: the poliadic deity, Athena. In these circumstances, it is more likely than not that at the very least (among priestly personnel) Athena's ritual substitute, the priestess of Athena Polias, would have participated at the *xenismos* of Dionysos at the Dionysia.[174]

If any of this is right, if a single priestess took part in the *xenismos* ritual, women had not been symbolically excluded from this ritual. The presence of one signifies that women were symbolically included, and that would entail that when the prototragic performance part of the rite moved outside, and ceased to be restricted to a small group, the audience would have included female, as well as male, spectators.

Lack of evidence, then, prevents us from proving that women had been present at the *xenismos* of Dionysos, but, I argued, the presumption

Chapter 2: [Re]constructing the Beginnings

is definitely in favor of their presence. However, even if we leave this problem aside, the fact that the minimum certainty is that women had been present in the procession of the Dionysia constitutes in itself an argument in favor of their presence in the dramatic performances. In the earliest stage of the festival, as reconstructed here, the procession had followed immediately after the *xenismos* at the prytaneion, so that there would appear to have been a seamlessly connected tripartite ritual nexus marking the [re]establishment of the present order: the sacrifice of the *tragos* at the prytaneion, then the procession, and finally, the installation of the statue (reenacting the installation of the cult) and the sacrifices, at the end of procession, which mark the completion of the reenactment of the first installation of the cult, and the beginning of normal time. This nexus had, in its turn, been interlinked with another, the ritual nexus that had marked the transition from abnormality and dissolution to the process of restoration of normality: *komos* (in abnormal time), *hypodoche*, *xenismos* at the prytaneion.

This would suggest that the fact that women participated in the middle and last part of the "establishment of order" nexus, the procession and the sacrifices at its culmination,[175] makes it less likely that they would have been excluded from the first, the *xenismos*. Even if the restricted dining inside the prytaneion in the earliest stages had included no women, when the performances had moved outside, women, who were to participate in the next stage that would follow, the procession, would have been present in the performances that had just preceded it.

A similar direct connection between the performances and the procession would have obtained when the performances had taken place in the Agora, in the sense that the performances, though now much more extensive, were part of the same nexus as, and may have been completed just before, the procession. In the form in which we know the festival in the classical period and later, the dramatic performances in the Theater of Dionysos followed the celebration of the establishment of the cult of Dionysos by the whole community, a celebration in which women were included. This new order of events provides, I suggest, an additional argument in favor of the view that women were present in those performances. For it would go against Greek ritual logic to imagine that they would have participated in the celebration of the [re]establishment of the cult of Dionysos, but would have been excluded from the dramatic performances that followed that celebration on the next days—unless the nature of the rite was such that would demand such exclusion. This is not the case with a public rite like the theatrical performances. We have seen that the reason why only males are members of the chorus is because, as it had been the men who had been more directly involved in the offense, and needed most to propitiate the god, in the original sacrificial chorus it had been men who had been the most appropriate, because the most directly involved, segment of the community to represent the whole community in singing hymns to the god. This had no implications for the presence of women. It is no different from choruses of girls or boys singing on behalf of the community at other festivals.

Thus, the fact that at the very least Athenian women participated in the procession of the Great Dionysia indicates that women were present in the dramatic performances. Let us now consider some further arguments in favor of this view.[176]

Let me summarize the main points.[177] First, there is conclusive and unambiguous evidence that women were present in the theater in later periods. It is methodologically unjustifiable to postulate a change, in the absence of any evidence, especially in the case of gender exclusion. For there are ritual reasons demanding the exclusion of certain groups from certain cults, men from some, women from others, foreigners from yet others, and so on. Since the religious nature of the cult of Dionysos in Athens did not change in the period involved, it would go against the ritual logic of the festival to reverse the exclusion of a group, in this case, women. For the exclusions of women from certain cults is not "political," is not connected with their exclusion from the political institutions; it is not different from the exclusion of men or of other groups, from certain other cults. In fact the exclusion of men would seem to be more common than that of women. Those scholars who believe that women were not present in the theater in the classical period, and who therefore are obliged to postulate a change, do so because explicitly or implicitly they see the occasion of the theatrical performances as above all political, and they think that such a change could have come about by the increased importance of women in the Hellenistic period. However, this is to misunderstand radically the nature of dramatic performances, which for the Athenians were fundamentally a religious occasion, at which they were also entertained, as at other festivals.

Evidence from the postclassical period refers to things happening in the classical period which assume the presence of women.[178] For example, there was a story that when the chorus of the Erinyes came in during the performance of Aeschylus' *Eumenides* they were so terrifying that pregnant women miscarried.[179] It could be argued that this is a later invention, based on the fact that in later periods women were present. But this, again, is no more than an a priori argument. Furthermore, there is much more decisive evidence. Plato has Socrates, in

Chapter 2: [Re]constructing the Beginnings

speaking of the theater, speak of a type of rhetoric directed at a public involving children together with women and men, slave and free.[180] And elsewhere,[181] in an imaginary address to tragedians—which was obviously based on real experience, here contrasted with the plans for the ideal city—he speaks of those tragedians haranguing women and children and the whole populace.[182] There are also some comic passages which indicate very strongly that women had been present in the audience.[183]

Henderson takes the fact that whenever the audience is addressed by the comic poet it is in the masculine form, and the (arguably even more significant) fact that when the constituent members of the audience are listed they are typically males in various age groups, to indicate not that women were not part of the audience, but that there was a difference between the actual and the notional audience.[184] I do not disagree with this; it is simply that I would locate the notional male audience more specifically as the audience implicated in the stage-audience metatheatrical exchanges and, by extension, other metatheatrical references. On the other hand, my explanation of the reasons why the notional audience was and remained male is somewhat different from that of Henderson's.[185] He accepts the older view that decorum may have been part of the reason for this, but he does not believe that this provides the whole explanation; he thinks it is possible that "the conventional invisibility of women in other public contexts held true of the theater as well." However, I hope to have shown elsewhere that women were not invisible in the religious sphere.[186] And however much modern scholars may overprivilege the "political" by focussing on the fact that the Athenian polis displayed itself to itself and to foreigners in the Great Dionysia in the ways we saw above, the context of this display was deeply religious, it took place in the course of a ritual occasion, in a sanctuary. The polis articulated religion and religion articulated the polis.[187]

In my view, there were two types of reasons why the audience implicated in the comic metatheatricality was exclusively male. First, there was a reason pertaining to the origins of comedy, to the creation of the matrix that shaped the developments of comedy; and second, there was a set of reasons involving symbolic distances. With regard to the first, if it is true that respectable Athenian women had not taken part in the *komos*, and if it is also true that the metatheatricality of comedy was ultimately derived from the exchanges between performers and male audience at the *komos*, it would follow that in the matrix that shaped the development of comedy only males were involved in the exchanges, and so also in the metatheatrical dimension in general. The second set of reasons (that reinforced the first) implicates, like the older interpretation about decorum, Athenian gender discourse, as well as symbolic distances. It may have been felt that respectable Athenian women should be kept at a distance from obscenity in mixed company, and also from the dramatic constructs that were the women impersonated by men on the comic stage, and generally kept at a distance from all other aspects of the comic discourse, especially since much comic discourse was political comic discourse, and from the polis political discourse women were excluded.

I will end this section with an illustration of the ways in which preconceived ideas can create readings of certain passages that appear to me to be doing violence to the text, by using as an example one of the (few) texts that have been adduced as evidence for the absence of women from the theater. In Aristophanes *Peace* 962-7 a sacrifice is enacted on stage, in preparation of which a slave throws barley groats to the spectators. When the slave tells Trygaios that he has distributed barley to the audience, Trygaios replies that the women didn't get any, to which the Slave answers that the men will give it to them tonight. This is an obscene play on the word for barley, *krithe*, which also means 'penis'. If there had not been any women in the theater the joke would be meaningless.[188]

In these circumstances, the presence of women in the theater cannot, surely, be doubted; only a determined bias can explain the persistence of the belief in their absence.

Notes

1. Restriction of space prevents me from engaging with earlier theories of the origins of tragedy, except when I consider it necessary or desirable, especially interesting discussions and those directly relevant to my argument. See the bibliography on the origins of tragedy: CHCL 175; Versnel 1993, 30 n. 29; Henrichs 1994/5, 91 n. 3; cf. also, on the origins of the tragedy and/or on the relationship between Dionysos and the theater: Bierl 1989, 43-58; Bierl 1991; Des Bouvrie 1993, 79-112; Aronen 1992, 19-37; Seaford 1994, 268; 281-2; 328-9; Stoessl 1987; Vernant 1986, 17-24; Henrichs, 1984, 205-40; Henrichs 1993, 13-43; Henrichs 1994/5, 56-111; Friedrich 1996, 257-83; Seaford 1996, 284-94; Zeitlin 1993, 147-82; Miralles 1989, 23-41.

2. For example, the rite of *xenismos* at the Delphic Theoxenia involved special sharing: various classes of people had a right to a portion from the sacrifice (cf. II.1 n. 142). This modality of ritual dining at *xenismos*/Theoxenia rituals, involving only a restricted number of people, would fit a sacrifice in which only one *tragos* was sacrificed.

3. Burkert 1990, 16-8.

Chapter 2: [Re]constructing the Beginnings 185

4. As Burkert pointed out (1990, 16), they amount to the same thing, since the prize animal would have been sacrificed to Dionysos. I will return to this below.
5. Polemon *ap.* Athen. 372a.
6. Plutarch *Moralia* 557F.
7. Or of the winning paean, if there had been a competition; Pindar may have won repeatedly.
8. Cf. Schol. Aesch. 1. 23; Harpokration s.v. *katharsion*; Hesych. s.v. *peristiarchos*; Phot., Suda s.v. *peristiarchos*; Istros *FGrH* 334 F 16; cf. Jacoby, commentary ad loc. (IIIb.1 pp. 639-40), where most of the sources are given; cf. Parker 1983, 21.
9. Gow 1912, 238 n. 142 raised the possibility that *peristia* (that is, the sacrifice of the pig at this purification rite) and *peristiarchoi* may reveal further traces of a hearth altar of Dionysos in which the dramatic performances had originally taken place—which he deduced from the consideration of the word *thymele* (cf. below). Because he did not identify this as being in the earliest stages the *hestia* at the prytaneion, he added that it may have been derived from the hearth in the prytaneion or the council chamber and not from the hearth altar of Dionysos.
10. On *thymele* cf. esp. Gow 1912, 213-38; Burkert 1990, 19-20, and 34 n. 32 with bibl.; Wiles 1997, 70-2, 75-6.
11. Cf. Burkert 1990, 19-20 and 34 n. 32. On *mel-* see Frisk, *Griech. Etymolog. Wörterbuch* p. 699 s.v. *thyo*.
12. Gow 1912, 213-38; what Gow calls a hearth, given the way he uses the word (as including the *hestia* in the prytaneion (cf. e.g. 222) and *escharai* (cf. e.g. 224 `, is equivalent to the more usual term 'hearth altar'.
13. Pratinas *TrGF* i 4 F 3 *epi Dionysiada polypataga thymelen*.
14. In the theater at Isthmia, built some time before 390, the altar stood slightly to the east of the central axis and near the proskenion (Gebhard 1973, 13). At Thorikos the surviving altar belongs to the theater's second phase, dated to the third quarter of the fifth century, but the fact that the east end of the cavea bends here to accommodate the altar shows that there had been another altar in that position in the theater's first phase. (Cf. Gebhard 1974, 431-2; Travlos 1988, 430-1, 437 fig. 550.)
15. Etym. Magn. 743.35.
16. Cf. Gow 1912, 234; Burkert 1990, 34 n. 32 on the meaning of *orchestra* here.
17. For other interpetations and bibl. cf. Burkert 1990, 34 n. 32.
18. Pollux 4.123.
19. Cf. Gow 1912, 234.
20. Cf. Gow 1912, 236-7. The meaning 'stage', *skene* (on which see Gow 1912, 234-5), is probably not unrelated to the meaning 'platform' (cf. *op. cit.*).
21. Etym. Magn. s.v. *thymele*.
22. Pollux 4.123.
23. Gow 1912, 236 also takes the view that *eleos* answers to the description of the table in Etym. Magn.

24. I do not include here as separate categories the meaning 'orchestra', which is derived from the meaning 'altar in the orchestra' by metonymy, or the meaning 'stage', another extension, we saw, from the the meaning 'altar in the orchestra' and probably connected with the meaning 'platform'.

25. Miralles 1989, 23-4 and n. 7 thinks that the leader of the chorus actually stood on the altar.

26. Cf. Burkert 1990, 19.

27. It is interesting that Gow, purely on the basis of his study of the meanings of *thymele* and its appearance in the theater, put forward a hypothesis about the history of the word which coincides with the relevant aspects of the reconstruction of the ritual and its development put forward here on the basis of a series of entirely different (and independent) arguments. Gow 1912, 238: "Hence if these performances originally took place at some spot where the god was worshipped at a hearth, not an altar, we should naturally expect to find a 'hearth' rather than an altar for him in the theater which is built as a substitute for the original scene of these celebrations." Wiles (1997, 70-2, 75-6, cf. also 176) associates *thymele* with the hearth and Hestia totally independently from the thesis developed here.

28. For paeans associated with Theoxenia at Delphi: Pindar Paean 6, on which cf. Rutherford 1997, 1-21; Rutherford forthcoming [a]; cf. Nilsson 1906, 161.

29. SIG^3 450.

30. From now on, I will be using the term "hymn" as a generic term, within which there are several species, such as *prosodion*, paean, dithyramb (Didymos *apud* Orion p. 155-6 Sturz; cf. Furley 1995, 31-2; cf. also Bremer 1981, 193).

31. Some sources (cf. Etym. Magn. s.v. *prosoidion*; Suda s.v. *prosoidia*) say that *prosodion* was a processional song accompanied by the *aulos* sung as processions were approaching altars and temples, others (Pollux 1.38) that *prosodia* were associated with Apollo and Artemis; this specialization is almost certainly a later development, but the question of terminology, as opposed to function, in any case does not matter for our purposes. I will be using the term *prosodion* here in the sense of processional song sung when approaching altars, temples, or a god's statue. In this sense paeans and dithyrambs can function as *prosodia*—which is what, in my opinion, may have been the early usage of the term. By contrast Grandolini 1991, 126-7 distinguishes the *prosodion* from processional dithyrambs and processional paeans.

32. Proklos *ap*. Photius 320a2.

33. Cf. Furley 1995, 32 on the fact that this expression does not mean that the others were not hymns.

34. Nordquist 1992, 144.

35. Cf. Nordquist 1992, 144-6.

36. Cf. Nordquist 1992, 155-6.

37. Cf. Bremer 1981, 197 and 201 n. 35.

38. Cf. e.g. Angeli Bernardini 1991, 87-8.

Chapter 2: [Re]constructing the Beginnings

39. Angeli Bernardini 1991, 88.
40. Cf. on this Gentili 1984-5, 31-2.
41. On the performance of paeans see Rutherford forthcoming [a].
42. Rutherford forthcoming [a]; for circular motion cf. Erythrai *LSAM* no 24 A 34-6.
43. Rutherford 1997, 1-21.
44. See on this Rutherford 1997, 17.
45. Not that the paean is impossible for Dionysos; Philodamos' paean was for Dionysos, but is thought to be the result of syncretism. But what the paean is to Apollo the dithyramb is to Dionysos. On dithyrambs see most recently: Zimmermann 1992; Privitera 1991; van der Weiden 1991, 1-29.
46. Some aspects of the relationship between tragic choral odes and choral lyric has been well discussed by Gentili 1984-5, 21-35, despite the fact that it is connected with the hypothesis (26) of Arion as the inventor of a new form (dithyramb structured as lyric dialogue, in which the chorus' interlocutor assumes the character of a mythological person) and new content (no longer Dionysiac), which is based on wrong premises: Gentili 1984-5, 22-3 considers the fact that Arion was believed to have given the dithyramb authoritative form and also to have invented tragedy as confirmation of the validity of Aristotle, *Poetics* 1449a11 that tragedy was born of the dithyramb, which he takes as confirmation of the genetic link between choral lyric and tragedy. I believe this genetic link does correspond to historical reality; however, the information about Arion has no evidential value for the very reason that, once the link between the dithyramb and the origins of tragedy had become established (whether because it was a memory of historical reality or as the result of successfully established inference [which may of course have been a successful reconstruction of a real historical development]), it would have been projected backwards, and affected the persona of any claimant to the role of inventor of tragedy, such as Arion.
47. The fictionality of the theory of the Dorian origin of tragedy has been convincingly demonstrated by Else 1965, 16-26.
48. On the content of hymns see esp. Bremer 1981, 193-215; Furley 1995, 29-46. On their definition, content, function, and form cf. also Pulleyn 1997, 43-55, cf. 105-6.
49. Grandolini 1991, 126-7.
50. The mythological part of the myth is an element of the worshipper's attempt to win divine favor and guide it in channels beneficial to him (Furley 1995, 43).
51. Cf. Rutherford 1997, 1-21.
52. Cf. most recently Calame 1994/5, 136; cf. 149 n. 1 for bibl.
53. Cf. Grandolini 1991, 132; Gentili 1984-5, 34-5.
54. On Ikarios see Flückiger-Guggenheim 1984, 108-12; Kearns 1989, 172, 167; Robertson 1986, 83-6; Shapiro 1989, 95-6.
55. Cf. Burkert 1983, 177-8. I should mention with regard to the history of Dionysos' cult a Linear B tablet from Chania, which mentions Dionysos in an unambiguously religious context: it registers offerings sent to Zeus and to Dionysos at a shrine of Zeus (Hallager, Vlasakis, and Hallager 1992, 76-81).

56. In Aelian fr. 73 Herscher.

57. On the relationship of this myth with the Anthesteria see Hamilton 1992, 25-6 with bibl.

58. Philochoros 328 F 5.

59. Cf. on this Nagy 1979, 303-8; Nagy 1990, 363-4 esp. 395-7; Privitera 1991, 144; Cf. SEG xv. 517. Nagy 1990, 397 notes the similarity of this to the aition of the City Dionysia.

60. Cf. Aristophanes *Acharnians* 259-60.

61. Cf. a survey of views on the meanings of the phallos, especially in connection with Dionysos, in Henrichs 1987, 96-8. He points out (97-8) that sexual stimulation is physiologically comparable to the excitement brought on by wine and the ecstasy of orgiastic cults of Dionysos.

62. Cf. Sourvinou-Inwood 1989b, 147-52.

63. As well as, no doubt, other ritual occasions.

64. On Pindar's *Paean* 6 cf. Rutherford 1997, 1-21.

65. Cf. also Privitera 1991, 145 against the notion that Arion's dithyrambs were mimetic and dramatic.

66. Until, we are told, Sophocles: cf. *TrGF* iv Sophocles T A1.21-2. The story may well be invented (as Lefkowitz 1981, 78 suggests), but the assumption behind it is that the poet had for some time been one of the actors.

67. Introduced by Aeschylus: Aristotle *Poetics* 1449a15-7; cf. also *TrGF* iv T R 97; *TrGF* iii T N 102.

68. *TrGF* i 1 T 1; cf. 1 T 15.

69. *TrGF* i 1 T 1: starting with rubbing white lead, through the use of purslane as covering, and ending with the introduction of the masks (cf. also *TrGF* i 1 T 16). The chorus had covered their faces with the dregs of wine or with plaster (*TrGF* i 1 T 14-5). On this developmental model cf. also the discussion in Calame 1986, 128-9.

70. *TrGF* i 1 T 17 (= Plutarch *Solon* 29.6).

71. I am leaving aside Pindar's Epinikia, over which there is controversy as to whether they were really choral; cf. esp. Lefkowitz 1991.

72. On first-person statements in Pindar see Lefkowitz 1991, 3-25; cf. also Goldhill 1991, 144-5.

73. On *exegetai* in Athens see Clinton 1974, 88, 89-93; Parker 1996, 48-9; 53; 130; 295-6.

74. On the term *hypokrites* see *DFA* 126, 131-2; Ghiron-Bistagne 1976, 115-9. Else 1965, 58-9, mentions earlier views and sets out a different one, which depends on a somewhat circular argument.

75. That the space around the prytaneion was not crammed is suggested by the story in Zenobius iv.93 that there was a *limou pedion*, a field consecrated to famine, behind the prytaneion.

76. Cf. Else 1965, 59-60.

77. Cf. Nagy 1990, 361-4.

78. Lonsdale 1993, 93-6.

Chapter 2: [Re]constructing the Beginnings 189

79. Else 1965, 62; 38-45 and passim; Herington 1985, 117-9. In rightly stressing the relationship to Solonian poetry Else took a negative position towards influences from religion; thus, he asserted (*op.cit.* 38) that tragedy did not inherit any model or pattern of exegesis from cult or any other religious source; but this ignores the fact that the ancient knowledge of the very existence of religious exegesis was part of the assumptions that shaped the perceptual filters through which they viewed related phenomena, and so could not easily be divorced from those phenomena, except by context; but in this case the context did not neutralize, but reinforced, the relationship. Unlike Else, I believe that both religious and literary models helped shape the generation of tragedy. The two fundamental points on which I agree with Else are, first, that tragedy emerged in Athens, the product of particular circumstances; and second, that it was not the result of a gradual organic development, but had involved creative leaps—which Else ascribes to Thespis and Aeschylus. In my view, the development was very complex, and the leaps had been shaped through the operation of many interacting factors, a very specific ritual context and also other ritual schemata, as well as poetic traditions other than those of choral lyric.

80. On which cf. II.1 n. 140.

81. Cf. also Cooper and Morris 1990, 70-1.

82. Cf. e.g. Euripides *Ion* 1129, and esp. 805-6, *paidos prothyson xenia kai genethlia, skenas es hieras*, where the taken-for-granted custom of ritual banquets in a *skene* in sanctuaries explains why Euripides can simply refer to it this way without any previous mention of such a tent.

83. On *kopis* cf. esp. Bruit 1990, 163-4.

84. Athenaeus 138F.

85. On *skenai* for ritual dining at festivals in sanctuaries cf. also Kron 1988, 144.

86. *Xenoi* at the ritual dining on *stibades* of ivy at the Athenian City Dionysia: Philostratos, *Vit. Soph.* 549.

87. Cf. Kolb 1981, 41-3.

88. Wiles 1997 (the most recent discussion of the *skene* and its meanings, 161-74) suggested (52-3, 58) that the *skene* was removed during the dithyrambic performances, so that the audience in the lower part of the theater could have an unobstructed view of the altar below. This may well be right, but this state of affairs would still be correlative with a a perception of this *skene* as a temporary structure.

89. I discuss the greater complexities in the use of the *skene* from the *Oresteia* onwards in part III below.

90. *TrGF* i T 6. Cf. also the commentary by Else 1965, 53-4.

91. This, and the fact that there are prologues and *rheseis* in early Aeschylean plays, does not entail (as Else 1965, 58-9 suggests) that one of the *hypokrites'* main functions in proto-tragedy had not been to both answer and expound to the chorus. On my reconstruction, the "linking" role that I suggested was played by the earliest *hypokrites* was reflected in the prologue, and was a separate part of his role, different from that in which he answered, and expounded to, the chorus.

92. Aristotle *Poetics* 1449a10-11.

93. Aristotle *Poet.* 1449a19-21 tragedy *ek satyrikou metabalein opse apesemnynthe* does not imply that he believed that tragedy developed from satyr play, but that he believed that early tragedy was more like satyr play is now.

94. This is the sense in which Liddell and Scott take it.

95. The overall development I am proposing is different from the view (which Else 1965, 54 describes as the standard view) that Thespis' addition of a speaker simply developed a potentially dramatic element, which was already present in the lyrical form of tragedy; this element would have been originally represented by the *exarchon* and perhaps later by the *coryphaeus*; Thespis converted him into an actor by separating him more distinctly from the chorus and giving him lines to speak. This is different from my view that what there had been in terms of potential for the *hypokrites* development in terms of form is first, the ritual context with the structure it imposed, including the nexus of hymns, and second, the bardic I; and that in changing circumstances other schemata came into play to reshape this nexus into new forms through bricolage. My view is also different from Else's thesis, according to which (cf. esp. 55-6) Thespis created a new genre and the actor's part and the choral part had never existed independently, but were invented together with and for each other.

96. Probably adopted from other rituals, in which they were used. For an example of the use of masks in other Athenian rituals see Kahil 1977, 91-3 (a woman, almost certainly the priestess of Artemis Brauronia, and a male wearing bear masks).

97. On masks see most recently Frontisi-Ducroux 1995; cf. also Calame 1986, 85-100.

98. The comparability in some of the forms of some of the *hypokrites'* utterances (e.g. the prologue) to messenger speeches in tragedy is not due to an attempt on my part to reproduce the schemata of the latter; I tried to shape this attempted reconstruction through the factors set out above. But it may not have been unaffected (at a nonconscious level) by the fact that I consider the messenger speech in tragedy to be a transformation (primarily through its incorporation in a different context) of this type of *hypokrites rhesis*. For a sophisticated analysis of Euripidean messenger speeches see de Jong 1991; cf. 61-2 for the differences in the focalization of messenger speeches in Euripides on the one hand and in Aeschylus and Sophocles on the other.

99. Is it a complete coincidence that one of the titles of the tragedies ascribed to Thespis (*TrGF* i 1 F 1c) is *Pentheus*? Of the three other titles we are given (cf. *TrGF* 1 i T 1), one has an explicitly religious title, *Hiereis* (*TrGF* F 1a), and a second, (1b), *Eitheoi*, has a title referring to an age group involved in initiatory rituals, and myths reflecting such rituals, of which that of Theseus' journey to Crete was the most prominent (on *eitheoi* cf. Jeanmaire 1939, 333-4). Both relatively substantial surviving fragments attributed to Thespis have a reli-gious content, one "theological" (F 3), the other ritual (F 4).

100. On the place of Thebes as a conceptual category in Athenian drama cf. Zeitlin 1990a, 130-67 (= Zeitlin 1986, 101-41); Easterling 1989, 13-4; Zeitlin 1993, 147-82. I discussed

Chapter 2: [Re]constructing the Beginnings 191

the ways in which the distances are manipulated in ch. I.2 and cf. Sourvinou-Inwood 1989a, 134-48 passim.

101. Clinton 1992, 131 suggests that the two goddesses were impersonated by their hierophantids. Mylonas 1961, 310-1 believed that both roles were taken by the priestess of Demeter. Obviously, the details are not relevant to my argument.

102. Plutarch *Moralia* 293C.

103. Cf. Nilsson 1906, 150-7; Brelich 1969, 387-414; Sourvinou-Inwood 1991, 194-5.

104. Later on in the same paragraph he uses the word *apomimesis*.

105. Plutarch *Moralia* 418A.

106. Strabo ix.3.12.

107. Plutarch *Moralia* 418A.

108. Plutarch *Moralia* 293D-F.

109. Clinton's hypothesis (Clinton 1992, 85 and n. 113) that the events represented in the sacred drama did not include the abduction is not very convincing.

110. That is, whether it had been mimetic from the very beginning, or, as suggested here, after a time in which the *hypokrites* had spoken *in propria persona*.

111. The third *hypokrites* was introduced by Sophocles (Aristotle *Poetics* 1449a18-9; *TrGF* iv T A 1.23; T A 2; T R 97-8). The notion that the third *hypokrites* was introduced by Aeschylus is found in *TrGF* iii T A 1.57-8; T N 101.

112. With regard to the political circumstances, cf. Parker 1996, chapters 4, 6-7 for a sophisticated, nuanced discussion of sixth-century religious policies. The other important factor, not of course unrelated to politics, was the development of the New Agora (see Parker 1996, 73; *Guide* 19-22; Shapiro 1989, 5-8).

113. Though not, for example, in Plutarch *Solon* 29.4.

114. Cf. on this above II.1.iii.

115. Cf. also West 1989, 251-4.

116. Cf. also West 1989, 254. But I argued above it may indicate that something to do with the Dionysia may have taken place at that time.

117. On Lasos see Privitera 1965; Privitera 1991, 146-7; Herington 1985, 92-3; Nagy 1990, 388-9; van der Weiden 1991, 5-8, 9-10, 14-5.

118. Suda s.v. Lasos; on this cf. also van der Weiden 1991, 14-5.

119. Schol. Aristoph. *Birds* 1403.

120. According to one view (cf. Privitera 1991, 147), it was Lasos' introduction of the agonistic element in the dithyramb performance that led later Greeks to credit him with the invention of the dithyramb, because the introduction of the agonistic element had transformed the dithyramb performances, made them into spectacle. Lasos is shown to have taken an interest in oracles by the story in Hdt. 7.6, according to which Lasos caught Onomakritos in the act of interpolating an oracle in the writings of Mousaios, and denounced him to Hipparchos.

121. Osborne (1993, 21-38), who discusses the date of the introduction, the context, and functions of competitions in Athenian festivals, especially Athenian dramatic festivals (see

esp. Osborne 1993, 24-37), believes that tragic competitions began under the tyranny, and dithyrambic competitions immediately after the fall of tyranny (see esp. p. 36).

122. On satyr drama see esp. now Easterling 1997c, 37-44. Recent discussions on the origins, functions, and history of satyr drama: Seaford 1976, 209-21; Seaford 1984, 10-33; Sutton 1985, 94-102; cf. also Seaford 1994, 268.

123. Cf. e.g. Sutton 1985, 102.

124. Easterling 1997c, 38.

125. Cf. esp. Easterling 1997c, 37-44.

126. Cf. Lissarague 1990, 233-6; Easterling 1997c, 38-44.

127. *TrGF* i 1 T 18.

128. On these traditions see Seaford 1976, 209; Seaford 1984, 11-12.

129. Pratinas *TrGF* i 4 T 1.

130. Aristotle *Poetics* 1449a19-21.

131. *TrGF* i 1 T 18.

132. For a review of theories on, and discussions of, the origins of comedy: Giangrande 1963, 1-24; Sifakis 1971, 15-22 (cf. 53-70 on the origins of the parabasis); West 1974, 35-7 (22-39 on iambic poetry); Csapo and Slater 1995, 89-95; Henderson 1991b, 15-29 passim; cf. also Seaford 1984, 15-6.

133. Since my concern is with setting out the parameters for the creation of Attic comedy, especially the ones determined by the ritual context, I am not interested in the so-called Doric farce (on which see Stoessl 1987, 108-15 with bibl.) and the nature of its contribution, if any, to Attic comedy. My reconstruction of parameters has "spaces" in which such contribution, if there had been any, would have been located.

134. Cf. e.g. Burkert 1985, 134-5.

135. E.g. the riders on men with animal masks on the black figure belly amphora Berlin F 1697 (ABV 297.17; Add 78; Green 1994, 28 fig. 2.7; Trendall and Webster 1971, 20-1 no I.9. On animal choruses on vases and in general see Sifakis 1971, 73-85.

136. Aristotle *Poetics* 1449 b1.

137. Janiform head kantharos London 786 (ARV 1537.3; Add 386; here pl. 4.1-2).

138. Cf. other vases with images of men's choruses: Green 1994, 28-33 passim, with illustrations; Trendall and Webster 1971, 20-4. The images showing the dolphin riders, warriors riding dolphins, most strikingly when an *aulos* player is represented (see e.g. Green 1994, 33 fig. 2.12), are, of course, constructed images in which conventionally naturalistic dolphins have replaced whatever had actually been used in the performance.

139. I speak of a general schema because it is futile to attempt to determine how the different elements were first put together, what converged with what, and so on. All I am concerned with here is parameters and the general schema.

140. Semos *FGrH* 396 F 24; discussed above in II.1.ii.

141. Aristotle *Poetics* 1449a11-13.

142. Philomnestos *FGrH* 527 F 2.

Chapter 2: [Re]constructing the Beginnings   193

143. On iambic poetry West 1974, 22-39; Henderson 1991b, 15ff. On the notion of iambic cf. Nagy 1990, 397-400.

144. Aristotle *Poetics* 1449a4-5.

145. Cf. e.g. Henderson 1991b, 17.

146. Athenaeus 621F. Cf. a survey of comments on Athenaeus 621 D-F (= *FGrH* Sosibios 595 F 7) in Giangrande 1963, 16-7.

147. *FGrH* 396 F 24 (= Athenaeus 622B).

148. West, as others before him, assumes that the performance described by Semos took place in the theater at Sikyon, but does not discuss this location (West 1974, 36). Presumably the assumption is based on the statement in Athenaeus 621F that the Sikyonians call these type of performers *phallophoroi*. However, as the list does not tell us that the Athenians called them something else, and as *phallophorein* is a common activity in the cult of Dionysos, most famously in Athens, this is not a good reason for the assumption, especially since we have seen very good reasons for the connecting the *ithyphalloi* with the Athenian City Dionysia. The notion that the chant of the *phallophoroi* is a parody of Eur. *Hippol.* 73ff (West op. cit.) obviously has no implications for the date in which the ritual activity in which the chant cited had been uttered had begun.

149. Athenaeus 622B-C (= *FGrH* 396 F 24).

150. In II.1.ii above.

151. That *ithyphalloi* were part of the *phallika* from the *exarchontes* of which Aristotle had derived comedy is hardly controversial (see e.g. the survey in Giangrande 1963, 11). Obviously, I do not accept the notions of phallophory and ithyphallophory being pre-Dionysiac fertility rites on which Dionysos was superimposed (cf. e.g. Giangrande 1963, 11). Cf. Giangrande 1963, 11, 18-21 for a brief survey of views on the relationship between Attic comedy and what is described by Semos.

152. That the *phallophoroi* and the *ithyphalloi* performed the kind of *phallika* from the leaders of which comedy originated is an old view (cf. Sifakis 1971, 18-20 and 112 n. 24). The difference with my interpretation is that I connect the *phallophoroi* and *ithyphalloi* to the Athenian City Dionysia through an argument that is not based on the assumption of a relationship between *phallophoroi* and *ithyphalloi* and comedy, but pertained to the reconstruction of the City Dionysia—also I am not trying to determine the particular contributions of these elements to a comedy which I see as having been in a flux and development until comedy as we (more or less) know it acquired its basic schema.

153. Cf. Taplin 1993, 102-3.

154. Taplin 1993, pl. 24.28, the only Attic vase representing Old Comedy.

155. Sifakis 1971, 69 thinks that the parabasis was not derived from performances like those of the *ithyphalloi* and *phallophoroi*. The reason he gives is "because the odes are addressed to a variety of gods among whom Dionysos is hardly prominent, and the main theme of the epirrhemata is not satire but the self-presentation and self-glorification of the chorus." But this argument is not valid when looked at from the point of view suggested here; because the whole point is that there has been a very significant transformation from

the disparate elements, to protocomedy, and then to comedy, and the enlargement of the canvas to include gods other than Dionysos would be fundamental in this, as in tragedy.

156. Henderson 1990, 271-313.

157. The reason why this question is discussed here and not in chapter 1 will become apparent in the course of the discussion.

158. Menander fr. 558 Kock= 382 Körte.

159. Schol. Aristophanes *Acharnians* 241.

160. On *kanephoroi* and their association with beauty and marriageability see Schelp 1975, 15-21, 54-5; Brelich 1969, 282-90.

161. *FGrH* 228 F 5.

162. Suda s.v. *askophorein* ("in the Dionysiac *pompai*," which must include this, the most important Dionysiac *pompe*).

163. Athenaeus 150A.

164. Undoubtedly a slave, and so not breaching the symbolic exclusion of the community's women.

165. Plutarch *Mor.* 391D.

166. Plutarch *Numa* 9.5-6.

167. Schol. Thuc. 2.15.2; Suda s.v. prytaneion; Pollux i.5-7. Malkin 1987, 127 accepts that there were two eternal fires in Athens, one at the prytaneion, but believes (Malkin 1987, 127 n. 68) that Plut. *Numa* refers to the flame at the Erechtheion, not the prytaneion, because he believes that the fire at the prytaneion was probably tended by men. But there is no evidence for such a belief; Aristotle *Pol.* 1322b26f simply speaks of the fact that some religious personnel derived their religious roles from their non-religious polis roles of representing a group, such as a deme, a fact expressed as the religious officials who derive their authority from the common hearth (on this cf. also Sourvinou-Inwood 1988b; 1988, 261); the mention of Naukratis is not helpful, as Malkin himself (129) lists Naukratis among the exceptional colonies in which particular adaptations were made in the transfer of the sacred fire owing to the particular circumstances of foundation. Graf 1985, 363 n. 48 also takes the women who tended the sacred fire in Athens to have been personnel associated with the cult of Hestia.

168. Cf. inscriptions and discussion in Merkelbach 1980, 85-7.

169. Cf. inscriptions and discussion in Merkelbach, 1980, 85-6.

170. As Graf 1985, 363 remarks, in some cities Hestia had a priest, but in others, for example, at Chalkis, she had a priestess (cf. *IG* xii suppl 651).

171. Wolters 1889, 321-2.

172. *LSCG* 8.16-8.

173. Though there was a certain fluidity as to who was included among the Twelve Gods in the different cities. Cf. on the Twelve Gods: Bruneau and Ducat 1983, 165-6; Shapiro 1989, 133-41.

174. It seems that in the procession to Eleusis priests and priestesses of important Athenian central polis cults took part and walked together with the Eleusinian priesthood; the

Chapter 2: [Re]constructing the Beginnings 195

priestess of Athena seems to have walked side by side with the priestess of Demeter and Kore (Clinton 1974, 35-6), a ritual enactment of the intimate relationship between the most important central polis cult and the most important periphery cult of the polis.

175. At the very least the minimum that can be proved is the participation of the *kanephoros*, which in itself proves that the female sex was not the symbolically excluded. But, of course, in terms of Greek ritual logic, it is absurd to even contemplate the possibility that women who had taken part in the procession as participants or spectators had been excluded from the sacrifices.

176. Henderson 1991a, 133-47 has made an excellent case for women's presence at theatrical performances. I do not find Goldhill's critique (Goldhill 1994, 347-69) of Henderson convincing. Since the precise ways in which the polis articulated itself in the Dionysia is one of the things that need to be carefully and systematically reconstructed, the structuring of the investigation through assumptions pertaining to this question—and to gender construction—involves methodological dangers. Another route through which the effect of culturally determined assumptions is maximized in this critique is through the implicit deployment of the concept of likelihood; the difference between Goldhill and the discussions he criticizes is in the assumptions that have shaped this (inevitably culturally determined) notion. I discussed very briefly the question of women's participation in the Dionysia in Sourvinou-Inwood 1994, 270-1 and n. 9. Goldhill's comment (164 n. 45) that I (in Sourvinou-Inwood 1994) "may not be cautious enough in using such late evidence to uncover fifth-century ritual" seems to be based on a slight confusion; I did not start with the presupposition that late evidence was relevant to the early period, but produced an argument for a development and change in the spatial articulation of the festival which makes sense of the later attested *eisagoge apo tes escharas*—whether or not ephebes formed the escort from the beginning is not relevant to my case. But it is worth stressing that on a more general methodological point, it is not more rigorous to assume that change has taken place in the absence of any evidence for such change than to assume it has not (the opposite point, against the opposite assumption than I made before; neither position is entitled to a presumption of validity). Indeed, when such assumption for change is formulated in the context of an investigation structured by prior assumptions, it is less rigorous.

177. The only thing that is new in the survey of arguments set out below (cf. especially the discussion in Henderson 1991a; cf. also *DFA* 263-5) is my explanation of the fact that women were not addressed in comedy despite the fact that, on the thesis accepted here, they were present in the performances.

178. On this cf. e.g. Henderson 1991a, 139.

179. *Vita* 9 (= *TrGF* iii T A 1).

180. Plato *Gorgias* 502d .

181. Plato *Laws* 817c.

182. The presence of women in the theater is also suggested in Plato *Laws* 658d.

183. Cf. the discussion in Henderson 1991a, 139-41.

184. Henderson 1991, 140.

185. The discussion in Henderson 1991a, 146-7.
186. Sourvinou-Inwood 1995b, 111-20.
187. Cf. Sourvinou-Inwood 1990a, 295-322.
188. Cf. the most recent comment on the passage, Csapo and Slater 1995, 291: "This passage is sometimes cited as proof that women did not attend the theater. It seems to us to demonstrate the opposite." Cf. also Henderson's excellent comments (1991a, 141-2).

II.3. The Great Dionysia and the "Ritual Matrix" of Tragedy

I will now sum up the main conclusions of the analyses set out in chapters II.1-2. On the reconstruction set out here, tragedy was generated as a result of a very complex process, not a unilinear one. It developed in particular circumstances in Athens some time in the last quarter of the sixth century, out of a performance of hymns, dithyrambs, at the sacrifice of a *tragos* in the course of a rite of *xenismos* of Dionysos that was an important part of the festival of the City Dionysia.

On my reconstruction, the Great Dionysia began some time in the third quarter of the sixth century as a festival focussing on a ritual *xenismos* of Dionysos, and the celebration of the establishment of his cult. Both in the earliest form of the festival, and in the ones in the classical period and later, before the rite of *xenismos* of Dionysos there was a *komos* involving ritual dining on *stibades* of ivy, and then a ritual reception of the statue, brought back from a shrine at the Academy, to which it had been previously taken. In the earliest form of the festival the *xenismos* of Dionysos took place at the prytaneion; it involved the sacrifice of a *tragos* accompanied by the singing of hymns, of a processional dithyramb as a *prosodion* and other dithyrambs at the altar. After the *xenismos* the procession escorted the statue from the prytaneion to the sanctuary of Dionysos Eleuthereus.

These rites reenacted the first *xenismos* of Dionysos, and the establishment of his cult in the mythological past, after the Athenians had offended the god by not receiving his cult with honor, and had been punished by an enraged Dionysos, who sent them a disease of the male sexual organs, and after they had been advised by the oracle to receive the god with honor. Thus, these were both rites in the present, in which the cult of Dionysos had an honored place, and reenactments of the first occasion of the establishment of the cult. The chorus of male citizens who sang at each *xenismos* were, above all, Athenians of the present singing in honor of Dionysos, but they were also, at the same time, invested with the persona of the Athenians of the mythological past, who had first offended the god, and then received him with honor and established his cult—the ritual act in the past that is also being reenacted in the present. This double identity of the participants in the ritual ended with the procession and sacrifices in the sanctuary, themselves both a reenactment of the establishment of the cult of Dionysos and a cultic act in the present.

Initially, this procession and sacrifices in the sanctuary had followed immediately after the *xenismos*. But eventually the performance part of the *xenismos* acquired a dynamic of its own, expanded, changed, and became spectacle. First prototragedy emerged, then tragedy developed, and eventually both tragic performances and dithyrambic performances became substantial competitions. At some point, the *xenismos* rite with the associated performances was moved to the Agora, near the Altar of the Twelve Gods, which was the alternative to the prytaneion center of the polis; the (increasingly expanding and important) performances had taken place by the *eschara*, a "doublet" of the *hestia* in the prytaneion. By this *eschara* by the Altar of the Twelve Gods, a *skene* had been erected (as was the case in other rituals of *xenismos*, and indeed other rituals) and the performances had taken place in front of this *skene*, which became one of the elements to be transferred to the Theater of Dionysos when the performances were moved from the Agora to the theater in the sanctuary of Dionysos Eleuthereus around, just after, 500. The *skene* in the new context took the form of a rectangular wooden structure, to fit the new spatial needs, but it still remained a temporary structure for a very long time. This far from self-explanatory fact suggests that the *skene*'s temporary, wooden nature was part of the assumptions associated with it.

On my reconstruction, the nexus of dithyrambs sung at the sacrifice of a *tragos* at the *xenismos* evolved into prototragedy in the form of a *hypokrites* speaking *in propria persona* and an unmasked chorus; this then changed into a fully mimetic prototragedy with masks; finally, tragedy as we basically know it emerged. These developments took place in interaction with, and as the result of the operation of, other ritual schemata, perceptions pertaining to the chorus leader-poet, and poetic models. A crucial factor that provided a fundamental impetus for these developments was the ritual context and festival myth which was reflected in the hymns' content. For this involved the complex paradoxes implicated in the myths of resistance to Dionysos, which, above all myths, exemplified the wider paradoxes of Greek religion in general, and invited religious exploration; the complexity of these explorations generated new forms, in interaction with various schemata, such as those of the poet as instructor; these forms then developed further, in interaction with other schemata, and, when the explorations came to implicate not simply the Athenians' own past, which had a direct relationship with the present in which it had been reenacted, but also stories such as that of Pentheus, involving greater distance from the chorus in the present, prototragedy became fully mimetic and eventually developed into tragedy.

Chapter 3: Great Dionysia and "Ritual Matrix"

When prototragedy became mimetic, as a mimetic performance in a ritual context, it could not but have come to be seen also in terms of the ritual schema of mimetic performances in which priestly personnel impersonated deities. This would have invested the *hypokrites* with some of the connotations associated with priests impersonating gods in such ritual mimetic performances; and this would have reinforced further the aspects of the perceptions associated with the chorus leader (who was, at least symbolically, even when not actually, the poet) that connected him with religious personnel. The fact that the number of *hypokritai* increased slowly, and never went beyond three, may be the result of such a conceptual association. As for the chorus, though in the mimetic forms of prototragedy and in tragedy they came to represent other collectivities, their identity as ritual performers, a chorus, in the present, did not disappear, though it was their mimetic persona, focussed on the mask, that was dominant.

It is possible that the great dithyrambic poet Lasos of Hermione, who was active in Athens, and, we are told, specifically at the Dionysia, at this time, under the Peisistratids, may have played an important role in the development of the dithyrambs that generated, and were part of, prototragedy. If Lasos had played such an important role in the shaping of the songs out of which tragedy emerged, the Doric elements, the Doric words and forms, in the tragic choruses, would have been the direct result of this important role played by Lasos, and not simply of the general influence of the choral lyric tradition of the Peloponnesians and Western Greeks.

If these analyses are right, the tragedy that was generated out of this process would have been characterized by the following parameters: some density of ritual content, religious exploration and problematization, and a form structured through hymns. To put it differently, its development would have been shaped by a ritual matrix, a dynamic ritual matrix, which would have set the parameters for the development and crystallization of tragedy, and would have involved the following elements. First, religious exploration, the setting out and exploration of problems pertaining to the world of the gods, and men's relationships with it, and appropriate behavior; then, some density of religious elements, of religious language, religious references, and so on; finally, a form structured by hymns, sung by a chorus, which represented a collectivity in the represented "other" locus, but was still perceived also as a chorus of Athenian citizens singing hymns in honor of Dionysos in the present: the parodos and stasima, reflecting an original schema *"prosodion* and stasima at the altar" and separating segments involving *rheseis* of the *hypokrites* and/or chorus-*hypokrites* exchanges; another formal characteristic of the matrix would have been a very important role for the chorus.

Besides hymn singing, other rituals would also have been important in this ritual matrix, reflecting the fact that, on this reconstruction, the ritual out of which tragedy emerged culminated in a procession, from the prytaneion to the sanctuary of Dionysos Eleuthereus, reenacting the establishment of the cult of Dionysos in Athens. This suggests that when prototragedy emerged it may have included either an enactment of a ritual establishing cult, or a narration, or prediction, of the establishment of a cult, or a combination of these. Given the exploration of religious problems, as well as the nature of the festival myth of the City Dionysia, there would have been some authoritative "answers"; the source, given Greek religion, and the history of tragedy as reconstructed here, could have taken one of two forms: prophecy or divine epiphany. I am sure that both forms had appeared in early tragedy, especially since prophecy had provided the answers in the festival myth of the City Dionysia, and divine epiphany was crucial in the Pentheus/Lykourgos-type myths, which, I suggested, had been crucial in the generation of tragedy.

The similarities between this reconstructed matrix and early tragedy are obvious—and the argument is not circular, since I did not take account of early tragic forms in my reconstruction, which was based entirely on ritual practice. I will be arguing in part III that the independent reading of the earlier Aeschylean tragedies shows that they have these characteristics, are shaped by such a matrix; and that this dynamic ritual matrix articulated early tragic forms, and was eventually transformed into a dynamic tragic matrix, with a larger canvas of more and more elaborate themes and greater complexities in the exploration of human relationships, which, however, still included elements of ritual articulation and also involved, among other things, but very importantly, religious exploration.

III. Religion and the Fifth-Century Tragedians

III.1. "Starting" with Aeschylus

III.1.i. *Introduction and Methodological Problems*

That Aeschylean tragedies are full of religion is surely an uncontroversial statement.[1] It would also be uncontroversial to say that these tragedies present a world in which the divine plays a determining role in human affairs and that this is foregrounded. In this chapter I will be arguing that these and other widely shared perceptions of Aeschylean tragedy are manifestations of the fact that Aeschylean tragedy was religious in ways more radical than usually believed. I will therefore be drawing attention to ritual elements and aspects of the play that are often taken for granted or considered in isolation, instead of as part of a dense religious framework. I will try to show that, given their place in the audience's assumptions, the strong clusterings of ritual elements in a context in which religious issues were important, against a background of dense religious references, in a performance at a sanctuary, in the course of a religious festival, placed the tragedies in a different category from that in which modern readers (and audiences) usually do, made them in important ways religious.

Various scholars have pointed out the ways in which religious language and religious elements, such as rituals, are deployed in the *Oresteia* in ways that create specific dramatic effects, most strikingly, the ways in which the language and conventions of sacrifice are perverted, a perversion corrected at the end of the *Oresteia*.[2] In my view, the focus on the complexity of the deployment of ritual elements and their dramatic effects in modern discourse has led to the marginalization, in the sense of the taking for granted, of the basic fact that Aeschylean tragedy is articulated through ritual and other religious elements, without consideration of the reasons why, and the implications of, this fact. Perhaps the reason for this is an unexamined a priori assumption that Aeschylus introduced those ritual elements *ex novo*, from outside, in order to achieve specific dramatic effects.[3] My eventual conclusion will be that the comparison of an independent reading of the earlier Aeschylean tragedies to the ritual matrix reconstructed in II.3 will show that Aeschylus had inherited this matrix, and developed it in complex ways that gave rise to what we consider fully mature tragedy.[4]

However, in order to avoid circularity, I will leave all this aside for the moment and attempt to reconstruct (as far as possible) the ancient readings of each Aeschylean tragedy independently of this reconstruction.[5] The main focus of these readings will be the attempt to reconstruct the ways in which these tragedies related to religion.

In trying to reconstruct the ancient readings I find myself in a difficult methodological position. For if my reconstruction of early tragedy is right, the neutral approach I am adopting would be distorting the results to the detriment of my interpretation. That is, if it is right that the early tragic performances at the Dionysia were generated by, and developed on the basis of, a dynamic ritual matrix which created various forms of religious exploration; if it is right that the forms, at least at the beginning of Aeschylus' career, before the introduction of the second *hypokrites*, were not radically different from those developed once *mimesis* had shifted the nature of prototragedy and generated early tragedy, there would be no reason to think that early Aeschylean tragedies were not seen as fundamentally religious, like the forms which had ultimately generated them, and every reason to think that the audiences had perceived these performances as in some significant way religious.

If that is right, if we approach the tragedies neutrally, without taking account of this religious framing, we would be leaving out an important set of asssumptions shaping the filters through which the ancient audience made sense of the tragedies, and we would thus be creating meanings different from theirs. On the other hand, if we did not approach these tragedies neutrally the argument would be circular. As I said before, in order to avoid the danger of cultural determination, it is desirable to have some control on our analyses and their results, and this can be provided through cross-checking the results of entirely independent, separately conducted, investigations. I will therefore keep the two parts of my case separate. However, I want to draw attention to the fact that what I will be presenting here may be radically *understressing* the religious dimension; and that if it is right that the group of earlier Aeschylean tragedies I will be first considering was even more strongly religious than is usually acknowledged, this reading could still be seriously underestimating the tragedies' religious nature in the eyes of their contemporary audiences.

To avoid structuring these readings through the Problematik established by modern discourse, which is inevitably shaped by modern assumptions, I will try, in attempting to reconstruct the ways in which Aeshylean tragedies related to religion, to bring out the *basic* building blocks through which Aeschylus constructed these tragedies, and the audience made sense of them. I will be arguing that religious matter,

Chapter 1: "Starting" with Aeschylus

and especially the deployment of ritual, the articulation of the tragedies through ritual, is a fundamental and basic category of such building blocks. Aeschylus' choices were shaped by parameters of selection shaped by assumptions he shared with his audience. Why, I shall be asking, does religion articulate Aeschylean tragedy in this way, and how did the audience make sense of this articulation?

I shall be discussing *Suppliants, Persai,* and *Septem* as one group. I will consider briefly the *Oresteia* separately.[6] One of the conclusions that will emerge from this analysis, if it is convincing, is that what has been perceived as "archaic stiffness" in *Suppliants, Persai,* and *Septem* is the mark of a very important state of transition: the transformation of a dynamic ritual matrix articulating tragic forms, and involving religious exploration, into a dynamic *tragic* matrix with elements of ritual articulation and involving, among other things but very importantly, religious exploration.

III.1.ii. *Suppliants*

I will begin with *Suppliants,* for, though it is not the earliest surviviving Aeschylean tragedy,[7] it is the most old-fashioned.[8] Or is it? The notion that *Suppliants* is the most old-fashioned of Aeschylean tragedies because the chorus is the protagonist[9] has been challenged by one particular approach which sprang up as a reaction to the discovery that *Suppliants* is later than *Persai* and *Septem*:[10] according to this argument *Suppliants* and *Eumenides,* in which the chorus is the protagonist, do not reflect archaic tragedy where the chorus was the protagonist, but were Aeschylean innovations, experiments; for in archaic tragedy the chorus had not been active, but only had a quantitatively more important role, which had consisted of singing choral songs which were juxtaposed to brief speeches. In my view, this thesis runs counter to very serious difficulties.

First, the notion that because *Suppliants,* in which the chorus is the protagonist, is later than *Persai* and *Septem,* in which it is not, suggests not only that in early tragedy the chorus was not the protagonist, but also that the early chorus was not active, and that its role was that of singing choral songs juxtaposed to brief speeches, may prima facie appear more neutral than its predecessor, but in fact relies on similar preconceived ideas: it replaces the old concept of linearity with a new one; instead of the old logical model of linear progression this thesis relies on another logical model, one which we may call a linear pattern with a blip, or perhaps a cyclical one: the chorus begins as nonactive and ends as nonactive; in between there are a few experiments in integration. This perception is no less culturally determined and a priori than the earlier one, and, in my view, does even more violence to the complex situation.

It is right that *Suppliants* is not simply a tragedy with old-fashioned features, and that the dramatic technique fits the period between *Septem* and the *Oresteia*,[11] and also that the role of the chorus in *Suppliants*, as a protagonist, is an innovation when compared to *Persai* and *Septem*. However, first, it could be an innovation in the sense that Aeschylus may have gone back to an earlier form, which he reshaped and deployed for his own purposes. After all, Euripides did precisely this in his *Suppliants*. And second, and most importantly, there are two distinct points involved, and this thesis does not distinguish between them: whether the chorus was the protagonist in early tragedy is a distinct point from whether the chorus was an active participant in, an integral part of, the action in that tragedy, or simply sang choral songs interspersed with speeches. The chorus as a protagonist would be simply one version of the chorus as an active participant in, an integral part of, the action; even if early tragedy did not have a chorus as a protagonist this would tell us nothing as to whether the chorus had been an integral part of the action.

Though, to avoid circularity I am not taking account here of the reconstruction of the early forms of tragedy offered in chapter II.3; I will simply point out that that reconstruction coincides with the conclusion that everything in the surviving early tragedies points to a close involvement of the chorus in the action in early tragedy, one version of which involvement was that which we see in *Suppliants*.

At the very general level, the fact that in the three early plays the main interactions are more between character and chorus than between characters[12] is surely indicative of a tradition in which first one *hypokrites* was interacting with the chorus, and then a second *hypokrites* was introduced; not of one in which choral songs had been juxtaposed to brief speeches. Then, as Taplin argued,[13] "The distinctive point about the handling of the chorus in Aeschylus, and not only in *Hik* and *Eum*—is that it not only has longer songs but it is also more consistently and more extensively integrated into the dialogue acts (epeisodia)." He rightly goes on to note that this must have been even more so in the days of one-actor tragedy. He also considers that the ways in which the chorus is given a larger part in the dialogue acts in Aeschylus are not irrelevant to what may be inferred about archaic tragedy.[14] He notes that while Sophocles and Euripides only use two techniques for the participation of the chorus, stichomythia and lyric dialogue, in Aeschylus, where lyric dialogue is also common, first, actor-chorus stichomythia is the norm, in contrast to later tragedy, and second, the additional technique of the epirrhematic dialogue structure is used. He

Chapter 1: "Starting" with Aeschylus

also suggests that the fact that while in later tragedy the chorus (or coryphaeus) had no more than two or three continuous spoken lines, longer "choral" speeches, found especially in Aeschylus, may illustrate another way in which the chorus may have been given a larger part in the epeisodia of early tragedy. I believe that the implication here,[15] with which I agree, is that this variety and richness of techniques for the participation of the chorus in Aeschylus constitutes an argument in favor of the view that the chorus had been fully integrated into the action in archaic tragedy.

At a more specific level, a comparison which seems to me to constitute implicitly a key argument for the "non-integrated archaic chorus" hypothesis is, in my view, seriously flawed. Garvie,[16] while noting that in *Suppliants* the chorus has a more important part, and the lyrics are far more extensive, than in any other extant play, and that the choral passages in *Persai* are only a little less extensive, stresses the differences between the two *choroi* in function and composition, and calls the chorus in *Persai* "anonymous and colourless" because while in *Suppliants* the chorus was "a group of people who are properly at home in myth, with an existence independent of their place in Aeschylus' play," one could not imagine any member of the *Persai* chorus becoming "a character in his own right in a later play of a trilogy."[17] He concludes: "It is absurd, then, to class the two plays together as evidence for an earlier stage of tragedy. One or other may be the more archaic: it is not immediately self-evident that the development is from *Supplices* to *Persae*."[18]

I suggest that the notion that this distinction (between a chorus made up of distinct mythological figures and a chorus made up of a group which is simply a group, a segment of a community which does not have a distinct mythological history) is significant is both culturally determined and dependent on the hypothesis that it is deployed to support. For it is only if one starts with the presupposition that the chorus began as a group singing choral songs juxtaposed to speeches that a distinction between on the one hand a chorus made up of distinct mythological figures, and on the other one made up of a collectivity such as the Theban parthenoi of *Septem*, or the Persian elders, seems significant; for in that case the former could be expected to be part of the action and would mark a "full involvement" version, while the latter would seem an in-between case.

However, in the ancient perceptions, a group such as "the Thebans in the time of Pentheus" did have a mythological persona as a collectivity, as a segment of the community, which is what a chorus above all was. It is certainly the case that the collectivity "the Athenians of the time when Pegasos introduced the statue of Dionysos to Athens" had a significant persona, and an important part, in the action of the festival myth of the City Dionysia. Even indepedently of the reconstruction of the emergence of tragedy offered in part II, in which this festival myth had a central place, this fact shows that in Athenian conceptual categories such collectivities were significant and could be involved in dramatic action.

This persona of the chorus as a collectivity directly involved in the action makes perfect sense in the context of, but does not depend on, my reconstruction in which the chorus of Athenians as representatives of the community in the here and now eventually (when prototragedy developed into early tragedy) came to impersonate other collectivities. Seen from this perspective, of the chorus as a collectivity directly involved in the action, the differences between the chorus of *Suppliants* and that of the other tragedies is less radical than has been argued.[19] The chorus of *Suppliants* is simply one of the versions of the early chorus' involvement in the action. Consequently, we may conclude that both *Persai* and *Suppliants*, and of course *Septem*, can be used as evidence for early tragedy, and in addition, that Aeschylus did indeed use old-fashioned features in *Suppliants*. I shall return to the question of the chorus in this tragedy; but now I must consider the question of the opening.[20]

There are two modalities of opening in the three early plays: with a non-choral prologue, in *Septem*, and with the parodos, the chorus opening the play in marching anapaests, in *Persai* and *Suppliants*. This latter modality is not found in Aeschylus' later surviving tragedies,[21] or in the extant tragedies of Sophocles and Euripides. As has been noted, there is no reason why one method of opening the tragedy should be chronologically earlier than the other, and early tragedy may well have used both.[22]

Both these forms of tragic opening can be related to my reconstruction of early tragedy, in that both schemata are closely connected to, and can be seen as having been derived from, the ritual matrix which, on my hypothesis, generated tragedy, which had involved the chorus entering singing a *prosodion*. When the performance became separated from the ritual, and the *hypokrites* came into play, this original ritual schema of the chorus entering singing a *prosodion* could be (and, I suggest, was) modified in two alternative ways to produce two alternative schemata. One of these two prototragic schemata would be a simple reflection of the original ritual schema, the performance beginning with the chorus' entrance, and the *hypokrites* taking the place of the sacrificial ritual acts, that is, replacing them in the structure of the performance. This would be something similar to the schema structuring *Persai* and *Suppliants*. The other prototragic schema would have

Chapter 1: "Starting" with Aeschylus 207

involved a more radical transformation of the ritual schema: it would have involved the *hypokrites*, to begin with *in propria persona*, opening the play with an address to the audience which, on my reconstruction, may also have performed the function of linking the performance to the sacrifice out of which it had developed and to the ritual occasion, in the way illustrated in the sample prototragedy I set out in chapter II.2. This would be very closely related to the schema involving a prologue spoken by an character, as is the case in *Septem*.

There can be very little doubt that *Suppliants* was part of a trilogy, that the generally accepted view that *Suppliants*, *Aigyptioi*, and *Danaides* formed a tragic trilogy, with *Amymone* as the satyr play of a full tetralogy, is right.[23]

As for what happened in the missing two tragedies,[24] the middle play, *Aigyptioi*,[25] would have been focussed on the sons of Aigyptos and their dealings with Danaos, who would have replaced Pelasgos, killed in battle, as king of Argos. Danaos made an arrangement which involved surrendering his daughters to his nephews for marriage; the murder would have taken place in the gap between *Aigyptioi* and *Danaides*. Hypermestra would probably have saved her new husband Lynkeus, because she was sexually attracted to him.[26] In *Danaides* Aphrodite appeared and delivered a speech which proclaimed the universal power of sexual love.[27] Given the myth, and the content of fragment 44, it is difficult to doubt that at the end of *Danaides* the other Danaids became reconciled to marriage through the agency of Aphrodite,[28] and were thus restored to normality.[29]

In Aeschylus' *Suppliants* there is one main, dominant, theme, treated in a complex way, supplication. This is not to deny the richness and subtlety of the tragedy; of course other themes do come into play, such as various aspects of gender discourse,[30] the notion of descent, and the claims that can be seen to be attached to it, of foreigners in the city, of the so-called "democratic" kingship. But all these are structured by, articulated through, the enactment of a ritual, and this centrality of the ritual is correlative with the belief that gods support suppliants, and the fear of offending the gods, which is central to the action. Thus, for example, the Danaids' claim on Argos on the basis of rather remote ancestral links, the validity of which is unclear, is interwoven with supplication and helps make its exploration more complex.

It is not until the end, when the supplication is resolved, and the Danaids are about to be integrated in the polis of Argos, that the theme of marriage, and refusal of marriage, begins to be focussed on, from lines 1034ff, and here also the articulation is religious. Until then, this theme remains in the background; it is in the rest of the trilogy that it will be explored further. In *Suppliants* the question of the refusal of marriage is subordinated to the theme of supplication: the ambiguousness of the Danaids' cause is one of the themes that complicate further the problems of supplication explored here.

The fundamental skeleton of the problems implicated in supplication, as it is explored here, is the conflict between divine rules and human self-interest. On the one hand the gods, especially Zeus, protect suppliants, and expect people to receive them; on the other, there are legitimate fears of the consequences from the suppliants' pursuers for one's own polis and safety. However, not to do what the gods want will bring divine punishment to the community. This problem is further complicated here, first, by the fact that the Danaids had greater claim on the protection of the gods, and especially Zeus, the protector of suppliants, because they are descended from him, which intensifies—or may intensify, Argos cannot know—the divine protection, and on the other by the Danaids' threat to bring pollution upon the city if they are not given protection, by killing themselves on the very statues of the gods—a polarized, visible, and much more powerful form of the offense against the gods involved in rejecting suppliants.

Aeschylus' *Suppliants*, focussed on, and articulated by, a supplication rite,[31] perceived by the ancient audience as a *mimesis* of an event in the heroic past, has a very much less complicated and less multifaceted canvas than Euripides' tragedy with the same title, which also involves a supplication rite, and which will be discussed in chapter III.3.

The ritual dimension in this tragedy is reinforced through an extraordinary density of religious references throughout; a great abundance of prayers and invocations, and praise of the gods, and the narration of myths explicating the chorus' divine descent, but also simply religious language imagery and references. From the very first words uttered by the chorus, *Zeus men aphiktor*, referring to Zeus protector of suppliants, there is an extraordinary density of religious language, imagery and references. Just in the opening anapaests, for example, after recounting their circumstances—an account which has religious connotations[32]—and the story that they are descended from Zeus and Io—which has a strong religious facet, for it involves divine-human interaction and gives the chorus a special connection to the world of the gods—the chorus refer to their ritual status as suppliants, which is at this moment beginning to be enacted, and pray[33] to the local divine powers presiding over the polis, the land, and its water, who are specified at 24ff as both Olympians and local heroes,[34] and to Zeus *soter*, to receive them as suppliants.

The long strophic song that follows the opening anapaests is teeming with religious references. Thus, in the first strophe they invoke

Chapter 1: "Starting" with Aeschylus

209

Epaphos, the son of Zeus and Io, and then, from the beginning of the third antistrophe (*theoi genetai, klyet'* 77) to the beginning of the fifth antistrophe (104), their song involves a very dense web of religious concepts and language, references to Zeus, his will, a description of his power, and what he does to mortals, and the unknowability of his will. The rest of the song also contains dense religious references, especially the final segment, lines 144-75. In this segment the chorus first express their wish that Athena may help them (*hagna m' epideto Dios kora*); then (154-61) they say that if she does not they will die. The formulations and language they use to say this are religious, and the future is presented as being entirely in the hands of the gods (cf. 156-61): *ton gaion, ton polyxenotaton Zena ton kekmekoton* (to be translated as: "the infernal, the most hospitable, Zeus of the dead") *hixomestha syn kladois artanais thanousai, me tychousai theon Olympion*.

Then follows a plea to Zeus for help, which is formulated in such a way that it involves at the same time religious problematization of myth. The chorus claim that it is due to Hera's hatred of Io that vengeance from the gods is pursuing them; and that Zeus could be open to the accusation of injustice that he dishonored his son by Io, Epaphos, if he does not listen to their prayers. The audience would not necessarily have seen the situation in this way, since they knew that their cousins were also descended from Epaphos, and taking women by force is not always marked as negative in Greek myth.[35] But that is another matter that cannot be pursued here. However, the fact that this question mark emerges as to the validity of the chorus' contention would, I suggest, have helped the audience's attention slide away from the problems evoked through the notion of Hera's hatred of Io, and of the possibility that the chorus is unjustly pursued by divine vengeance because of it, and the notion that Zeus' own actions, his erotic exploits, can lead to human misery, and that this is not just. These notions have been stated, or rather sketched, but they are not here dwelled upon.

Religious elements, ritual action language and other religious elements continue to be dense and important throughout the tragedy, as I will now show through a brief and selective survey of some of the most important relevant passages.

There is, of course, a high density of religious language and action when at 189ff Danaos instructs the chorus to take refuge at the altars,[36] which they do, and to invoke Zeus and other deities. At 418ff they continue to appeal to Pelasgos to accept them on religious grounds,[37] and at 461ff they make a threat that would involve pollution: they threaten to hang themselves from the statues of the gods. At 468ff Pelasgos expresses the problem that arises when suppliants arrive: on the one hand, if a community accepts these suppliants this may lead to having to fight, to men's blood being shed for women's sake (itself a problematic notion); on the other hand, reverence towards the gods demands that the suppliants be accepted: for a variety of reasons, piety to the gods demands the protection of the suppliants, to avoid pollution, and because Zeus looks after suppliants (478-9: *homos d' ananke Zenos aideisthai koton hikteros*).[38]

In Scott's view,[39] the first, second, and third stasima are introduced as prayers: 521; 625-9, 772-3. The first stasimon (524-99) is a hymn to Zeus. The first strophe and the first antistrophe are an invocation of, and prayer to, Zeus; from the second strophe to the end of the fourth antistrophe they tell the myth of the chorus' descent from Io (stressing the divine actions), thus establishing their descent from Zeus, and relationship to the land to which they have come as suppliants. In the fifth strophe and the fifth antistrophe they set out their special claim for protection from Zeus, and describe his power; the fifth antistrophe in particular places Zeus theologically, and describes his sovereignty and power.[40] After they were granted asylum, the chorus (625-9) announce that they will call blessings in prayer for the Argives and invoke Zeus Xenios.

The second stasimon (630-709) is presented as, and consists of, prayers on behalf of the Argives, in thanksgiving for the grant of asylum. This ode is in fact multifunctional; thus, in the first antistrophe they present their case as involving male versus female, with Zeus being on their side. But what is interesting is that all this is articulated through a prayer sung by the chorus, with a great density of religious references. Among them the invocation of, or references to, the gods, both as a group (cf. 630-1: *theoi diogeneis, klyoit'*; and 704-6: *theous d' hoi gan echousin aei tioien*) and individually.

Zeus is most centrally mentioned, as the sovereign god, and their protector, both as their ancestor, and in virtue of his persona as Zeus Xenios. The other gods mentioned are Ares (636, 665-6, 682, 702), Aphrodite (664), Artemis-Hekate (676), Apollo (686), Dike (709).[41] Dike is of course of central importance to the chorus' case. The frequence of references to Ares is correlative with the danger of war brought about by the acceptance of their supplication.

One of the things they pray for is that Artemis, here with the epithet Hekate,[42] may protect women in childbirth. The chorus are women, so it may be seen as women voicing women's concerns. But things are more complex than this. First, because the birth of healthy children also concerns the polis as a whole; and second, because these particular women are refusing marriage, and so also childbirth, and this refusal may have been evoked, for the audience, by their very prayer.

Chapter 1: "Starting" with Aeschylus

So this invocation may have been taken to suggest an acknowledgment by the Danaids of the importance of marriage, and so help strengthen their claim that they are only refusing this particular marriage. Aphrodite, who was involved with marriage and whose importance to the events will be manifested in the third play of the trilogy, is only mentioned en passant here: Ares is called *Aphroditas eunator* at 664-5. The fact that it was Artemis Hekate that they invoke for protection in childbirth, where Athenian women would probably have invoked Artemis Brauronia, may be part of a slight distancing between the audience's cultic reality and the prayer on the stage performed by Athenian men impersonating Aegyptian women praying for Argos.

A stronger distancing from the world of the audience is created by references that distance the characters from ordinary mortals, such as the recurring references by the chorus to their claim that they (and Danaos) are descended from Zeus, and Pelasgos' statement (250) that his father Palaichthon was *gegenes*, 'earth-born'. The formulation at 693, *to pan d' ek daimonon lachoien*, is at the same time as a prayer also an expression of the perception that all things do come from the gods; and this perception helps put religion at the center of this tragedy. Similarly, at lines 707-9 (*to gar tekonton sebas triton tod' en thesmiois Dikas gegraptai megistotimou*) something which is perceived to be important for the proper order of society, and which is going to be crucial for the future action of this trilogy, is presented as decreed by divine law.

According to Scott,[43] the third stasimon is also introduced as a prayer at 772-3. This is perhaps a bit too strong a way to describe the formulation *sy de phronei men hos tarbousa me amelein theon*, when we compare it to the "introduction as prayers" of the first and second stasima, at 520-1 and 625-9, but it certainly helps place the ode that follows in a religious frame. The first part of the ode, 776-807, includes religious language, but the content is not religious; it is focussed on the chorus' fear, and their desire to escape from marriage to the sons of Aigyptos. The second part, 808-24, is a supplication of the gods and especially Zeus, whom they invoke by name as *gaiaoche pankrates Zeu* at 816 and about whom, and whose power, they make a theological statement at 822-4: *son d' epipan zygon talantou. ti d' aneu sethen thnatoisi teleion estin?*

The centrality of the gods continues, and this is expressed in a variety of ways. For example, it is made clear that the herald's disregard of the fact that the suppliants are under the gods' protection is not due to his holding a competing view of the world, in which there are things that are more important than what the gods want. He states that he thinks that he does not need to fear the local gods of Argos, who were not the gods who nurtured him: 893-4,[44] 921-2. But what of Danaos' statement (980-2) that they must now pray, sacrifice, and pour libations to the Argives as to Olympians, because they were their saviors? Does this not raise doubt as to whether it was the gods on whom the Danaids' salvation depended? I suggest that when this was made sense of through fifth-century assumptions, the fact that it was because of the fear of offending the gods that, first the king, and then the Argives, had offered protection would have been strongly felt, and this would have stressed the role of the gods. The fact that at 1014 the chorus asks the Olympians to send them good fortune would have further foregrounded the perception that the gods are responsible for good and bad fortune.

The tragedy ends with a procession to Argos, which may have begun to form at 1018.[45] The long ode that begins at 1018 has a great density of religious elements. One segment (1018-29) involves thanksgiving to the gods of the city; then, within the first antistrophe, the theme of marriage begins to be focussed on, in religious terms. First (1030-3) the chorus address a prayer to Artemis, the protector of *parthenoi*. Aphrodite comes into play already at 1032, and then again, more emphatically, at 1034ff: *Kypridos <d>' ouk amelein, thesmos hod' euphron, dynatai gar Dios anchista syn Herai; tietai d' aiolometis theos ergois epi semnois.*[46] This continues with references to Pothos, Peitho, Harmonia, and Erotes. Thus, in these verses—whoever had sung them[47]—the themes of acceptance or rejection of love and marriage are articulated in religious terms, presented in terms of paying honor to the goddess in whose sphere love falls, Aphrodite. Hera, of course, was the deity protecting marriage par excellence, the protector of marriage as an institution, in the Greek world, and the mention of her name at 1035 would have evoked this, in this context in which it is Aphrodite and her retinue, and the concept of erotic love, that are to the fore—a deity and a concept that will be central in the final part of the trilogy. This is very important; what our own culture would consider to be lifestyle choices are here presented as focussed on respecting the power and honor of the deities who preside over the relevant spheres.

The importance of the gods', especially Zeus', will is foregrounded again at 1047-9: *ho ti toi morsimon estin, to genoit' an. Dios ou parbatos estin megala phren aperatos*; and again at 1052-3: *ho megas Zeus apalexai gamon Aigyptogene moi*. The conclusion of the tragedy, from the beginning of the third antistrophe at 1057 to the end of the ode, and of the tragedy (at 1073), is densely religious. This densely religious concluding segment of the ode starts with a statement of the unknowability of the divine will, here specifically of the mind of Zeus, continues with statements about the proper relationship of mortals to immortals

Chapter 1: "Starting" with Aeschylus 213

(cf. 1061: *ta theon meden agazein*), then with a prayer to Zeus, and concludes with a statement, presumably sung as the end of the procession was moving off, which, again, foregrounds the religious dimension (1071-3): *kai dikai dikas hepesthai, xyn euchais emais lyteriois machanais theou para.*

It is clear, then, that there is an extraordinary density of ritual action, religious language, imagery, and references, and that this is correlative with the fact that the tragedy is structured through a rite of supplication, and explores the religious problems implicated. This is precisely my point: that this tragedy, whatever else it may be exploring, is above all what we may call a "religious" tragedy, exploring a question of behavior of the individual and the collectivity as a religious question, in a religious structure, through religious language in a religious context. It is exploring problems pertaining to the relationships between mortals and gods, and also relationships between mortals, which here are presented as above all depending on relationships between mortals and gods.

This coincidence between the religious nature of its forms and of its exploration and problematizations, helps challenge the approaches which marginalize the importance of the religious nature of the tragedy. I will illustrate this tendency with one example. Garvie argues as follows against the argument that Aeschylus' lyrics show a gradual liberation from the restrictions of the prayer form: "If all the lyrics of the *Supplices* contain prayers, this does not mean that Aeschylus could not at this stage write any other kind of lyric (he had, after all, the whole of Dorian choral lyric before him), but only that prayer is the natural activity of the Danaid chorus, as the name of the play indicates."[48] He is, of course, right that it is not the case that Aeschylus' lyrics show a gradual liberation from the restrictions of the prayer form. He is also right that the lyrics of the *Supplices* do not suggest that Aeschylus could not at this stage write any other kind of lyric. However, another part of his argument presents some problems, because it begs important questions. He states that prayer is the natural activity of the Danaid chorus;[49] and that[50] "[t]he *Supplices* is full of prayers and the traditional forms of prayers not because it is an archaic play, but because the theme demands it"—having stated[51] that the existence of threnodic forms in tragedy tells us nothing about the origins of tragedy, for the subject matter of the plays requires many laments, and so it requires threnodic forms of expression, and that the same is true of cult in general.

This is not exactly wrong, but the implicit marginalization of the significance of the density of religious forms begs two important questions. First, why it should be the case that these subjects which demand such an important ritual element should have been chosen for tragedy—especially early tragedy, since we are focussing on the greatest density here. In other words, this position implicitly assumes that the possibility must be excluded that the very choice of such subjects may have been significant. Second, it implicitly assumes that the subjects chosen virtually dictated the forms of the tragedy, that the particular choices made were, as it were, necessary choices; that because it makes sense to us to have the myth of the Danaids treated in this way, now that our perception of it has been shaped by Aeschylus' tragedy, which involved all these prayers and other cult acts, this was the only possible choice of presenting this myth; in other words, again, that the possibility can be excluded that these choices were made because the tragic matrix that helped shape them was religious.

Not only are these assumptions flawed as the basis of an argument because they are a priori and culturally determined, but they are also not convincing in themselves. First, it is easy to think up several different scenarios for a tragedy focussed on the Danaid myth that would not involve articulation through the ritual of supplication, religious problematization, and extraordinarily dense concentrations of religious elements. Second, as we shall see, the two other early Aeschylean tragedies also have a great density of religious matter, though their subjects were very different from each other, and from *Suppliants*, and their structuring through religious elements even less of a necessary choice. No one would, surely, claim that the religious structuring that, we shall see, articulated *Persai* is an obvious, let alone a necessary, choice in a tragedy about the Greek victory at Salamis. That this religious articulation of the early tragedies was not a simple "coincidence" (a notion highly implausible in itself) is shown by the fact that, we shall see, this religious dimension continues in later tragedy—to a greater or lesser extent in the different tragedies, and combined with a stronger element of other explorations and problematizations. In addition, these religious explorations and problematizations are not the *necessary* corollary of dealing with subjects with a religious component. The fact that they take place in tragedy suggests that tragedy invited such religious exploration.

Ultimately, what is important is the fact that all three early tragedies made the choices to structure their very different subjects through religious stuff, and to have religious problematization and a great density of religious references, all of which makes them into "religious" tragedies. To focus on *Suppliants*, one way of describing this tragedy is as a performance in the course of a festival, in honor of the deity honored in the festival, in a place located in that deity's sanctuary, centered on the enactment of a ritual, in which the chorus plays the most

Chapter 1: "Starting" with Aeschylus 215

important role—a chorus the identity of which as also a chorus in the present is not wholly narcotized, though the perception that this was above all a mimetic performance was dominant—and setting out and problematizing religious questions through religious language imagery and behavior. This, then, could not but have been perceived by the fifth-century audience as a *ritual* mimetic performance. For (even without taking account of my reconstruction and its implications for the audience's perception of these tragedies), it is clear that there was nothing to weaken, let alone neutralize, the religious nature of the tragedy constructed through the strong ritual context, the ritual nature of the chorus, the fact that the performance was centered on a ritual, the extraordinary density of religious references, and the fact that it problematized religious questions through religious language, imagery, and behavior.

Modern commonsense readings which do not see this as a religious tragedy, which see the religious dimension of the tragedy as one among many aspects of it, implicitly rely on the deployment of a "secular drama" model; but for the ancient audience there was no such conceptual schema that would have come into play, competing with the "religious performance" one to weaken, let alone neutralize, this perception of it as religious performance. On the contrary, the nearest schema, which may indeed have helped shape some of the perceptual filters through which the early fifth-century audience had made sense of these tragic performances, was "ritual mimetic enactments" in other festivals. These were, of course, different; they enacted the central myth of the cult, focussed on the cult's main deity or deities; and we have no reason to think they had problematized any aspects of the cult.

In the Eleusinian Mysteries sacred drama coexisted with a "revelation" by the hierophant and the hierophantides, and with exegesis.[52] Tragedy does not involve revelation and exegesis, but, I shall be arguing, it appropriated some aspects of both, integrated into itself transformations of both. Whether or not my hypothesis that the schema "mimetic ritual enactments" may have come into play in the generation of tragedy, may have helped inspire the shift into *mimesis* is right, it cannot be doubted that in the early fifth-century audience's assumptions these "mimetic ritual enactments" provided the conceptual schema nearest to the tragic performances, and so would have helped color their perception of such performances; this would have confirmed and reinforced the religious nature of the tragedy.

But, it may be argued, what of *Persai*, and the other historical tragedies? Surely, their existence demonstrates that none of the above remarks is right; that by the time of Aeschylus' *Suppliants* tragedy was not religious tragedy. I will be arguing below that this objection is invalid; but it is necessary to defer this discussion until after that of *Suppliants* and *Septem*. For since no earlier tragedy has survived, we need to look at them to gain an idea of the type of tragedies, and audience perceptions of tragedies, that had been performed before the experimentation with historical settings began; for only thus can we glimpse an approximation of the perceptual filters through which these historical tragedies were perceived by the ancient audiences, for they would have been perceived and made sense of with the help of the perceptual filters shaped by their assumptions about, and experiences of, those earlier tragedies. I am not, of course, suggesting that we should apply those filters, approximately reconstructed with the help of *Suppliants* and *Septem*, that we should use them for reading *Persai*, the one historical tragedy that survives; for that would expose the argument to the danger of circularity. But we do need them as eye openers, to compete against, and block, the implicit and by default deployment of modern culturally determined assumptions of what a historical tragedy was.

To return to *Suppliants* and the trilogy of which it was part. The rest of the trilogy also involved significant religious explorations. The murder of the sons of Aigyptos raised a serious religious problem. The Danaids may or may not have been justified in one way to kill their bridegrooms, who had tried to force them into marriage using violence; but, not only was the murder of a husband by his wife especially abhorrent in Greek collective representations, but also, and most importantly, it involved violation of the rules of hospitality, in that the grooms had come as *xenoi*, and therefore they were under the special protection of Zeus Xenios. And this in its turn would have brought pollution to the city of Argos as a whole.[53] Thus, the Argives avoided the pollution of the threatened suicide of the Danaids at the altars (in *Suppliants*), only to be polluted by the actions of the same Danaids at the instigation of their father who, what is worse, is now the king of Argos. This impious plot would have been hatched in the course of *Aigyptioi* and would have been accomplished, and so the wrath of Zeus Xenios and the pollution would have been perceived by the audience to have been incurred, by the beginning of the *Danaides*.

What then happened, whether or not there had been a trial, and if so who would have been tried, are, I believe, unanswerable questions.[54] I find the view that the trilogy ended with the foundation of the Thesmophoria convincing.[55] The way the Thesmophoria relate to the rest of the trilogy and the similarities with the end of the *Oresteia* have been set out by Zeitlin.[56] It is true that it is not legitimate to assume that we can extrapolate rules governing Aeschylean trilogies on

Chapter 1: "Starting" with Aeschylus 217

the basis of just the one surviving trilogy, the *Oresteia*. But the notion that the Thesmophoria was founded at the end of the Danaid trilogy, in the context of a reconciliation of the Danaids to marriage, through the mediation of Aphrodite, fits not only the modality of the *Oresteia*, but tragic modalities in general. For it would fit such modalities to have a trilogy, which begins with a rejection of marriage and ends with its acceptance, link this acceptance to the foundation of a festival, the Thesmophoria, which (in Athens, and probably also elsewhere)[57] was ritually and symbolically connected with the status of married woman, and because of this it was a very important part of, and could symbolize, the important ritual contribution of married women to the religion of the polis, and so also to the prosperity and very existence of the polis.

This does not mean that we can be certain that the Thesmophoria was founded at the end of the Danaid trilogy; but it does suggest that it is likely, especially since in the assumptions shared by Aeschylus and his audience there was a close link between the Thesmophoria and the myth of Persephone's abduction by Hades, which was, among other things, a paradigm for marriage, which also involved, albeit in a very different and nontransgressive way, violence and compromise.[58] Also in favor of the view that the foundation of the Thesmophoria was announced at the end of the trilogy is the fact that there is a symbolic correlation between on the one hand the Danaids killing their husbands and then, after a period of marginalization and separation from the normal community, remarrying, and reentering normality, and on the other the respectable wives celebrating the Thesmophoria by abandoning their husbands and homes to go and camp out with other women in a place forbidden to men in a festival that included abnormality and mourning.

If it is true that the trilogy had ended with the foundation of the Thesmophoria, presumably announced by Aphrodite, because the Thesmophoria was a festival celebrated all over the Greek world, including Athens, its foundation would have zoomed the whole tragedy more directly to Athens as part of the Greek world, and the rituals of today to the heroic past in which they were anchored, an anchoring—among other things—explored and enacted on the stage.

Whether or not these hypotheses concerning the trilogy are right, there can be no doubt that the *Suppliants* is a "religious" tragedy in the way described here—and also that Aphrodite appeared on the stage in the third play of the trilogy.

Let us now return to the tragedy's structure. The fact that the choral element is greater in proportion to the whole than in any other Aeschylean tragedy and in any other extant tragedy[59] can be seen as a stronger, more extreme, form of the general characteristic of all Aeschylean tragedy to have a choral part greater in proportion to the whole than was the case in later tragedy.[60] The relatively restricted use of the second actor, though not, as some had thought in the past, resulting from lack of ease in the handling of an innovation, entails nevertheless, in conjunction with the important role of the chorus, which is its correlative, that we have a form de facto nearer to pre-second-actor tragedy in which the chorus had a central role.[61]

Of course, the notion of proximity to the forms that preceded the introduction of the second actor is only relative. Though we do not know how early in his career Aeschylus had invented the second *hypokrites*,[62] if it is true that he did,[63] and I believe that it is, his earliest surviving tragedies have developed away from the early forms in significant ways. For, besides the obvious and important ways in which the second *hypokrites* both changes the forms of tragedy and opens up new possibilities, I will now argue that the introduction of the second *hypokrites* marked a significant change in another way.

It is, in my view, significant that it cannot have been less that twenty-five to thirty years from the beginning of tragedy to the introduction of the second actor. Given, first, that *mimesis* would have invited at least a second actor, second, that the flexibility of the second actor would have offered great dramatic advantages, and third, that impersonation of more than one character by more than one person had taken place in ritual, for example, in the Eleusinian Mysteries, so that the model was available, I believe that a factor needs to be postulated that was strong enough to discourage this introduction, but was not of a nature to block it eventually—when the forms of tragedy presumably reached a point that made such introduction more pressingly desirable, especially in the hands of a great innovative poet.

On the reconstruction of the ritual origins of tragedy I proposed in part II there was indeed such a factor inhibiting, but not prohibiting, the introduction of the second actor: the very close connection between the role of the poet as framer and expounder and the role of the *hypokrites*, which, the inhibition to break the bond would suggest, persisted after the poet had ceased to perform *in propria persona* and put on the mask of another. Aeschylus' introduction of the second actor as a sort of duplication of the poet began to break the bond which eventually disappeared after the poet had ceased to perform in his own plays, and the third actor was introduced, both innovations our sources mostly attribute to Sophocles.[64] Until Aeschylus the requirements of the genre had involved only the chorus and the poet—which may suggest a certain strength in the perception of the tragic performers as a ritual chorus with its poet in the here and now. In any case, this state

Chapter 1: "Starting" with Aeschylus

of affairs suggests, I submit, that it was not until Aeschylus that the parameters determining the generation and development of tragedy set by the very earliest forms of tragedy changed.

In *Suppliants* the chorus is the protagonist, in *Eumenides* deuteragonist, and one of the characteristics of Aeschylean tragedy is that generally the chorus is at least emotionally involved in the action. I will now consider further the different ways in which Aeschylean choruses in the surviving tragedies are involved in the action, taking as a criterion how directly the chorus themselves are affected by that action.

At one end of the spectrum we have the type represented by *Suppliants* and *Eumenides*. Then, I would suggest, there is a group comprising *Agamemnon*, *Persai*, and *Septem*, in which the chorus is directly affected by the action to a greater or lesser degree, and with an ascending degree of urgency and immediacy. Each of these is a group of citizens which represent the whole polis—or, in the case of *Persai*, the best of the nation. While in *Agamemnon* the polis is represented by an important and central segment, elder citizens, in *Septem*, we shall see, the choice of the chorus of *parthenoi* allows the terror at the prospect of the sack of one's city to be openly expressed, without deconstructing the notion of manly virtues.

The third type of Aeschylean chorus involvement is that in *Choephoroi*, where, in my view, the chorus is not directly affected by the action; however, this does not mean that this chorus was not an integral and important part of the tragedy. On the contrary, first, they are the actors in the ritual action on which the first part of the tragedy is focussed. Second, they interfere in the action (766-72) and so play a vital part in the plot.[65] The combination of being at the less affected end of the spectrum, with playing an important part in the plot would, in my view, confirm that this is one of the transformations of an earlier state of affairs in which the chorus was an integral part of the action. Insofar as involvement in the action is concerned, the chorus in *Choephoroi* seems to be an early manifestation of a type of chorus involvement that will become more common in later tragedy. Thus, all three types of chorus involvement appear in Aeschylus, though the third less commonly, and in the "more involved" version. Later on this third type becomes much more popular, and the first type extremely rare. Thus, some forms of chorus involvement and role appear in the earlier tragedies, while others do not appear until later, and some forms become the preferred choices later. This state of affairs fits best the hypothesis that in early tragedy the chorus was an integral part of the action.[66]

To return to *Suppliants*. This tragedy is basically structured by a simple schema, that of a ritual, implicating a question pertaining to behavior between mortals, explored in terms of relationships to the divine and its ordained rules, set in the heroic age, and involving a collectivity on stage and a collectivity embodied in a king, and exploring the religion of today through explorations set at the time in which the rituals were set up. Human relationships are not explored in their own right, but primarily in connection with relationships between human and divine.

These religious explorations involved a very densely religious fabric of prayers, invocations, religious imagery, and the like, and generally are articulated through forms that are not very different from those of the ritual matrix I reconstructed in chapter III.3. Therefore, *Suppliants* can be seen as the result of Aeschylus' choice to revert to a form of tragedy that is basically not very far removed from a transformation of the dynamic ritual matrix which, on my reconstruction, had generated tragedy. If this is right, it would offer some confirmation for the validity of the reconstruction of that matrix. It would also show that Aeschylus' tragedies straddled, and probably effected, the transition from a dynamic ritual matrix articulating tragic forms, and involving religious exploration, into a dynamic tragic matrix with elements of ritual articulation, and involving, among other things, but very importantly, religious exploration.

III.1.iii. *Persai*

I now turn to *Persai*. It is a fact, rather than a modern assumption, that *Persai* is "experimental"; it deploys an experimental type of distancing, which does not involve the heroic past, as the preferred choice did. Despite this difference, *Persai* shows many of the characteristics identified in the preferred choice and the ritual matrix.

The overt theme of *Persai*, the battle of Salamis, seen from the Persian viewpoint,[67] is interwoven with a certain amount of Athenian and generally Greek self-presentation.[68] In modern eyes the most striking aspect of the play may be the sympathy and empathy with which the enemy other is presented and explored[69]—though this would have been less striking in ancient eyes, since in their collective representations next to the schema "the other as alien barbarian presented as the negative opposite of self," there was also the modality of presenting the other as like the self.[70] What is interesting for our purposes is the ways in which the tragedy's overt theme is articulated.

To begin with, as is generally recognized,[71] the most important strands in the play involve human relationships to the divine.[72] My argument is that these relationships were problematized in the play, that the tragedy does not simply present the Persian defeat as pun-

Chapter 1: "Starting" with Aeschylus   221

ishment for offensive behavior and warn against hybris; it also problematizes the notion of hybris and the transgression of the human limits. That the Persians had offended against the gods, and how, only becomes clear eventually. For example, yoking the Hellespont was not self-evidently hybristic. Dareios had, after all, yoked the Thracian Bosporos[73] and also the Danube.[74] This problematizes the proper limits of human intervention on the landscape. On my reading, through this exploration that takes place at a distance, in the world of the defeated enemy, problems pertaining to the Athenian religious discourse were explored. It was not simply a warning against hybris; it also set out the unknowability and uncertainty of the human limits.

Persai is permeated by the very strong recurrent theme that everything is determined by the gods, the version foregrounded being that the outcome of the Persian expedition is in the hands of the gods.[75] Lines 93-101 articulate the notion that mortals cannot avoid being deceived by god:

> dolometin d' apatan theou
> tis aner thnatos alyxei?
> tis ho kraipnoi podi pedematos eupeteos
>   anasson?
> philophron gar potisainousa to proton paragei
> broton eis arkystat' Ata.
> tothen ouk estin hyper thnaton alyxanta
>   phygein.[76]

So here we have the notion of the basic unknowability of divine will, which is frequently expressed in tragedy, here presented very negatively. This statement is directly related to the present situation in the verses that follow, when the chorus go on to say, from the third strophe onwards, that in old times Fate, ordained by the gods, had ordered the Persians to engage in wars, and now they have crossed into Europe and the old men are afraid. They are afraid that by crossing the sea into Europe they may have gone beyond what had been divinely sanctioned. A comparable notion is expressed at 157-8, when they address Atossa, *theou men eunateira Person, theou de kai meter ephys / ei ti me daimon palaios nyn methesteke strato*. Besides the distancing from the world of the audience produced by these verses, a distancing first stressed through the chorus' prostration in front of the Queen at 152,[77] these verses bring up explicitly as a possibility the notion of change in fortunes. The Queen herself expresses her fear of the possibility of a reversal of fortunes at 163-4, where she stresses that Dareios' prosperity was achieved through the favor of one of the gods.

222   Part III: Religion and the Fifth-Century Tragedians

The notion that a change in the Persian fortunes has taken place is expressed by the chorus at the conclusion of the stasimon sung after the departure of Dareios' ghost, between the Queen's exit and the entrance of Xerxes, in which, after they had sung of past glories during Dareios' reign, the chorus speak of now suffering a reversal of fortunes brought about by the gods (903-4). A similar notion, in the personalized form that the gods have changed course against him, is expressed by Xerxes at 942-3.[78]

Another strand of this theme is the notion that in the past a *daimon* had brought military success and power to the Persians, and this had created the expectation and confidence, above all in Xerxes, that this would continue to be so; this was, of course, a foolish attitude, not least because, as we learn from Dareios' ghost (739-42), oracles had foretold bad things—though they did not specify when they would happen. These oracles are important. For they bring up one of the most important notions problematized in Greek tragedy, as part of the exploration of the Greek religious discourse, the notion of preordained fate and the limits of free will.

If disasters had been foretold by the oracle, to what extent is Xerxes' hybris responsible for them? Dareios sketches the possibility of a partial answer: he had been hoping that those things would happen in the far future, but *hotan speude tis autos cho theos synaptetai*. It is important that, as will become clear below, Dareios' ghost does not speak with the authority of deities in epiphany in the other tragedies. He can only speculate about this.[79] The question is always left open, because there was no definitive answer in the Greek collective representations; so it is left open in the sense that all the people involved in such situations in Greek tragedy are presented as having contributed to their downfall.

Xerxes, in any case, had become overconfident, which is not something wise men should do; for, we saw, the chorus earlier articulated the idea that the divine is potentially malicious or at least deceitful[80]—and express the worry that things will cease to be as they had been so far. But when does confidence become overconfidence that leads to hybris? Xerxes had not been the first to cast his eye on Greece. Atossa's words at 472-7, at the very time she is blaming a *daimon*, activate the audience's knowledge that it had been the good king Dareios who had first attacked Greece, and that Xerxes was trying to avenge the Persian defeat at Marathon.[81]

Xerxes' overconfidence resulted in presumptuous pride and impiety. Presumptuous pride was wrong in itself, and also led to his transgression of the human limits, when he yoked the Hellespont, a transgression that both expressed, and polarized, his overweening confidence

Chapter 1: "Starting" with Aeschylus

that led him to overstep the human limits. He disregarded the divine nature of the landscape, and assumed that he was entitled to tame it through human ingenuity, thus attempting to gain mastery over Poseidon and the other gods. This brought divine punishment in the form of the Persians' defeat at Salamis. And, Dareios prophesied, the Persians would be defeated again, in punishment for their impiety, the sacrileges committed by the army who had invaded Greece, and who had showed no respect to the gods, but had burnt their temples, destroyed their altars, and overthrown their statues.

To this Persian impiety and presumptuous pride is contrasted Greek piety, illustrated in the description of the preliminaries to the battle (388-405), which stresses the ritual framing of the Greeks' going into battle, and the religious dimension of the Greek cause. As they themselves announced, the Greeks were fighting for their country, their wives and children, and most importantly, for their gods and their ancestors' graves. And it is the gods who gave them victory.[82]

This is the main framework of the tragedy. Of course, there are also other important themes, but they are woven into this main strand, and help explore it. For example, the mother-son relationship helps bring out the tragic aspects of the results of the hybris. The tragedy is not simply setting out a religious and moral framework; it is also problematizing at least implicitly the question of hybris and transgression: the fact that the chorus, though they did not share in his overconfidence, had not been aware of the transgressive nature of Xerxes' behavior, articulates implicitly the notion that it is not always clear when confidence slides into hybris and the overstepping of the human limits. That is why, in my view, the *Persai* is not a study in black and white lacking subtlety, as it has been accused of being.[83]

It is in creating a conceptual map of what went wrong, and what was hybristic, that Dareios' ghost plays a role comparable to that of gods in some Greek tragedies, in that he offers a supernatural authority for the assessment of the situation. Thus, the ritual of the invocation of the ghost of Dareios provides this correlative to the tragedies set in the heroic world, in that it offers a supernatural authority for the assessment of the situation—all this distanced in a world which is fundamentally other from that of the audience. It is in this way that the question of unknowability, and the consequent need to be cautious and thoughtful in one's actions, lest they overstep the proper limits, comes into play here—at a distance.

The role played by Dareios' ghost is comparable to, but not the same as, that of gods in those tragedies in which deities appear. I will now try to show, and refine, this by attempting to reconstruct the ways in which the ritual of the raising of Dareios' ghost would have been perceived by the audience.[84]

This ritual is made up of Greek ritual elements,[85] but it would have been perceived by the audience as non-Greek. The Persians are presented as partly sharing in the religious universe of the Greeks, in that they are presented as worshiping the same gods. This was necessary if the religious explorations in the tragedy were to have any relevance to the Athenian religious discourse. The audience, or part of it, may have perceived the fact that the Persians are presented as worshiping the same gods in a straightforward way; at least some may have seen this as a result of a "translation" of the Persian gods, an identification of Persian gods with the equivalent Greek ones. This is less important than the fact that, in the audience's perceptions, the Persians did not share the same religion as themselves; for only Greeks shared the same religion.

It is striking that the Persians' communication with the supernatural does not take place in the part of their religious world that (in this tragedy) they partly and superficially shared with the Greek audience; it takes place in a facet of the Persians' religious world that is totally separate from that of the Greeks. The otherness of that world would have been further stressed in the eyes of the audience by the fact that Dareios resided in the Underworld, though he was said to be a *theos*.[86]

The kletic hymn succeeds, and Dareios' ghost appears,[87] but his appearance did not have the same authority as the appearance of deities in other tragedies, precisely because this is not the world of the Greek heroic past. I am arguing in this book that the appearance of deities in the "canonical" tragedies set in the heroic age would have been perceived by the audience as having a certain degree of authority—which I am attempting to define. If this is right, the situation would be very different as far as *Persai* is concerned. The apparition of Dareios, which took place in a religious universe not shared by the Greeks, would not have been perceived as invested with such authority. On the contrary, the contrast between this and the "canonical" tragic setting, which was part of the audience's heroic past, in which the gods appeared and, for example, instructed heroes to found certain cults, would have made them perceive Dareios' ghost as even more definitely lacking that authority. Exactly how they perceived this apparition we cannot even try to reconstruct. But what, I submit, we can reconstruct, is that it was perceived differently from the ways in which the gods' appearances in other tragedies were perceived. On the other hand, I suggest that, partly because of the assumptions associated with supernatural apparitions in the other tragedies, and partly because they

Chapter 1: "Starting" with Aeschylus 225

fitted the audience's conceptual, and especially religious, world,[88] the audience would have understood the positions expressed by Dareios to be right. Dareios' prophecies are based on interpretation. Now that he knows that the oracles refer to the present situation, Dareios is interpreting the oracles as a skilled interpreter.[89]

There is a dissonance between the statements and ideology articulated by Dareios' ghost and the Athenian audience's knowledge of the live Dareios' behavior, knowledge activated within the tragedy, not least when the chorus' presentation of the old king as blameless would have evoked the audience's knowledge that it had been Dareios who had begun the aggression against Greece, which had resulted in the Persian defeat at Marathon, which is what Xerxes was trying to avenge.[90] Also, as critics have noticed,[91] the act that is here presented as major *hybris* by Xerxes, the "yoking" of the Hellespont, is not very different from Dareios' own actions: for Dareios had yoked the Thracian Bosporos—and also the Danube.[92] Again, at least a part of the audience would have been aware of this fact, and their knowledge would have been activated when at 746 Dareios mentioned *Bosporon rhoon theou*. And this activation would have raised questions for the audience. For why should Poseidon have been less offended by the bridging of the the Thracian Bosporos than by that of the Hellespont? So how would the audience have made sense of this dissonance and of these questions?

On my reading, since the dubious behavior was associated with the live Dareios, and the wise counsels with his ghost, one way in which the audience might have made sense of the wisdom of Dareios' ghost would be in terms of his new status after death. If that is right, one of the meanings this would have created would have been to deconstruct further the contrast between the foolish Xerxes and the good king Dareios, which the tragedy has set up; and this would have had the result of reinforcing the notion that it is not easy to know what behavior is hybristic. Presumably, Dareios' behavior had not been hybristic, but the reasons for this become less clear when the idealized Dareios set out in the tragedy is deconstructed, when the audience make sense of that presentation through filters shaped by their knowledge and assumptions concerning Dareios' behavior in life.

Winnington-Ingram thought that the fact that the chorus returns to the themes of the first part of the play in the last scene, and speaks in terms of unforeseen disasters (cf. 1005-7) and a daimon of destruction shows that they have not taken in Dareios' explanation and moral guidance, that the disasters were caused by hybris and hybristic actions that had offended the gods.[93] But in my view, the situation is more complex than this, because the tragedy is problematizing as well as setting out some (complex and ambivalent) answers. Understanding that these disasters have been the result of Xerxes' hybris does not necessarily entail that the notion of unforeseen disaster and of a *daimon* which brings destruction disappears. For (I submit this tragedy is suggesting) it is not always unproblematic when one has slid into hybris. Clearly, the destruction of temples and stealing of the gods' statues is unequivocallly hybristic, and that is why ultimately there is no question about Xerxes' behavior. But what about the rest? What Dareios had done in the past is not here presented as hybristic. How different would Dareios' behavior have been perceived to have been from Xerxes'? Furthermore, is there any guarantee that when mortals do not behave hybristically no unforeseen disasters take place? After all, the chorus themselves had not done anything hybristic, but they are sharing in the suffering of their nation. I submit that these remain open questions in *Persai*. But such openness is located in the minds of the enemy other, and so articulated but distanced from the Athenian audience.

The fact that the ritual of the invocation of the ghost of Dareios structures a significant part of the tragedy adds ritual weight to the religious dimension of the tragedy—despite the fact that this is Persian ritual. Also, there is a very significant density of religious references in this tragedy: references to prophetic dreams, rituals, and the great lamentation concluding the play,[94] the expression of thoughts and fears concerning the workings of the divine, and also references that bring out the religious dimension of the Greek landscape (see for example 447-9), or expressing things through religious language, as in the way the notion "when the Greeks had won" is expressed in verses 454-5.

The question of overweening pride and overstepping the limits was not only relevant to the Persian kings. At the time of the production of the *Persai* it might have seemed to some at least that the Athenian polis may have been in danger of transgressing in the same way. Thus the exploration of this overconfidence and transgression, here distanced to, and located in, the enemy other, was of direct relevance to Athens.

In these circumstances, I submit that, despite its experimental nature, the *Persai* displays (besides the obvious grandness and formality of language and style which lead in the same direction) the following characteristics—which, on my thesis, had also characterized the dynamic ritual matrix that generated, and shaped the early development of, tragedy. One, a substantial part is focussed on the performance of a ritual. Two, the human-to-divine relationships are central. Three, religious themes are explored. Four, the relationship between the

Chapter 1: "Starting" with Aeschylus 227

world of the audience and the world of the play involved a double perspective, but of a different type than that of all other tragedies. The distanced world is geographically and culturally distanced, and is also part of the audience's world in that it is its enemy other—as opposed to it being the ancestors and cult recipients, as is the case in the usual form of the double perspective. Five, Dareios provides a supernatural source of "answers," "assessments," comparably to what gods do. Six, there is density of religious references of all kinds. Seven, the chorus plays a large part and is seriously involved in, and directly affected by, the action; it represents a politically and symbolically central segment of the community affected by the action. Finally, eight, the canvas is not complicated.

I submit that, therefore, this tragedy appears to have been shaped by that ritual matrix, can still be perceived as a transformation of a developed form of that matrix.[95]

III.1.iv. *Septem*

Septem, the Aeschylean part of which ended at line 1004,[96] was the last tragedy in a trilogy, the first two plays of which were *Laios* and *Oidipous*.[97]

The first part of *Septem* is dominated by the danger to Thebes, the second by Oidipous' curse and its fulfilment in the death of his sons at each other's hands. Without going into the details of what we can reconstruct about the plots of *Laios* and *Oidipous*, among the themes involved the following were inevitably included: the notion of oracles, obedience to oracles, and the question of whether their fulfilment can be avoided; inherited guilt and divine punishment; curses. A question that traverses these themes is the extent to which mortals are able to shape their own fate, and the constraints on that ability. The related question of human versus divine responsibility for the outcome of events is posed at the very beginning of *Septem*, with reference to the outcome of the war: in the prologue, Eteokles says, at the very beginning of his opening speech (4-5), that if things go well it will be thanks to the gods; but if disaster were to strike the citizens will blame him.

That the gods will determine the war's outcome and the city's fate is a given throughout the play; it is a strong and recurrent theme, and the whole tragedy, especially in its first part, with the prayers to, and supplication of, the gods, articulates this perception. What is not clear, what is being explored, is human responsibility and the human ability to alter the course of events. The answer given by the play is ambiguous. The one certainty is that improper behavior towards the gods will ensure punishment, and that in this case proper behavior towards the gods ensures their protection for the city. But for Eteokles himself things are more complicated.

It is clear then, that *Septem* is concerned with, sets out and problematizes, questions of major religious importance. In addition, a large part of the play is concerned with ritual matters, the performance of rituals, especially prayers, most strikingly by the chorus in the parodos,[98] in a physical setting full of ritual structures such as altars and statues.[99] The tragedy also includes references to rituals,[100] a discussion of the appropriateness of particular rituals; omens, oracles, and prophecies and curses are central in it. *Septem* ends with the performance of a ritual, a long lamentation which evoked ritual echoes, since it made use of ritual patterns from real lamentations.[101] There are, of course, also very frequent references to, and invocations of, the gods throughout.

Let me illustrate briefly how the tragedy is articulated by religion. In the first part of the play the articulation of the theme of the siege, and the danger of destruction, of Thebes is focussed very strongly on religion, and on human relationships with the divine. As I mentioned, Eteokles at the very beginning of his opening speech (4-5) says that if things go well it will be thanks to the gods, and then (8-9) he invokes the help of Zeus *alexeterios*. The rest of this speech (10-38) is also full of religious references of various kinds.

The messenger speech that follows launches almost immediately into the description of a ritual (42-8) and is followed by Eteokles' prayer at 69-77. Then the chorus, in the parodos, perform a prayer ritual; they invoke, pray to, and supplicate, the gods, the statues of whom are on the stage, especially Thebes' *poliaochoi* gods and goddesses; they stress their kinship to Ares and Aphrodite, the parents of Harmonia, the wife of Kadmos, the founder of Thebes. Their formulations evoke the language of solemn prayer.[102] Their prayers and supplication are followed by the long passage about the proper way of asking the gods' help at this particular point, with Eteokles berating the chorus over its supplication of the gods, which was suggestive of premature terror and despair, and urging them to utter the form of prayer he considers appropriate for the circumstances, which should involve an *ololygmon hieron eumene* (268).

This is a substantial section that foregrounds the importance of the performance of the right ritual, so that the gods' help is ensured without sapping the morale of the city's human defenders. Clearly, the latter is important; it is a mistake to think that as long as one trusts the gods nothing else matters. This passage, and the contrast between a hysterical female chorus and a measured male leader, has often been seen in terms of a contrast between male and female ethos. In my view,

Chapter 1: "Starting" with Aeschylus

this gender-based contrast, and the underlying perceptions about women, are deployed in order to articulate the notion of terror in a threatened polis, without suggesting that it is ever possible that the central part of the polis, its male defenders, could be abandoned to such terror. The negative has, as so often, drifted to the female, so that extreme fear could be expressed, without deconstructing the notion of manly virtues, and thus threatening official ideology.[103] Moreover, the women's powerlessness, in anything except the religious sphere, emphasizes the plight and fear of a besieged city in an even more extreme manner. Because extreme negative feelings are involved, the community is represented by a female chorus.

The description of the shields characterizes the enemy leaders; all except the seer Amphiaraos, who is presented positively, and who himself frames negatively Polyneikes and the expedition, are seriously hybristic, impious, and blasphemous towards the gods.[104] Polyneikes in particular is presented by Amphiaraos as a prospective sacrileger and enemy of the gods; and this negative framing by the positively characterized Amphiaraos makes the audience understand that later on Eteokles is right in his characterization of Polyneikes and in claiming that Polyneikes did not have Dike on his side.

The figure of Amphiaraos is also a focus for the exploration of the problem that it is an empirically ascertainable fact that good people can suffer dreadful disasters. Eteokles' answer is that it is because they find themselves in what we may call the catchment area of bad people. But of course, this answer itself raises more questions. Through the imagery of the shield of Hippomedon, which places the Seven on the same side as Typhon, the challenger to Zeus' rule, and Eteokles' comment, which aligns the Thebans with Zeus and the other gods, the fight between the Thebans and the Argive army is identified with the battle of the gods against the savage challengers to their rule, such as the Giants and Typhon. Another struggle that was presented in similar terms in the Greek ideology of that time was the Persian wars, and the alignment of the mythological paradigm brought somewhat to the fore for the ancient audience the alignment between the prospective Sack of Thebes, articulated in various segments of the play, and the actual Sack of Athens and the destruction of its temples and sanctuaries by the Persians.[105] It is this plane of reference that has shaped the stress on the alienness, as well as savagery and barbarity of behavior, of the invading Argive army. Contrasted to the Argives' hybris and impiety is the piety of the Thebans, demonstrated through their prayers and rituals.

In the area most directly relevant to the audience's everyday reality,[106] the tragedy explores but ultimately reassures. To the question,

"Do the gods really abandon a captured city? Is that how cities are captured?" adumbrated at 217-8, no answer is given, but the fact that the impious are shown to be punished and the pious saved is reassuring. Everything is in the hands of the gods, but the gods punish the overbearing and hybristic and protect those who have not done bad things, provided—and this is the exploration into which the second part of the play slides, returning to the themes of the first two plays of the trilogy—that they are not under a curse, or have inherited guilt, or both.

From 677 onwards, following Eteokles' decision to place himself at the seventh gate, in opposition to his brother, the chorus tries to stop him and warns of the pollution of fratricide. Eteokles is convinced that the fulfillment of his father's curse cannot be prevented, and since the gods have decided that this will happen, he will let it happen. The chorus urge him to resist and express the possibility that with the help of the gods one could perhaps resist a curse and get rid of the Erinys.[107] This optimistic perception is not tested in this tragedy; it is in a way deconstructed by Eteokles' view that the gods are no longer interested in Oidipous' sons; the only thing they want from them is to see them destroyed. This articulates the notion that, once one is cursed, and sees the curse beginning to be fulfilled, one believes that the gods intend his destruction and he is not going to try to escape anyway.

The question of the ability to act as one wishes, and the extent to which supernatural agents constrain this ability, is articulated in 718-9. To the chorus' question, "Are you willing to harvest your brother's blood?" Eteokles replies that you cannot escape ills sent by the gods. In the gap between the two the ancient audience would have mentally supplemented "It is not a matter of being willing; I have no choice"; "You cannot escape ills sent by the gods." This is not, as Hutchinson thought,[108] an evasive answer involving human weakness. In ancient eyes this was an exploration of an important problem. Can someone escape a curse? The victims of a curse believe that they cannot, so they do not try.

To this and, more generally, the question of how far the ability of mortals to act as they wish is constrained and determined by supernatural forces, the play does not give definite answers; it suggests possibilities. The perception that ultimately the answers are unknowable is left hanging in the air. However, the more negative articulations are situated at a distance from the world of the audience. The articulation of the notion of maximum supernatural constraint on one's ability to shape one's life has drifted to manifestations distanced from the audience, and involving gross offenses against the gods as with the doomed Labdacids.

Chapter 1: "Starting" with Aeschylus

Myths articulated, and were articulated by, Greek perceptions of the cosmos, the gods, the relationships between men and gods and men and men. By exploring problematic areas in these myths, problematic in the sense that they generated questions and potential anxieties, tragedy explored problematic areas in the Greek religious system, and the human relationships that were grounded in that system, which was not based on dogma, and acknowledged, though it did not foreground, the ultimate unknowability of the divine world.

As tragedy developed, I suggested, the exploration of human behavior, and what we may call, schematically, "human character" became increasingly important. In *Septem* we do not find, in my view, explorations of relationships between mortals, except with reference to relationships to the divine. The fratricide is articulated in terms of the curse, and Polyneikes' impious nature, which is correlative with his threat to the city and its gods. Given the characteristics of the tragedy I have set out here, which, again, are very similar to those of the ritual matrix reconstructed in chapter II.3, I suggest that *Septem*, like the other two early Aeschylean tragedies, was shaped by a transformation of that matrix that had generated, and shaped the early development of, tragedy.

III.1.v. *Oresteia*

That the *Oresteia* deals with major religious issues and problems is a well-established fact. I will not rehearse those aspects of this trilogy's theology and religious explorations that have been discussed many times before. Thus the centrality of the religious explorations and the theological issues are too well established to need further discussion. The presence of the gods is an aspect I will discuss later on. What I want to stress is, first, something that I shall consider further, the fact that the three tragedies articulate, and are articulated by, rituals in different ways. Then, that the *Oresteia* also overflows with religion in the sense that there are very many religious themes and references throughout the plays, which give the trilogy a religious texture and which, in the eyes of the audience, would have contributed to its being preceived as something religious in itself, and not simply framed by religion.

While a very considerable part of *Choephoroi* is articulated by ritual, this is not the case with *Agamemnon*, with which I begin. In *Agamemnon* there are many religious references, and also several ritual segments and descriptions of rites by the chorus.

The tragedy begins with a ritual segment, the watchman's opening words of prayer, *Theous men aito*, though the rest of his speech does

232   *Part III: Religion and the Fifth-Century Tragedians*

not sustain this religious beginning. The strongly religious flavor of the parodos is clear and incontrovertible. It is especially important to note the performance of rituals by the chorus, such as the singing of the hymn to Zeus, and the reports of rituals. In the anapaestic part of the parodos, at 88-96, there are references to rituals being performed in the city. More important, and more sustained, reports of rituals which were of central significance to the tragedy are found in the lyrical part of the parodos (104-257).[109] There the chorus describe the portent sent to the Atreidai at Aulis and Kalchas' interpetation of this portent, and also the sacrifice of Iphigeneia (218-49). In between they sing a hymn to Zeus (160-84).[110] This hymn singing is itself a ritual act, as is the recital of a thanksgiving hymn for victory, addressed above all to Zeus, in the anapaestic prelude of the first stasimon (355-66). The lyrical part of the first stasimon (367-488) would not have been perceived as a religious hymn, but as a more complex ode that contained hymnic segments, such as the first strophe (367-84), and also religious references of various types.[111]

I will add one remark about the rituals reported in the parodos. I am arguing in detail elsewhere[112] that the chorus' report of the sacrifice of Iphigeneia had a more important, and more complex, role in the trilogy than is normally assumed. In that paper I offer additional arguments in favor of the view that the formulation *krokou baphas d' es pedon cheousa* in the description of the sacrifice of Iphigeneia in *Agamemnon* 239 had evoked the Brauronian *arkteia* ritual,[113] thus zooming the world of the tragedy to the world of the audience, and activating the ritual knowledge that, despite what the characters in the world of the play thought, Iphigeneia had not died; for in the audience's ritual reality, activated by verse 239, Iphigeneia had not died at the altar; she had lived and become the priestess of Artemis at Brauron.

Besides hymn singing by the chorus another type of ritual act also performed on stage in the *Agamemnon* is prayers: the herald invokes, and addresses a prayer to, a set of gods,[114] Klytemestra prays to Zeus Teleios.[115] The Kassandra scene (1072-1330) includes segments of ritual actions, Kassandra invoking Apollo, Kassandra prophecying and Kassandra uttering cries of lamentation. The chorus evoke the Delphic oracle, and implicitly compare Kassandra to the Pythia, when at 1255 they say, in answer to her response to the fact that they do not understand her prophecies that she speaks Greek well, *kai gar ta pythokranta; dysmathe d'homos* ("so do the Delphic oracular responses; but still they are difficult to understand"). Other ritual acts performed on stage are the chorus' lament for Agamemnon[116] and Klytemestra's idiosyncratic oath;[117] there is also a report of Thyestes' curse.[118]

Chapter 1: "Starting" with Aeschylus

Choephoroi, like *Agamemnon*, begins with a prayer.[119] But unlike the prayer in the earlier play this one is sustained and significant to the tragedy's action. In *Choephoroi* the first part of the tragedy is focussed on a ritual, a complex chthonic ritual. After the prayer to Hermes Chthonios, with which it begins, it continues with the arrival of the bearers of chthonic libations, and then the pouring of these libations, together with Electra's invocation of Hermes Chthonios—whom she asks to summon the chthonic gods, while she herself invokes her dead father, while pouring libations to the dead, and addresses a prayer to him. This is followed by lamentations by the chorus, and the discovery of the Orestes' offering of hair to their father's tomb. At 246-63 there is Orestes' prayer to Zeus; at 269-99 his report of Apollo's oracle, which includes the enumeration of the punishments inflicted by the infernal powers to those who do not avenge their kin. This is followed by the *kommos* (306-478),[120] itself followed by a segment in which religious references abound, as it includes further addresses to the dead Agamemnon, invocations of, and prayers to, chthonic deities, and the recounting of Klytemestra's prophetic dream. The libation rite is central: its original purpose as intended by Klytemestra was perverted and turned against her. It is a sophisticated deployment of a ritual, but this must not obscure the simple fact that a considerable part of the tragedy is structured by, and articulated through, ritual. When we are trying to reconstruct the perceptual filters that Aeschylus shared with his audience, we need to begin at a very basic level, and not take for granted the basic schemata which were the building blocks through which complex meanings were constructed.

The first two triads of the second stasimon consist of a prayer to Zeus and other gods who are significant in the tragedy.[121] At 855-68 we have a prayer by the chorus; at 900-2 we have a significant religious reference that affects the course of action, Pylades' reminder to Orestes of Apollo's oracular command.[122] The third stasimon (935-71) is in effect the victory song which the chorus had previously said they wanted to sing, sung to celebrate that Dike has come, a song of victory and thanksgiving.[123] What follows after 973 can be considered a scene of supplication, since Orestes is holding the suppliant's bough.[124] At 1029-39 Orestes, having mentioned that it was Apollo's inducements that led him to kill his mother, announces that, on Apollo's instructions,[125] he is now going to Delphi as a suppliant to be purified. At 1048 he begins to describe his vision of the Erinyes, whom no one else sees. At 1057 he invokes Apollo, and the chorus urge him to go to Apollo at Delphi. He then exits fleeing, to go to Delphi, pursued, the audience will understand, by the Erinyes.[126]

234   *Part III: Religion and the Fifth-Century Tragedians*

A very considerable part of *Choephoroi*, then, is articulated by ritual, and there are religious references everywhere. The Delphic Apollo had a central role.[127]

Eumenides differs from both *Agamemnon* and *Choephoroi* in that it is full of gods who interact with mortals, there is a ghost, an *eidolon*, and the chorus consists of deities, the Erinyes-Eumenides were divinities,[128] who have an important role in the play. Thus, the world of this tragedy is very different from that of the audience. The tragedy is articulated by a ritual quest, for purification and liberation from persecution by the deities who form the chorus.

The tragedy begins in the Delphic oracle; the *skene* represents the temple of Apollo at Delphi;[129] then it seems to represent the temple of Athena Polias in Athens.[130] That is, after two tragedies in which the ultimate mainspring of human action was divine requests and instructions, the *Eumenides* begins in a religious setting, and with a ritual, the oracular consultation of Apollo at Delphi through the Pythia, familiar to the audience from practiced cult, which entails that they would have zoomed the world of the tragedy to their own world, they would have made sense of it as a particular representation of cult practices of which their own were later versions and descendants.

Like *Agamemnon* and *Choephoroi*, *Eumenides* also begins with a prayer; but this is a religiously more significant, as well as longer, prayer, for it is uttered by the Pythia before she enters the temple to prophesy. In the course of this prayer, she narrates the myth of the Previous Owners of the Delphic oracle in the friendly transfer version,[131] which, it has been noted[132] foreshadows the play's conclusions. This myth and the connotations it evoked concerning divine succession and the relationships between the older and darker and the younger, celestial, gods, would have signalled to the audience that this tragedy was not only about human action, in interaction with the divine, but also about the gods themselves. The opening of the tragedy also made clear that Apollo and the Delphic oracle were important in the play; in fact, in this play Apollo's credibility seems to be at stake, the authority of his oracle.

To return to the opening ritual, the Pythia also speaks of, as well as prays to, the other Delphic gods, and to the *teleion hypsiston Dia* (28) and then enters to prophesy, having called on those who wished to consult the oracle to enter, in a turn determined by lot. All this would have zoomed the world of the tragedy to the audience's own world and ritual practices. For example, a statement like (19), *Dios prophetes d' esti Loxias patros*, was simple religious fact in the world of the audience, and so would have helped zoom the two religious worlds. The activation of this religious fact, which was to be reactivated by

Chapter 1: "Starting" with Aeschylus 235

Apollo himself later on in crucial moments of the tragedy, at 616-18, when he says that he prophesies only what is commanded by Zeus, and again at 713-4, entailed that, given the assumptions of the audience, it was a foregone conclusion that Apollo's, and so also the Delphic oracle's, authority would be validated.

One element in the Pythia's speech, her statement in 9-14, that Apollo travelled from Delos to the coast of Attica and from there to Delphi, escorted by Athenians, an Attic version of the myth, according to which Apollo travelled on the road which in the historical period was taken by the Pythias, the Athenian *theoria* to Delphi,[133] would have zoomed the world of the play even more closely and specifically to Athenian cultic reality, through evoking both the myth and the cultic practice, the *theoria*.

After the ritual beginning with the Pythia comes a disruption of the ritual of oracular consultation; the Pythia rushes out of the temple, after seeing a horrible scene inside, a scene involving another ritual, Orestes' supplication in the presence of hostile supernatural agents, the Erinyes, whom she describes. She concludes with a statement (60-3) that set out the main problem of Apollo's power and its possible limits:

> *tantheuthen ede tonde despotei domon*
> *autoi melestho Loxiai megasthenei.*
> *iatromantis d' esti kai teraskopos*
> *kai toisin allois domaton katharsios.*

At the same time, these lines, by evoking Apollo's functions in cult, zoom the god of the tragedy to the god worshiped by the audience. Then the *ekkyklema* reveals the interior of the temple and the scene she described, with the addition of Apollo, at the back of the *ekkyklema*.[134] By this time, then, the audience's perception of the god is as a representation of the god they worship in cult.

Orestes prays to Apollo,[135] and Apollo gives him reassurances of further support; he also expresses his negative perception of the Erinyes, and instructs Orestes to go to Athens, and supplicate the old statue of Athena, promising that there he will find release. Apollo stresses the fact that his own authority is at stake at 84 when he says that it was he that persuaded Orestes to kill his mother.

The song in which the Erinyes accuse Apollo of misbehavior over Orestes includes the accusation, at the beginning of the second antistrophe (162-3) that the younger gods in general act beyond their authority: *toiauta drosin hoi neoteroi theoi, / kratountes to pan dikas pleon.* One of their accusations against Apollo is that he stained his sanctuary with pollution, another that he acted *para nomon theon brotea men tion, palaigeneis de moiras phthisas* (171-2). The audience would not have understood these accusations against either Apollo or the younger gods in general to be "the truth," simply the Erinyes' perception—in the way they would have understood Apollo's earlier evaluation of the Erinyes to have been his own.

When in the course of the confrontation the issues of blood kinship on the one hand and the marriage bond on the other, come into play, Apollo's articulation of the issue is through the divinities connected with marriage. He claims (214-8) that the Erinyes, through privileging blood kinship over marriage, dishonor the divinities whose realms are marriage and erotic love: Hera, Zeus, and Aphrodite. These divinities were younger gods, and included Zeus. Consequently, when at 224 Apollo announces that Orestes' trial will be watched over by Athena, I suggest that the audience would have had its earlier expectations that Apollo's authority would be validated further reinforced. They would have assumed that whatever happened, and by whatever route, Athena would take the same side as Apollo. On my reading, it was never an issue for the audience whether or not Apollo's authority would be upheld. I suggest that making sense of the play through their assumptions they would have been taking for granted that it would; the issue was how this would come about, and above all, how the Erinyes would be dealt with. This is one of the ways in which the myth of the Previous Owners at the beginning of the tragedy, in a version almost certainly created by Aeschylus,[136] foreshadows the outcome.

The scene moves to Athens, to another temple, the temple of Athena Polias, where Orestes begins another supplication ritual, by clasping the ancient image of Athena. This setting, in combination with the fact that in the audience's ritual assumptions Orestes had come to Athens after the matricide,[137] would have zoomed the setting of the tragedy to their own world, the sanctuary of Athena Polias in the heroic age.

After the Erinyes enter in pursuit, Orestes reports a rite, the rite of purification he underwent at Delphi, and enacts ritual, a supplication and a prayer to Athena. Then comes the chorus' enactment of a ritual: the Erinyes sing the *hymnos desmios* (306), a binding song intended to put Orestes in their power, a *hymnos ex Erinyon desmios phrenon* (331, 344). This is a very strongly ritual segment, the ritual character of which is further reinforced by choral self-referentiality.[138] As Henrichs noted,[139] in the anapaestic prelude (307-20) to the first stasimon (321-96) the Erinyes begin their dance-song with an emphatic articulation of choral self-referentiality (307-11), and then, in the lyric parts, they draw attention to their identity as performers in choral dance, both through their words and their actions, such as the fact that they

Chapter 1: "Starting" with Aeschylus 237

were stamping their feet on the orchestra floor as they cursed Orestes.[140]

This self-referentiality entails that the ritual was perceived by the audience as being performed not only in the world of the play, but also in the here and now. This double nature of the song is important; at one level it is correlative with the fact that, in this stasimon, the Erinyes, among other things, sing a hymn to themselves, about themsleves. That is, in the same way that normal ritual hymns present a deity's powers, their functions and *timai*, and so on, here the Erinyes are doing it themselves in their own hymn. This is correlative with the fact that the audience would not have perceived this hymn to be sung only by the Erinyes in the world of the tragedy, but also, because of the activation of the persona of the chorus as a chorus in the here and now through choral self-referentiality, by the chorus of Athenian men in the here and now. This is important; for in the world of the audience, of the here and now, the Erinyes were indeed worshiped, and this fact was inevitably activated through the chorus' singing of this hymn straddling the world of the tragedy and the here and now in the orchestra. This, I will be arguing, has important consequences for the relationship between the world of the tragedy and the world of the audience when the Erinyes threaten Athens.

The cursing segments[141] would probably have evoked curse rituals in the world of the audience.[142] This would have enhanced the ritual character of the scene.

It is in this strongly ritual context, in which the world of the audience has permeated the world of the tragedy, that Athena appears. This context, and also the framework of real cult, and of Apollo as a representation of a god of cult, as well as the zooming of the sanctuary of the tragedy to the sanctuary of Athena Polias in real life, would have made the audience perceive the Athena who appeared on stage to be a representation of the goddess they worshiped in cult.

It is beyond my present scope to discuss what follows or indeed the trial and its procedures,[143] so I will only mention two points. First, the second stasimon (490-565) articulates the persona of the Erinyes as embodiments of justice.[144] This is a very important aspect of their persona, and it is, of course, very important in the tragedy. This is their role, and this is how they see themselves as acting here; the question is, are they right, or is Apollo's perspective of justice the right one? My second point is not wholly unrelated: at 476-9 Athena recognizes that the Erinyes do have a role; she also states that they may take revenge on Athens if they lose, their poison will fall on the ground and bring pestilence. The Erinyes themselves threaten to damage the land at

711-2 and 719-20, if they are dishonored, if they do not receive justice as they see it.

After his acquittal, and before he departs, Orestes takes an oath that, in gratitude, he will protect Athens from any future attack by Argos after his death, when he will have the powers of a hero.[145] In other words, his future heroic status in the audience's present is activated.

After their defeat the Erinyes threaten to blight the land.[146] This marks a grave danger for Athens in the world of the tragedy. But, I would argue, the audience is "insulated," protected from feeling this danger symbolically too close, and threatening their present. For, as we saw, choral self-referentiality before, and in, the first stasimon activated the persona of the chorus as a chorus in the here and now, which entailed that the audience would have perceived the hymn about the Erinyes to be sung also by the chorus of Athenian men in the here and now. This, in turn, entailed both an act of reverence to the Erinyes in the here and now, and the activation of the knowledge that in the world of the audience the Erinyes were indeed worshiped. So the threat of the Erinyes does not affect the world of the audience; it was a danger in the past that has been overcome. It is Athena who had, once more, protected the city; in this case she eventually, after a sustained effort of persuasion,[147] convinces the Erinyes not to harm Athens and promises that they will receive worship by the Athenians.

The new relationship between the Erinyes and Athens is immediately enacted. At 902 the Erinyes ask Athena what blessings they should invoke upon Athens, and she gives a list which includes blessings that correspond to the curses uttered in 780-7,[148] and then she herself gives Athens the blessing of victory at war. Then the Erinyes deliver those blessings in song,[149] interspersed with comments from Athena, who stresses their power to curse and bless, and admonishes the Athenians to give them proper honor.[150] Athena's comments would have zoomed the world of the tragedy to that of the audience. Athena's description of the powers of the Erinyes at 950-55 would have corresponded to the audience's perception of the power of these goddesses, whom they worshiped in their everyday life. Above all, the statement at 993-95, that if the Athenians honor the Erinyes their city will be righteous and glorious, would have zoomed them to their own religious reality, in which they did honor and worship the Erinyes—and this would have brought up the expectation of the fulfilment of this promise.

The tragedy ends with a ritual: its exodos[151] is a procession establishing the cult of the Eumenides in Athens.[152] It included, among other things, torches (1005), sacrificial victims (1006), the cultic personnel of Athena (1024).[153] Though this procession is not a representation of the actual ritual of the cult of the *Semnai theai*, but a construct deploying a variety of ritual elements, including elements evoking the Panathenaia,[154] it would have zoomed the world of the tragedy to the cultic reality of the audience. For in the perceptions of the audience the distance between this rite in the heroic age, in which both the deities being honored and the poliad deity took part, and the cult they practiced would have accounted for the differences.

Kavoulaki rightly notes[155] that the connection with the Panathenaia has been overstressed, and that the *phoinikoun* color of the metics' processional garments, which has been correctly connected[156] to the Eumenides' *phoinikobapta esthemata* (1028), is not particularly Panathenaic, but generally processional, and is certainly associated with Dionysiac processions.[157] This is important; if this procession had evoked the Dionysia procession, it would have zoomed the world of the tragedy not simply to the cultic reality of the audience, but also more specifically to the cultic occasion in which they were taking part, of which this performance was part. This strong self-referentiality, I submit, would have greatly strengthened the perception of the tragedy as a religious performance. In these circumstances, I suggest that this enactment, this representation of the cult's grounding, had an authority partly comparable to, though not nearly as high as, that of ritual enactments in sacred drama.

On my reconstruction of the generation of tragedy set out in part II, this is how the ritual out of which tragedy emerged was completed, with a procession reenacting the establishment of a cult: the procession from the prytaneion to the sanctuary of Dionysos Eleuthereus, which reenacted the establishment of the cult of Dionysos in Athens. This would suggest that when prototragedy emerged it may have included such a procession, an enactment of a ritual establishing cult. It is therefore conceivable that in this respect *Eumenides* may be reflecting a schema of prototragedy and early tragedy.

As we saw, the ritual matrix shaping tragedy would have included prophecy, a consultation of Delphic oracle. This could have taken two possible forms, a representation of consultation of the Delphic oracle enacted mimetically, or a report of a consultation. The pre-mimetic forms of the performances inevitably involved the latter. The mimetic forms are likely to have included both, in different performances. If this is right, it would follow that both reports of oracular consultations, by the *hypokrites*, or in choral song, and enactment of rituals, would have been part of the ritual matrix shaping prototragedy and early tragedy. If it is correct that the myths of Lykourgos and/or Pentheus were the first myths to be the subject of prototragic and/or early tragic performances, the presence of gods, the interaction of gods and mortals, would have been another element in this matrix—a source of authoritative answers alternative to prophecy. If we compare this cluster of elements that, I suggested, were aspects of the ritual matrix that shaped early tragedy, with the three tragedies of the *Oresteia* we get some interesting results.

Agamemnon takes place in the world of mortals, with prophecy the only way of communicating with the gods; hymn singing, but also lamentations, and prayers, are the main ritual acts enacted on the stage; most other rituals are reported in the chorus' song. This seems close to what, on my reconstruction, was clearly one schema produced by the ritual matrix shaping early tragedy, that in which, as in *Agamemnon*, many narrative elements, including rituals, were reported in the chorus' songs.[158] A very considerable part of *Choephoroi* is structured by ritual. Ritual enactment would have been part of the early tragic schemata, though it is likely that much of it would have involved hymn singing. The world in the first two tragedies of the trilogy is similar to the world of the audience, in that the gods are absent, distant. It is also similar to the world of the festival myth of the City Dionysia. Communication with the gods in both these two tragedies, and in this myth, is similar to that in the world of the audience, through prophecy.

The audience knows that prophecies in tragedy come true, their knowledge and assumptions tell them so, but in the world of the tragedy the characters do not; it is not very different from the world of everyday reality, in which people know that the god speaks the truth, but human fallibility may intervene and distort the message—except insofar as the assumption of greater closeness to the gods in the heroic age in the audience's perceptions, though not activated in these two tragedies, may have distanced it somewhat from their own reality. In *Eumenides* the assumption of closeness between mortals and immortals in the heroic age is activated, and so the otherness of that heroic world is stressed. This is a world in which mortals and immortals interact freely and directly. The change of register is signified by the fact that while before the Erinyes were only visible to Orestes, now they are physically present on the stage. Such interaction, I suggested above, would also have been part of the ritual matrix, one of the schemata generated by this matrix. In *Eumenides* it is combined with the articulation of rituals, and of the tragedy through rituals.

If this is right, the *Oresteia* is structured by a complex combination of various versions, and transformations, of prototragic and/or early tragic schemata, all shaped by the ritual matrix reconstructed here. It would follow that Aeschylus deployed these schemata in order to

Chapter 1: "Starting" with Aeschylus

achieve the complex dramatic effects that he does achieve in the *Oresteia*.

First, in *Agamemnon* events are seen from a human perspective; this tragedy's world is comparable to the world of the audience, in which access to the divine is only through prophecy. The most significant prophecy—in the sense that it led to action in the play's past, which was a fundamental factor in unleashing action in the play's present, the sacrifice of Iphigeneia—is reported by the chorus. Kassandra's inspirational prophecy distances the world of the tragedy from that of the audience, for it was the result of the personal relationship between Kassandra and Apollo. This, then, activated the facet of the heroic age which involved a closeness between mortals and immortals. However, the distance was itself somewhat deconstructed. First, because Kassandra was perceived as someone apart in the world of the play. And second, the fact that the chorus evoked the Delphic oracle, and implicitly compared Kassandra to the Pythia, would have evoked the perception that there *is* a correlative to Kassandra's inspiration in the world of the audience, prophecy by the Pythia—and one which had credibility and could be acted upon.

Similarly comparable to the world of the audience is the world of *Choephoroi*. Again, it is the human perspective that is presented. Again, the only access to the gods is, as in the world of the audience, through prophecy. However, Orestes has been given detailed guidance and advice. Prophecy here no longer involves (a report of) the distant interpretations of omens, or Kassandra's visions of inescapable horrors, as in *Agamemnon*. There is direct divine guidance—even if it involves the advice to do the dark deed of matricide. *Choephoroi* is structured by ritual; that mortals communicate with the divine world, and it is not clear whether or not that communication will lead to the achievement of the mortals' desires. The same chthonic ritual fails for Klytemestra, who had ordered it, but succeeds for Electra and Orestes, who had performed it.

The modality of direct human-divine interaction was deployed in *Eumenides* to widen the perspective beyond the sphere of ordinary mortal understanding, to offer the divine perspective on the problems pertaining to the human action of both preceding plays. However, what it shows is that there is not one divine perspective, but more than one. Apollo's perspective, the Erinyes' perspective, and Athena's. And this not only gives a cosmic dimension to the events that took place in the first two tragedies, and the problems they gave rise to, but also leads to further, and more complex, religious explorations.

These explorations involve issues pertaining to the divine world—and so also to the human which (in Aeschylean tragedy, as in

Greek perceptions) is dependent on the divine. The explorations pertain to a variety of issues, including to the relationships between older and younger gods, which are intertwined with the notion of divine succession, and also to the complex and ambivalent nature of polytheism, and ultimately cosmic order as perceived by Greek polytheism, in which there is a supreme god, but also different divinities have their own sphere of competence and power.

Some of the questions explored in this tragedy, which pertain to this basic aspect of religion and are of direct concern to the audience, seem frightening: What happens when gods disagree? Are there really different divine perceptions of Dike? And if there are, what should mortals do? However, when these explorations are perceived through the fifth-century audience's assumptions they become more manageable. When viewed through those ancient assumptions, in which Apollo spoke for Zeus—a perception activated in the play by the Pythia and by Apollo himself—and Athena was one of the younger gods, the daughter of Zeus, one of those divine perspectives was right; the other was inferior, destined to be subordinated to the dominant one; subordinated but not annihilated; earlier dark chthonic gods are not annihilated in Greek mythology, they become integrated in a subordinate position. The tragedy offers one possible representation of how this came about in this case, and how the human world, in this case Orestes, was affected. It also explores the darkness of, and the danger presented by, one group of dark dangerous chthonic powers; it explores their possible relation to humanity; and it shows how and that they came to be accommodated in the Greek conceptual universe and, correlatively, in the religion of the Athenian polis.

I am not going to discuss all the religious explorations and theological issues which have been discussed many times, or, indeed any of the issues involving social institutions, gender politics, or the question of contemporary political references.[159] I am not offering a comprehensive reading of the *Oresteia*, only a discourse on its religious nature. But there is one issue that I need to discuss, since it involves a fundamental aspect of the religious explorations and it affects some of the views I expressed above: the hypothesis that Zeus himself changed within the trilogy. Let me consider a recent formulation of this view by Sommerstein.[160] His argument, as I see it, is, in summary, that in *Agamemnon* the Erinyes are emissaries of Zeus and the Olympians, while in *Eumenides* "the Erinyes and the 'younger gods' are at daggers drawn."[161] The Erinyes have not changed, so it follows that it is Zeus who has changed. Also,[162] if Zeus was from the beginning so benevolent and so wise, "Why did he, through Apollo, compel the morally innocent Orestes to kill his mother. . . ?"

Chapter 1: "Starting" with Aeschylus 243

To begin with the latter question, I would argue that it reflects modern assumptions, it is implicitly shaped by perceptions of justice and fairness which are not those of the ancient Greek collective representations. A fifth-century Athenian would have answered the question unproblematically: "Because that is how things are; because once one gets involved in a bad situation, like a cycle of revenge, this is what happens." Zeus' *dike* ensures that Orestes will be free in the end; but the Greek perception of Zeus was not that of a scrupulously fair kindergarten supervisor; it is the ultimate order that he safeguards, and the ultimate order that matters. This is related to the fact that "The purposes of Zeus are inscrutable to mortals."[163]

To turn to the first point, I would argue that the fifth-century audience, given their religious assumptions, would have perceived Apollo to be in conflict with the Erinyes over this specific issue; and his claims to be speaking for Zeus would have been accepted by the audience as true—on the basis of their assumptions over the Delphic oracle. Athena eventually sides with Apollo. The Erinyes present this in terms of a conflict with the younger gods. But in fact the audience would have seen this as an adversarial oversimplification of a more complex situation. Apollo spoke for Zeus in urging Orestes to kill his mother; in the actual conflict Apollo takes on the role of combatant, and by the time the action moves to Athens, it is Athena, the poliadic deity, who takes on the role of spokesman for Zeus.[164] And Athena acknowledges that the Erinyes do have a legitimate role as well as power. The fact that their cult is installed in Athens means that their role is now officially integrated.

I submit that the ancient audience's perceptions of the conflict would have been shaped by the following parameters. The Erinyes are not normally in conflict with Zeus and the younger gods. A situation arose which created dissent, and a crisis, between, on the one hand the Erinyes, who want to pursue the murderer of kin whatever the circumstances, and who put the *drasanta pathein* law[165] at the center of justice, and on the other Zeus, who, through Apollo, wants to act to safeguard the institution of marriage—as perceived in the Greek collective representations, which privileged the male. Zeus, as the supreme ruler of the universe, must preserve an order and balance between different competing aims and claims, represented by the different divinities who are responsible for each completing area. It is he who has to order the priorities.

That Zeus would be concerned to safeguard the instituion of marriage is made almost explicit by Apollo at 214-8, when he comments that the Erinyes, through implicitly underestimating the seriousness of the murder of a husband, dishonor the divinities whose realms are marriage and erotic love: Hera, Zeus, and Aphrodite. Thus, a crisis arose, which involved issues of more general relevance than the fate of Orestes; this entailed that new arrangements needed to be made in order to resolve it, and ensure that a sustainable order that will not lead to future crises is set in place. On the one hand, at the human level, arrangements involving justice and punishment: the Areopagus is set in place, so that the community of mortals takes responsibility for the punishment of murder; on the other a cult to the Erinyes is instituted, so that what they stood for, and their *timai* and power, are both revered, and taken account of in the conduct of human affairs. This is the justice of Zeus.

Zeus has not changed since *Agamemnon*; it is the circumstances that changed with the murder of Agamemnon in that tragedy, and this led to a variety of unpleasant things, until eventually the new order is put in place. This is not a perfect order; for human justice cannot be guaranteed to be always right—a perception articulated in the fact that Athena's intervention is needed to lead to a decision about Orestes. But it is an order that is now guided by the new, superior, order in polis religion, in which the Erinyes have become recipients of cult, albeit in a position clearly subordinate to that of Athena and Apollo—let alone Zeus. Through this, their dangerous power is acknowledged, and, it is hoped, propitiated and turned to the good, as it is in the play; also, their position in the cosmos is articulated in the cult: powerful, but subordinate to Zeus and the younger gods.

Finally, in the ancient audience's assumptions there would be nothing in Zeus' position in *Eumenides* to suggest that he "progresses morally" within the trilogy. In their perceptions Zeus' reign began with the new values of consensus and persuasion, as well as force: in Hesiod's *Theogony* 881-5 Zeus becomes ruler not only because of his strength and intelligence, which led him to defeat Kronos, but also by the consensus of the other gods. This—among other things—also expresses the notion that this is a new value that comes into play in the reign of Zeus. Zeus is a complex and ambivalent figure, but his reign is presented as just from the beginning.[166]

The audience of the *Oresteia* knew (because their religious assumptions told them so) that the outcome would be such as to validate Apollo's authority, and the authority of his oracle, which entailed also the release of Orestes. It is in the world of the tragedy, for Orestes, that the outcome is an issue. This is, then, for the audience, an exploration at a safe distance, that will not lead to anomic terror, since the audience know that Apollo's authority and the authority of his oracle would be validated. This is comparable to the second stasimon of Sophocles' *Oidipous Tyrannos*, in which the chorus' anxiety over the

Chapter 1: "Starting" with Aeschylus 245

possibility that oracles mean nothing is put in a wider perspective through the audience's knowledge that in the case of Oidipous the oracles will prove true.

From the point of view of the audience, Orestes' experiences, which involve problematizing Apollo's authority, are a metaphor for the audience's own experiences. First, experiences pertaining to prophecy and oracular guidance, since, in the audience's world it is not clear if the oracles will come true, or whether human fallibility may have interfered and corrupted the divine word. Then, it is also a metaphor for the general unknowability of the divine world and will, which includes a positive outcome, and is thus a reassuring representation. In addition, as we saw, Orestes' experiences involve certain religious problematizations that are religious explorations for the audience as well: the dangers represented by the dark chthonic powers, whom Greek religion acknowledged as part of the divine world, and also the ways in which the situation described (that is the mythological schema structuring myths) in *Theogony*, and the hostile version of the myth of the Previous Owners, of the older and darker deities becoming integrated after their defeat into the new order in a subordinate position, came to be.

To return to basics. The audience made sense of these three tragedies through perceptual filters shaped by the fact that this was a performance in religious time, a festival in honor of Dionysos, a fact strongly activated in the last play, and in a religious place, in a sanctuary. They saw a trilogy exploring a variety of religious and theological issues, through religious schemata, with religious references everywhere, with a very considerable part of *Choephoroi* being articulated by ritual, and with ritual also articulating *Eumenides*, in which the gods dominated the action, and with hymn singing and other prayers, prophecy, and reports of rituals structuring *Agamemnon*. I suggest that they would have perceived these tragedies as being above all a type of "religious" drama, exploring religious problems—as well as some other things, to which I will return. In their eyes, I am suggesting, these tragedies did not present human action against a divine backdrop, but human action presented above all in religious terms, in terms of human-divine interaction and what the gods consider appropriate behavior.

However, I also want to stress that the "other things" that are explored here, human relationships, including social institutions and gender ideologies, are developed very much further in the *Oresteia* than in the three early extant Aeschylean tragedies. The *Oresteia* represents a very significant development of such aspects, and so a very significant movement away from the schemata of the three early extant tragedies, which were still, I argued, shaped by the ritual matrix that generated tragedy. There are four ways in which the *Oresteia* represents a very significant movement away from that matrix when compared to the three earlier plays. First, the *Oresteia* has a much more complex canvas. Second, and most importantly, in the *Oresteia* there is much greater stress on, and complexity in, the relationships between humans, which are also explored more in themselves and not only primarily in terms of relationship to divine. Third, the religious explorations are also much more complex. Finally, the ritual and the religious dimension in general are deployed in much more complex and sophisticated ways than in the earlier tragedies. I suggested that Aeschylus was deploying a variety of earlier schemata in different versions to achieve his complex dramatic effects.

One (inevitably oversimplifying) way of clarifying the distinctions I am trying to make, by exaggerating them, would be to say that the *Oresteia* is the earliest surviving example of a tragedy not shaped by the ritual matrix but deploying material that originated in that matrix, originated in the earlier tragic schemata generated by that matrix, to create what we may crudely call fully developed tragedy.

III.1.vi. *The* Skene *in the* Oresteia

The masterly and highly complex use of the *skene* in the *Oresteia*, and the complex symbolic meanings it helps create by contrasting inside and outside, inner and outer space, the hidden and the revealed, are well known and I will not repeat them.[167] I want to say something about one particular aspect of the use of the *skene*. Taplin had accepted the view that the *skene* had been invented between the latest of the earlier Aeschylean plays and the production of the *Oresteia*, while the earlier tragedies did not have a *skene*.[168] He would not now[169] wish to exclude the possibility that there may have been a skene before the *Oresteia*, but if so it had not been exploited in its full potential as it is in the *Oresteia*. This last point is undoubtedly correct. However, I would argue that there had been a *skene* in early tragedy, from its very beginning—though it was not used in complex or sophisticated ways.

As we saw above in II.2.i, there are very good reasons for thinking that a *skene*, in the word's ritually common meaning of "a tent erected in the open air for ritual dining at a festival," was erected for the ritual *xenismos* of Dionysos in the Agora; and also that it is not unlikely that the *hypokrites* had come out of that tent when the dramatic performances had taken place in the Agora. We also saw that the ritual schema "*skene* as a temporary structure erected for a mimetic per-

Chapter 1: "Starting" with Aeschylus

formance at a festival" existed in at least one other Greek ritual, in which it represented a palace.[170] In these circumstances, I suggest that the name, basic function, and temporary nature of the theatrical *skene* can best make sense if it is seen as emerging out of these ritual beginnings; that the *skene* in the theater originated in, emerged out of the transformation of, the tent *skene*, when the dramatic performances moved to the Theater of Dionysos. In addition, if there had been no *skene* in earlier tragedy there would have been no definition of the performance area. The early orchestra had not been round, and had not been a clearly defined area; it was an area of vaguely rectangular shape between the cavea and the *skene*.[171]

The most complex uses of the *skene* in the *Oresteia* are in the scenes of the murders in *Agamemnon* and *Choephoroi*, where it represents the palace, and in the scene set at Delphi in *Eumenides*, where it represents the Delphic temple; when the action first moves to Athens, it represents perhaps the temple of Athena Polias—while it is ignored in the second part of the play as it had been in the first part of *Choephoroi*.[172] In *Agamemnon* cries are heard from within, Agamemnon's cries as he is being killed, and eventually the inside opens up through the *ekkyklema* to reveal horrible things, the murdered bodies of Agamemnon and Kassandra; the same revelation through the *ekkyklema* of the murdered bodies of Klytemestra and Aigisthos takes place in *Choephoroi*. In *Eumenides* the *ekkyklema* reveals the scene inside the adyton of the temple which had been described a little earlier by the Pythia, Orestes by the omphalos and the Erinyes, with Apollo at the back of the platform.

The notion of the *skene* as an inner space in which secret things are happening—which are then brought out, and revealed when the *skene* opens up through the *ekkyklema*, bringing to light what was in the darkness—is not a modern construct; it is confirmed by the formulation of Pollux that the *ekkyklema* reveals the *aporrheta* things that had taken place in the houses inside the *skene*.[173] The schema of a structure in which secret things are taking place, and from the inside of which cries are heard, prior to its being opened up, and the secrets that were hidden inside being brought outside and revealed, corresponds to the ritual schema centered on a structure that seems to bear a significant physical resemblance to the *skene* and which was a major part of a major Athenian cult: the Anaktoron inside the Telesterion at Eleusis.[174] The resemblance can be seen to be significant, once the fundamental difference between the two settings is taken into account, the fact that while the *skene* was in the open air, the Anaktoron was situated in an inner space. The difference is correlative with the differences in the basic cults of which the two schemata are part. But both were theatrical spaces in which mimetic and ritual performances were enacted.[175]

Let me describe very briefly what has been reconstructed with regard to the function of the Anaktoron.[176] In the Anaktoron, which, of course means 'palace', were kept the *arrheta hiera*, the cult's secret sacred things.[177] Only the hierophant could enter it.[178] At some point in the initiation ceremony the hierophant was inside the Anaktoron, which was closed, and his voice was heard from inside. The importance of this rite is shown by the fact that *hai ex anaktorou phonai* could be used as a synonym for *hierophantia*.[179] Then, the doors of the Anaktoron were opened, and the hierophant emerged from inside, lit in brilliant light, and exhibited the *hiera* to the initiates.[180] If we ignore the context—since one of the things I am trying to investigate here is whether or not the contexts were similar to the Athenians, whatever they may appear to us—I suggest that the similarity in the two action schemata is clear and unambiguous.

I submit that—again, leaving aside the question of whether tragic performances were seen in a comparably religious light—the similarity would have been clearer to fifth-century Athenians because in their assumptions the cults of Demeter and Dionysos, which form the wider frames of the two phenomena, were very closely associated. First, there was a close cultic connection between the Attic cults of Demeter and Dionysos, the precise nature of which is a controversial matter, which I cannot discuss here, but the existence of which is undoubted. Second, the two cults are comparable, they have common elements; both involved the bringing of an important agricultural product into Athens; the third element of the triangle, the olive tree, was not brought from the outside, but was given by Athena as a gift, and was a sign of the "contract" between Athens and Athena as its poliad divinity; and both involved *xenismos* rituals. Finally,[181] the rites of the Eleusinian Mysteries had included singing and dancing and impersonation of the goddesses by religious personnel, *mimesis*. Also in the Eleusinian Mysteries, as in tragedy, the initiates underwent certain experiences, that may be crudely described as of a psychological nature; *pathein* and *paschein pathos* are among the expressions mentioned in connection with the Mysteries.[182]

Of course, there were also fundamental and radical differences between the two rituals, pertaining both to the nature of the deities, and also of the two relevant cults, the Eleusinian Mysteries on the one hand, which were closed and secret, and accessible through individual initiation, and the City Dionysia on the other. But the Eleusinian Mysteries was also an Athenian polis cult, part of Athenian polis religion.[183]

Chapter 1: "Starting" with Aeschylus

I would like to suggest the possibility that the Eleusinian Anaktoron operated as a model, through similarity and differentiation, for the more complex use of the *skene* by Aeschylus. I suggest that the similarities are very real, and that this is what is important. But in any case, the perception that there was a connection between Aeschylean performances and the Eleusinian Mysteries is an ancient one,[184] as is shown by various stories about it. First there was a story according to which Aeschylus had created theatrical costumes of such *euprepeia* ('comeliness') and *semnotes* ('dignity') that the Eleusinian hierophants and the *dadouchoi* changed their costumes in imitation of them.[185] Whatever, if anything, this story may reflect, it reveals a perception of a connection between Aeschylean *hypokritai* and the hierophant.

Then, there are various attestations of the story that says that Aeschylus was accused of impiety for revealing certain features of the Mysteries.[186] One version says that he was acquitted by claiming that he was not an initiate, and therefore could not have revealed secrets he did not know were secrets. Whatever the validity of the story of the accusation,[187] it is extremely unlikely that Aeschylus was not an initiate. There is every reason to think that the large majority of Athenians were initiated, and the fact that Aeschylus was an Eleusinian increased the likelihood of his being an initiate very greatly. In addition, and most importantly, Aeschylus' invocation of, and prayer to, Demeter in Aristophanes *Frogs* 886-7 seems to me to be shaped by the assumption that Aeschylus was not simply an Eleusinian, but an initiate of the Mysteries. It seems perverse to deny that something other than the accurate reflection of a historical event lies behind the story; but what, if anything, that may have been is beyond our grasp. If the hypothesis I am proposing here is right, it would offer one possible scenario for the sort of thing that the story might conceivably be reflecting: a little unease may have been created by the fact that the schema based on the Anaktoron and the revelation of the *hiera* was used to reveal murder and corpses.

One of the major differences and differentiating parameters between Anaktoron and *skene* pertains to the permanent nature of the Anaktoron and temporary nature of the *skene*. As mentioned in chapter II.2, the fact that the *skene* in the Theater of Dionysos did not acquire stone foundations until the mid-fourth century is far from self-explanatory, and may suggest that the *skene*'s temporary, wooden nature was part of the assumptions associated with it, as it is in the interpretation of its origins offered here. If the *skene* began as such a temporary structure in the way suggested here, the contrast with the Anaktoron may well have been a factor strengthening the importance of its temporary nature, and keeping it unchanged for such a remarkably long time.

If the use of the *skene* first seen in the *Oresteia* had been modelled on, or inspired by, the function of the Anaktoron in the Telesterion at Eleusis at the Mysteries, this would testify to a perceived close semantic connection between the Eleusinian Mysteries and the tragic performances at the City Dionysia—not simply in the frame of the performances, but in the dramatic enactment. This would reinforce further the thesis that what took place in the tragedies was part of the religious discourse of the polis. But even if this use of the *skene* had not been inspired by the Eleusinian Anaktoron, even if the similarity between the two is due to a coincidence, that very similarity would have evoked for the fifth-century Athenians—the large majority of whom, I assume, were initiates of the Eleusinian Mysteries—religious echoes of those Mysteries—at whatever point in the conscious-unconscious spectrum of meaning creation and reception. And this, I suggest, would have reinforced even further the religious dimension of the performance, and in particular the notion that things are shown in the theater which involve serious enactment and teaching pertaining to the religious sphere, something almost akin to revelation—but revelation in the Eleusinian Mysteries sense, in which things are shown and things are told; not in the sense of an absolute truth revealed from the gods.

III.1.vii. *Conclusions: Aeschylean Tragedy and Religion*

Let me sum up the central conclusions of these analyses. Aeschylean tragedies were in fundamental ways religious tragedies. Their religious setting (religious in both time and space), the centrality of religious explorations in them, their presentation of human issues in terms of human relationships to the divine, the fact that they are structured through ritual acts, the density of religious language and of religious references, all these are not separate things, somehow put together, partly accidentally and partly deployed for dramatic effect by Aeschylus who imported them from the outside, from the separate world of religion—itself a higly implausible interpretation, once it is made explicit. They are all manifestations of a perception, shared by Aeschylus and his audience, of tragedy as in fundamental ways religious. It is something certainly different from ritual enactments of a central myth, such as took place at the Eleusinian Mysteries, but, on my interpretation, something which the ancient audience would have perceived through filters that were nearer to those through which they had perceived such reenactments than they are to basically "secular"

Chapter 1: "Starting" with Aeschylus

filters, comparable to those through which modern audiences make sense of Greek tragedy.

Besides (like other Greek public rituals) honoring the god in whose festival it took place, and entertaining the audience, tragedy had another religious function: it explored a myth's interstices of religious Problematik, and, through this, questions directly relevant to the audience's reality. To put it differently, it was a locus in which religious Problematik about conduct in life, and beliefs about the gods worshiped by the polis, could be explored, through the enactment of a myth which gave rise to the same Problematik, and the exploration of those problems, the exploration of the problematic interstices of myth, and, through this, the interstices of polis religion. Though *Persai*[188] did not involve a myth, it still involved religious explorations: as well as presenting the Persian defeat as a punishment of hybris, it problematized hybris and showed, at a symbolic distance, that though some acts, like destroying temples, are clearly and unequivocally transgressive, it is not always, and in all circumstances, easy to know when one has crossed the line into hybris.

A comparison of the basic schema structuring *Suppliants, Persai,* and *Septem* with the ritual matrix that had shaped earliest tragedy, as I reconstructed it in chapter II.3, suggests that these three tragedies were shaped by that ritual matrix. Since the readings of the tragedies on which this conclusion is based were independent of that reconstruction, this coincidence, I submit, provides a little confirmation for the reconstruction set out in part II of the developments that generated tragedy.

The *Oresteia* represents a very significant development away from that ritual matrix, most significantly, in the fact that in this trilogy there is much greater stress on, and complexity in, the relationships between mortals, which are also explored more in themselves, and not only primarily in terms of relationship to divine. Also, the tragedies' canvas is much more complex, as are the religious explorations and the deployment of ritual elements. Aeschylus, I suggested, was deploying, in complex ways, a variety of earlier tragic schemata, that had been generated by the ritual matrix, to achieve complex and sophisticated dramatic effects. But ultimately, he was still, above all, composing "religious" tragedy.

Notes

1. Cf. e.g. Winnington-Ingram 1983, 1. Also, for example, Else, who does not believe that tragedy began in ritual, nor that it had anything to do with religion, let alone Dionysos, "except that Pisistratus attached it . . . to his festival of the Greater Dionysia" (Else 1965, 30), nevertheless states the following with regard to Aeschylus (Else 1965, 4): "The plays of Aeschylus are obviously religious in the profoundest sense. Dealing with the ultimate mysteries of fate, suffering, the relation of man to god, they grip us with an overwhelming intuition of forces out of scale with human power, of titanic combats embracing earth, hell and heaven." He the goes on, "What more natural than to suppose that this religious drama grew out of religious ritual? Yet the inference is not necessarily valid. Aeschylus uses inherited religious forms in his plays, but their form as a whole cannot be understood as a reflection of any ritual." And elsewhere (Else 1977, 75) he states that Aeschylean plays are permeated with ritual elements from one end to the other.

2. Zeitlin 1965. Zeitlin 1978, 149-84=1996, 87-119) has also argued that the *Oresteia* is structured as a rite of adolescent initiation. Else 1977, 70-87 argued that Aeschylus uses ritual in order to create feelings of fear, grief, and uncertainties in the audience, to involve it deeply in the feelings of the chorus and the dramatic characters. Cf. also Goldhill 1986, 21-3 for the complexity and sophistication with which prayers and the language of prayer are deployed in the *Oresteia*. Bowie 1993b, 10-31 has argued that rituals (and myths) provide filters to help the audience explicate the political codes of the *Oresteia*. Cf. also Bowie 1993b, 19 for references to other suggestions of deployment of religious practices in the *Oresteia*.

3. Cf. e.g. Else 1977, 70-87, esp. 78-9, 83, 87.

4. Phrynichos' contribution is impossible even to begin to speculate about; however, the interaction between them is clear, and therefore, for the purposes of reconstructing the basic parameters of early fifth-century tragedy (other than in the areas, like the setting, in which Phrynichos' contribution can be separated) Phrynichos' contribution can be subsumed into an intertextual construct "Aeschylus."

5. Because of obvious limitations of space, I cannot offer systematic readings of the Aeschylean tragedies under discussion.

6. I will not consider *Prometheus* at all; in my view it is not Aeschylean, and its consideration would introduce distortions into the discusion. On the question of the authorship of *Prometheus* see Schmid 1929; Herington 1970 (defense of authenticity); Griffith 1977; Taplin 1975, 184-6; Taplin 1977, 460-9 (who argues against the assumption that this play was part of a trilogy with *Prometheus Lyomenos* and *Prometheus Pyrphoros*); West 1979, 130-48 considers the whole trilogy non-Aeschylean; West 1990, 51-72 argues that the author of the trilogy was probably Aeschylus' son Euphorion. Cf. also bibl. on the authorship of *Prometheus* in Des Bouvrie 1993, 187-8 n. 2.

7. On the date of *Suppliants* cf. *TrGF* iii T 70 (= Did. C 6 [*TrGF* i p. 44]); Taplin 1977, 195-8 expresses some reservations with regard to the generally accepted view that *Hiketides*,

Chapter 1: "Starting" with Aeschylus

Aigyptioi, and *Danaides* formed a tragic trilogy, with *Amymone* as the satyr play of a full tetralogy (for it is *Danaides* and *Amymone* that the papyrus fragment dates, to sometime between 467 and 456). In my view the reservations are not justified (see below).

8. Cf. Taplin 1977, 194-5, 207, 209.
9. Cf. bibliography on this view in Garvie 1969, 107 n. 5.
10. Cf. esp. Garvie 1969, 106-40. There is much which I find convincing, and from which I have learnt, in this excellent discussion. It is only with the notion that the early chorus sang songs juxtaposed to brief speeches and the arguments connected with it that I disagree, and this is why I am here focussing on the negative rather than the multifaceted positive. This view is accepted by Conacher 1996, 76, 150.
11. Cf. Garvie 1969, 139.
12. Cf. e.g. Taplin 1977, 86-7.
13. Taplin 1977, 207.
14. Taplin 1977, 207-8.
15. Cf. Taplin 1977, 209.
16. Garvie 1969, 106-7.
17. Garvie 1969, 106.
18. Garvie 1969, 106-7.
19. Cf. Garvie 1969, 109.
20. Cf. also on this Garvie 1969, 120-3; Taplin 1977, 61-5.
21. Aeschylus' *Myrmidones* also began with marching anapaests (cf. Taplin e.g. 1977, 64, 424; West 1990, 8) and so did *Prometheus Lyomenos*, which West considers non-Aeschylean (cf. n. 6 above). *Myrmidones* was probably early, if it is right that some elements on some early fifth-century vases reflect the influence of this trilogy. On the relationship between Aeschylus' trilogy *Myrmidones, Nereides,* and *Phryges* or *Hektoros Lytra,* see Boardman 1976, 13-4 (with earlier bibliography), whose (somewhat tentative) doubts about the similarities being due to Aeschylean influence on vases do not appear to me to be justified in this case. It is, of course, only a matter of reflection, partial inspiration channelled through the idiom of vase painting that is at issue here. Taplin (1977, 63) calls the *Myrmidones* "probably . . . an early play." If *Prometheus Lyomenos* is Aeschylean we do not know its date; if it is not the author was imitating the Aeschylean choral opening.
22. Cf. Garvie 1969, 121 ("Thespis" is how he puts it). Cf. also Taplin 1977, 61-5.
23. On this question cf. Winnington-Ingram 1961, 141-52=Winnington-Ingram 1983, 55-72; Garvie 1969, 163-233; West 1990, 169-72. Taplin 1977, 195-8 expresses some reservations with regard to the generally accepted view that *Hiketides, Aigyptioi,* and *Danaides* formed a tragic trilogy, with *Amymone* as the satyr play of a full tetralogy (for it is *Danaides* and *Amymone* that the papyrus fragment dates, to sometime between 467 and 456). In my view, the reservations are not justified. I see no problem with envisaging a middle play *Aigyptioi* or *Aigyptos,* focussed on the sons of Aigyptos who were the chorus; the murder would have taken place between *Aigyptioi* and *Danaides* (as suggested by Winnington-Ingram 1961, 142 = 1983, 57-8). As to the notion that this would be the only trilogy known to have

had the same chorus in two plays, *Hiketides* and *Danaides*, as Taplin himself admits (196-7), Aeschylus "may well have had a special artistic point in bringing back the same chorus contrary to convention." Indeed, the transformation of the frightened suppliant virgins of the first play to the murderous wives/brides of the third seems to be sufficient motive. This, we saw, this was a period of experimentation in the tragic forms. Some scholars (cf. Winnington-Ingram 1961, 146=Winnington-Ingram 1983, 64; Gantz 1993, 204-5) think that the Danaids were the main chorus in *Aigyptioi* also, and that the tragedy took its name from the supplementary chorus, which is what, on this hypothesis the sons of Aigyptos were (Winnington-Ingram 1983, 64), or because they were the prime agents in the drama and the difficulty in finding yet a third title to refer to the same chorus (Gantz 1993, 204). The latter hypothesis seems to me somewhat culturally determined, as even I can think of titles referring to the Danaids in the same modality as *Hiketides* and *Danaides*, such as, to give but two examples, *Metics* or *Parthenoi*. With regard to the notion that the sons of Aigyptos were the supplementary chorus, this may well be right; but in that case why, once again, was the title not taken from the main chorus as in the first and the last tragedy? It seems to me much more plausible that rather than the chorus of the sons of Aigyptos entering late, the tragedy was focussed on them. This would fit both the title of the play and the fact that in Greek mentality a marriage had at its center a transaction between the bride's father (or other *kyrios*) and the groom. On the chorus of *Aigyptioi* see esp. Garvie 1969, 191-7; 201-2.

24. Cf. a survey of sources for the myth and of proposed reconstructions of the trilogy in Garvie 1969, 163-233; cf. also Conacher 1996, 104-9.

25. On the title see Garvie 1969, 189-90; on the reconstruction of the plot see Winnington-Ingram 1983, 55-72, esp. 56-66 (=Winnington-Ingram 1961, 141-52 esp. 142, 145-6, 147); Garvie 1969, 197-204; West 1990, 169-72. Cf. also Gantz 1993, 204-5.

26. Cf. Winnington-Ingram 1983, 65-6; Garvie 1969, 225-6; cf. also Gantz 1993, 205.

27. *TrGF* iii F 44 Cf. Winnington-Ingram 1961, 142=Winnington-Ingram 1983, 58.

28. Winnington-Ingram 1961, 143-4 = Winnington-Ingram 1983, 58-61.

29. On the reasons for the Danaids' rejection of marriage to their cousins cf. Garvie 1969, 215-23; also Winnington-Ingram 1983, 59-60 (= Winnington-Ingram 1961, 143-4); Zeitlin 1990b, 106; 113 n. 7; Zeitlin 1996, 125; 128; cf. 153.

30. Up to a point this tragedy, more the trilogy as a whole; cf. esp. Zeitlin 1990b, 103-15; Zeitlin 1992, 203-52= 1996, 123-171.

31. To illustrate the fact that this is not a loaded and prejudiced formulation let me quote, as an example, Taplin 1977, 193: "In Aeschylus' *Hiketides*, *Eumenides* and Sophocles' *Oedipus at Colonus* the entry of the suppliant is also his arrival at a particular holy place and his approach to the sacred ground is itself the beginning of the supplication. . . . The very first stage movement of the play (i.e. Aeschylus' *Suppliants*) represents the Danaids arrival, the rest of the play will be about the circumstances in which they will leave the sacred place, and the very last movement of the play is their departure to the city."

32. Since they describe as *asebe* any wedding with the sons of Aegyptos (9).

Chapter 1: "Starting" with Aeschylus

33. On the textual problems here see West 1990, 126-7.
34. On this reading cf. West 1990, 127.
35. This is a long and complex story that is beyond my scope here; I have discussed this question in Sourvinou-Inwood 1991, 65-70, 85-7, and passim.
36. On the staging of this play see Wiles 1997, 195-7.
37. The religious basis of their supplication, which was in any case obvious to the ancient audience, is stressed again and again; e.g. by Pelasgos 413-6.
38. Cf. 347: *barys ge mentoi Zenos hikesiou kotos*. Cf. also 616 (*hikesiou Zenos koton*), where the danger of incurring the wrath of Zeus was a decisive factor in the decision to grant them asylum, a fact stressed at 624 (*Zeus d' epekranen telos*).
39. Scott 1984, 165.
40. On the text of 598-9 see West 1990, 147-8.
41. They are mentioned in a variety of ways, as gods in a straightforward way, or in different tropes.
42. Given the existence of the cult of Artemis Hecate in the religious reality of the Athenians and other Greeks (cf. e.g. Henrichs 1996b, 672), this is how the audience would have understood the word, as an epithet of Artemis.
43. Scott 1984, 165.
44. On the text and its meaning see West 1990, 164-5.
45. Cf. Taplin 1977, 239.
46. On the text and its meaning see West 1990, 167-8.
47. Whether a supplementary chorus of handmaidens, or a different supplementary chorus, or one of two hemichoruses (cf. the discussion in Taplin 1977, 230-38; cf. West 1990, 167).
48. Garvie 1969, 43 n. 2.
49. Garvie 1969, 43 n. 2.
50. Garvie 1969, 93.
51. Garvie 1969, 92-3.
52. On the Eumolpid *exegetai* cf. Clinton 1974, 89-92; Parker 1996, 295-7.
53. Cf. Winnington-Ingram 1983, 63-4 (=Winnington-Ingram 1961, 145-6).
54. Cf. the discussion in Garvie 1969, 204-11, 224-33; cf. also Winnington-Ingram 1983, 66-70. Garvie 1969, 206-8 sets out the serious objections against the hypothesis that there was a trial of Hypermestra in the *Danaides*. Garvie 1969, 208-10 discusses the difficulties with having a trial of the other Danaids. I would like to make a tentative suggestion starting with the ending which is widely accepted. If it is right that the Danaids became reconciled to marriage—probably through the intervention of Aphrodite—the problem arises of who the grooms would be and where they would come from. My suggestion is that it is the version of the myth reported in Schol. Eur. *Orestes* 872 (a), which brings into play a group of males, whether present on stage, or simply conceptually present, that reflects the Aeschylean *Danaides*. (This is different from the version in Phrynichos *TrGF* i 3 F 1 according to which Aigyptos had gone to Argos with his sons, as he had in Euripides fr. 846).

According to this Aigyptos comes to Argos to punish the murder, Danaos wants to fight, but Lynkeus convinces them to settle the dispute, and they set the best of the Egyptians and the best of the Argives as judges. (Cf. also Eur. *Orestes* 872-3: Danaos gathered the people *dikas didont'*, making amends, or granting arbitration, to Aigyptos). If this was the Aeschylean version, it would solve the problem of how the Danaids' grooms would materialize out of the blue; they could have been a supplementary chorus, or simply a mute group, whose identity had been established before they were needed as bridegrooms. For the notion that only an announcement of marriages to be arranged signified the Danaids marriages to be (cf. Garvie 1969, 226) would provide a weaker integration into normality than the presence of a group of males as husbands-to-be of the chorus, after the latter have been purified. If, as is more likely, the adjudication took place off stage (cf. Winnington-Ingram 1983, 68-9, who is thinking of a somewhat different trial, an assembly of Argives off stage, which, he thinks, had been asked by Danaos to condemn Hypemestra, but instead condemned the polluted Danaos and the other Danaids) Aphrodite may have made her speech to the Danaids, after the verdict. Another argument that may be in favor of this version being Aeschylean is that Lynkeus played a conciliating role, and this would fit the fact that in this Aeschylean tragedy, and, it would seem, trilogy, in which persuasion, *peitho*, is an extremely important, indeed crucial, concept. (Cf. Winnington-Ingram 1983, 59, 62, 71; Zeitlin 1996, 136-43, 158, 170.)

55. Herodotos 2.171 says that the Danaids introduced the Thesmophoria from Egypt and taught the rites to the Pelasgian women, and this has been taken by some scholars (see bibliography in Garvie 1969, 227 n. 6) to suggest that the trilogy ended with the foundation of the Thesmophoria. Garvie 1969, 227-8 does not agree with this view. But he appears to underestimate the association of the festival, at least in Athens, with the state of married woman, an association which creates a direct link between the situation of the Danaids who are to be reconciled to marriage and the festival. A strong case in favor of the view that the trilogy ended with the foundation of the Thesmophoria has recently been made by Zeitlin (Zeitlin 1996, 163-9). Cf. also Detienne 1989, 43-4, 56-7.

56. Zeitlin 1996, 163-71.
57. On Thesmophoria cf. Deubner 1969, 50-60; Parke 1977, 82-8.
58. On Persephone as a paradigm of marriage cf. Sourvinou-Inwood 1991, 67-8, 152-75 passim.
59. Cf. Lloyd-Jones 1990, 267; Garvie 1969, 106.
60. Cf. Lloyd-Jones 1990, 276.
61. Cf. above.
62. Cf. e.g. Conacher 1996, xi.
63. Cf. e.g. *TrGF* iii T 100, 102.
64. Cf. *TrGF* iii T 1.58-9=*TrGF* iv T 98 (Aeschylus or Sophocles introduced the third actor); *TrGF* iv T 1.20-3, T 95, T 97.
65. Cf. Garvie 1969, 139.
66. I shall return to the question of tragic choruses in III.2.

Chapter 1: "Starting" with Aeschylus 257

67. For the relationship between tragedy and historical events cf. most recently Pelling 1997a, 1-9 (with bibliography); cf. also on the play in general Hall 1996b, 1-25 (with a survey of views and bibliography).

68. On the presentation of the Persians as other in the *Persai* cf. Hall 1989, 57-100. On the ideology and Athenian self-presentation Pelling 1997, 9-19; Hall 1996b, 11-13; 16-7.

69. The relationship between self and other in the *Persai* is subtly discussed by Pelling 1997, 13-19.

70. I have discussed this question in Sourvinou-Inwood 1997c, 296 cf. 294-6.

71. In the *Persai* the events are presented in terms of divine causation: cf. Goldhill 1988, 189 and n. 4 with earlier bibliography. Cf. also Buxton 1988, 42 on divine motivation and human motivation.

72. As Lloyd-Jones (1971, 88) put it, in *Persai* the defeat of Xerxes is the punishment of hybris by Zeus and Dike (cf. 88-9). The privileging of modern perceptions sometimes intrudes in the assessment of this state of affairs: Conacher 1996, 8, having rightly said that the theme of the play is "the demonstration of divine nemesis," then calls this "the ethical theme," marginalizing its central religious dimension.

73. Hdt. 4.83, 85.

74. Hdt. 4.89. I shall return to this below.

75. The way Hall 1996b, 15 puts this is that the Greek victory over Persia was divinely sanctioned, "indeed this is the overarching theological argument of the play. The Persian catastrophe is multiply over-determined, for numerous contributory factors are adduced besides the ubiquitous *daimon*." But she has conflated different categories of things when listing those factors (15-6), such as gods, acts offensive to gods, and Xerxes' personal characteristics without considering the relationhips between them. She concludes on this that the gods "became hostile for a complex series of interconnected misdemeanours, and not least because they were the protectors of the city of Athens." My argument is that the tragedy explores the question of the ways in which Persian behavior was assessed by the gods and the relationship of this, and of the contrasting Greek behavior, to the Persian defeat.

76. On the text at line 99 see West 1990, 77-8. This is also the text adopted by Hall 1996b for 99.

77. On *prospitno* see Broadhead 1960, 58 ad 152; Hall 1996b, 119-20 ad loc.

78. Cf. also on this Winnington-Ingram 1983, 13-4.

79. Dareios' own prophecies (discussed in Broadhead 1960, xxi) are based on interpretation. Now that he knows the oracles refer to the present situation, Dareios is interpreting the oracles as a skilled interpreter.

80. And indeed this is how the characters subsequently perceive what happened: cf. e.g. at 361 the messenger speaks of *ton theon phthonon* in connection with Xerxes being deceived before the battle; at 472-3 the Queen says *o stygne daimon, hos ar' epseusas phrenon Persas*. On the concept of the *phthonos* of the gods in the *Persai* see Winnington-Ingram 1983, 7-9.

81. Scholars have commented on the the idealization of Dareios in this tragedy; cf. e.g. Broadhead 1960, xvii-xviii. But what I am interested in is what meanings would have been created by the audience, who would have made sense of the presentation of Dareios in this tragedy through their own assumptions, which included knowledge of Dareios' historical actions. In my view, they would have made sense of the idealization as located in Persian perceptions; the persona of Dareios' ghost is a more complex matter which will be discussed below.

82. Cf. e.g. 345-7; 532-4. Cf. also Broadhead 1960, 116-7 ad 345-6.

83. Cf. e.g. Winnington-Ingram 1983, 15.

84. On the raising of Dareios' ghost cf. also Broadhead 1960, xxxvi-viii; 302-90; 156-72 ad 598-680.

85. Cf. Hall 1989, 89-93; Hall 1996b, 15.

86. The question of the divinity of Dareios in the *Persai* is discussed in Hall 1989, 90-93.

87. Cf. Pelling 1997a, 14 and n. 63; Taplin 1977, 115.

88. As Hall 1989, 70 notes, Dareios gives a theological explanation for the disaster in distinctively Greek terms; cf. Broadhead 1960, xxix; Pelling 1997a, 15-6.

89. If one applies pedantic logic, the prophecies would appear too detailed to be simply the result of interpreting oracles, the meaning of which had been unclear before. But the audience would not have applied such logic in the process of making sense of the tragedy.

90. The contrast between land warfare pursued by Dareios and sea warfare associated with Xerxes (Rosenbloom 1993, 190-1) would not have corresponded with the Athenians' knowledge either, but this would probably not have registered as strongly as the other conflicts—whether or not Rosenbloom (1993, 190-2) is right that the presentation of the Persians in *Persai* would have recalled, in this and in other respects, the Athenian experience. On the presentation of Dareios' career in *Persai* cf. also Conacher 1996, 29-30.

91. Cf. most recently, Pelling 1997a, 15.

92. Thracian Bosporos: Hdt 4.83, 85; Danube: Hdt. 4.89.

93. Winnington-Ingram 1983, 13-5.

94. Cf. on this lamentation Else 1977, 75-80.

95. This has nothing to do with the old question whether or not *Persai* is really tragedy. Of course it is tragedy (cf. e.g. Broadhead 1960, xv-xviii; Hall 1996b, 16-9); what I am concerned with here is what early tragedy was like.

96. Cf. on this Hutchinson 1985, xliii-xliv, 209-11.

97. It was, of course, a tetralogy, but I am only interested in the tragedies here. On the tetralogy cf. Hutchinson 1985, xvii-xxx. On *Laios* see *TrGF* iii pp. 231-2; on *Oidipous* see *TrGF* iii pp. 287-8.

98. Cf. Hutchinson 1985, 55-7 ad 78-181.

99. Cf. Hutchinson 1985, 55 ad 78-181. On the staging of the play cf. also Wiles 1997, 197-200.

100. For example, in the messenger speech at 42-8.

Chapter 1: "Starting" with Aeschylus 259

101. Cf. the discussion in Hutchinson 1985, 178-81. On this lamentation and the beginning of the funeral procession cf. now Kavoulaki forthcoming.
102. Cf. Hutchinson 1985, 60 ad 87; 67 ad 128-50.
103. Cf. also on this modality chapter I.2.
104. On the descriptions of the shields and their meanings in the context of the play see Vidal-Naquet 1986a, 115-147; see also Hutchinson 1985, 103-7 with further bibliography; Conacher 1996, 47-51.
105. Cf. Rosenbloom 1993, 188-9.
106. In my view, the notion (cf. Winnington-Ingram 1983, 52) that the Athenian audience would have seen in *Septem* a dramatization of the notion of a *genos* endangering the polis, reflecting the political process of the Athenian polis disengaging from the power of the aristocratic *gene*, is not convincing. It is only in abstract and from the viewpoint of a modern perspective that the two may seem related. The ancient audience's perceptual filters, and the two tragedies that had preceded this, would have directed their reception in entirely different directions.
107. See 699-701; cf. also Hutchinson 1985, 157 ad 698-701.
108. Hutchinson 1985, 160 ad 719.
109. Cf. Fraenkel 1950, vol. ii.57 and n. 1; cf. p. 27 ad 40-103.
110. On this hymn cf. Fraenkel 1950, vol. ii.112-4.
111. See e.g. 396, 462-3, 469-70, 478. In this notion of religious references I also include religious language, tropes based on religious concepts, and so on. The second stasimon (681-781) is also full of religious references of various kinds (698, 701-16, 735-6, 748-9, 770-76), as is the third (990-1, 1015-6, 1018-29).
112. In Sourvinou-Inwood forthcoming.
113. I first made this connection in Sourvinou-Inwood 1971, 340, and, in a more developed form, in Sourvinou-Inwood 1988, 132-3.
114. 509ff. On *daimones . . . antelioi* (519) see Fraenkel 1950, ii. 264-5 ad loc.
115. At 973-4; cf. on this Fraenkel 1950, ii. 440-1 ad 973. Agamemnon's speech (810ff), in which he said that it was right that he should first address the gods who had helped him, did not, I believe, constitute a prayer in the eyes of the audience. It was a speech of thanksgiving, not a ritual prayer. The gods a major concern in his speech also at 844-6.
116. See esp. 1489-96 = 1513-20, 1537-50.
117. 1431-6; cf. on this Fraenkel 1950, iii. pp. 674-5 ad loc.
118. 1601-3 (and a reference to it at 1565-9).
119. On the text of the opening lines of *Choephoroi* see West 1990, 229-34.
120. On which cf. Garvie 1986, 122-5 ad loc.
121. 783ff. Cf. Garvie 1986, 255 ad 783-837.
122. Cf. on this Garvie 1986, 293-4 ad 899, 900, 901, 902.
123. Cf. on this Garvie 1986, 303-4 ad 935-71.
124. Garvie 1986, 340 ad 1035 comments that either Orestes or an attendant brought in the suppliant's bough when Orestes entered. Taplin 1977, 359 thinks that when he en-

tered Orestes had probably held a sword in one hand and the suppliant's bough in the other, a view with which I agree.

125. Undoubtedly to be understood as part of the original oracular response.

126. On this final scene cf. also Taplin 1977, 359-61.

127. The role of the Delphic Apollo in the *Oresteia* has been discussed by Roberts 1984; Bierl 1994, 82-92. Cf. below passim for some important aspects of this role as I see them.

128. On the relationship between the Erinyes and the Eumenides and on the cult of the Semnai Theai/Eumenides see now the definitive studies by Henrichs: Henrichs 1991, 161-201, esp. 164-8, 171-9; Henrichs 1994, 36-54. On the Erinyes in epic and tragedy cf. also Padel 1992, 164-92.

129. Cf. Sommerstein 1989, 33.

130. Cf. Sommerstein 1989, 33, 123 ad 235-98.

131. I discussed this myth in Sourvinou-Inwood 1991, 217-43. On the version in *Eumenides* cf. esp. 232-3.

132. See bibliography in Sourvinou-Inwood 1991, 242 n. 68. Cf. also Bowie 1993b, 14-5.

133. Ephoros *FGrH* 70 F 31b; cf. Sommerstein 1989, 81-2 ad 10. On this passage cf. also Bowie 1993b, 15-6.

134. Cf. Sommerstein 1989, 94 ad 64. Hermes was not present on the stage: Taplin 1977, 364-5; Sommerstein 1989, 93-4 ad 85-7.

135. If it is right that 85-7 should be transposed (cf. Sommerstein 1989, 93-4 ad 85-7; Taplin 1977, 363-4).

136. Cf. Sourvinou-Inwood 1991, 232-3.

137. As manifested, for example, in the festival of the Anthesteria, in one of the rituals at the Choes and its aetiological myth (see Hamilton 1992, 15-26) and in one of the versions of the Aiora myth (see Kearns 1989, 167). On Orestes and Athens cf. also Kearns 1989, 190. On the Anthesteria and the *Oresteia* see Bowie 1993, 22-4.

138. Cf. Henrichs 1994/5, 60-65; cf. also Wilson and Taplin 1993, 306ff.

139. Henrichs 1994/5, 61.

140. Cf. Henrichs 1994/5, 62-3, 64.

141. Cf. 328-33=341-6.

142. The relationship between the Erinyes' binding song in Eumenides and Athenian curse tablets aiming at affecting, at binding, one's opponent's ability to think clearly and speak effectively in court has been discussed by Faraone 1985, 150-54.

143. Cf. Sommerstein 1989, 221-26 for a survey of the discussion on the question of how many jurors there were and whether Athena voted as one of the jurors. I am not focussing on this debate from the viewpoint of the relevance of the trial scene to the contemporary political reality concerning the Areopagus because I cannot, for reasons of space, encompass a discussion of the political resonances dimension of tragedy. I will only say that, in my view, problematization affecting political matters in tragedy did not have, in the eyes of the ancient audience, the centrality often assumed by modern critics. They were interested in the modern echoes and resonances, but in their eyes these tragedies involved a lot

Chapter 1: "Starting" with Aeschylus

of other problematizations; and, in my view, the "political" was not perceived to be as important as the religious. Indeed, in *Eumenides* the political debate does not effect a solution, because it does not bring reconciliation. It is in, and through, the religious dimension that the integration and reconciliation takes place.

144. On the second stasimon cf. Lloyd-Jones 1971, 92-3; Sommerstein 1989, 171-2 ad 490-565.

145. Cf. on this passage Sommerstein 1989, 236-8 ad loc. On the Argive alliance in the world of the audience cf. Sommerstein 1989, 31.

146. 780-7=810-17.

147. As well as making a veiled threat that she may use Zeus' thunderbolt against them at 826-9; cf. also Sommerstein 1989, 246 ad loc.

148. 907-9; cf. Sommerstein 1989, 258 ad 907-9.

149. As Lloyd-Jones 1971, 92 puts it, "they sing a majestic hymn of benediction upon the city."

150. On the blessings cf. the discussion in Sommerstein 1989, 260-2 ad 916-1020.

151. On the question of who sings 1032-47 cf. West 1990, 292-5; and Kavoulaki forthcoming.

152. On this procession see Kavoulaki forthcoming.

153. Cf. on this Kavoulaki forthcoming; cf. also Sommerstein 1989, 279 ad 1024.

154. Cf. esp. Kavoulaki forthcoming; on the Panathenaia cf. also Bowie 1993b, 27-8, 30.

155. Kavoulaki forthcoming.

156. By Headlam 1906, 268-77.

157. Cf. also above chapter II.1.

158. On another, not unrelated, aspect of this tragedy, its economy, Winnington-Ingram commented that it is "austerely archaic" in its use of actors (Winnington-Ingram 1983, 73).

159. Cf. a brief survey of opinion on politics and the *Oresteia* in Bowie 1993b, 10-2. I must however, signal my position by noting my disagreement with Meier 1993, 110, 112-3, 114-6, who pursues parallels between the tragedy and political events that implicitly end up by privileging this alleged political discourse above all other aspects.

160. Sommerstein 1989, 22-3.

161. Sommerstein 1989, 23.

162. Sommerstein 1989, 23 n. 78.

163. Lloyd-Jones 1971, 88.

164. On Athena speaking the will of Zeus see Winnington-Ingram 1983, 126-7.

165. On which cf. Sommerstein 1989, 20, 23.

166. I discuss this further in Sourvinou-Inwood 1997d, 10-1.

167. Taplin 1977, 458-9 and n. 2; cf. 322-3. On this use of the *skene* in general see Gould in *CHCL* 13. On the *skene* as internal space and its relationship with outside space: Padel 1990, 343, 354-65. The *skene* and the meanings of its inner space are now also discussed in Wiles 1997, 161-74.

168. Taplin 1977, 452-9, cf. esp. 454-5.

169. Personal communication.

170. Cf. the structure which Plutarch (*Moralia* 418A) calls *kalias*, which can mean 'hut' or 'shrine', and Strabo (ix.3.12) calls *skene*, that was erected for the festival of the Septerion at Delphi, and represented, according to Plutarch, a palace, which was burnt down in the course of the ritual. Cf. also on this above chapter II.2.

171. Cf. esp. Gebhard 1974, 428-40.

172. Cf. Sommerstein 1989, 33.

173. Pollux 4.128.

174. Cf. an illustration of a reconstruction in Travlos 1988, 135 fig. 158.

175. For the ritual enactment of the myth of Persephone at the Eleusinian Mysteries cf. above II.2 with bibliography.

176. Cf. Mylonas 1961, 83-91, 261-79; cf. also Clinton 1974, 46-7. Clinton 1992, 89 and 126-32 has revived the old theory that the Anaktoron is to be identified with the Telesterion (cf. on the Anaktoron within the Telesterion Mylonas 1961, 78-88). Mylonas 1961, 85-7 had already argued against this theory, and I do not find Clinton's reformulation more convincing. I cannot here set out a systematic critique which would need both a lengthy critical part (to explain, for example, why, in my view, the usual interpretation of Plutarch *Moralia* 81D-E, which assumes the *anaktoron* [*anaktora*] is inside the Telesterion is the only one that can make sense in the context) and a positive one. I will simply point out that, first, some of the arguments Clinton adduces to support this interpretation have already been criticized by Mylonas, such as on his testimonium 5 (Mylonas 1961, 86)—to which it may be worth adding that what would have been perceived as impiety would have been erecting a throne for a hetaira by the Anaktoron, inside the Telesterion, where thrones of priestly personnel are in "normal" Greek temples, not outside the Telesterion; and even if she was in a good position to see the hierophant emerging from the Telesterion, this was hardly worth much compared to the things that would have gone on inside, hardly worth alienating opinion for. Second, the fact that according to *IG* II² 3764 a *hierophantis* is said to have revealed the *teletai* of the goddesses *par' anaktora Deous* (a description that Clinton himself in 1974, 89 correctly translates as 'beside the anaktora of D.') entails that the Anaktoron was a structure inside the Telesterion; for if it had meant 'by the Telesterion' the revelation would have taken place outside, which is in conflict both with what we know of the cult and with its ritual logic. The revelation of the *teletai* would have taken place inside the Telesterion; this was surely what the Hall of Initiations was for. Clinton 1992, 89 and 131 no 12 refers to this inscription but does not explain this point. Then, besides some wholly inconclusive testimonia (such as his no 7, *IG* II² 1552a), which seem to me to point against Clinton's theory rather than in its favor, most of the arguments adduced to support it disappear, once it is realized that they are based on a misreading of tropes, the mistaking of, above all, *pars pro toto* metonymies, aimed at stressing proximity to the most sacred part of the complex, for literal language. It may also be worth adding that, in my view, the fragment of Aelian (fr. 10) which says that only the hierophant was permitted to enter the Anaktoron, which would be consistent with the Anaktoron being a structure

Chapter 1: "Starting" with Aeschylus

inside the Telesterion, but not with it being the same as the Telesterion, cannot convincingly be interpreted to mean that this prohibition only pertained to part of the ceremony only. It is true that the text is not wholly secure, but in its present state it points in the same direction as a variety of other evidence. This convergence, I believe, builds up a case against the identification of the Anaktoron with the Telesterion.

177. Cf. Mylonas 1961, 84.

178. Cf. Mylonas 1961, 86. Cf. also supra n. 174.

179. Cf. Philostratos *Lives of Sophists* 600.20; cf. on this Clinton 1974, 40, 46.

180. Cf. e.g. *IG* II² 3811; *IG* II² 3709. Clinton 1974, 46-7.

181. In chapter II.2 I had suggested the possibility that the Eleusinian Mysteries may have offered one of the models that helped shape the developments out of the hymnal nexus associated with the sacrifice of a *tragos* into the earliest forms of tragedy, but I want to leave this possibility out of the argument, for otherwise there would be a danger of circularity.

182. On the *pathos* experienced by the initiates, sharing the suffering of Demeter and Kore and eventually their joy: Burkert 1987, 69, 89-90, 114; Clinton 1992, 94-5.

183. I discussed this double nature of the Eleusinian Mysteries in Sourvinou-Inwood 1997b, 144-53.

184. Some modern scholars have argued that there are Mysteric allusions in the *Oresteia*, above all to the Eleusinian Mysteries; cf. bibliography and brief discussion in Bowie 1993b, 24-5 (to which add Seaford 1994, 373-4); Bowie himself sets out a case for the Mysteries being a metaphor for Orestes' experience.

185. Athenaeus i. 21 D=*TrGF* iii pp. 66-7 T 103. Mylonas 1961, 87 accepts this as fact.

186. *TrGF* iii pp. 63-4 T 93a-d, 94.

187. Cf. on this story Lefkowitz 1981, 68, 173.

188. The distancing of which I discussed here and in chapter I.2.

III.2. From Phrynichos to Euripides: the Tragic Choruses

In chapter III.1 I discussed some questions relating to Aeschylean choruses, that also pertained to earlier tragic choruses. In this chapter I shall discuss some further aspects of fifth-century tragic choruses.

The chorus is a collectivity and represents a collectivity. But what sort of collectivity do fifth-century tragic choruses represent? In Aeschylus' *Persai, Septem,* and *Agamemnon* the chorus is a segment of a community, polis, or nation. Their identity is derived from the fact that they are such a segment, Argive elders or Theban *parthenoi*. In Aeschylus' *Suppliants* and *Eumenides* the collectivity of the chorus is not a segment of a community, but a particular group with its own identity, the Danaids and the Erinyes. This was probably also the case in Aeschylean tragedies like *Trophoi*, where the chorus appear to have been the nurses of Dionysos, and *Toxotides*, where the chorus were the attendant nymphs of Artemis. But in the case of *Suppliants* this group with a distinct mythological identity is also a group defined by their ritual role. In *Choephoroi* the chorus consists of slave women, defined by their ritual action of bringing chthonic libations. In Sophocles' surviving tragedies all choruses are segments of a community: elders of Colonus, in *Oidipous at Colonus*, elders of other poleis in *Oidipous Tyrannos* and *Antigone*, Salaminian sailors, in *Ajax*, Neoptolemos' sailors in *Philoctetes*, Greek women of other poleis in *Trachiniai* and *Electra*. In some of Sophocles' fragmentary tragedies the chorus appears to have been a segment of the community, in some it is not possible to judge, while in the case of *Manteis* it would appear to a group of prophets, that is, a group defined by their ritual role.[1]

Of the seventeen surviving Euripidean tragedies only the chorus of *Suppliants* has a distinct mythological identity. But this chorus, as well as having a distinct mythological identity, is also a group with a specific ritual role, that of suppliants, but also that of mourning mothers, whose duty is to perform the lament and other appropriate rites for their sons.[2] In eleven tragedies the chorus represents a segment of a community in the straightforward sense.[3] In one, *Bacchai*, the chorus can be seen as a kind of segment of a conceptual community, the community of Dionysiac worshippers; but they are, of course, also, and above all, a group defined by its performance of a ritual. In the remaining four, *Phoenissai, Iphigeneia in Tauris, Ion,* and *Helen,* the chorus is not quite a segment of a community, because they are a particular group, but they do not have a distinct mythological identity; they are simply defined by their role. The chorus of *Ion* also de facto performed a ritual role, in that they are in a *theoria* to the Delphic sanctuary. In the case of the chorus of *Phoenissai* it is their ritual action, their being sent as *hierodouloi* to Delphi, that gives them a specific identity. In this they are comparable to the chorus in Aeschylus' *Choephoroi*, a chorus of slave women who were defined by their ritual action. In the other three Euripidean tragedies the chorus are attendants of the main female character, and their main role is above all with reference to that character. These tragedies are late, and perhaps this type of chorus represents a particular Euripidean choice at a particular stage in his career. A chorus with a particular ritual identity is also found in early Euripides: his *Cretans* had a chorus of priests.

It would appear, then, that the chorus representing a segment of a community is the predominant schema in tragedy. The distinct mythological identity seems to have been a very rare occurrence, mostly clustered in Aeschylus' tragedies. The schema "group defined by its performance of a ritual role" is also found. This state of affairs would fit excellently my reconstruction of the generation of tragedy and its beginnings. In my reconstruction the tragic chorus began as a segment of the Athenian community representing the whole polis, and when prototragedy developed into a mimetic genre the chorus began by representing a segment of another community, in the heroic past. The chorus with a distinct mythological identity, which can be made sense of as a development out of the "segment of a community" type of chorus, may have been, like the contemporary setting, an experiment that did not become the preferred option—though it was not totally abandoned. The group defined by its ritual identity schema can also be seen to fit excellently within the parameters of the generation and development of early tragedy as suggested here, focussed on religion, ritual, and religious problematization.

If so, the fact that the chorus representing a collectivity that is a segment of a community remained the predominant option in Greek tragedy for most of the fifth century would suggest that, in that respect at least, the parameters shaping choices (and shaped by assumptions about the role of the chorus) had not changed drastically, at least not with regard to the perception that a chorus representing a segment of a community fulfilled the perceived requirements for a tragic chorus.

In order to try to extract as much information as possible to try to reconstruct the filters through which the ancient audience perceived the chorus we need to reconsider certain things that we take for granted, such as the fact that some tragedies take their name from the chorus and others do not. Whatever the precise significance of this fact, there can be little doubt that in the former tragedies the chorus was in some way focussed on; at the very minimum in the sense that a tragedy

Chapter 2: From Phrynichos to Euripides 267

called *Hiketides* would have been thought of as a tragedy in which the chorus were suppliants, *Trachiniai* that in which the chorus took on the persona of women of Trachis, *Persai* that in which the chorus took on the persona of Persians. Indeed, I would suggest, they would have been thought of as the tragedy in which the chorus the polis has put forward in honor of Dionysos takes on the persona and role of suppliants, women of Trachis, Persians.

We need to consider whether there is any significant pattern in the usage of titles, any shift in that usage, and if there is, whether that change is significant and how.[4] Obviously, the last two questions are closely related, since the answer to the first depends on the answer to the second, and both are vulnerable to cultural determination. However, it is no less culturally determined, and a strategy conducive to a distortion of the ancient realities, simply to assume that there is no pattern in these titles, or that the pattern has no significance. It may appear superficially more rigorous to do so, because, we saw, the apparently sceptical approach appears deceptively more rigorous, but in reality it is simply a licence for the unfettered—as opposed to maximally controlled—intrusion of modern assumptions.

Among the few titles ascribed to the earliest tragedians a few are derived from the names of characters, such as *Pentheus*, attributed to Thespis, and *Alope*, to Choirilos, but the validity of this attribution is highly dubious. Such attributions tell us something about later perceptions of early tragedy, rather than reflect earlier reality. It is with Phrynichos and Aeschylus that we begin to be on firm ground.

Of Phrynichos' tragedies we know of five the name of which is derived from the chorus: *Aigyptioi, Danaides, Dikaioi* or *Persai* or *Synthokoi, Pleuroniai, Phoinissai*;[5] of one with two titles, one derived from the name of a character and one from the chorus: *Antaios* or *Libyes*; three tragedies have a name derived from the name of a character: *Aktaion, Alcestis, Tantalos*; and one has a title which indicates its subject: *Miletou Halosis*. The sample is very small; but, for what it is worth, it is clear that a majority of the surviving titles of tragedies by Phrynichos is derived from the chorus, a more substantial majority when we add those with two names, one of which is derived from the chorus.

Of Aeschylus' six surviving tragedies, four, *Persai, Hiketides, Choephoroi, Eumenides,* derive their names from the chorus, while *Agamemnon* and *Septem* do not. Aeschylean tragedies with a title derived from the chorus[6] that have not survived are the following: *Aigyptioi* and *Danaides,* which formed a trilogy with *Hiketides*;[7] *Aitnaiai; Argeioi; Bacchai;* the three tragedies of the *Lykourgeia*: *Edonoi, Bassarai* or *Bassarides,* and *Neaniskoi; Eleusinioi; Heliades*;[8]

268 Part III: Religion and the Fifth-Century Tragedians

Threissai; Hiereiai; Kabeiroi; Kressai; Lemniai or *Lemnioi; Myrmidones*, which forms a trilogy with another tragedy the name of which was also derived from the chorus, *Nereides*, and with a third which has two titles, one derived from the chorus and another denoting the tragedy's subject: *Phryges* or *Hektoros Lytra; Mysoi; Xantriai; Perrhaibides; Propompoi;*[9] *Salaminiai; Toxotides; Trophoi;*[10] *Psychagogoi*. The following tragedies have two titles, one derived from the name of a character and one from the chorus: *Kares* or *Europa; Semele* or *Hydrophoroi; Phryges* or *Hektoros Lytra* has one title derived from the chorus and another denoting the tragedy's subject.[11] Leaving aside the six surviving Aeschylean tragedies, there are, then, at a conservative estimate, twenty-five surviving titles of Aeschylean tragedies which have a name referring to their chorus; in addition, three more have two names, one of which is derived from the chorus. This is about half of the surviving titles of tragedies by Aeschylus.

Of Sophocles' surviving tragedies, only *Trachiniai*, a tragedy the general consensus on which is that it is early,[12] has a title derived from the chorus. Let us now consider the fragmentary tragedies, and those of which only the title survives. Of these there are at most about fifteen with a name derived from the chorus:[13] *Aichmalotides; Kamikioi;*[14] *Kolchides; Lakainai; Larissaioi; Lemniai;*[15] *Mysoi; Poimenes;*[16] *Rhizotomoi;*[17] *Skythai; Skyrioi; Tympanistai;*[18] *Hydrophoroi;*[19] *Phthiotides;*[20] *Phryges.*[21] Then there are five tragedies with two or three names one of which was derived from the chorus: *Manteis* or *Polyidos;*[22] *Atreus* or *Mykenaiai*, which may be the same as one of the three plays by Sophocles called *Thyestes; Dolopes*, which may have been the same as *Phoinix;*[23] *Aithiopes*, which may have been the same as *Memnon*, and perhaps *Mousai*, which may have been the same as *Thamyras* and presumably would have had a chorus of the Muses. There are about sixty-five titles of Sophoclean tragedies derived from the name of a character;[24] there is also a very small number which derive their title from their subject: *Helenes Apaitesis; Helenes Harpage* or *Helenes Gamos; Niptra.*[25]

Because of the uncertainties noted above, including the uncertainties as to the identity of plays with two, or sometimes more, titles, it would be misleading to attempt to give precise numbers or proportions. But what is clear is that this is a different pattern of title usage from that observed in Aeschylus and Phrynichos, since well under one-third of Sophocles' tragedies derive their title from the chorus. And it is possible that three of these (one-fifth of the tragedies with a title derived from the chorus), *Kolchides, Rhizotomoi*, and *Skythai*, may have formed a trilogy.[26] Given the extreme paucity of evidence available for the dating of Sophoclean tragedies, all that, I believe, can be said

Chapter 2: From Phrynichos to Euripides 269

is that there are some reasons for thinking that at least some of the Sophoclean tragedies the title of which was derived from the chorus were early; and to speculate that such tragedies were bunched early in Sophocles' opus.

The situation is more complex in the case of Euripides. Of the surviving Euripidean tragedies four have names derived from the chorus: *Suppliants, Troades, Phoinissai, Bacchai*. Among Euripides' tragedies that have not survived, or of which only fragments have, the following have titles derived from the chorus: *Kressai; Kretes; Skyrioi; Mysoi*.[27] The title of forty-five is derived from the name of a character, and in two cases, *Peliades* and *Temenidai*, it is unclear whether the name is derived from the characters or subject, or the chorus; for though the numbers of the daughters of Pelias and the sons of Temenos were too small for a chorus, we cannot exclude that they had indeed formed the chorus, since there are cases such as Euripides' *Suppliants* and Aeschylus' *Eumenides*, where a small number of mythological characters are multiplied to form the chorus. Of these the *Peliades* at least is a very early tragedy, produced at 455.[28] Of the four tragedies that definitely had titles derived from the chorus, one, *Mysoi*, may not be a Euripidean tragedy.[29] *Kressai* is early, produced at 438,[30] and *Kretes* is almost certainly also early, perhaps near *Kressai* in date.[31]

There can be little doubt, then, that the pattern shows a shift in the choice of titles. From a predominance of titles derived from the chorus in the early period, to a rarity of such titles in later fifth-century tragedy. What little we can glean about the choice of titles by the minor fifth-century tragedians seems to confirm this. In the case of most minor fifth-century tragedians we do not have enough titles of tragedies to attempt even an approximate assessment. The five for which we do have a few titles are Ion, Achaeus, Philocles I, Agathon, and Kritias. Their surviving titles are as follows.[32] Titles of tragedies by Ion:[33] *Agamemnon, Alkmene, Argeioi, Eurytidai, Kaineus* or *Phoinix, Laertes, Mega Drama, Teukros, Phoinix* or *Kaineus, Phoinix 2, Phrouroi*. By Achaeus:[34] *Adrastos, Azanes, Alphesiboia, Erginos, Theseus, Katapeira, Kyknos, Momos, Oidipous, Peirithous, Philoktetes, Phrixos*. By Philocles I: *Erigone, Nauplios, Oidipous, Oineus, Penelope, Priamos, Tereus* or *Epops*. By Agathon:[35] *Aerope, Alkmeon, Anthos* or *Antheus, Thyestes, Mysoi, Telephos*. By Kritias: *Peirithous, Rhadamanthys, Sisyphos, Tennes*. Here also, then, the same pattern as that identified in the case of the major tragedians seems to emerge—though, of course, its reconstruction is less securely based in the case of the minor ones.

Before attempting to assess the significance of this pattern, if any, we need to consider the surviving tragedies. Is there any significance in the use of titles derived from the chorus?

Starting with Aeschylus, the case of *Persai, Hiketides,* and *Eumenides* is straightforward. It cannot be doubted that in *Suppliants* and *Eumenides* the chorus play a major role, in the former that of protagonist. In *Persai* also, with its very extensive choral passages and the chorus' direct emotional involvement, the chorus is very important. It is the collectivity of the Persians that is represented here, by its most honored segment, and this collectivity is set next to the members of the royal family, Atossa, Xerxes, and Dareios' ghost. They are central in the presentation of the disaster of the enemy other. Their role is in every respect much more central than the role of the chorus in *Septem*, who are also emotionally very affected by the action. No tragedy in this trilogy derived its name from the chorus; *Septem* derived it from its subject, *Laios* and *Oidipous*, from the names of their central character.

In the *Oresteia* the titles are a mixture. That of *Eumenides* is correlative with the fundamentally important role of the chorus, that of *Agamemnon* with the centrality of the character of Agamemnon. But what of *Choephoroi*, the chorus of which does not fit the same categories as the other three Aeschylean tragedies the title of which is derived from the chorus? This chorus is not very strongly affected by the action. The chorus in *Choephoroi* by its interference plays a vital part in the plot at 766-73.[36] But is this the full correlative to the choice of title? It may be; or it may be a random choice, though this is not very likely, since the mixture of both types of titles here suggests deliberation over the choice of each. But it is also possible that the greater or lesser role of the chorus may not be the only correlative inspiring a choice of title derived from the chorus. For, like *Suppliants*, this tragedy is named after a chorus defined in terms of its ritual role. So, as the title of *Suppliants* defined it as the tragedy in which the chorus performed a supplication ritual, so *Choephoroi* is that in which the chorus have the role of chthonic libation bearers. As we saw, the chorus consisting of a group defined by their performance of a ritual role is a significant category of fifth-century tragic choruses. This type of naming after the chorus focusses attention on the rite, which is presented as central to the tragedy.

Turning to Sophocles' *Trachiniai,* I cannot see any special aspect of the role of chorus that would explain the choice of a title derived from the chorus. I would like to suggest that this choice of chorus and of title may have been an intertextual reflection of an earlier tragedy, which had dealt with an earlier part of the story of Heracles and Deianeira,

Chapter 2: From Phrynichos to Euripides

Phrynichos' *Pleuroniai*. In my view, Phrynichos' *Pleuroniai* almost certainly dealt with the wooing of Deianeira by Acheloos and her eventual marriage to Heracles, events to which Deianeira refers to in the prologue (6-27) of Sophocles' *Trachiniai*; it seems clear that this tragedy had dealt with events after the death of Meleager,[37] and of these the wooing of Meleager's sister Deianeira by Acheloos, and her eventual marriage to Heracles, are the most significant.[38] If this is right, Phrynichos' *Pleuroniai*, which had dealt with the beginning of the marriage of Heracles and Deianeira, had a chorus consisting of women of Pleuron, where the events took place, which gave it its name, and Sophocles' *Trachiniai*, a tragedy which dealt with the end of Deianeira's and Heracles' life and marriage at Trachis, and which referred to that beginning at its very opening, had a chorus consisting of women of Trachis, where the events were taking place, which gave it its title. I suggest that this is unlikely to have been coincidental. If it is right that Sophocles' choice of title for *Trachiniai* had an intertextual inspiration, the implication would be that, at that time at least, there was no perceived connection between the title of a tragedy being derived from the chorus and a special role for the chorus.

The earliest of the four surviving Euripidean tragedies with titles derived from the chorus is *Suppliants*. The fact that the name is derived from the chorus is correlative with the central role of the chorus in this tragedy. In this it resembles Aeschylus' *Suppliants* and *Eumenides*; it comes near enough to them in the role of the chorus. It is difficult to doubt that Euripides chose the title deliberately, to echo Aeschylus' *Suppliants*, as part of a complex play of intertextuality. As for his latest tragedy with a title derived from the chorus, *Bacchai*, the choice of title can be seen as correlative with the fact that the chorus is of central importance in this play, not least as one visible manifestation of the Dionysiac ritual at the center of the tragedy. It may also not be irrelevant to this choice that *Bacchai* was also the title of a tragedy by Aeschylus,[39] and may also have been the title of a tragedy by Sophocles.[40]

In the case of *Troades* the title is correlative with the fact that the chorus of captive Trojan women play a significant role and are the most visible and powerless victims of war. It is they who represent most vividly the sacked city, which is the focus of the tragedy. Hecabe, the main character, and two other characters, Kassandra and Andromache, were, like the chorus, Trojan Women—in the same way as in Aeschylus' *Choephoroi* Electra was also a *choephoros*, performed the most important part of the chthonic libation rite. The centrality of the chorus of *Troades* becomes sharper when this play is compared to *Hecabe*, where Hecabe is manifoldly, and much more strongly, foregrounded, set off from the chorus in ways that make that collectivity less important than in *Troades*, correlatively with the fact that the main focus there is not on the destruction of the city.

At first glance *Phoinissai*[41] would appear to invalidate this picture that has been emerging so far, that in the extant Euripidean tragedies a title derived from the chorus suggests some sort of centrality of the chorus. *Phoinissai* was produced probably some time between 411 and 409 B.C.[42] The function of this chorus and the reasons for its choice are not unproblematic. Mastronarde[43] argues that Euripides made this choice in order to give the tragedy resonances of parallels with, and causation derived from, the Kadmos story, and also because he liked to concentrate the action, and the strongest emotional stresses, on the actors, and accordingly, favors in general powerless choruses, sympathetic, but not too intimately tied to the fate of the protagonists.[44] The first point is undoubtedly right, though it is the ways in which such resonances worked for the audience that are especially important, and which ultimately, I suggest, invalidate Mastronarde's second point. For not only is it arguable that the chorus might have been perceived to have been de facto intimately tied to the fate of the protagonists, since if Thebes had been sacked they would not necessarily have themselves been unaffected, but also, and most importantly, the chorus (who stress their kinship to the royal family of Thebes)[45] explicitly state in the parodos that, because of this kinship, they share in the Thebans' suffering (245-9). And this affects the audience's perception of the extent to which they are emotionally involved. The chorus is not simply "other" and uninvolved; it is both very foreign to the audience and to the world of the play, and also very close to the world of the play. Their otherness was obvious, and was probably stressed by their costumes. Their nearness and kinship is stressed by their statements. They stress their Phoenician origin, and their close ancestral links to Thebes, and so also the fact that Thebes had been founded by a Phoenician, and that the Theban royal family, this polluted family that has brought disaster to the city, are of Phoenician origin: as Jocasta mentions at lines 5-9: Labdakos, Laios' father, was the grandson of Kadmos.[46]

One of the effects of this choice of chorus was that the Theban royal family appears totally isolated from the collectivity of the Thebans, no segment of which, not even one as noncentral as *parthenoi*, are shown on stage. The collectivity of the Thebans is kept away, and are only presented in others' discourse; of these the most authoritative is Teiresias, and in Teiresias' discourse the collectivity of the Thebans are the victims of the royal family's pollution and doom (867-9; 881-8). Instead, it is a foreign collectivity that is flanking the royal family, stressing the latter's foreignness, and distancing it further from the audience.[47] For the stressing of Thebes' Phoenician connections, of the royal family's Phoenician origin, had the effect of distancing this Thebes, and the events that take place there, even further from Athens.

The fact that (negative) distancing from the world of the audience is important in this tragedy is confirmed by Teiresias' statement at 852ff, that he had just come from Athens, where he has given victory to the Athenians over Eumolpos. Mastronarde is right that this anachronism alludes to the story pattern of patriotic self-sacrifice, evoking Euripides' *Erechtheus*, in order to provide a specific intertextual standard to be applied to Menoikeus' sacrifice, and that it also endows Teiresias' present prophecy with greater authority;[48] but the scholion ad loc. is also right that the anachronism constituted praise of the Athenians, in the sense that the contrast between the two would have operated as praise of the Athenians. The reference almost certainly evoked Euripides' *Erechtheus* for that part of the audience who had been at its performance, and in any case undoubtedly activated the myth of the sacrifice of the daughter of Erechtheus, and this would have constructed a series of contrasts: Thebes was polluted when in danger of being sacked, while Athens had not been; in Thebes a male will eventually refuse to sacrifice his child to save the city, in Athens a woman willingly sacrifices hers for the polis. The Athenian sacrifice of a *parthenos* was "normal," this is who one offered as a human sacrifice to save the polis or other collectivity; the sacrifice of a virgin male is "abnormal."

Another effect of the identity of the chorus is also important. In the first strophe of the parodos the chorus explain that they have been sent as *hierodouloi* to Apollo at Delphi, and this, and to some extent their presence throughout, brings the Delphic oracle, whose role in this story that is now coming to an end was decisive, to the fore of the audience's perceptions.

Phoenissai includes a compendium of motifs and religious problematizations from the Theban saga. It includes stuff[49] presented in Aeschylus' *Septem*, Sophocles' *Antigone*, *Oidipous Tyrannos* (and also a reference to Oidipous' end which was to be set out a few years later in *Oidipous at Colonus*)—with extra bits as well, and a variety of religious problematization, including the question of human sacrifice, the working of the Erinys, the fulfillment of curses, the notion of preordained fate and the role of the Delphic oracle, the refusal of burial to Polyneikes. Euripides chose to stress one element of the Theban saga, the Phoenician origin, through the chorus, with important effects. Thus, their identity as a collectivity of Phoenician maidens was very important, and this is why the title focusses on the chorus. The use of the title derived from the chorus is significant, but in a more complex way than before. In these circumstances, we may conclude that the four surviving Euripidean tragedies with titles derived from the chorus have in common a certain emphasis on the chorus as a collectivity.

Can we reconstruct the situation, and the perceptions, behind these fragments of evidence pertaining to the naming of tragedies after the chorus? Generic comments about the diminished importance of the chorus and the greater importance of individual characters as tragedy developed are, in my view, too simplistic to provide a full answer, since they do not explain the choice of titles in the surviving tragedies. For if that was all there was to the situation, a generic diminution of randomly chosen chorus-based titles, how do we explain the choice of such titles both in the early, and in the later, periods? If the titles were randomly chosen, with just a vague notion of chorus-based ones cropping up when the chorus is especially important, as in Aeschylus' *Suppliants* and *Eumenides*, why did Aeschylus give a character-based title to *Agamemnon* and a chorus-based one to *Choephoroi*? Moreover, such a hypothesis cannot explain the pattern of Euripidean titles, *Suppliants*, but also the other tragedies, perhaps especially *Phoinissai*.

I suggest that the situation we are trying to reconstruct was complex. The fact that in early tragedy titles derived from the chorus were very common, and then they became rare, suggests that naming a tragedy after the chorus was a main naming modality in early tragedy, perhaps the default modality. To judge from *Persai* and *Suppliants*, this was correlative with a centrality in the role of the chorus.[50] Such naming would not appear to have been the default modality by the time of the production of the *Laios, Oidipous, Septem* trilogy. In the *Oresteia* Aeschylus appears to have chosen, and differentiated, his titles with deliberation. In the case of Sophocles' *Trachiniai* there does not seem to be any correlation between the title and the role of chorus; I suggested that the choice was intertextually inspired. With regard to Euripides, we can make no judgment concerning his early, nonextant tragedies, such as *Kressai* and *Kretes*, but by the time of *Suppliants*, and to the end of his career, we can detect significant, albeit complex, relationships between title derived from the chorus and the role of the chorus in the tragedy. In the case of such titles the chorus appears to have had some centrality.

Euripides, then, made conscious and deliberate choices of such titles. The fact that this entailed a centrality of the chorus would confirm that the early frequency of titles derived from the chorus was indeed correlative with the greater centrality of the chorus in early tragedies. I am not suggesting that there was a rule about this. On the contrary, I am suggesting that early tragedies routinely[51] derived their

Chapter 2: From Phrynichos to Euripides

title from the chorus because the chorus was perceived to be central, that this gradually changed, as the characters gained in importance, and that Aeschylus, at least for a certain point onwards, used titles deliberately, correlating titles and role of the chorus. Either this did not become general practice, or if it did, it lapsed, since Sophocles did not appear to have felt bound by it when he named the *Trachiniai*. Euripides then revived, refined, and extended this correlation.

The notion that early tragedies had routinely derived their title from the chorus would fit well with the fact that the chorus was, and was perceived to be, institutionally central in the tragic performances,[52] since the terminology used by the Athenians to speak of tragedy defined tragedy through the chorus, and also the chorus was, and remained, central in the organization of the production. If this reconstruction is right, it tells us that in early tragedy the chorus, the collectivity, was perceived to have been central in the tragedy. This means that the chorus was not only institutionally central, that is, as the chorus in the here and now, but was also central as the collectivity impersonated by this chorus of Athenian men. If it is right that in the perception of the audience of early tragedy the chorus was central, it would mean that collectivities, and so things to do with collectivities, were central in early tragedy.

This would fit well with my reconstruction of the generation and early history of tragedy. On that reconstruction, collectivities were indeed very important in very early tragedy, and this had nothing to do with democracy, and everything to do with the religious discourse of the polis.

Let us now consider another aspect of choral identities. As we saw in the discussion of extant Euripidean tragedies with titles derived from the choruses, there were context-specific reasons that shaped the choices of the chorus of Phoenician *parthenoi* in *Phoinissai*, of Trojan women in *Troades* and of Asiatic *bacchai* in *Bacchai*. This leads to the question of the alleged preference for otherness in tragic choruses, and to the related topic of the authority of the choral voice.

The question of the relationship of the chorus to the audience, and the authority of the choral voice, has been the subject of many discussions.[53] A very influential discussion has been that of Vernant,[54] who saw the chorus as a "personnage collectif et anonyme incarné par un collège officiel de citoyens, et dont le rôle est d'exprimer . . . les sentiments des spectateurs."[55] Vidal-Naquet agrees that the chorus expresses, in the face of the hero characterized by excess, the collective truth, middle truth, the truth of the city, but at the same time adds that, though the chorus is the vehicle for collective and civic expression, it is only very exceptionally that it consists of adult males of military age, what he calls "citoyens moyens."[56] Vidal-Naquet only considered the extant tragedies. He included *Rhesos* in his account. Leaving aside *Rhesos*,[57] he counts only two tragedies as having a chorus consisting of men of military age, Sophocles' *Ajax* and *Philoctetes*. Then he counts nine as having a chorus of women, sometimes slave women. So he subsumes free and slave women into one category and justifies this by saying that free or slave women were outside the city, not citizens.[58] Others scholars also emphasized this notion of the otherness of the chorus. Hall speaks of a prevalence of foreign choruses, and suggests that the reason for what she sees as the prevalence of foreign choruses may originally have been connected with the ritual form from which tragedy emerged.[59] But, she argues, as tragedy developed, the foreign chorus became conventional in its own right—especially the female barbarian chorus—because of its role as a plural lyric voice, distanced from the individual actors; while at one level the chorus is the voice of the collective, whose well-being is dependent on the individual characters, it is also estranged from the central pathos, rarely participates in or influences decisions and events, for its members remain marginal, their role—usually that of social inferior—to sympathize and lament. The choruses' relation to the central figures, dependent and marginalized, is almost a cultural paradigm of the relation in the Greek polis of women, slaves, and metics to the body of male citizens. For Gould, with two exceptions, the chorus in extant plays enacts the response, not of the representatives of the citizen body, but of the marginal or excluded.[60] He argues[61] that the otherness of the chorus resides in its giving collective expression to an experience alternative, even opposed, to that of the "heroic" figures; they express not the values of the polis, but far more often the experience of the excluded, the oppressed, and the vulnerable.[62]

I will be arguing that this emphasis on the alleged otherness of the tragic choruses is wrong. First, because several of the principles on which is based the classification of many choruses as "other" are flawed. First, in my view, it is wrong to subsume free and slave women into one category on the basis of the argument that both free and slave women were outside the city, not citizens. For this classification, implicitly based on a privileging of the political, does not correspond to the ancient perceptions, in which citizen women were significantly different from noncitizen women in a variety of ways, above all in the sphere of religion.[63] The same is true of choruses made up of old men, whom Vidal-Naquet classifies as consisting of super-citizens, because old men were privileged in the Assembly.[64] The notion of "citoyens moyens" on which this classification is based is not a valid ancient category; citizens of military age is a valid ancient category, in con-

Chapter 2: From Phrynichos to Euripides

texts in which such distinctions are relevant. In the context of decision making and assessing even this was not a relevant concept, and old men were indeed perceived as part of the central category, male Athenian citizens. Furthermore, the strategy of only counting surviving tragedies inevitably introduces a bias towards later tragedies, and towards Euripidean tragedies, and it is not legitimate simply to assume implicitly that this is not methodologically significant. Thus, this procedure is flawed, for its validity depends on the validity of the a priori assumption that the bias is not significant and does not introduce distortions.

Let us now consider the identities of the tragic choruses in detail, and not deal in generalities, and let us also try to take account of the fragmentary tragedies. First, we need to define the different distances between the audiences and the choruses. Second, we need to consider and compare these distances in the tragedies of each of the three tragedians, to see whether or not there are any differences between their choices, and what, if anything, this may imply about these choices.

The fifth-century tragic audiences were not, of course, homogeneous in civic status or, I argued, gender; but the symbolically central part of the audience were the Athenian male citizens. Let us consider the distances between this symbolically central part of the audience and the various tragic choruses. One type of distancing is common to all the choral identities discussed here, except that in Aeschylus' *Persai*: all those choral identities were located in the heroic age. The choral identities that are most distanced from that audience are those of slave women, as, for example, in Aeschylus' *Choephoroi*,[65] and foreign women, as, for example, the Danaids in Aeschylus' *Suppliants*, or the Asiatic *bacchai* in Euripides' *Bacchai*.

The identities that are closest to that audience are those of Athenian elders: elders of Colonus in Sophocles' *Oidipous at Colonus*, of Marathonian elders, in Euripides' *Herakleidai*, and of Athenian elders in the *asty* in Euripides' *Erechtheus*. The title of Aeschylus' *Eleusinioi*[66] tells us that its chorus also consisted of Athenian male citizens, whether elders, as in these three plays, or, perhaps (for all that we can tell) of young or mature age. A choral identity involving men of military age is that of the Salaminian sailors in Sophocles' *Ajax*. In the world of the audience Salaminians are Athenians, but it was part of their assumptions, their "historical" knowledge that this was not so in the time of Ajax. Nevertheless, the distance between audience and choral identity would not have been perceived to have been very great—and was perhaps, to some extent, ambiguous. An identity partly comparable to this, in that it involved sailors, men of military age, but was further distanced, is that of Neoptolemos' sailors that were the chorus in Sophocles' *Philoctetes*. Another type of choral identity, that is further distanced from the Athenian males (and to some extent also from the quasi-Athenian Salaminians), is that of elders in other poleis which make up the chorus in, for example, Sophocles' *Oidipous Tyrannos* and *Antigone* and in Aeschylus' *Agamemnon*. To judge from their titles, the following tragedies also had a chorus consisting of males, which in fifth-century terms would have been perceived as male citizens, of a Greek polis or *ethnos*. Aeschylus' *Argeioi*, *Myrmidones*, Sophocles' *Larissaioi*, *Skyrioi*, *Manteis* (or *Polyidos*), *Dolopes* (which may have been the same as *Phoinix*); Euripides' *Kretes*; *Skyrioi*. Some of these poleis or *ethne* are central, and what we may call "almost (though not quite) culturally equivalent" to Athens, such as Aeschylus' *Argeioi*, some marginal, such as Sophocles' *Dolopes*. The chorus of Aeschylus' *Myrmidones* at least would have consisted of men of military age.[67]

In the extant Aeschylean tragedies we find the following types of distances. At the most distanced end of the spectrum are slave women in *Choephoroi* and the Danaids, foreign women, in *Suppliants*; in *Persai* the distance is different from all the others: the chorus are foreign elders in the world of the present, but in an "other" place. Radically distanced from the audience, but in a different modality from that of the preferred options for choral identities, is the chorus of the *Eumenides*, consisting of divine beings. At the less radically distanced from the symbolically central audience end of the spectrum are the Argive elders in *Agamemnon*, and to a lesser extent the Theban *parthenoi* in *Septem*. That Aeschylus also gave choral identities that were very close to the symbolically central audience is shown by his *Eleusinioi*. And that he also gave choral identities involving men of military age is illustrated by his *Myrmidones*. Among his fragmentary tragedies, a group of foreign women with a particular ritual identity, Thracian and Phrygian and Lydian *bacchai*, formed the chorus of *Bassarai* or *Bassarides*, one of the tragedies of the *Lykourgeia*.[68] Its other two tragedies, *Edonoi* and *Neaniskoi*, had a chorus consisting of foreign (Thracian) men.[69] There was a chorus of foreign captive women in *Threissai*.[70] It is possible that *Threissai* was part of a trilogy of which *Salaminiai* or *Salaminioi* was the last play,[71] the chorus of which, as with the case of the chorus of Sophocles' *Ajax*, would have been perceived as not far removed from their Athenian counterparts. If so, there would be the same mixture of differently distanced choruses in this trilogy as in the *Oresteia*.

There does seem to be one difference between the identities of Aeschylean choruses and those of other choruses. Some Aeschylean choruses consist of minor deities.[72] The Erinyes in *Eumenides*, and, among the fragmentary tragedies about which we have, or can legitimately deduce, sufficient information to be able to judge, in *Kabeiroi* a chorus of Kabeiroi,[73] in *Nereides* a chorus of Nereides, in *Toxotides* a chorus of Nymphs companions of Artemis; in *Trophoi* the chorus consisted of Nysaean Nymphs, who were Dionysos' Nurses, in *Prometheus Lyomenos*, if it is Aeschylean,[74] a chorus of Titans.[75] Subsequently, there seems to have been a chorus of the Muses in Sophocles' *Mousai*, which was probably the same as *Thamyras*, and which, I am arguing in chapter III.4, was early. As far as I am aware there are no choruses consisting of deities in later tragedy.

In Sophocles' extant tragedies the choral identities that predominate are close to, or at least less distanced from, Athenian males: first, Athenian elders, elders of Colonus, in *Oidipous at Colonus*; second, quasi-Athenian men of military age,[76] the Salaminian sailors, in *Ajax*; third, non-Athenian Greek men of military age: Neoptolemos' sailors in *Philoctetes*; fourth, elders in other poleis: in *Oidipous Tyrannos* and *Antigone*; and finally, Greek women of other poleis in *Trachiniai* and *Electra*. Among his not extant tragedies, some, such as *Aichmalotides, Kolchides*,[77] and *Lemniai*, did have choruses consisting of the more radically distanced category, but not, it would seem, very many.

Let us now consider Euripides. Of his seventeen surviving tragedies, one, *Herakleidai*, has a chorus consisting of Athenian elders, of old men of Marathon. Two, *Herakles* and *Alcestis*, have a chorus consisting of elders of another Greek polis. Many more choruses in the extant Euripidean tragedies consist of women. In *Ion* the chorus consisted of female attendants of Kreousa, who were free and probably Athenian. In seven (*Medea, Iphigeneia at Aulis, Suppliants, Hippolytos*,[78] *Electra, Orestes, Andromache*) the chorus consists of *parthenoi* or women citizens of other Greek poleis. In two it consists of Greek girls, who are, during the action of the tragedy, captive attendants of the main character: *Iphigeneia in Tauris; Helen*. In four, *Troades, Hecabe, Bacchai, Phoenissai*, it consists of foreign, barbarian women, two of these with a specific ritual role.

Let us now consider the identities of the chorus in a random sample of Euripides' fragmentary tragedies to try to assess whether they suggest that the picture presented by the extant tragedies would seem to reflect Euripides' opus in general. First, there is one instance, in *Erechtheus*, in which the chorus is at the least possible[79] distance from the audience, since it consists of heroic age Athenian elders at the very center of the *asty*. The following fragmentary tragedies had a chorus consisting of elders of another Greek city: *Telephos*, which had probably a chorus of Argive elders;[80] *Antiope*, which had a chorus of old men, Attic shepherds;[81] *Kresphontes*, which had a chorus of Messenian elders.[82] In *Palamedes*, produced together with *Troades* at 415, the chorus consisted of Greek soldiers.[83] In *Kretes*, which, we saw,[84] was an early play, the chorus consisted of Cretan priests.[85] In the following two tragedies the chorus consisted of women of another Greek polis: *Kressai*, an early play,[86] in which the chorus presumably consisted of Cretan women, and *Hypsipyle*, a late play, in which the chorus consisted of Nemean women.[87] In the following two it consisted of foreign women: in *Alexandros*, which had been produced together with *Troades* and *Palamedes* at 415, the chorus probably consisted of Trojan women;[88] in *Phaethon* it consisted of servant girls of an Aethiopian (presented as in a fairy tale world) palace.[89]

In this randomly chosen sample, then, the number of choruses consisting of males, elders of a city (in a few cases Athenian ones) and other central males, and of choruses consisting of women, is more or less the same; in fact there are slightly more elders than women. This would suggest that perhaps the pattern of choral identities in his extant tragedies may not necessarily reflect Euripides' opus wholly accurately.

It is clear, in any case, that a detailed consideration of the evidence shows that the view that fifth-century tragedy had a predilection for choruses which are "other" is mistaken. There are many choruses consisting of males, even a few of Athenian males. When assessing the "otherness" of choruses, it must be kept in mind that there are two distinct things that must not be confused or blurred. First, how central or marginal the collectivity represented by the chorus is in the world of the tragedy; and second, how near or distanced they were with reference to the Athenian audience. In the world of the audience Theban elders are at some distance from the Athenian citizens; in that of the tragedy they are at the very center of the polis, and so they are closely correlative with the Athenian audience, with its symbolically central part. It is this interplay of the worlds, and the shifting distances, that allow the exploration of problems relevant to the audience at a distance.

Another conclusion is that there are differences among tragedians, with Sophocles apparently having a greater preference for male choruses than Euripides. But Euripides' preferred choruses are not radically "other"; his preferred choruses are Greek citizen women; and for the Athenian audience Greek, and especially Athenian, women were not perceived as "other" in the way that barbarians are other. Above all, and most importantly, they were not "other" to the polis discourse, which gave women a very important, active place in the central sphere of religion.

Chapter 2: From Phrynichos to Euripides 281

In the world of the play the citizen women of Trachis, or of Corinth, or of Argos, or of Phthia, were equivalent to Athenian women in the world of the audience. In both cases, women were not central, they were in a weak position, vulnerable. This is one of the things that Euripides especially explores, hence the choice of a chorus of citizen women in some of the tragedies. For, of course, there are different reasons in the different plays, why Euripides chose a chorus of citizen women, correlative with his specific dramatic concerns. Thus, I have argued elsewhere[90] that in *Medea* the exploration of "woman," through a polarized version of a "bad woman," was effected through, among other things, a series of textual strategies that in different places zoomed Medea to, and distanced her from, the Athenian normative discourse's perception of "normal woman," and that the chorus of Corinthian women played a significant part in these strategies. In the case of *Troades* the presentation of the aftermath of war from the viewpoint of the women of the vanquished side polarizes the suffering, the negative aspects of war, by focussing on the most vulnerable and powerless among the enemy. The choice of Phoenician girls in *Phoenissai* was discussed above; we also saw that in *Bacchai*, the reasons for the choice of a female chorus of *bacchai* are self-evident, while their foreignness was part of the alienness and disorder that seemed to Pentheus to have been threatening the order of the polis.

There is, then, no privileging of "otherness" in fifth-century tragic choruses, only a variety of choral identities. As we saw in chapter I.2, the persona of the chorus as a chorus in honor of Dionysos in the here and now was never fully narcotized for the ancient audience, and this persona was focussed on through choral self-referentiality. Insofar as the chorus was perceived as also a chorus in the present, it was a representative of the polis at the ritual level. And this does give the voice of the chorus a certain limited authority.[91] But this authority is variable. In the parodos of *Antigone*, where, we saw,[92] the chorus would have been perceived to have been singing a hymn in the here and now as well as in the world of the play (though the latter was dominant), I suggest that its authority would have been perceived as being comparable to that of a polis chorus singing hymns to gods on a solemn ritual occasion. But things are more complex in the case of the second strophe and second antistrophe of the second stasimon of *Oidipous Tyrannos* (883-910). In this segment of the ode, as Henrichs' subtle analysis has shown,[93] choral self-referentiality evokes the persona of the chorus as a chorus in the present; the religious problematization of the chorus is located above all in the world of the tragedy, but it is not irrelevant to the world of the audience, and the complex and ambiguous relationship between the chorus' two personae allows this religious problematization to take place at a distance, in a context in which the audience's knowledge about the play would lead them to give reassuring answers. For the questions have been articulated, simultaneously in both worlds, but the audience's knowledge allows them to place the questions the chorus ask in the world of the play in their proper perspective. When the chorus ask, if people act without fear of Dike and without reverence for the gods and get away with it, "Why should I dance?" that is, worship the gods through being a member of a chorus, and say that they will not visit the oracles any more if oracles do not come true, and when they pray to Zeus not to allow this to escape his power, the audience knows that nothing will go unpunished and that the oracles will come true—in this case.

I must stress that the distances between the audience, the symbolically central male Athenian citizens, and the chorus in the dominant mimetic facet of their persona is not static in each tragedy, but they shifted in the course of the performance. For example, the distance between male Athenian citizens and the chorus in their persona as Corinthian women in *Medea*, is complex. Since, we saw, in the world of the play the citizen women of Corinth were equivalent to Athenian women in the world of the audience, the distance between male Athenian citizens and the chorus in their persona as Corinthian women was determined by the parameters of the distance between male Athenian citizens and Athenian citizen women on the one hand, and fifth-century Athens and Medea's Corinth on the other. But this distance shifted in the course of the tragedy, as the collectivity of women that the chorus represented was zoomed to, or distanced from, the normative ideology of "good woman" in the Athenian polis discourse. For example, in the first stasimon the chorus articulate the notion that since men break oaths with impunity, and the gods no longer police these oaths, the proper order of things has been upset, and a reversed world has been created, in which it is women who will have good fame and honor, and they will no longer be dishonored by slanderous songs. The notion that oaths must not be broken is correct religious discourse. But the rest would have activated for the audience the mythological and conceptual schema "women in charge," the schema of a reversed world, in which women are on top, and enjoy what in the real world—perceived as the properly ordered world—are the privileges of men.[94] This is an image of serious disorder, which would have colored the chorus negatively in the eyes of the Athenian males, distancing them negatively from the schema "good woman," and so also of their ideological perception of "normal Athenian woman."[95]

Consequently, in my view, the relationship of the chorus to the collectivity of the audience was very complex, differed from one tragedy

Chapter 2: From Phrynichos to Euripides

to the other, depending on the choral identities, and was not static within each tragedy. The same was true of the authority of the chorus, which depended on the same parameters.

It is a fact that the chorus can be mistaken, take the wrong positions, even when they are a collectivity central in the world of the play, and not symbolically very distanced from the world of the audience (from the symbolically central part that were the male Athenian citizens), as the Theban elders in Sophocles' *Antigone* were.[96] On my interpretation, this very fallibility is central to tragedy; for it is a reflection of the limitations of the polis discourse, and of the ultimate unknowability of the divine world and the cosmos. This is part of what tragedy was about, the exploration of problems that arose in the interstices of the religious discourse of the polis—for it is the polis (or *ethnos*) that sets in place the religious systems of communities in the Greek world.[97] Hence the preference for a setting in other Greek cities of the heroic age; it allowed such problems to be explored at a certain distance, a distance which itself shifted continuously within each tragedy.

The choices of choral identities, and their fallibility, make perfect sense in the context of my reconstruction of the generation and early development of tragedy as set out in II.2-3 above. On that reconstruction, the fallibility of the collectivity, as manifested in the festival myth of the City Dionysia, was at the center of the generation of tragedy. As for choral identities, choruses at the pre-dramatic Dionysia had been above all choruses in the here and now, though in receiving Dionysos each year they were also reenacting the actions of the Athenians of the heroic age, who had initially rejected Dionysos and subsequently accepted him with honor. The distance between their dominant persona in the here and now and the "reenacting of the past" facet of their persona was not great, as befitted this nonmimetic performance. The closest distance between tragic choruses and their audience, as seen in tragedies such as *Erechtheus*, *Oidipous at Colonus*, *Herakleidai*, and *Eleusinioi*, is comparable to that distance in the ritual: men of the present/men of the heroic past. The fact that this type of close distance between audience and tragic chorus was rare, for mostly the distances were greater, befits a genre that included, and crystallized when it embraced, *mimesis*.

On my reconstruction, "other male Greeks of the heroic age" was the identity the newly mimetic choruses of early tragedy would most commonly have assumed, starting with "Thebans of the time of Pentheus." This "other Greek males of the heroic age" is a common type of identity for the tragic choruses of fifth-century tragedy. The emergence of "female" and even "foreign female" choral identities can also be accounted for on my reconstruction, in which tragedy began with mimetic representations and problematizations of Dionysiac myths, in which the earliest choruses would have impersonated Theban men (the Pentheus myth), Thracian men and perhaps women (the Lykourgos myth), and Maenads, including Asiatic Maenads—since both indigenous maenads and foreign bacchants are important, and so potential choral choices, in the myths of resistance to Dionysos, which, on this reconstruction, was where earliest tragedy began.

In conclusion, I suggest that this investigation (besides having, I hope, illuminated certain aspects of the tragic chorus and its developments in the fifth century) offers a little further support for the reconstruction of the generation and early history of tragedy proposed here. For the early dramatic centrality of the chorus (as well as its continuing institutional centrality), and its identities and authorities, are correlative with, make perfect sense in the context of, that reconstruction.

Notes

1. If it is not a satyr play (cf. Lloyd-Jones 1996, 207).

2. Cf. Kavoulaki forthcoming for an excellent analysis of the complexities of the ritual roles of the mothers in the death ritual in Euripides' *Suppliants*.

3. *Med., IA, Hrkldai., Her.; Hipp., Alc.; El., Tro., Hec., Or., Andr.*

4. I am assuming that the titles we have were the original titles given by the tragedians (cf. also Taplin 1975, 185 with bibl.). There is no reason that I can see to doubt this. It is in any case a neutral strategy to examine the evidence to see whether any significant differences, any pattern, emerge; the fact that the patterns are so different for the different tragedians is in itself an argument in favor of the view that we have the titles given by the dramatists. For no alternative theory can explain why, for example, character-based titles were given less to Aeschylus' plays and more to the others', or any of the other significant patterns. Sometimes arguments against particular titles depend on certain assumptions; Brown's case (1984, 268-9, cf. 260-81) concerning the title *Eumenides*, which depends, above all, on certain assumptions concerning the divine names and personalities of the Erinyes-Eumenides; cf. on this Henrichs 1991, 164-5 n. 9, 167-8.

5. On the relationship between *Persai* and *Phoinissai* cf. chapter I.2 n. 7.

6. I am only including those titles which seem more or less certain to belong to Aeschylean tragedies. To avoid distorting bias I am erring on the side that underestimates the number of plays whose title was derived from the chorus. (Why this is avoidance of distorting bias will become clear subsequently.) Thus, for example, I am not including titles that may conceivably have belonged to satyr plays, such as *Thalamopoioi* (on which see *TrGF* iii pp. 193-4), or even *Ostologoi* (on which see *TrGF* iii pp. 291-94), which in my view was almost certainly a tragedy and not a satyr play—because the latter is a possibility, not a wild improbability as in the case of *Xantriai* (on which see *TrGF* iii pp. 280-87). Similarly, I

am not including titles that are not certain to have belonged to a separate tagedy, such as *Phrygioi* or *Phrygiai* (on which see *TrGF* iii p. 370).

7. Didascalia a 465/59 (*TrGF* i p. 5); cf. Did C 6 (*TrGF* i p. 44); cf. chapter III.1 n. 23.

8. On chorus consisting of Heliades cf. *TrGF* ad loc. (vol. 4 p. 185).

9. That this may have been a satyr play is a wholly a priori speculation (see *TrGF* for the evidence for, and bibliography on, this play); it seems to me that the reference in Alkiphron 3.12 (whether or not reporting a fictitious story) would lead us to conclude that *Propompoi* was a tragedy.

10. I see no reason why this should have been a satyr play; I am assuming that the chorus consisted of Nysaean Nymphs, who were Dionysos' Nurses (cf. *TrGF* iii pp. 349-51).

11. One possible explanation for the double title is that at a subsequent stage in the tragedy's history the titles *Kares*, *Hydrophoroi*, and *Phryges* came to be considered too vague to indicate the subject and a second explanatory title was added in each case, *Europa*, *Semele*, *Hektoros Lytra*.

12. On the date of *Trachiniai* see Easterling 1982, 19-23.

13. I am not taking account of those titles for which there is a possibility that they may have belonged to satyr plays, such as *Nausicaa* or *Plyntriai*, as I am not taking account of such plays when considering titles derived from the name of a character (e.g. *Inachos*), or indeed in any other category for which there is a similar possibility (for example, *Syndeipnoi* or *Syndeipnon*, which may have been the same play as *Achaion Syllogos*, may have been a satyr play [cf. Lloyd-Jones 1996, 280-1; *TrGF* iv pp. 425-6]), or the existence of which is problematic, or the authorship by the older Sophocles uncertain (cf. e.g. *Iberes* [cf. *TrGF* iv p. 247 ad loc.]). But I have included more doubtful examples among the titles derived from the chorus than in any other category, in order to show that even if the sample is biased in favor of maximizing of such titles, the proportion of titles derived from the name of the chorus is much smaller than in the case of Aeschylus and Phrynichos.

14. It cannot be totally excluded that it may have been a satyr play; on this play see Lloyd-Jones 1996, 178-81; *TrGF* iv p. 310.

15. For this play also the suggestion has been made that it was a satyr play: see *TrGF* iv p. 337.

16. This is extremely unlikely to have been a satyr play; there are reasons for thinking it was an early tragedy; see on the play Lloyd-Jones 1996, pp. 256-7; *TrGF* iii T 70.

17. For the hypothesis that this may have been the same as the *Kolchides* see Lloyd-Jones 1996, p. 269.

18. For this play also the suggestion that it was a satyr play has been made; cf. *TrGF* iv pp. 458-9.

19. We have no way of knowing whether or not this was a satyr play. On this title see Lloyd-Jones 1996, 322-3; *TrGF* iv p. 473.

20. It has been suggested that this was the same play as *Peleus* or *Hermione*; see Lloyd-Jones 1996, 330-1; *TrGF* iv p. 481; 390-2.

21. If there had been a tragedy *Phryges* by Sophocles, which is not certain; see Lloyd-Jones 1996, 338-9; *TrGF* iv p. 493.

22. For this play also the suggestion has been made that it was a satyr play: see Lloyd-Jones 1996, 207.

23. It is unlikely to have been a satyr play; on this question see the brief discussion in Lloyd-Jones 1996, 68-9; on *Phoinix* cf. *TrGF* iv pp. 490-1.

24. This includes titles such as, for example, *Philoktetes at Troy*, which, like, for example, Euripides' *Iphigeneia at Aulis*, are derived from the name of a character described as being located in a particular place, which is comparable to titles derived from the name of a character described as being in a particular state (cf. e.g. Sophocles' *Odysseus Mainomenos*); so both relate also to titles describing the tragedy's subject.

25. I take this tragedy to have been separate from *Odysseus Akanthoplex*. On this question cf. *TrGF* iv pp. 373-5; Lloyd-Jones 1996, pp. 236-7.

26. Cf. Lloyd-Jones 1996, p. 275. That is, if *Kolchides* and *Rhizotomoi* were not titles of the same play (cf. above n. 17).

27. It is not certain that there was a Euripidean tragedy of that name; cf. Nauck ad loc.).

28. *TrGF* i p. 6: Did a. 455.

29. Cf. Nauck ad loc.

30. *TrGF* i Did C 11.

31. Cf. Collard, Cropp, and Lee 1995, 58.

32. Listed in chronological order of the tragedians.

33. Who was born in the 480s.

34. Who started producing tragedies between 447 and 444.

35. Who was born after 450.

36. Cf. Garvie 1969, 138.

37. See *TrGF* i p. 75, commentary ad 3 F 6. It may have included Meleager's death (see Lloyd-Jones 1996, 213).

38. It may have included, but is highly unlikely to have consisted only of, an account of their mother Althaia's death.

39. *TrGF* iii p. 137.

40. Cf. *TrGF* iv p. 170; Garvie 1969, 9.

41. On the textual problems and the question of interpolation see Mastronarde 1994, 39-49 and passim, cf. esp. 591-4; Diggle 1994, 341-61 (353-61 is a review of Mastronarde 1994). I discuss the tragedy in more detail below in chapter III.3.

42. Cf. Mastronarde 1994, 11-14.

43. Mastronarde 1994, 208-9.

44. He mentions (Mastronarde 1994, 209) the other reasons that have been suggested to explain this choice of chorus, such as, for example, the opportunity to display the exotic, and considers them of minor importance, if any, in comparison with these literary/dramatic motivations. Among them he mentions a "cryptic (and, I would say, point-

Chapter 2: From Phrynichos to Euripides

less) allusion to Phrynichos' *Phoenissai*." The fact that any allusion to Phrynichos' *Phoenissai* may appear cryptic and pointless to us is not a good argument for dismissing the hypothesis that it may have played some role in that choice, since the exiguous surviving sample of the early play does not provide an adequate basis for such an assessment—which would be in any case in danger of being culturally determined even under the best circumstances.

45. See e.g. 291-2.

46. Lines 4-6: *hos dysteche Thebaisi te toth' hemera aktin' ephekas, Kadmos henik' elthen gen tend' eklipon Phoinissan enalian chthona.*

47. Mastronarde 1994, 5-6 has noted the separation of the polis and the royal family in that he has noted the separation of the salvation of the polis, achieved through Menoikeus' sacrifice, from that of the royal family, but does not relate this to the identity of the chorus, to the fact that no segment of the Theban collectivity is visible.

48. Mastronarde 1994, 399 ad 854-5.

49. On self-consciousness about the relationship of *Phoinissai* to literary tradition, as in other contemporary plays of Euripides see Mastronarde 1994, 9-10.

50. In the case of *Suppliants*, and almost certainly in the whole Danaid trilogy, there is a significant relationship between the titles and the central role of the chorus.

51. Though not necessarily universally; it is impossible even to speculate.

52. As we saw in chapter I.2.

53. Cf. esp. Vernant 1972, esp. 25-8; Vidal-Naquet 1986b, 159; Gould 1996, 217-43; Goldhill 1996, 244-56; Cf. a survey of earlier discussions in Gould 1996, 215-9.

54. Vernant 1972, esp. 25-8.

55. Vernant 1972, 27.

56. Vidal-Naquet 1986b, 159-60.

57. Which I consider to be fourth-century. Cf. ch. III.4.

58. Vidal-Naquet 1986b, 160.

59. Hall 1989, 115.

60. Gould 1996, 219-20.

61. Gould 1996, esp. 221-4.

62. Goldhill 1996 offers a sophisticated critique of some aspects of Gould's argument; I agree with a lot of what he says.

63. Cf. esp. the discussion in Sourvinou-Inwood 1995b, 111-20.

64. Vidal-Naquet 1986b, 160.

65. On their status see esp. Garvie 1986, 53-4; for a different view cf. Hall 1989, 116.

66. *TrGF* iv pp. 175-6. The action of the play took place in the time of Theseus, at the same time as Euripides, *Suppliants*, the aftermath of the expedition of the Seven against Thebes. So not only would Eleusinian men have been Athenian citizens in fifth-century Athens, they would also have been perceived to have been Athenian citizens in the world of the play also.

67. On Aeschylus' *Myrmidones* see *TrGF* iii pp. 239-57.

68. On Aeschylus' *Lykourgeia* see West 1990, 26-50.
69. On the chorus of *Neaniskoi* see West 1990, 46-7.
70. See *TrGF* iii pp. 205-6.
71. See *TrGF* iii pp. 333-5 (s.v. *Salaminiai*).
72. On this cf. below III.4.
73. In view of Athen. 10.428F I find it difficult to understand how some scholars can consider *Kabeiroi* to be a satyr play. Cf. on this play *TrGF* iii pp. 214-5.
74. Cf. III.1 n. 6.
75. See *TrGF* iii p. 307.
76. The Salaminian sailors would have been, in (the audience's) present-day terms, Athenian citizens.
77. Which may have been the same as *Rhizotomoi*; see Lloyd-Jones 1996, 269.
78. The subsidiary chorus of which consisted of huntsmen who were servants (cf. Barrett 1964, 167-8 for other subsidiary choruses).
79. Given the parameters of tragedy discussed in chapter I.2.
80. See Collard, Cropp, and Lee 1995, 20. *Telephos* was produced in 438 B.C.
81. See Page 1941, 62; the play was produced in, or about, 408 (op. cit. 61).
82. See Collard, Cropp, and Lee 1995, 122; for a presentation of earlier discussions cf. Harder 1985, 13. It was probably produced between 427 and 421 (see Collard, Cropp, and Lee 1995, 125).
83. See Scodel 1980, 55.
84. Cf. above n. 31.
85. They may have been partly distanced as "other" because they abstained from living food (fr. 472 v. 20; this fragment has been much discussed; see bibliography in Collard, Cropp, and Lee 1995, pp. 68-70 esp. 70); but, as in other respects they could be seen as an extreme version of priests of ordinary cults, and the deities and rites involved are not sectarian, their practices would probably have been perceived as normal practices of Cretan priests at the time of Minos; distanced from the present, partly through the deployment of elements that in the present belonged to sectarian practices, perhaps as a way of stressing the perceived (by the Greeks in general) religious authority of Cretan religious personnel in the past.
86. Cf. above n. 31.
87. See e.g. Page 1941, 79.
88. I agree with Scodel 1980, 26 on this; Koniaris 1973, 87 follows the view that we are in doubt whether the chorus consisted of Trojan men or Trojan women. The subsidiary chorus of *Alexandros* consisted of shepherds (see e.g. Coles 1974, 24).
89. Aethiopia as fairy tale world, in which mortals and immortals live in close proximity: cf. Collard, Cropp, and Lee 1995, 200-1. Cf. also below III.4. *Phaethon* was perhaps produced in, or soon after, 420 (see Collard, Cropp, and Lee 1995, 203).
90. In Sourvinou-Inwood 1997c, 254-62.
91. Goldhill 1996, 253 takes a not vastly dissimilar position.

92. Cf. ch. I.2
93. Henrichs 1994/5, 65-73.
94. Pembroke 1965, 217-47; Pembroke 1967, 1-35; Vidal-Naquet 1983, 267-88; Zeitlin 1978, 153-60.
95. Cf. my analysis in Sourvinou-Inwood 1997c, 254-62.
96. The position articulated by Goldhill 1996, 253 is not vastly different from my position, but I locate this situation in the religious sphere which, on my thesis, is where it all began.
97. Cf. Sourvinou-Inwood 1990a, 295-322.

Neck amphora Oxford 1965.126. Courtesy Ashmolean Museum.

Neck amphora Oxford 1965.126. Courtesy Ashmolean Museum.

Neck amphora Oxford 1965.126. Courtesy Ashmolean Museum.

Neck amphora Oxford 1965.126. Courtesy Ashmolean Museum.

Neck amphora Oxford 1965.126. Courtesy Ashmolean Museum.

Cup Oxford G.262 (V.516). Courtesy Ashmolean Museum.

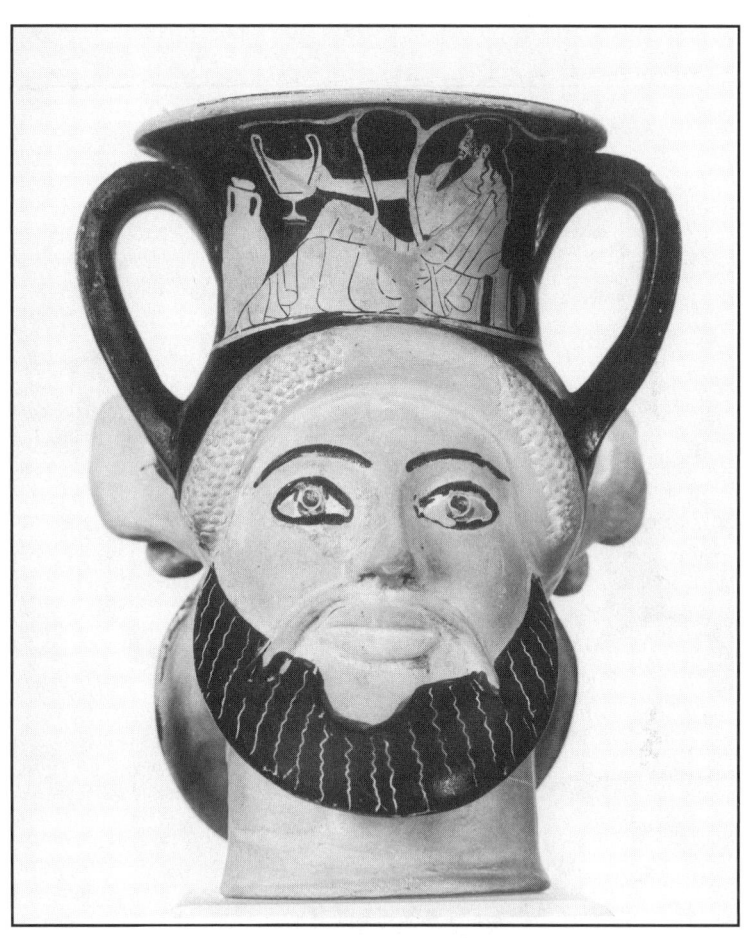

Janiform head kantharos Ferrara, Museo Nazionale di Spina, 9410 (T 256 B VP). Courtesy Soprintendenza Archeologica of Emilia Romagna.

Janiform head kantharos Ferrara, Museo Nazionale di Spina, 9410 (T 256 B VP). Courtesy Soprintendenza Archeologica of Emilia Romagna.

Janiform head kantharos London 786. Courtesy British Museum.

Janiform head kantharos London 786. Courtesy British Museum.

III.3. Euripidean Tragedy and Religious Exploration

III.3.i. *Euripidean Tragedy and Religion; Problematik, Methodology, and Euripides' Reception*

1) *Introduction, Problematik, Some Methodological Remarks*

In chapter I.2 I discussed the ways in which divinities were perceived by the ancient audiences in a few Euripidean tragedies and also some of the problematic areas of religion that those tragedies explore. I will develop some of these questions in greater depth here and consider several others, in the context of an attempt to reexplore radically the relationship between Euripidean tragedy and religion.[1]

Much of the discussion of this relationship has focussed on Euripides' theology. The reconstruction of this theology is especially vulnerable to cultural determination, to judgments made on the basis of modern assumptions and perceptions. This, I believe, is the reason why various scholars have interpreted the role of the gods in Euripides in a variety of ways over the generations. Many had read Greek tragedy, and made sense of the gods in Euripides, through their own perceptual filters,[2] that were shaped by assumptions which were not sympathetic to those of the Greek religious universe. In my view, much of the discourse on Euripidean tragedy and religion is still structured, at least implicitly, by questions (or at least by multiform seepages from questions) that had been asked at an earlier age, in which, first, perceptions of Greek religion were implicitly affected by culturally determined judgments shaped by the assumptions of a Western Christian liberal tradition and/or a rationalizing cast of mind that privileged religious scepticism; and second, readings of tragedies were less informed by the awareness of the cultural determination of perception. Onto this type of structuring schema has sometimes been grafted another, reflecting our own times' postmodern perceptual cast, which privileges the subversive, ironic, and self-deconstructing mode, and this symbiosis has kept alive, albeit not unchallenged, certain types of reading of Euripidean tragedies which, in my view, are very different from those which the ancient audiences constructed during the performances, which were shaped by parameters of determination constituted by the cultural assumptions which the audience shared with the tragedian.[3] I must stress again that the fact that the audience was not homogeneous (that different segments may have had different assumptions concerning, for example, sophists) does not affect the fundamental fact that they shared basic cultural assumptions, which shaped perception, and which were fundamentally different from ours; this diversity of the audience must not be used as an alibi for the unwillingness to relinquish "direct," culturally determined readings.[4]

In order to make sense of deities in Euripidean tragedies in ways that are as close as possible to those of the ancient audience we need to reconstruct their relevant perceptual filters. One of the most fundamental aspects of those filters was the relationship between the divinities on the stage, in epiphany, and also the divinities are presented in the words of the characters and implicated in rituals, and the religious reality of the audience. I hope to have shown in chapter I.2, and will be arguing in much more detail in the discussion of the individual tragedies here, that the deities in Euripidean tragedies were zoomed to the cultic reality of the Athenian audience in complex ways, and so were perceived by the audience to be representations of the gods of cult.[5]

Furthermore, since, we saw, the tragic chorus was also perceived as a chorus of Dionysos in the here and now, tragedies were perceived by the ancient audiences as shot through by present-day ritual, which would in itself have led them to perceive gods in epiphany as a serious representation of the divinity—unless otherwise indicated, which it was not; in fact the case is the opposite: the zoomings produced a strong identification. Most importantly, the institution of cults is one of the main things gods in epiphany do. In the context just described, of a performance shot through with ritual in the present and the identification produced by the zoomings, it is impossible to imagine that the institution of cults (which included, we saw, in *Erechtheus*, the most central cults of the Athenian polis), and was zoomed to the audience's cultic reality, was understood in anything but the most serious way. Nor is there any reason to understand any other epiphany differently.[6] On the contrary, as I will be arguing in chapter III.4, there are very strong reasons for thinking that in the eyes of the ancient audience epiphanies were charged with religious significance. But I will keep that argument separate, so that the convergence of the conclusions can be seen to add validity to my case. I also argued in chapter I.1 that Aristotle *Poetics* 1454a39-b8 provides support for my view that the *apo mechanes* deities were not perceived as empty or ironic gestures of closure, but as representations of the audience's gods.

It is a culturally determined perception that the fact that gods in epiphany sometimes turn the action in unexpected ways entails that such endings are ironic. For such turnabouts are the correlative of the important Greek religious notion of unknowability, of the fact that the wider picture of things is presented as being unclear to the dramatis

Chapter 3: Euripidean Tragedy and Religious Exploration 293

personae of these tragedies, who, until the revelations of the gods in epiphany, have no more access to the gods, and thus also to knowledge of what would be appropriate behavior, than a fifth-century audience—for they do not know that the prophecies that they have received are always right; the same human potential of human fallibility distorting the god's message that had existed for the audience obtained for the tragic characters as well; it was the audience who knew that prophecies in tragedy are always right. As I have argued, this notion of unknowability is an important category in Greek religion. In tragedy it is stressed in a variety of ways, not least, in Euripides, through the floating epilogues in *Medea* 1415-9 and, with a different first line, in *Alcestis* 1159-64, *Andromache* 1284-8, *Helen* 1688-92, and *Bacchae* 1388-92, which will be discussed in the context of the relevant tragedies and also in appendix 1 to this chapter. Here I will only say that these epilogues express precisely this general perception, they articulate the ultimate unknowability of the will of the gods, while they acquire their full meaning in context each time.

Another argument against the view that (at least in the eyes of the sophisticated segment of the audience) divine epiphanies were used ironically and subversively by Euripides, is the fact that Sophocles used such an epiphany in *Philoctetes* at 409; for if these epiphanies had been subverted by an ironic deployment by Euripides,[7] Sophocles, pious and beloved of the gods (a reputation in the tradition which is confirmed by the available historical evidence concerning his life), would not have used a strategy of closure that was tainted with impiety.

It is important to stress that, if we start with certain presuppositions about Euripides, we will inevitably structure the discourse in ways that will fit those presuppositions, which will thus appear to be validated, while in fact this pseudo-validation would be the result of a circular argument.[8] This is why critics who believed Euripides to be an atheist were able to read the plays in such a way that this belief was not invalidated. The same is true for those who expected irony to govern Euripidean tragedies, especially where religion is concerned.

Scholars who still believe in Euripidean "atheism" or "rationalism" would argue that theirs is the right interpretation, based on ancient perceptions of Euripides, and that therefore there is nothing wrong with giving it a central place in the interpretative discourse. Leaving aside the fact that the validity of this thesis is at the very least arguable, it is not the methodologically neutral approach to base the validity of one's analyses on the validity of an a priori thesis, however convincing this thesis may appear to be. In fact this particular thesis has been shown to be wrong, above all by Lefkowitz,[9] and I will be adding some further arguments to this discussion. It had appeared convincing because it had fitted the rationalizing cast of mind of the time. And this, the corruption of the discourse through cultural determination, is a major danger in interpretative strategies that are less methodologically neutral than they might have been; for instead of helping minimize cultural determination, such strategies place it at the very center of the discourse.

2) *The Reception of Euripides: "Atheism" and Aristophanes*

I will now discuss briefly this notion of Euripides' atheism and generally the question of Euripides' reception by his contemporaries. The previously accepted perception that Euripides had been unpopular, isolated, and persecuted was challenged by Stevens,[10] who concluded that it was wrong, and that in the eyes of his contemporaries he had been, after Sophocles, the most distinguished dramatist of his day. Subsequently, Lefkowitz[11] criticized decisively the view that the ancient tradition that Euripides had been associated with sophists and that he had been prosecuted for impiety shows Euripides' scepticism towards traditional religion. She showed that the argument is ultimately circular, for certain readings of Euripidean tragedies have led to a construct of an impious Euripides, the associate of sophists, and this construct then structured the modern readings of Euripidean tragedies. She also showed[12] how comedy was the source of many stories purporting to describe the reception of Euripides, while others[13] were modelled on the biographies of other poets, how the stories of his association with sophists and of his alleged trial were constructed, and how this constructed Euripides has structured the readings of Euripidean tragedies.

There can be no doubt that the Aristophanic presentation of Euripides has played a major role in structuring readings of this kind.[14] It may be argued that this is valid evidence about Euripides' contemporary reception; that, above all, the woman's allegation in *Thesmophoriazousai* 450-1 that Euripides through his tragedies had persuaded people that there are no gods suggests that this is how Euripidean tragedies were understood. But it is not legitimate to take this joke at face value, for Aristophanic comedy does not describe Athenian perceptions of tragedy, or at the very least, it cannot be assumed to do so, since so often we can see that it sets out a comic distortion of common perceptions; and it is this, surely, that makes it comical. We may only be able to have a partial perception of ancient humor, for humor, of course, is not transcultural,[15] but it is up to a point possible to recon-

Chapter 3: Euripidean Tragedy and Religious Exploration 295

struct the underlying assumptions, what needs to have been the case for the joke to work.[16]

If the audience's assumptions were that Euripides really did teach people not to believe in gods, there is nothing funny for an Athenian audience about a woman, the widowed mother of five children, whose husband was killed in a military campaign,[17] claiming that she lost a lot of her business, and is having difficulties to make ends meet because people no longer brought garlands, having been persuaded by Euripides that there are no gods. So, the joke must be located there, in the notion that Euripides persuaded the Athenians that there are no gods; such a distortion would make the widow a comic figure—while if she were reporting common assumptions about Euripides she would have been a sad figure. I suggest that what needs to have been the case for this to function as a joke is that Euripidean tragedies should not have been perceived to be aiming at convincing people that there were no gods, but that they should have included material that made such a comic distortion possible.

This would fit well with my readings as will be set out below. If, as I will argue, Euripides had contributed to the polis religious discourse, but in his own idiom, which included asking difficult questions, and which can be comically distorted into "Euripides through his tragedies persuaded people that there are no gods," that would be funny in a way comparable to that in which Aristophanes' distortion in the same play of Euripidean gender discourse is comical. For the description of Euripides' representation of women presented as a popular perception in *Thesmophoriazousai* is a radical comic distortion of the actual representations of women in the surviving tragedies—which are less inaccessible to us than the religious representations. The fact that, on my reconstruction of the religion joke, the two are comparable offers support to this reconstruction.

Let us consider two other passages which have helped shape modern perceptions of Euripides. In Aristophanes' *Frogs* 888-94 Euripides prays to the aether, the tongue, intelligence, and the nostrils, the tongue indicating a versatile tongue, the nostrils sharpness and subtlety of perception.[18] He is, in other words, shown privileging things that "intellectuals," at least as constructed in the popular perceptions that shaped *Clouds*, do. This fits with what the chorus say about Euripides at 1491-9, but we must be careful not to impose meanings here, and construct a tidy picture which distorts the ancient realities. At 1491-9[19] the chorus express the view that one of the reasons why Aeschylus has won was because Euripides had sat by Socrates and talked, discarding poetry and leaving out the things that matter most in tragedy; and he spent his time theorizing and quibbling nonsensically, which they consider insane. But the fact that they associate Euripides with Socrates does not mean that they thought Euripides worshiped new gods or was an atheist. First, it is far from certain that those were perceived as serious accusations against Socrates at the time of the production of *Frogs*—any more than they had been at the time of the production of *Clouds*. The years between the former production and Socrates' trial[20] were few, but they were significant and traumatic. Second, what both passages show Euripides doing is privileging intellect, thinking. His prayer at 888-94 would have been understood as a joke, a comical polarized distortion of Euripides' tendency to intellectualize, which is what the chorus accuse him of at 1491-9; it is not legitimate to assume it expresses the perception that he worshiped new gods or was an atheist. It is crucial to remember that Dionysos had originally gone to Hades to bring back Euripides.

Let us, then, consider briefly first, what is at issue in *Frogs*, and second, what perceptions of tragedy in general, and Euripidean tragedy in particular, are expressed in this comedy—keeping in mind that these perceptions are here structured through binarily opposed conceptual schemata, to which the two poets have been assimilated, above all, "old vs. new" and "Aeschylus' age::Athens powerful vs. Euripides' age::Athens in decline."[21] There are commonly agreed assumptions in the comedy about what makes a good tragedian: *dexiotes* and *nouthesia*, and, related to *nouthesia*, admonition, making people better.[22] The contest is an *agon sophias*, and Dionysos found it difficult to choose between Aeschylus and Euripides. Dionysos' own concerns are expressed at 1418-21:

> *ego katelthon epi poeten; tou charin?*
> *hin' he polis sotheisa tous chorous agei.*
> *hopoteros oun an tei polei parainesein*
> *mellei ti chreston, touton axein moi doko.*[23]

If some modern perceptions of Euripidean tragedies, and of Aristophanes' perceptions of Euripidean tragedies, were right, it would be very difficult to understand Dionysos' difficulties in adjudicating between the two. Another passage of *Frogs* shows us, I suggest, where the jokes are coming from, what it is about Euripidean tragedies that Aristophanes polarizes into those jokes. At 1052-6, to Euripides' defense of truth concerning the myth of Phaedra Aeschylus responds by accusing him of showing bad things which he ought to conceal, stating that they, as tragedians, are *didaskaloi*, and therefore they must *panu chresta legein*. Aeschylus' continuing attack at 1078ff on Euripides is based on the same grounds: Euripides has done (comically presented)

Chapter 3: Euripidean Tragedy and Religious Exploration 297

damage to the polis by showing, among other things, women giving birth in sanctuaries (which was sacrilegious), women sleeping with their brothers, and so on. Aeschylus is not suggesting that Euripides showed approval of such behavior in his tragedies; what was bad is that he showed it at all.

This is very close to what I am suggesting; that Euripides' religious discourse could be turned by Aristophanes into the joke that Euripides persuaded people that there were no gods, because Euripides showed the darker side of the gods more explicitly than others, and asked more disturbing questions, and included elements derived from sophistic and Anaxagorean thought.[24] This explanation fits precisely the chorus' description of the reasons for disapproval of Euripides at 1491-9. I will be arguing that Euripides deploys these so-called Anaxagorean and sophistic elements in the context of responding to the religious needs of the time. Here I will only stress that what is important was how he had deployed those elements. Lefkowitz has shown[25] that they are used to express the unconventional views of particular characters: several characters express doubts over the existence, or the justice, of the gods, but these people prove to have been wrong at the end.[26] Thus, the criticisms have been articulated only to be invalidated.[27] This, even on a culturally determined reading that does not involve attempting to reconstruct the ancient assumptions, should have led modern critics to the conclusion that Euripides was "answering" criticisms of the gods; that he was articulating criticisms and fears that were felt and expressed in real life and was giving positive, reassuring, albeit complex, answers.

3) *Modern Criticism and Ancient Audiences*

Why, then, has the expression of such critical views been taken by so many to be evidence for Euripides' "atheism" or "impiety," or something at any rate more in tune with mid-twentieth-century "rationality"? Obviously, one part of the answer is that, unless a deliberate effort is made to reconstruct the ancient perceptual filters, modern filters, shaped by modern assumptions, structure the understanding of a text by default, and in this case inevitably privileged the reading that made Euripides more like "us," Euripides the critic of traditional religion. Another part of the answer also results from the deployment of modern culturally determined assumptions, in symbiosis with the ancient tradition—privileged precisely because it fitted those assumptions. The fact that the bleakness of the problematization of religious matters in some Euripidean tragedies has often been interpreted as involving criticisms of the gods is the result of the implicit intrusion of the assumptions of twentieth-century liberal Christianity.

A comparable intrusion of culturally determined assumptions has led to the creation, and privileging, of the notion of Euripidean irony. Irony is an elastic concept, which has often been used in Euripidean studies as a strategy for making sense of something that clashed with the culturally determined reader's expectations. Thus, rationalists, who "knew" that Euripides could not possibly have believed all that rubbish about the gods, explained what to their eyes would otherwise appear to be naive and credulous in terms of irony. The fact that irony has acquired an especially privileged status in our culture has given new impetus to ironic readings of Euripides. These more recent, superficially sophisticated versions of Euripidean irony are also based on a priori presuppositions, and so are no less flawed methodologically than their predecessors—though the culturally determined nature of such readings, which ignore audiences and make no attempt to reconstruct an ancient text's ancient meanings, is given, explicitly or implicitly, false methodological respectability by postmodernism.[28] I will argue that such ironic readings are modern constructs in the discussion of *Orestes*, the tragedy considered par excellence ironic. Here I will say only that this type of reading, like that involving Euripides the atheist, is based on intentionalism. The radical flaws of intentionalism are now taken for granted in literary criticism. I will only stress that, not only are "intentions" a vague concept that ignores the complexity of selections made at various points of the conscious-unconscious spectrum, and shaped by parameters determined by cultural assumptions, not only are an author's intentions in general unknowable, but also, in the case of fifth-century tragedians, they are totally beyond our grasp. What is important, and what can, up to a point, be reconstructed in its main lines, is the ancient audience's assumptions, and so the main parameters of determination shaping the process of that audience's meaning creation. Within these parameters, we saw, individual responses are possible.

Critics have (some explicitly, others implicitly) focussed too much on the supposedly "enlightened" part of the audience. Whether a segment "enlightened" in the ways postulated (explicitly or implicitly) by such critics ever existed, or if it did whether it did so in other than the minutest numbers, is debatable; but even if it did, why should this be a more important segment than the majority of the audience in Euripides' parameters of selection? The judges whose judgment would have determined victory were statistically unlikely to have been part of such a segment, and more significantly, judgments were influenced by audience reactions. It is only because critics have read the Euripidean

Chapter 3: Euripidean Tragedy and Religious Exploration 299

plays in ways that fitted those rationalist antireligious presuppositions that perceptions of the audience have been implicitly made to fit such readings.

All Athenians took part in the intensive ritual life of the polis; thus, they all shared the emotional charge associated with rituals—whatever the exact nature of this may have been. For many Athenian men, and at least some Athenian women, performance in rituals, above all in choruses and dances, had been part of their education in their formative years. The large majority of Athenians believed in the gods of the polis, believed that the survival and prosperity of both polis and individuals depended on ensuring these gods' benevolence through ritual. This is suggested by their religious behavior, of the polis and of individuals, and also by their religious discourse.[29] In any case, I think that too much emphasis has been put on beliefs in the modern discourse, the result of the fact that many influential figures who structured the scholarly discourse on these matters had been brought up in the Protestant tradition. (The Orthodox Church, whose emphasis is more on ritual than dogma or spirituality gives a different perspective.) The participants in a ritual are seriously involved in the religion. The fact that in Athenian perceptions religion was at the very heart of the polis, articulated the polis and was articulated by it,[30] would have increased the emotional commitment in the rituals.

At the "enlightened" pole of the Athenian citizen population there may have been a group who, in another context, other than that of their involvement in ritual practice, may well have asked questions about the nature of gods, such as whether the divine really take the forms of the traditional gods.[31] But since the ultimate unknowability of the divine was a fundamental category in Greek religion, such problematization was not perceived to be a challenge to traditional religion. For this reason, there was no dichotomy between such problematization and the participation in rituals; whatever the forms of the divine, this is the form in which we offer worship to this divine. This may sound like a culturally determined assertion, but it is in fact based on Xenophon's presentation of the one individual who we know was prosecuted and put to death for impiety, Socrates.[32] In his rebuttal of the charge of impiety against Socrates, Xenophon says that the guidance Socrates was given by his *daimonion* was divine guidance no different from that offered by traditional divination, and that Socrates stressed the unknowability of much of the divine will, and the fact that there are limits to what the gods will allow mortals to know;[33] he also performed rituals for the gods and advised others to worship according to the rituals of the polis, not as "empty gestures," but as acts of piety towards the gods.[34]

At the other, the majority, end of the spectrum worship of the gods, and belief in the gods of traditional religion, does not imply a simple acceptance with no problematization. We are told by Thucydides, for example, that during the plague the Athenians felt that turning to the gods was useless, and since the plague struck indiscriminately, people were not restrained by fear of god or human law.[35] Consequently, all sections of the audience were interested in religious problematization, in differing degrees and depth, and all were involved in ritual in significant ways. The rituals of everyday life had a significant place in everyone's conceptual and emotional universe, and were of fundamental importance at the very least to the large majority of the Athenian audience. This, I will be arguing, has important implications for the reconstruction of the ways in which the ancient audience made sense of Euripidean tragedies.

Rituals are deployed in complex ways in Euripidean tragedies, to help create particular meanings and particular dramatic effects. To quote Easterling,[36] "Ritual was able to provide tragedy with a range of particularly potent metaphors—which tragedy likewise expressed in words, music and action—because it was intimately concerned with all the most important perceptions and experiences of the community." Here I want to go back to a basic question: Why is this consistently done through rituals? Why is Euripidean tragedy so often articulated through the deployment of rituals? Of course, rituals were part of the audience's shared experience, which could be used as a basis for creating meanings and particular dramatic effects; but it should not necessarily be assumed that this is the whole answer, especially since this, often dense, deployment of rituals goes together with the emphatic presence of gods, and the exploration of religious themes.[37] I argued in chapter III.1 that the articulation of Aeschylean tragedies through rituals, and their religious problematization, were aspects of the ritual matrix which had shaped the generation and development of early tragedy. I will be arguing here that Euripidean tragedies have not lost all connection with this ritual matrix; that different versions of further developments out of that matrix helped structure, in different ways, several Euripidean tragedies. I shall be returning to this question, after I have considered the deployment of ritual in a few Euripidean tragedies.

Chapter 3: Euripidean Tragedy and Religious Exploration   301

III.3.ii. *The Tragedies: Part One*

1) *Iphigeneia in Tauris*

I will begin with *Iphigeneia in Tauris*, for I have already discussed a major aspect of its religious problematization and explorations in some detail in chapter I.2. Here I will bring out the dense ritual framework that structures the tragedy, and show how religious problematization is intertwined with, and partly articulated through, this framework.

The tragedy takes place in front of the temple of Artemis in Tauris (34, 69-75). As it became clear in chapter I.2, much of this tragedy is, in one way or another, structured by ritual, above all human sacrifice. This, we saw, was intertwined with the problematization of human sacrifice. Three different types of human sacrifice come into play. First, a reported ritual, the sacrifice of Iphigeneia, aborted by the goddess, who replaced Iphigeneia with a deer. This sacrifice is repeatedly mentioned: at 8-30, where it is followed by a description of Iphigeneia's present ritual duties as priestess of Artemis in Tauris (34-41; cf. 53-9), and in many other places,[38] including at 358-60, where it is intertwined with other ritual acts, for Iphigeneia includes a report of her supplication of her father (361-71), which had included a mention of the wedding rites that her mother and the Argive women were performing for her thinking that she was being married.

Second, the past sacrifices that had been regularly performed in the Tauric cult of Artemis are repeatedly mentioned.[39] Finally, and more significantly, a ritual of human sacrifice is expected, and begins, to be enacted. Some of the preliminaries are enacted, or announced, or partly enacted. First, there is, at 241-5, the announcement of the arrival of new appropriate sacrificial victims, and the first mention of *chernibas* and *katargmata* that need to be prepared. This is repeated in another form at 335, where the herdsman says that the king is sending Iphigeneia the human victims *eis chernibas te kai sphagei'*. The use of religious terms from the audience's ritual reality, animal sacrifice, would have created a disconcerting effect, both relating it to the audience's religious practices and sharply distancing it from them.[40]

Some ritual acts are enacted in connection with the human sacrifice, a preliminary prayer (463-6) and ritual preparations (468-71). Others are mentioned in anticipation. At 617-35 Iphigeneia says that it is to her that falls the ritual duty to sacrifice Orestes, and explains what she does, and how other parts of the rite take place, and what she will do for his corpse in his death ritual. The preparations for the human sacrifice eventually become intermeshed with, and blur into, Iphigeneia's plan of escape, which involves further rituals. First, the pretense that the human sacrifice must be preceded by a special purification rite that has to be performed because the victims were especially polluted, which involves a cluster of ritual acts and religious terms (1033-1049). Iphigeneia tells Thoas that she is taking the statue to be purified in the sea because it had turned miraculously because of the victims' pollution. Second, the carrying off of the statue for the purposes of installing it in a new sanctuary, on Apollo's instructions, constitutes a ritual act, the foundation of a new cult.

The beginning of the purification ritual, the start of the procession, is enacted.[41] This is the beginning of the purification ritual as far as the Taurians are concerned, and elements from real purification rituals were included to convince the Taurians that this is what it was. So, for the audience, this was, at one level, part of a purification rite. But at another level it was part of the escape plan, which involved the carrying off of the statue, which in the audience's eyes was also, in a way, part of a ritual. The audience first heard of the plan to carry off the statue at 85-91, where Orestes addressed Apollo and mentioned the oracle given him to come to this sanctuary of Artemis and remove her statue which had fallen from heaven and take it to Athens, and again as part of Orestes' report of the oracle at 977-81.[42] A significant statement about this act, the validity of which will be confirmed later on in the tragedy, is made by Orestes, who tells Iphigeneia at 1012-5 that if Artemis was against the removal of her statue Apollo would not have ordered him to take it. He correctly assumes that Apollo's oracle reflects something approved of, certainly by his sister, and perhaps also, the implication may be, by all the gods, for, after all, Apollo spoke the will of Zeus.

When Thoas comes to inquire about the progress of the human sacrifice (1152-4) Iphigeneia appears, carrying the statue of Artemis. The sight of the cult's priestess carrying the statue would have evoked for the audience a ritual involving the manipulation of a cult statue, with both ritual components, the purification and the cult foundation, present in their perceptions, since, in their eyes, both were to be enacted. After giving various instructions on how to avoid pollution from the strangers whom she is claiming to be taking to be purified (1205ff) Iphigeneia instructs Thoas to purify the temple. At 1222 she announces the appearance of the victims, says that she will purify them, and makes a ritual proclamation for people to move away so that they are not defiled by this pollution. She then prays to Artemis, a cryptic, polysemic prayer that covers both what Thoas expects to hear and Iphigeneia's real hopes.

The ritual enacted at the surface level evoked real life rites, such as the purification of the statue of Athena Polias in the sea during the

Chapter 3: Euripidean Tragedy and Religious Exploration 303

festival of the Plynteria, a rite which, like the one which Iphigeneia claims will perform, was secret and had a gloomy element—the day in which it was celebrated was inauspicious.[43] The ritual enacted at the level of the real intentions of the chief participants, known to the audience, involved taking a statue from one sanctuary to a new sanctuary, and this would have evoked a ritual of cult foundation which in religious practice involved a procession.[44]

Other ritual acts also take place as part of the escape plan: Iphigeneia supplicates the chorus not to reveal the plan (1068-70) and the chorus swear by Zeus that they will not (1077); Iphigeneia prays to Artemis for her help, and in her prayer is intertwined the notion that if she does not, Apollo's prophecies will no longer be believed by mortals because of her (1082-8). At 1289-92 and 1313-6 the messenger announces, and at 1327-1419 he describes, and comments on, the flight of Iphigeneia, Orestes, and Pylades and the theft of the statue.[45] At 1331-8 he reports the ritual actions performed by Iphigeneia as part of the purification ritual aiming at deceiving the Taurians. At 1388-1403 he reports that Iphigeneia addressed a prayer to Artemis, and the sailors answered with a paean. He ends his report with the hope that they will catch the fugitives with the help of Poseidon, whom he believes to be hostile to the Pelopids, and the characterization of Iphigeneia as a traitor who is ungrateful to Artemis who saved her at Aulis—with the implied belief that Artemis would be hostile to her. Thoas makes explicit the belief that Artemis will be on the Taurians' side (1425-6). But Athena appears at 1435 and makes clear that the escape and removal of the statue was preordained by Apollo's oracle, and that Poseidon, at Athena's request, is helping this escape. She then orders Orestes to take the statue to Halai Araphenides in Attica, and build a temple to, and institute the cult of, Artemis Tauropolos, part of the ritual of which she describes; Iphigeneia is to be the first priestess of Artemis at Brauron, where she will be buried and receive heroic cult. I discussed the zooming to the audience's realities through Athena's speech in chapter I.2, where, we saw, the fact that the cults of Artemis Tauropolos at Halai Araphenides and of Artemis Brauronia at Brauron are presented as having been instituted on the orders of Athena symbolically anchored by the authority of the poliadic deity—as well as explored certains aspects of the cults of Artemis.[46]

Thoas' response at 1475-6 characterizes as wrong thinking to hear the words of the gods and disobey, and adds (1478-9) *ti gar pros tous sthenontas theous hamillasthai kalon?* At 1480-1 he uses the religious word *kathidrysainto*, which confirms and stresses the perception of the taking of the statue as a ritual: *itosan eis sen syn theas agalmati gaian, kathidrysainto t' eutychos bretas.* Athena replies (at 1486):

*aino; to gar chreon sou te kai theon kratei.*⁴⁷ She thus brings up the difficult notion of *to chreon*, which the gods must also obey. Insofar as this notion can be seen as at least partly absolving the gods of what may appear unfeeling behavior towards mortals, this could function as a[n at least partly] reassuring representation. But insofar as this notion is unfathomable, and its operations difficult to grasp and articulate, it is a frightening notion. However, this sinister facet of the *to chreon* may itself have been deconstructed in the audience's perceptions through the possibility that in this case *to chreon* may have been the will of Zeus, which Apollo had spoken; this would have been a reassuring representation.

These questions are, I believe, left open in this tragedy; no easy answers are given, for in the Greek perceptions there were no easy answers. What, I would argue, this tragedy does with Athena's last words is shift the focus, displace it, from this unfathomable notion to the gods; first to Athena's help to Iphigeneia, Orestes, and Pylades, and then to the audience's own realities, by evoking, through *semnon bretas*, which are her very last words, the worship of the gods, especially, through the mention of this cult statue, the audience's cult of Artemis Tauropolos. Cult, especially a cult founded on Athena's instructions, is the reassuring aspect of religion.

The tragedy ends with a reference to the audience's own cult activities. The epilogue, if, as I believe, is authentic,⁴⁸ draws attention to the nature of the chorus as a chorus for Dionysos in the present, and so reinforces this shift to ritual, the ritual of the present, and in general strengthens the tragedy's ritual dimension further; and this would have reinforced the authority of the aetiology.

Let us now return to the beginning of the tragedy, to explore another major strand of this tragedy's ritual skeleton, also intermeshed with religious exploration, the strand that pertains to prophecy. The first appearance of prophecy is in its lowest form, and presents it as confusing and misleading: Iphigeneia has a dream, which the audience knows was prophetic (though it only told part of the truth), but which she has misinterpreted (44-60). A higher form of prophecy makes its first appearance, at 85-91, where Orestes addresses Apollo, and mentions the oracle the god had given him, instructing him to come to this Taurian sanctuary of Artemis, take her statue and bring it to Athens. In his opening words (78-9) Orestes expresses some dissatisfaction with Apollo's instructions. The theme of prophecy returns at 569-75, where Iphigeneia, on learning that Orestes is alive, assumes that her dream was false. In response, (the still unrecognized) Orestes expresses his belief that not only dreams, but the gods themselves (meaning the oracles they give) are deceitful, and that those who believe the oracles perish. At 711-5 he repeats more explicitly and forcefully that Apollo deceived him. Pylades at 719-22 tells him that the oracle may yet prove right, and things may turn out differently from the way they look at present, but Orestes is not prepared to accept this possibility. The theme of the oracle Apollo gave to Orestes resurfaces at 937, and then again at 976-86.

The third stasimon (1234-83) is a hymn to Apollo, and includes the myth of the Previous Owners of the Delphic oracle.[49] In the version presented here Apollo took over Themis' oracle after killing the dragon who had guarded it; to avenge her daughter, Gaia sent prophetic night dreams which made Apollo's oracle redundant; Zeus, whose help Apollo sought, removed the night dreams' truthfulness, and restored men's confidence in Apollo's prophecies. In this version of the myth, then, the pair Gaia-Themis is implicitly compared with, and presented as inferior to, the pair Zeus-Apollo. This myth, part of a song praising Apollo at a crucial moment in the action, foreshadows the happy outcome, for it suggests that Orestes' doubts were mistaken, and Apollo's guidance was right. For stressing that Apollo's prophecy is guaranteed by Zeus was equivalent to confirming its validity, and thus indicating the tragedy's happy ending.

The validity of prophecy has been repeatedly connected to the outcome of Orestes' travails in this tragedy; so the happy outcome can be seen to confirm the validity of prophecy, at least of Apollo's prophecy at Delphi. That prophecy is uncertain and vulnerable to misinterpretation was something the audience were all too aware of, and this perception is articulated in this tragedy. But through the myth of the Previous Owners, these negative characteristics of prophecy gravitated to Gaia's prophecy, which is defeated in myth, and proved conducive to misinterpretation within the play—because Iphigeneia's dream had only told part of the truth. For in the myth the prophetic dreams sent by Gaia are negatively characterized: they are born of malice, they come unbidden (and so are uncontrollable), and they are associated, through language and content, with darkness and night. Thus, in both myth and play, the dark side of prophecy drifts to Gaia, and this allows Apollo's prophecy to emerge as wholly positive. Prophecy's dark side has been articulated, but it came to drift to the defeated and superseded Gaia, so it has not contaminated Apollo's oracle. On the contrary, Apollo's oracle has contributed to the dark prophecy's defeat, and is thus presented as its opposite, strengthened by the other's failure.

The tragedy's outcome demonstrates that Orestes' doubts and scepticism were mistaken, the prophecies were true, and Apollo had given him excellent guidance, which proved beneficial beyond Orestes' expectations, and led to the foundation of two cults beneficial for all time. The ways of the divine were more difficult to fathom than Orestes thought.

Human sacrifice and prophecy are the two major rituals structuring the tragedy, and they articulated two major areas of religious exploration. But there are also many other ritual references and enacted ritual acts, which I will now set out, in order to show the density of this tragedy's ritual skeleton.

I begin with rites pertaining to funerary ritual, of which there are three clusters. In the first, Iphigeneia announces that she will pour chthonic libations, for Orestes who she thinks is dead (61-3); she pours them at 159-72, and mentions two mourning rites that she will not be able to perform at his grave, lament, and the offering of locks of her hair. At 178 the chorus take up the lament.[50] The fact that the audience knew that Orestes was alive would have made them see this as not a proper part of a death ritual; but this perception did not alter the fact that the play was articulated also through the performance of ritual acts that were part of the death ritual in the audience's reality. Later on, at 617-35, we saw, Iphigeneia informs Orestes of what she will do for his corpse in the death ritual. Finally, at 702-3 Orestes, who thinks he is going to be sacrificed, asks Pylades to erect him a cenotaph and put up a grave monument and for Electra to perform lament and bring locks of hair to this grave.

Another major nexus of ritual, and generally religious, references pertains to Orestes' persecution by the Erinyes. Its first appearance is at 267-8, a report of Orestes' vision of the Erinyes, followed by a prayer by a Taurian 268-74, and then a description of Orestes' vision of the Erinyes (281-300). The second major cluster begins with another reference to the Erinyes at 931-5; then, at 940ff Orestes tells the whole story of his travails with the dread goddesses and his sojourn in Athens, or rather a version of it that includes the aetiology of a particular ritual in the Choes at the Anthesteria (which zoomed the world of the tragedy to the world of the audience),[51] and also the institution of the shrine to the Erinyes, which had the same effect. The twist in the myth here (which involves further ritual references) is that not all the Erinyes had accepted the judgment, and those who did not are now persecuting Orestes, who had returned to Delphi and supplicated Apollo for salvation; Apollo had sent him to the land of the Taurians to remove the statue of Artemis and take it to Athens.

There are also other ritual references of various types. At 221-8 Iphigeneia expresses the normality she has been robbed of through the ritual duties she is not performing, as she would have done, as a normal *parthenos* in her homeland, celebrating Hera with song and dance, and

Chapter 3: Euripidean Tragedy and Religious Exploration 307

weaving the image of Athena in the Titanomachy, and contrasts them with the bloodthirsty rite she is in fact performing in her present life. The worship of Hera at Argos is the obvious cultic service for the daughter of the king of Argos to be performing. The reference to weaving the image of Athena in the Titanomachy inevitably evoked for the Athenian audience the weaving of the peplos of Athena to be presented at the Panathenaia by the *Ergastinai* and the *Arrhephoroi*,[52] and this would have partly zoomed what would have been Iphigeneia' normal fate to the reality of the Athenian audience, whose virgin daughters wove Athena's peplos as *Arrhephoroi* and especially and more relevantly to Iphigeneia's age group, as *Ergastinai*.[53] At 735-752 Iphigeneia and Pylades swear an oath, she by Artemis, he by Zeus, that each will do as they promised. At 798-9 the chorus says to Orestes ... *ou dikaios tes theou ten prospolon chraineis athiktois peribalon peplois chera*. At 818-9 there is a reference to a part of the wedding ritual that had been performed at Aulis for Iphigeneia. At 778 Iphigeneia threatens Orestes in her letter, as she tells it to Pylades, that if he does not come to take her away she will become *araia* in his house.

The third stasimon, we saw, was a hymn to Apollo. Other choral songs also involve ritual and the evocation of ritual. The parodos begins at 123 with the ritual injunction *euphameit'* and contains an address to Artemis. In the first strophe of the second stasimon (1089-1105 cf. especially 1097-1105) the chorus express longing for an Artemis firmly placed in the Delian cultic context;[54] this zooms the world of the tragedy to the religious realities of the audience, to Artemis' Delian cult. In the first antistrophe they mention their present situation, in which they serve *tas elaphoktonou theas amphipolon*, Iphigeneia, and the altars on which it is not sheep which are sacrificed. This reference to Artemis' Taurian cult at 1112-6 effected a distancing of the world of the tragedy from that of the audience. In the second strophe, they sing, among other things, that Apollo will lead Iphigeneia, Orestes, and Pylades to Athens, while they, the chorus, will be left there. In the second antistrophe[55] the chorus wish that they could be at their home, and that they would be taking part in dances with their contemporaries, in a vivid description that would have evoked *parthenoi* dancing at weddings and other occasions, in the audience's realities. Finally, as we saw, the epilogue draws attention to the nature of the chorus as a chorus for Dionysos in the present, and so strengthens further the tragedy's ritual dimension. There are also other religious references that do not involve ritual.[56]

It is clear, then, that *Iphigeneia in Tauris* has a very great density of ritual and dense religious problematization. I discussed in chapter I.2 the complex problematization and exploration of human sacrifice, and of certain present-day rites that may appear related to it, and of the fact that myths of human sacrifice are closely related to present-day cult, and here I discussed the other major exploration of a religious issue in the play, prophecy; a minor strand involves the aetiology of the Anthesteria. Both major explorations also involved explorations of the nature of the gods. All these religious explorations, including the exploration of the nature of the gods, were intertwined with, and articulated partly through, a dense ritual framework that structures the play. It follows, then, that any attempt to discuss these questions outside this framework will inevitably produce readings different from those of the ancient audience, who had made sense of them in that framework, and through filters constructed in interaction with that framework.

If we scrape off all the accretions resulting from the discourse about tragedy that began with Aristotle, it becomes clear that the situation at the performance of this tragedy was as follows. The audience were in a religious space, a sanctuary, at a religious time, a festival, watching a performance, in which the identity of the chorus as a chorus in the present performing in honor of Dionysos was not neutralized, representing a world full of religion, with constant ritual references, and references to deities that were identified as representations of the deities they themselves worshiped, with some references connecting the world of the play directly and significantly with the world of the audience, through zoomings to, and especially the representation of the institution of, their own cults, a performance which problematized and explored religious matters. In their assumptions those gods were real, and the mortals' relationships to them, of the kind represented, problematized and explored in the tragedies, were of fundamental importance; I therefore find it very difficult to understand how it is possible to believe that the audience did not perceive this as a "religious" play, a locus in which problems to do with religion—as well as other things—were explored in ways that enriched the polis religious discourse.

2) *Medea*

Of course, not all tragedies have this ritual density or this depth and intensity of religious problematization. I will now consider a tragedy that belongs to the other end of the spectrum of ritual density and religious problematization from *Iphigeneia in Tauris, Medea*.[57] No significant part of *Medea* is structured by ritual. Of the rites that are enacted in the tragedy most are invocations of divinities; thus, for example, after an invocation of Zeus by the chorus at 148-50, which

Chapter 3: Euripidean Tragedy and Religious Exploration

then turned into an address to Medea, that included the statement *Zeus soi tade syndikesei* (158), at 160 Medea calls on Themis and Artemis as witnesses to her sufferings and asks them to avenge her against Jason who broke his oaths. Another rite enacted on the stage is the supplication of Kreon by Medea (324-56);[58] another is the oath taking by Aigeus (752-5)—which also evokes Jason's oath now broken. As for ritual references, at 1053-5 Medea deploys what Page calls a "macabre metaphor"[59] of sacrifice for the infanticide.[60] At 1377 Jason asks to bury the children, and at 1378-83 Medea, in the chariot of the Sun, announces that she will bury them in the sanctuary of Hera Akraia, and she will institute a festival in their honor.[61]

Though there is no great ritual density in this tragedy, rituals are of crucial importance in the plot: Medea's and Jason's wedding, Jason's oath, Jason's new wedding to Kreon's daughter; there is also the report of Aigeus' consultation of the Delphic oracle.

Medea's distancing to the divine sphere at the conclusion of the play, created, I have argued elsewhere,[62] the ideological space in which she escapes punishment for her deed. But this did not neutralize the fact that in this tragedy a bad woman escapes punishment. I hope to have shown that in the eyes of the ancient audience, this would have been perceived as problematic, but it would also have beeen seen as correlative to Jason's betrayal of his oaths.[63]

Medea ends with the so-called floating epilogue (1415-9), which also occurs, with a different beginning, at the end of *Alcestis, Andromache, Bacchai,* and *Helen.* I discuss these epilogues in appendix 2. Here I want to note first that verse 1415 occurs only in this tragedy, and differs from the beginning of the other four epilogues, which begin *pollai morphai ton daimonion,* in that it emphasizes the role of Zeus:

pollon tamias Zeus en Olympoi,
polla d' aelptos krainousi theoi;
kai ta dokethent' ouk etelesthe,
ton d' adoketon poron heure theos.
toiond' apebe tode pragma.

And second, that in this tragedy, in the eyes of the ancient audience, this epilogue articulated the ultimate unknowability of the will of the gods, and generated at least the possibility of the meaning that the success of Medea's revenge and successful escape was the will of the gods, and that this was correlative with Jason's betrayal of his oaths.[64] The notion is explored in this play that if men break oaths, an institution that helps create order in society, if they abuse their position of power over women, it will be their own fault when catastrophe follows, and the gods will not necessarily be on the men's side. The importance of oath taking had been stressed by the chorus, who in the first stasimon articulated the notion that if oath breaking remains unpunished serious disorder will follow; that since men break oaths with impunity and the gods no longer police these oaths, the proper order of things has been upset and a reversed world has been created.

Consequently, though in this tragedy enacted ritual plays a smaller role than in most, and though the center of the explorations and problematizations in *Medea* pertains not to religious discourse, but to gender discourse, ritual, and above all the reported ritual of oath taking was of crucial importance, and it was religion that provided the framework and mechanisms through which the tragedy was articulated and gender discourse explored. This is not a matter of "empty convention." For it is only because religion and the actions of the gods would have been perceived by the audience to have been central, in the world of the play and in their own, that those complex explorations could have taken place, and the disturbing position about gender relations mentioned above could be articulated. Without these religious perceptions *Medea* would be a simpler, cruder tragedy, with an ending that, given Greek cultural assumptions, would have been nonsensical.

This tragedy, then, is considerably distanced from the ritual matrix which, on my reconstruction, had shaped the generation and development of early tragedy. This is a particular version of the tragic matrix (that had developed out of the ritual matrix), in which religious explorations are not central, and there are fewer rituals, but in which nevertheless those rituals are crucial, and religion is of central importance.

3) *Suppliants*

In *Suppliants*, by contrast, religious problematization is important, there is a great density of religious references, and ritual plays an important part. In general, the play has a significant religious dimension, a fact accepted even by those who stress the play's political aspects.[65]

Suppliants begins, and a substantial part of it is structured by, an enacted ritual of supplication, a supplication at the altar in the court of the sanctuary of Demeter and Kore at Eleusis. At 28-31 it becomes clear that the audience would have understood that the occasion on which Aithra was being supplicated was that of a festival, specifically, that she had come to sacrifice at Eleusis in the context of the festival Proerosia.[66] The ritual of supplication, then, intersects with, and disrupts,[67] a ritual which would have been perceived to be part of a festi-

Chapter 3: Euripidean Tragedy and Religious Exploration 311

val celebrated in the world of the audience, and this would have zoomed the world of the tragedy to that of the audience's reality. Within the framework of the visually articulated supplication the tragedy begins with a prayer, by Aithra, which zoomed the tragedy to the audience's realities by zooming it through words, as well as visually,[68] to the Eleusinian sanctuary:[69] lines 1-3,

> Demeter hestiouch' Eleusinos chthonos
> tesde, hoi te naous exchete prospoloi theas,
> eudaimonein me Thesea te . . .

and again at 28-31, when, we saw, Aithra says she went to Eleusis to make a sacrifice *elthous' . . . pros tonde sekon, entha prota phainetai phrixas hyper ges tesde karpimos stachys*. Then she goes on to articulate verbally the rite of supplication and again refers to a feature of the sanctuary of Demeter and Kore at Eleusis that would have again zoomed the tragedy to the audience's reality: 33-4: *meno pros hagnais escharais dyoin theain Kores te kai Demetros*. The object of the supplication is itself a religious matter, to obtain burial for the Argives killed in the expedition of the Seven against Thebes.

In the first part of the parodos (42-70) the chorus articulate verbally the rite of supplication; in the second they lament (71-86).[70] Theseus refers to this lamentation, and to other parts of the death ritual, at his entrance (87-9), and then he describes the supplication ritual as he sees it, stressing the ritual elements that shows the suppliants to be mourners, and also the ritual elements that one would normally expect to see, thus defining an identity for participants in a ritual appropriate to the sanctuary, *theoria*.[71] At 114 Adrastos defines himself as a suppliant of Theseus and of Athens. But it soon becomes clear that this supplication involves more complex religious problems than is at first apparent. For in the discussion between Theseus and Adrastos that follows the latter's request[72] it emerges that Adrastos had made religious mistakes. First, he had misinterpreted an oracle concerning the marriage of his daughters,[73] which evokes that past ritual of prophecy; more seriously,[74] he did not consult seers or take omens before embarking on the expedition (155-6); Theseus' reaction to this information is to comment that Adrastos had not embarked on the expedition with the gods' *eunoia*; at which point Adrastos reveals that it was even worse than that, that he had, in fact, gone against the advice of Amphiaraos who was a seer (158); Theseus' reaction, expresses, I suggest, the audience's perception of such behavior: *houto to theion rhadios apestraphes?* Adrastos and the others, then, had brought their fate upon themselves, but this does not necessarily mean that Theseus can ignore their plight. As his mother Aithra tells him, when pleading for the mothers, at 301-2 *ta ton theon skopein keleuo me sphales atimasas*. She then refers to the burial of the dead as being a part of the *nomima* of all Greece (311).[75]

Thus, supplication is one issue of religious importance problematized in this tragedy. Does one grant everyone's supplication, and if not, should one help someone who brought their misfortunes on themselves, by behaving in a way that courted divine displeasure? But what about those who were innocent victims of the situation? And shouldn't one help when the cause is just and pious, even if the people involved had brought these things upon themselves? This problematic supplication also brings in, and problematizes, the issue of the right to burial.

At 524-7 Theseus says that it was the common law of Greece to bury the dead.[76] He says it in reply to the herald, whose emphasis on the sacrilegious aspect of the actions of the Seven (496-9, 504-5) reproblematizes the issue. After he had invoked the common law of Greece, Theseus reinforces the position he now takes that to bury the dead is what is the religiously right thing to do: at 559 he says *thapsai doth' emin tois thelousin eusebein* and at 563 that not to bury the dead is to disobey an ancient law of the gods. Before he goes off to fight he invites the gods' support[77] at 595-8 and expresses the belief that without the gods' goodwill men cannnot win victory, which cannot be achieved through valor alone.

The possibility that the justice of a cause may not necessarily ensure the support of the gods is adumbrated by the chorus in the second stasimon, at 610-2:

> First hemichorion: *dikaious daimonas sy g' ennepeis*.
> Second hemichorion: *tines gar alloi nemousi symphoras?*
> First hemichorion: *diaphora pollon brotoisin eisoro*.

But the reply by the second hemichorion at 614-6 is unequivocally positive, reaffirming the justice of the gods; 615-5 (*kakon d' anapsychas theoi brotois nemousi, panton term' echontes autoi*) also evoked the notion of the unknowability, the fact that mortals cannot always fathom how the end of all things will turn out—with the implication that this is why they may not see the gods' ultimate justice.

At the end of the the second stasimon, at 625-33, the chorus pray, and their prayer is answered by the messenger's news of the Athenian victory. The messenger reports the ritual of the burial of the other Ar-

Chapter 3: Euripidean Tragedy and Religious Exploration 313

gives (other than the Seven) by Theseus (756-9), and of Theseus washing and laying out the corpses of the Seven (765-6). Then, the corpses of the Seven are brought on stage.[78] After an anapaestic prelude (announcing the return of Adrastos with the corpses) the lamentation takes place over them, the first *kommos* with Adrastos (798-837). Adrastos gives an *epitaphios* speech (857-917);[79] then a funeral procession takes the corpses to the pyres; their cremation is almost enacted, in that it takes place just off stage, in a space presented as an extension of the stage, as when, for example, Euadne throws herself on Kapaneus' pyre. Eventually there is the procession of the dead men's sons carrying the ashes in funerary receptacles, over which they, as a secondary chorus, and the chorus of mothers, lament the final *kommos* (1114-64).[80]

After that Theseus sends off the Argives, asking them to remember Athens' benefaction to them, invoking Zeus and the Olympians as witnesses (1165-75). But Athena appears in epiphany and urges Theseus to bind the Argives through an oath ritual in which they will swear that they and their descendants will never attack Athens, on pain of destruction. The oath ritual will involve the Delphic oracle, which stresses explicitly the Panhellenic dimension of religion. The sacrificial knife will be buried near the burial pyres, and this will stop any future Argive invasion.[81] Athena also orders the institution of *temene* in the place where the corpses were burnt,[82] and prophesies the Sack of Thebes by the Epigonoi. The play concludes with a funeral procession carrying the ashes.

This tragedy, then, has a great ritual density, with significant parts being articulated by ritual, and it includes the appearance of a deity. The tragedy zoomed the world of the play to that of the audience from the beginning, through the sanctuary and the religious occasion, with the strongest focus being on the sanctuary. This focus emerged in the opening words of the play, and was visually articulated, and so ever present, as well as being repeatedly mentioned.[83] It has been suggested[84] that there is some clash between the setting in the Eleusinian sanctuary of Demeter and Kore and the tragedy's focus on burial, corpses, and the death ritual. This is wrong; it is a culturally determined notion that ignores cultic facts as well as complexities. First, death is inextricably connected with the Eleusinian sanctuary and cult, one of the two main goddesses of which is the Queen of the Underworld, and in which Hades and Persephone were worshiped, as Plouton and Kore in their personae relating to fertility, and as Theos and Thea in their personae as rulers of the Underworld, which presented the gods of the dead in a more benevolent and approachable form.[85] The two personae of each of these two deities may be separately articulated, but each is present in the other. The whole point about the eschatological/soteriological facet of the Eleusis cult is the presence of death, but a death and afterlife articulated in more reassuring terms.

Second, the nexus of attitudes pertaining to the sadness of death, which are expressed in the death ritual, is complementary to, not in conflict with, the hope in a happy afterlife offered by the Eleusinian Mysteries. The fact that epitaphs in the archaic period and private epitaphs in the fifth century do not reflect mysteric beliefs in a happy afterlife, but stress the sadness of the death, despite the fact that at the very least many of the Athenian dead commemorated in those epitaphs were (extremely likely to have been) initiates, illustrates that different aspects of the complex attitudes towards death were expressed in different contexts; and the sadness at the loss of life need not be contradictory with the belief in a happy afterlife.[86] The exception was, in the fifth century, the Athenian war dead, for they were perceived, at this time, to have gained immortality,[87] and it was not appropriate to express sadness at their death. But in one epitaph for the Argive war dead who fell in the battle of Tanagra, set up in Athens, the word *penthos* is mentioned.[88] So the Seven, and the Argive dead in general, were distanced in the eyes of the audience from their own war dead, for whom it was not appropriate to express sadness, because they were Argives, because they had lived in the heroic past, and also because they were fighting against the advice of the gods. It is in this context that the Athenian audience would have placed the spectacle of lamentation for these war dead. Nevertheless, through this lamentation, the notion that the death of men in battle entails a tragic loss to the family is also expressed; it is articulated, and so acknowledged, but at a symbolic distance, so that the ideology of good death in the service of the polis is not threatened or challenged.

To return to the role of the Eleusinian sanctuary in the creation of meanings in this tragedy, it follows from what we have seen that there is no incongruity between the setting and the play's content, and no "assault" on the Eleusinian rites;[89] if there is tension, it is an explicit articulation of the tension between the different facets of Athenian attitudes to death. And this helps create interesting meanings: in the middle of all this focus on death, corpses, and the death ritual, the Eleusinian sanctuary setting reminds the audience—at whatever segment of the conscious-unconscious spectrum of meaning creation—of the further dimension of death, the possibility of a happy afterlife, and so provides a framework of hope.

We cannot be certain how deeply and how widely the belief in the immortality of the war dead, constructed by Athenian polis ideology, was held. But in any case, the juxtaposition of the Eleusinian sanctuary

Chapter 3: Euripidean Tragedy and Religious Exploration 315

with its connotations of happy afterlife and of the grief associated with death in war, and the death ritual for those "other" war dead, would have created a representation of reassurance, by framing death in war and grief through images of a happy afterlife. This representation, then, in this tragedy, would have helped sustain the ideology of death at war which may have been coming under pressure.

A date in the late 420s is most probable for the production of *Suppliants*.[90] It has been argued that it was inspired by a contemporary event, the Theban refusal to return the Athenian dead after the battle of Delion,[91] an incident discussed at some length by Thucydides.[92] Bowie[93] has argued that *Suppliants* refracted these events in complex ways, and through that complex refraction[94] presented that event in certain particular terms which offer some hope for the future.[95] Whether or not the conclusion of this subtle analysis is right, there can be no doubt that, if the tragedy had indeed been produced after Delion, it would have evoked the real life situation, and therefore zoomed the world of the tragedy to a serious matter of the audience's realities, especially since, comparably to the fact that Adrastos had not embarked on his expedition with the gods' consent, the Boeotians had accused the Athenians of sacrilege.[96] The tragedy ultimately offers divine approval of the decision to privilege the right to burial, even of people whose religious conduct had been questionable, and thus confirms the notion that the right to burial is divinely sanctioned.

In this tragedy, then, great ritual density goes together with dense religious exploration. Supplication, the right to burial, the religious dimension of death, attitudes towards death, and the relationship of those attitudes to polis ideology, are some of the themes in these explorations. Furthermore, by urging Theseus to ask the Argives to take an oath, Athena also problematized the notion of *charis*[97] in human relationships, when not underpinned by divine guarantees—which is what the oath ritual brings about, the policing of the agreement by the gods. This, of course, also helps stress further the importance of religion in the conduct of human affairs, an attitude that has been expressed repeatedly in this tragedy: one should behave piously, in the ways in which the gods expect one to; pious behavior can bring rewards, since only the gods can give victory in war and guarantee order. In this context the Panhellenic religious dimension is presented as a crucial locus for relationships between different poleis, in the same way that it was crucial in the relationships between cities in the audience's reality.

Let us now compare this tragedy with its great ritual density and religious explorations to Aeschylus' *Suppliants*. The most striking difference is that the Euripidean tragedy has a much more complex canvas. As we saw, in Euripides' *Suppliants* the supplication is complicated by the fact that the expedition had been mounted against the divine will;[98] associated with this are the themes of overweening pride and divine punishment. Other themes are also included in the tragedy; among others, the notion of entitlement to proper burial; a debate about democracy;[99] an *epitaphios* speech; the mother-son relationship and the theme of the mothers in mourning and mothers lamenting,[100] to which is juxtaposed the figure of the mourning father; conjugal love and the notion of the wife who cannot live without her husband, and a married woman's relationship to the natal family;[101] the theme of the orphan sons and of the legacy of vengeance.

It is clear even from this brief comparison that in this tragedy human relationships are explored for their own sake and in complex ways. A trend towards both greater complexity of the canvas and greater development of human to human relationships, is also found, we saw, within Aeschylus' work, distinguishing the *Oresteia* from the earlier extant tragedies; now these tendencies have developed very much further. Another, related, difference between the two suppliant tragedies is that the Euripidean tragedy does not have the same density of religious references as Aeschylus' *Suppliants*. This less strong foregrounding of the religious goes together with the much greater development of the human-to-human facet. This tragedy, then, looks like a descendant of the ritual matrix via the early tragic matrix seen in the *Oresteia*, but with even greater complexity of canvas and richer developments of various aspects of human relationships.

III.3.iii. *The Religious Dimension: Some Remarks*

Clearly, Medea on the one hand and Iphigeneia in Tauris and Suppliants on the other represent two ends of the spectrum as far as the presence of the religious dimension in Euripidean tragedies is concerned. But it is significant that, even at the minimum end of the spectrum, in Medea, the religious dimension is crucial. A sceptic may claim that no significance should be attached to this, that this minimum religious presence is what we would expect in Greek tragedy. But first, such a view cannot account for the crucial role of this religious dimension to the tragedy, crucial because without it the tragedy would not make much sense when read through the ancient perceptual filters. Second, and most importantly, such a view begs the question of why this should be so; of why there is no known Greek tragedy with no religion, especially no known one by Euripides. The presence, and frequent strength, of the religious dimension is not the inevitable result of the fact that tragedies were set in the heroic age; and in any case, as we saw in

Chapter 3: Euripidean Tragedy and Religious Exploration 317

chapter I.2, the tragedies' heroic setting was a preferred choice because it fulfilled the tragedies' perceived "needs"; if another setting could have better fulfilled the needs of another type of tragedy, then that setting would have been chosen instead.

Are we to believe that the strength of the religious dimension in Euripidean tragedy was the result of contingent accumulation? On the one hand the influence of the conventions of the tragic tradition, and on the other of the deployment of ritual elements because rituals were part of the audience's shared experience, which could be used as a basis for creating meanings and particular dramatic effects? For this seems the only alternative to the interpretation that tragedy, including Euripidean tragedy, was also, and very significantly, a discourse of religious exploration—and developed out of a ritual matrix in which religious exploration had been central. Besides the a priori implausibility of the theory of contingent accumulation, its inevitable implication would be the assumption that Euripides was deploying (however skillfully) the conventions of an empty tradition. This may satisfy those who privilege ironic self-deconstructing readings, but it cannot stand close scrutiny. For, if we leave aside culturally determined assumptions which ultimately rely on the intentionalist fallacy, and instead try to reconstruct the meanings which the ancient audience would have created in the course of the performance, we find that in many Euripidean tragedies religious problematization was, first, very important, and second, significantly intertwined with ritual elements—as, we saw, was the case in *Iphigeneia in Tauris* and *Suppliants*. Finally, this theory of contingent accumulation would not explain the varying pattern of the strength of the religious dimension in the different Euripidean tragedies, which will emerge below. Nor would it explain the nature of the religious dimension in Euripidean tragedies, for example the density of cult institutions, especially by deities.[102]

In the next section I will consider the deployment of ritual and the articulation of religious exploration in the extant Euripidean tragedies not yet discussed, starting with the earliest, *Alcestis*, produced at 438.[103]

III.3.iv. *The Tragedies: Part Two*

1) *Alcestis*

In *Alcestis* no deity appears in epiphany at the end, but Apollo and Thanatos appear in the prologue, on an empty stage.[104] Apollo sets out the story which is the framework of the play, a purely religious framework; the dialogue between Apollo and Thanatos,[105] which fol-

318   *Part III: Religion and the Fifth-Century Tragedians*

lows, develops this, in that it explores the frontiers between Apollo's powers and the *timai* due to Thanatos and the Nether Gods. The theme of snatching people who belonged to the Nether Gods would already have been evoked in the audience's perceptions by Apollo, when he mentioned at 3-4 that Zeus had killed his son Asklepios with the thunderbolt; for the audience knew that Zeus did this to punish Asklepios for resurrecting dead people. Thus, the prologue sets out the play's religious canvas and touches on a religious question.

Many of the ritual acts enacted, or reported, in this tragedy are centered on death. They include, first, pre-death mourning, in various forms: the chorus in the parodos enumerate the features the absence of which indicates that Alcestis is not yet dead (100-6)—and so describe some of the rites that follow after a death; there is also mention of Alcestis' and others' acts of ritual preparation for her death, that included prayers and the decoration of altars with wreaths by Alcestis (148-9, 159-61, 162-72), and Admetos' reported lament before her death (199-202). Second, rites of mourning after her death, after 392: Eumelos' lament, the announcement of the future burial and lament by Admetos, a declaration by Admetos of public mourning in the lands over which he rules, and a description of the ritual acts involved in this mourning (420-31); ritual acts of mourning by the palace servants, shorn hair and black robes, are mentioned later (818-9), but would have been visible before.

The ode at 435-75 is an ode of praise addressed to Alcestis.[106] Praise is one of the main themes in archaic and fifth-century epitaphs, and was undoubtedly also part of the death ritual songs. An important part of the death ritual enacted on stage is the funeral procession—to be more precise the beginning of this procession (605-746).[107] The procession is interrupted by the arrival of Admetos' father Pheres bearing burial gifts, which Admetos rejects (614ff). This incident, besides all its other meanings that pertain to the *oikos*,[108] allows the articulation of some of the play's problematization concerning attitudes to death, such as fear of death and an exploration of the disruption of the succession of the generations, of the normal pattern "sons die after fathers," to be conducted during, and be structured by, a ritual: the ritual which articulates the death at the center of the problematization, and which is the visible expression of an attitude towards death different from those of Pheres and Admetos, one that involved sacrificing one's life for the sake of a loved one. As well as adding pathos to the debate, the presence of Alcestis' corpse illustrates the (potential) superiority of conjugal love. At 746 the chorus exits, following the funeral procession; their participation, which involved a (rare) abandonment of the orchestra by the chorus, stresses the centrality of this ritual.

Chapter 3: Euripidean Tragedy and Religious Exploration 319

They return after 860, after the burial, with Admetos and the rest of those who had been part of the funeral procession, and at 861 begins a *kommos* by Admetos and the chorus.[109] In the course of this Admetos mentions that he was prevented from throwing himself into Alcestis' grave (897-9) so as to die with her. The ritual expression of the desire to join the deceased was part of the Greek death ritual.[110] This does not entail that the audience would have necessarily assumed that "he did not mean it," but the fact that this was part of the established ritual in their assumptions would entail that they would not have necessarily have assumed that Admetos had changed his mind about the wisdom of accepting Alcestis' sacrifice, and had tried to kill himself. At 914-25 Admetos remembers his wedding ritual and contrasts it to the present mourning ritual;[111] it is only after these ritual expressions that he sets out his distress and future unhappiness in reasoned argument.[112] Eventually, Heracles fights with Thanatos and rescues Alcestis; he tells Admetos that this is what he had done at 1140-2; at 843-54 he had described what he had been going to do, and said that if he missed Thanatos he would go to Hades and ask Kore and Hades to release Alcestis. This, then, is a supernatural world, in which Heracles, whose identity as son of Zeus Admetos stresses at 1136, in the middle of the revelation of what had happened, has a certain access to the world of the gods, interacts directly with gods. However, this interaction is not shown on stage.

To return to the ritual skeleton, there were also other rituals acts, such as various invocations of the gods (see e.g. 213-4, 220-5); and Admetos' proclamation of a celebration in the land involving choruses and sacrifices (1154-6). Lines 962-94 of the choral song sung at 962-1005 are an ode to the power of Ananke, who is presented as a goddess who has no cult through which men can propitiate her. Her power is such that even when Zeus decides something, he has to accomplish it with her—a representation that evoked, without problematizing, the complex question of the relationship between Zeus and the elusive related concepts of fate, necessity and the like.[113] In 995-1005 (the second antistrophe of this ode) the chorus ascribe a higher than normal status to the dead Alcestis, they say that she will be considered a *makaira daimon*, and address her with *chaire*, which is like an acclamation of deification.[114]

The inescapability of death is a theme that pervades this tragedy. As we saw, it was brought up in the prologue, which explored the frontiers between Apollo's powers and the *timai* due to Thanatos and the Nether Gods, and in which mention of the death of Asklepios had also evoked the fact that all men must die. In the second strophe and second antistrophe of the parodos the chorus sing of the inescapability of death and evoke the fact that when Asklepios had been alive he had resurrected the dead before Zeus had killed him (112-30), thus picking up the theme raised in the prologue.

Defeating death by bringing to life people who had died, then, is policed by Zeus. This may appear to problematize the fact that Heracles brought Alcestis back from the dead. But of course, it is made clear from the beginning that this was only a temporary reprieve (cf. 52-6), and in the eyes of the audience the fact that Heracles succeeded in defeating Thanatos suggested that the gods, and especially Zeus, had agreed—indeed in some versions of her myth it was the gods who had returned Alcestis to life in admiration of her self-sacrifice,[115] and in *Alcestis* Heracles' alternative plan of action if he had not found Thanatos had been to supplicate Hades and Persephone.[116] Nevertheless, the problematization does not entirely disappear. Why should Heracles have been allowed to bring about the result that had caused Asklepios' punishment? Both were sons of gods, albeit Heracles was the son of Zeus, and both became gods.[117] I suggest that the audience would have made sense of this difference as follows. Asklepios, by extending his healing a step beyond its proper limits to resurrecting the dead,[118] had brought about a blurring of the frontiers between the world of the living and that of the dead, while, in my view, it was fundamentally important to the Greek perception of the cosmos that those borders had to be clear, and the two worlds had to remain separate.[119] Thus, this blurring would have been perceived as threatening to the cosmic order. While Heracles' one-off defeat of one of the agents of the transition did not have the same effect of pernanently transgressing limits, and so was allowed to happen. For this happy outcome does not, of course, alter the fundamental inescapability of death. This is a postponement of death.

Nevertheless, this postponement is exceptional. And it is, I suggest, in this context of exceptionality that the floating epilogue (which this tragedy shares with *Andromache*, *Bacchai*, and *Helen* and, with a different beginning, with *Medea*) acquires its specific meanings.[120]

>*pollai morphai ton daimonion*
>*polla d' aelptos krainousi theoi;*
>*kai ta dokethent' ouk etelesthe,*
>*ton d' adoketon poron heure theos.*
>*toiond' apebe tode pragma* [*Alc.* 1159-63].

Alcestis' return from the dead is exceptional. Though temporary, it *could* have been seen to be disturbing the important boundaries between life and death. Heracles' bringing Alcestis back from the dead may

Chapter 3: Euripidean Tragedy and Religious Exploration 321

have seemed similar to the actions of Asklepios which were punished, but it turned out they were not. This is what the chorus is commenting upon here.

The notion that death is the inevitable fate of mortals is only very partially deconstructed by the notion that some mortals may achieve a higher status after death. That Alcestis will have done so is the chorus' judgment. Heracles' deification is part of the audience's cultic reality. This does not offer much reassurance for ordinary mortals; but, I suggest, the tragedy offered another reassuring representation. One of the things placed at the center of this tragedy is the notion of knowing that one is about to die, the certainty of one's imminent death. Through this situation in which Alcestis found herself the tragedy explores the fear of death in general, and the notion of dying, and the fifth-century Athenian visualization of the transition from life to death. This transition is presented in reassuring terms, for it involves the benevolent and reassuring figures of Hermes Chthonios and Charon,[121] after the initial trauma represented by the violent agent of death, Thanatos.

Other themes explored in this tragedy are: the fear of death, the value of life to young and old, the notion of sacrificing one's life for someone else and the question of the replaceability of a loved one; and, intertwined with these, the exploration of interpersonal relationships, especially gender discourse, and most particularly the construction of the "good wife," conjugal love, the father-son relationship, guest relationships. The attitude carpe diem for tomorrow we may die is also expressed (782-89), but it is somewhat deconstructed by the fact that it is expressed by Heracles, who, the audience knows, after his death will become a god.

This tragedy, then, is articulated by quite a lot of ritual, and the religious dimension is important in it. But the ritual and religious elements are deployed above all as the framework of explorations that are only very partially, and not primarily, religious;[122] they are deployed, in a world in which men and gods interact directly, to explore things that pertain above all to the human condition and to human relationships. But these distinctions are not always stable; thus, the fear of death is partly calmed through the notion that the divine beings implicated in this experience will be benevolent.[123] Some religious issues are also set out, but their explorations were not central: besides the notion of the *timai* of the different gods, which here pertains to the theological underpinning of the inescapability of death, another important religious issue brought up in the tragedy is the notion of *charis* between gods and mortals, the notion that gods acknowledge a relationship of *charis* with mortals. Here this *charis* involved direct interaction between god and mortal, and this polarized both *charis* and the god's gift, and at the same time distanced it for the normal *charis* between gods and mortals, which was established by sacrifices and other acts of worship towards gods who, it is hoped, will acknowledge the relationship. Nevertheless, despite this distancing, this representation and exploration of *charis* sets a hopeful model for the ordinary relationship of *charis* between gods and mortals established by cult.

Ritual plays a significant role in this tragedy, and there is a significant religious dimension, and some religious problematization and exploration; but the main explorations do not pertain to the relationships between gods and mortals, but to human relationships and human fears. *Alcestis*, then, like *Medea*, is a version of the tragic matrix which focussed on the exploration of primarily human relationships; but the version of the tragic matrix in *Alcestis* is closer to the ritual matrix out of which the tragic matrix had developed than that in *Medea*.

2) *Herakleidai*

Herakleidai[124] has significant ritual density; it starts with a ritual of supplication,[125] within which there are many reports of other rituals. After announcing the performance of *thysia* sacrifices to obtain omens for the battle at 340, Demophon reports the preparation of the *sphagia* for prebattle sacrifice (which will be performed at 819-22), and the performance of the *thysia* sacrifices to obtain omens for the battle;[126] he also announces the prophecy that in order to achieve victory and the salvation of Athens, which is now bound up with the suppliants since the Athenians had accepted them, it is necessary to sacrifice a highborn *parthenos* to Persephone.[127] From then on and until 629 the theme of human sacrifice structures the tragedy (in combination with the continuous enactment of the supplication ritual), but in this tragedy, at least as the text now stands, human sacrifice structures an almost self-contained segment, and is forgotten thereafter. The daughter of Heracles leaves in a procession after 596.[128]

At 673 the *sphagia* for the prebattle sacrifices which had been mentioned earlier are now said to have been brought forward. The third stasimon consists of a prayer; it is an ode calling upon the gods to support Athens against the Argives. At 819-22 the sacrifice by the *manteis* of the *sphagia* is reported. At 851-9 is reported Iolaos' prayer to Zeus and Hebe to rejuvenate him for one day, and its miraculous outcome: two stars came to rest on the yoke of the chariot and covered it with a cloud; the wise men said it was Hebe and Heracles, and out of the cloud came Iolaos rejuvenated. At 869-72 a short thanksgiving prayer is uttered to Zeus by Alcmene, in which she takes the reported miracle to be proof of Heracles' deification. At 936-7 it is reported that a victory

Chapter 3: Euripidean Tragedy and Religious Exploration 323

trophy is being erected for Zeus. There is a different kind of religious reference at 989-90, where Eurystheus claims that it was Hera who had afflicted him with the enmity towards Heracles. At 1010-3 he says that his killing will pollute the killer and that the Athenians were wise to spare him, honoring the gods more than their hatred of him. Finally, at 1028-44 Eurystheus reports an oracle of Apollo, on the basis of which he turns himself into an enemy hero protector of Athens, who will in the future defend the Athenians against the invading descendants of the Heraclids, the Spartans.[129]

As Wilkins noted,[130] if the text of the end of the play is sound, the speech of Eurystheus stands in place of an *ex machina* speech. This, of course, does not mean that it is the same as an *ex machina* speech. On the contrary, here the voice of the god is heard indirectly, from the mouth of a future hero, Eurystheus, who, at 1026ff, says that, because the Athenians had spared him, he will make them the gift of a prophecy of Apollo: they should bury him before the sanctuary of Athena Pallenis, and he will become an enemy hero, he will protect Athens against the Heraclids' descendants, when they invade Attica. Another, more direct, but not enacted, contact with the divine world is the reported epiphany of Heracles and Hebe, followed by the miracle of the rejuvenation of Iolaos;[131] this established in the eyes of the characters of the play Heracles' divinity, as is shown by the fact that in the final stasimon the chorus denies Heracles' death and sing of his marriage to Hebe on Olympos.[132]

So this is a world in which miracles happen offstage, but in other respects, and certainly as far as what is shown onstage is concerned, it is not far removed from the world of the audience. It is not a world in which men and gods mingle onstage.

This play also involves a problematization of supplication, here intertwined with human sacrifice.[133] How far does the host's obligation to the suppliants go? Fighting for the suppliants is a regular theme in tragedies problematizing supplication; so why not offer one's daughter for sacrifice?—which the Athenians in *Herakleidai* are not prepared to do.[134] Human sacrifice as a religious issue is not problematized here.[135] It is simply presented, in terms of a prophecy revealing that the sacrifice of a highborn virgin to Persephone is necessary for victory in battle; the only question is who shall be sacrificed, and the reasons why Makaria offers herself. It is not impossible that, the fact that the Athenians in the tragedy were ready to sacrifice their young men in war to protect the suppliants, but not offer the sacrifice of one virgin girl, may also have problematized both types of death. However, because in the eyes of that audience war was part of normality, and the fact that men died in it was simply part of the package, while human sacrifice was not part of normality, the position of the Athenians in the tragedy may have appeared to the ancient audience perfectly natural.

Another religious theme set out in this tragedy is that of the enemy hero. As we saw, Eurystheus turned himself into an enemy hero who will in the future defend the Athenians against the Spartans, the descendants of the Heraclids. This notion is comparable to that in Aeschylus' *Eumenides* 762-4, where Orestes says that in death, as a hero, he will protect Athens from any future attack by Argos.[136] It is also found later, in Sophocles' *Oidipous at Colonus* 1520-34, where Oidipous tells Theseus that if the place where he will die remains secret, its presence will protect Athens from the Thebans. A comparable idea, we saw, occurs in Euripides' *Suppliants*: the sacrificial knife used in the oath ritual will be buried near the burial pyres of the Seven, and this will stop any future Argive invasion. Kearns rightly connects these instances in tragedy in which the foreign hero, perhaps an enemy, certainly potentially hostile, becomes in death the city's protector with the religious practice of attempting to win over the enemy's heroes to one's cause.[137] An example of a story structured by the religious schema "appropriation of the enemy hero" is that of the Athenians' enmity with the Aeginetans, and the oracle received by the Athenians, which said that they should not attack the Aeginetans immediately, but wait for thirty years and on the thirty-first set out a shrine to Aiakos and begin the war with Aegina.[138] For Aiakos was, above all, Aegina's hero. This tragic schema, then, is a transformation, or, rather, its different versions are different transformations, of this religious schema. Whether or not the cults involved had been practiced before the production of the tragedies, the notion of the enemy hero protecting Athens is a reassuring representation, precisely because it was based on a religious schema, it relied on, deployed, and activated, religious elements structured by religious logic.

In *Herakleidai*, produced at this particular time (whether before or after the first major Spartan invasion),[139] the notion that Eurystheus protected Athens from Spartan invasions, which was connected to an oracle, would have been charged with special significance, and functioned as an especially potent construct of reassurance. This religious reassurance is not about religion in itself, but about how religion affects life, about danger at war and supernatural protection. The fact that this notion was deployed in this Euripidean tragedy at this particular moment is one of the many arguments that shows that such religious elements and religious reassurances were perceived by the audience to be serious, not ironic. For the ironic interpretation, if it is to be consistent, would have to have applied also to this Euripidean reassuring

Chapter 3: Euripidean Tragedy and Religious Exploration 325

closure; and, I would argue, the notion and the reality of the Spartan invasions were too serious to be ironic about and play games with, at that particular moment of maximum fear and trauma for all Athenians.

This argument, that the concept of the enemy hero functioned as a serious schema of reassurance, is further strengthened by the fact that the notion of the enemy hero protector is intertwined with an important element of Athenian ideology. In these tragedies the notion of the enemy hero protector is connected with the concept of *charis* owed to the Athenians, the notion, which was important in Athenian self-perception, and self-presentation, that they had been a haven for refugees and other suppliants in the past. This ought to have entitled them to an acknowledgment of the resulting relationship of *charis*. It follows from this that the citizens of those cities whose ancestors the Athenians had succored in the heroic past are in the wrong whenever they are hostile to Athens, for they do not show the appropriate gratitude. In the Greek world, in which events in the heroic past can provide arguments relevant to situations in the present,[140] this creates a framework in which to locate present-day hostilities with those cities, a framework in which the Athenians occupy the high moral ground. This aspect would have been especially potent in *Herakleidai*, early in the war with Sparta. Indeed, in *Herakleidai* the notions of *charis* and ingratitude are stressed. As we saw, Eurystheus acknowledged a relationship of *charis* with the Athenians; because they had spared him, he made them the gift of a prophecy, which involved mention of the fact that the Heraclids' descendants will not honor the gratitude that they ought to have for the fact that the Athenians have, at this very moment in the tragedy, saved their ancestors,[141] but, on the contrary, will invade Attica; then the present enemy will turn friend to help against their present friends who will then be their enemies.

Prophecy may also have been problematized in the eyes of the audience. For Eurystheus explains that he came to Attica though he knew the oracle he just told the Athenians, *Heran nomizon thesphaton kreisso poly, kouk an prodounai m'* (1039-40). This brings up the possibility that prophecy may not necessarily be telling what will happen, if another deity intervenes. This possibility seems superficially to have been refuted through the outcome: Eurystheus was wrong, and the prophecies did come true. But in ancient eyes this may not have given an unambiguous answer; for after his death Hera had became friendly to Heracles,[142] and so had no reason to support Eurystheus against Heracles' children. The mention of Heracles' marriage to Hera's daughter Hebe would have activated that knowledge for the audience, and so for them it would have remained unresolved whether or not Hera would have been stronger than the *thesphata* if she had so wished.

There are also other themes set out and (to a greater or lesser extent in the different cases) explored in this tragedy, which do not concern us here; for example, the notion of revenge, and above all a woman's and mother's vengeful attitude, and the notion of a democratic king.[143] The notion of self-sacrifice is explored through Makaria's self-sacrifice to save her siblings—above all her brothers; she sets out her reasons for offering herself in purely pragmatic terms; she examines her options and sets out the consequences of each course of action for herself.

To sum up, the religious dimension of *Herakleidai* is very significant.[144] In this tragedy, unlike in *Medea* and *Alcestis*, ritual density goes together with significant religious problematization. But the religious explorations here are not very deep or very probing, and they are, above all, focussed on war. It is difficult to doubt that this focus reflects concerns arising from, and offers religious reassurance for, the Spartan invasions of Attica.

3) *Hippolytos*

Hippolytos was produced at 428.[145] The prologue by Aphrodite and the concluding segment, in which Artemis appears in epiphany are strongly religious, in that they focus on relationships between divinities and mortals. The prologue begins with Aphrodite's self-presentation, in which she includes the information that it is important to the gods to receive worship from mortals, since, she says, they rejoice in it. Aphrodite then sets out the situation, Hippolytos' neglect of her worship, and announces the punishment she reserves for him. The prologue, then, places ritual, above all the absence of ritual, of Hippolytos' worship of Aphrodite, at the center of the play. Aphrodite refers to Artemis (15) as *Phoibou th' adelphen Artemis Dios koren*, thus evoking invocation forms, and zooming Artemis towards the audience's cultic reality, evoking Artemis as a recipient of cult in the audience's everyday reality. Then Aphrodite refers to Artemis as *parthenos*, and presents her as associating with Hippolytos in hunting in the woods. This is the most fundamental core aspect of Artemis' divine persona, the virgin huntress roaming the woods, and this had the effect of sustaining the zooming to the audience's cultic reality.

Aphrodite concludes by announcing the approach of Hippolytos, who, with his companions, is singing hymns to Artemis. This is indeed what follows; the action at the human level begins with a ritual, in which Hippolytos and his band of huntsmen offer worship to Artemis; they sing a hymn, and Hippolytos offers her a garland. When they

Chapter 3: Euripidean Tragedy and Religious Exploration 327

entered, Hippolytos urged them to follow him singing of the daughter of Zeus, *ouranian Artemin*, "in whose care we are" (58-60). This last statement corresponds to the audience's cultic reality, in that they are ephebes and hunters, a group who is indeed in the special care of Artemis. Since, to my knowledge, Artemis did not have the cult title Ourania, while the cult of Aphrodite Ourania was an important Athenian cult, I submit that, though of course all Olympian divinities were *ouranioi*, 'heavenly', in this context Hippolytos' use of the epithet *ourania*, which was a cult title of Aphrodite, to refer to Artemis would have registered with the audience as illustrating his unbalanced privileging of Artemis at the expense of Aphrodite that Aphrodite had just spoken of.

After this ritual there is a discussion about the fact that Hippolytos is not offering worship to Aphrodite; that is, a discussion about ritual, intertwined with theology. The second strophe of the parodos (141-50) is full of religious references. The chorus ask whether Phaedra is ailing because she is possessed by Pan or Hekate or the Corybantes or the Mountain Mother or (145-7) whether she is "wasting from some fault concerning Diktynna of the wild things," for neglecting to offer a bloodless offering. "For she ranges over the Mere and across the dry land of the open sea [that is a sandbar], amid the wet eddies of the brine." Diktynna is a Cretan goddess who is often perceived as a persona of Artemis in her function of goddess of the wild. The references to the Mere and the sandbar zooms this Diktynna to the Troezenian cult of Artemis, for the Mere is a lagoon behind the shore north of Troezen on the shore of which there was a sanctuary of Artemis Saronia.[146] Thus this reference zoomed the Artemis of the tragedy to real-life cult and also reinforced the aspect of Artemis' persona that involved her association with wild things and places. But in the epode, in 166-9, a different function of Artemis is articulated, when the chorus recall past occasions in which they had invoked Artemis in her persona of protector of women in childbirth, *eulochon ouranian toxon medeousan auteun Artemin*[147]—and Artemis responded.[148] This function of Artemis as protector of women in pregnancy and childbirth was an important facet of the goddess. It may have evoked for the audience more generally her role as protector of women, the most important cult of which in Athens was that of Artemis Brauronia—which was also associated with hunting and wild animals and with the transition of girls to marriageable *parthenoi* through the *arkteia*.[149]

At 713-4 the chorus swear by Artemis, to whom they refer as *semnen Artemin Dios koren*, thus evoking the goddess as a whole, and this choice may have brought to the fore in the eyes of the audience again Artemis' role as a women's goddess.[150] This ritual, then, and the earlier evocation of a ritual in the epode of the parodos, would have been important in evoking and presenting Artemis' divine persona, which was more complex and multifaceted than Hippolytos' one-sided perception of her. This deployment of ritual and evocation of cultic realities would have led the Athenians to perceive the Artemis conceived and worshiped by Hippolytos as a polarization of one aspect of the goddess Artemis. And so they would have understood Hippolytos as having a one-sided perception of Artemis, which is what allows him to see Artemis in opposition to Aphrodite, and overprivilege the former while underprivileging the latter. Hippolytos constructed an Artemis that excluded an important facet of the goddess' persona, her concern with the transition into adulthood and full maturity which is an important aspect of her Attic persona, and which, in the case of the transition of *parthenoi* into *gynaikes*, is related with her protection of childbirth.

This facet of Artemis is related to Aphrodite. In the context of cult, which is a context of cooperation, Artemis' role in the transition to maturity and Aphrodite's concern with the erotic sphere drift together and are articulated as complementary.[151] The potential tension involved in this type of cultic complementarity is activated and transformed into conflict and hostility in this context of perversion of normality, of disorder, that is created by Hippolytos' refusal to abandon the status of young huntsman, of ephebe, and embrace erotic love and the status of maturity, marriage and reproduction, and the proper order of things. It is only by restricting and polarizing Artemis that Hippolytos can overprivilege her while underprivileging Aphrodite. All these complex meanings were constructed for the Athenian audience through the deployment of ritual.

Among the reports of ritual acts in the tragedy are references to the oath taken by Hippolytos not to reveal what the nurse told him; of these most interesting is the reference by Hippolytos at 656-7, which makes explicit the religious nature of the oath: *toumon s' eusebes soizei, gynai; ei me gar horkois theon aphraktos heirethen*. Among the enacted ritual acts is the chorus' brief lament for Phaedra at 811-6, which is followed by Theseus' lament for Phaedra (817-51)—interrupted by the chorus at 834-5.[152]

At 887-90 Theseus invokes his father Poseidon and asks him to grant him one of the three curses[153] he had promised him and destroy Hippolytos on that same day. It is, then, through ritual that the action moves towards disaster. At 1025-31 Hippolytos swears an oath to Theseus by Zeus Horkios and by the earth that he did not dishonor his father's marriage. Other minor ritual acts in the tragedy are invocations,[154] and Hippolytos' reported prayer (1190-3). There are also

Chapter 3: Euripidean Tragedy and Religious Exploration

other religious references of various kinds,[155] and especially many references to Aphrodite, who is referred to as Kypris.[156] In addition, the first stasimon (525-64) is a hymn to Eros and Aphrodite, and the fourth stasimon (1268-82) a hymn to Aphrodite and Eros.

At 1283 Artemis appears and, in a segment dense with religious matter, reveals Hippolytos' innocence to Theseus and tells him about Aphrodite's responsibility; she also informs Theseus that Poseidon had no choice but to grant Theseus' request as he had been bound by his pledge, but that he, like herself, consider Theseus to be *kakos*, for not examining the accusation and not consulting prophets. This includes a reassuring representation, the notion that a god is bound by his pledge; for though this notion did not have direct relevance to the audience's reality, for they were not the sons of gods, and did not have the same relationship with the divine world, it could nevertheless function as a paradigm of a type of relationship in which a god does not carelessly break trust with a mortal.

Artemis then explains why she herself could not act to help Hippolytos, in a statement to which I will return. Eventually, in addressing the dying Hippolytos, she institutes a cult in his honor. She promises him that she shall give him *timas megistas* in the polis of Troezen; that a cult will be instituted to him, in which the Troezenian girls would cut their hair before they married and dedicate it to him; there would also be mourning rites for Hippolytos, and songs sung by *parthenoi*.[157] This announcement of the institution of a cult to Hippolytos zooms the world of the play to the world of the audience in two ways; by evoking in an indirect way the Athenian cult of Hippolytos,[158] which was different from the one described in the play, and, by zooming the play directly to the Troezenian cult, which, though not Athenian, was a real present-day cult.[159]

Thus ritual again moves to the center; it is through ritual that Hippolytos will be "compensated." This particular rite, which pertains to the transition of Troezenian *parthenoi* into womanhood through marriage, evoked Artemis' role as goddess supervising this transition,[160] and thus also the perception that Hippolytos' Artemis was only partial. The fact that this is evoked by Artemis' own words here would have deconstructed in the eyes of the Athenians Artemis' own presentation of the case, which omits Hippolytos' guilt in neglecting Aphrodite and refusing to make the proper transition, thus offending against the divine order and the proper order of things. She only mentions Aphrodite's malice. This, I suggest, would have been perceived by the audience as reflecting Artemis' partiality. At the same time, the fact that Hippolytos will be the recipient of this rite, in a way, compensates for his failure to acknowledge the need for the transition to full adulthood and the married status in his lifetime: he himself did not make that transition, but he is now, after his death, forever implicated in it.

Artemis' pronouncements set out several things pertaining to gods and divine-mortal interaction: besides the issues mentioned above, also, for example, at 1433-4: *anthropoisi de theon didonton eikos examartanein*, and 1437-8: *emoi gar ou themis phthitous horan, oud' omma chrainein thanasimoisin ekpnoais*. Her explanation of why she could not act to help Hippolytos (1327-34) is part of the religious problematization in *Hippolytos*. That there is strong religious problematization in this tragedy cannot be doubted—though, of course, this is far from being all there is. Neglect of the worship of a particular deity is a serious transgression; it was well rooted in the Greek collective representations that the deity most directly offended by a human transgression acts most directly to inflict punishment, but [s]he acts on behalf of the divine and cosmic order, backed up by the power of the divine order represented by Zeus. This in *Hippolytos* is explored through the rivalry between Aphrodite and Artemis. But this rivalry is restricted by the religious perception that the underprivileged deity is in the right, and so her punishment of the guilty mortal cannot be hindered by the overprivileged one. This is presented by Artemis in 1328-31 as a principle of noninterference, resulting from a *nomos* presented as being policed by Zeus, that no immortal is allowed to interfere in the plans of another. The Athenian audience would not have understood this as a general principle of noninterference, but as pertaining to situations in which the deity against whom a mortal has transgressed is exacting revenge for what ultimately is an offense against the whole divine order.

This has implications for the perception of Aphrodite in *Hippolytos*. Knox[161] thinks that the Euripidean gods are different from those in Sophocles and Aeschylus, that they are like mortals, torn, capricious, "naked passion unrestrained by any sense of moderation."[162] Aphrodite in *Hippolytos* is, he implies, a very striking manifestation of this. He does not think it is likely that Euripides believed in these gods "with the literal acceptance and religious awe of the archaic time that gave them their shape";[163] these gods served him as dramatic incarnations of the capricious irrational forces which his tragic vision saw as the determinants of the fate of mankind.

However, first, while Euripides' "real" beliefs and intentions are beyond our grasp—and it is doubtful that they were within his own—the fact that (as I hope to have shown) the audience perceived the deities in this tragedy to be representations of the deities, above all Aphrodite and Artemis, whom they themselves worshiped, entailed that in the ancient audience's process of meaning creation they

Chapter 3: Euripidean Tragedy and Religious Exploration 331

could not be incarnations of irrational forces, but the deities of lived religion—whose nature (and so also possible capriciousness) is explored here (and whose personae may or may not have included the perceptions that they were incarnations of irrational forces). This is a world in which the power of love *is* the power of Aphrodite, of Kypris—not an all-pervasive sex instinct defined by psychoanalysts, for which Aphrodite can be a metaphor. Moreover, it follows from what we have just seen that the presentation of Aphrodite as cruel did not entail that capricious irrational forces determined the fate of mankind—however much Aphrodite's rhetorical self-presentation may mislead modern readers into thinking that Aphrodite could do as she liked. On the contrary, *Hippolytos*—among other things—articulates an exploration of the empirically observable fact that the world is a cruel place, and people suffer, in intelligible terms, and suggests that there is a cosmic order, a divine order, and also that human life should reflect this order—as Hippolytos' did not. In addition, presenting a deity as cruel did not entail, for the Greeks, criticism of polis religion:[164] in a religion without a devil gods have a dark and dangerous, as well as a benevolent, side; for the same gods and cults articulated the dark and dangerous side of the cosmos, which Greek religion acknowledged and articulated, as the benign and positive one. The dark, dangerous, threatening, arbitrary side of gods is one particular articulation of the perception that the world is dangerous and man's life very precarious.[165] Individuals and cities performed rites in honor of the gods in order to propitiate them and persuade them to show their benevolent side. I may add that the notion that Aphrodite is especially cruel because she destroyed Phaedra, who was an innocent victim, since she had no choice, is not a perception that would have been shared by the ancient audience. Not only is it at the very least arguable—in fact likely—that in ancient eyes Phaedra did have a choice,[166] but also the very notions "innocent victim since she had no choice" and "cruel because destroying an innocent victim" are unstable cultural constructs. The most important thing is that this exploration in *Hippolytos* suggests that, despite the fact that the world is dangerous, and man's life very precarious, the cosmos has rules and a fundamental order, a notion that guards against the despair generated by the fear of cosmic *anomie*.

Hippolytos gives a good illustration of the fact that tragedy presents this reassuring image of an ordered cosmos, policed and guaranteed by Zeus. So that, whatever any of the individual deities who appear on the stage may be tempted to do, in pursuit of their own perception of their duties or their *timai*, the cosmos will not be unbalanced, ultimate order and ultimate justice will prevail, because Zeus guarantees it.

To sum up, then, in *Hippolytos* ritual is at the center of the tragedy in various ways, and helps articulate the problematization. Though this tragedy's ritual density is significant, it is not as great as that of some others; but the place of ritual in it is very important; ritual and other religious elements form the skeleton of the play; ritual, the worship of Aphrodite, is central to the action and the religious problematization of the tragedy, and ritual helps construct significant meanings, such as the one-sidedness of Hippolytos' perception of Aphrodite, which are crucial to the tragedy in general and its religious problematization in particular. Religious problematization, concerning worship, divine punishment and divine attitudes towards mortals, the interaction between a god-sent *mania* and human will, the concept of *philia* between deity and mortal,[167] are extremely important in this tragedy—though, of course, many other issues, pertaining to human relationships, are also explored.

4) *Andromache*

Andromache was perhaps produced soon after *Hippolytos*.[168] A substantial part of *Andromache* is structured by a ritual of supplication enacted on the stage, by Andromache at Thetis' altar. Andromache verbalizes her situation as a suppliant at Thetis' statue at 115-6.[169] There are also many other references to this supplication.[170] At 411 she gets up from her crouching position of suppliant and abandons the altar, at or just after, 424. She refers to her former supplication when, at 565-7, she tells Peleus that she was torn away from the altar of Thetis.[171] Another part of the tragedy is structured by Peleus' and the chorus' lament over the corpse of Neoptolemos, a *kommos* (1173-1225). The fact that dead bodies were brought on the stage had the effect of enhancing the dramatic effect and arousing the audience's emotions further; but it also entailed the enactment of a ritual of lamentation similar to that over a dead body in real life, which it thus inevitably evoked. Other ritual acts also take place on stage: Molossos' supplication of Menelaos at 537-8; Andromache's supplication of Peleus at 572-6; Hermione's supplication of Orestes at 892-5. There are also several significant religious references.[172]

Crucial to the plot in *Andromache* is a reported ritual, Neoptolemos' pilgrimage to Delphi, his request of forgiveness from Apollo for his previous arrogance towards the god, and his sacrifice, in the course of which he was attacked.[173] Earlier on in the play, Hermione's pseudo-self-lamentation (825-7, 829-31, 833-5, 837-9) and Orestes' pretense

Chapter 3: Euripidean Tragedy and Religious Exploration 333

that he was on a visit to the oracle of Dodona (886-7), prefigure as in distorting mirrors the real lamentation for Neoptolemos that resulted from his real consultation of the Delphic oracle.[174]

Neoptolemos' pilgrimage to Delphi is first referred to by Andromache at 50-55 where she says that he went to Delphi where *didosi diken* to Apollo for his *mania*, which had made him ask Apollo for redress for killing his father Achilles, in the hope of turning the god benevolent towards him for the future; that is, he went to Delphi to make amends for his past transgressions. She refers again to Neoptolemos being at Delphi at 76. And Hermione at 926 refers to his being at Apollo's oracle. At 998-1008 Orestes tells Hermione of his plot to have Neoptolemos killed at Delphi (en passant referring to oaths taken by his friends and allies at Delphi) and says (1002-6):

pikros de patros phonion aitesei diken
anakta Phoibon; oude nin metastasis
gnomes onesei theoi didonta nyn dikas,
all ek t' ekeinou diabolais te tais emais
kakos oleitai.

As Orestes sees it, Apollo does not forgive, and he, Orestes, and Apollo are, as it were, collaborators in Neoptolemos' downfall, which, as far as Orestes is concerned, he brought upon himself. He concludes at 1007-8: *echthron gar andron moiran eis anastrophen / daimon didosi k'ouk eai phronein mega.*

The choral ode that follows, the fourth stasimon, begins in a way evocative of a hymn. The first strophe and the first antistrophe are addressed to Apollo and Poseidon. In the first strophe the chorus sings of their building of the walls of Troy. As Stevens rightly noted,[175] verses 1014-8 express the notion "why did you abandon your handiwork to destruction in war," and the answer is provided by the myth,[176] which would have been evoked by the audience by the mention of Apollo's and Poseidon's building of the walls of Troy, that Laomedon, Priam's father, had refused to pay Apollo and Poseidon their wages for their year of service building the walls, but instead sent them away with threats. Laomedon was punished for this, but this does not mean that the *hybris* had been cancelled out, any more than Neoptolemos' *hybris* towards Apollo could have been cancelled out by his attempt to make amends. For both Laomedon and Neoptolemos were guilty of the serious offense of *hybris*.[177] When perceived through the filters of Greek religion Neoptolemos' transgression was more serious than may appear to the modern reader. For in asking redress of him for Achilles' death Neoptolemos had treated Apollo as though Apollo were a mortal, as though the two were equal; in other words he had transgressed the human limits, and offended Apollo's divinity. This ode constructs a comparability between Troy's destruction and Neoptolemos' destruction.[178]

In the first antistrophe, in which the Trojan War is presented as being the gods' responsibility, the end of Troy is expressed through the notion of the cessation of sacrifice, in Greek religion the most important ritual through which men relate to gods: *oud' eti pyr epibomion en Troiai theoisin lelampen kapnoi thyodei* (1024-6). The second strophe and the second antistrophe deal with the suffering of the victors. The second strophe is addressed to Apollo, or at least, it concludes with an address to Apollo; it is possible that until that time the audience may have perceived the addressees to have been both Apollo and Poseidon. This strophe deals with the murder of Agamemnon by Klytemestra, and of Klytemestra by Orestes at the oracular behest of Apollo, and concludes, *o daimon, o Phoibe, pos peithomai?*

This choral ode, then, among other things, prefigures Neoptolemos' punishment; for the fact that Troy eventually paid for the *hybris* of Laomedon would have suggested that Neoptolemos would too. At the same time the ode would have stressed, for the ancient audience, the hubristic nature of Neoptolemos' offense, through the implicit comparison with the well-known *hybristes* Laomedon.[179] In addition, reference to the end of Troy, in which Neoptolemos had played such a prominent role, and especially the evocation of the suffering of Andromache and her *philoi* at 1041-2, would have evoked Neoptolemos' behavior at the Sack, and, above all, the fact that he had personally committed sacrilege when he had killed Priam at the altar of Zeus Herkeios. All this, then, would have put in perspective, would have created a conceptual framework in which the audience would have placed and made sense of, Apollo's enmity, that was soon to be confirmed, and the death of Neoptolemos that was soon to be announced.[180]

After the fourth stasimon Peleus enters, and the chorus informs him of the plot at Delphi, stressing the sacred nature of the place, and so also the fact that the murder would be committed during a ritual, by referring to Delphi (1065) as *hagnois en hierois Loxiou*; the same modality of reference, now stressing the ritual nature of the place is used by Peleus at 1067: *Pythiken pros hestian*.

The messenger arrives, announces the murder of Neoptolemos, and describes what happened in a long passage (1085-1165).[181] He first describes the situation of suspicion they found when they arrived at Delphi, in a passage which includes many references to "the god" and "Phoibos." Mention of their arrival, and also of features like *en*

Chapter 3: Euripidean Tragedy and Religious Exploration 335

peristylois domois, would have zoomed the reported action to the audience's religious reality, the Delphic sanctuary which many would have visited, and which played an important role in the lives of all. At 1100 the messenger begins to describe the ritual, which, first, set the reported action in a ritual setting, and second, would initially (until Neoptolemos' statement particularized the situation and set it apart) have zoomed it to contemporary religious reality. This zooming to place and ritual would have brought the god Apollo of the play, the god who, it will turn out, was responsible for Neoptolemos' murder, near the god Apollo of the audience's religious reality, would have made the play's Apollo be perceived as a representation of the god Apollo worshiped by the audience.

When the messenger described how Neoptolemos was attacked in the middle of the ritual, while he was praying, a perversion of the ritual, the audience would have perceived this to have been with the connivance of Apollo. Indeed it is Apollo whom the audience would have understood to have uttered the strange and thrilling cry[182] that, we are told at 1147-8, came from the temple's adyton, and gave impetus to the Delphians and turned the battle around. The messenger (1161-5) ascribes the murder to Apollo,[183] and blames the god for taking revenge and remembering all wrongs, he *ho tois alloisi thespizon anax, ho ton dikaion pasin anthropois krites*. He concludes: *pos an oun eie sophos?* I shall return to this. In the description that follows the first attack on Neoptolemos, until Neoptolemos was killed, and his body taken away by his comrades, various features of the Delphic sanctuary are mentioned, and this would have had renewed the zooming to the religious realities of the audience.

At 1231 there is an epiphany of Thetis, at whose altars the initial supplication had taken place, and who, the audience had been repeatedly reminded,[184] was Peleus' wife and Achilles' mother, and so Neoptolemos' grandmother and Molossos' great-grandmother. She announces that Andromache must marry Helenos and live in Molossia, where Molossos will be the founder of the royal dynasty of the Molossians. She also announces that Peleus will become a sea god in virtue of their marriage; she also mentions the fact that their son Achilles is in the paradise island of Leuke. Then she instructs Peleus to bury Neoptolemos at Delphi. Mention of Neoptolemos' burial at Delphi would have evoked the audience's knowledge of Neoptolemos' grave in the Delphic sanctuary, and his cult at Delphi.[185] The funeral procession taking his corpse to Delphi will have started at or after 1278.[186] Thetis had made clear in her speech that all that will be accomplished is the will of Zeus.[187] This presents the world as an ordered cosmos, policed and guaranteed by Zeus—which is a reassuring representation.

The floating epilogue expresses the perception of the unknowability of the will of the gods. What would have been perceived as unexpected in the world of the play[188] is Peleus' deification, but above all, the new relationship between Neoptolemos and Apollo, initiated by the latter's burial at Delphi, which marks a reversal of their hostile relationship in Neoptolemos' lifetime. This explicit expression of the notion of unknowability, the notion that things are not what they appear when seen from the limited mortal perspective, is, in some way, also a comment, the chorus' judgment, on the messenger's criticism of Apollo, and also, in some way, correlative with the appearance of the deity *ex machina*, who directs the plot in a particular way, which may appear different from that in which it had so far been going, and who reveals unexpected things. Thus, the close connection between epiphany and floating epilogue here is the result of an organic relationship between the two. The goddess reveals certain things, and the chorus comments on this, from the (now more enlightened) human perspective, and explains that the reason why these things appear unexpected from this pespective is because the divine will cannot be easily gauged by mortals. This perception is, on my interpretation, central to Greek tragedy; central to its beginnings, on my reconstruction of those beginnings, and central to the continuing importance of religious exploration in fifth-century tragedy.

In any case, since unknowability was a central category in Greek religion, both the expression of those perceptions in the epilogues, and the appearance of the *ex machina* deities, would have tapped into, and activated, significant religious feelings, and thus would have been perceived as serious religious manifestations; what to the modern mind can appear as contrived endings, to the ancient audience would have been significant religious representations.[189]

In *Andromache*, then, we have a very considerable amount of ritual structuring the action and helping articulate significant religious explorations and problematization. A central aspect of this problematization concerns the notion of enmity between god and mortal, divine hostility, and the exploration of the notion of divine attitudes towards repentance and attempted atonement, of the notion that the gods are harshly vindictive. This exploration is intertwined with the notion of *hybris*, and also with the notion of the heroization of the mortal enemy of the god. In this tragedy Neoptolemos had repented for his behavior, but Apollo did not forgive him. The messenger attacks Apollo for this. How would the audience have perceived this situation?

I suggest that they would have perceived Neoptolemos' punishment as inevitable. For, when perceived through the filters of Greek religion, Neoptolemos' transgression was more serious than may appear to

Chapter 3: Euripidean Tragedy and Religious Exploration 337

the modern reader. In asking redress for Achilles' death Neoptolemos had treated Apollo as though Apollo were a mortal, as though the two were equal; he had transgressed the human limits and offended against Apollo's divinity.

What of the fact that the murder perverted the ritual, and the god whose sanctuary and ritual this was had connived in this perversion? I suggest that the Athenians would have perceived this through filters shaped by the assumption that Neoptolemos, who had been guilty of serious impiety towards Apollo, had desecrated the sanctuary and the rites, by entering the sanctuary and taking part in the rites, since in Athens if someone was guilty of relatively mild impiety towards a deity they were prevented from entering that deity's sanctuary on pain of death.[190] Consequently, his murder would have been perceived as a manifestation of the well-established phenomenon of impiety quickly punished.[191] This divinely condoned perversion, then, would have been perceived as rectifying the desecration.

The messenger's articulation of the thought that a wise god who gives guidance to all about justice might have accepted the atonement expresses what might have been perceived as desirable from the human viewpoint—though the harshness of this divine justice is correlative with that of human justice on religious matters. But even if it was felt to have been desirable by most Athenians, this desirability would have been deconstructed by the perception that Apollo was safeguarding the cosmic order in punishing an offense that involved the transgression of the human limits. Thus, the notion that it would have been nice if the gods accepted atonement, and the fact that Apollo does not here, is expressed, and the harshness of this articulated, and through this, implicitly the desire of a more merciful god is constructed as a possibility—though not necessarily an unambiguously desirable one, since if the gods did not police the cosmic order ruthlessly, there was a danger of disorder. The fact that Neoptolemos' was an offense against the cosmic order would have entailed that the audience would have seen this harsh treatment as inevitable and the desirability for mercy as not unambiguous and unproblematic. Because of the nature of Neoptolemos' offense, the possibility was left open that in other cases, which do not represent a threat to the cosmic order, repentance may lead to the god accepting atonement.

The ambivalence of Neoptolemos' relationship to Apollo as presented here is resolved in a positive way after his death. In the audience's perceptions Neoptolemos was to be heroized. Consequently, Neoptolemos' ambivalent behavior towards the god resulted in a bad outcome for him while he was alive, his murder, and a positive one after his death: he received heroic cult. Neoptolemos' ambivalent nature fits, of course, the ambivalent nature of Greek heroes.

Another religious issue explored here is deification resulting from marriage to a goddess. I argued elsewhere[192] that erotic unions between mortals and immortals were perceived to have been potentially dangerous to mortals—a perception activated in, and articulating, some of the myths pertaining to such unions; and also that the marriage of Peleus and Thetis was an exception, because it had been instigated by the gods, and for that reason Peleus had counted as a sort of honorary immortal. His deification in *Andromache* represents a further development of this persona: here he actually becomes a god.

The notion that mortals have choices, and prophecy can help them make the right ones, is articulated in the first stasimon (274-308). The chorus starts singing of the Judgment of Paris, and the latter's choice, which led to the Sack of Troy; they connect Andromache's present misery with the misery of the Trojan War, and sing that none of those miseries would have happened if Hecabe or any of the other Trojans had killed the baby Paris when Kassandra foretold the ruin he would bring. Thus, here prophecy gave a cruel choice, and Hecabe and Priam chose the usual compromise; they did not kill the baby outright, but exposed it (something not mentioned in the ode), and the result was disaster. Paris is presented as being beguiled by Aphrodite, but this is not dwelt upon; it happened; but the Trojans had the opportunity to avert the catastrophe, and they had not taken it.

Issues pertaining to human relationships that do not involve the gods are of greater importance in this tragedy. The most important are: gender discourse, especially the rich and complex discourse on the good versus bad wife, which is here much more complex and ambivalent than may appear on the surface;[193] maternal love, the giving and taking in marriage, the father's role and the couple's feelings; Greek versus barbarian.[194]

The version of the tragic matrix structuring *Andromache*, then, is quite close to the parameters of the ritual matrix out of which it had ultimately developed as regards the deployment of ritual structuring the tragedy, and more generally the religious conceptual framework that articulates it. Religious exploration is important, but not exclusively so. The choices made here created a tragedy which resembles the ritual matrix more than *Alcestis*, and very much more than *Medea*, two tragedies in which gender discourse is also of central importance.

5) Hecabe

No gods appear in *Hecabe*,[195] but the prologue is spoken by the *eidolon* of Polydoros on an empty stage.[196] Two rituals are important in this prologue: burial, Polydoros' desire for burial, and human sacrifice, the reported demand by the shade of Achilles, who appeared over his tomb, that they sacrifice Polyxena to him at his grave.

Hecabe's speech, which follows the prologue (68-97), contains a series of invocations of the gods, mention of a dream, which the audience understands to be prophetic, and another mention of Achilles' *phantasma* asking for the sacrifice of a Trojan woman. A fuller account of Achilles' apparition and demand for human sacrifice, and the debate that followed among the Greeks, is given by the chorus (104-43), who then urge Hecabe to pray to, and supplicate, the gods, and also to supplicate Agamemnon. As they report it, the decisive argument for the decision to offer the human sacrifice was to honor Achilles, and honor the relationship of *charis* between him and the rest of the Greeks. After expressing her anguish at some length, Hecabe tells Polyxena at 188-90 that the Greeks want to sacrifice her to Achilles. Polyxena expresses her distress, and then Odysseus arrives to take her to be sacrificed. At 220-4 Odysseus gives some ritual details, he will be *pompos* and *komister* of the girl, and Achilles' son Neoptolemos will be the *epistates* and *hiereus*. This perverted echo of real-life ritual practices would have connected the world of the play to that of the audience through contrast, which distanced the human sacrifice and the world in which it took place from the audience's realities.

The ritual of supplication, which had been urged on Hecabe by the chorus, comes into play when Hecabe reminds Odysseus of, and describes, his past supplication of her at 245-6, and at 273-95, where that report of the past supplication is followed by Hecabe's present enacted supplication of Odysseus. Odysseus refuses her supplication, and gives the same reason as that which, according to the chorus' report, he had given at the debate, the desire to honor the dead hero, and repay the Greeks' debt of gratitude to him. Failure to do so would undermine the ideology of good death for Hellas. Supplication again comes into play at 339-41, where Hecabe urges Polyxena to supplicate Odysseus. Odysseus tries to prevent her from doing so, and Polyxena tells him she does not intend to supplicate him, he is safe from *ton emon hikesion Dia* (342-8). She has decided she will allow herself to be sacrificed. Hecabe offers herself to be sacrificed in her stead, but Odysseus rejects the offer, since it was Polyxena's sacrifice that Achilles had requested, as he rejects her subsequent offer that she should be sacrificed in addition to her daughter. That would be an unnecessary excess of death. Polyxena, Odysseus, and perhaps attendants, depart for the sacrifice in a procession after 440,[197] a combination of sacrificial and funerary procession.

In the first stasimon which follows the captive Trojan women agonize about their future, and wonder where in Greece they will end up (444-83). In the first antistrophe they envisage the possibility that they will be taken to live in Delos, and they mention the sacred palm tree and the sacred laurel tree, and the ritual singing of the Deliades, with whom they imagine they might be singing. In this, presumably, the Athenian audience would have perceived them to be mistaken, since foreign slaves would not, one assumes, have been perceived to be taking part in such hymn singing together with citizen women, even in the heroic age. The references to Delos, the palm tree, and the laurel tree would have zoomed the world of the play to that of the audience's religious reality, but at the same time the erroneous nature of their imaginings would have distanced them from the audience. This is especially true for the reference to the weaving of the peplos of Athena which follows. For in the second strophe they speculate that they may be taken to Athens, where they imagine that they may be involved in the weaving of the peplos of Athena, of the Gigantomachy or the Titanomachy. This would have zoomed the world of the play to that of the audience's religious reality. But in that reality the peplos was woven by Athenian girls and male professionals,[198] so this is another distorted ritual image, which distanced the chorus from the audience's realities at the same time as the tragedy had zoomed to those realities.[199] Another effect of these two misperceptions would be have been that the audience would have seen the chorus as even more pathetic, since in fact things would be even worse than they are imagining, they would be excluded from the cultic roles which they are imagining they would be performing.

In the second epeisodion, after this ode, there is mention of the burial of Polyxena, and then a return to the human sacrifice, for Talthybios describes the performance of this ritual in detail (518-82). The ritual had included a prayer by Neoptolemos to Achilles, after he had poured the chthonic libations, asking for favorable winds to gain safe return home. At 609 Hecabe begins the preparations for the death ritual she is to perform for Polyxena. In the second stasimon that follows (629-57) the chorus ascribe their doom to Paris' abduction of Helen and the judgment of Paris, and then sing of the disaster that befell them, and by doing so they lightly adumbrate (for an audience who knew the story) the notion that Hecabe, whose terrible plight and reversal of fortunes has been repeatedly commented upon, was not without her share of responsibility for not killing Paris, either as a baby, instead of

Chapter 3: Euripidean Tragedy and Religious Exploration 341

exposing him, or as an adult, when his identity became known. They end their song with a description of the ritual mourning of mothers whose children are dead (652-5). This is a counterpoint to the constant motif of Hecabe the uniquely miserable mother; other mothers grieve too, and they were not in any, even remote, way responsible for the disaster.

In the third epeisodion a corpse, and burial rites, become the focus of the action, not, as Hecabe initially assumes (670-3), Polyxena's corpse brought to be buried, but Polydoros'. For in the course of the ritual preparations for Polyxena's burial (678-80) a servant discovers the corpse of Polydoros, as a result of which two major ritual acts follow, which structure this epeisodion. First, from 684 Hecabe begins a sung lament, which is interspersed with single trimeters spoken by the chorus and the servant.[200] Within this segment of the epeisodion is also contained another religious reference, to Hecabe's prophetic dream (702-11). The rest of the epeisodion is structured through a supplication rite, the supplication of Agamemnon by Hecabe,[201] which aims at obtaining Agamemnon's support in her revenge on Polymestor. At 894-7 she asks Agamemnon to delay the burial of Polyxena, so that she and Polydoros can be buried together. At 1297-8, just before the end of the play, Agamemnon urges Hecabe to bury Polyxena and Polydoros. So what follows after 897 can also be seen as a segment framed between the announcement of the double burial and the first steps towards its performance. In the epode of the third stasimon (943-52) the chorus curse Helen and Paris.

In the segment that follows the action is focussed on the accomplishment of revenge.[202] The concluding part of the tragedy is articulated by prophecy: Polymestor tells Hecabe and Agamemnon what is going to happen to them, he foretells the manner of their death, and of that of Kassandra (1259-1284),[203] as he knew it from a prophecy given by Dionysos.[204] Hecabe will be transformed into a dog and fall into the sea.[205] After the prophecy Agamemnon urges Hecabe to go ahead and bury Polyxena and Polymestor. I argue elsewhere[206] that this burial would have been perceived by the audience as a perverted death ritual, because it would have been conducted by women, while in the audience's ritual reality, and indeed in other tragedies, burial was conducted by men—women had important ritual roles in other parts of the death ritual; and that this is one more expression of the disordered world of this tragedy.

Significant religious references, interspersed throughout the tragedy, express two major perceptions. First, that gods are responsible for the bad things that happen;[207] and second, that the gods support justice, and police transgressions,[208] and so they, the characters, act accordingly.[209]

It is clear, then, that in *Hecabe* ritual articulates a significant part of the tragedy,[210] indeed ritual is one of the major foci of this tragedy, which also explores a series of questions, especially questions pertaining to human relationships and justice (such as *charis*, grief and suffering, greed and the transgression of *xenia*,[211] revenge),[212] in ways that bring in the gods and their role in this justice.[213]

In this tragedy the human sacrifice is a case limit of horror: the girl will be sacrificed not to a god, but to a dead enemy; not to save her community or social group, but to allow her living enemies to honor their dead enemy hero. It does not involve religious problematization, as it does in *Iphigeneia in Tauris* and in *Erechtheus*. This is correlative with the fact that this human sacrifice does pertain not to the gods, but to the relationship between the living and the dead, above all dead heroes. The notion of good death is central; Achilles died a good death, in the service of Hellas, and this entitles him to certain privileges. This pertains to the ideological dimension of the exploration, to the ideology of good death; but a religious dimension is also included in this, and is stressed by the formulation at 136-40, which imagines a scene in Hades in the presence of Persephone. For this makes clear that it is not simply the honor bestowed on the social persona of the deceased[214] that is at stake here, but also—a notion intertwined with that of honor to the social persona—the feelings of the shade in Hades.

One of the questions explored, then, is the notion of honoring the dead who died for their country, *charis* between the dead and the living—and the fact that sometimes this can have a high cost, which has to be paid. The notions of good death and bad death is a significant theme in this tragedy: Polyxena also died a good death, by taking charge of her own sacrifice. By contrast, her brother Polydoros died a bad death: he was treacherously killed, and his corpse was thrown into the sea.

Revenge and justice are, of course, central in this tragedy's explorations; they are intertwined with the notion of maternal love, and with an exploration of the grieving mother in the form of avenging mother. As far as the grieving mother aspect of Hecabe is concerned, she suffers immensely, but is she a wholly blameless victim? I argued that she would not have been perceived to have been so by the audience. It is as a mother that she suffers above all, as a mother who loses her last children, and it was as a mother that Hecabe had acted, wrongly, when she had not killed, but exposed, Paris as a baby, and received him back into the royal house when he was recognized as an

Chapter 3: Euripidean Tragedy and Religious Exploration 343

adult—ignoring the prophecy. It is as though by refusing to lose a part of her motherhood, one of her children, she lost all of them—and caused untold suffering to others. It was, in the circumstances, an excess, and excess was in any case negatively colored in Greek perceptions. This, when perceived through modern perceptual filters, seems unbearably harsh; and this is why such modern filters must be excluded from the readings of Greek tragedy. Excess characterized Hecabe also in her persona as avenging mother. As an avenging mother she wreaks a horrible, excessive revenge involving the death of Polymestor's innocent sons. In the audience's perceptions, though revenge was justified, and the cautious go-ahead of Agamemnon gave it legitimacy, the murder and blinding of males by a group of women in an internal space would have evoked negative schemata of threatening, destructive women.[215] The males were barbarian, but so where the women, and this made it equivalent to Greek women attacking Greek men.

Let us now consider the audience's perceptions of Hecabe's metamorphosis and death. It is difficult to doubt that in the eyes of the Athenian audience one of the meanings of the metamorphosis was that it was the physical correlative of Hecabe's savage behavior,[216] and that it was also correlative with, and added to, her misery. More recently, the aspect that involves assimilation to an avenging Erinys has been stressed.[217] It is likely that this was one of the meanings of this metamorphosis, that her metamorphosis into a dog was, at least partly, inspired by her assimilation to an avenging Erinys. But does this entail that there are positive elements in this metamorphosis? That the metamorphosis offers Hecabe escape from a degraded status and endows her with fierce grandeur?[218] Not, I would suggest, in the eyes of the ancient audience. For in Greek perceptions to die as an animal, and to have the *sema* of an animal, is a very bad thing. That this was so in the assumptions shared by Euripides and his audience, and that this is how this death would have been understood by that audience, is shown by Hecabe's reaction at 1274:[219]

> P: . . . *tymboi d' onoma soi keklesetai.*
> H: *morphes epoidon, e ti, tes emes ereis?*
> P: *kynos talaines sema, nautilois tekmar.*
> H: *ouden melei moi sou ge moi dontos diken* [1271-4].

This demonstrates clearly that dying in the form of a dog was perceived by the ancients as the (bad) price Hecabe had to pay for her excessive revenge.

The appearance of ghosts and metamorphoses into animals did not happen in the audience's real life—though some members of that audience may have disputed this as far as the ghosts are concerned. But otherwise, and specifically insofar as the relationship with the gods is concerned, the world of the tragedy is not very different from that of the audience.

As Segal noted,[220] the remoteness of the gods is presented from the perspective of the human victims. For the audience this remoteness was, above all, correlative with the gods' remoteness in their own world. As we saw in chapter III.1, both a world basically, but not wholly, like the audience's, and a world in which the gods are present, correspond to schemata originating in the ritual matrix which (on my reconstruction) had shaped tragedy, and which had been deployed in an advanced form in Aeschylus' earlier surviving tragedies. Each of these schemata, which occur in different variants, in which the heroic world of the tragedy was nearer or further away from the world of the audience, explores problems pertaining to religion and to mankind's place in the cosmos, and also problems of human relationships, from different perspectives, nearer or further away from the world of the audience. In *Hecabe* the choice was to present a world as near to that of the audience as possible. This is why access to the gods is closely comparable to that of the audience's religious reality. The prophecy uttered by Polymestor does reproduce correctly a god's utterance, for it will, of course, come true, as prophecies do in Greek tragedy, and as confirmed by the fact that, the audience knows, it speaks of events that will happen. But the characters in the play do not know this, so their own perception of their access is similar to the audience's real life access.

Consequently, while in the world of the tragedy there was no certainty—as there was not in the audience's lived reality—in the world of the audience there was certainty as far as the world of the tragedy was concerned:[221] they knew the prophecy would come true, and this validated prophecy, and the possibility of true divine guidance. It also invalidated Talthybios' tentatively expressed speculation, as a possible alternative to the gods watching over human affairs, that it may be random *tyche* that governs human affairs (488-91).[222] For the fact that, the audience knows, Dionysos' prophecies will come true shows that human affairs were not governed by random *tyche*. Therefore, the fifth-century audience would have not perceived the world of the tragedy as a disordered world in which no sense could be made, and anything went. On the contrary, one of the perceptions articulating this tragedy is that, though mortals may transgress against the most basic rules on which human intercourse is based, like that of *xenia*, for the basest of motives, like greed, this does not go unpunished. There are victims, above all Polymestor's children; but then, life as the

Chapter 3: Euripidean Tragedy and Religious Exploration 345

Greeks perceived it included cruel things, a fact acknowledged by their collective representations, while it is marginalized and elided in ours. And the fact that despite the disordered world, and despite the fact that the characters do not see any certainty, or the possibility of a direct contact with the gods, the audience knows that there is ultimate order, and that the gods do give true guidance, gives some reassurance that the same is true in their own world, even if this is not immediately apparent to them when they find themselves in certain situations.

In this tragedy, then, a dense web of ritual elements is intertwined with the exploration of problems pertaining to fundamental questions of human relationships which are ultimately sustained by a divine order. Thus, as far as form is concerned, the version of the tragic matrix structuring this tragedy is not very far removed from the ritual matrix; however, the nature of the explorations is somewhat different, in that the center of gravity has here shifted towards the human side of relationships—though within a framework of a world ruled by the gods and their ordinances, a fact that is clearer to the audience than to the characters in the play.

6) *Electra*

I will now consider *Electra*,[223] starting with the rituals that are less crucial to the plot, in the sense that they are not part of the central segment of the main ritual skeleton articulating the tragedy (though some of them are very important), in order to illustrate the density of the ritual references. The following are some of the rites of this type that come into play in *Electra*, some enacted, some spoken of: Electra's informal lament in verses 112-66;[224] the reference (at 167-97) to the forthcoming festival of Hera, aspects of which are evoked by both chorus and Electra;[225] a double report of a ritual in the old man's account to Electra of his visit to the tomb of Agamemnon: he mentions his own lament and the fact that he offered a libation and deposited myrtle branches, and also reports that he saw evidence of a previous ritual, a sacrifice of sheep and offering of hair.[226] A rite enacted on stage is the prayer by Electra, Orestes, and the Old Man at 671-82. There is also a prolonged reference to the sacrifice of Iphigeneia by Klytemestra (1011-50).

Both stasima contain ritual and/or other religious references. In the second antistrophe of the second stasimon (737ff) the chorus express their disbelief of the story that (after Atreus' faithless wife had given the golden lamb to her lover) the sun had changed its course, to the misfortune of mankind for the sake of mortal justice; they add that frightening stories are profitable to men in furthering the service of the gods; and that Klytemestra, not remembering such stories, killed her husband. This, as Stinton has conclusively shown,[227] is not Euripides the rationalist sceptic putting rationalist, cynical, sceptical thoughts in the mouth of the chorus. Whether or not the incredulity was directed at the harshness of divine justice, which brought misfortune to mortals by changing the course of the sun,[228] the passage affirms the gods' intervention in human affairs on the side of justice, and it is this that Klytemestra should have remembered. For the chorus' comment concerning Klytemestra shows that the notion of "frightening stories conducive to piety" is not presented by the chorus with a rationalist's sneer, but as something good, since they remind people of the existence of divine justice.

Let us now move on to the main ritual skeleton articulating the tragedy. Crucial to the plot is a ritual reported by a messenger in detail, at 783-851, the sacrifice performed by Aigisthos, in the course of which he was murdered by Orestes, a sacrifice corrupted by murder.[229] This sacrifice had been referred to before its description, and will be referred to again, by Klytemestra, after the murder, of which she is ignorant. At 825-29 we are told that when Aigisthos took the omens the organs were abnormal and diseased, that is, the omens were bad. They came to pass very soon, as the disguised Orestes almost immediately afterwards killed Aigisthos.

A corrupted sacrifice is not a good thing, and since I argued in chapter I.2 that there was some permeability between the world of the tragedy and the world of the audience, I should note that this corrupted sacrifice is very distanced from the world of the audience. First, the sacrifice is reported, it is not enacted on stage; second, and most importantly, it is not part of the Athenians' heroic past, since it happened "elsewhere"; moreover, this was a sacrifice for the benefit of a closed unit, an *oikos* sacrifice to the Nymphs by Aigisthos, who prayed for the well-being of himself and his wife and ill fortune for his enemies. The sacrifice is corrupted by his murder, and this both brings about, and signifies, the destruction of his *oikos*.

The messenger reports that when Orestes revealed his identity the palace servants raised the ritual cry of triumph and crowned him with a wreath.[230] When the messenger departs the chorus performs a victory dance and invite Electra to join in the dancing and singing (859-65). In fact, Electra will fetch a wreath to crown her brother, but will leave the *choreia* to the chorus.[231] The chorus at 874-9 refer to their singing and dancing in a way that will have zoomed the audience's perception to their identity as a chorus in the present.[232] This zoomed the world of the tragedy to the world of the audience; this happened between

Chapter 3: Euripidean Tragedy and Religious Exploration 347

the corrupted ritual and the next disturbing enacted ritual, Electra's crowning of Orestes at 880-9, a disturbing victory celebration, given the circumstances;[233] for the killing of Aegisthos, which could have been presented as a legitimate act of punishment, is made problematic in this tragedy through the outrage of the ritual order during the sacrifice;[234] also potentially disturbing is the fact that the corpse of Aigisthos is brought on to the stage and treated with disrespect.[235]

The murder of Klytemestra involves deception centered on a ritual. At 1124-38 Electra tricks Klytemestra by requesting her to perform a rite for her, the sacrifice performed on the tenth night after childbirth. Klytemestra goes into the house believing she will perform the role of sacrificer, while in fact she will be the sacrificial victim.[236] When, after the murder, Orestes and Electra come out of the house, appalled at their actions, they continue with religious language. Electra expresses her perception of her situation by asking *tin' es choron, tina gamon eimi* (1198-9).[237] This would have evoked her earlier statement of isolation resulting from her exclusion from ritual: in 309-13 she had mentioned that she was deprived of participation in festival and dances, for she avoided the group of which she is supposed to be a member, that of married women, since in reality she was a *parthenos*. Now, as she sees it (wrongly as it will turn out), she is excluded both from the ritual role of the *parthenos* in choruses and from marriage.

Orestes invokes first Gaia and Zeus (1177-8) to look upon his deeds, and then, in 1190-93, Apollo: *io Phoib', anymnesas dikai' / aphanta, phanera d' exepra- / xas achea*. This most telling cri de coeur reflects the mortal's view of the unfathomability of the divine will, which seems to demand suffering. One can see the suffering, the justice one cannot see.[238] It is one of the problems that tragedy explores.

Finally, there is the epiphany of Kastor and Polydeukes.[239] Kastor, among other things, urges Orestes to go to Athens to supplicate the statue of Athena there, and she will protect him from the Erinyes; he then says (1266-9) that Orestes will be saved, for Apollo will take on the blame to save Orestes, since it was he who instructed Orestes to kill his mother; after their defeat, the Erinyes will sink into a chasm making a venerable oracle for pious men.

Let us now look at 1245-8, spoken by Kastor.

Phoibos de, Phoibos- all' anax gar est' emos,
sigo. sophos d' on ouk echrese soi sopha.
ainein d' ananke tauta. tantheuthen de chre
prassein ha Moira Zeus t' ekrane sou peri.

After this follow instructions for the future, including those mentioned above. Those instructions and predictions, then, have the authority of Zeus and Moira. But the comments about Apollo are presented as Kastor's own. The audience's perception of Kastor's words would have been that his viewpoint was both partial and biased;[240] that he is expressing a partial view, shaped by his kinship to Klytemestra, and by the fact that in this version of his story (312-3), before he had become a god, he had courted, and wanted to marry, Electra. His view was inferior to that of Apollo; as Kastor acknowledges, Apollo is his master, and the audience's knowledge, also activated by that statement, was that at Delphi Apollo spoke the will of Zeus. So Apollo's was the more authoritative voice; and it was Apollo who had a special concern for order.[241]

That the Dioskouroi, who had been mortals and are now gods, are not quite like other, Olympian gods has been acknowledged;[242] but one of the implications of this that has not been considered is that the authority of Kastor's statement when he is speaking for himself (and Polydeukes, we may assume) as when he criticizes Apollo, is affected by their status. There are degrees of unknowability and access to Zeus' will and plans. At one end are the mortals, whose access is limited. At the other end, Zeus: only Zeus in Euripidean tragedy knows Zeus' will; but of the other gods Apollo has privileged access, while the formerly human Dioskouroi would have been perceived to have less access, and therefore also lesser authority in their judgments. This allowed a perception of the events that would have been nearer the human perception to be articulated, the suffering to be stressed, without destabilizing the authority of Apollo and the Delphic oracle. Thus, gods in epiphany were not interchangeable, and there was a hierarchy in the authority of their pronouncements, as there was a hierarchy among the gods.

The fact that Apollo will take on the blame to save Orestes (1266-9) does not mean that he was wrong or unwise to tell him to kill his mother. What it means is that Apollo stands by the man who followed his instructions.

This tragedy problematized several things pertaining to religion—it also deployed complex explorations of human relationships, passions, behavior patterns, and characteristics, but this is not my concern here. It problematized matricide, the notion of avenging one's father by killing one's mother—which involved human relationship issues as well as ones involving rules policed by the gods, pollution and divine punishment. But it surely also problematized the notion of revenge in general, suggesting the possibility that it is in itself a corrupting act. For the killing of Aegisthos involved the corruption and pollution of sacri-

Chapter 3: Euripidean Tragedy and Religious Exploration 349

fice, and so, while it could have been presented as a legitimate act of punishment, it is made problematic through this outrage of the ritual order.[243] Of course, all this involved problematizing the role of Apollo and the Delphic oracle, above all through the explicit statements of Kastor in epiphany. However, I suggested that the ancient audience would not have been perceived this as "criticism" of Apollo and his oracle, but as an illustration of the dark side of life; once one is caught up in a cycle of destruction such as that of the Atreids, a lot of suffering will come about. But ultimately Orestes will be saved, Apollo will take on the responsibility. So, at the end, if one acts on divine instructions, even if they make no sense, or seem wrong, there may be intense suffering, but there will be an end to the suffering and an end to the self-perpetuating cycle of destruction. This is a reassuring position, and one relevant to the Athenian audience's own realities. Incidentally, I should note that, in my view, through becoming an oracle themselves, the Erinyes are reaffirming the validity of prophecy.

Orestes' suffering would have been perceived by the ancient audience as at least partlty correlative with his own actions; for it was his own decision (the old man suggested it, but it was his decision) to kill Aigisthos at a sacrifice, and so pollute the ritual and pervert the ritual order, as well as offend against the laws of hospitality, and so also against Zeus Xenios. In the circumstances, Orestes got off lightly for this offense, which he committed of his own free will.

The tragedy ends with a pronouncement by Kastor on the modus operandi of the Dioskouroi as *theoi soteres*, which reinforces the notion that good behavior, the type of behavior approved by the gods, is conducive to better fortune. At 1346-56 Kastor offers a mini-self-presentation of the Dioskouroi as gods who are saviors at sea; he states their function and adds that they do not help those who are polluted, that they save those who respect what is just and holy, *chalepon eklyontes mochthon*—because in the Greek collective representations holding dear what is just and holy is not, of course, a guarantee that one will be spared suffering. So, he continues, no one should do wrong willingly, nor should he sail together with men who have perjured themselves.[244] Kastor's last words, *theos on thnetois agoreuo* (1356) confirms the authority of this statement.

The chorus' last words return to the notion evoked by *chalepon eklyontes mochthon*; they express the perception that it is extremely rare for mortals not to suffer, that misfortune is inevitable.[245] This, it submits, puts the suffering of Orestes in a wider perspective: suffering is the lot of mankind; but at least, the play shows, there is order, and Zeus is the guardian of that order; and though being just and pious does not guarantee freedom from suffering, it is more conducive to good for-

350 Part III: Religion and the Fifth-Century Tragedians

tune; and following divine guidance, again, though it does not guarantee freedom from suffering, brings about, in this case, ultimate divine protection and eventual release from suffering. For an Athenian audience who had gone through ten years of war and the plague this is not bleak perception, but a reassuring one.[246]

To sum up. In *Electra* there is a significant density of ritual elements, intertwined with deep and rich religious problematization. This tragedy, then, like some others,[247] can be seen as being structured by what we may call a new version of the developed tragic matrix, which had ultimately emerged out of the ritual matrix, in which a new and intense type of religious exploration is central.

7) *Troades*

Troades was produced in 415, together with, and following, *Alexandros* and *Palamedes*. It most strikingly articulated the horrors of war, of the destruction of a city, focussed on the suffering of the women. I will be arguing here that this tragedy has an extraordinary ritual density, and that through this density of ritual elements is articulated a dense and significant religious exploration and problematization.

The prologue involves deities, Poseidon, subsequently joined by Athena, in the presence of Hecabe, who is sleeping and unaware of their presence. Poseidon mentions the sacrileges committed by the Greeks when Troy was sacked. Athena tells him of her purpose to bring cheer to the former enemies, the Trojans, and a grim return home to the Greeks, because sacrilege was committed against her shrine when Ajax raped Kassandra and the Greeks did not punish him. She describes the punishment that they will suffer on the way home, if Poseidon consents *hos an to loipon tam' anaktor' eusebein eidos' Achaioi theous te tous allous sebein* (85-6). Poseidon consents to this. He concludes by saying that he who, in sacking cities, lays waste the temples of the gods and the graves of the dead is foolish, and will perish. This, then, is a clear-cut message of retribution for sacrilege, and at the same time an explanation for the unhappy fate of the Greeks returning from Troy. Insofar as it is an explanation it is reassuring, for it establishes cause and effect and validates the notion of an ordered universe.

After the gods' exit Hecabe sings a lament (98-152). Then there is the complex parodos, the first part of which is sung by Hecabe and the chorus divided in two hemichoria,[248] and includes a lament, and the second a choral ode. Hecabe has the shorn hair of mourning,[249] and probably the chorus did too. They are in a state of mourning for their dead; Kassandra mentions at 315-7 that Hecabe is lamenting for her dead husband and mourns for their country. The women mourn and lament not

Chapter 3: Euripidean Tragedy and Religious Exploration 351

only for their dead, but also for Troy, and also lament over their bad fortune. The lamentations over their bad fortune, especially by Hecabe, would probably not have been perceived as proper death ritual, lamentations, but some expressions of grief (in whatever form and meter), for example Hecabe's at 279-81,[250] would have had very strong echoes of the ritual lamentations for the dead, because of the similarity of their actions to those death ritual lamentations. In some cases, as in the *kommos* at 577-607, a *kommos* involving Hecabe and Andromache, the lament for their bad fortune is intertwined with a lament for Troy and for their dead.

In these circumstances, and given that lamentations articulate the tragedy throughout, and especially given the ritual mourning appearance of Hecabe (and probably the chorus), it is possible to see the whole play after the prologue as, in a way, a ritual of mourning for the Trojan dead and for Troy. Within that framework, other, more specific and focussed rituals are enacted in, and structure, the tragedy, two of which are major ritual nexuses, one involving Kassandra, and the second a segment of the death ritual. At 251-8 Talthybios tells Hecabe that Kassandra (of whom Hecabe speaks as Phoebus' virgin, to whom the golden-haired god had given a virgin life) will be Agamemnon's concubine—he refers to her as *entheos kore*. On hearing this Hecabe, referring to Kassandra's priestly office, exclaims (256-8) *rhipte, teknon, zatheous kledas, apo chroos endyton stepheon hierous stolmous*, in other words, throw off your priestly emblems, your life as a priestess is over.[251]

With the entrance of Kassandra, at 308, begins a complex ritual nexus. The somber mourning ritual coloring of the post-prologue opening segment was not altered by Talthybios' entrance at 235; on the contrary, it was strongly activated and reinforced by Hecabe's self-invitation to lament at 279-81, which, we saw, would have evoked very strong echoes of the death ritual.[252] But at 308 the death ritual framework is jarred through the eruption of a disturbing ritual amalgam in which are combined wedding ritual elements and prophetic *mania* elements with Dionysiac overtones. Kassandra in a state of frenzy bursts onto the stage holding two flaming torches and sings a perverted wedding hymn, thus performing, while in a state of divine possession, a perverted version of a segment of the wedding ritual, for her pseudo-marriage to Agamemnon.[253] She speaks of herself as *entheos* (366) and speaks of *baccheumaton* (367). The others refer to her as *mainas* (349, 415), *baccheuousan* (342). Hecabe had already earlier on referred to *ekbacheousan Kasandran . . . mainad'* (169, 170), and she had referred to her as *mainas* when announcing her arrival at 307. And at 500 Hecabe addresses her now absent daughter *o symbacche Kassandra theois*.

352 *Part III: Religion and the Fifth-Century Tragedians*

At 408 Talthybios tells her *ei me s' Apollon exebaccheusen phrenas*. Thus, in one way, her bacchic state is metaphorical. But Kassandra herself cried *euan euoi* in her song, and the metaphorical and the ritual bacchic references merge into each other, so that the ritual enacted by Kassandra had bacchic, as well as wedding, elements.[254] The other facet of this *mania* is its prophetic nature, which will soon be activated, and its Apolline origin, stressed when Kassandra addresses Apollo and declares that she is sacrificing in his temple at 329-30.[255] And of course all this is intermeshed with Hecabe's and the Trojan women's mourning.[256] Indeed Kassandra herself interweaves mourning and wedding when, in the course of her song, she addresses her mother, and tells that since she, Hecabe, is lamenting for her dead husband and her country, Kassandra lit the torches herself—while in normal weddings it would have been her mother who did this.[257]

Hecabe begins her response at 343 with an invocation of Hephaistos; she comments on the negative nature of this pseudo-marriage, and takes the torch from Kassandra, *ou gar ortha pyrphoreis mainas thoazous'* (348-9). Kassandra responds by telling her mother to crown her victorious head and to rejoice on her royal wedding; then she says *ei gar esti Loxias*, she will take her revenge, and starts prophesying, telling, in an allusive manner, of the future disasters that will befall Agamemnon and his family. In her long speech she mentions, among other things, the fact that the Trojans who died for their country received the appropriate death ritual (388-90); she concludes (404-5) that she will destroy her and her mother's most hated enemies *gamoisi tois emois*—and this is a prophecy. Talthybios' response begins (408) *ei me s' Apollon exebaccheuses phrenas*. In her reply Kassandra says, among other things, referring to Hecabe going to Odysseus' palace at 428-30, *pou d' Apollonos logoi, hoi phasin auten eis em' hermeneumenoi autou thaneisthai? talla d' ouk oneidio*. We know, as the audience did,[258] that others did not believe Kassandra's prophecies; but here she herself seems to express a doubt about the veracity of one of them, doubt which is, however, immediately deconstructed by the fact that she goes on to prophesy on other matters with confidence.[259] She prophesies what will happen to Odysseus (431-44), and returns to Agamemnon's future death and her own, and mentions that their corpses will not be buried, but will be thrown into a ravine, and her body will be given to the animals, *ten Apollonos latrin* (450). Then at 451-4 she says farewell to the garlands of her most beloved god, which she characterizes as *agalmat' euia*, the garlands that were the marks of her priesthood, and which she now throws away, adding that she has already abandoned *heortas*, in which she had previously taken delight, and concludes with various religious references, including an

Chapter 3: Euripidean Tragedy and Religious Exploration 353

address to Apollo (453-4). Thus, the end of her life as a Trojan princess and priestess is expressed through the final stage in her abandonment of ritual normality, which included her ritual attire. The perversion of ritual normality manifested in Kassandra's "wedding ritual" is correlative with, and symbolizes, not only the end of her own religious office as priestess of Apollo at Troy, but also the end of Troy's ritual life altogether.[260]

The second major ritual nexus structuring *Troades* is the one involving a segment of the death ritual; it comes later on in the play. In between these two major ritual nexuses there is a variety of other ritual acts, some more significant than others.[261] After Kassandra's exit, in her long speech that begins at 466, Hecabe, before going on to enumerate her misfortunes, invokes the gods, and then makes the bleak comment (469-71) *o theoi; kakous men anakalo tous symmachous, homos d' echei ti schema kikleskein theous, hotan tis hemon dystyche labei tychen*. In the course of the enumeration of her misfortunes she mentions some of the rites she had performed as part of the death ritual for her dead and the sacrilegious murder of her husband on the altar of Zeus Herkeios (480-3).

In the first stasimon (511-67)[262] the chorus sing an *epikedeion* song about Troy's ruin, which includes the story of the Trojan Horse, in the telling of which the religious nature of the snare (the dedication of the horse of which it is said at 525 *tond' hieron anagete xoanon*) is stressed.[263] After the first stasimon, Andromache enters in a cart that, in the context, which includes the fact that Andromache was being taken to be Neoptolemos' concubine, evoked the marriage cart which in ritual reality took the bride to her new husband's house.[264]

In the course of this ritual-evoking scene Andromache raises questions that pertain to the causes of the destruction, which implicates the role of the gods, and touches on the question of the extent of the Trojans' own responsibility. At 595-600 Andromache says that Troy's miseries were the result of the gods' hostility, when Paris (*sos gonos* is how Andromache, addressing Hecabe, refers to him) escaped death *hos lecheon stygeron charin olese pergama Troias*, so that now *haimatoenta de theai para Palladi somata nekron gypsi pherein tetatai*. This is important. For it activated the audience's knowledge of Hecabe's responsibility. Having watched the *Alexandros*, they would have perceived the disasters to have been, first, predictable and predicted, and second, ultimately brought about by the fact that, when it came to it, the Trojan royal family, Hecabe above all, probably supported by the chorus of Trojan women,[265] had ignored the prophecies of the disaster that her newly recognized son Paris Alexandros would bring to the city and welcomed him. That may have been perceived to be an understandable reaction, but in the eyes of the ancient audience it would have made Hecabe (and perhaps to some extent, by symbolic extension, the Trojan women of the chorus) far from wholly blameless. The events in the *Alexandros* would have helped shape the filters through which the audience perceived the misery of the defeated Trojans in the *Troades*, and that knowledge would have been activated again by Helen's claim at 919-22[266] that the people responsible for Troy's downfall are, first Hecabe, who gave birth to Paris, then Priam for not killing the baby.

At 884-8 Hecabe invokes Zeus in a prayer which has been considered to be one of the loci reflecting Anaxagorean or sophistic thought in Euripidean tragedy.[267] Though the form of the prayer is by then traditional,[268] it alludes to contemporary philosophical systems, especially Anaxagoras', and Menelaos' reply at 889 demonstrates its novelty. But, as Lefkowitz noted,[269] this prayer is uttered by Hecabe, who, in dire straits, doubts that the gods care about the fate of Troy, while the audience knows that her doubts are mistaken, having heard in the prologue Athena explain how revenge will be taken on the Greeks, which is what Hecabe desires. I shall return to this question below. Here I would like to stress that the Anaxagorean elements are part of Hecabe's religious discourse, which will be proved partially wrong.

Most of the exodos is structured by the death ritual for Astyanax, the rest by a lament for Troy and a ritual attempt to make contact with the dead. It begins at 1118 with the arrival of Astyanax's corpse, announced by the chorus. From 1156 is enacted part of the death ritual for Astyanax, the dressing and adornment of his corpse, with laments and the mourning ritual of hitting one's head (1235-6). The ritual density is further intensified by other ritual references. At 1181-4 Hecabe mentions the promise Astyanax had made her that he would visit her grave, bringing locks as offerings and leading a group of his friends. At 1219-24 she says she is clothing his corpse with the robes which he ought to have worn at his wedding, and adorning with a wreath the shield of Hector on which Astyanax will be buried. Both passages stress the abnormality of the situation: first, the grandmother performing part of the death ritual of the grandson, instead of the other way around; and a boy, whose ritual transition to be celebrated ought to have been his wedding, is being buried. The ritual being enacted is not perverted or distorted; it is the circumstances in which it is being performed that are negatively abnormal; this is brought out through the comparison of the ritual being enacted to the rituals which will never be performed, as they would normally have been, Astyanax's visit to his grandmother's tomb, and his wedding. At 1234 Hecabe says

Chapter 3: Euripidean Tragedy and Religious Exploration 355

to Astyanax that his father will take care of him in the land of the dead. This, I suggest, would have appeared a "commonsense" statement to the audience, and the evocation of a life after death in which familial relationships continue would have evoked an image of reassurance.[270] The funeral procession started at 1246, and would have left at 1250,[271] after Hecabe had commented that in her view it does not make much difference to the dead if they have rich funeral honors, that is a vain subject of boasting for the living.

This enacted ritual had been preceded by a discussion of the death ritual for Astyanax,[272] and a lamentation by Hecabe preceding his death; she had lamented at 790-8, just after Astyanax has been taken away to be killed, beating her head and breasts. It had also been preceded by reports about other parts of the death ritual. At 1134-46 Talthybios, who brought Astyanax's corpse on stage, reports to Hecabe Andromache's instructions for the burial; at 1147-8 he offers to perform the burial, once Hecabe ritually prepares the corpse, and erect the grave monument; he then tells her that one of the ritual duties usually performed by women, the washing of the corpse, he has himself performed already. He then departs to dig the grave.[273]

After the funeral procession had left, Hecabe articulated her resentment of the gods through a ritual (1280-1): she invoked the gods and then said, *kai ti tous theous kalo? kai prin gar ouk ekousan anakaloumenoi.* This, then, is a more despairing comment than the one she had made earlier at 469-71 in her invocation of the gods. Nevertheless, it is significant that she continues to invoke them, even if only to complain and castigate them. In the course of a lament for Troy by Hecabe and the chorus, which begins at 1287 and goes on to the end of the tragedy, she (1288-90) invokes Zeus in his persona as ancestor of the Trojans, father of Dardanos, and asks him whether he sees the suffering of Dardanos' race, to which the chorus responds at 1281 *dedorken.* I shall return to this. Hecabe and the chorus kneel and beat the ground with their hands to make contact with their dead (1305-9), before lamenting for, and commenting on, the final death of Troy (1317ff); then they leave for the Greek ships.

Besides these two major ritual nexuses there are also some other reported rituals and other ritual references in this tragedy. Thus, at 263-70 and 622-3, 628 there are references to the sacrifice of Polyxena, without a description of the ritual acts. At 626-7 Andromache says that she performed certain ritual acts for Polyxena's corpse. The possibility of Hecabe cursing the Achaeans is raised at 734.

That everything is the work of the gods is the underlying implication in several places in this tragedy.[274] On the other hand, to what extent one's actions are one's own responsibility, and to what extent one can blame the gods is a question raised, debated, above all in the *agon* between Helen and Hecabe,[275] and ultimately left open in the play. At 919ff Helen claims that the people responsible for the Trojan War are, first Hecabe, who gave birth to Paris, then Priam for not killing the baby; then she tells the story of the judgment of Paris, and she says that she was sold for her beauty—by Aphrodite. Then (at 940ff) she says that Paris (whom she calls Hecabe's Alastor) arrived at their house accompanied by Aphrodite; it is Aphrodite whom she blames for the fact that she left Menelaos to follow Paris; it is the goddess he should punish, she tells Menelaos, and so become more powerful than Zeus, who has power over the other gods, but is the slave of Aphrodite (cf. also 964-5). Hecabe begins her reply at 969 with the statement that she will become an ally to the goddesses, for she does not believe the version of the Judgment of Paris that Helen has just told,[276] and puts forward logical arguments for her belief, as she does in order to ridicule the notion that Aphrodite went to Sparta with Paris. According to Hecabe, Helen was seduced by Paris' beauty, and made her yearnings into Aphrodite, as men are wont to do, calling their own folly Aphrodite. The distinction is not as clear-cut as it may seem; for one way of describing what would have happened if, as Hecabe claims, Helen had been seduced by Paris' beauty, is that she had come under the power of Aphrodite. Does that mean that Aphrodite herself is personally involved every time a person comes under her power? It is not necessary to believe this, in order to see erotic love as the result of the power of Aphrodite. So what Hecabe says cannot invalidate Helen's claim, except that her claim involved the goddess' strong personal commitment. One distinction may be located in the person's power to resist; but even this is unstable, since it is not clear in the Greek collective representations that Aphrodite's power means that the person has to act on it, that they have no freedom to resist.[277] Hecabe is on safer ground when she claims that Helen was attracted by the love of luxury and gold—a stereotypical accusation against women. But her point that Helen did not protest or cry out is dishonest rhetoric, for Helen had not claimed that she had been taken from Sparta by force, but that she had been swayed by the power of Aphrodite.[278] So the question of human responsibility is left open. Menelaos' comment at 1038-9 means that his conclusion from the debate at least is that Helen had a choice. But there is no clear-cut answer.

In the second stasimon (799-859) the chorus sing of Troy's past history, an exposition which includes several religious references, including an address to Ganymede and one to Eros, and the statement (845-6) *to men oun Dios ouket' oneidos ero*, where *to men* seems to refer to the love affair between Zeus and Ganymede, and to the fact that, despite

Chapter 3: Euripidean Tragedy and Religious Exploration 357

that relationship, Zeus did not protect Troy—any more than Eos did, whose husband, and father of her children, Tithonos, was a Trojan, as the chorus goes on to remark.[279] They conclude (858-9) Troy's charms over the gods are gone.[280] The audience would not have perceived this expectation of special favor on those grounds justified, since there was hardly a place in the Greek world that did not have one or more figures in the heroic age whom some deity had loved, mated with, and usually had a child with.

But the third stasimon (1060-1117) did raise some disturbing questions, above all, whether the gods do honor, whether there is any meaning in, the relationship of reciprocity established by cult, and whether the gods care about human affairs. The whole ode is full of ritual and religious references, but it is the first strophe and the first antistrophe that are of primary concern to us here. Of the rest I will only mention that at 1113 a reference to the temple of Athena Chalkioikos at Sparta zooms the world of the play to present-day religious realities.[281]

The chorus addresses the first strophe and the first antistrophe to Zeus, beginning (1060-3),

> *houto de ton en Ilioi*
> *naon kai thyoenta bo-*
> *mon proudokas Achaiois,*
> *o Zeu, kai pelanon phloga*

and continuing with the same emphasis on ritual; the section beginning *phroudai soi thysiai choron t' / euphemoi keladoi* (1071-2), through enumerating the cultic acts that will no longer be performed in Troy, because Troy no longer exists, reminds Zeus of what they had in the past offered to the gods as part of their worship, and so stresses further the absence of reciprocity of which they accuse Zeus. And at 1076-80 they sing of their concern as to whether Zeus cares about these things, as he sits on his heavenly throne and on the aether while Troy perished.

Here, then, the notion is expressed that the gods betrayed their obligation of reciprocity, and also the notion that the gods may not care about human affairs.[282] How would the audience make sense of this discourse? Would they have agreed that Zeus had betrayed the bond of reciprocity that had been established by the cult offered by the Trojans? And would they have considered it likely that the gods may not care about human affairs? It is, of course, significant that both these possibilities are articulated, that it is a conceivable thing at this time that this could be so. But having been articulated, these bleak possibilities would have been to a very large extent rejected by the audience. First, because the audience knew that the notion that the gods may not care about human affairs is wrong, for they had seen Poseidon and Athena in the prologue, and they knew that they did take an interest, and a hand, in human affairs.[283] Then, because, the principle of reciprocity between gods and mankind had been presented in the prologue, in its negative form, that involved the gods punishing impiety and sacrilegious behavior.[284] In addition, though the audience would have been sympathetic, and also disturbed by the fact that the principle of reciprocity between gods and mankind does not guarantee the survival of a polis that had offered cult, the following factors would, I suggest, have colored their perception of the chorus' discourse as being (understandably) partial. First, the fact that in the second stasimon the audience would have perceived the chorus' expectation of special favor as unjustified, and therefore the chorus' discourse on these matters as partial; second, the fact that the chorus did not consider that they, the Trojans, had done anything wrong, anything to deserve the destruction of their city, while in Greek eyes it was at least arguable that they had.

Hecabe's complaint at 1240-2 begins in the same vein, the accusation that the gods did not acknowledge their part of the relationship of reciprocity established through the cult offered by the Trojans: she says that there is nothing of any concern to the gods except her miseries,[285] and Troy whom they loathed; in vain we sacrificed (1242). But then, she continues (1242-5) in a different vein, saying that if they had not had this terrible fortune from the gods, they would not have been remembered in song by subsequent generations, as they now will be. So, through their misery, they have gained memory survival, which was a very important thing in the Greek collective representations.[286] Again, the fact that the audience had seen the gods in the prologue taking an interest in the affairs of humanity would have framed the audience's perception of Hecabe's complaints.[287]

To sum up, then, this tragedy has a very great ritual density, and also a density of religious references[288] and very significant religious problematization. The problematization is articulated through the deployment of the rituals, as are also the tragedy's main structural lines. To refocus on the main ones, in the case of the segment of the wedding ritual, its perversion corresponds to the bad end that awaits both "bride" and "groom," as was revealed in the prophesying rite with which the perverted wedding was combined, and also to Troy's overthrow and general disasters, while the prophecy revealed that justice will be done. The death ritual is not perverted but abnormal, in that the grandmother performs part of the death ritual for her grand-

Chapter 3: Euripidean Tragedy and Religious Exploration 359

son, which is a reversal of the natural order of things (a natural order evoked the mention of rites that will not now be performed), while the other part of the death ritual for Astyanax will be performed by a member of the group of his enemies who killed him. This abnormality expresses the notion of the utter desolation and destruction of Troy, and the notion of the end of the line of the Trojan royal house.

Other rituals, the invocation of gods, and the singing of songs to them, are used to articulate Hecabe's and the chorus' resentment of the gods who had abandoned them. This notion of the gods abandoning a city, and not acknowledging the reciprocity established through the cult, is explored in this tragedy in very complex ways. The resentment of the gods expressed by the Trojan women in this tragedy is comparable to the Athenians' feelings during the plague, when, according to Thucydides, turning to the gods was useless, and since the plague struck indiscriminately, people were not restrained by fear of god or human law.[289] Religious practice and the perception of the centrality of religion in Athens recovered, if it had ever become shaky. I will be returning to this question. But it is possible to see *Troades*, at the safe distance of several years later, rearticulating some of the questions that had been asked then, when some Athenians at least may have felt that the gods had abandoned them, and that they had worshiped them in vain. In fact, Athens had not been abandoned by the gods, while here we have the exploration of the case limit: Troy had indeed been abandoned by the gods, the worship that the Trojans had offered them did not ensure the city's survival.[290]

Would the audience have understood this tragedy to be saying that reciprocity means nothing to the gods? I suggest not. It is true that the gods abandoned Troy, despite the fact that that city had offered them worship. However, the tragedy brings up three very important considerations which, first, provide an explanation for the Trojans' sufferings that did not entail a simple cruelty of indifferent gods who did not recognize the relationship of *charis*, and second, provided some compensation for the suffering. As a result, in my view, in the eyes of the fifth-century audience this tragic representation of Troy's abandonment did not present the gods as cruel and indifferent, and did not constitute a challenge to the religious discourse of the polis, did not make the worship of gods seem pointless.[291]

First, the Trojans are presented as responsible for their sufferings, which they (at least partly) brought upon themselves, by ignoring the warning of prophecy and letting Paris live. The gods had given the Trojans a warning, and the Trojans chose not to act on it. The notion of human responsibility for disasters people attribute to gods is explicitly brought up in the debate over Helen's responsibility for the Trojan

War. It is not answered in a totally clear-cut way, but the fact that human action is a very important factor emerges clearly.

Second, justice will be done, the justice Hecabe craves for, since the Greeks will be punished for their sacrilegious behavior. This shows that the gods are not indifferent to human behavior, and it also entails that there is order in the world. The audience's perception of what happens in the tragedy was framed, and shaped, by this knowledge, that the Greeks will be punished. The Trojan women do not, of course, know that the gods have decided this; but they have heard from Kassandra how Agamemnon and Odysseus will suffer; Kassandra is not believed, but given that she has proved right in the past, above all in her prophecies in *Alexandros*, which have come to fruition now, they ought to have believed her, or at least seen it as a possibility. This does not neutralize their suffering, but it does restore justice; suffering is part of life in the Greek perceptions, and the possibility that a polis may be destroyed is acknowledged in this tragedy. But the Greeks' punishment shows that there is order in the world, and justice prevails.[292] Third, as Hecabe states, the Trojans, because of their suffering, will be remembered in song by subsequent generations. They gained memory survival, which, in Greek perceptions, is very important.

The Greek collective representations acknowledged that the world is cruel and precarious; the important thing is that there should be order and, in the main lines, justice guaranteed by the gods; and *Troades* says that there is. It explores very difficult questions in the light of harsh realities; but the image presented is ultimately reassuring. Though the fact that in this case the Trojans were not innocent victims leaves open the question of whether a polis can be utterly destroyed though its citizens were innocent of any offense against the gods. Equally, the fact that it was difficult to be certain of the gods' will always left open the possibility of inadvertent offense, and all this to some extent deconstructed the reassuring nature of these perceptions—deconstructed, but not challenged or undermined.

Parker rightly comments that in tragedy the issues of justice or injustice of the gods are raised, and the characters demand explanations;[293] the worst possibility is explored, above all in *Troades*, where the ultimate disaster, the sack of a city is shown; the gods abandon the captured city. He notes that Poseidon says that it was the hatred of Hera and Athena that destroyed the city; in Parker's view, "Whatever the content of the two previous plays in the quasi-trilogy which *Troades* concludes, it is hard to believe that any theological justification offered there for the Trojans' fate would have withstood the tide of pathos that sweeps through the final play."[294] I do not disagree; but I do feel that it did make a difference in the audience's "placing" of the

Chapter 3: Euripidean Tragedy and Religious Exploration 361

pathos and the misery that, having watched the *Alexandros*, they would have perceived these woes to have been, first, predictable and predicted, and second, ultimately brought about by the fact that when it came to it the Trojan royal family, above all Hecabe, probably supported by the chorus of Trojan women, ignored the prophecies of the disaster that her newly recognized son Paris Alexandros would bring to the city, and welcomed him. Hers may have been perceived to be an understandable reaction, but in the eyes of the audience it would have created two very important meanings that would have affected their perception of the misery of *Troades*. First, that there is order in the world—which reinforced the message of the prologue, where they learnt that the Greeks will be punished for their impiety. Second, that Hecabe, and by symbolic extension, the Trojan women of the chorus, are not wholly blameless. This fact, while not neutralizing the pain, makes it not only intelligible but also, though not perhaps, or not necessarily, justified, at least motivated. Both these meanings had the effect of distancing Troy symbolically even further from Athens. Parker is basically right that though the city the gods did not save is not Athens, "the spectator would have been complacent indeed who did not feel that it might have been."[295] But I believe that the symbolic distance between this Troy and the audience's Athens was greater than may appear; that the events in *Alexandros* (activated within *Troades* in the ways suggested above) would have helped shape the filters through which the audience perceived the misery of the defeated in *Troades*, and this would have increased the symbolic distance from their own reality.[296]

8) *Heracles*

Heracles[297] was probably produced in the last decade of Euripides' career.[298] One way of summarizing this tragedy is to say that it shows a good man going mad, and committing dreadful deeds, as the result of divine hostility and malice. This would appear to vindicate the notion of Euripides as a critic of the gods. But, I am arguing here, this summary is misleading, and the tragedy presents a much more complex picture.

The opening segment of the tragedy, until the exit just before the first stasimon (which begins at 348), is structured by a ritual enacted on stage, the supplication by Amphitryon, Megara and Heracles' sons, at the altar of Zeus Soter (cf. 48-54); for Lykos, the new king of Thebes, wants to kill them.[299] The world of the play is sharply distanced from the world of the audience at the very beginning, through Amphitryon's first words: *Tis ton Dios syllektron* . . . (1). He then identifies himself as Heracles' father, but the mention of his sharing the same bed as Zeus would have qualified this in the eyes of the audience as meaning social father, Zeus being Heracles' biological father.[300] Within that supplication, and within Amphitryon's speech, there is a reference to a past ritual which is significant for the play, Heracles' wedding to Megara (10-12).

In this segment, which is structured by the supplication, there are also various other elements of religious significance. At 62 Megara says that none of the gods' actions are clear to mortals,[301] thus expressing, and activating, the notion of the unknowability of the divine world. In replying to Lykos' abuse, Amphitryon says at 170-1 that he leaves it to Zeus to defend Heracles' divine paternity;[302] he then invokes divine witnesses for Heracles' bravery, Zeus' thunderbolt, and the chariot[303] in which Heracles rode when he helped the gods defeat the Giants, and when he sang and danced the victory hymn and dance with the gods; he also bids Lykos to ask the Centaurs, whom Heracles had defeated, who they think is the bravest man (176-84). All this, and especially the fighting, and the singing and dancing with the gods, would have had the effect of distancing Heracles, and so also his family and the world of the tragedy, from the world of the audience.[304] At 309-11 Megara says that it is foolish to struggle against the *tychai* sent by the gods; *ho chre gar oudeis me chreon thesei pote*. So here the *tychai* sent by the gods do not seem to be distinct from *to chreon*.

Lykos prepared to burn the suppliants at the altar—which respects the letter, but not the spirit of supplication.[305] When the suppliants became convinced that they would die, Megara asked Lykos to let her go into the palace to dress her children in the appropriate clothes and wreaths for the dead. Lykos allows her to; the expressions used by both Megara and Lykos would have evoked the dressing and adorning of the corpse after death in the course of the death ritual. After Megara left the altar with her sons and entered the palace, Amphitryon invokes Zeus, and berates him for not helping Heracles' children, saying *aretei se niko thnetos on theon megan* (342) and concluding *amathes tis ei theos, e dikaios ouk ephys* (347); he then exits.[306]

The first stasimon (348-440) is a *threnos* for Heracles, whom the chorus consider dead, a *threnos* which takes the form of a hymn to Heracles.[307] At 442-50 the chorus announces the entrance of Amphitryon, Megara, and the children in funeral clothes; this is followed by their entrance. So this is like a perverted part of the death ritual. At 451-3 Megara's words (*tis hiereus, tis sphageus ton dyspotmon . . . hetoim' agein ta thymat' eis Haidou tade*) evoke a perverted human sacrifice, which is what will in fact happen eventually, at the hands of Heracles. The perverted death ritual continues, when at 497 Amphitryon

Chapter 3: Euripidean Tragedy and Religious Exploration 363

urges Megara to do the appropriate death rites. At 498-502 Amphitryon prays to Zeus, concluding that he is praying in vain. But Heracles arrives very soon after, and this seems to prove wrong Amphitryon's doubts, and his earlier accusations against Zeus. This invalidation of Amphitryon's accusations against Zeus here would have activated the audience's perception that mortals do not see the whole picture, and that their reproaches against the gods can be misguided.

Heracles comments on the fact that his children are attired in the dress of the dead (526; cf. also 548-9). He urges them (562) to throw away *Haidou tasde peribolas komes*; there is another reference to this attire at 702-3 by Lykos, who does not yet know that Heracles has returned. This segment of the play, then, evokes, and refracts, the death ritual.

Given that *kallinikos* was a common epithet of Heracles in cult, as well as in literature, Heracles' formulation at 581-2, *ouk' ar' Herakles ho kallinikos hos paroithe lexomai*, would have activated the audience's knowledge that he is a god in their religious realities. This activation, here and in other parts of the tragedy, was, we shall see, very important for the audience's perception of the play.

At 607-9 Heracles says that he will salute the gods of his house: *chronoi d' anelthon ex anelion mychon / Haidou Kores <t'> enerthen ouk atimaso / theous proseipein prota tous kata stegas*. This articulation has the effect of presenting Heracles' return from Hades also as a movement from the jurisdiction of Hades and Persephone to that of the gods of his house, who, in the audience's perceptions, in this context, would metonymically stand for the Upper gods in general. At 612-3 there is a reference to the Eleusinian Mysteries and to the myth of Heracles' initiation before his descent to Hades.[308] This would have zoomed the world of the tragedy to the world of the audience's religious realities. At 615 there is a reference to the grove sanctuary of Demeter Chthonia at Hermione. This would also have zoomed the tragedy to the present, but not to the Athenian religious realities.

The second stasimon (637-700) is a paean.[309] The second strophe and the second antistrophe take the form of a hymn to Heracles, and involve, above all the second strophe, strong choral self-referentiality, which activates the persona of the chorus as a chorus in the present,[310] in which Heracles is a god, and the recipient of hymns. It is in this context of choral self-referentiality, which situated the statement in the present, that the audience would have understood the chorus' view that Heracles is worthy of paeans in the same way that Apollo is worthy of paeans; and it is in this context that the chorus, who in the first stasimon were not certain whether Heracles is the son of Zeus or of Amphitryon, now declare at 696 that he is Zeus' son.

364   Part III: Religion and the Fifth-Century Tragedians

At 715-6 there is a false report of a ritual action as part of a deception: Amphitryon tells Lykos that Megara is sitting as a suppliant at the hearth altar of Hestia; Lykos believes it and responds appropriately. The third stasimon follows soon after. Verses 735-762 are a prelude rather than the stasimon proper, which begins at 763 (763-814).[311] In the course of the prelude the chorus affirm the power of the gods, when they sing, while Lykos is being killed inside, at 757-9:

> tis ho theous anomiai chrainon, thnatos on,
> aphrona logon ouranion makaron katebal',
> hos ar' ou sthenousin theoi?

This notion is rearticulated in a different form in the stasimon proper, at 772-3: *theoi theoi / ton adikon melousi kai / ton hosion epaiein*, and again at 811-14, at the end of the ode. So the chorus express a theodicy in this ode of triumph before the catastrophe,[312] which has clear ritual echoes.[313]

This theodicy is articulated in a context of choral self-referentiality, which would have activated the persona of the chorus as a chorus in the present. For the transition from the prelude to the stasimon proper is marked by choral self-referentiality. The prelude ends with (761) *pros chrous trapometha*, and the stasimon proper begins with (763) *choroi choroi*.[314] This context of choral self-referentiality zoomed the theodicy more directly to the audience's reality.

In the first stasimon (353-4) the chorus were uncertain as to whether Heracles was the son of Zeus or of Amphitryon. In the second (at 696), in the context of choral self-referentiality, which situated the statement in the present in which Heracles is a god, they called him Zeus' son. In the third, at 801-808, they acknowledge him as Zeus' son in their persona as Theban elders, who had earlier had doubts about the story, but now see that Heracles' deeds prove him to be the son of Zeus.

This happens just before the epiphany of Iris and Lyssa, which takes place at 817. In response the chorus invoke *onax Paian* to avert sorrows from them.[315] Iris reassures them that the city will not suffer, only Heracles' house. She explains that while he was performing his labors he was saved by fate, and Zeus would not let her or Hera harm him.[316] But now Hera wants him to be stained with the blood of his kin, to kill his children. She urges Lyssa to drive him mad so that he will do so. She concludes (840-2),

> gnoi men ton Heras hoios est' autoi cholos,
> mathei de ton emon; e theoi men oudamou,

Chapter 3: Euripidean Tragedy and Religious Exploration

ta thneta d' estai megala, me dontos diken.

This notion has puzzled scholars. The suggestion that Heracles has committed *hybris* has been made, and generally rejected, but no satisfactory interpretation of these verses has been given.[317] In my view, it is imperative to focus on how the audience would have made sense of these verses at this particular point in the play. I suggest that the formulation at 841-2 would have directed the audience's perception towards the notion of transgression of human limits. This would have inevitably activated any relevant information they may have had from their knowledge of the myth; and they did have relevant knowledge: the knowledge that Heracles had come dangerously close to exceeding the human limits when he fought against the gods. The best known of these fights is that with Apollo over the prophetic tripod.[318] This direct offense against Apollo had followed after another dark deed of Heracles, which had offended the gods in a different way: the murder of Iphitos, which had offended the gods, especially Zeus, either because Iphitos was Heracles' guest-friend,[319] or because Heracles had killed him by treachery.[320] Iphitos' murder had caused Heracles to suffer a disease, and he went to the Delphic oracle to find out how to be cured.[321] The fact that in the biographical accounts of Heracles' exploits these incidents would have taken place after the murder of Megara and their children is not relevant. For what I am talking about here is the audience's knowledge of Heracles' myth, which would have been activated nonlinearly by the creation of the posssibility that he may have overstepped the limits—especially since the order of his various exploits varies in the different versions of his myth,[322] and since the variability of variants of myths in general, and the order of events in particular, was part of the audience's taken-for-granted assumptions.

Heracles had also fought against other deities. Pindar *Ol.* 9. 29-35 tells us that Heracles fought against Poseidon, Apollo, and Hades. Homer *Iliad* 5.392-402 speaks of Heracles wounding Hera and Hades. Hera was wounded in her right breast; the circumstances are unclear, but it is likely that Heracles had intended to wound her, especially since other sources mention Heracles also fighting against other gods, Poseidon and Ares.[323] Since Heracles was still a mortal when he quarrelled with Apollo and fought against the other gods, his behavior involved lack of respect for the proper limits between man and god, which is bad. However, because of his participation in the Gigantomachy, on the gods' side, the limits had been somewhat blurred as far as Heracles was concerned, or could be perceived as having been blurred, and his behavior would probably have seemed to be more a form of excess, another form of the excess, which, we shall see, characterized him, rather than impiety and an offense against the cosmic order.

Thus, I suggest, the audience would have understood Iris' words to be referring to a transgression of human limits by Heracles; but they would also have understood that this was how Iris, on her own and on Hera's behalf, presented things, but that this presentation was biased. If Heracles had truly committed *hybris*, Hera would have been entitled to punish him. For, we saw, when an offense of this kind is committed, the god directly involved carried out the punishment, and Hera was indeed one of the deities directly involved, since Heracles had wounded her. But in the audience's perceptions Heracles would probably not have been perceived as having truly committed *hybris*, and Iris' implicit claim about Hera's and her own motivation would have been perceived as biased, since the audience's knowledge of the myth, their knowledge of Hera' jealousy and persecution of Heracles, would have made Iris' implicit claim at the very least suspect. And yet, I suggest, it would not have been perceived by the audience to be a total fabrication. Their knowledge would have been activated that Heracles, at the very least, had come close to *hybris*, and in any case was characterized by excess. I shall return to his association with excess below.

Lyssa is reluctant to unleash herself on Heracles, and pleads with Iris and Hera to reconsider, claiming that he had tamed the earth and he restored the honors of the gods when they had been brought down by unholy men. This is normally seen as Lyssa's defense of Heracles as a pious supporter of the gods.[324] This is not a wrong perception, but it is a partial one. For the very notion of men overthrowing the honors of the gods, so soon after Iris' implicit claim, which would have activated knowledge of Heracles' fighting against gods, would have reactivated that knowledge and deconstructed Lyssa's claim. Nor would the coloring of their perception have been unaffected by the fact that it is Lyssa who puts Heracles' claim, and Iris the case against him. For, in their assumptions, Lyssa was colored negatively, and Iris positively. A modern reader sees her intervention on Heracles' behalf only in terms of "even Lyssa is reluctant to harm such a man"; but, I suggest, the ancient audience's assumptions, in which these figures were representations of their religious realities, would have structured their perception differently: it is Lyssa who puts forward the case for Heracles, while it is Iris who is acting as Hera's ally and executive arm.[325] In any case, when Iris tells her that she must obey Hera, Lyssa has no option but to comply. She enters the palace at 873 as Iris goes up to Olympos.

Chapter 3: Euripidean Tragedy and Religious Exploration 367

At 890-5 (cf. 899) the chorus use a Dionysiac ritual as the basis of a metaphor to describe the workings of Lyssa.[326] At 904-5 they describe an earthquake that she has produced. At 906-9 Amphitryon addresses Athena, who is not visible to the audience, but who, it will eventually become clear, has hurled a boulder at Heracles to stop him (1002-6).[327]

At 922-1015 we have the report of a perverted ritual: the messenger describes the sacrifice that was being performed by Heracles with his wife and children and Amphitryon at the hearth altar of Zeus to purify the house, when he was struck by madness, and turned the sacrifice into the murder of his sons and wife, thinking they were the sons of Eurystheus. Before he could kill Amphitryon, Athena appeared and hurled a rock at Heracles' breast; this stopped his frenzy and sent him to sleep. The murder of his children and wife at the altar may evoke the rite of human sacrifice, but it is perverted even as human sacrifice, for that rite had involved[328] a preparation of the victim and consecration to the appropriate deity. There is a further reference to Heracles' going mad during the sacrifice at 1144-5, where Amphitryon is telling Heracles what had happened.

It has been claimed[329] that with the murder of the children the theodicy articulated earlier dissolves completely. In my view, this is not right. For the emphasis in Greek perceptions of theodicy seems to be on the punishment of the wicked and unjust. There is no evidence known to me to suggest that the suffering of the innocent invalidated the notion of divine justice. The perception that it does is, in my view, dependent on modern (Western liberal) assumptions, in which it is considered an injustice when an innocent man is jailed, but it is not considered an injustice (at least in opinion-forming circles) when a guilty man goes free.[330] Nor can it be claimed that the particular expression of theodicy in *Heracles* is invalidated by Hera's revenge on Heracles.[331] For neither *to dikaion theois et' areskei* (813-4) nor *ton adikon melousi kai ton hosion epaiein* (772-3) implies that the innocent do not suffer, since *epaiein* does not imply that the *hosioi* do not suffer. In addition, I am claiming, there was, almost certainly, a doubt in the audience's perception, as to whether Heracles was really *hosios*.

At 1016-24 the chorus[332] compare Heracles to women who had murdered their husbands or their children, to the Danaids, who killed their husbands, and to Prokne, who killed her son. For the murder of his children may be seen as a female crime, since it is usually women who killed their children, sometimes when in a state of madness. There are also other connections between Heracles and femininity. While a slave to Omphale he wore women's clothes, and did womanly tasks, like holding a basket of wool, and even carding and perhaps spinnning wool. This is not, as it used to be thought, a Hellenistic invention, for this version of the myth is represented in at least one classical image.[333] Other connections between Heracles and femininity also concern women's clothes. Thus, on the island of Kos the priest of Heracle wears women's clothes at various points in his career.[334]

This connection between Heracles and femininity coexists, in his myth, with its opposite, excess of virility and attendant sexual excess,[335] for he slept with countless women, and had a vast number of children. The myth of the deflowering of Thespios' (or Thestios') fifty daughters crystallizes his sexual excess. In one version[336] Thespios had arranged for Heracles to sleep with one of his daughters each of the fifty nights Heracles spent with him, because he wanted grandchildren from Heracles; Heracles was under the impression that it was the same woman every night. In other versions it took him fewer nights, and he was aware of the girls' identity. The most extreme version[337] combines sexual excess with excessively arrogant behavior: Heracles slept with all fifty daughters of Thespios in one night, except for one daughter who refused to sleep with him; Heracles was insulted and condemned the girl to be a virgin all her life, serving him as a priestess. All the others had sons by him, two of them twins. Heracles' excessive virility goes with his great power, but in the human world this excessive virility is ambivalent. Because it is excess, it is bad. But it is also good, since it is a manifestation of Heracles' power, and it also meant that he had many descendants, some of whom were important actors in the heroic past, and had descendants in the present.[338] This was good for the alleged descendants, and also provided a genealogical link with the heroic past and the children of the gods, which was reassuring. But this did not alter the fact that in Greek mentality excess itself was bad. Another manifestation of Heracles' excess was his legendary excessive eating. In general, Greek heroes, though benefactors of humanity, were believed to have been in danger of overreaching themselves, indulging in excess, which was a very bad thing. Heroes should have excellence but not excess; but the danger is that from the excellence they may slide into excess. Heracles, who was the greatest Greek hero, was strongly associated with, and characterized by, excess. He cannot be the greatest hero without excess, of strength and power, and so also masculinity, violence, and so on.

At 1028 the *ekkyklema* begins to wheel the bodies, and Herakles, who is bound, onto the stage.[339] Amphitryon enters separately, and urges the chorus to let Heracles sleep. They reply that they are lamenting for him, Amphitryon, and for the children, and for Heracles. Amphitryon urges them to move further away and, in order not to wake up Heracles, *me ktypeite, me boate* (1047-8), thus evoking the ritual lament of the death ritual. Then they lament, interrupted again by

Chapter 3: Euripidean Tragedy and Religious Exploration 369

Amphitryon, who urges them to make even less noise in their *threnos*, lest they wake Heracles, which will bring danger. At 1064-6 there is a short liturgical *threnos*.[340] At the end of the lyric exchange, at 1087-8, just before Heracles wakes up, the chorus invoke Zeus, and ask him why he has shown such hatred of his son that he had brought him such suffering. This is how things appear to the chorus in the world of the tragedy; but the audience knows that there is a wider picture, in which Heracles' suffering will be "compensated" through great rewards. For in the audience's realities Heracles was a god, and the very notion that Zeus hated Heracles would have activated the knowledge that this was the opposite of the reality known to the audience.

At 1127-8 Amphitryon invokes Zeus and asks him if he sees what has come from Hera's throne. So here the notion of Hera's hostility is expressed through the ritual of invocation. This notion of Hera's hostility is expressed also in other statements, most strongly at 1303-10. Before we discuss this, I should note two further ritual elements, a small one at 1207-9, where Amphitryon supplicates Heracles to unveil his head; and a more significant one at 1281-4, where Heracles presents his pollution in terms of exclusion from ritual activity in Thebes (1283-4): *es poion hieron e panygerin philon eim'? ou gar atas euprosegorous echo.* Amphitryon's perception that it was a deity who was responsible for the disaster is expressed also at 1234-5; Heracles asks who killed his children, and Amphitryon replies, "You, and your bow *kai theon hos aitios.*" At 1192-4 Heracles is again distanced from ordinary mortals by Amphitryon's statement that he fought with the gods at the Gigantomachy.

At 1243-5 Heracles says that the god is *authades*,[341] and so he will be the same towards the gods. This statement would have created the perception for the audience, and evoked the earlier activated notion, of his overstepping, or, rather, being in danger of overstepping, the human limits, of committing *hybris*, a perception that would have been further reinforced by Theseus' reaction, for he urges Heracles to restrain his mouth, lest, *mega legon*,[342] he suffers worse woes, to which Heracles replies that he is full of woes already and there is no room for more. His hostility towards the gods is expressed in a different way at 1263-5, where he says that Zeus, whoever he may be,[343] begat him an enemy to Hera, and he considers Amphitryon more a father to him than Zeus. Then, he goes on to recount the story of Hera sending the snakes in his cradle to kill him when he was a baby. The first effect of all this was a sharp distancing of Heracles from the audience's realities; for this passage stresses the fact that his special misfortunes were directly connected with his special nature. The second effect of his telling the story of the snakes would be to bring up clearly, to zoom to, the "malicious" nature of Hera's persecution, and to marginalize the notion that she is punishing him for overstepping the human limits.

At 1303-10 Heracles expresses the notion of Hera's joy at having accomplished his downfall through the image of her dancing; then he goes on to ask who should pray to such a goddess, who, jealous of the fact that Zeus slept with a mortal woman, destroyed Greece's benefactors though they themselves were not guilty of anything. Would the audience have shared Heracles' perception? Would they have thought that what he said was true? I suggest that they would have seen the situation in a much more complex and ambivalent way, because of the following (interacting) reasons. First, they would not have perceived Heracles to be entirely innocent. For, we have seen, the tragedy shifts perspectives in complex ways, zooming towards, or being distanced from (not only the audience and its realities, but also) the notion that Heracles overstepped, or came near to overstepping—it is probably ambiguous—the human limits, and this is correlative to his suffering; and correspondingly being distanced from, or zoomed towards, the perspective that privileges the notion that Hera punished Heracles out of jealousy and malice. Second, in the eyes of the audience Hera was not simply, as Heracles presents her, a jealous wife who took revenge on her husband's mistresses and illegitimate children to satisfy her wounded pride. She was also, and very importantly, the goddess of marriage, the divine protector of marriage as an institution. Therefore her actions were, in a way, within her own sphere of competence; she was also defending her *time* as a goddess, which, we saw, was entirely legitimate. This would have introduced a certain ambiguity in the perception of her actions. Third, the audience knew that her hostility will cease after Heracles' death, when he will become a god, and that she will symbolically adopt him, and also give him her daughter Hebe in marriage.[344] Consequently, not only will Heracles' suffering be "compensated" by this blessed fate, but also Hera's hostility towards him will be "compensated" by a great benevolence.[345]

In response to Heracles' statement, Theseus repeats that the disasters were Hera's work (1311-2).[346] Then he goes on to say that none among the mortals has unmixed fortunes, nor among the gods, if the bards do not tell lies. This to some extent deconstructs the notion of Hera's malice being alone responsible for Heracles' misfortunes, and constructs the notion that, since Heracles had had an excess of good things, in being the son of Zeus and brave and strong and all that, this would have been balanced by an excess of bad fortunes. What follows continues to deconstruct the notion that Hera's malice was the only factor involved. For Theseus goes on to say that the gods have slept with

Chapter 3: Euripidean Tragedy and Religious Exploration 371

each other unlawfully, and they (meaning Zeus) dishonored their fathers by putting them in chains for the sake of sovereignty (1318-21):

   ...*all' oikous' homos*
   Olympon eneschonto th' hamartekotes.
   kaitoi ti pheseis, ei sy men thnetos gegos
   phereis hyperpheu tas tychas, theoi de me?

The views expressed by Theseus, and especially the word *hyperpheu*, would have triggered off the notion of excess, would have associated the notion of excess with Heracles, and so evoked his general and strong association with excess. This evocation of his strong association with excess here would have had the effect of connecting his present misfortunes with this excess.

But what would the audience have made of Theseus' statement about the gods? Looked at superficially, to a modern reader, at least one part of this statement may seem religiously subversive, or at least like a criticism of the gods for lawless and immoral behavior, put in the mouth of the greatest Athenian hero. But this, I submit, is not how the the ancient audience would have made sense of it. On the contrary, Theseus framed this comment by statements about the gods also having to endure their share of bad fate. So their "guilt" is here elided, it is aligned with Heracles' bad behavior while in the throes of madness. The notion of fate, and the ways in which it operates with regard to the gods, is unfathomable. One factor that may have come into play as far as the notion of Hera's malice is concerned is the fact that, in a way, she could have been understood as almost obliged to persecute Heracles and Zeus' other illegitimate children and lovers, because of her function as the goddess who protected marriage. More crucially, in the ancient assumptions Zeus had been forced to dethrone his father, and put him initially in chains,[347] because Kronos, in swallowing his children when they were born, had upset the order of the generations (which had already been established by then), and so subverted the cosmic order, which it is the gods' role to guarantee, and thus forfeited his position as sovereign god.[348]

Theseus goes on (1323ff) to offer "solutions," both parts of which involve rituals. First, he will purify Heracles in Athens, and then, he will give him *temene* which will bear Heracles' name while Heracles is alive; but (1331-3) when Heracles goes to Hades they will honor him with sacrifices (*thysiaisi*) and stone erections.[349] This, and especially the word *thysiai*, zoomed the world of the play to the world of the audience, and to the audience's religious realities. It activated their knowledge that Heracles did not go to Hades, but he was deified, and that he received cult in the audience's world.[350] This, I suggest, was a very important element in the audience's perception of the play.[351] The fact that he became a god did not erase Heracles' suffering, but it put it in a wider perspective.

In his answer to Theseus, Heracles returns to the question of the gods' immoral behavior, including the fact that they have sex *lektr' ha me themis*, and declares that he does not believe such tales,[352] nor does he believe that one god was born the master of another; *deitai gar ho theos, eiper est' orthos theos, oudenos*.[353] All those stories, he thinks, are the bards' pernicious tales.[354] But what exactly would the audience have understood him to be saying? That the Olympian gods are not like this? Or that the Olympian gods are not proper gods? The notion of the possible untrustworthiness of traditional tales told by poets was familiar, and would have been activated. The fact that such a view would be contradicting Heracles' own asserted belief that he was the son of Zeus, which did involve having sex *lektr' ha me themis*, does not mean that the audience would have blocked such interpretation; for they would not have assumed that he could not be contradicting himself, let alone that he is here expounding a coherent theological vision. I suggest that, given the mention of the bards' pernicious stories, this perception, that he is saying that he does not believe that the Olympian gods are like this, would have been dominant for the ancient audience. However, given Heracles' expressed hostility to the Olympian gods, it is possible that the notion that they are not proper gods may also have been constructed as a possibility; not that there are other, more proper gods; but that the Olympians are not as gods ought to be.[355] I suggest that the audience may not have been entirely clear exactly what Heracles was claiming, but would have seen these views as representing what Heracles thought when he was a mortal and only saw part of the picture, and he was in despair and angry with the gods.

The notion of divine self-sufficiency (on which, on Heracles' account, his disbelief of the poets' tales partly depends) was expressed by Antiphon the sophist, having been earlier formulated by Xenophanes.[356] I suggest that the audience would have perceived all these views expressed by Heracles to be deconstructed by the play. In the world of the play Heracles' very existence showed that Zeus had slept with someone else's wife, and Hera had persecuted Heracles. In the world of the audience the fact that Heracles is a god and receives cult shows that his belief was mistaken, that Zeus had slept with Alkmene, and that gods are not self-sufficient—but also that they are not unjust and incapable of recognizing reciprocity, as Heracles is assuming; or at least, if they are self-sufficient, at some higher level, this is not the facet they show to mortals. For not everyone in the audience would have necessar-

Chapter 3: Euripidean Tragedy and Religious Exploration 373

ily rejected the notion of divine self-sufficiency. The central notion of unknowability in Greek religion allowed speculation of this type to be unproblematically articulated. Ultimately, for all the audience *knew*, the gods may have been self-sufficient, but they did not show themselves to humans in that light, not as far as mortals could perceive. The notion of self-sufficient deities *could* have been accommodated in Greek religion as a possibility;[357] the possibility that the gods were, at some level, self-sufficient, but that this was not the facet that mortals saw.[358] For the mortals needed the gods to interact with them, to accept the gifts that established reciprocity, and even to have children with mortals, to create heroes. And the gods, who are really of a higher order, have accommodated these human needs.

At 1360-4 Heracles asks Amphitryon to perform the death ritual for, and burial of, his sons and wife. So this future ritual will complete the perverted death ritual enacted earlier, in which the present dead had been attired in funerary clothes while still alive. The perverted ritual will now take a "normal," nonperverted form, though it will be abnormal to the extent that the grandsons will be buried by the (social) grandfather, which is a reversal of normality; and also in that the father and husband (the burial by whom in the case of the children would itself have been abnormal for the same reason) cannot bury them himself because he was their murderer.[359]

At 1367-85 Heracles addresses his dead wife and sons, laments them, and embraces their bodies, thus evoking the death ritual, though in a somewhat perverted form, since the mourner is their murderer. At 1390-2 he asks the whole of Thebes to cut their hair in mourning, and share his grief, and lament both for the dead and for him—a sort of modification of public ritual, here for the living, as well as for the dead. At 1419 Heracles returns to the question of the burial (as he does once more at 1422), and asks Amphitryon to bury his sons as he had requested. At 1419-20 Amphitryon asks who will bury him, Amphitryon, and Heracles replies that he, Heracles, will.[360] This future death ritual will mark the restoration of ritual normality, in that a son will bury his (social) father, which is as it should be. Heracles' speech concludes soon after (1425-6), with a *gnome* praising the importance of friendship,[361] echoed by the chorus' statement, which concludes the tragedy, that they lament the loss of a friend, *ta megista philon*, Heracles (1427-8).

This tragedy, then, has a very significant ritual density. Actions and opinions are, to a very great extent, embedded in, and articulated through, ritual. Since everything acquires meaning in context, this ritual context contributed very significantly to the ways in which the ancient audience made sense of both the actions and the opinions that were expressed. Thus, it is methodologically illegitimate to wrench those off from this ritual context, and discuss them without reference to it; for if this happens the meanings created would be very different from those constructed by the ancient audience.

All important actions in this tragedy depend on, and/or are expressed through, rituals. It was through the ritual of supplication that the threatened death of Heracles' family was delayed for long enough for Heracles to return. It was through a perverse ritual that the fact that their death was imminent was expressed, the decking out of living people with the *kosmos* of the dead. It appeared, at the superficial level, that the death ritual was interrupted, and they threw off the attire of the dead. But in reality the interruption was very short, and the *kosmos* of the dead they had worn had also been an expression of their imminent death. It was at a sacrifice that those for whom the death ritual had begun while they were still alive, and then was interrupted. The future completion of the death ritual is announced at the end of the play, bringing closure to this interrupted ritual sequence which began as a perverted ritual and will be accomplished as a nonperverted, if "abnormal," one—"abnormal" in the sense of the wrong generation burying the wrong generation—that will be followed by another death ritual which will be normal in that a son will bury his (social) father. Finally, and very importantly, the 'solution' of the tragedy, is expressed, for the audience, through a reference to another future ritual, that activated the knowledge that Heracles was a god in the audience's world, a fact which had important consequences for their perception of the tragedy, and of religion and the gods in the tragedy. As we saw, many other important actions were also articulated through ritual, such as the falsely reported ritual through which Lykos was ambushed, or the Dionysiac ritual used by the chorus as the basis of a metaphor to describe the workings of Lyssa.

Besides this dense ritual skeleton, the tragedy also has a nonritual religious framework. The less important facet of this involves Heracles' descent to Hades and his return, which forms a significant element of the plot. The more important facet of the religious framework, which structures a very significant part of the tragedy, and is at the center of its action and problematization, is Hera's hostility, physically expressed through the epiphany of Iris and Lyssa. This tragedy problematizes the notion of divine hostility and shows the tragic results of divine persecution.

I will now pull together and crystallize the main points set out above concerning this religious problematization in *Heracles*, and suggest that, far from this being a tragedy of unmitigated bleakness about divine malice, it is a very complex, but ultimately reassuring, explora-

Chapter 3: Euripidean Tragedy and Religious Exploration 375

tion of the concept of divine malice, and of the empirically observed phenomenon of things going very wrong for an apparently undeserving mortal.

First, Heracles would not have been perceived, as he is by modern readers, as a wholly innocent victim of divine malice, but in a much more complex and ambivalent way, for the following reasons. One, the play had activated the audience's knowledge that Heracles had come dangerously close to exceeding the human limits. Two, he was strongly associated with excess; this was an inseparable part of his personality, and was in any case activated in the play. Greek mentality privileged moderation, so Heracles' excess, including his good fortune of being the son of Zeus, and the greatest and most powerful hero, is "balanced" by an excess of suffering; Heracles suffered in his lifetime and died a bad death. One way in which the ancient audience would have perceived the murder of his children in this tragedy would have been as follows: Heracles, under the sway of Lyssa, directed one aspect of his excess, excess of violence, at the wrong target, and brought upon himself an excess of suffering, to balance the positive excesses. Three, Hera would not have been perceived as being motivated only by malice. As the goddess of marriage, she would have been understood as being almost obliged to persecute Heracles, and Zeus' other illegitimate children and lovers, defending the institution she had the duty to protect, and also her *time* as a goddess, which, we saw, was entirely legitimate. This would have introduced a certain ambiguity in the perception of her actions. The tragedy shifts perspectives in complex ways: it zooms towards, or distances itself from, the notion that Heracles came near to overstepping the human limits, and that this, and his excesses, are correlative with his suffering, and correspondingly distances itself from, or zooms towards, the perspective that privileges the notion that Hera punishes Heracles out of jealousy and malice.

One facet of the notion that Heracles' excess of suffering was correlative with his excess of good fortune is the fact that the reason for the divine hostility that led to the suffering was correlative with his good fortune that distanced him from ordinary humanity: Heracles was Zeus' son—and the greatest hero. This distance is an important aspect of the persona of Heracles in *Heracles*; he is distanced from ordinary humanity, and so from the audience. This distance was activated and stressed in the play, above all through the stress on his divine birth, and the repeated mention of the fact that he had fought with the gods in the Gigantomachy, and also through the fact that he has just returned from Hades. The distance does not remain stable throughout the play, but it shifts, zooming Heracles towards, or distancing him from, ordinary humanity, and so the audience. One particular distancing of Heracles from the audience involves a strong zooming to that audience's reality, the activation of the knowledge that in that reality Heracles was a god. The tragedy stresses Heracles' divinity and close relationship to the gods, also through choral self-referentiality. Because this aspect of Heracles would have been perceived by the audience as being correlative with his extraordinary suffering, ordinary humanity, the audience was distanced also from his status as victim of divine hostility. A second effect of the activation of the knowledge of Heracles' divinity is to create the notion that Heracles' great suffering was "compensated" by his deification. The fact that he became a god did not erase his present suffering, but it put it in a wider perspective.[362]

The Greek collective representations, and the myths and religious beliefs that articulated them, acknowledged the fact that dreadful things do happen in life. This tragedy explores one such instance, which allows it to explore the whole phenomenon, but at a distance. The explanation that it offers for the phenomenon of a good man going mad and doing dreadful things, a shifting and complex explanation, with the emphasis now on one, now on another, facet of a complex phenomenon, and indeed even the notion of divine malice, are more satisfactory and less terrifying than anomic disorder, in which such things, which do happen, are seen as random, have no explanation, are part of a world with no intelligible meaning, or any meaning at all. It is that which is terrifying. Of course, this does not make Heracles' suffering any less tragic, or his fate any less bleak. But it does offer some ultimate reassurance of order, at least to the audience, who are distanced from the world of the tragedy. The fact that, by stressing Heracles' divinity and close relationship to the gods, the tragedy presents his extraordinary suffering as being correlative with his distance from ordinary humanity, and so from the audience, made this religious exploration crystallized in, and explored through, myth, less threatening. The play does not say ordinary humans can never undergo extraordinary suffering, or be victims of divine malice—if it did it would not be directly relevant to the audience's realities; but what it is exploring is a case in which this happened to someone who was not ordinary. In this way it explores the empirically observed fact that dreadful things can happen to those who appear undeserving in a way that deactivates the potential symbolic terror.

To sum up. Through a complex series of shifts in perspective, through complex zoomings and distancings, the problem of great undeserved suffering is explored, in combination with that of a malicious deity; but they are explored at a distance, in a way that is, ultimately, reassuring, when seen from the perspective of a religion, and of a conceptual

Chapter 3: Euripidean Tragedy and Religious Exploration 377

universe, which acknowledged the empirically experienced darkness of the cosmos and precariousness of the human condition.

9) Phoinissai

Let us now consider *Phoinissai*,[363] some aspects of which I have already discussed in chapter III.2.

In the prologue Jocasta reports a series of past ritual acts which have structured the past history she is recounting: at 13-20 the fatal consultation of the oracle by Laios and Apollo's reply, at 34-5 she refers to Oidipous' consultation of the oracle, at 68-70 to the curse Oidipous pronounced against his sons; she ends (84-5) with an invocation of Zeus, asking him to bring about her sons' reconciliation. The scene that follows includes a series of invocations by Antigone (182-92) and is interspersed with various religious references.[364] In the first strophe of the parodos the chorus explain that they have been sent as *hierodouloi* to Apollo at Delphi, and the reference to their service to Apollo continues in the first antistrophe; subsequently the explanation is repeated to Polyneikes at 282-4; this, and to some extent their presence throughout, brings the Delphic oracle, whose role in this story that is now coming to an end was decisive, to the fore of the audience's perceptions.

The first epeisodion, which follows the parodos, has many ritual and other religious references, of varying importance. Less significant are references to sacred structures (274, 367). More significant is Jocasta's use of ritual to articulate emotions. At 322-6 she expresses her distress at Polyneikes' absence and says that she was so upset that she has adopted the ritual mode of mourning in her dress, and in cutting her hair. At 344-9 she mentions the ritual acts she had not performed at his wedding,[365] and those ritual acts that would have been performed at Thebes for that wedding if he had not been married abroad.[366] She ascribes responsibility for the misfortunes of the family of Oidipous to the gods (379, 382). I suggest that the ancient audience would not have taken her claim to be "the truth"; they would have seen it as a way of expressing despair and powerlessness, marginalizing or even eliding, human responsibility; as an articulation that polarized one side of a nexus of causation that was perceived to be complex and ambivalent, the operation of the divine, and minimized the importance of human choices. For in the perceptions articulating myths, even in case limits, of which Oidipous is probably the most extreme version, human choices did exist. I shall return to this question below.

The motif of the god directing human action comes up again at 413,[367] where Polyneikes says, in response to a question by his mother *ho daimon m' ekalesen pros ten tychen*, to which Jocasta responds *sophos gar o theos* (414).³⁶⁸ This was framed by the report of a ritual action, prophecy: Polyneikes explains (409-423) that he married Adrastos' daughter because of the oracle given to Adrastos; he then (432-3) swears by the gods that it is unwillingly that he is attacking his parents.³⁶⁹ At 467-8 Jocasta prays for some god to be *krites* and *diallaktes* between Eteokles and Polyneikes; at 586-7 the chorus ask the gods to avert this evil.³⁷⁰ At 491-3 Polyneikes invokes *daimonas* as witnesses that while he always behaved justly, *dikes ater aposteroumai patridos anosiotata*.³⁷¹

There are also other religious references of various kinds. At 506 Eteokles calls Tyrannis *ten theon megisten*.³⁷² More importantly, at 571-6 Jocasta asks Polyneikes how, if he sacks his own city, he will put up trophies to Zeus, and how he will sacrifice. And how will he inscribe the spoils, saying that Polyneikes, having burnt Thebes, dedicates these shields to the gods? At 604 Polyneikes begins to pray to the gods, or rather, he begins by invoking the altars of the ancestral gods, which prompts Eteokles to point out that he wants to sack those very altars, and tells him to pray to the gods at Mycenae. Sacking a city means (at least potentially and symbolically) sacking the altars of the local gods, since religion was at the center of each polis' identity; since one's main cultic relationships are with the gods of one's city this presents problems for the man who attacks his own city, like Polyneikes.

At 624 Jocasta, on hearing that her two sons will face each other in battle asks *patros ou pheuxesth' Erinys?* At 626-7 Polyneikes calls upon the land that nurtured him, and upon the gods to be witnesses that he has been driven *atimos* from his homeland, and at 631-5 addresses, among others, Apollo Agyieus and the altars³⁷³ of the gods, and expresses his belief that with the gods' help he will win and become king of Thebes. The first stasimon includes³⁷⁴ a reference to the oracle which had guided Kadmos to found Thebes, a reference to the birth of Dionysos in Thebes, who, they sing, is worshiped with dances by Theban *parthenoi* and *gynaixin euiois*,³⁷⁵ and a narration of Kadmos' killing of Ares' dragon, when he had gone to the spring *epi chernibas* (662),³⁷⁶ in order to perform a sacrifice, and also of the aftermath of the killing; they say that Kadmos had acted on Athena's advice when he had sowed the dragon's teeth. Finally, they pray to their ancestor Epaphos, and Persephone and Demeter, to protect Thebes. They conclude (689) *panta d' eupete theois*.³⁷⁷

The notion of the gods controlling men's destiny comes up again at 705: Kreon tells Eteokles that they must leave things in the hands of the gods. Rituals are mentioned in Eteokles' instructions to Kreon;³⁷⁸ he asks Kreon to take care of the wedding of Antigone and Haimon, he mentions his father's curse, and he says they must resort to prophecy, consult Teiresias; he instructs that the corpse of Polyneikes must never

Chapter 3: Euripidean Tragedy and Religious Exploration 379

be buried on Theban soil if the Thebans win[379] and concludes (782-3): *tei d' Eulabeiai, chresimotatei theon, / proseuchomestha tende diasoizein polin.*[380] The chorus then begin the second stasimon with an invocation of Ares and a description of his cruelty, full of references to Dionysiac rituals, which are contrasted to Ares' "rites" of war. At 788-800 they exclaim how terrible a goddess is Eris, who devised these miseries for the Labdacids. The rest of the ode deals with the story of Oidipous and other aspects of Thebes' perceived history.

The religious dimension is foregrounded with the entrance of Teiresias (with his daughter and Menoikeus) at 834. At 838-40 Teiresias mentions aspects of the divination he practices:

> klerous te moi phylasse . . .
> hous elabon oionismat' ornithon mathon
> thakoisin en hieroisin, hou manteuomai.[381]

At 852-7 he says that he has just come from Athens, where he gave victory to the Athenians over Eumolpos, and he is wearing a visible sign of his success, a golden wreath which he received as *aparchai* of the enemy spoils. He does not mention what prophecy he had given to the Athenians which ensured victory, but the audience knew that it involved the sacrifice of the daughter of Erechtheus. This reported ritual of Teiresias' prophecy to the Athenians and its successful outcome zoomed the world of the play to that of the audience in complex ways; firstly to their own heroic past, then (for some at least) to the performance of Euripides' *Erechtheus*. In the eyes of the audience, this would have brought up the contrast between Athens and Thebes: when in danger of being sacked, Thebes was polluted, and was being attacked as a result of fratricidal strife; Athens had not been polluted, and had been unjustly attacked by external enemies.[382] Kreon replies that he considers Teiresias' triumphant wreath an omen, and asks what they should do to save the city.

Teiresias gives a long reply. His main points are that he had withheld the oracle from Eteokles when he had enquired, but he will now tell Kreon. The Thebans are the victims of the royal family's pollution and doom (867-9; 881-8); the land *nosei* ever since Laios begat Oidipous *biai theon*, and Oidipous' sons erred, "as though they could escape from the gods."[383] Oidipous cursed them and they are doomed. According to Teiresias (870-1), the blinding of Oidipous was a contrivance by the gods to give a visible demonstration to Greece[384] (that is, according to the scholiast,[385] so that it is shown to everyone that they must not disobey the gods). But now the polis is in danger; unless Kreon takes certain actions to save it, Thebes will be destroyed. The first of these is that no descendant of Oidipous must stay in Thebes *hos daimonontas kanatrepsontas polin* (888). The second *pharmakon soterias* Teiresias hesitates to reveal, but eventually (911, 913-4) he informs Kreon that he must slay his son Menoikeus; to save Thebes it is necessary for Menoikeus to be slaughtered, and offer his blood as chthonic libations to the earth,[386] as Ares' revenge for the killing of his earth-born dragon; the sacrifice must be a virgin male descended from the Spartoi, and that means Menoikeus. If they do this Ares will be their ally. At 954-9 Teiresias concludes his speech before he exits as follows:

> ... *hostis d' empyroi chretai technei,*
> *mataios; en men echthra semenas tychei,*
> *pikros kathestech' hois an oionoskopei;*
> *pseude d' hyp' oiktou toisi chromenois legon*
> *adikei ta ton theon. Phoibon anthropois monon*
> *chren thespioidein, hos dedoiken oudena.*

This (besides giving a leading prophet's point of view), problematizes prophecy, by showing one of the ways in which the human status and nature of the seer may intervene and distort the words of the god, one of the ways in which, though the god speaks the truth, the prophecies one gets may not be trustworthy.

The segment that follows Teiresias' exit focusses on the prophecy and Kreon's reaction to it, which is to urge Menoikeus to run away. That this comment, and his plan, do not imply disregard of prophecy—only the desire to save his son, even at the expense of the city of Thebes—would have been made clear to the ancient audience by the central place Kreon gives to the two great Greek oracles, Delphi and Dodona, and to the action of the gods in his plan: he starts his description of the suggested itinerary *Delphous perasas* (980) and then he tells him to go to Thesprotia, at which point Menoikeus asks (982) *semna Dodones bathra?* Kreon replies in the affirmative, and when Menoikeus asks what his safeguard will be, Kreon replies *pompimos ho daimon* (984), which the scholia take to indicate that Zeus will guide him through prophecy at Dodona.

At 991-1018, before exiting to go and sacrifice himself, Menoikeus explains why he will not follow his father's plan, but will offer himself in sacrifice. He exits alone, and this lone exit, unaccompanied by ritual, completes the series of "abnormalities," of differences in this human sacrifice from others, "normal," in the sense of usual ones. The most important of these abnormalities is that the victim is a male, not, as is "normally" the case, a female, virgin. These abnormalities mark the polluted, sick nature of the society in which this sacrifice is taking

Chapter 3: Euripidean Tragedy and Religious Exploration 381

place. At the same time, the fact that the victim is a virgin male constructs the comparison between human sacrifice to save the city and the young males' good death in battle. This comparison, we saw in chapter I.2, was also made elsewhere in Euripidean tragedy, even when the required victim was female. Different meanings are created through the different comparisons between the death of a sacrificial victim and the death of young men in war in the different tragedies; the male-to-male comparison in the *Phoinissai* elides the differences, for the sacrifice of Menoikeus is a sacrifice of a young male to the god of war without the usual ceremonial of human sacrifice, and the closeness of the two is articulated explicitly in a statement by Menoikeus, who says that it would be *aischron* if he refused to sacrifice himself while (999-1002)

> ... hoi men thesphaton eleutheroi
> kouk eis ananken daimonon aphigmenoi
> stantes par' aspid' ouk oknesousin thanein,
> pyrgon paroithe machomenoi patras hyper.

This elision of the differences between human sacrifice to save the city and the death in battle of young men to save the city (an elision which allowed a further explication of the relationship of the sacrifice of a *parthenos* with the death of young men in war) could not but affect the perception of the notion of the cruelty of the gods who demand human sacrifice, it would have radically diminished this perception of cruelty; at the same time it lightly problematized, in the sense of showing the pain attendant on, good death in battle.

This tragedy, then, explores the question of human sacrifice,[387] briefly, but in a way comparable to that in *Erechtheus*; human sacrifice is problematized, but so also, implicitly, is death in battle. Not, of course, that the ideology of good death for one's country is challenged; but, as elsewhere, the human cost is sketched.

In the third stasimon that follows the chorus sings of the myth of Oidipous and the Sphinx and also tells the rest of the story until the present moment, in a narration teeming with religious references, which become especially dense in the concluding part of the ode. Especially interesting for our purposes are the references to ritual lamentations (for the victims of the Sphinx) at 1033-5, which probably evoked the traditional style of ritual lamentation,[388] and also the invocation of Athena at 1061-2.

In the fourth epeisodion the messenger begins his report from the battlefield with a reference to Menoikeus' self-sacrifice. His report contains hardly any religious references[389] until the hybristic boast made by Kapaneus (1172-86), who *emaineto*, that not even Zeus' fire can stop him; as he put his head over the ramparts Zeus killed him with a thunderbolt—*hybris* is punished on the spot. Having seen this, Adrastos realized that Zeus was hostile to his army, he took them out of the trench, while the Thebans attacked, having seen this favorable omen from Zeus. The messenger concludes (1197-9) that now it is up to the gods whether Thebes will have good fortune in the future; for it was one of the gods that saved her today. The chorus' and Jocasta's comments in response to this are in the same vein: they concern the favor of the gods.[390] Here, as elsewhere, in times of crisis, especially of danger to the city, the outcome is perceived to be in the hands of the gods.

In the messenger's second *rhesis*[391] religious references are not dense; there is one briefly reported oath ritual at 1241;[392] a reference (1250-1) to a reported mention (an exhortation for the achievement) of a future erection of *Zenos . . . bretas tropaion*; at 1255-8 a report of a divination ritual in connection with the sacrifice of sheep;[393] and finally a mention of *philtr' epodon*, the possibility of using them, at 1259-60. Then, in calling Antigone to come out of the house, Jocasta mentions (1265)[394] the things that would normally bring a virgin out of the house, *choreiai* and *partheunemata*, the pursuits of virgins—some of which, at least, would also have been understood by the audience to have been connected with ritual activities—and adds that this is not where the fortunes established by the gods may proceed for her, that is the gods and fate do not now demand of Antigone her normal behavior.[395] She tells Antigone which ritual activity she wants her to perform at 1278, where she announces that she will supplicate her two sons to stop their single combat and asks Antigone to join her in that supplication.

In the fourth stasimon the chorus anticipates the mourning that will result from the duel and concludes, *apotmos apotmos ho phonos henek' Erinyon* (1306-7). After this ode there is another mention of Menoikeus' sacrifice, by Kreon, who then reports the rite of lamentation over the corpse that is taking place at his house, and adds that he has come to fetch Jocasta to have her perform for Menoikeus those ritual duties that are the responsibility of the nearest female relative (1313-21). His concluding statement (1320-1)[396] expresses the perception that the performance of the appropriate rites for the dead honors not only the individual dead person, but also the gods of the Underworld, in whose realm the dead belong.

In the second messenger scene there are two lyric outbursts by the chorus, at 1340-41,[397] and 1350-1, and one by Kreon at 1345. At 1350-1 the chorus urged raising the wailing and (making the ritual mourning gesture of) hitting the head with the hands, and thus evoked ritual lament. The long messenger speech at 1356-1424 contains the following reported rituals. First, Polyneikes' prayer to Hera (1364-8) and Eteokles' prayer to Athena (1372-5). Then (1432-6), the report of Jocasta's and Antigone's lament over the bodies of Eteokles and Polyneikes, who are not yet dead; which would have evoked echoes of the death ritual; ritual is also mentioned in his report of Polyneikes' dying words: he had asked to be buried in Thebes, and asked his mother to perform the ritual act of closing his eyelids. Finally, the messenger reports that the Thebans had won the final battle and so 1473: *Dios tropaion histasan bretas*, and mentions the procession carrying the corpses, which enters at 1485.

The segment that follows the entrance of the procession can be considered as a version of a prothesis, as being articulated by a ritual of prothesis.[398] At 1485 begins Antigone's long lyric lament.[399] Of special interest for the ritual aspect of this aria is the fact that, near the beginning, she says of herself *pheromai baccha nekyon*, and that she acts the ritual mourning gestures of unveiling her hair, to tear it, and disarranging her dress, to beat her breasts (1489-91).[400] The religious dimension of the deaths is brought out at 1503, when she refers to the three corpses as *charmat' Erinyos*.[401] Later on, in talking to Oidipous Antigone says (1555-7) that his (Oidipous') *alastor* was responsible for the death of Eteokles and Polyneikes, the destructive demon whom Oidipous' curses had aroused.[402] At 1579-81 Antigone expresses the perception, which had been expressed before, that a god has caused these miseries.

The part that follows includes some interpolations, above all the segment after 1736, to the end.[403] I will only discuss the parts and verses that are not inauthentic. At 1584-94 Kreon says that they must now think of burial, and then announces some of Eteokles' last wishes; he refers to the forthcoming wedding of Haimon and Antigone, and tells Oidipous that, in accordance with Teiresias' prophetic advice, he cannot allow him to stay in Thebes *dia . . . tous alastoras tous sous dedoikos me ti ge pathei kakon* (1593-4). Oidipous begins his response by blaming his fate, then goes on to say how Apollo had prophesied before he was born that he would kill his father, and then goes on, summarizing the rest of his unhappy history. At 1611 he states that he passed on to his sons the curse of Laios,[404] for he would not have been so stupid as to bring about these horrible things against his own eyes and his own sons *aneu theou tou* (1614). He is, then, denying all responsibility for his actions.

Would the audience have understood him to be right? I suggest not. When he was recounting his misfortunes the audience would not have understood that Oidipous had had no free will, but that he was eliding, and now he is denying, his own contribution to the disasters, above all his cursing of his sons. The Greek collective representations, as articulated in the tragic explorations of myths, gave ambiguous replies to the question of free will; for in the case limits of people like Oidipous, the people who cannot escape the doom that had been foretold them are always shown to have committed serious errors. So here too the "rule" of double motivation, the divine operating through human weakness and error, applies. The question that is never asked, the possibility that is never articulated, is "What would have happened if such mortals had not committed errors?" Was it possible for them not to have done, or is it the inevitable result of their foretold doom that they do? To that extent the question ultimately remains open.

At 1627 Kreon focusses on burial; he announces that Polyneikes, who had come to sack his motherland, will be thrown unburied outside the frontiers of Thebes, and mentions the ritual acts that it is forbidden to perform for his corpse. He then invites Antigone to abandon her ritual role in the death ritual.[405] There follows a heated discussion, in which Antigone challenges the notion that Polyneikes is a traitor, claiming that in attacking Thebes he came to claim his own. This claim is unlikely to have convinced the audience that he was not a traitor; in Athenian assumptions such treatment of traitors was perceived as legitimate, for traitors' bodies were thrown unburied out of the borders of Attica. After Antigone had announced her determination to bury Polyneikes, the issue is articulated in religious terms at 1662-3: KREON: *ekrin' ho daimon, parthen', ouch ha soi dokei.* ANTIGONE: *kakeino kekritai, me ephybrizesthai nekrous.* Kreon reiterates that he will not allow him to be buried, and does not answer the religious point. The fact that he himself had earlier expressed the view (1321-2) that the performance of the appropriate rites for the dead honors not only the deceased, but also the gods of the Underworld, may have echoed with the audience, but not decisively, not so that it would support Antigone's claim with regard to Polyneikes, since, in their assumptions, traitors were excluded from ordinary considerations, and their bodies[406] did not deserve the honors of proper burial in their homeland. So the question of the gods' attitude is left open here. In the course of the debate various ritual acts that were part of the death ritual are mentioned, as is mentioned Antigone's wedding, which was supposed to take place, but which she now renounces.

At 1703-7 Oidipous mentions an oracle of Apollo which said that he will die in Athens, where he will be received at *hieros Kolonos, domath' hippiou theou.*[407] This zooms the world of the tragedy to the world of the audience, and lightly brings up the notion of Oidipous' future heroization. The Delphic oracle, which, we saw, had been

Chapter 3: Euripidean Tragedy and Religious Exploration

brought to the fore of the audience's perceptions early on in the play, and whose role in this story was decisive, is here also providing the "closure."

At 1728-31 Oidipous mentions the epinician song that had been sung when he had solved the riddle of the Sphinx. This past glory is contrasted by Antigone to the unhappy present. But her last words at 1736, *thanein pou*, would have reactivated the oracle, and the audience's knowledge, that Oidipous will die in Athens and will be heroized.[408]

The tragedy, then, ends with an emphasis on Oidipous, and Antigone. I suggested above that Oidipous' suffering would not have been understood by the audience to have been inflicted on a wholly innocent man by cruel gods. The same is true, albeit by ricochet, for Antigone. In the ancient perceptions she was, as women often were, in reality, as well as in the collective representations, as much a victim of the actions of the male members of her family as of fate. The activation of the knowledge of Oidipous' heroization in the audience's religious realities would have been perceived to have in some ways "compensated" for Oidipous' suffering. The perception of the suffering was not neutralized or marginalized, but, as in the other cases we saw, somehow or other balanced—a perception that also had the effect of symbolically distancing further Oidipous' suffering from the audience's world. This exploration of doom, suffering, and freedom of will took place at a symbolic distance from the world of audience; the audience were distanced from the polluted patricide and incestuous husband and from Antigone, the child of a doomed incestuous union of a patricide and his mother. In addition, as we saw in chapter III.2, the stress on the Phoenician origin of the polluted Theban royal family distanced this doomed group further from the audience's realities.

Phoinissai has a significant density of ritual and other religious references—though they do not occur uniformly throughout the play. This deployment of ritual is intertwined with religious problematization, the exploration of a variety of religious issues, including loyalty to one's ancestral, local gods and the religious dimension of attacking one's city; the question of human sacrifice; and the complex nexus of notions involving the working of the Erinys, the fulfillment of curses, the notion of preordained fate and the role of the Delphic oracle, the notion of the gods control human destiny, prophecy. The issue of the right to burial is taken beyond where it had been taken in Sophocles' *Antigone*. Here the exploration starts with the fact that we know (through *Antigone*) that it is wrong to expose a corpse;[409] though Kreon speaks of the body becoming food for the dogs (1650), this is symbolic, a polarized expression for "not proper burial"; what is lightly problematized here is the notion of throwing traitors' bodies out of borders, which is the treatment Athens reserved for traitors' bodies. The problematization is very light; for the religious dimension of the issue is not pursued, and the issue is not resolved; Antigone does not bury the body within the tragedy, and the audience would have made no assumptions about what would happen afterwards.

The religious problematization in *Phoinissai*, then, is dense, in the sense that there is a lot of it, but it is not deep, not sustained and profound on any one issue.

10) *Orestes*

Let us now consider *Orestes*.[410] The prologue is spoken by Electra who, in her opening words, tells of the precarious nature of, and the potential suffering in, human life; there is nothing, however terrible to tell, nor calamity sent by the gods, that humanity may not have to bear; for Tantalos, who was once blest, and who, they say,[411] was the son of Zeus, is now suffering after his death because, having been admitted as a tablemate by the gods, though he was a mortal, he had a licentious tongue. Electra's opening words, then, speak of a simple example of reversal of fortune, but the paradigm would have been perceived by the audience as an example of *hybris* against the gods, a paradigmatic *hybris*, which made Tantalos one of the "cosmic sinners," eternally punished.[412] The *hybris* he commits here is spoken *hybris*,[413] and it has been argued that Athenian myth making of the time had connected Tantalos with blasphemous sophism, and with *asebeia* concerning *ta meteora*.[414] In any case, this is a man who brought disasters upon himself, and who, like some modern thinkers, committed verbal *hybris*, and it is this man who provides the paradigm that frames the audience's perception of Orestes. Thus, the *gnome* concerning the precarious nature of, and the potential suffering in, human life sent by the gods uttered by Electra is deconstructed by her choice of paradigm. By using Tantalos as an illustration, the play overturns the apparent meaning of the *gnome*. The audience understands all too well why Tantalos should suffer. It was entirely his own fault. I suggest that the *gnome* would have activated, at least for a part of the audience, intertextual knowledge, the tragic articulations in which mortals suffer reversals of fortunes and woes, for which they blame the gods, and deconstructed them through the presentation of Tantalos as the paradigm for such reversals, and so also a paradigm for, a way of looking at, the tragic characters who complain about the gods. Whether or not this is right, this tragedy certainly framed the action, and Orestes' and the other mortals' complaints against Apollo, through this perception "mortals blame the gods for their sufferings, but in fact it is their own fault."

Chapter 3: Euripidean Tragedy and Religious Exploration 387

This would not entail that Orestes' sufferings, or the problem of divine responsibility, were elided; but they were, I suggest, put in a wider, more complex, perspective.

In addition, I suggest that the hint of potential *hybris* may have been evoked, and created a frisson every time the characters blame Apollo. In this respect the Tantalos paradigm was deceptive, one of the several strands of the plot's movement towards calamity which prove deceptive. For it will turn out that Orestes had not been guilty of *hybris*, and that, unlike Tantalos, he will eventually be free of suffering. But though the potential for *hybris* is not fulfilled, it did place the relationships between gods and mortals in the play in a framework of seriousness and danger.

The notion that gods cause troubles and woes to humans is repeatedly expressed in this tragedy,[415] starting with Electra at (12-3). At 1545-8, the perception that it is the gods, here *daimon*, who are responsible for what happens to mortals is combined with the notion of an *alastor* or *alastores* extracting payment from Pelops' descendants for the death of Myrtilos.[416] Another theme that appears in the prologue, and will recur later, is that mortals think they know how the gods feel, but they are proved wrong: at 19-20, Electra expresses her belief that the gods hate Helen; this will prove wrong. This type of false perception is one of the many things that marks the distance between human understanding and divine realities and will.

At 28-31 there is a reported prophecy; Orestes killed his mother on Apollo's orders; Electra begins this report saying *Phoibou d' adikian men ti dei kategorein?*, and this ambiguously worded "attack" on Apollo is characteristic of this tragedy, in which Apollo is repeatedly blamed for Orestes' matricide.[417] At 34-48 Electra mentions Orestes' "illness" and the Eumenides,[418] and she refers to her mother's burial, and to the isolation of the polluted killers. She then explains that the Argives are going to decide whether or not to put her and Orestes to death. Helen, soon after her entrance, at 75-6, expresses the view that Orestes is not a polluted killer who can pollute her, because it is Apollo who was responsible for the misdeed.[419]

A rite woven through much of the tragedy is the offering of locks of hair and of chthonic libations to the tomb of Klytemestra. Helen mentions wanting to send locks of her hair and chthonic libations to the tomb, and at 94-8 she asks Electra to go on her behalf. Electra refuses, saying that she cannot look at her mother's grave, and when Helen remarks that it would be shameful to send servants to perform these rites, Electra suggests that Helen's daughter Hermione should go. Helen summons Hermione and gives her the locks of her hair and the chthonic libations—which means she had been carrying them, and so, that, in a way, an informal part of the death ritual of postburial offerings to the dead was enacted. This is reinforced by the fact that Helen tells Hermione not only what to do at the tomb, but also what to say to the dead Klytemestra, an address that includes the request for Klytemestra to be well disposed towards Helen and her family, and also towards Orestes and Electra, whom the god had destroyed (105-24). At 128-30 Electra refers again to Helen's performance of the rite of cutting off her hair to offer at Klytemestra's grave, to criticize her by saying that she had only shorn her hair along the edge, to avoid spoiling her beauty. Then Electra curses Helen. The performance of the offering ritual at Klytemestra's grave is referred to again at 1185-7, where it becomes part of the plan involving Helen's murder. Also, at 1321-2 Electra asks Hermione whether she has come having put garlands on Klytemestra's grave and poured chthonic libations to the dead.

In the parodos, which involves a lyric dialogue, the chorus refer to Orestes' deeds as godsent, and then Electra claims, at 162-4, that Apollo spoke unjustly when he decreed Klytemestra's murder, sitting on Themis' tripod. This expression is even more aggressive towards Apollo than most, in that she implicitly contrasts Themis, who is associated with *dike*, with what she claims were the unjust utterances of Apollo, who, according to the myth of the Previous Owners of the Delphic oracle,[420] had replaced Themis as the prophetic deity at Delphi.[421] Other ritual references in the parodos are Electra's invocation of Nyx at 174-9,[422] and at 191-4 the deployment of a metaphor based on ritual: Electra says that Apollo, in decreeing the matricide, *exethysen* them, made them into sacrificial victims.[423]

Orestes awakes at 211.[424] At 255-7 he begs his dead mother not to unleash the dreadul Erinyes onto him, and then (260-1) he invokes Apollo, saying that the dread goddesses will kill him. At 264-5 he addresses one of the Erinyes who is grabbing him.[425] At 268-79 he asks for the bow which Apollo had given him, to defend himself against the Erinyes, and then, in a demented state, shoots at them with an imaginary bow.[426] He finally urges the Erinyes to fly to the aether and accuse Apollo's oracular responses. At 285-7 Orestes again blames Apollo, who, having induced him to do a most unholy deed, cheered him with words, but not with deeds. Orestes and others repeatedly say that Apollo was responsible for Orestes' actions. Thus, at 416-20 Menelaos says of Apollo, *amathesteros d' on tou kalou kai tes dikes*,[427] and Orestes responds *douleuomen theois, ho ti pot' eisin hoi theoi*—a traditional, not impious, expression.[428] Also, at 591-5 Orestes says that it was Apollo whom he obeyed in killing his mother, and they should therefore consider Apollo *anosion*, not him. At 955-6 the messenger tells Electra that the Pythian Apollo who sits on the tripod was of no use to her, but he destroyed her. These references to the Delphic oracle, especially references which evoked specific features of the Delphic sanctuary, such as this, and the one at 329-31,[429] would have evoked the audience's own consultation of the oracle; in this way the Apollo of this tragedy was zoomed to the audience's religious realities. So the god Apollo who is consistently blamed for Orestes' act of matricide would have been perceived by the audience as a representation of the god Apollo whom they worshiped. Thus, it is the god they worshiped that they would have perceived as being problematized.

The first stasimon (316-47) includes a "lamenting address" to the Eumenides,[430] whom the chorus implores to release Orestes from his raving; the reference to Orestes receiving the prophecy at Delphi at 329-31, which evoked specific features of the Delphic sanctuary, and an invocation of Zeus at the beginning of the antistrophe. Then there is an address to Orestes, with concepts and language that evoke ritual: there is mention of an *alastor*, they sing that his mother blood *anabaccheuei* him, and a double *katolophyromai*. The rest of the antistrophe develops the theme that great prosperity among mortals does not last, because some *daimon* destroys it. This is exemplified by Tantalos' descendants—though they came from divine stock.[431] The mention of Tantalos would have activated, I suggest, the notions constructed at the beginning of the prologue.

In the segment that follows there is a cluster of references to past rituals, and also some enacted small-scale rites. At 362-7 Menelaos refers to the prophecy given him by the god Glaukos, son of Nereus, who rose from the waves. This report of Glaukos' appearance distances the world of the tragedy from that of the audience. At 382-4 Orestes supplicates Menelaos. At 422 there is a reference to Klytemestra's funeral pyre. At 429-30 Orestes tells Menelaos that he has not undergone the purification ritual. At 456-8 the chorus describes Tyndareos' appearance in the ritual attire of mourning, with a shorn head and black clothes. Tyndareos enters and explains that he had been at the grave of Klytemestra, pouring chthonic libations. At 611 he says that he came to Argos to tend Klytemestra's grave. Before that, at 500-2 he said[432] that Orestes ought to have aimed for religious correctness[433] in punishing his mother for the murder of his father, and thrown her out of the house. At 512-7, Tyndareos describes how one is supposed to behave towards the polluted murderer according to the ancestral custom. Like Electra in the prologue, Tyndareos believes that he knows the gods' will; he says (531-5) that the fact that Orestes wanders in the grip of *maniai* and terrors shows that he is loathed by the gods. At 624 Tyndareos urges Menelaos not to shield Orestes *enantion theois*.

At 579-84 Orestes invokes the gods, *pros theon*, and then adds that it was not appropriate to call on the gods, when judging murder, thus activating and stressing the prayer aspect of the expression, as well as drawing attention to the fact that murder is polluting and abhorrent to the gods. Then, he says that if he had condoned his mother's murder of his father by his silence, it would have been his father who would have sent him Erinyes—the expression he uses is based on ritual: *anechoreu' Erinysin*.[434] More ritual (and other religious) references follow. At 618-20 Tyndareos says that Electra had been inciting Orestes to murder their mother, reporting her dreams of Agamemnon and the adultery with Aigisthos, may the hatred of the Nether Gods fall on it. At 658-9 there is a reference to the sacrifice of Iphigeneia. Then there is a series of references to the belief that good and bad things come from the gods at 667-8 and 684-8; in the latter passage Menelaos manipulates this notion, stating "if god provides the means," to justify his unwillingness to help Orestes. At 708 also he uses a pious expression to justify himself (the god hates excessive displays of zeal). At 796-8 Orestes says that he will go to his father's grave to supplicate him, while he does not want to see his mother's grave.

The second stasimon (807-43) begins with a return to the theme of reversal of fortunes; the strophe refers to the misfortunes of the Atreids, which it presents as a legacy from their earlier misfortunes, the events surrounding the golden lamb and the cannibalistic meal offered to Thyestes. The antistrophe deals with Orestes' matricide. At 823-5 the chorus claim that *to d' eu kakourgein asebeia poikila kakophronon t' andron paranoia*, in other words, that the notion that the matricide can have been justified, and be a good thing, is considered by the chorus to be sophistical impiety. This, then, aligns Orestes with sophism and impiety, an alignment that can be seen as to some extent a continuation of his partial alignment with his ancestor Tantalos. The epode mentions Orestes' persecution by the Erinyes, whom they refer to as Eumenides; again ritual language is used to describe his state: *bebaccheutai maniais*. Language pertaining to ritual is also used in the metaphor at 842: *sphagion etheto matera*.

The messenger's report on the assembly that decided the fate of Orestes and Electra is generally empty of religious references, with a minimal exception at 923-5, where it is reported that the farmer who supported Orestes said that they should crown Orestes, for killing a bad and impious woman. Thus, in this tragedy, when the focus is on the political debate, the religious dimension is kept away.[435] The verdict of death passed by the Assembly must not be assumed to have been perceived by the audience as simply unjust.[436] Their perception would have been more complex. The death penalty for a matricide would not

Chapter 3: Euripidean Tragedy and Religious Exploration 391

have been seen as unreasonable. The negatively colored process through which the verdict had been reached[437] may have partly deconstructed its validity, but the fact that the report is delivered by a partial, rather than a neutral, observer, an old retainer of Orestes' family, may have itself colored the audience's perception of that negative coloring. In any case, the verdict, given Greek assumptions, was one possible, commonsense, response to the murder of a mother, the person with whom the Athenians believed a man had the closest possible blood relationship—though he owed the greatest loyalty to his father, for it was that relationship that was socially crucial.[438]

The fact that the Athenian audience would not have perceived a death sentence against a matricide to be unreasonable would have been one element that would have gone into their perception of this verdict;[439] another would have been the negatively colored process through which the verdict had been reached; yet another important element was their knowledge of the myth, in which the gods, in one way or another, had "in reality" secured Orestes' acquittal. The audience also knew—or, at least, some of them did—that the human jurors in Aeschylus' *Eumenides* were equally divided, and it was Athena's casting vote that acquitted Orestes.[440] At a later point in *Orestes*, we shall see, Apollo will announce that Orestes will stand trial with the gods as judges, and will be acquitted. Thus, the audience would have perceived a disjunction between the human verdict and the divine actions known to them at the time of the report of the debate—and, eventually, with the future divine verdict enunciated by a god. But this would not necessarily make them see the assembly's verdict as clearly unrighteous. For the disjunction between the human verdict and divine actions would have been seen as correlative with the fact that in Greek perceptions the ways of the cosmos and the divine are unknowable; human intelligence can only see and understand so far and no further.

At 960 begins a *kommos*, a ritual lament (960-1012); there is no general agreement as to who initiates it, Electra or the chorus.[441] The lament is accompanied by the actions that were performed at the death ritual, scoring the cheeks and beating of the head, that is said to be the due of the Queen of the Dead. The lament is for Electra and Orestes who, it is believed, are about to die, bringing to an end Pelops' lineage—or so it is claimed, but it is not in fact true, since Menelaos lives. Two things are blamed, *phthonos* ... *theothen* (974) and the people's murderous vote. At 982-96 Electra mentions the murder of Myrtilos by Pelops as the event from which first came an *ara polystonos* to her house;[442] this led to the quarrel between Atreus and Thyestes, and all the other misfortunes, culminating in those of Agamemnon and Electra (1010-12). The segment that follows contains some ritual references. At

1053-5 Electra and Orestes speak of their future grave. At 1065-7 Orestes asks Pylades to lay out their bodies and bury them in their father's grave. At 1078-80 Orestes mentions the wedding that Pylades will not now have with Electra, and the future one that Orestes urges him to have with someone else. While they are plotting to kill Helen Pylades says that if they do kill her there will be an *ololygmos, pyr t' anapsousin theois* and there will be prayers asking for blessings for them (1137-8). When Electra mentions that she thinks she has found salvation for them, Orestes replies, *theou legeis pronoian* (1179).[443]

As we saw, Hermione's visit to the grave bearing ritual offerings becomes part of the plot at 1185-7. At 1209-10 Pylades expresses the wish that he may still celebrate his wedding with Electra, that she may come to the community of the Phokians, honored through beautiful wedding songs. Then there is enacted ritual with some further evocations. At 1225-30 Orestes invokes his dead father and asks for his help. At 1231-4 first Electra and then Pylades also invoke Agamemnon, and the invocation by all continues until 1239, and includes the offering of a libation of tears by Orestes, and of laments by Electra, a metaphor[444] based on the ritual practice of accompanying prayers with libations, which therefore evoked for the audience real-life rituals. At 1241-3 Pylades says that if prayers can go inside the earth Agamemnon hears them. Then he invokes, and prays to, Zeus and Dike.[445] At 1299-1300 Electra invokes Zeus, and asks for his help. Before that the expression *sphagia phoinissein*[446] at 1285 would have evoked ritual language.

Hermione enters, and at 1321-2 Electra asks her whether she has come having put garlands on Klytemestra's grave and poured chthonic libations; Hermione replies that she has, and that she has obtained Klytemestra's benevolence. At 1332 Electra tells Hermione that Orestes had fallen suppliant to Helen's knees, and then she asks her to join in the supplication. The false supplication is reported by the Phrygian at 1410-5. This corrupt use of supplication in the plot to murder Helen is a perversion of a ritual comparable to that in *Electra*, where Orestes had chosen to kill Aigisthos during the performance of a sacrifice. The short choral intermezzo that follows after Electra and Hermione had gone inside includes the comment, at 1361-2, *dia dikas eba theon nemesis es Helenan*, justly has the (wrathful) dispensation of the gods proceeded in respect of Helen.[447] I suggest that the word "nemesis" would have evoked for the audience the goddess Nemesis,[448] and probably also the knowledge that, according to one version of her myth, Helen was the daughter of Zeus and Nemesis;[449] this would have activated for them the knowledge that, on this version, she was of double divine parentage, and so perhaps raised some doubt as to whether what appears to have happened has in fact happened.

Chapter 3: Euripidean Tragedy and Religious Exploration 393

The Phrygian enters at 1369, and at 1395 he begins a lament with *ailinon ailinon*,[450] a traditional exclamation of lament,[451] explaining that this is what the barbarians say when someone royal dies, that is, at the beginning of a royal death ritual. There is a ritual evocation at 1431-6, where the Phrygian describes Helen as spinning to prepare purple clothes from the Phrygian spoils to adorn Klytemestra's grave monument. At 1440-3 Orestes asks Helen, whom he is supplicating, to go to Pelops' ancient hearth seat, that is, to the central hearth of the house, the hearth altar of Hestia, which was the most appropriate place for a supplication. At 1453-4 the Phrygian invokes the Idaean Mother;[452] at 1492-3 he uses a simile based on Bacchic ritual.[453] Eventually, and after he had reported her murder, at 1495-9 he reveals that Helen, to whom he refers as "Zeus' daughter" had miraculously disappeared; he invokes Zeus, Ga, the Sun, and Nyx, and says that she disappeared—he does not know how; he considers the possibility of witchcraft and also the possibility that she was stolen by the gods. These events surrounding Helen's "murder" and disappearance, then, were not narrated by the usual type of messenger, but sung by a Phrygian slave.[454] The song, being a more emotional medium, fits the present circumstances of the Phrygian, who described the events in response to the chorus' questions.[455] These choices, of a Phrygian and of song, also allowed the events to be reported in more emotional terms, and so make the final revelation even more surprising, and perhaps also, less immediately trustworthy than it might have been. It is possible that the suspense as to Helen's fate may have encompassed, for the ancient audience, the question whether she had really disappeared, as well as how, and what that disappearance meant. But I do not share the view that the incongruity of having articulate and high-flown language used in the song by such a character "is part of the humour of this delectable scene."[456] Since we know that the ancient audience did not automatically find Oriental nameless characters in tragedy comical,[457] the fact that the Phrygian's language is typical of late Euripidean lyric would have directed the audience to perceive him as a noncomic character, as would the circumstances in which the scene takes place. West calls him "semi-comic, ludicrous in his unmanly fear and his native lack of dignity," but in fact the Phrygians had tried to save Helen, and some had died in the process (1473-89). The audience would have perceived this Phrygian as an exaggerated, inferior version, a negative polarization expressed through, and marked by, his Orientalism, of this tragedy's unheroic Orestes, who placed the highest value on the saving of his life.[458] This is a case of "the other" being an exaggerating mirror of the self, here of a particular version of the Greek hero.

394   *Part III: Religion and the Fifth-Century Tragedians*

The choral antistrophe that follows the Phrygian's exit and Orestes' return to the palace includes the statement *telos echei daimon brotois, telos opai thelei; megala de tis ha dynamis kai alastor* (1545-6); this is followed by the statement that this palace is falling because of Myrtilos' fall—the fall which had led to his death, and for which Pelops had been responsible, hence Myrtilos' curse.

Menelaos does not believe that Helen disappeared miraculously, and asks Orestes to surrender her body; Orestes replies that he should ask the gods for it (1586). A little earlier he had said that he wishes he had killed Helen, but he was robbed by the gods (1580). After Orestes had declared that not only does he want to live, but also to be king, Menelaos tells him, at 1601-3, that as he is a polluted killer he will not be able to touch the lustral vessels, or perform the prebattle sacrifices, and so he cannot rule Argos, since a leader needs to do these things. Not long after that, when disaster is about to take place, at 1625, Apollo appears in epiphany, accompanied by Helen. Throughout the tragedy, Apollo had been zoomed to the world of the audience's religious realities, through references that would have evoked their own consultation of the oracle, so that they would have identified the Apollo of the tragedy with their own god; they would have therefore perceived the god who appeared in epiphany to be a representation of the Apollo they worshiped.

Apollo's first pronouncement puts a stop to the violence that was about to take place; he announces the deification of Helen, who, by virtue of being Zeus' daughter, will be immortal, and together with Kastor and Polydeukes will be a savior to seamen. In the audience's religious realities, the Dioskouroi received cult in Athens, and it is likely, albeit not certain, that Helen also did.[459] It is in any case clear that the Athenians were aware of her Spartan cult.[460] We do not know whether this function of Helen as marine savior corresponded to any religious realities.[461] In these circumstances, the cult announced by Apollo zoomed the world of the tragedy to the present—though possibly at a little distance from the audience's own present, if she had not had a cult in Athens. At 1639-42 Apollo states that the gods had used Helen to bring about a war, because there were too many people, and it was necessary to lighten the burden of the earth. This seems a cruel notion, but it is a traditional explanation of war, also found in the Epic Cycle;[462] in a world in which the prospect of overpopulation was terrifying, the concept seems perfectly reasonable from a purely utilitarian point of view. Apollo's statement deconstructs Helen's strong and persistent vilification, which was based on the assumption that she was entirely responsible for the Trojan War. But for the ancient audience Apollo's statement did not exonerate Helen entirely; for the notion of

Chapter 3: Euripidean Tragedy and Religious Exploration 395

the double motivation of events, caused by the divine will, but also human character and action, would have come into play when they made sense of this statement, especially since the notion of her guilt had been articulated.

Then Apollo gives instructions to Orestes, who must eventually go to Athens to stand trial for the matricide against the three Eumenides;[463] he will be victorious at this trial at the Areopagus, in which the gods will be the judges.[464] Apollo also tells him that he is destined (*peprotai s'*) to marry Hermione, and that Neoptolemos, who thinks he will marry her, will not, for his fate is to die at Delphi, where he will go to ask Apollo for recompense for his father's death. Apollo concludes at 1664-5, promising that he will reconcile Orestes to Argos, he will set right Orestes' relations to the city, because, he says, *exenangassa*,[465] 'I forced', Orestes to kill his mother. The fact that *exenangassa* is Apollo's last word in this speech—though he will speak again subsequently—gives it a special emphasis. Throughout the tragedy, Apollo was repeatedly blamed for the matricide, which was characterized as *anosion*, unholy, and for its consequences, and here he accepts that responsibility. But things are not as simple as that. There are, we shall see, good reasons why Apollo should have stressed his own responsibility here, and this was clear to the audience. They would have perceived the notion that Apollo was alone responsible for the matricide as one possible way of presenting a complex situation, but not the whole picture. The Greek—and tragic—perception of double motivation, divine and human, in which the gods will something but mortals' actions bring it about, would have deconstructed the notion that the god alone was responsible. More importantly, there is another recurrent theme in this tragedy, which also deconstructs the notion of Apollo's sole responsibility: the notion that these disasters were the result of Myrtilos' curse that afflicted Pelops' descendants, and the consequent operation of an *alastor*, an avenging demon. This complicates the picture, and affects the way in which the audience would have made sense of the notion that Apollo had forced Orestes to kill his mother. If it was perceived by the audience that an *alastor* triggered off by Myrtilos' curse was operating, then it was inevitable that Orestes should have suffered. Seen in this context, Apollo's command was good advice on how to deal with a dreadful situation. And this is surely how the audience would have made sense of this. Apollo stresses his own responsibility very strongly, focusses on his own role, because he is stressing that Orestes obeyed him, a god, and because he wants to marginalize Orestes' choice in this context, in which he is speaking of reconciling him to the people of Argos; it is as though he is presenting the case here for Orestes that he will make to the Argives.

So the superficial impression that Apollo is to be blamed for Orestes' matricide was modified, in the eyes of the audience, through their perception that Orestes had ultimately made his own choices, and also, very importantly, through the perception of the workings of the *alastor* who had been set in motion by the curse. Nevertheless, Apollo was responsible, and if he himself perhaps overstresses his responsibility, what he says would have been perceived by the audience to have been largely true. He had ordered Orestes to kill his mother. Does this entail that the audience would have perceived Apollo to have been wrong, and worthy of criticism? Surely, gods should not instigate matricide. I suggest that these are culturally determined questions. Clearly, for the ancient audience Apollo was right, in the sense that the fact that Orestes followed the god's advice has led, after suffering, to the present situation, in which it has become apparent that order will eventually be restored, and Orestes' sufferings will come to an end. This does not alter the fact that his guidance involved committing an *anosion* deed. The theme of vengeance, and the notion of reacting to injustice and wrongdoing with further injustice and wrongdoing are explored in many tragedies. The answer is not simple. The ideology of the society in which tragedy was generated led to a hierarchy of wrongness. In Greek discourse the father and the father-son bond were privileged, and a woman who betrayed and killed her husband was perceived, as she is described in this tragedy, as a threatening figure, representing the dangers of complete disorder. But the matricide is also presented in very negative colors, and the murder of the mother also threatens disorder, of a different kind, and it is also policed by divine powers—albeit ultimately less powerful ones than Apollo and his peers. Because of this hierarchy of wrongness, at the end a matricide will be restored to order. But the other side is also strongly articulated. And, of course, the prospective happy ending does not obliterate Orestes' suffering which the audience has witnessed; on the contrary, the very fact that it will continue after the end of the tragedy stresses this.

The question is whether the audience would have perceived that there were alternatives to what Apollo had advised Orestes to do. From the human perspective Tyndareos believes that there were. But in the assumptions through which the ancient audience made sense of the play, the human perspective is limited. The ways of the cosmos beyond the human experience are unfathomable. So, the audience's perception, I suggest, would have been that in those circumstances, only part of which are intelligible to mortals, Apollo's command revealed what was the best way to deal with a terrible situation—however awful that remedy may have been.

Chapter 3: Euripidean Tragedy and Religious Exploration

One of the perceptions articulated in this tragedy, then, was that the ways of the gods are unfathomable. But this is interwined with the perception that, even when people think that the gods have abandoned them, this is not necessarily true, not if they have followed the gods' will. Ultimately the gods help those who obey them, whatever it may look like; there is suffering, and this suffering is not annihilated by what will happen in the future, but the future is better, eventually the suffering will come to an end, and things will work out. This is a reassuring message. However, this reassurance is partly deconstructed, as far as the world of the audience is concerned, by Orestes' reply. For, in response, Orestes addresses the god and acknowledges that he is a true prophet. His fear had been that it might have been a false oracle, not Apollo's voice, but an *alastor* demon attempting to deceive him (1666-69). This evokes the fact that in the audience's reality people did not know if the prophecy they received was right, for there was always the danger, in their perceptions of prophecy, that human fallibility may interfere to distort the god's message.

Orestes assures Apollo that he will obey his orders; at 1673, Menelaos addresses Helen with *chaire*, marking her divine status.[466] Then Apollo urges both to go and to do as he ordered them, and to dissolve their strife; both agree. Apollo then at 1682-90 urges then to honor Eirene, Peace, whom he calls *ten kallisten theon*, the fairest of deities. The cult of Eirene[467] appears not to have been established in Athens until 375 B.C., though she was thought of as a goddess in literature, including in fifth-century tragedy and comedy.[468] In the audience's realities, then Peace was honored, but not with a cult. The relationship between the *stasis*, the discord, in *Orestes* and the political turmoil that had recently taken place in Athens is a complex question;[469] the part that concerns me is that by the time of Apollo's epiphany, the specifically political dimension of *stasis*, the exploration of problems inherent in democracy, constructed through the debate, has been left behind. Consequently, Apollo's promise that he will set right Orestes' relations to the city brings a reassuring closure to this *stasis*. Insofar as the audience had felt any resonances of their own situation in the tragedy,[470] the promise of healing dissent in Argos given by Apollo in the tragedy, who was perceived as a representation of their god, would have constructed the possibility that the god Apollo will also heal the scars of *stasis* in Athens, and protect the city from dissent, so that it could enjoy unity and order. For one of the most important characteristics of Apollo in the religious assumptions of the audience was that he was the god who par excellence established order. The placing of the cessation of strife at the religious register was further strengthened by Apollo's injunction to Orestes and Menelaos to honor Eirene, *ten kal-*

listen theon. This confirms that, as we move on towards the tragedy's closure, the solution of *stasis* is located at the religious register; it has become distanced from its earlier political matrix. This, I suggest, helped create a reassuring closure as far as the Athenian audience is concerned.

The importance of the religious dimension is confirmed by an intertextual evocation. For *ten kallisten theon Eirenen* evokes *Eirena bathyploute kai kallista makaron theon*, the opening lines of fragment 453 from Euripides' *Kresphontes*, which had been produced before 421.[471] This fragment gives us part of one of the tragedy's main stasima, and is an invocatory hymn to Eirene, Peace, with many of the standard elements of such a prayer.[472] This evocation would have strengthened the notion that Eirene guards against *stasis*; for the antistrophe of this invocatory hymn in *Kresphontes* begins *Tan d' echthran Stasin eirg' ap' oikon tan mainomenan t' Erin* (10-11). *Stasis* may have been a significant dimension in *Kresphontes*.[473]

It may be asked for whom the expression in *Orestes* would have evoked the hymn in *Kresphontes*, who would have remembered and recognized this expression after many years. This question is not easy to answer. It is possible that, because of its novelty, a hymn to Eirene may have been remembered over the years by many. If not, the evocation would only have worked for those who knew Euripides' tragedies well. For any spectators for whom verses 1682-3 evoked the hymn to Eirene in *Kresphontes*[474] the serious religious dimension of the healing of stasis would have been reinforced. But, most importantly, even if no one in the audience had registered it, this intertextual connection can still help confirm that the solution of the *stasis* in *Orestes* is presented as being located in the religious dimension, and also confirm the serious religious coloring of the closure of this tragedy; for the intertextual connection of this *Orestes* passage with an invocatory hymn to Eirene suggests that in the assumptions helping to shape Euripides' choices, the parameters determining his selections, this *Orestes* passage, far from being ironic, had indeed belonged to the serious religious dimension.

The play ends with a choral address to Nike. I am discussing all such lyric epilogues in detail in appendix 2 below. Here I will only say that if, as there is every reason to believe, it is genuine, besides being a strategy of closure, it would have created important meanings. As we saw in chapter I.2, the tragic chorus had a double identity; its dominant identity was as a chorus of, in this case, Argive women, in the world of the play, its weaker one as a chorus of men for Dionysos in the present; the latter was strengthened in certain places through choral self-referentiality. The zooming to the chorus' persona as a chorus for

Chapter 3: Euripidean Tragedy and Religious Exploration

Dionysos in the present through the tailpieces addressing Nike can be seen as a strong, polarized variant of choral self-referentiality. One effect this zooming would inevitably have had for the ancient audience was to stress the context of the performance, *agones* in the course of a festival for Dionysos, and so also to stress and strengthen the religious dimension of the performance. In *Orestes* it follows Apollo's last pronouncement, in which Apollo had first urged everyone to honor Peace, and then spoken further of Helen's deification and future cult and function, in association with the Dioskouroi. Thus, the strengthening of the religious dimension here through the zooming to the chorus' identity as a chorus performing in a Dionysiac festival in the present gives greater authority not only to the notion of Helen's deification, but also, and especially, to the recognition of Apollo's authority, and the validity of his oracle, and to his admonitions with regard to civil strife which was directly relevant to the Athenian audience.

This, then, is a tragedy with a serious religious dimension. Ritual played a significant role in structuring *Orestes* for the fifth-century audience, ritual and other religious references created the framework through which the tragedy's fabric and the tragic explorations were woven, and sustained a world in which the relationships between mortals and immortals were important, both in themselves and in helping shape human relationships. They are not the only thing that was important in this tragedy; human relationships of various kinds were also very important, and they were explored, such as, for example, the notion of *stasis*, of democracy, of *philia*, and the human cost of war (here displaced onto the figure of Helen). Religious problematization is important, though it is only one facet of the play's complex problematization and explorations. But ultimately, at least some nonreligious problems also come to be located and tackled at the religious register. This is correlative with the Athenian (and generally Greek) perception that religion is at the heart of the polis and articulates, and sanctions, legitimates, and ultimately guarantees, all relationships.

In these circumstances, I find it difficult to understand how modern critics could have imagined that this ancient audience would have made sense of the tragedy's ending other than in a straightforward way, not as an ironic construct:[475] a god, who had been zoomed to the audience's religious realities, so that he was perceived as a representation of the god they worshiped, and who was the god par excellence involved in the establishment of order, established order in the world of the tragedy, a complex and not unproblematic order, but order nevertheless, and some kind of "answers" to the religious problems explored in the tragedy—albeit again complex and not easy "answers." Consequently, the audience would not have thought that the ending shows that there is no sense in the cosmos, or that confusion characterized the divine as well as the human world; but that the divine world is unknowable—with the more reassuring representations of protection from the gods for those who obey them—a notion itself rendered somewhat problematic by the raising of the issue of the potential unreliability of prophecy.

The fact that there is a happy ending for both Orestes the matricide and Helen the destroyer would not have created a problem in ancient eyes. Both had suffered, and Orestes will go on suffering. But, ultimately, things will be alright because Orestes had obeyed Apollo and also because, ultimately, what he did was, however awful, the right thing in those appalling circumstances. Helen also suffered; she suffered a virtual death; but in her case, despite her destructive history, the good outweighs the bad: she becomes deified. This is correlative with the activation of her divine parentage;[476] even her destructiveness is placed in a cosmic perspective and drifts towards almost divine destructiveness.

If we think intertextually, as the Athenian audience did, in the sense that their perceptions of the myths were shaped, among other things, through earlier tragic performances, we may consider how Kastor's criticism of Apollo's role in the matricide at the end of *Electra* relates to the satisfactory state of affairs brought about by Apollo at the end of *Orestes*. It can be claimed that Apollo in *Orestes* makes explicit, and confirms, the perception of the audience in *Electra* that Kastor's pronouncement was partial and biased. The fact that Apollo spoke the will of Zeus at Delphi, would have led the audience to perceive that the representation of the god in tragic epiphany would be doing the same. Kastor, on the other hand, only spoke Zeus' will when he stated that he was reporting that will; his own perspective was more circumscribed. He knew and understood more than mortals, but less than Apollo. Apollo in his turn knew and understood less than Zeus. Zeus, the ultimate source of authority and order, did not appear in epiphany in Euripides, or if he did, extremely rarely, it was more as a character involved in the story and less as the sovereign god.[477] He is distanced, and his ultimate plan is only partially glimpsed at through the words of other gods. The gods in epiphany reassure the mortals that there is a plan, and give some partial answers that allow an assessment, if a complex and open-ended one, of the problems that were explored in the tragedy. They also anchor symbolically some cults, thus reassuring mortals that they do indeed embody a correct way of relating to the divine.

Euripides did not represent Zeus on stage precisely because what is being conveyed is that even through gods in epiphany mortals can only

Chapter 3: Euripidean Tragedy and Religious Exploration 401

have a partial sight of the divine will. It is correlative with the notion of unknowability that the god who is in control, and who knows everything and has a plan, does not appear, so that the audience only gets partial views of "the truth." Of course, the notion that Zeus is in total control needs to be qualified by the perception that fate is stronger than Zeus. This perception is correlative with the zooming of the gods into more or less comprehensible anthropomorphic beings; the more they are presented like that, the more the ungraspability of the cosmos drifts to something else which is ungraspable, this notion of fate. This would suggest that when the divine takes physical form in front of the audience, the graspable becomes dominant, and the ungraspable marginalized. Whether or not this is right, when the focus is on Zeus' overall plan, the dominant assumption would be that he is, effectively, in control.

The fact that Zeus does not appear is a further argument in favor of the religious significance of gods in epiphany. The fact that we never see Zeus makes sense if we understand the gods in epiphany to have been perceived by the ancient audience as representations of the gods of lived religion. It cannot be made sense of if gods in epiphany are empty closure devices.[478]

I am arguing against the view that Orestes was an ironic and/or comic tragedy below in appendix 1. Here I want to make a positive point about the tragedy's idiosyncracies. What is different in *Orestes*, when compared to the earlier tragedies I have discussed, is the degree in which various things occur in *Orestes*: the very great density of intertextual references, the extent of the plot innovations, the strength of the resonances of contemporary reality, the in-your-face nature of the deployment of the multifunctional Tantalos paradigm, the explicitness of Apollo's explanation and assumption of responsibility, and the virtual explicitness of the intertextual answers he gives to problems raised in an earlier tragedy, the stress on Orestes' desire to live, whatever he has to do to achieve this aim, the extent of the plot's movement towards calamity which proves deceptive. This density and intensity does not make the play comic or paratragic or even bizarre. It is part of the play's self-reflexivity. It is a culturally determined perception that self-reflexivity and sophistication must involve a sceptical, rationalizing, or self-deconstructing "message." As we saw, what Euripides himself believed, whether he belonged to that "Enlightenment" in which many modern commentators have placed him—another culturally determined concept which carries distorting connotational luggage—is beyond our grasp. What, I have argued, is not, are the basic parameters shaping the main parameters of meaning creation by the audience—parameters which had inevitably also shaped Euripides' choices, at whatever point of the conscious-unconscious spectrum each of those was located. And it is on these that I have tried to focus. The reconstructions based on that strategy show that religious problematization had, in varying degrees, a significant role in Euripidean tragedies, a religious problematization which involved an ultimate, if complex and not unproblematic, reassurance.

The tragedy's self-reflexivity intensifies the depth of the problematization, especially the religious problematization. It brings up many of the problematizations articulated in other plays and attempts to deal with them. An instance of this strategy is the Tantalos paradigm, which would have created, at the very beginning, the message "mortals always moan about the gods, but in fact their misfortunes are their own fault." This in-your-face verdict, based on an extremely polarized case, is then deconstructed, modified, and refined, in complex ways.

There is a correlation between the strength of the contemporary resonances and political problematization in *Orestes* and the political turmoil of the audience's life experiences. It is possible that a synergy of an authorial dynamic towards greater self-reflexivity and the intensity of the political turmoil, which is reflected in the play's political problematization, created a matrix of intensification which generated this partly intertextually constructed intensity of religious problematization. The intensity of the problematization leads to ultimately reassuring "answers." The restoration of order in this tragedy, as in other Euripidean tragedies, is complex, and it leaves questions open. But it does ultimately reassure, having raised serious issues of religious nature and of *stasis*, issues that were important to the Athenians. As Parker noted,[479] in tragedy difficult questions are asked. They are asked in *Orestes*, and the harsh realities are put in an ultimately reassuring framework. This does not necessarily entail that every Athenian spectator would have adopted a naively optimistic view of the world as a result. But however complex and sophisticated some Athenians' perception of the cosmos may have been, the raising of difficult questions and placing them in an ultimately reassuring framework may have reinforced an ultimately reassuring conceptual map, whatever the details of that map may have been in individual cases.

11) *Ion, Helen, Bacchae, Iphigeneia at Aulis*

Restrictions of space force me to end my discussion of individual tragedies here. Since it is not important for my case to claim that all tragedies involved a significant religious discourse, absence of completeness does not affect my case. The four tragedies I have not discussed are *Ion*,

Chapter 3: Euripidean Tragedy and Religious Exploration 403

Helen, Bacchae, and *Iphigeneia at Aulis.* I will mention very briefly those aspects of their religious dimension that are apparent without need of discussion. That *Bacchae* is structured by ritual and involves religious problematization is obvious. *Ion* is located at the Delphic sanctuary and structured by the ritual of *theoria,* which includes the consultation of the oracle; Apollo had had sex with one of the characters and is the father of another; the prologue is spoken by Hermes and Athena appears in epiphany at the end, the poliadic deity of Athens, the polis at the center of the plot. *Ion* also involves religious problematization, but as this requires a complex disscission I will not go into it. *Helen* has a supernatural framework (divine intervention ensured that it was Helen's *eidolon* that went to Troy; she herself had been brought to Egypt by Hermes), and involves a prophetess as an important character, and also several rites; most importantly, the performance of a ritual is crucial for the plot, as it provides the excuse that allows Helen and Menelaos to escape; finally, the Dioskouroi appear in epiphany and announce Helen's future deification. The one aspect of the religious dimension of *Iphigeneia at Aulis* that is clear without need for discussion is the fact that the tragedy is focussed on human sacrifice.

III.3.v. *Conclusions: Differences, Patterns, and Meanings*

These analyses have shown that religion has a very important place in Euripidean tragedy, though the degree of its importance varies in the individual tragedies. Rituals have a very significant place; they are deployed in, and help articulate, Euripidean tragedies, differently, and to a varying extent, in the different tragedies; at one end of the spectrum they play a relatively small part, at the other a major one. But even when rituals play a minor part, they are always present. The deployment of rituals is intertwined with religious problematization, or problematization with a religious dimension; for problematization pertaining to human relationships very often has a religious facet. Explorations and problematizations of religious issues are articulated, again differently, and to a varying extent, in the different tragedies.

In terms of my reconstructions, then, this state of affairs can be formulated as follows: the basic schema of the ritual matrix that had generated the tragic matrix has not totally disappeared; Euripidean tragedies are articulated by various transformations of that matrix, some of which are nearer, and some further away, from the ritual matrix.

The tragedy with the least significant religious content (in terms of my reconstruction the one furthest away from the ritual matrix) is one of the earliest extant ones, *Medea*. So whatever it is we are dealing with is not a linear movement away from the religious dimension. I am not suggesting anything simplistically linear here. For in *Kretes*, which is early,[480] the religious dimension is very important, since Minos had offended Poseidon, and the god punished him by inspiring in his wife Pasiphae erotic *mania* for a bull, with whom she copulated, and gave birth to the Minotaur; furthermore, the chorus consisted of Cretan priests. What I am suggesting is considering whether perhaps certain choices were becoming privileged in certain circumstances, and, if so, what were those circumstances.

Among the earlier surviving tragedies, the religious dimension is significant in *Herakleidai*, in which ritual density goes together with important religious problematization. But religious exploration in this tragedy is not very deep or very probing, and it is above all focussed on war. *Andromache* is quite close to the parameters of the ritual matrix as regards the deployment of ritual structuring the tragedy, and more generally the religious conceptual framework that articulates it. Religious exploration is not at the very center of the tragedy, other explorations are, but it still has a not unimportant place, and it is significant religious problematization. Consequently, this tragedy in which gender discourse is important, is much nearer the ritual matrix than *Alcestis* and especially *Medea*. Gender discourse is also very important in *Hippolytos*, but there it is closely intertwined with religious problematization which is central. *Hippolytos* does not have a very great ritual density, though ritual and other religious elements do form the skeleton of the play, but ritual, the worship of Aphrodite, is central in the action and to the rich religious problematization of the tragedy. *Suppliants* has a great ritual density and involves religious problematization and exploration—albeit not of a very deep kind. In *Hecabe* a density of ritual elements is intertwined with the exploration of problems pertaining to fundamental questions of human relationships which are ultimately sustained by a divine order. In form this tragedy is not very far removed from the ritual matrix, but the center of gravity of the explorations has shifted towards the human side of relationships—within a framework of a world ruled by the gods and their ordinances. In *Electra* there is a significant density of ritual elements, intertwined with deep and rich and serious religious problematization, exploring some of the most serious questions pertaining to Greek religion. This is among the tragedies that can be characterized as most strongly articulating, and being articulated by, a discourse of religious exploration. It can be seen as a new version of the developments out of the ritual matrix, in which a new and intense type of religious exploration is central.

Chapter 3: Euripidean Tragedy and Religious Exploration 405

In these circumstances, it is clear that, far from Euripidean tragedies moving further and further away from the religious sphere (on my reconstruction further and further away from the versions of the tragic matrix which retained the religious dimension of the ritual matrix), as would have been the case if at least part of the religious dimension in Euripides was the result of inherited (even if reinterpreted) conventions, we see a certain shift towards expanding the nonreligious dimension in the earlier tragedies, a greater and varying concern with religious explorations in the tragedies produced at c. 430 and in the early 420s, and (not, I stress again, in terms of a linear progression, but of preferred choices) a new and increasingly deepening focus on religious exploration in the tragedies produced in the late 420s. *Erechtheus*, which was produced at the end of the 420s, would appear to fit this pattern since, insofar as it is possible to tell, it involved, we saw in chapter I.2, ritual density, significant religious problematization, an epiphany of Athena, and the foundation of cults by the goddess.

I will now set out a crude classification of the tragedies discussed above,[481] though this straightjackets their richness and diversity, simply in order to be able to talk about patterns without needing to list every tragedy. Type 1 tragedies have a significant density of ritual elements, intertwined with deep and rich religious problematization; they can be seen as being structured by what we may call a new version of the developed tragic matrix, with a deep and intense type of religious exploration. The following tragedies belong here: *Hippolytos* (ritual density not as great as in some in this category), *Andromache* (considerable ritual density), *Electra* (great ritual density), *Troades* (great ritual density), *Iphigeneia in Tauris* (great ritual density), *Heracles*. Type 2 includes tragedies which have a significant density of ritual elements, and important religious problematization, which is, however, less deep and probing. The tragedies belonging to this type are *Herakleidai* and *Suppliants* (which has more significant religious problematization than in *Herakleidai*). Type 3 includes tragedies which have significant density of ritual elements, while the religious problematization is indirect and implicit: *Hecabe* is the one tragedy which belongs to this type. Type 4 includes tragedies which have ritual density, a significant religious dimension, but have only limited religious problematization and exploration. *Alcestis* belongs to this type. Type 5 includes tragedies which have lesser ritual density and hardly any significant religious problematization. One tragedy belongs to this type: *Medea*.

Most of the surviving tragedies, then, belong to type 1, with a significant density of ritual elements and deep and rich religious problematization; only one belongs to type 5 at the other end of the scale;

types 2 and 3 share a significant density of ritual elements, and a significant presence of religious problematization, which is either not very deep, or implicit and indirect. Type 4 can be seen as lying between types 2 and 3 on the one hand and type 5 on the other. Type 1, then, was, or became, Euripides' preferred choice. Its earliest appearance is in *Hippolytos*. This may be an accident of survival; but the development of the tragedies suggests that Euripides was developing and refining the type at that time. That this was the case is suggested, first, by the development from *Hippolytos*, the ritual density of which is not as great as in some type 1 tragedies, to *Andromache*, with a considerable ritual density, and then to *Electra*, *Troades*, and *Iphigeneia in Tauris*, with its great ritual density. Second, the surviving tragedies suggest that the type of matrix with little or no religious problematization was, if not abandoned (it may have been, but we cannot know, given the proportion of surviving tragedies), at the very least made into a nonpreferred choice—we have enough tragedies from this segment of Euripides' career to be able to say that. Furthermore, the distribution of types 2 and 3 suggests experimentation with a significant density of ritual elements, and important religious problematization, starting with *Herakleidai*, and continuing with *Suppliants* and *Hecabe*; eventually, it is the forms deployed in *Hippolytos* and *Andromache* that become the preferred choice. I am not, I stress again, talking of linear development, but of clustering of preferred choices.

If this is right, then a tendency had begun at around 430, intensified very strongly by 428, to articulate tragedies through a dense deployment of rituals, and to intensify the religious problematization, an intensification first seen in *Hippolytos* and further developed in *Andromache*. In *Herakleidai* the religious explorations, not very deep or very probing, were, above all, focussed on war. It is difficult to doubt that this focus reflects concerns arising from, and offers religious reassurance for, the Spartan invasions of Attica. In both *Hippolytos* and *Andromache*, with their significant religious explorations, the notions of a deity's hostility towards a mortal is explored, together with the possibility of divine malice; and very complex, but ultimately reassuring, answers are given. In *Hecabe* we see a bleak world. The frightening possibility that it may be random *tyche* that governs human affairs is raised, but is shown to be wrong; the world proves to be ordered and governed by the gods.

Is this pattern significant? Perhaps not. But if we ask, "Were there any circumstances in the relevant years conducive to the choice to deploy versions of the tragic matrix with an increasingly strong and significant religious dimension?", the answer is yes. We must not fall into the trap of *post hoc ergo propter hoc*; but neither must we assume that

Chapter 3: Euripidean Tragedy and Religious Exploration

it is more rigorous to claim that a set of circumstances directly related to a particular phenomenon is not relevant, than to explore the possibility that it might be. For it is not; scepticism of this kind sounds superficially more rigorous because it sounds like scholarly caution; but in fact it relies on an implicit a priori assumption: that to exclude something from a phenomenon even if there are good indications that it was part of that phenomenon does not distort the reconstruction of the phenomenon, while to consider a possible relationship would. This assumption is fallacious, since every element in a whole, a play, a tragedian's oeuvre, a social phenomenon, acquires significance through its interactions with the other elements and with the whole.

I suggested in the discussion of *Troades* that the resentment of the gods expressed by the Trojan women was comparable to that which, according to Thucydides, the Athenians had expressed during the plague, when, he says, turning to the gods was useless, and, since the plague struck indiscriminately, people were not restrained by fear of god or human law;[482] and that *Troades*, at the safe distance of several years later, was rearticulating some of the questions that had been asked then, when, some Athenians at least, may have felt that the gods had abandoned them, and that they had worshiped them in vain.

In general, the cultural context in which the surviving Euripidean tragedies were generated had involved some form of religious "turbulence" and anxiety.[483] It is not unlikely that at 432 Diopeithes proposed a decree against impiety, and it is possible Anaxagoras was indicted for impiety.[484] Thucydides' report of the plague indicates disillusionment with religion. This is one observer's interpretation; what he describes is a kind of moral panic; but the notion that this catastrophe had undermined religion, rather than created a climate of insecurity and perhaps religious anxiety, is deconstructed by his own report of the popular debate concerning oracles. Religious practice and the perception of the centrality of religion in Athens recovered, if it had ever become shaky, which is highly doubtful. But in one way or another, there was a certain climate of anxiety. A few years later anxiety was reactivated by two impious acts, the mutilation of the Herms and the Profanation of the Mysteries, however short-term the effects of the panic they created may have been. This climate of intermittent insecurity, and intermittently reactivated religious sensitivities (further fuelled by the volatile circumstances), may have been an important factor in the arousal of hostility towards certain ideas that came to be perceived as dangerous, so that, as Parker puts it, "speculative thought was perceived by some as a threat."[485] This eventually led, ultimately, and in combination with the fact that some of Socrates' associates had been involved in antidemocratic actions, to Socrates' trial.[486] While earlier philosophical thought could be appropriated by, and integrated into, the traditional religious system, probably partly for reasons internal to the systems, and partly in symbiotic reaction to a general climate of possible anxiety, Anaxagorean and generally the natural philosophers', reflections were perceived as a challenge to polis religion. I suggest that the "Anaxagorean" and sophistic elements in Euripidean tragedies articulate that challenge, and defeat it. These tragedies face the challenge and explore further, but eventually reaffirm, the religious system of the polis, through articulations that acknowledge the darkness and the unknowability of the cosmos and the divine, but set it all in a wider, and ultimately reassuring, perspective.

This view, which sees the sophistic elements in some Euripidean tragedies as part of the construction of a misguided discourse that will prove wrong, makes these tragedies in one sense comparable to (though even in this respect much richer, more complex and subtle than) Aristophanes' *Clouds*, which deployed the tragic schema of deities punishing wrongdoers, to construct the meaning "these philosophers miss the point, their speculations are puny efforts in the context of a complex cosmos that is that of traditional religion." It is possible to see this discourse of religious exploration in Euripidean tragedies, which acknowledges the darkness, but presents complex but ultimately reassuring "answers" as part of the process that sustained and healed any problems in religious and moral stability.

The modern and postmodern perceptual casts privilege the assumption that Euripidean sophistication was deployed in order to take an ironic view of religion, and block the possibility that all this sophistication and complexity may have been deployed in the service of reinforcing religion. This is clearly a problem relating to modern thinking and modern hierarchies. It cannot be sustained with ancient evidence, since, we saw, the view that it can has been shown to be wrong. It reflects modern rationalism, which, even if now renounced by many, has seeped, or rather implicit assumptions and hierarchies derived from it have seeped, into postmodernist discourse, where they formed a symbiotic relationship with the privileging of the deconstructive and subversive, to create a cast of mind in which it is assumed that, unless it is proven conclusively and beyond reasonable doubt—which so little can for the ancient world—Euripidean tragedies cannot be serious religious discourse. I hope to have shown that, when made sense of through the ancient audience's perceptual filters, Euripidean tragedies do indeed involve—among other things—a serious religious discourse of exploration.

Chapter 3: Euripidean Tragedy and Religious Exploration

It is my argument here that tragedy explored the interstices of polis religious discourse, and so also explored areas of religion that appeared somehow problematic. On my reconstruction, tragedy began as a locus of religious exploration, then it became a locus of general exploration and problematization, of all aspects of polis discourse, interpersonal relationships and so on, in which religious discourse was one, sometimes small, part. Eventually, Euripidean tragedies more and more frequently gave an important place to religious discourse, exploring problematic areas in the myths, areas that generated questions and potential anxieties, and thus exploring problematic areas in the Greek religious system, and the human relationships that were grounded in that system. Several Euripidean tragedies are articulated by a particular type of religious exploration, in which the darkness and bleakness are articulated, and "answers" are offered, which were ultimately, and in complex ways, reassuring.

Euripidean tragedies explored recurrently, among other things, the empirically observable fact that the world is a cruel place, and people suffer. I suggest that these tragedies were shaped, among other things, but very importantly, by the interaction between the nature of tragedy, which, I proposed, included its identity as a locus of exploration of the religious discourse of the polis, and this climate of moral and religious anxiety; and that several characteristics of Euripidean tragedy can be seen as correlative with that climate: the bleakness of the problematization, the "Anaxagorean" and sophistic elements, but also the stress on the unknowability of divine plans, which indicates a wider picture which, if only one knew it, would put everything in perspective. This would not neutralize the suffering, but show that it was not senseless.

It is in this context that we should understand the fact that in Euripidean tragedies the religious exploration is often so dark. These tragedies problematize men's relationships with the divine through both plot and statements made by the characters. This is one of the factors behind the density of human sacrifice in Euripides. Human sacrifice is one of the areas of major problematization because of what it may suggest about the nature of the gods. This is not the only problematization articulated through the theme of human sacrifice; as we saw, there were others, including the exploration of the very notion of "young men dying for their country." The question of the cruelty of gods in tragedy, and also the more general question of the relationship of the gods in tragedy to the gods of civic religion, has been discussed most recently by Parker.[487] His general thesis on the relationship of the gods in tragedy to the gods of civic religion is not very different from that argued here. He argues, against the view that the gods of civic religion as manifested in oratory and comedy are different from those of tragedy, the former benevolent, the latter cruel, that the differences result from their different contexts; that the tragedies raise the issues of justice or injustice of the gods, and the characters demand explanations; given the basic unknowability of Greek religion, the tragic poet can be viewed as a kind of honorary seer, capable of conveying what might be true about the divine world.[488]

Another characteristic of Euripidean tragedies, the heavy concentration of cult institutions, which, we saw, anchored symbolically those cults, can also be seen as correlative with a climate of religious anxiety and disquiet.

The most terrifying thing is a world that has no meaning, no order, and no plan. Euripidean tragedies show that the world does have order and meaning, and works on a plan of Zeus. By our standards, that order and that plan were often cruel, and not the mark of a benevolent divine order. But the world is not always kind and just and fair, and the Greek perception of the cosmos acknowledged this fact. It is this perception that is articulated in those tragedies which, to modern eyes, have often appeared to be criticizing the gods. They were not criticizing; they were articulating the problems, and the human suffering, and exploring possible ways of accounting for, and making sense of, both. Ultimately, they articulated the notion that there is an order and a plan, often difficult for mortals to gauge; and that although the divine is ultimately unknowable, there are certain rules that almost guarantee their benevolence. Above all, the performance of cults, which, this type of tragedy above all others reassures his audience, has the approval of the gods.

Appendix 1: Other Views on *Orestes*: A Brief Critique

It is clear that I disagree with those modern critics who believe that the ancient audience would have seen the ending of *Orestes* as "unconvincing," or would have thought that Apollo announces what he does, as Knox put it, "in what seems to be a deliberately banal fashion" future marriages and apotheoses "which seem incongruous with the desperation portrayed in the body of the play."[489] Knox[490] continues that it is hard to see what else Euripides could have done, since his realistic treatment has destroyed the heroic and moral values underlying the myth, and no ending which could reidentify the Orestes and Electra of these plays with their heroic prototypes is conceivable; perhaps he thought it best to underline, by the deliberate artificiality of the form of his ending, the irrelevance of its content.

Chapter 3: Euripidean Tragedy and Religious Exploration

On the first point, I find it difficult to see how these concepts could have been relevant to the ancient audience, in whose eyes a god, who had been zoomed to their religious realities, appears in epiphany with a character whose deification he announces, Helen, whom the audience knew as a goddess; also in their assumptions Apollo speaks the will of Zeus. Why should the unexpectedness of the happy ending, the change from the earlier bleakness, create problems? One of the points about deities *ex machina*, we saw, is that they bring about what to the ancient audience were unexpected developments, instructions, and predictions, correlatively with the notion of the unknowability of the divine will.[491] This happy ending comforms with what the audience's assumptions led them to expect, that Orestes' sufferings will eventually come to an end. What is different here, and what disturbs modern critics, is first, the sharpness of the contrast with the earlier despair and deceptive moves towards disaster; and second, the unheroic nature of the characters. With regard to the first, this is no more than a polarized, intensified version of the unexpected development, reflecting the unknowability, that occurs in many tragedies; as we saw, intensification is characteristic of *Orestes*. As for the unheroic nature of the characters, it was not a consistent Greek expectation that heroic age characters should only be shown in heroic colors. I will illustrate this with an example of a comparable shift in distances in a different medium, Athenian vase painting. Let us look at two different representations of the Dioskouroi. On the first, the stamnos Oxford 1916.68, of c. 440 B.C.,[492] the Dioskouroi are represented as serene and dignified, distanced from the everyday world—in fact they reflect very closely the sculptures of the Parthenon. On the late fifth-century hydria London E 224[493] the Dioskouroi are chubby, flabby, and undignified; the one who is still on foot seems to be almost spaced out; they both look more like playboys out on the razzle than distanced and dignified figures descended from, and consorting with, gods. This comparison shows that a movement towards a lesser distancing of heroic figures from everyday reality in the construction of the characters is a choice sometimes made in another medium in the late fifth century.[494] Thus, the unheroic nature of the characters in *Orestes* was not something the audience would have perceived as needing to be remedied, or as impinging on the credibility of the closure. On the contrary, that unheroic nature brought the characters nearer to the audience, and this made the (ultimately) happy ending more directly reassuring (in the complex ways that it was reassuring).

Reinhardt saw the ending of *Orestes* as ironic.[495] He claimed that when Apollo orders Orestes to marry the girl he was about to kill, and Orestes consents, it becomes difficult for us to take the solution seriously.[496] He remarked that the girl is not asked about this. He asked whether Euripides is ironically bowing to the theatrical convention, and continued: Is therefore the healing so absurd, that thereby theater undermines itself? The ending shows how things should be, not how they are. Confusion without measure dwells in the divine as well as in the human. Where does there remain any sense?

This, in my view, is a culturally determined judgment. We do not know what Euripides thought; but we can, up to a point, reconstruct the ways in which his audience would have made sense of the tragedy, through filters shaped by their cultural assumptions. To start with a simple point, the fact that Hermione's consent was not asked, is part of the Athenian gender discourse. Whether or not in reality a girl had any input in the choice of her future husband, in normative ideology her marriage was a transaction between men. Then, when the audience "judged" what Apollo said, they did so in a conceptual framework in which, first, Apollo had been zoomed to the world of the audience's Apollo, whose representation the Apollo of the play would have been perceived to be; and second, unknowability, and the distance between human understanding and divine will were important representations. Consequently, I suggest, they would not have seen the ending as Reinhardt did; they would not have thought that it shows there is no sense in the cosmos, or that confusion characterized the divine world; but that the divine world is unknowable—with the more reassuring representations of protection from the gods for those who obey them—a notion itself rendered somewhat problematic by the raising of the issue of the prophecy's potential unreliability.

What, then, of the allegedly comic aspect of the play? The hypothesis attributed to Aristophanes the grammarian says that this drama *komikoteran echei ten katastrophen*. The scholion ad 1691 tells us that tragedies end either with a lament or with *pathos*, while comedies end with treaties and reconciliations, and therefore, this tragedy has an ending belonging to the genre of comedy. The scholiast then goes on to deconstruct this simplistic binary opposition he had set out, by citing examples of tragedies that do not fit it. I would go much further and claim that, though the very notion of what constitutes a happy ending is culturally determined, there are several tragedies that can be considered to fall into this category, including *Electra*[497] and *IT*, which are thematically closely related to *Orestes*. In any case, it is clear that all the hypothesis is doing is making a point about genres, which we know to be based on a simplistic perception of a dichotomy, the result of a critic's attempt to systematize.[498] Even this comment, simplistic though it is, only pertains to the type of ending. It

Chapter 3: Euripidean Tragedy and Religious Exploration 413

does not sanction any claim about the tragedy being comic, or having comic elements.

Modern critics have gone much further. For example, Willink[499] claims that "the pervasiveness of the 'comic' elements needs to be recognized throughout the play ... in scenic handling, in topicality, and in countless passages (even lyric ones) with a faintly but unmistakably paratragic flavour."[500] In my view, this is a culturally determined perception of the play. We saw that the topicality of *Orestes* is no different from that of other tragedies in nature or modality, a matter of complex resonances,[501] albeit in this case very strong ones, and that the distances from the world of the audience are no different from those in other tragedies. The topicality of comedy was radically different in nature and modalities. I cannot discuss all relevant *Orestes* passages here, but I tried to show in the discussion of the scene with the Phrygian that it is not comical, and the audience would not have perceived an incongruity between the character and his language. The implicit (and, in my view, culturally determined) assumption at the center of this discourse is that if something in a tragedy is faintly similar to something in comedy the audience would have perceived it to have been comic. Another culturally determined perception that implicitly sanctions and legitimates for modern critics the comic element in this tragedy is Shakespearean plays, in which it is indeed the case that comic elements are found in plays that would otherwise be considered tragedies.

I suggest that the fact that *Orestes* had elements which appear slightly similar to elements that, in a totally different framework, in comedy, are comic would not have led the fifth-century Athenian audience to perceive this tragedy as comic, or even as containing comic elements. For the Athenian audience the context of performance, the fact that this play was a tragedy, was a determining parameter of their perception of the play. Closely connected with this is the fact that the sets of elements that seem slightly similar to modern critics, had belonged to different wholes, and since meaning is created through the interaction of elements with each other, and with the whole to which they belong, apparently similar elements can be understood very differently when not wrenched from their proper context and when read through the appropriate assumptions, which the dramatic poets had shared with their contemporary audiences.[502] Even if it is true that "some of the characteristics of comedy 'infiltrate' tragedy towards the end of the century,"[503] about which I am not convinced, this would not affect the audience's parameter of perceptual differentiation. It is even arguable that if such generic blurrings had taken place, they could have done so precisely because this parameter of perceptual differentiation allowed this to happen unproblematically. If this is right, readings that depend on the assumption that *Orestes* contains comic or paratragic elements would be invalid. What is involved here, I argued, is intensification, of intertextuality and other things, not parody, or undercutting of religious authority.

I hope that it has become clear, first, that, unless we make the presumption of irony, assume that Euripides must have been ironic here, and (explicitly or implicitly) read the tragedy in that light, the notion that this is an ironic play does not arise; and that it is not methodologically justified to make this presumption of irony. I hope to have shown that, when we try to reconstruct the ways in which the ancient audience would have made sense of *Orestes*, in performance, through filters shaped by cultural assumptions they shared with the tragedian, the ironic reading does not work; on the contrary, this tragedy involved serious problematization, including religious problematization, and serious, if complex and difficult, and often open, "answers" were given by the god in epiphany, who was perceived by the audience as a representation of the god Apollo they worshiped.

Appendix 2: Euripidean Endings: Strategies of Closure and Ancient Audiences

Euripidean endings have come under special scrutiny recently, under the influence of studies in literary criticism that focus on closure.[504] Knowledge derived from such studies can be useful, in alerting us to questions and possibilities, such as the possibility that there may (or may not) be common modalities of closure, which may help locate the individuality of one's object of study, perhaps by alerting us to nuances, and also by making explicit the culturally determined nature of both the generation of closure in individual texts, and its assessment by individual critics operating within certain cultural climates.[505] But there are also serious dangers, above all the implicit projection of assumptions derived from modern closures to those of tragedies, and the marginalization of the fact that the relationship between the world of the play and that of the audience in Greek tragedy is unique.

I will be arguing that the studies of Euripidean endings as strategies of closure have succumbed to these dangers, and that their thesis that deities, aetiologies, and epilogues are simply closure devices, the contents and meanings of which are determined by the demands of closure and plot organization, is wrong. For, I will be arguing, these studies have forced Euripidean endings into simplistic schemata, thus emptying them of the significant meanings which they had for the ancient

Chapter 3: Euripidean Tragedy and Religious Exploration 415

audiences. Before discussing specific cases, I should stress that it is methodologically dangerous to privilege a priori one aspect of the tragedies, in this case the plot, over all others. The only argument explicitly presented in support of this approach is the authority of Aristotle.[506] However, as we saw,[507] it is dangerous to structure our understanding of tragedy through Aristotle's views; in this particular case, the notion that a genre which, even in late Euripides, is structured through choral odes, is plot driven is less than plausible, and thus it is especially dangerous methodologically to place it at the center of an investigation.[508]

In the analyses set out above I have, I hope, shown how complex and shifting the relationship between the world of the tragedy and the world of the audience was in each tragedy, and how, as a result of these shifting relationships, the audience perceived, among other things, the deities in epiphany to be representations of their own deities worshiped in cult, and the aetiologies to be zooming to, and have direct relevance for, their own lived religion. To complete my case I need to take on, and demonstrate the fallacy of, the approach centered on the thesis that deities in epiphany, aetiologies, and epilogues are simply closure devices. I will be arguing that this view is only sustainable when tragedies are considered in abstract, as floating texts; that the fact that it is fallacious becomes clear once the attempt is made to reconstruct (even approximately) the ways in which the ancient audience would have made sense of the tragedies in performance, through filters shaped by assumptions which they shared with Euripides, whose parameters of selection were shaped by those shared assumptions.[509] For what is important is how these endings would have been perceived by the ancient audience, in whose religious realities the cults referred to were real cults, and for whom the deities were representations of deities whom they worshiped, and on whom depended their prosperity and indeed survival.[510] I will discuss, engage with, and try to demonstrate the fallacy of the recent comprehensive discussion of Euripidean closures by Dunn.[511]

Dunn begins with lyric epilogues, which he says are closural devices;[512] he believes that Euripides' "closing morals" are not particular, but general, and might fit anywhere.[513] Let us consider the epilogue of *Alc., Andr., Hel., Bacch.,* and, with a different first verse, *Med.,* both versions of which were cited above.[514] Dunn claims that "The gnomic quality of such reflections does not offer up the truth or the lesson of a particular drama; instead it is a general or generic cue that the play is over and that the time has come to reflect upon it as we may."[515] Subsequently (after briefly mentioning some views of some of the scholars who rejected these epilogues, and of some of those who tried to make sense of their deployment),[516] he says, "Rather than reject lines deficient in dramatic meaning, or rescue them by trying to find meaning in them, we need to revise our premises. As Deborah Roberts points out, the last words need not be charged with special meaning."[517] Then, he states, "The closing anapaests should be read less for significant content than as a gesture or ritual of closure."[518]

Here, then, Dunn has moved from the assertion that last words *need not* be charged with special meaning to the presumption that closing anapaests *do not* have any such meaning. This argument is methodologically flawed. In addition, the fact that unknowability was a central category in Greek religion entails that the expression of these perceptions in these epilogues would have tapped into, and activated, significant religious feelings. Finally, as we saw in the discussion of the relevant tragedies, these epilogues were indeed charged with specific significant meanings; each acquires its specific meanings in the specific context of each tragedy; I discussed these meanings with regard to the three tragedies for which I have offered readings above, in the relevant places. With regard to *Bacch.*, without discussing it in detail, all I can say is that this play, above others, articulates the unknowability of the divine world, and the divine will, in a multifaceted and complex way, including in the central myth which, I have argued, above all expresses it strikingly in ways that, I suggested in chapter II.3, were conducive to explorations that ultimately led to the generation of tragedy. As for *Hel.*, I will only point out that its epilogue is comparable to that in *Andr.* in its relationship to the revelations of the *deus*, in the case of *Hel.* the Dioskouroi.

As for the repeated use of the same epilogue, I have argued that the notion that the divine will cannot be easily gauged by mortals is central to Greek religion and especially tragedy; central to its beginnings, on my reconstruction, and central to the continuing importance of religious exploration in fifth-century tragedy. If this is right, since no one would doubt the sophisticated intertextuality of Euripidean tragedies, the explicit and repeated deployment of an articulation of this central perception, in ways that both create specific meanings in each tragedy, and draw attention to the fact that this is one of the central perceptions articulating tragedy, ceases to be a problem and, on the contrary, can be seen to fit the established Euripidean meaning-creation modalities. If this epilogue was first used in *Alc.*, it was then redeployed in a modified form in *Medea*, where we saw, it served a different purpose. *Andromache*, one of the early tragedies in the cluster with intense religious exploration, would be the earliest surviving instance of the "stressed through intertextuality" use of this epilogue.

Chapter 3: Euripidean Tragedy and Religious Exploration

Even the floating tailpieces addressing Nike and requesting a prize in *Orestes, Iphigeneia in Tauris,* and *Phoinissai,* and in some manuscripts of *Hippolytos* after the play's own tailpiece[519] were not, for the audience, a closure gesture wholly empty of any specific meanings other than those of closure: they ended the tragedy with a zooming to the chorus' persona as a chorus for Dionysos in the present. Throughout the tragedy, we saw, the tragic chorus had a double identity; its dominant identity was as a chorus of, for example, Phoenician women, in the world of the play, its weaker one as a chorus of men for Dionysos in the present; the latter was strengthened in certain places through choral self-referentiality; the zooming to the chorus' persona as a chorus for Dionysos in the present through the tailpieces addressing Nike can be seen as a strong, polarized variant of choral self-referentiality. As for the meanings of this epilogue in the individual tragedies, since the text of the end of *Phoinissai* is corrupt, we cannot exclude that in this particular case the tailpiece may be interpolated. It was almost certainly interpolated in *Hippolytos*, which had its own tailpiece. This leaves *Iphigeneia in Tauris* and *Orestes*. As we saw, in both these tragedies the zooming to the chorus' persona as a chorus for Dionysos in the present, which stressed the ritual context of the performance, and so stressed and strengthened the religious dimension of the tragedy, had created significant effects and meanings. Thus, in the two instances in which there are no reasons for doubting the epilogue addressed to Nike, this epilogue adds something important to the tragedy's ending. These epilogues, then, are not "empty" gestures of closure.

Let us consider deities in epiphany.[520] I have argued that in several tragedies the deity who appears in epiphany at the end had earlier been zoomed to the audience's religious realities, and was therefore perceived as a representation of the deity of their lived religion. Dunn, in his consideration of deities *ex machina*, makes various assertions. Thus, for example, he claims that the assurances that the *deus* is acting in accordance with Zeus and the fates are "largely formulaic . . . conventional platitudes rather than signs of a grand design."[521] This is a simple assertion; no evidence is offered to support it, and no attempt made to show how these statements would have been perceived by an audience to whom "Zeus" and "fate" are significant forces and not abstract concepts. Many of these assertions are demonstrably based on culturally determined judgments and the application of culturally determined categories. I will try to illustrate how they are often dependent on an implicit measuring of the tragedies against an underlying perception of an implicit canon of a tight linear plot. For this is the implication of the fact that he takes anything not directly driving the plot forward in a linear manner as being somehow empty, without significance. Thus, in his view,[522] the commands issued by the gods in epiphany are an empty gesture, unless they alter radically the course of events, which, he says, only happens in *Orestes*. "The divine command has a direct and tangible effect only when the result it produces is least plausible."[523]

I suggest that the notion of a tight linear plot coming into play in assessing tragedies is highly questionable. I will try to illustrate, with one example, how this (plot-driven) assessment distorts the reading of the tragedies. One of the examples Dunn gives of a divine command with a least tangible effect, a type of command which, as he sees it, simply ratifies events on stage, is Thetis' injunction to Peleus to bury Neoptolemos. Dunn thinks this injunction is totally predictable and (by implication) meaningless:[524] "[S]ince the body of Neoptolemos has been brought on stage, Thetis reminds his grandfather to give him burial (*Andr.* 1240)."[525] However, this is not what in fact happens in *Andr.* 1240. What Thetis tells Peleus to do is to bury Neoptolemos at *Delphi*, and this, we saw, in the eyes of the ancient audience, was of fundamental importance.[526] Dunn's assessment of the role of the *deus* here, then, depends on a reading that distorts the ancient realities and ignores the complexity of the process of meaning creation through the deployment and activation of the audience's cultural assumptions. Another example of this is his discussion of Kastor's epiphany in *Electra*; he rightly sees that it is significant that Kastor, as a semigod, is inferior to Apollo, but says that if Kastor cannot explain or condone what his master Apollo had prophesied, there was little reason for mortals to take seriously his warnings that they must obey Fate and Zeus.[527] This is a culturally determined judgment which falsifies the ancient realities by assuming that in the audience's perceptions either Kastor was wholly right or wholly wrong. I suggest that the audience's perceptual filters, shaped by their religious assumptions, would have led them to a more nuanced perception. Kastor knew more than mortals, but less than Apollo. When relating to mortals his persona drifts to its divine pole, and he speaks things that mortals do not know. When relating to Apollo his persona drifts towards its "formerly human" pole and shares some of the human limitations of perception. Dunn also downgrades the importance of what he calls the gods' "explanations."[528] Thus, he uses the term "essentially irrelevant" to describe, for example,[529] the fact that in *Orestes* Apollo says he saved Helen at Zeus' command. This may be irrelevant to the development of a linear plot, but it was important to the ancient audience, and the ways in which they made sense of this tragedy, that Apollo was Zeus' instrument.

Eventually,[530] the discourse becomes explicitly intentionalist, or rather, an underlying intentionalism is presented as the only alterna-

Chapter 3: Euripidean Tragedy and Religious Exploration 419

tive to Dunn's approach. After presenting a brief survey of the different approaches to the *deus* in modern criticism[531] he concludes that "whatever the playwright's views on traditional religion, we need to take a new approach, examining the *deus* as one among several closing gestures in Euripides and paying attention to what we may call the rhetoric of closure." There are several problems with this. First, it is not Euripides' views (which are, in any case, beyond our grasp) that matter, but how the audience made sense of a *deus* in performance. Second, Dunn has not shown that for the audience a god *ex machina* was not fundamentally different from other closures, surely a necessary prerequisite to avoid distortion in assuming that the *deus* can be considered as simply one among several closing gestures in Euripides. Then, we saw, that the readings on which Dunn's understanding of the *deus* in Euripidean tragedies is based are culturally determined, radically different from the ways in which the ancient audience would have made sense of those tragedies and those endings. For Dunn the role of the *deus* in Euripidean tragedies is that of a closure schema generating radical subversion. He suggests that "the disruptive *deus* serves to expose" (what in an earlier passage he describes as) the tragedies' incompleteness, "an unfinished performance and an incomplete plot."[532] And this disruption, he continues, challenges "not just the aesthetic unity of the play, but the privileged role of tragedy as a literary and cultural model. The god on the machine is the most spectacular agent of this subversion"; he presents his detailed case for this in later chapters. I hope that my analyses have shown this view to be wrong on all counts.

Turning to aetiologies, Dunn rightly considers the aition to connect explicitly the past enacted in the drama and the audience's present.[533] But in assessing this, he does not take account of the fact that such zoomings take place throughout each tragedy, and are not limited to the aetiologies at the end. He argues against the religious significance of aetiologies,[534] by arguing against the notion that the aition is a vestige of the ritual origin of tragedy: "Yet many aitiologies have nothing to do with ritual. Several are clearly invented, and most appear only in Euripides, the playwright furthest removed from the 'origins' of tragedy."[535] The second view of aetiologies very briefly considered by Dunn is the approaches, such as Foley's, that see a homology between tragedy and ritual, made explicit through aetiologies.[536] The fact that these two simplistic ways of perceiving the religious dimension of aetiologies are easy targets cannot invalidate the notion that, as we saw, aetiologies had religious significance for the ancient audiences. This significance does not depend on the ritual origin of tragedy. As it happens, I have argued that the ritual origin of tragedy does relate to the religious significance of aetiologies, but not as a vestige; it was the context in which tragedy was generated that had made religious discourse part of tragedy—rather, it was one of the parameters that did that, continuing "need," which renewed the importance of religious discourse as one of the things tragedy did, being another. This is why aetiologies are common in Euripides; because one of the things Euripidean tragedies did was to shape a new type of tragic religious discourse. Nor, we saw, does the fact that some aetiologies may be invented entail that they did not have a religious significance.

Dunn's analysis of the aition in *IT* illustrates his approach.[537] He comes to the following conclusions. "We thus have two faulty connections: one between Euripides' aition and what little we know of contemporary practice, and the other between Euripides' aition and events of the play."[538] And, "At the end of the performance, as the audience takes leave of the enacted past, the aition offers the promise of a stable, objective and familiar end in the contemporary world. Yet it fails to deliver such an end, not just by marking the gap between past and present, but by confusing them. If rhetoric becomes ritual and culture becomes text, as they do in *Iphigeneia*, then neither is a stable ground that will serve to secure the other."[539] I submit that these conclusions are based on the neglect of the process of the creation of meanings by the ancient audience. For the ancient audience had not come to Athena's speech cold; they did not perceive the Artemis cults Athena spoke of in isolation from the rest of the tragedy. I hope to have shown in chapter II.1 how the Artemis of *IT* had been zoomed to the Artemis of Athenian cult, especially the Brauronian cult, from the beginning. Thus, when Athena speaks of Iphigeneia as becoming Artemis' first priestess at Brauron the connection between the Brauronian cult of the audience's reality and that of the play had already been established, and Athena's words reinforced it strongly by zooming the former onto the latter.

If there had been differences between their everyday cult practices and what Athena describes, the audience would have made sense of them within this frame, in which the identity of the two was established. If, for example, there had been no actual cult practice of dedicating the clothes of women who died in childbirth to Iphigeneia,[540] the audience may have perceived the divergence, the fact that Athena mentions it as a practice, as the result of the distance between the present and the earliest practices in the heroic age which have now lapsed, but which they would have perceived as making sense. For they stressed a homology which would have been perceived by the Athenians as such: Iphigeneia did not make the transition to the state of *gyne*; for women who did, the transition was completed with the birth of the first child;[541] thus, women who died while giving birth to

Chapter 3: Euripidean Tragedy and Religious Exploration 421

their first child did not fully complete the transition. This failed transition would have created a homology with Iphigeneia. Since Artemis was associated with successful transitions, failed transitions would have become associated with the other *parthenos* involved in the cult, Iphigeneia, who had herself "failed" her transition. The connection with all deaths in childbirth would have been the result of a drift, attracting the whole category to Iphigeneia.[542] So, whether this had been an established cult practice, or had been invented by Euripides, the association between Iphigeneia and women who died in childbirth made sense in terms of Athenian religious realities. Second, Dunn is critical of scholars who postulate that the rites specified by Athena had been part of the cults of Halai and Brauron, and then proceeds to assume that we can know that they were not, simply on the basis of the fact that for some things there is no other evidence to show that those specific rites were practiced, despite the fact that all these rites make sense in terms of what we do know independently about these cults.[543] Familiarity with the primary evidence makes one more aware of the fragility of these *ex silentio* arguments. In fact, some of Dunn's assertions are simply wrong. It is not true that there is no evidence for offerings to Iphigeneia at Brauron. On the contrary, that Iphigeneia received cult at Brauron is a fact.[544]

I will end with some remarks on his readings of the ending of *Heracles*, which both form a chapter of Dunn 1996 and are published as a self-contained discussion in Dunn 1997. Dunn[545] reviews very briefly the various positions concerning the final part of *Heracles* and suggests that the critics who have defended the value of this part tried to read too much into an inconclusive ending, while his discussion asks "why the play ends with an ending erased, with an epilogue that lacks the compelling gestures and redeeming transformation that may give meaning and coherence to the whole."[546] I will not continue with his elaboration of this, and his answers, for, in my view, there is a fundamental misconception here that invalidates all that follows. In the eyes of the ancient audience the tragedy did not have an inconclusive ending; the ending may have been complex and also bleak—a bleakness the audience would have placed in its wider perspective, but not inconclusive. Dunn's belief that it was inconclusive is based on a series of assumptions. The most crucial of these is the misreading of the role of Theseus, and of Theseus' promises of *temene* and future sacrifices to Heracles. This misreading is made up of several components; the first is the overprivileging of generic conventions and schemata, which leads him to take the view[547] that Theseus is playing the role of the *deus ex machina*, but a *deus* without the power or authority that this role requires.[548] I suggest that it is only when one privileges plot and closure at the expense of Theseus' wider persona[549] that it can seem reasonable that these totally different categories may be subsumed into one. I suggest that the ancient audiences would not have seen Theseus in that light; they would not have had set expectations about his role, and thus would not have judged, as Dunn does, Theseus against the yardstick of a *deus* and found him wanting.[550]

Much more important is the way Dunn misreads the actual promise of *temene* and future sacrifices to Heracles by, first, again, measuring them against the characteristics that they ought to have had—if they had been delivered by a real *deus*; then, missing the important point that Theseus does not know that Heracles will be deified. No one knows this in the world of the play, which remains bleak; but the audience's knowledge that Heracles will become a god, that he is a god in their realities, is activated by the word *thysiai*. Dunn also sees a problem in connecting these future honors with the play, since, he says, they cannot be honoring him for the actions in the play, not for his earlier labors since he has disowned them and his madness has overturned them.[551] This pedantic examination of his honors is, I suggest, irrelevant to the ancient audience's perceptions. In their world Heracles was a god and a hero, and this was the starting point in their perceptions of him; in the play they saw him as a suffering man; his apotheosis is activated to put the suffering in a wider perspective. It is on readings of this kind, irrelevant to those constructed by the ancient audience, that is based this conclusion which Dunn offers on *Heracles*: "Overturning familiar ends, yet failing to define new beginnings, *Heracles* explores the unpredictable process of living—one that is governed, if at all, not by divine ends, but by vagaries of chance, and that speaks to the humble and unheroic experience of private, not public individuals. It is the curse and the blessing of everyday, ordinary people (1248) to live their lives in the time in-between."[552] I am surely not alone in being shocked at the idea that fifth-century Athenians would have seen Heracles, and Heracles in *Heracles* in particular, in that light.

Restrictions of space prevent me from attempting a full critique of Dunn's whole book. But I hope to have shown that the notion that for the ancient audiences deities, aetiologies, and epilogues are simply closure devices, empty of religious meanings, is unsustainable.

Chapter 3: Euripidean Tragedy and Religious Exploration

Notes

1. Pressures of space force me to illustrate the ways in which I see Euripidean tragedies operating as—among other things—discourses of religious exploration, without offering the full detailed readings of the tragedies that would have been ideally desirable.

2. Heath, who argues (1987, 49-64) that Euripides was a religious traditionalist, also points out how certain expectations about Euripides have structured the readings of Euripidean tragedies, despite the fact that the meanings of the text point in the opposite direction (cf. e.g. Heath 1987, 50, 54).

3. I have given an example of the ways in which common assumptions and diversity of audience interact, and construct different reactions within common parameters of perception, in Sourvinou-Inwood 1997c, 257-8.

4. Another "alibi," or rather, another modality of false methodological respectability for those who do not want to bother with trying to reconstruct an ancient text's ancient meanings, is the postmodernist professed belief that texts have no meanings other than those created by the reader; for if that were so there would have been countless ancient meanings, and they can never be reconstructed, so why bother? In practice, critics who adopt this position do not always consistently present their readings as their own modern readings, and the distinction is often blurred between these modern readings and the ancient meanings, and claims of "truth" are made, explicitly or implicitly. Anyone who really believes that we can never reconstruct ancient meanings should be prepared to accept the idea that for the fifth-century Athenians Euripides' *Orestes* was a tragedy about a technologically advanced extraterrestrial called Apollo, who fooled the naive Greeks of the heroic age into worshiping him as a god, and doing terrible things because he told them to. Of course no critic would accept this, because it involves concepts alien to the Greeks. In other words, even postmodernists would implicitly rely on the notion that we *can* reconstruct *some* ancient meanings if we take account of the ancient assumptions.

5. Representations does not, of course, entail identification (cf. Sourvinou-Inwood 1997a, 182). Thus, this is not in conflict with Easterling's statement (Easterling 1993b, 79) that in tragedy "the characters identified as gods might be perceived as only partial or oblique reflections of true godhead and not fully representing the true 'reality' of divine beings."

6. I will be setting out a critique of the view that the epiphanies of deities in Euripides were simply gestures of closure in the appendix to this chapter. The earlier view that the gods who end so many Euripidean plays seem mechanical and lifeless, a dramatic convenience or a bow to convention rather than a religious epiphany, was rightly challenged by Knox (Knox 1985, 72). Some commentators underplay more subtly the centrality and primacy of the religious dimension in those facets of the speeches of deities in epiphany that concern religion. For example, the interpretation by Goff (Goff 1990, 111) involves among other things, a distinction in the founding of rites by deities in epiphany according to which only *Med.*, *IT*, and *Hipp.* envisage rituals "that can be seen to repeat the content of the play concerned and thereby to act as prolongations or perpetuations of the play." And of these only *Hipp.* "ends with a rite that includes a reference specifically to music.

The rite and song thus establish at the outset a claim to be considered as self-conscious comment on the play." With regard to the last point, Greek rites involved music, and in the eyes of the audience, mention of a sacrifice, or the foundation of a cult, would have been enough to evoke it. So this distinction is culturally determined. As for the rest, why should the repeating of the content of the play be privileged? Of course the rites founded by the deities in epiphany are connected to the play, and this is true for other foundations as well, such as in *Erechth.*; that is the whole point; when the focus is on these cult foundations, they turn the tragedy into, among many other things, an exploration of an aetiological myth of a cult. In the eyes of the Athenians the rites founded by deities in epiphany would not lose their primacy, would not be seen as primarily a comment on the tragedy, at the expense of the religious dimension, as is implicitly assumed by such hypotheses. They were a closure for the tragedy, and in this way a comment on it, but they were *also*, very importantly, foundations of a cult, and this dimension would never have been marginalized by the rites' relationship with the tragedy, however self-referentially this is constructed.

7. For irony in Sophocles, and a definition of irony in Greek tragedy see Hester 1995, 14-43.

8. I have discussed how presuppositions and hypotheses structure the investigation (which is why the building and testing of models is a flawed method) in Sourvinou-Inwood 1995, 413-4.

9. Lefkowitz 1987, 149-66; Lefkowitz 1989, 70-82.

10. Stevens 1956, 87-94.

11. Lefkowitz 1987, 149-66; Lefkowitz 1989, 70-82.

12. Lefkowitz 1987, 150-3; Lefkowitz 1989, 71-2.

13. Lefkowitz 1987, 153-4.

14. Stevens 1956, 92-3 had already considered the question of Aristophanes' attacks on Euripides, and rightly concluded that *Frogs*, which is considered by some to be the most serious attack, is not in fact any such thing, and does not suggest that Euripides was unpopular and isolated—though he thinks it is arguable that Aristophanes personally may have preferred Sophocles and Aeschylus to Euripides.

15. The shifts in the perceptions of the humorous and funny are illustrated, for example, in the essays in Bremmer and Roodenburg 1997.

16. Cf. on this question Pelling forthcoming.

17. Cf. e.g. Sommerstein 1994, 185 ad 446.

18. Cf. on this Dover 1993, 303-4 ad 892f.

19. Cf. Dover 1993, 20-2 on these verses.

20. On the trial of Socrates see esp. Parker 1996, 199-217.

21. Cf. Dover 1993, 22-4.

22. Cf. e.g. Dover 1993, 12; cf. also op. cit. 21

23. It is true that in his original conversation with Heracles at the beginning Dionysos had said that he wanted to bring back a *dexios* poet from Hades. But this does not mean that Dionysos is "economical with the truth" as the development of the plot requires, as

Chapter 3: Euripidean Tragedy and Religious Exploration 425

Dover 1993, 370 ad 1418 states. For Dionysos in *Frogs* is a comic construct, and different facets of his relationship to tragedians and to his quest for a tragedian come up in different contexts.

24. Cf. also Heath 1987, though he thinks that Euripides was using sophistic ideas for stylistic, emotive purposes, while I will be arguing that he used them, above all, as one of the strategies through which he constructed his religious discourse.

25. Lefkowitz 1987, 163-5; Lefkowitz 1989, 72-80.

26. Cf. esp. Lefkowitz 1989, 72-4.

27. I should mention in this context that the fragment *TrGF* i 43 F 19 does not show that tragedy challenged the religious discourse of the polis; for comparable apparently "subversive" statements in extant tragedies are subsequently deconstructed. But the fact that such a statement could be articulated in a tragedy is itself significant; it reflects the fact that the later fifth-century Athenian discourse encompassed such possibilities in a way that made it conceivable for such a statement to be articulated in a tragedy. (Recent discussions have centered on authorship; on this fr. cf. Davies 1989, 16-32 with extensive bibl.)

28. Cf. n. 4 above.

29. On what I consider to be religious behavior and religious discourse relevant to this point cf. e.g. Parker 1996, 184-6; 200-1; cf. 214; Sourvinou-Inwood 1990a, 303-7; Sourvinou-Inwood 1988, 264-7, 273.

30. Cf. Sourvinou-Inwood 1990a, 295-322.

31. On the various kinds of religious speculation in the late fifth century and on the reconcilability of most with traditional religion see esp. now Parker 1996, 210-14.

32. On the trial of Socrates see esp. now Parker 1996, 199-217.

33. Xenophon *Mem.* esp. I.i. 4, 8, 9, 13.

34. Cf. Xenophon *Mem.* I.i.2; I.iii. 1-4.

35. Thuc. 2.47.4, 2. 53.4. Cf. Parker 1996, 200.

36. Easterling 1988, 108-9.

37. Jouanna 1992, 406-34 accepts that tragedy was marked by religion more than epic through its origin and the circumstances of its performance (407), but states (406-7) that the presence of rituals in the tragedies must not be connected to the cultic origin of tragedy; he does make a connection between the sacred space of the performance and the representation of sanctuaries in the world of the tragedy (408-9), but he does not investigate the nature of the relationship, and only focusses on the dramatic uses of rituals, such as their deployment to mark entrances and exits and to create spectacular scenes.

38. Cf. 211-17; 338-9; 563-5; 770; 783-5; 852-61.

39. Cf. 53-4, 58, 72-5; 225-8; 490-1; 585-7; 775-6; 1116.

40. Something which, we saw in ch. I.2, this exploration of human sacrifice generally does with regard to the distance between the Taurian ritual and the audience's religious realities.

41. On this cf. Kavoulaki forthcoming.

42. The taking of the statue is also mentioned (by Iphigeneia) at 1000-1.

43. On the Plynteria see esp. Parker 1996, 307-8 (esp. n. 63 on the reasons why the statue involved is unlikely to have been the Palladion); cf. also Deubner 1969, 18-22; Parke 1977, 152-5; N. Robertson 1996, 48-52. The relationship between the Plynteria and the rite in *IT* is discussed in Kavoulaki forthcoming.

44. Nilsson 1951, 177.

45. Cf. esp. on the statue 1359; 1383-5.

46. Cf. also the appendix to this chapter, where I show that the view that there was a disjunction between the cults described by Athena and the cults in the audience's reality is mistaken.

47. On this verse cf. Platnauer 1938, 179-80 ad loc.

48. I discussed these recurring epilogues in III.2 n. 132 and I shall return to them below in appendix 2 and in the discussion of the relevant tragedies.

49. I have discussed this myth in Sourvinou-Inwood 1991, 217-43.

50. On *antipsalmous* cf. Platnauer 1938, 75 ad 178-81.

51. Hamilton 1992, 24-5, argues that Euripides is distorting the Choes practices. Some of the arguments on which this view is based are culturally determined, for example, the notion that (Hamilton 1992, 118) "The implication that the contest is a somber affair fits ill with the general atmosphere of a contest (especially one that must end in drunkenness)." But in any case, for my present purposes what matters is that this passage would have zoomed the tragedy to the audience's religious realities.

52. On the weaving of Athena's peplos see Barber 1992, 112-16; Ridgway 1992, 123-4.

53. The fact that it is the Titanomachy rather than the Gigantomachy (as in the peplos offered to Athena at the Panathenaia) that Iphigeneia would have been weaving marks the fact that what is at issue is partial zooming, not identification; the double distancing, non-Athenian and of the heroic age, is not elided, simply diminished.

54. Cf. Platnauer 1938, 152-3 on the various references.

55. On the text see Platnauer 1938, 156-7.

56. Some of the most important are the following: at 692-4, where it is clear that Orestes considers the gods responsible for his misfortunes; references to the notion of the unhappy fate of the Tantalidai, especially Iphigeneia; 199-207; 865-7; and finally 476-8 on the unpredictability of the future.

57. Which I have discussed in Sourvinou-Inwood 1997c, 254-62, 288-96. Kovacs 1993, 51-67 has set out, and discussed the role of, religious references in Medea, especially to the gods. He takes a view (Kovacs 1993, 45-70) comparable to mine in that he argues that there is a theological background based on the traditional Greek perceptions of divine workings in the world.

58. Cf. on this Gould 1973, 85-6.

59. Page 1938, 148 ad 1054. On the verses op. cit ad 1053, 1054.

60. The infancticide is also presented as a perverted sacrifice in some of the images representing it (cf. Sourvinou-Inwood 1997c, 271-2). Cf. also McDermott 1989, 75-8 for a discussion (with bibl.) of the murder as perverted sacrifice.

Chapter 3: Euripidean Tragedy and Religious Exploration 427

61. On this rite cf. Page 1938, xxviii-ix and especially Brelich 1959, 213-54; Brelich 1969, 355-65.
62. In Sourvinou-Inwood 1997c, 260-1.
63. Sourvinou-Inwood 1997c, 260-2.
64. The notion that *Medea* ends in moral chaos (McDermott 1989, 70-1, 115, 118) is culturally determined, dependent on modern perceptions of a simpler "moral order." Kovacs 1993, 45-70 expresses a view not dissimilar to mine with regard to the role of the gods. Both McDermott 1989, 111-2 and Kovacs 1993, 65-7 consider the epilogue significant.
65. Bowie 1997, 45 n. 58 (cf. p. 45: "historical events viewed though not exclusively through religious filters"). Cf. also Zeitlin 1990a, 146-7. (Cf. also Zeitlin 1993, 166-7 n. 42 on Dionysiac motifs in *Suppl.*). The most recent discussion of *Suppl.* by Mills 1997, 87-128 (cf. esp. 104-28), which is focussed on Theseus, and ideological Athenian self-presentation, is learned, but does not, in my view, add new insights; it follows the Zeitgeist in stressing ambivalence and the pessimistic side. One sentence from the concluding part may summarize the author's general position (128): "Human nobility and care for other humans is often set against divine detachment, and sometimes cruelty, by Euripides." But the basis on which the notion of the alleged divine ambivalence is constructed in this tragedy is very flimsy. It is said to be the result of a combination of elements (cf. esp. p. 113). The first of these is the notion that Theseus at 549ff brings into doubt the optimistic perception of relations between human and divine because he says *trypha d' ho daimon*, which Mills takes to mean the god is capricious. However, one, this is one of the two possible alternative meanings of this expression (cf. Collard 1975, 254-5 ad 552-5a), the less plausible one; for a meaning "and this situation is all right for the gods, they gain from it," fits the verses that follow the way "the god is capricious" does not. Two, it is the non-fickleness of the divine that is articulated in this tragedy (cf. below). The second element which, for Mills, contributes to the creation of divine ambivalence is the suffering of Adrastos and others. But this is a culturally determined perception. Adrastos, it will become clear below, would have been perceived to have brought suffering on himself; and the suffering of the mothers, though tragic, and arousing a lot of empathy, would have been perceived as "collateral damage" (Sourvinou-Inwood 1997a, 185-6). Third, "the mysterious oracle whose true interpretation we never learn." This is the oracle given to Adrastos, and Mills' perception of its significance is simply a very much milder version of earlier scholarly discussions (cf. 112-3 for a correct critique of some of these), which are themselves dependent on a rationalist central perception of Euripides as an atheist. For if we focus on the ancient audience, we would conclude that they would not have been disturbed by the fact that they are not told what the oracle meant, nor would this have colored the gods in any way ambivalently. For ambivalence and obscurity are inherent in Greek perceptions of prophecy, and what one does is try to maximize clarity by consulting more than one oracle, and/or deploying more than one type of divination, on more than one occasion before embarking on a major enterprise. If Adrastos had taken prophetic advice before the expedition, above all, if he had followed the seer Amphiaraos' advice, the catastrophe would not have taken place. So, for all the audience knew, the oracle may not have been misin-

terpreted by Adrastos—though he thinks it was. This interpretation and the marriages may not have led to disaster if Adrastos had acted wisely thereafter. The final element which, according to Mills, contributes to the creation of the alleged divine ambivalence in *Suppliants* is "Athena's enigmatic appearance at the end of the play." But this is a circular argument; I see nothing enigmatic about Athena's appearance, nor, I would suggest, would the Athenian audience. To quote Collard "Athena's abrupt and unannounced epiphany at *Su.* 1183 is typical" (Collard 1975, 408).

66. Collard 1975, 112 ad 28-31 formulates this as "E. models Ae's sacrifice on the Proerosia"; Parke 1977, 74 puts it as follows, "Clearly the occasion which Euripides suggests is the Proerosia." On the festival Proerosia cf. Parke 1977, 72-5; Deubner 1969, 68-9; Parker 1987, 141; Parker 1996, 143 n. 85, 225.

67. Cf. 63-4 and Collard 1975, 124 ad loc.

68. The staging of this tragedy has been discussed by Collard 1975, 14-7.

69. That is, by making clear the identity of the sanctuary setting, if it was not already clear through the staging.

70. On the metrical change between the two segments see Collard 1975, 116-8.

71. Cf. 97; cf. Collard 1975, 138 ad 95-7.

72. On this cf. also Bowie 1997, 48-9.

73. 132ff. This is presumably what the audience would have understood from his explanation *Phoibou m'hypelthe dystopast' ainigmata* at 138. Bowie 1997, 48 also takes it in this way.

74. Cf. line 156.

75. Cf. Collard 1975, 190 ad 308-12a.

76. Cf. Collard 1975, 249 ad 524-7.

77. On *hosoi* cf. Collard 1975, 262 ad 594-6a.

78. Bowie 1997, 51-2 sees the last third of the play as closely recalling Athenian public funerals. Cf. also on this Pelling 1997, 230-33. The complexity of the ritual resonances is brought out very persuasively by Kavoulaki, forthcoming.

79. On the funeral speech by Adrastos in (857-917) cf. esp. Pelling 1997b, 230-33.

80. Cf. Collard 1975, 390-6.

81. Cf. on this Collard 1975, 416-7 ad 1208-9.

82. Cf. Collard 1975, 417-9 ad 1211-12.

83. Cf. e.g. 88, 173, 271, 290, 392, 619; cf. 63-4; cf. also expressions that draw attention to the sanctuary buildings represented by the *skene* at 938, 982, 988.

84. Cf. Rehm 1994, 115: "The incogruity of mourning and burial rites in a sacred place associated with fertility and regeneration makes explicit the tension between the drama and its setting"; and on p. 111, "an even more damaging assault on the rites associated with Eleusis."

85. Cf. Clinton 1992, 51-2, 114-5, with a critique of earlier discussions; cf. also 112.

86. Cf. Sourvinou-Inwood 1995, 173-4.

87. Cf. Sourvinou-Inwood 1995, 191-5 with bibliography.

Chapter 3: Euripidean Tragedy and Religious Exploration 429

88. The epitaph Hansen 1983, no 135; cf. also Sourvinou-Inwood 1995, 193 n. 335 with bibl.

89. As Rehm 1994, 111 claims.

90. On the date cf. Collard 1975, 8-14; Bowie 1997, 45.

91. Cf. most recently (with bibl.): Collard 1975, 1013-4, who took the view that the production of the tragedy followed soon after Delion, at the Dionysia of 423; Bowie 1997, 45-56 (on whose discussion cf. below in the text). The question is also discussed by Hornblower 1996, 89-93; and Mills 1997, 91-7 (who takes a sceptical view). The relationship between historical reality and tragedy is an extremely complex topic, to which a recently published book has been dedicated: Pelling ed. 1997c. Cf. esp. the conclusions by the editor Pelling 1997b, 213-35.

92. Thuc. 4.89-101; cf. Hornblower 1996, 286-317 ad loc.

93. Bowie 1997, 45-56.

94. He also takes the view (Bowie 1997, 54-5) that the tragedy had also evoked, and was also seen in terms of, the festival myth of the Eleusinian Mysteries, the abduction of Persephone. On this notion cf. also Rehm 1994, 112-3.

95. Cf. esp. Bowie 1997, 55.

96. Cf. the view put forward by Mills 1997, 94 that "Euripides' emphasis on the impiety of the Argives makes it impossible for an Athenian audience to identify themselves with the Argives, rather than with the representative of their city who proves himself superior to both cities. The Athens of the play is not the real city of 424 but the idealized Athens of the *epitaphioi*." This is somewhat simplistic, for it implicitly relies on three unarticulated (and incorrect) assumptions. First, that the relationship between the world of the play and the world of the audience remains static and inert throughout the play. Second, that it is either a matter of conscious identification or nothing, while in fact there is a whole spectrum of loci from the conscious to the unconscious poles, and a whole spectrum of relationships between the world of the play and that of the audience, from the pole of identification to that of perception of nonrelevance. Third, intimately connected with the first and second, that an audience can "identify" with only one "side" in a play. Finally, and related to all the above, that only one perception of Athens would be presented in the tragedy, and the audience would be limited to that perception, and would not complement, or deconstruct it.

97. Cf. Theseus 1169: *charin memnemenous*.

98. Cf. above; cf. also on this Bowie 1997, 48-9.

99. On this cf. esp. Pelling 1997b, 233-34 with bibl.

100. Cf. on this Bowie 1997, 51-2. Foley 1993, 117-29 discusses the occurrence of lamentation in Eur. *Suppl.* Her discussion is not, on the whole, fundamentally unsound, but it is somewhat marred by the overall perception informing the paper (Foley 1993, 101-43): that while the Athenian social system had tried to control the public behavior of women, especially at the death ritual, tragedy allowed the politics of the past, whether real or imaginary, to reemerge on stage and to reenact the type of social scenarios that may have led to the earlier funerary legislation; this was bolstering the ideology of the public funeral; the

fact that it needed bolstering suggests opposition to, or doubts about, these policies; these plays nevertheless make public and assertive female funerary behavior serve an important cause, or make the attempt to control it at least partially ambiguous, and so raise questions about similar issues in democratic society (pp. 142-3). This, in my view, is a vastly oversimplified and culturally determined perception of a hugely complex presentation of women's connection with the death ritual in tragedy, a perception resulting from readings which deploy by default the culturally determined filters of modern gender discourse. I cannot discuss this here. (I have discussed Antigone's behavior in Sophocles' *Antigone* in: Sourvinou-Inwood 1989a, 134-48; Sourvinou-Inwood 1987-1988, 19-35; Sourvinou-Inwood 1990c, 11-38; I am discussing some other aspects and tragedies in 'Women and the death ritual' in *WRT*, in preparation [cf. ch. I.2 n. 59]). Here I will only mention briefly some of the parameters governing that culturally determined perception, especially the fact that it ultimately depends on implicitly conflating developments that took place in different periods and contexts, as well as on overprivileging the perception of woman as "other," which is only one of the two dimensions of Athenian perceptions of women. In reality, and in the Athenian perceptions of that reality, the limitations on women's excesses at the death ritual were part of the general tendency to lower the tone of the death ritual in the archaic period; because women were ritually and symbolically associated with the more excessive aspects, the limitation drifted to them (cf. Sourvinou-Inwood 1983, 33-48 esp. 47-8; cf. also Sourvinou-Inwood 1995, 344-5; Sourvinou-Inwood 1997b, 163 n. 63 (my reply to Seaford 1994, 79-83); cf. also my review of G. Holst-Warhaft, *Dangerous Voices. Women's Laments and Greek Literature*, CR 44 1994, 67-9). But in controlling women men also controlled themselves, and in being controlled, women were responding to desiderata in social attitudes to death that were not only male. In addition, this limitation of women's participation that took place in the archaic period is a different matter from their marginalization at the public funerals of the war dead in the fifth century, an ideological construct of particular circumstances in the fifth century, and it is not methodologically legitimate to conflate these different things into an undifferentiated whole. These public funerals could only function as they did if the polis took on a role equivalent to that of the family in private funerals, and if it marginalized grief; since the higher emotional tone in the death ritual was associated with women, women were inevitably more marginalized. This is very different from the situation in the archaic period, when grief and lamentations were unproblematically associated with the war dead, as is shown in their epitaphs (cf. Sourvinou-Inwood 1995, 191-5, cf. 173-9).

101. On this episode cf. Seaford 1987, 121-2; Rehm 1994, 111-15; Collard 1975, 354-5; cf. also Loraux 1985, 44-6; Zeitlin 1993, 166-7 n. 42; Foley 1993, 125-6. I am discussing the episode in *WRT*, in preparation.

102. Of course the "ironists" offer their own interpretations of such phenomena. Foley's (Foley 1985) recent version of Euripidean irony and ritual reflects the 1980s Zeitgeist: she acknowledges the importance of rituals and cult institutions, but (implicitly) divorces them from the gods who institute them, and whom, we saw, the audience would have seen as representations of their own gods; for she thinks (Foley 1985, 22; cf. 20-1) that Eu-

Chapter 3: Euripidean Tragedy and Religious Exploration 431

ripides insists on the preservation of ritual performance "while debunking theological superstructure." In her view (Foley 1985, 64), the references to cult that close Euripides' tragedies offer the audience the opportunity to reenact and to reconsider perpetually both the remedies offered by myth and the disasters heroically faced by the tragic protagonists. Tragedy and ritual are linked by a common claim to offer therapy and immortality, despite a reality that may be incommensurate with them. Whatever the cost to the characters in the dramas, citizens can bring the heroism of Heracles and Alcestis into their lives through festival and hero cult. It is part of my own perception that tragedies, through religious exploration, can enrich the perception of rituals, but this cannot happen in Foley's conceptual framework, in which the gods have been debunked. So the implication must be that tragedy somehow replaced religion as the "ideology" of the rituals. It also inherent in Foley's analysis and conclusions that, in watching tragedies, the ancient viewers were blank pages, from which their own religious realities had been blanked out—in fact their religious realities, ritual and theology intertwined, structured their perception of the tragic references to all cult and religious exploration. The fact that Foley does not attempt to reconstruct the ancient perceptual filters makes her readings largely irrelevant to those of the ancient audiences. Thus, to give one illustration, she thinks that (Foley 1985, 18) in the final scenes in *Herakles,* Heracles' "rejection of suicidal despair implicitly denies the repellent and vengeful anthropomorphic Olympians that the audience has just witnessed on stage in the peripety. The play thus concludes by turning against its own mythical tradition." I hope it will be clear in my discussion of this play below that this perception is wrong, based on a culturally determined understanding of a very complex picture, in which no account is taken of the fact that the fifth-century audience did not come to the performance as blank sheets, but made sense of what they saw through filters shaped by their assumptions, in which Heracles was a god; so their understanding of the ending would have been the result of a complex interplay between what happens in the world of the tragedy, and their own knowledge of the wider perspective, which the characters in the tragedy do not have, and which, we shall see, was activated by Theseus' words.

103. *Alcestis* was produced after three other tragedies, in place of a satyr play (cf. Dale 1954, xxxix). Scholars have seen satyric aspects, or at least traces, in the play; the author of one of the hypotheses to *Alc.* goes further, and claims that the play is *satyrikoteron*; he singles out *Alc.* and *Orestes* as unfitting the tragic genre because of their happy ending. I will not discuss this question (cf. the brief discussion in Knox 1979, 255), since it does not affect my argument. I discuss the question of happy endings with reference to *Orestes*.

104. On the prologue of *Alcestis* cf. Segal 1992, 97-8. He notes that this prologue is a particularly clear example of the Euripidean mixture of suspense and prediction in the prologue.

105. On Thanatos and his role in Alcestis' death cf. Sourvinou-Inwood 1995, 306-7, 306 n. 20, 320-1, 321 n.82.

106. Cf. Dale 1954, 87-93.

107. On this procession cf. Kavoulaki forthcoming.

108. Cf. e.g. Rehm 1994, 90-92.

109. 861-934. On the form of this *kommos* cf. Dale 1954, 114 ad 861-934.
110. Alexiou 1974, 178; Sourvinou-Inwood 1983, 38; Sourvinou-Inwood 1981, 26.
111. Cf. on this Rehm 1994, 88-9.
112. At 934-61. I am not concerned with the ways in which Admetos' character is constructed (on which cf. e.g. Dale 1954, xxii-xxviii; Pippin Burnett 1965, 240-55; Conacher 1981, 5-9; Segal 1993, 55-6, 59-62; Rehm 1994, 86-94 passim).
113. Cf. Dale 1954, 121 ad 978.
114. Cf. Sourvinou-Inwood 1995, 195-8, 216.
115. Cf. Apollodoros 1.9.15 (Kore); Plato *Symposion* 179b.
116. Cf. on these alternatives Sourvinou-Inwood 1995, 307 n. 22. The same alternatives of defeating Thanatos by violence or persuading the Nether Gods also occur in the myth of Sisyphos, in alternative versions of his myth: cf. Sourvinou-Inwood 1986, 48-9. But Sisyphos had tricked them, and was punished for it; Heracles planned to persuade them through supplication.
117. Though the cult of Asklepios had not yet been introduced to Athens from Epidaurus when *Alcestis* was produced; on this introduction cf. esp. Parker 1996, 175-85; cf. also Garland 1992, 116-35.
118. Cf. Pherekydes 3 F 35; cf. also Pindar *Py.* 355-8; Stesichoros 194 *PMG*.
119. Cf. Sourvinou-Inwood 1995, 61-6, 304-21.
120. Cf. appendix 2 below and also above n. 105.
121. On their roles in *Alc.* cf. Sourvinou-Inwood 1995, 306-7, 306 n. 20, 320-1, 321 n. 82.; cf. op. cit. 303-56, esp. 338-9, 343-6, 353-5 on Hermes Chthonios and Charon as figures of reassurance.
122. Segal expresses this as follows (Segal 1993, 73): "*Alcestis* uses death rites and hospitality rites to create a visual concretization and perhaps a critique of Athenian society's sharp division of sexual roles and values." I would not necessarily go quite as far as this, but I would agree with the basic concept.
123. Charon and Hermes in the transition from life to death, but also the Nether Gods in Hades, Hades and Persephone. One of the soteriological facets of the Eleusinian Mysteries, to which it is likely that the vast majority of Athenians would have been initiated, was to establish a relationship of benevolence between worshippers and the Underworld gods.
124. On the problems concerning the text cf. Wilkins 1993, xxvii-xxxi; Diggle 1994, 51-8, 220-8, 169-70, 11-13.
125. On suppliant prologues see Segal 1992, 99-100.
126. 399ff. On the performance of sacrifices to obtain omens for the battle and on *sphagia* cf. Wilkins 1993, 101-2 ad 399-409. On sacrifice before battle in general cf. Jameson 1991, 197-227.
127. 403-9; for the text cf. Wilkins 1993, 103 ad 402; Diggle 1994, 222-24.
128. Cf. Kavoulaki forthcoming for a discussion of this procession and its distinct nature.

Chapter 3: Euripidean Tragedy and Religious Exploration 433

129. On this cult of enemy hero: Kearns 1989, 48-50, 164; Wilkins 1993, xix-xx, xxiv-xxv, 177-8 ad 928-1055, 190-1 ad 1040-2; Seaford 1994, 126-9. Cf. also below.

130. Wilkins 1993, 188 ad 1026-44.

131. 849-65.

132. 892-927. On the status of Heracles in *Hkld*. cf. Wilkins 1993, xxv.

133. On this sacrifice cf. Wilkins 1993, xix, who says that this anonymous daughter of Heracles may have been created by Euripides, who may have based his heroine on an anonymous local heroine, and named her Makaria and linked her with the spring in the lost lines at the end of *Hkld*. Cf. Larson 1995, 107-9, 156.

134. Cf. ll. 410-24.

135. As it is, we saw in chapter I.2 and above, in other tragedies.

136. On this passage cf. Sommerstein 1989, 236-8 ad loc.

137. Kearns 1989, 46-8 and cf. 48-53.

138. Hdt. 5.89.

139. Cf. on this Wilkins 1993, xxxiv.

140. Cf. e.g. Hdt 9.26-27. In 9.27 the Athenians tell the myth of their offering refuge to the Heraclids articulated in *Hkld*., as well as the myth which is the subject of Euripides' *Suppl*.

141. Cf. 1036-7: *charin prodontes tende; toiouton xenon proustete*.

142. Cf. e.g. Hes. fr. 25.26-33 M-W.

143. Cf. e.g. 423-4.

144. I am not alone in considering the religious dimension of *Hkld*. to be significant. Cf. Wilkins (Wilkins 1993, xxii) who says that this "is a text of great religious importance," both for the presentation of mythical human sacrifice before a battle and for the institution of the "enemy hero."

145. I have discussed aspects of this tragedy in Sourvinou-Inwood 1997a, 175-84. Here I will only mention those parts of that discussion that are directly relevant to our concerns here.

146. Cf. on all this Barrett 1964, 190-1 ad 148-50, whose translation I am also using here.

147. Barrett 1964, 193 ad 166-8 noted that the series of epithets echoes the language of ritual invocation. The use of *ouranian* here would have been perceived to have been different from that by Hippolytos earlier because here the adjective is separated from the name, and so does not unavoidably function as an epithet—and also because here the context is neutral, rather than charged with an Artemis versus Aphrodite contrast as the earlier one was.

148. On the tense used cf. Barrett 1964, 193 ad 168-9.

149. Cf. Sourvinou-Inwood 1988.

150. On Artemis as a women's goddess in this passage cf. also Zeitlin 1985, 69-70.

151. This is exemplified by e.g. the sanctuary of Artemis Mounichia, in which there is a significant number of figurines and scenes on vases, that belong to the cycle of Aphrodite (cf. Palaiokrassa 1991, 62; 68; 70; 73; 82-4; 92 n. 269; 94).

152. On this lament cf. Barrett 1964, 319-20 ad loc.

153. On the use of the word *arai* here cf. Barrett 1964, 334 ad 887-9, 166 ad 43-6.

154. Cf. esp. of Artemis by Phaedra 228-31; of Zeus by Hippolytos 616ff; cf. also 1092-4; 1169-70.

155. Cf. e.g. 241, 476: both: this situation was caused by a deity; 675; 831-3; 940-1; 948-53; 995-6; 1060-63; 1258-9.

156. Cf. e.g. 401; 443-61, an exposition of the power of Aphrodite over mortals and immortals; 642; 725; 969.

157. Cf. Barrett 1964, 412-3 ad 1423-30. The institution of this rite, and its place in *Hipp.*, is discussed by Goff 1990, 113-29.

158. On the Athenian cult of Hippolytos cf. Kearns 1989, 173; Aleshire 1989, 22 and n. 4. For the association of Hippolytos with Aphrodite in Athens cf. esp. Pirenne-Delforge 1994, 40-6.

159. Cf. Barrett 1964, 3-4.

160. Artemis' promise that she shall give Hippolytos *timas megistas* in the polis of Troezen implies that the cult that will be instituted to him will be within her own cultic sphere, which the transition of *parthenoi* to womanhood through marriage was, in Athens and elsewhere.

161. Cf. e.g. Knox 1985, 72-3.

162. Knox 1985, 73.

163. Knox 1985, 73.

164. Heath 1987, 51 has pointed out in this connection that the rest of Greek literature also contains examples of people complaining about the gods' behavior towards them.

165. Kovacs 1987, 75-6 is thinking along similar lines when he notes with reference to the gods in *Hippol.*, and more generally in Greek literature, that the presentation of the world as not one designed for the satisfaction of human aspiration, a fact confirmed by experience, has a positive role to play in helping people to cope with life, given man's precarious condition.

166. Cf. Sourvinou-Inwood 1997a, 180-2.

167. Though there are strict limits to this *philia*: Hippolytos cannot see Artemis, a fact that stresses the distance between mortal and immortal. On his inability to see Artemis cf. also Segal 1988a, 58; Segal 1988b, 268-9. Cf. also ch. III.4 below.

168. On the date of *Andr.* see Stevens 1971, 5-19. It is impossible to be certain as to whether the information that *Andr.* had not been produced in Athens, given by Schol. Eur. *Andr.* 445, is reliable, and if it is, whether or not it had been destined for a non-Athenian audience when written; cf. on this question of the place of production Stevens 1971, 19-21. But these uncertainties do not affect my argument, since the religious realities implicated in this tragedy were Panhellenic ones.

169. Cf. on these lines Stevens 1971, 109-10 ad 115, 116.

170. Cf. 129-30, 135, 161-2, 253-4, 257-68, 311-5, 357-8, 380.

171. Cf. Stevens 1971, 165 ad 565ff.

172. Cf. at ll. 246; 269-70; 439-40; 603; 680; 860; 900-903; 921; 1203.

Chapter 3: Euripidean Tragedy and Religious Exploration

173. Cf. on this pilgrimage Rutherford forthcoming b, which discusses the theme of pilgrimage in Greek dramatic poetry.

174. Stevens 1971, 193 ad 825ff notes that sometimes in this scene the thought and language recall earlier and later tragic laments. He gives his own interpretation of this, which I cannot discuss here. What is relevant to my argument is the fact of the deployment of tragic schemata reflecting ritual schemata to create these distorting mirrors.

175. Stevens 1971, 215 ad 1014-8.

176. Cf. Hom., *Il.* 21.450-7. Hellanikos *FGrH* 4 F 26; Apollodoros 2.5.9 and cf. also Frazer ad loc.

177. Whether or not Laomedon was unaware of the gods' identity in all versions of the myth, *hybris* was committed.

178. As Stevens 1971, 213 rightly saw; but his formulation ("[T]he reference to Apollo as one of the gods who built the walls of Troy and in the end abandoned them to destruction may have been suggested by the same god's unrelenting enmity to Neoptolemus, as described by Orestes at the end of the preceding scene")—besides the fact that, unlike mine, does not focus on the audience—puts the emphasis on Apollo's hostility, while in fact, as he himself notes (Stevens 1971, 215 ad 1014-8) Apollo had been far from consistently and unrelentingly hostile to Troy.

179. Cf. Hellanikos *FGrH* 4 F 26; Apollodoros 2.5.9.

180. Yunis claims that (Yunis 1988, 91) at 1036 (*o daimon, o Phoibe, pos peithomai?*) the chorus are hesitant to believe any of the indications of Apollo's perfidy that had just been mentioned: the betrayal of Troy; the complicity in matricide, and the apparent complicity with the lying, matricidal scoundrel in the ambush of Neoptolemos. This view is based on a series of culturally determined assumptions: on the first point, it ignores the fact that, we saw, for the audience the chorus' perception concerning Troy was partial, indeed mistaken; on the second it ignores the fact that, however horrendous the matricide, it was ultimately perceived as a necessary tough choice, in an ideology in which the wife killing the husband is a dreadful and threatening thing, and the son is expected to privilege the father over the mother. As for the final point, it ignores the fact that it is Apollo who is using Orestes, and so Apollo's will that is being executed; the moral qualities of the instrument of Apollo's will was not an issue.

181. Cf. on this Rutherford forthcoming b.

182. Cf. on this Stevens 1971, 233 ad 1147, 1148; Rutherford forthcoming b, who convincingly suggests that this represented the epiphany of the deity which is the culmination of the pilgrimage—a negative and dark epiphany.

183. Cf. also Peleus at 1212; cf. 1194-6.

184. Cf. e.g. 17-20, 565-6.

185. Cf. on this Burkert 1983, 119-20 with bibl.

186. Cf. Kavoulaki forthcoming.

187. Line 1269; cf. on this Stevens 1971, 245 ad loc.

188. Stevens 1971, 246 ad 1284ff states that this, and the other instances of the epilogue except that in *Alc.*, are not particularly appropriate as a comment to the play, but have a

more direct relevance to the divine arrangements announced by the deity in epiphany; the fate of Andromache and her child and Peleus' immortality are *aelpta* and *adoketa* to those concerned.

189. I discuss this in appendix 2, and provide further arguments in favor of the positive side of this statement throughout this chapter and in ch. III.4.

190. Cf. Andoc. 1. 30 with 33.

191. Yunis discusses the messenger's reproach together with the fourth stasimon (Yunis 1988, 88-93); I argued above (cf. n. 179) that his comments on that ode were dependent on culturally determined assumptions. As for his overall conclusions, (even leaving aside the fact that he speaks of Euripides' intentions [89 n. 21]) they are, I suggest, wrong, because they are dependent on culturally determined assumptions. He claims (91) that the execution of the murder shows the god to have contributed to the desecration of the rites and purity of his own sanctuary and that "the god, aiding the assailants, corrupts the pious standards of his worship at Delphi in the mean pursuit of revenge." The latter notion is based on a misconception concerning the severity of Neoptolemos' offense of *hybris* and transgression of the human limits; as for the general point, that the fact that the murder perverted the ritual in the audience's perceptions was a manifestation of impiety quickly punished, since Neoptolemos had desecrated the sanctuary and the rites through his participation. Consequently, his remarks (91-2) on the messenger's reproach of the god are not, I submit, relevant to the ways in which the ancient audience would have made sense of the play.

192. Sourvinou-Inwood 1991, 48-9, 66-7.

193. Andromache was the over-the-top fantasy wife, at least in her self-presentation; Hermione was far from a simple example of a "bad wife." I discuss this in WRT.

194. Cf. e.g. Hall 1989, 180-1, 222.

195. On the date of this tragedy cf. Collard 1991, 34-5.

196. On this tragedy's setting and its significance cf. Zeitlin 1996, 172-75.

197. Cf. on this Kavoulaki forthcoming.

198. The *arrhephoroi* and the *Ergastinai* wove the peplos offered every year at the Lesser Panathenaia; the large peplos, offered at the Great Panathenaia every four years, was woven by professional male weavers (on the weaving of Athena's peplos cf. Barber 1992, 112-6; Ridgway 1992, 123-4).

199. As we saw above, a comparable distancing within a zooming took place in *IT* 221-8.

200. 683-725, on which cf. Collard 1991, 166 ad 658-904.

201. On 726-904 cf. Collard 1991, 166. Cf. esp. 752, 787-8; 839-40; 851.

202. On Hecabe's revenge cf. most recently Segal 1993, 157-90 passim; Mitchell-Boyask 1993, 116-34; Mossman 1995, passim; Zeitlin 1996, 172-216 esp. 176-7, 188-92, 199-200, 213-6.

203. Wilkins 1993, 188 ad 1026-44 compares the prophecy in *Hecabe* 1259ff to *Medea* 1378-88 and *Herakleidai* 1026-44.

204. On the role of Dionysos in this tragedy cf. esp. Zeitlin 1996, 172-216, esp. 176, 178-83, 194-5, 210, 214-6.

Chapter 3: Euripidean Tragedy and Religious Exploration 437

205. On the metamorphosis cf. Forbes Irving 1990, 207-10; Collard 1991, 197-8; Mossman 1995, 199-201; Zeitlin 1996, 183-6, 189.

206. In *WRT*, forthcoming.

207. 199-201; cf. 232-3; 721-2; 958-60.

208. 790-4; 799-805; 852-3; 1028-30; cf. 1234-5.

209. Cf. 852-3.

210. The absence of ritual where its performance would have been appropriate, or desirable, is also marked: when the shade of Polydoros at 30 says he is *aklaustos, ataphos* (cf. also 796-7); and, in almost a mirror image when Polyxena says at 416 that she will die unmarried, *anymphos anymenaios*.

211. On Polymestor's transgressions cf. also Zeitlin 1996, 214.

212. On the themes pertaining to the human relationships explored in *Hecabe* cf. also Collard 1991, 25-31; Zeitlin 1996, 208-9.

213. Segal 1993, 224-5 states, "Whatever justice from the gods Euripides intimates, then, is qualified by their remoteness and inscrutability. . . . The gods, invisible and anonymous, *may* be viewed as creating the circumstances that favor this process of retributive justice, but Euripides leaves the question open. Here, as elsewhere, he does not give us an unambiguous theology." But since, we saw, characters express the view that the gods support justice and police transgressions, I believe that this statement needs perhaps to be qualified by the fact that in the perceptions expressed by the characters the world, justice and retribution are ultimately guaranteed, and so policed, by the gods. Cf. also below on justice and the gods.

214. On the social persona of the deceased cf. Sourvinou-Inwood 1995, index, s.v.

215. Already evoked by Hecabe's comparison of herself and her women to the Danaids and the Lemnian Women (886-7) on which cf. Segal 1993, 179; cf. op. cit. 179-82 for the Dionysiac facet of these women's behavior. On one reading (cf. Zeitlin 1996, 172-216, esp. 215-6) this is a Dionysiac plot, in which women take over power and destroy children, a specifically Dionysiac revenge. This is convincing, but I would stress that the fact that here the women, not the god, were the ultimate instigators as well as the instrument, for private, not religious, reasons would have appeared a decisive difference to the ancient audience, so that they would have perceived this as a perversion, rather than a version, of a Dionysiac revenge.

216. Cf. esp. Segal 1993, 161-2. As Nussbaum 1986, 414 stresses, this is not vague bestiality, but specifically traits associated with dogs, including absence of regard for community.

217. Cf. Mossman 1995, 199 with references. Nussbaum 1986, 416 sees the process of Hecabe's transformation to a bitch as a reversal of the Erinyes' transformation into Eumenides in Aeschylus' *Eumenides*.

218. Cf. e.g. Mossman 1995, 199 with references.

219. On this *sema* and these verses cf. also Segal 1993, 159.

220. Segal 1993, 225.

221. It is by (among other simplifications) ignoring the complexity of the relationship between the two worlds that critics reach the conclusion that *Hec.* can be seen as under-

mining ethical certitudes and making problematic the institutions that the polis needs for stability, and as giving answers that were not reassuring (cf. e.g. Mitchell-Boyask 1993, 116, 130).

222. On which cf. Collard 1991, 156-7 ad loc.
223. On the date cf. Cropp 1988, l-li.
224. Cf. on this Cropp 1988, 107-8.
225. Cf. on this Henrichs 1994/1995, 89. Cf. also Zeitlin 1970, 645-69.
226. I am not here concerned with the intertextuality of this passage (on which cf. Goldhill 1986, 247-50)—or indeed of any other; what I am concerned with is its ritual content as part of the ritual skeleton articulating this tragedy.
227. Stinton 1976, 79-82; cf. also Cropp 1988, 152 ad 743-4.
228. Cf. Stinton 1976, 81-2.
229. On this sacrifice cf. Easterling 1988, 101-8; cf. also Henrichs 1994/1995, 86; cf. also on this passage: Cropp 1988, 153-7 ad 747-858. A comparable revenge killing in the course of a sacrifice had taken place in Eur. *Kresphontes* (cf. Harder 1985, 8; Collard, Cropp, and Lee 1995, 122).
230. According to Henrichs 1994/1995, 86 the wreath and the *alalage*, with sacrificial as well as epinikian connotations, mark the transition from the violence of the contaminated sacrifice to the communal celebration of Orestes' victory, in which the chorus is about to take an active part.
231. Cf. Henrichs 1994/1995, 87.
232. On the choral self-refentiality of this passage cf. Henrichs 1994/1995, 87-8.
233. On this crowning and its symbolic power cf. Easterling 1988, 106-7.
234. Cf. Easterling 1988, 101.
235. On the lack of ritual respect to the corpse of Aigisthos which has been brought on the stage cf. Easterling 1988, 107.
236. Cf. on this Easterling 1988, 107-8.
237. Cf. also on this Cropp 1988, 180 ad 1198-1200.
238. I have no doubt that this is the correct meaning of the sentence. Cf. on this Cropp 1988, 179-80 ad 1190-3.
239. On the epiphany cf. also Cropp 1988, 181-3 ad 1233-7, 1238-91, though I do not agree with Cropp 1988, 183 ad 1238-91, 1245-7, that "Apollo's unwisdom has no ultimate justification," as I will argue in a moment.
240. Cf. also 1302, 1296-7.
241. That is why I do not agree with Goldhill 1986, 163 that the divine support for Orestes' action is undercut by 1245-6.
242. Cf. Cropp 1988, 182.
243. Cf. Easterling 1988, 101.
244. For the divine punishment of such perjurers through shipwreck, which may also implicate their innocent fellow travellers, cf. references in Cropp 1988, 191 ad 1355. Oaths were very important in Greek society and policed by the gods.
245. Cf. Cropp 1988, 191 ad 1357-9.

Chapter 3: Euripidean Tragedy and Religious Exploration 439

246. Cf. Cropp 1988, l-li for the view that c. 420/19 is the most likely date for the production of *Electra*.

247. Cf. section iv below (p. 405) for a list of the tragedies belonging to this category.

248. Cf. Lee 1976, 91 ad 153ff on the question whether it is each hemichorion as a whole or the coryphaeus that sings.

249. Cf. lines 142, 279.

250. Where Hecabe "invites herself to begin the *kommos*, the ritual lament" (Lee 1976, 121 ad 279ff).

251. This is how, in my view, the audience would have made sense of this, as an exclamation of despair, not as a rational exhortation, motivated by the desire to avoid ridicule or prevent the desecration of the emblems (cf. Lee 1976, 117 ad loc.).

252. Croally's statement (Croally 1994, 73), "Kassandra's speech (308-40) shifts the play's focus on ritual," ignores the ritual dimension of what preceded it.

253. The language of Kassandra's song has many words with religious meanings and connotations; as Barlow (Barlow 1986, 174 ad 308-40) noted, this language is narrow in range, repeatedly stressing marriage within the context of religious observance.

254. Cf. Zeitlin 1996, 212; Barlow 1986, 174 ad 308; Croally 1994, 133-4, 243-4.

255. Cf. on this Lee 1976, 130-1 ad 329-30; cf. also Schol. Eur. *Tro.* ad 330; cf. ad 310.

256. Cf. 351-2; cf. also Rehm 1994, 130.

257. Cf. Oakley and Sinos 1993, 26.

258. And had had that knowledge reinforced by what they had seen in *Alexandros* (for bibliography on which cf. Coles 1974, 59-61; cf. also Scodel 1980), the first of the two tragedies produced by Euripides with *Troades*. For though this was not a connected trilogy, the events of one play could not have been cut off, excluded from the process of meaning creation in a later play; on the contrary, they would inevitably have helped shape the filters through which the audience perceived the latter.

259. The notion that in *Tro.* it is not clear when Kassandra is speaking the truth, and that Euripides uses Kassandra to challenge the mythic tradition and Aeschylus' Kassandra, and presents her as a critic of mythical truth (Croally 1994, 230-1, cf. 125-6) is based on the notion, in my view mistaken, that what Kassandra says about the Trojans being the real victors would have been perceived by the ancient audience as challenging the mythical tradition. What it might have been seen as challenging, as Croally says elsewhere (cf. e.g. 124ff), is aspects of the ideology of war, a matter that would have been perceived to pertain to her own viewpoint, not to foreknowledge resulting from prophetic inspiration. For the ancient audience who were familiar with the parameters of prophecy, Kassandra's views would not have been in danger of challenging the validity of her prophetically inspired knowledge of the future.

260. Kassandra's ritual abnormality is also correlative with the ritual abnormality which she ascribes to the Greeks: that is why, I believe, it is she who mentions that (cf. Croally 1994, 74) war brought about disturbance of burial rites for Greeks: they have not had their wives' ritual ministrations, their graves are in a foreign country (376-9), and their parents at home have no one to perform the appropriate ritual at their graves (381-2).

261. Among the less significant ones: at 1042-3 Helen supplicates Menelaos on her knees (cf. Lee 1976, 243 ad loc.).

262. On which cf. Lee 1976, 161-4; Barlow 1986, 183-4.

263. Cf. also: 535-6, 538-41; 544-7, 551-4, 561.

264. Cf. Rehm 1994, 131. This is developed and closely argued in Kavoulaki forthcoming.

265. Cf. hypothesis to *Alexandros* l. 32 (Coles 1974, 12).

266. On these verses cf. Stinton 1965, 35-9; Lee 1976, 229 ad loc.; Barlow 1986, 210-1 ad 921, 922. Cf. below on the debate between Helen and Hecabe.

267. Cf. Schol. Eur. *Tro.* 884. On this prayer cf. e.g. Barlow 1986, 209 ad 884; Croally 1994, 80; but cf. esp. Lefkowitz 1987, 154, 163-4; Lefkowitz 1989, 72-4.

268. Cf. Lefkowitz 1987, 163; Barlow 1986, 209 ad 884; Croally 1994, 80.

269. Lefkowitz 1989, 73-4; Lefkowitz 1987, 163-4.

270. Fantham 1986, 272-3 states, "Whether Euripides or his public believed in an afterlife or not, the line offers the comforting image of a child returned to his father's loving care." Leaving aside the fact that the notion that "Euripides' public" might not have believed in an afterlife is culturally determined, if she were right, and the audience believed that there was no afterlife, not only this would not have been a comforting image, but, on the contrary, like in all situations in which the "reader" does not share the ideological framework of the "text," the dissonance would have drawn attention to the absence of an afterlife and so stressed the greater hopelessness of dying.

271. Cf. on this ritual Kavoulaki forthcoming.

272. The issue of his future burial had been raised at 736-8.

273. Kavoulaki forthcoming rightly argues (*contra* Croally) that the absence of Trojans in the procession is a sign of incompleteness, but not of ritual disorder.

274. Cf. e.g. 612-3; 696; 775-6; cf. also 867 (*edoke syn theois diken*). Hecabe speaks often of her bad fate and reversals of fortune: cf. e.g. 98, 101.

275. On this agon (characterized by rhetorical, and generally sophistic, elements) cf. most recently Lloyd 1992, 99-112, cf. 35; Croally 1994, 135-162.

276. On this interpretation, on the fact that Hecabe rejects Helen's version and the motivation she ascribes to the goddesses, but does not reject the notion that the Judgment took place, cf. Stinton 1965, 35-9; Stinton 1976, 71.

277. Cf. Sourvinou-Inwood 1997a, 181-2 on Aphrodite's power over Phaedra in *Hippolytos*.

278. The *bia* in her claim *bia gamei* at 962 had resulted from the power of Aphrodite; cf. Barlow 1986, 211-2 ad 959-60.

279. On this cf. Barlow 1986, ad 845.

280. I follow Lee 1976, 219 ad 858-9 here·for the rendering of *philtra*.

281. Cf. Schol. Eur. *Tro.* ad 1113.

282. Yunis (Yunis 1988, 81-7) makes a distinction between Poseidon abandoning Troy only after his cult had died and Zeus' repudiation of the Trojan worship as expressed in this choral ode, which cannot, I believe, be sustained. All the gods' cults are desolate at the

Chapter 3: Euripidean Tragedy and Religious Exploration 441

beginning of the tragedy, and they are being destroyed, with the rest of Troy, at its end. The departure of Poseidon (and Athena) stands for the departure of all the gods; they can still hear the Trojans' prayers, but they are no longer present in the city. And, I am arguing here, it cannot be assumed that the audience would have taken the chorus' claim that Zeus had betrayed the Trojan worship as being the objective truth.

283. It may be argued that what the audience had seen in the prologue was two actors impersonating Poseidon and Athena; but it is, after all, a group of Athenian men impersonating Trojan women who are claiming that Zeus betrayed the reciprocity established by the cult offered by the Trojans. In other words, insofar as the chorus' anguish is constructed in the world of the play, the world of the play gives a reassuring answer; and insofar as the chorus' anguished questions had resonances in the world of the audience, the audience's perception of the questions would also have been shaped by those reassuring answers that were given before those questions had been formulated.

284. For punishment as an application of the principle of reciprocity cf. Burkert 1996, 133-4.

285. Cf. Schol. Eur. *Tro.* ad 1240.

286. Cf. Sourvinou-Inwood 1995, index, s.v. memory survival.

287. Here and at 1280-1, where she had invoked the gods and then said *kai ti tous theous kalo? kai prin gar ouk ekousan anakaloumenoi*. Yunis (Yunis 1988, 86-7) has taken the passages 1240-2, 1280-1 and also 1288-90 together, and out of their full context, and (on p. 87) he claims that the fact that the gods did not reciprocate the cult led to (as he claims [p. 83] it did with the chorus) a lapse of belief; he claims that Hecabe's belief that divine reciprocation is not forthcoming has led her at 1280-1 to forego the prayer she might have uttered; she has reached the point where she declines to worship the gods. At 1281, by suggesting that the gods did not even hear the appeals made to them, she doubts the belief that the gods pay attention to human affairs. In my view this interpretation is wrong. First, *ouk ekousan anakaloumenoi* surely does not mean that they did not hear, but that they did not listen to her prayers, they did not respond in the way Hecabe had asked them to. And she does not refrain from addressing the gods ever again after 1280-1; on the contrary, she does so, as Yunis admits, at 1288-90; and when at 1290 Hecabe asks Zeus *tad' hoia paschomen dedorkas?*, to which the chorus responds at 1281 *dedorken*, it is not part of her doubt of the belief that the gods pay attention to human affairs, she does not doubt whether the gods even see the Trojans' suffering; it is, surely, a less insolent version of a "Do you see what you have done now?" type accusation. This is on the same lines as 1240-43, where Hecabe had expressed the belief that the gods do take an interest in human affairs, but that they hated Troy, but then again, they had done the Trojans a favor by giving them immortality in memory.

288. There are also some other religious references in this tragedy. For example, at 766 Andromache says she cannot believe that Helen, whom she calls a *ker* to Greeks and barbarians, is the daughter of Zeus.

289. Thuc. 2.47.4, 2. 53.4. Cf. Parker 1996, 200.

290. In Aeschylus also there is failure of reciprocity between men and gods (cf. Aesch. *Agam.* 1168-71). But in *Tro.* this failure of reciprocity, of *charis*, is a central concern, very strongly stressed and explored. This, and other elements are, I will be arguing, aspects of Euripides' religious discourse.

291. It is clear that I disagree with Croally's view (Croally 1994, 84) that *Troades* dramatizes how divine self-interest conflicts with the notion of reciprocity, which conventionally governs human-divine relations; and that the power of the gods is apparent, but it is not clear that that power can be worshiped, and thereby brought over to worshippers' side; that the play not only shows women questioning the value of the gods to mortals, but also doubts about the difference of gods from men; that it suggests that, if the gods are self-interested, if they can change allegiance at will, if they are subject to human flaws such as vanity and stupidity, then in what sense are they different from humans? I believe that, when made sense of through the ancient filters shared by Euripides and his audience, the tragedy does not suggest any such thing. It explores very difficult questions in the light of harsh realities; but the image presented is ultimately reassuring.

292. What I am suggesting happened here, the ways in which the audience would have made sense of this failure of reciprocity, is what, as Burkert (Burkert 1996, 142) remarks while commenting on the Delphic oracle's reply to Kroisos' accusation of failure of reciprocity, happens when Greeks were faced with an apparent failure of reciprocity by the gods; the council of piety is to take a selective yet optimistic view. (Burkert 1996, 141-45 discusses failure in, and criticisms of, reciprocity.)

293. Parker 1997, 143-60.

294. Parker 1997, 155.

295. Parker 1997, 154-5.

296. If it is right that the presentation of the sacked Troy through its women's suffering would have evoked for the audience, in however unfocussed a manner, and at whatever point of the conscious-unconscious spectrum of meaning creation, the destruction of Melos by the Athenians in the previous year (on this question cf. esp. most recently Croally 1994, 231-4; cf. also Cartledge 1997, 31-2), this may have helped increase the symbolic distance between Athens and the destroyed city in the tragedy, by aligning the Athenians more closely with the Greek victors—and thus distancing them from the victims. This would have helped distance the sacked Troy from Athens. The tragedy was indeed disturbing, but also distanced. The perception of the enemy as like oneself is one of the modalities of thinking about the other in the Greek collective representations, and therefore the distance would be unstable; but, I argued, there were various factors that prevented that distance from collapsing.

297. On the text of *Herakles*: Diggle 1994, 90-108, 171-5; Bond 1981, xxxii-v.

298. I.e. 415-406; cf. Bond 1981, xxx-xxxii.

299. On the ways in which the myth articulated in this Euripidean tragedy differs from other versions of Heracles' myth cf. most recently Bond 1981, xxvi-xxx; Mills 1997, 131-6.

300. This is not altered by Lykos' claim at 148-9 that Zeus' paternity of Heracles was an empty boast by Amphitryon. Cf. Amphitryon's reply at 170-1.

Chapter 3: Euripidean Tragedy and Religious Exploration 443

301. On the text cf. Bond 1981, 78 ad loc.

302. Cf. Wilamowitz 1959, iii, 46-8; Bond 1981, 112 ad 170-235; 113 ad 170.

303. According to Wilamowitz 1959, iii, 48 ad 177 Zeus' chariot.

304. There are also other references involving the divine world and its interaction with humanity in this segment. At 211-2 Amphitryon says that *ei Zeus dikaias eichen eis hemas phrenas* Lykos would have been killed by us, who are Lykos' betters. And then at 215-6 he advises Lykos not to do violence, lest he himself suffer it, *hotan theos soi pneuma metabalon tychei.*

305. On such violations and threatened violations cf. Bond 1981, 126 ad 240ff.

306. Yunis 1988, 142 notes that Amphitryon inverts the traditional elements of prayer diction in the service of reproach rather than praise.

307. Cf. Bond 1981, 146-7; cf. also 150-2. Bond notes (Bond 1981, 147) that this ode "has several formal features which suggest that Euripides had hieratic forms in mind."

308. Cf. references to ancient sources and bibliography on this myth in Bond 1981, 218-9 ad 613, to which add Sourvinou-Inwood 1997b, 144, 153. Seaford 1994, 378-9 argues that Heracles' return and the salvation of his kin that this achieves is "described in language evocative of the mystic transition" (op. cit. 378).

309. Cf. e.g. Bond 1981, 243 ad 687, and cf. esp. Rutherford 1994/5, 124-5.

310. Cf. also Wilamowitz 1959, iii, 148-9 who, however, thinks of this (or rather, of the part of the choral self-referentiality he identifies) as a break in the illusion.

311. Cf. Bond 1981, 255 ad 734-62.

312. Bond 1981, 263-4 ad 763-814.

313. Bond 1981, 265 ad 763ff.

314. On the case for deleting 762 cf. Bond 1981, 263 ad 762.

315. Cf. Rutherford 1994/5, 125.

316. On this combination of fate and Zeus cf. Bond 1981, 282 ad 828f.

317. Cf. Bond 1981, xxvi, 285 ad 841f. with bibliography and critical discussions.

318. Cf. Apollodoros 2.6.2; rationalizing version in Pausanias 10.13.8. This myth's first extant representation is on a bronze tripod leg of c. 700; it was popular in Attic vase painting of the second half of the sixth century (cf. Gantz 1993, 437-9).

319. Cf. Homer *Odyssey* 21.13-38 (cf. Russo, Fernandez-Galiano, Heubeck 1992, 150 ad 13, 131-2); cf. also Apollod. 2.6.2.

320. Cf. Soph. *Trach.* 270-9. On the different variants cf. Gantz 1993, 434-7.

321. Cf. e.g. Apollodoros 2.6.2.

322. For example, in this tragedy the Gigantomachy took place before the completion of the Twelve Labors, as it did in Diodoros Siculus (4.21.5-6), while in Apollodoros it happens a significant time after that completion (Apollodoros 2.7.1).

323. On Heracles' confrontations with gods cf. Gantz 1993, 454-6.

324. Cf. e.g. Bond 1981, xxvi; Yunis 1988, 151. But cf. also Silk's remarks (1985, 16-7) on Heracles' connection with Lyssa.

325. Lyssa has a special connection with Heracles because he is associated with madness: cf. Silk 1985, 16-7 on this connection.

326. Cf. also 1119, 1122.

327. Cf. Bond 1981, 304-5 ad 906-9.

328. In the perceptions reflected in "proper" human sacrifices represented in tragedies.

329. For example, by Bond 1981, xxii.

330. An opinion expressed (in a personal conversation) by an internationally eminent jurist. In fact, even with the deployment of modern assumptions, whether a deity is judged unjust for making the innocent suffer depends on the general assumptions through which a text is approached, and on where the weight of the story is seen to lie; Job's suffering has not led to the perception that the god of the Old Testament was unjust.

331. As thought, for example, by Bond 1981, xxi-xxii.

332. Wilamowitz 1959, 217 considers 1016-27 as like a stasimon, or, rather, truly a stasimon.

333. Cf. on this myth with references to texts and images Gantz 1993, 439-41.

334. Cf. Plutarch, *Greek Questions* 58 with an aetiological myth.

335. According to Loraux's interpretation (1990b, 21-52), Heracles' excess of virility is connected to his association with things feminine. His excess of virility leaves his strength in constant danger of being exhausted; so it is appropriate that he should occasionally return to a more reasonable level of male energy. But Heracles cannot be moderate, nor can moderation balance the excess; he can only acquire this equilibrium by balancing one excess against another: against an excess of masculinity feminine elements that are, for a male hero, an excess of femininity.

336. Cf. Apollodoros 2.4.10.

337. In Pausanias 9.27.5-7.

338. For example, the kings of Sparta and of Macedon.

339. Cf. Bond 1981, 329 ad 1028ff.

340. Cf. Bond 1981, 332 ad 1042-87.

341. A word denoting both wilfulness and remorselessness. Cf. also Wilamowitz 1959, iii, 252 ad 1243; Bond 1981, 379 ad 1243.

342. Cf. on this expression Bond 1981, 379 ad 1244.

343. *hostis ho Zeus*; on the use of this expression here cf. Bond 1981, 383-4 ad 1263.

344. Cf. on this mytheme Loraux 1990b, 41-6; Gantz 1993, 460-3.

345. Yunis 1988, 156 seems to take Heracles' pronouncements as "the truth," which Heracles has now realized, and says that any meaningful reciprocity with Hera and also (op. cit. n. 29) Zeus is impossible. I suggest that the audience, making sense of this passage through filters shaped by the assumptions set out here, would have perceived Heracles' pronouncements in a much more complex way, and would not have assumed that reciprocity with Hera and with Zeus is impossible.

346. Theseus had correctly guessed that Heracles' madness was Hera's work at 1191.

347. According to an almost certainly post-Hesiodic passage in *WD*, 173a-b (on which cf. West 1978, 194-5 ad 173a-e), eventually Zeus freed Kronos and made him the ruler of the Islands of the Blest.

Chapter 3: Euripidean Tragedy and Religious Exploration 445

348. That is why in Aeschylus *TrGF* iii F 281a it is unequivocally the case that Zeus had justice on his side.

349. On this expression cf. Wilamowitz 1959, iii, 269 ad 1332; Bond 1981, 396 ad 1331-3. On the mytheme that Theseus gave some of his shrines to Heracles cf. Parker 1996, 169.

350. It is interesting to note that there was a story (Diod. Sic. 4.39.1) acording to which the Athenians had been the first to honor Heracles as a god with *thysia* sacrifices.

351. It has been suggested on the basis of 1331-3 that Heracles "is apparently to die" in Athens (Mills 1997, 134-5, who thinks this is an invention of Euripides which not even the Athenians took up). This is a mistaken inference; the implication may be that Theseus expects that Heracles will die in Athens, though even this would not have been unequivocally so perceived by the audience; but then Theseus also thinks that Heracles will go to Hades, and the ancient audience, in whose world Heracles was a god, will have known that Theseus was mistaken about this.

352. This part of the statement, and the ascription of the stories to *aoidoi*, is close to Xenophanes DK 21 B 11, in which he says that Homer and Hesiod have attributed to the gods things that among men bring reproach and blame, adultery, stealing, and mutual deception. Cf. Stinton 1976, 83-4.

353. On this passage, which has excited much interest, cf. Bond 1981, 399-400 ad 1341-6, who rightly insists on the significance of the context.

354. On this meaning of *dystenoi logoi* cf. Bond 1981, 401 ad 1346.

355. This is the position, that Heracles is not denying the stories told by the poets, but expressing his disapproval, saying that gods should not behave like this, taken by Stinton 1976, 83; cf. also Yoshitake 1994, 147.

356. Cf. on this Wilamowitz 1959, iii, 271 ad 1346; Bond 1981, 400 (ad 1341-6).

357. The story (Aristotle *Rhetor.* B 23.27 1400b) that Xenophanes had been consulted by the people of Elea as to whether they should offer *thysia*, "sacrifices," and laments to Ino Leukothea, and he had replied, that, if they think that she is a goddess they should not lament her, and if they think she is mortal (i.e. a heroine) they should not offer her *thysia*, "sacrifices," indicates that even Xenophanes had been appropriated, integrated into the religious mainstream, in the sense that the collective perceptions of him were such that a construct "Xenophanes" was deployed as a means of problematizing a traditional ritual from a rationalizing perspective. (Cf. also [Xenophanes to the Egyptians about deities in general]: Plut. *Mor.* 171D-E, 379B; Xenophanes to the Egyptians about Osiris: 763D). Interestingly, this consultation and reply is elsewhere associated with Lykourgos and Thebes (Plut. *Mor.* 228E; *Lykourgos* 26).

358. Yunis (Yunis 1988, 159-62), who believes that in this passage Heracles is concerned with a philosophical understanding of divinity, thinks that *tous theous* at 1341 does not refer to the Olympians (for it would be absurd for Heracles to deny that Zeus committed adultery) but to the proper gods defined at 1345-6. So the Olympians exist and can do harm, but they are not proper gods. This view is, first, dependent on the a priori presupposition that a tragic character has to have a consistent and logical viewpoint throughout. Then, given that Heracles himself, as well as Hera and the other Olympians, were cult

recipients in the world of the audience, I find it very difficult to see how the audience could have made this jump of comprehension, instead of understanding what Heracles says in terms as being what Heracles thought (when he was a mortal and only saw part of the picture). I am suggesting that the gods' self-sufficency could have been seen as possibly one aspect of the truth, by at least one segment of the audience, and so could have been accommodated in the traditional religious framework. Yunis does not attempt to reconstruct the ways in which the audience would have made sense of this passage, and in addition appears to be talking of Heracles as though he were a real person who had a doctrine—at least, this is the impression given by the formulation (Yunis 1988, 163): "It must be confessed that Heracles does not say enough about his notion of divinity for us to understand thoroughly the positive doctrine he is propounding." The flaws derived from this lack of attempt to focus on the audience continue. For he goes on to say that (164-166) Wilamowitz and others have been wrong in thinking that Heracles is positing a deity whose absolute self-sufficiency puts it out of contact with mankind. According to Yunis, what Heracles wants is just reciprocity; as Plato did in the *Laws*, Heracles demands gods with a morally exacting standard of reciprocation, rather than abandoning the idea of reciprocation altogether. However, this is not what Heracles says. And the audience, unlike Yunis, had not read Plato's *Laws*, and did not scour the philosophical literature to find a matching doctrine through which to interpret this statement, nor did they assume that Heracles was propounding a coherent alternative theology, which became progressively clearer through the play (cf. Yunis 1988, 149-50). And, I suggest that an ancient audience, accustomed to relationships with deities based on reciprocity—even if it is not perfect reciprocity, and sometimes it takes forms that are not immediately intelligible to humans, which is, in my view, the way they would have perceived Heracles' case—would have understood that what was implied by the notion of self-sufficient gods would be gods not involved in any reciprocity.

359. On the meaning of 1361 cf. Bond 1981, 405 ad 1361.

360. On the text of 1420 cf. Bond 1981, 414-5 ad 1420f.

361. The widespead notion (cf. brief discussion in Bond 1981, 416 ad 1425f) that this *gnome* expresses the main moral of the tragedy, that it is the only positive thing in it, depends on a reductionist view of the complexities of *Heracles*, and above all on a culturally determined perception of the ways in which the ancient audience would have made sense of the gods, and of religious issues in general, in this tragedy. For, I am arguing, these perceptions were neither as simple, nor as uncompromisingly negative and bleak, as it appears to modern readers.

362. Silk 1985, 14-5 perceives a more linear shift in Heracles' persona, in that he thinks that "for the rest of the play" after 921, Heracles is a man. I hope to have shown above that this is incorrect, and that his distance from ordinary humanity, and the evocation of his deification continue, with the latter, constructed in Theseus' speech, playing an important part in the tragedy's meaning creation.

363. On the textual problems and the question of interpolation cf. Mastronarde 1994, 39-49 and passim, cf. esp. 591-4; Diggle 1994, 341-61 (353-61 is a review of Mastronarde 1994). On the date cf. Mastronarde 1994, 11-4.

364. Cf. 109-10, 151-2, 154-5, 174-7.

365. Cf. on 344-6 Mastronarde 1994, 247 ad 345, 346.

366. Cf. on 347-8 Mastronarde 1994, 247-8 ad 347-8.

367. On the order of lines at 408-14 cf. Mastronarde 1994, 264 ad 408-14.

368. On these verses cf. Mastronarde 1994, 265-6 ad 412, 413.

369. Mastronarde 1994, 269 ad 433 says that "the traditional nature of Pol.'s values is suggested by the number of times that he invokes and refers to the gods" while "Et. refers to the gods only in mocking repartee (604-8) and in his prayer to the abstraction Eulabeia (782-3n.), though there is a reported prayer in 1372-5." In other words, he thinks that character is constructed also with the help of the deployment of ritual—though I would see Polyneikes' character construction as indicating persona presented rather than values held.

370. Mastronarde 1994, 280 ad 467-8 notes that Jocasta's prayer at 467-8 and the chorus' at 586-7, which are both futile, frame the formal *rheseis* of the *agon*.

371. Cf. Mastronarde 1994, 286-7 ad 491, 492, 493.

372. On Tyrannis as a goddess cf. Mastronarde 1994, 292-3 ad 506.

373. The meaning "altars" is more likely than "statues," given the expression *theon te deximel' agalmata*, but the "statues" cannot be wholly excluded; cf. Mastronarde 1994, 328 ad 632.

374. For the ways in which these myths relate to the tragedy cf. Mastronarde 1994, 330; on the links between the parodos and the first stasimon and the notion that the choral odes of *Phoin.* form a song cycle cf. Mastronarde 1994, 330-1 with bibliography.

375. On this use of *euiois* cf. Mastronarde 1994, 339 ad 656.

376. Cf. on this Mastronarde 1994, 340 ad 662.

377. Cf. on this Mastronarde 1994, 345 ad 689.

378. 757-83. Mastronarde 1994, 364 ad 757-65 rightly notes that Eteokles, who was the sole *kyrios* of his *oikos*, is passing this responsibility on to Kreon.

379. On the authenticity of these lines cf. Mastronarde 1994, 368-70 ad 774-7.

380. Mastronarde 1994, 371-2 ad 782-3 takes this (because it involves the personification of the abstraction *eulabeia* and the enthusiasm of the superlative as well as the criterion of usefulness) to be unconventional, which is true, but also, by implication, through the comparison to Men. fr. 614.3-4 K-T, cynical. I think what we have here is a complex trope, based on metonymy—despite the fact that it was not recognized as such by the scholiast ad Eur. *Ph.* 782, whose explanations as to why they should pray to Eulabeia are consequently lame (so that they should attack without fear, or so that she should put fear in their enemies). I suggest that the Athenian audience would have made sense of it in the way suggested here—without necessarily consciously unpacking the trope—because for them the following assumptions will have come into play in the process: "It is the gods who can choose to save the city; piety can ensure the help of the gods to save the city;

therefore piety is useful—an explication of the reciprocity that governs the relationship between gods and mortals; we pray to the gods to save the city." These, through the personification of piety, have generated the trope "we pray to piety, the most useful of the gods to save the city." But, it may be asked, what this trope be saying? If piety is thought of as a goddess Eulabeia, praying to her would involve offering her honors, acknowledging her *time*, thus acknowledging the importance of piety towards the gods, and, implicitly, the possibility that the person's, or the polis', piety may have been somewhat deficient until now. Thus, the audience would not have perceived Eteokles' prayer as cynical, but as humble. On Eulabeia and this passage cf. also Willink 1990, 183-5, 190.

381. On 840 cf. Mastronarde 1994, 395 ad 840.

382. Cf. chapter I.2.

383. For the case against the excision of 869-80 and 886-90 cf. Mastronarde 1994, 400-1 ad 865-95.

384. Cf. on these verses Mastronarde 1994, 402-3 ad 871.

385. Schol. Eur. *Ph.* 871.

386. I am less certain than Mastronarde 1994, 416 ad 939 that at 933 the chthonic ritual suggests a general sense "earth" rather than Ge.

387. The comments on the sacrifice of Menoikeus by Foley 1985 (in a chapter that also contains some perceptive comments on individual points) are, in my view, culturally determined constructs, as the following statement (from p. 133) illustrates: "If Menoeceus' sacrifice was, as most scholars think, a Euripidean addition to the myth, in the *Phoinissai* Thebes is 'saved' through the poet's intervention. The death of Menoeceus is indeed, as Tiresias characterized it, a *pharmakon* (893), a cure that salvages a plot in which the characters are, as Oedipus was said to be when he cursed his sons, sick (66), or unable or unwilling to listen to a divine voice." This comment undoubtedly appeals to the modern reader, but in its irrelevance to the ancient audience it is, I believe both an illustration of, and a metaphor for, the culturally determined nature of the reading. For this approach governs Foley's reading of the tragedy, in which the emphasis is on (a 1980s perception of) Euripides, and the ancient audience is totally ignored.

388. Cf. Mastronarde 1994, 441 ad 1034-5.

389. But it does have, for example, a reference at 1110-1 to the prophet Amphiaraos, who carried *sphagia*, sacrificial animals for the prebattle sacrifice, in his chariot. This has created difficulties for commentators who believe that by that time the *sphagia* would have been already sacrificed; the scholiast (ad loc.) gives an explanation that fits the modalities of the culture, that he carried them so that he could slaughter, and take omens from, them immediately, if a need for prophecy arose; Mastronarde (1994, 461 ad 1110) does not find this plausible, and opts for carelessness, by Euripides or an alleged interpolator.

390. On the problems concerning the exact meaning of 1200-1 cf. Mastronarde 1994, 482-3 ad 1200-1.

391. On the textual problems cf. Mastronarde 1994, 486 ad 1217-63.

392. Cf. Schol. Eur. *Phoin.* 1241.

Chapter 3: Euripidean Tragedy and Religious Exploration 449

393. Cf. Mastronarde 1994, 496-9 ad 1255-8.

394. For the authenticity of 1265-9 cf. Mastronarde 1994, 501 ad 1265-9.

395. Cf. on this Mastronarde 1994, 502-3 ad 1266.

396. There is no reason to doubt the authenticity of these lines; cf. Mastronarde 1994, 520 ad 1320-1.

397. For this distribution cf. the discussion in Mastronarde 1994, 524-5 ad 1340-3.

398. On prothesis cf. Sourvinou-Inwood 1983, 39 and bibl. in n. 35; Sourvinou-Inwood 1995, 187, and bibl. in n. 313, 217-8.

399. On which cf. Mastronarde 1994, 553, and 554-5 on its authenticity.

400. Cf. Mastronarde 1994, 563-4 ad 1489-90, 1490-1. On female ritual mourning gestures see Sourvinou-Inwood 1983, 37-8.

401. That is, as the scholiast (Schol. Eur. *Phoin.* 1503) explains it, the work of the Erinys, in which (i.e. work and so the deaths that work brings about) she delights.

402. Cf. Mastronarde 1994, 583 ad 1556. On *alastor* cf. below section 10 (p. 387).

403. I follow Mastronarde 1994, 590-4, 627-8, 635-7 ad 1736-57, 642-3 ad 1758-63, in considering the play to have ended at 1736, with the iambic part of the exodos (1582-1709) being genuine except for some lines, and the lyric tailpiece (1710-36) being genuine. But as regards the epilogue, though this particular epilogue may or may not be interpolated, the reasons Mastronarde 1994, 645 ad 1764-6 gives against its authenticity are not, I suggested (ch. I.2 and n. 132), convincing. I will return to these epilogues in appendix 2 below. Mastronarde 1994, 637 takes the view that there may have been some choral statement after 1736, now lost.

404. I am not taking any position as to exactly what this means; cf. the discussion in Mastronarde 1994, 603-4 ad 1611.

405. I accept Mastronarde's (Mastronarde 1994, 610-1 ad [1637-8]) argument against the authenticity of 1637-8.

406. Which would have been buried eventually by someone (I discussed this in Sourvinou-Inwood 1989a, 147).

407. Mastronarde 1994, 626 ad 1703-7 rightly defends these lines.

408. The interpolated parts (which appear to have been in the Alexandrian edition [cf. Mastronarde 1994, 636]) are full of ritual, which suggests that in the interpolator's perception ritual was significant in the Euripidean tragedy. After Antigone had reiterated her determination to cover Polyneikes' corpse with earth (at 1743-6), there is a short exchange centered on ritual (1749-57): Oidipous urges Antigone to supplicate at the gods' altars, to which she replies that they have had their fill of her misery; he then urges her at least to go to Dionysos' *abatos sekos* on the mountains. In her reply (1753-7) she expresses the expectation that worship established a relationship of *charis* with the gods, and her disgust that, as she sees it, in her case the gods did not honor the relationship. Is the interpolator here, then, operating on the assumption that it would fit Euripides' tragic composition to suggest that there is no point in worshiping the gods? I suggest not. First, such an attitude would have involved the elision of human responsibility, while in the ancient perceptions Antigone was as much a victim of the actions of the male members of her family as of fate,

since even in this case limit the double motivation is valid; and there was no contract with the gods that said if one worshiped them they would be taken care of whatever the circumstances, and whatever other people did. And then because of the perception articulated in last words that the interpolator gave Oidipous at 1763, that mortals have no choice but to bear whatever the gods choose to send.

409. I argued (Sourvinou-Inwood 1989a, 146-8) that this is what Kreon had done wrong, and this is the difference between Kreon's error in *Antigone* and Athenian practice.

410. On the text cf. Diggle 1994, 362-99. For a survey of views on *Orestes* cf. briefly, Willink 1986, xxii-xxviii; xlvii-lii; and esp. Porter 1994, 1-44. The intertextuality of *Orestes* has been explored by several scholars; cf. esp. Zeitlin 1980, 51-77 with bibl.; Porter 1994, 93-7 with bibl.

411. On this disclaimer at 5 and that at 8 cf. Willink 1986, 81 ad 5 and 8-9; but though he acknowledges that such "disclaimers" are traditional, and do not display scepticism, he suggests (1986, 81 ad 8-9) that the repetition gives the disclaimer "a decidedly ironical flavour." I do not see how irony would work here. If it is right that the repetition modified the usual meaning for the audience, this modification would surely operate by activating the scepticism of the disclaimer, marginalizing its conventionality; this would have had the effect of aligning Electra with the sceptics/sophists evoked by her Tantalos paradigm.

412. I discussed Tantalos as a cosmic sinner in Sourvinou-Inwood 1986, 37-58 (with bibl.); Sourvinou-Inwood 1995, 67-70.

413. On the version of the myth here cf. Willink 1986, 79-80 ad 4-10; Willink 1983, 30-3.

414. Cf. Willink 1986, 79-80 ad 4-10; and esp. Willink 1983, 25-33. Contra: West 1987, 180 ad 10.

415. Cf. 160, 393, 667-8; cf. also 685, 687.

416. Cf. on these verses and their textual problems Willink 1986, 337-9 ad loc.; West 1987, 286 ad 1546. On *alastor* cf. Jameson, Jordan, and Kotansky 1993, 118-20; cf. also Burkert 1985, 181.

417. Cf. 28, 75-6, 416-20, 590-99, 955-6, cf. also 329-31.

418. At 37-8, *onomazein gar aidoumai theas Eumenidas*. As Henrichs 1994, 50-1 has pointed out, it was Euripides in *Or.* who first amalgamated the mythical and cultic identities of the Erinyes and the Eumenides, referring to the Erinyes of the Orestes myth repeatedly as Eumenides, and equating them with the Semnai Theai.

419. I follow West's translation of *hamartia* here (cf. West 1987, 187 ad 76).

420. On the different versions of the myth of the Previous Owners cf. Sourvinou-Inwood 1991, 217-43.

421. Cf. also, on this passage Willink 1986, 111-2 ad 162-5; West 1987, 192-3 ad loc.

422. Cf. also, on this passage Willink 1986, 114-5 ad 174-9, 174-8; West 1987, 193-4 ad loc.

423. Cf. on this metaphor Willink 1986, 116-7 ad 191; West 1987, 194 ad 191.

424. Willink 1986, xlvii-li, reacting against what he considers an overemphasis of the negative aspects of Orestes, stresses the pity, the fact that even before he awakens we are supposed to feel sympathy for him and pity him because of the terrible situation in which

Chapter 3: Euripidean Tragedy and Religious Exploration 451

he found himself. I think there is an element of cultural determination in both approaches. Of course the ancient audience (not "we"; "we" do not come into the construction of meaning) would have felt pity for Orestes, but that does not mean that they would not have perceived the negative elements in his constructed character. On the contrary, I suggest, the Tantalos paradigm would have shaped their expectations towards registering the negative very strongly.

425. On Erinyes cf. also e.g. 408-12, 791, 834-8.

426. Cf. on this Willink 1986, 129-30 ad 268-74; West 1987, 200 ad 268.

427. Cf. on this Willink 1986, 154 ad 417.

428. Cf. West 1987, 212 ad 418; Willink 1986, 154-5 ad 418.

429. And elsewhere; cf. e.g. 591.

430. Willink 1986, 138 ad 316-23.

431. Cf. West 1987, 206 ad 346 on this descent.

432. Porter discusses Tyndareos' speech (Porter 1994, 101-30), and Orestes' *apologia* and second reply (Porter 1994, 130-72).

433. For this interpretation of *hosian* here cf. West 1987, 217 ad 501.

434. Cf. on the expression West 1987, 222 ad 582.

435. The political debate was an important element in this tragedy (cf. on this Pelling forthcoming, ch. 9), but it was not the main focus. In my view the audience's focus dwelled on this problematization of democracy (at a multiple distance) for a certain time, and then moved on to other issues, of which the religious dimension is of fundamental importance, and we shall see, will also provide a kind of solution to the stasis. But by the time Apollo appeared the emphasis was not on the problematization of democracy, and that is why, in my view, the Athenian audience would not have shared modern critics' perception of Apollo's inadequacies; because the shift has moved away from the particular problematization of political debate and democracy, Apollo's promise that he will make sure Orestes' relations with the polis will be restored brings a reassuring closure to this problem.

436. Reinhardt 1960, 248, sees it as the opposite of what is righteous, contrasting the trial in Aesch. *Eum.* to this, which he sees as a topical mirror in a heroic frame. I will be arguing that intertextuality here works in more complex and subtle ways.

437. On which cf. e.g. Wolff 1968, 144.

438. Cf. Isaeus 11.17.

439. A fact which, incidentally, would have partly deconstructed the "critique" of democracy constructed in the debate.

440. Cf. Sommerstein 1989, 221-6 for a survey of discussion on the number of jurors and the question on whether Athena had voted as one of the jurors.

441. Cf. Willink 1986, 240-1 (Electra, antiphonal arrangement); West 1987, 249 ad 960-81 (chorus).

442. Myrtilos had cursed Pelops and his descendants; cf. on this curse Willink 1986, 249-50.

443. I am not sure that we can reconstruct the precise way in which the ancient audience would have made sense of this and of the remainder of 1179-80 (cf. the comments in West 1987, 264 ad 1179 and Willink 1986, 278 ad 1179-80). But it is significant that the notion *theou pronoia* has been brought up.

444. On this metaphor cf. Willink 1986, 285 ad 1239-40; West 1987, 268 ad 1239.

445. On the intertextual relationship of this invocation to comparable ones in A. *Cho.* and E. *El.* cf. West 1987, 266-7 ad 1225-45.

446. On which cf. Willink 1986, 293 ad 1285; West 1987, 271 ad 1283-5.

447. This translation is by Willink 1986, 304 ad 1361-2.

448. It is not without interest in this respect that one of the scholia ad E. *Or.* 1361 explains this expression as follows: *dikaios he Nemesis ten Helenen etimoresato.*

449. Cf. references to the ancient sources and discussion in Gantz 1993, 319-21.

450. Cf. Schol. Eur. *Or.* 1396.

451. Cf. Willink 1986, 313 ad 1395-6.

452. Cf. Willink 1986, 320-1 ad 1453-4.

453. Cf. on this Willink 1986, 327-8 ad 1492-3; West 1987, 282 ad 1492.

454. Cf. Porter 1994, 173-213 on the scene involving the Phrygian, with special reference to his function as a messenger.

455. Cf. West 1987, 277.

456. West 1987, 277 ad 1369-1502.

457. For otherwise neither, for example, *Tro.* nor *Phoin.* would have worked with their choruses made up of such characters.

458. Cf. on this Willink 1986, li. Zeitlin 1980, 59 sees the Phrygian as a reverse doublet of Kassandra in *Agam.*, as well as a mirror of Orestes (Zeitlin 1980, 63, 75 n. 35).

459. In favor: Larson 1995, 69; contra: West 1987, 294 ad 1688. Notwithstanding the local flavor of the cults, the fact that in the Thorikos calendar (ll. 37-8; cf. Parker 1987, 145) Helen (part of the name is restored, but the restoration seems virtually certain) is associated with the Dioskouroi in their persona as Anakes and receives a sacrifice, makes it likely that she also had a place in the central polis cult of the Anakes.

460. Cf. e.g. Aristoph. *Lys.* 1314-5 and Sommerstein 1990, 224 ad 1314. On the announcement of Helen's apotheosis in Eur. *Hel.* 1666-9 cf. Kannicht 1969, 432-3 ad 1666-9.

461. On this question cf. West 1987, 291 ad 1637.

462. *Cypria* F 1 Davies.

463. Cf. Henrichs 1994, 50-1.

464. 1648-2; cf. on this Willink 1986, 354-5 ad 1648-52; West 1987, 292 ad 1650.

465. Cf. on the word Willink 1986, 357 ad 1664-5.

466. On the use of *chaire* in Greek tragedy and the archaic and classical world in general cf. Sourvinou-Inwood 1995, 180-216.

467. On the cult of Eirene in Athens cf. Parker 1996, 229-30 with references and bibl. A different view in West 1966, 407 ad 902.

468. Cf. e.g. Aristoph. *Peace*, Eur. *Bacch.* 419-20.

Chapter 3: Euripidean Tragedy and Religious Exploration 453

469. It has been discussed many times. Cf. Willink 1986, xxii-xxvii; West 1987, 36; cf. the most recent, very brief, discussion by Cartledge 1997, 32, and for a discussion of the complex relationship between this tragedy and Athenian political realities cf. esp. now Pelling forthcoming, ch. 9.

470. The fact that the characters in this tragedy are what has been called "unheroic" (cf. e.g. Willink 1986, li) would have helped the *stasis* in tragedy to evoke echoes of, to have resonances of, *stasis* in the audience's world, since it entailed that the former involved characters, and concomitant situations, not so radically distanced from those familiar to the audience from their everyday experience. In other words, the nature of the characters, whose unheroic nature was stronger in some cases than in others, would have functioned as a recurrent zooming device, bringing the world of the tragedy nearer the world of the audience. On this unheroic nature cf. also appendix 1 below.

471. Cf. Collard, Cropp, and Lee 1995, 125.

472. Cf. Collard, Cropp, and Lee 1995, 144 ad fr. 453. Cf. also Harder 1985, 105-6 ad fr. 453.1-2.

473. Cf. Collard, Cropp, and Lee 1995, 125, 144.

474. The story of this tragedy is thematically related to the Orestes myth: cf. Harder 1985, 14-8.

475. Cf. appendix 1 below for a very brief illustration and critique of a sample of readings based on the perception of this tragedy, and especially of its closure, as an ironic construct.

476. 1634-5, cf. 1673.

477. He may have appeared in *Alkmene*; this hypothesis is discussed in ch. III.4.

478. I set out in detail below, in appendix 2 to this chapter, the case against the view that gods in epiphany and other elements were just closure devices.

479. Parker 1997, 158.

480. Cf. Collard, Cropp, and Lee 1995, 58.

481. Into types that only pertain to, and address, a few aspects of the tragedies, those directly relevant to this discussion.

482. Thuc. 2.47.4, 2. 53.4. Cf. Parker 1996, 200.

483. Cf. the excellent discussion of this so-called religious crisis in Parker 1996, 199-217.

484. Plutarch *Pericles* 32. Cf. Parker 1996, 208-9.

485. Parker 1996, 210.

486. On this whole question of religious crisis, cf. Parker 1996, 199-217.

487. Parker 1997, 143-60.

488. Cf. esp. Parker 1997, 158-9.

489. Knox 1985, 80.

490. Knox 1985, 80.

491. A comparable divine intervention, in another late, or at least latish, Euripidean tragedy, is that of Hermes in *Antiope*, on which Nightingale (Nightingale 1992, 130) has taken the same line concerning the unexpectedness of the divine command and its significance as I am doing with regard to these extant tragedies: "[T]he *deus ex machina* . . .

unveils a divine perspective on the events of the drama that runs counter to that achieved by the human characters."

492. By Polygnotos; CVA Oxford 1 pl. 29.1; ARV 1028.6; Add 317.

493. By the Meidias Painter; Burn 1987, pl. 6a; ARV 1313.5; Add 361.

494. In sculpture the situation is more complex. Though a tendency away from the dignified and serene representations of the third quarter of the century can be perceived in the fussier, and more sensual, drapery, the restless composition, with more dramatic gestures, and a very weak movement of the modelling in the direction of a very slightly greater proximity to reality, which, especially in the face, involves more planes, a greater distancing, the strong idealization of both heroic and generic everyday figures, is maintained.

495. Reinhardt 1960, 256 (the discussion of Orestes: pp. 243-56).

496. Reinhardt 1960, 256. In his reading of the play he has marginalized elements that do not fit his interpretation. Thus, in his view (Reinhardt 1960, 249) in *Or.* inescapability of faith does not come into play—and he contrasts this with Soph. *OT*; he thinks in *Or.* there is a godless inescapability created by humans. However, we saw, the theme of the *alastor* resulting from Myrtilos' curse is important in *Or.* and the Athenian audience, in whose realities *alastores* were a fact, not an abstract concept, would not have marginalized this important element.

497. Goldhill 1986, 245 calls *Electra* a late play; but cf. Cropp 1988, l-li.

498. On the generic differences between fifth-century tragedy and comedy cf. Taplin 1986, 163-74; cf. op. cit. 163-4 for a brief review of modern approaches to this question, with bibl.

499. Though he acknowledges (Willink 1986, lvi n. 95) that the *hypothesis'* comment that the denouement is more of the comic type need mean no more than that the play has a happy ending.

500. Willink 1986, lvi-lvii.

501. Cf. Pelling forthcoming on the topicality of *Orestes*.

502. I have discussed the dangers of assuming that apparently similar elements have the same meaning in different contexts with regard to iconography in Sourvinou-Inwood 1991, 29-57.

503. Taplin 1986, 165.

504. Cf. a very brief survey of the concept of closure in modern criticism in Dunn 1996, 9. Cf. also the essays in a recent collection focussing on closure in classical literature: Roberts, Dunn, and Fowler 1997; cf. esp. Fowler 1997.

505. For an extreme version of this cf. Fowler 1997, 5.

506. Roberts 1987, 56, who views endings in terms of closure strategies, puts it as follows: "And if we hold with Aristotle that plot—the structure of events—is the very soul of tragedy, then it is the outcome of the story, the working out of the narrative, that is the most important aspect of the ending."

507. In chapter I.1.

Chapter 3: Euripidean Tragedy and Religious Exploration 455

508. I discussed the ways in which a priori notions function as organizing centers for structuring an investigative discourse in Sourvinou-Inwood 1995, 414-5.

509. That meaning creation by the ancient audience does not concern critics of Euripidean tragedy who treat Euripidean closure in this way is shown by their language the fact that the questions at the center of their enquiry are concerned with the response of an atemporal "we," such as, how "do we 'read' this new and more formal rhetoric of closure? How does this rhetoric shape our response to individual plays?" (Dunn 1996, 7).

510. Though the critics espousing the approach I am criticizing here acknowledge that the role of the readers and their knowledge is of fundamental importance in constructing the ending beyond the ending (cf. e.g. Roberts 1997, 269-71), this does not include taking account of cultural constraints, such as those shaped by the audience's religious realities, in the process of meaning creation throughout the tragedy's performance, which shaped their perception of the ending and of the ending beyond the ending. Nor is it methodologically rigorous not to keep the consideration of tragic performances in fifth-century Athens in the course of the Dionysia distinct from other texts of all periods, as Roberts and Dunn do.

511. Dunn 1996; cf. also Dunn 1997, 83-111.

512. And before him Roberts 1987, 51-64, who defends the authenticity of the choral codas (or rather [cf. p. 63] argues not that all our extant endings are genuine, but that they should not be automatically suspect or automatically despised) on the basis of the notion that they do not need to have any specific significance for the specific play to have significance; she sees them as markers of the end of the tragedy, a convention of closure, part of a strategy of closure.

513. Dunn 1996, 16-7.

514. This chapter, iii. 2, iv.1.

515. Dunn 1996, 17-8.

516. Dunn 1996, 24-5.

517. Dunn 1996, 25.

518. Dunn 1996, 25.

519. Cf. Barrett 1964, 417-8 ad 1462-6. I discussed briefly these epilogues in ch. I.2 and n. 132, where I argued that arguments against the authenticity of these tailpieces are based on an unsophisticated perception of choral identity in tragedy.

520. Cf. a survey of earlier studies in Dunn 1996, 41-2; Collard 1975, 407; Schmidt 1964, 23-8. I discuss deities in epiphany again, from a different perspective, in chapter III.4.

521. Dunn 1996, 32.

522. Dunn 1996, 33.

523. Dunn 1996, 33.

524. Cf. also Dunn 1996, 33: "[T]he god's authority is squandered upon empty and ineffectual commands."

525. Dunn 1996, 33.

526. When he returns to that speech (Dunn 1996, 52) Dunn does mention the burial at Delphi, but without allowing this to affect his earlier judgment of Thetis' instructions,

because here he has focussed on this passage as an aetiology; this treatment is not very satisfactory either. It takes no account of the fact that *hos apaggellei taphos* includes the notion that it will be doing so also in the future; and, in addition, it misses the main significance of the instruction in the process of meaning creation, and instead focusses on a false opposition, on the assumption that for the ancients either the tomb testified to Neoptolemos' *hybris* or to Orestes' and the Delphians' violence (contrived with Apollo's help), while in fact, first, both go to make up the persona of Neoptolemos as a hero, with varying emphases in the different versions; and second, *Andr.* is a much more complex play than Dunn assumes, and does not involve a "rehabilitation" of Neoptolemos that eliminates his *hybris*—though, of course, Thetis stresses the aspect of her grandson as Orestes' and the Delphians' victim.

527. Dunn 1996, 32.

528. Dunn 1996, 34-5. He seems unaware of the fact that by calling them "explanations," and giving them the baggage this term carries in modern discourse, he assesses what the gods say through inappropriate criteria.

529. Dunn 1996, 34.

530. Cf. Dunn 1996, 42.

531. Cf. Dunn 1996, 41-2.

532. Dunn 1996, 42.

533. Dunn 1996, 45-52.

534. Dunn 1996, 60-1.

535. Dunn 1996, 61.

536. Dunn also considers very briefly (Dunn 1996, 61) the rhetorical uses of aetiologies with reference to the view that by connecting the dramatic action with shrines and cult practices aetiologies makes the play believable (cf. also on this Collard 1975, 407). This relies on intentionalism, and presents aetiologies as external religious elements imported into the tragedy; I hope to have shown that for the ancient audiences the religious dimension was interwoven into the tragedies' fabric.

537. Dunn 1996, 62-3.

538. Dunn 1996, 63.

539. Dunn 1996, 63.

540. Dunn is not alone in assuming that the Brauronian aetiology in *IT* misrepresents Brauronian cult practice. Hamilton 1992, 118-9 also took this view, on the basis of the argument that, according to the Brauron inscriptions and epigrams in *Anthologia Palatina*, the mothers survived. With regard to the latter evidence, it is illegitimate to use evidence from Artemis cults in general for a particular local cult; as for the inscriptions, the garments they mention were dedications to Artemis, preserved in the sanctuary, like other dedications; their existence does not exclude a different rite of dedication, for Iphigeneia, on behalf of the women who died in childbirth, which may, for example have been burnt in honor of Iphigeneia, or set up in the sanctuary outdoors until they fell to pieces. A less extreme position is taken by Wolff (Wolff 1992, 308-34), who thinks that there were tensions between the play's construction of dramatic myth and its evocation of real-life ritual.

Chapter 3: Euripidean Tragedy and Religious Exploration 457

He (Wolff 1992, 323) notes the absence of a specific mention of the *arkteia*, and that what is mentioned is dedications on the occasion of failure and (p. 324) claims that there is a tension between the play's action and its aetiological conclusion. He thinks that the latter marks a discontinuity between the humanized and the sacral Iphigeneia, between an Iphigeneia "who insists on a pure Artemis untouched by human bloodshed, birth or death (380-91; cf. 1228)" and one who is recast in her service and as a figure of heroic cult has the closest association with Artemis still connected with bloodshed, and, through Iphigeneia, to death in childbirth. Then he remarks that Euripides' choice to make such an elliptical and muted representation has an unsettling effect, which he relates to the notion of female power and its subordination. This is a culturally determined interpretation, based on idiosyncratic readings. At 380-91 Iphigeneia does not insist "on a pure Artemis untouched by human bloodshed, birth or death"; she points out the contradiction of Artemis on the one hand barring those who have killed or who have touched a woman who has just given birth, or have touched a corpse, from approaching her altars because they are defiled, and on the other rejoicing in human sacrifice—allegedly, rejoicing; this is what is at issue here (cf. above I.2). Birth and death are normal forms of pollution which lead to the exclusion of those involved from worship for a period (cf. on this passage Parker 1983, 34, 37); there is nothing special to Artemis or to Iphigeneia's reference to Artemis. The ancient audience would not have perceived this to mean that Iphigeneia's ideal Artemis would not have been connected to death and birth, especially since they knew, and would have assumed Iphigeneia also knew, that Artemis was connected with childbirth, and caused the death of women. Line 1228 is wholly irrelevant: there Iphigeneia warns people to get away lest *they* be polluted. Once the Braur onian cult was evoked, Artemis' persona as women's goddess whose sphere included childbirth, and (as with all deities, who both protect and destroy) death in childbirth, would have been evoked. Since what is being announced is that Iphigeneia will be the heroine associated with the goddess in this cult, and since, this is made clear, and zoomed to the audience's cultic realities, through the mention of the fact that she will be buried in the sanctuary, it would have made ritual sense to the audience that what is mentioned here is a death-related aspect of the cult. The association with the *arkteia* was correlative to Iphigeneia's sacrifice; this ritual knowledge, which would have helped shape Euripides' parameters of selection, also shaped the filters through which the audience made sense of the play. Therefore they would not have registered an absence or an exclusion in Athena's discourse on the cult. The rite mentioned would have been perceived as appropriate here, since it involves death, and Iphigeneia's future death is ritually important; she will have a heroic cult, the chthonic character of which is correlative with this association with death.

541. Cf. King 1983, 121-2.
542. I discuss this aspect of Iphigeneia in *RWT*.
543. On Halai cf. Graf 1979, 33-41; Lloyd-Jones 1983, 96-7.
544. Cf. e.g. Themelis 1971, 24-6; and Sourvinou-Inwood 1997d, 19 n. 46.
545. Dunn 1996, 120-1.
546. Dunn 1996, 121.

547. The view that Theseus is playing the role of a *deus* is not confined to Dunn; cf. bibl. for earlier expressions of this view in Mills 1997, 146 and n. 77.

548. Cf. e.g. Dunn 1997, 89; Dunn 1996, 117, 119.

549. Which was much wider than the persona of Theseus as ambassador of the city that Dunn 1996, 121-2 allows him as the second, also ineffective, facet of his persona in *Her*.

550. Cf . Dunn 1997, 107: "It is because Theseus fails as a *deus* that he is able to approach Heracles as one man to another; and it is because he fails as a statesman that he is able to be a friend."

551. Dunn 1996, 118.

552. Dunn 1997, 107-8.

III.4. Walking among Mortals? Modalities of Divine Appearance in Aeschylus, Sophocles, and Euripides

III.4.i. Divine Appearances in Tragedy and in Lived Religion

I will now consider the ways in which divinities appear, and interact with mortals, in the different tragedies and the different tragedians.[1]

In Aeschylus there was direct interaction between deities and mortals; in the extant Euripidean tragedies there is no direct interaction between human and divine characters, nor were there any choruses consisting of deities, as there were in Aeschylus. When gods appear in the extant Euripidean tragedies they appear at a distance; either in a spatially distanced epiphany, sometimes on the roof, sometimes on the crane,[2] or in the prologue, on the stage, but unseen by the tragic characters, normally because no human character is present, once because the human character present is asleep.[3] These deities, then, invisible and inaudible to the mortal characters, could be seen by the audience as visible articulations of an invisible real-life situation: fifth-century Greeks know that deities have various plans, but one does not see them making the plans; just like the gods in the Homeric poems, they plot things about mortals which mortals do not know. The other main Euripidean modality of divine appearance involves the deities appearing at a higher level. Like the gods on an empty stage, the gods on high are separate from mortals; they are not shown mingling with them. Gods on high and gods on an empty stage make up the category which I will call "distanced interaction." These two categories, "direct interaction" and "distanced interaction," will function as two poles, with any other possible modalities being defined through their relationship to these poles.

But first, I will try to reconstruct the ways in which the fifth-century audience had made sense of these divine appearances, and to show that in their eyes there was a significant difference between, on the one hand a deity who suddenly appears on high at the completion of a Euripidean tragedy, giving instructions and "answers," and on the other a deity who is implicated in the tragedy's action, as, for example, Apollo in *Eumenides*, or Apollo and Artemis in Sophocles' *Niobe*, or even Athena in Sophocles' *Ajax*. In order to reconstruct the ancient audience's relevant perceptual filters, we need to consider divine appearances in lived religion, since it was such knowledge and assumptions, shared by audience and tragedians, that would have shaped the filters through which sense was inscribed in, and made of, divine appearances in tragedies.[4]

There were three basic types of what we may call "divine appearance" in lived religion, very different in nature. First, straightforward epiphany; second, impersonation of a deity by priestly personnel; and third, the ritual in which the arrival of a deity is enacted through the arrival, or the "finding," of the cult statue which had been removed from its usual place.[5]

"Real-life" epiphanies[6] took place when mortals believed that a deity had appeared to them.[7] Though this was hardly a regular occurrence, deities were believed to appear to mortals occasionally, and they gave them instructions, as a result of which very often a cult was instituted.[8] These real-life epiphanies encompass two categories: dream epiphanies, in which the deity appeared when the person was asleep, and "real" real-life epiphanies, when the person was awake. Interestingly, one of the tragedians was associated in the tradition with a dream epiphany that led to a cult foundation. According to *Vita Sophocles* 12, Heracles had appeared in a dream epiphany to Sophocles and informed him where to find a golden wreath that had been stolen from the Acropolis; when it was found Sophocles received a reward, which he used to found a shrine of *Heracles Menytes*. Sometimes the deity or hero did not make themselves known but performed a miracle,[9] or some other action.[10]

The second type of divine appearance in lived religion involved the impersonation of divinities by priestly personnel in the course of ritual, and sometimes sacred drama.[11] Such ritual acts may conceivably also have included an "enacted" epiphany,[12] in which the priest[ess] impersonated the deity, the divine manifested itself in the priest[ess]. The third category of divine appearance took place in the course of festivals of advent,[13] which sometimes had names like Theophania[14] and Katagogia,[15] and in which the arrival, the epiphany, of a deity is enacted through the arrival, or the "finding," of the cult statue, which had been removed from its usual place. The bringing in, or "finding" of the statue is a visible articulation of the deity's advent. It is not that the deity is embodied in the statue, but that the statue's arrival and presence gives material manifestation to the deity's arrival and presence. The City Dionysia, which involved the arrival of the statue of Dionysos in Athens, the reception of which, I argued in part II, was the context in which tragedy was generated, belongs, we saw, to this same category of festivals that involved a variant of epiphany. The notion of divine appearance is, therefore, central in the ritual context of the dramatic performances, and this is visually expressed through the presence of the statue of Dionysos in the

Chapter 4: Modalities of Divine Appearance

theater, which is the physical expression, the visual articulation, of Dionysos' presence in the theater.

The nearest real-life equivalent to divine appearances of the *Eumenides* type was, for the audience, divine appearances in sacred drama, in which the deities were impersonated by cult personnel; as far as it is possible to tell, in sacred drama deities and mortals interacted directly.[16] The world of the tragedy in such cases involved a condensed, polarized version of the "men walked with gods" facet of the heroic age. Perceptions pertaining to the heroic age involved a spectrum of modalities of interaction between deities and mortals, with the intimacy of the erotic contact between deity and mortal who will have a child by the deity at one end, and mortals who never had any closer contact with a deity than the ordinary people of fifth-century Athens at the other. So the tragic poets had a wide choice as to where within this spectrum they would locate their characters. The world of the tragedy in *Eumenides* is at one end of the spectrum, that in Euripides' *Phoinissai* at the other.

Deities that appeared on high at the conclusion of Euripidean tragedies resembled, and thus evoked, deities in 'real-life' epiphanies, in which a god appears, gives instructions, and as a result a cult is instituted. Thus, the audience would have seen these *dei ex machina* as deities in epiphany to the tragic characters—in the world of the tragedy. In the reality of the audience's own world what was happening was that an actor wearing a divine mask impersonated a god in a mimetic performance taking place in a sanctuary during a festival; this, I suggest, could not but have evoked the ritual schema "masked impersonation of deities by cult personnel."

In these circumstances, we may draw the following conclusions. First, the distinctions in the modalities of divine appearances set out above were indeed significant for the ancient audience. Second, divine appearances evoked, and would have been made sense with the help of, schemata of divine appearances in lived religion. Moreover, it is clear that the two modes of distanced interaction, "epiphany" and deities in the prologue on an empty stage, which are found in, and characterize, Euripidean tragedies, are directly comparable to the audience's reality.[17] They involve more distance between deities and the mortals of the world of the tragedy than the Aeschylean modalities of divine appearance. The direct interaction model involves closer contact between mortals and immortals, and thus inevitably also greater distance from the world of the audience—since there is no real-life equivalent to deities being visibly implicated in the tragedy's action, like Apollo in *Eumenides*. I shall return to these questions. First I will consider the modalities of divine appearances in the different tragedies in a little detail.

III.4.ii. *Aeschylus*

In the one surviving Aeschylean tragedy in which gods appear on stage they truly walk among men and interact with them on the same level, through "direct interaction," not through the Euripidean "distanced interaction."[18] As we saw in chapter III.1, the world in the first two tragedies of the *Oresteia* is similar to the world of the audience in that the gods are absent, and communication with, and guidance from, them is similar to that available to the audience: only through prophecy. In *Eumenides* gods appear on the stage and interact with mortals. This tripartite schema allows a certain circumscribed comparability between the world of the tragedy and the world of the audience in the first two tragedies, that makes explorations in the former relevant to the latter. On the other hand, the activation of the "other" side of the heroic age in *Eumenides* allows some (complex and ambiguous) answers to be given, that are presented as anchored in the authority of the gods, and a cult and ritual to be instituted, on the authority of the poliadic deity, which will protect the polis from a host of bad things and bring it blessings. The same schema, two plays from which the gods are absent and a final one in which at least one deity is present, may also have occurred in the Danaid trilogy. Certainly Aphrodite is one of the characters in *Danaides*,[19] in which she probably delivered a speech for the defense at Hypermestra's trial. However, even if this is right, it would not necessarily entail that Aphrodite's role in *Danaides* was close to that of Athena in *Eumenides*.

That deities had different roles in the different Aeschylean tragedies seems to be confirmed by what we are able to gauge concerning their appearances in those fragmentary tragedies in which the evidence allows us to set in place at least the parameters for the reconstruction of the interactions between gods and mortals. As we shall see, different patterns of interaction and intervention seem to be structuring the different tragedies; however, insofar as it is possible to judge, the interaction between human and divine characters was always direct: gods walked among mortals.

Let us consider the *Lykourgeia*, starting with its first play, *Edonoi*. First, I must make clear that epiphany described in the fragment *Edonoi TrGF* iii F 58, *enthousia de doma, bakcheuei stege*, does not describe Dionysos on the roof, but is a metaphor for the notion that the god's presence caused an earthquake that made the house shake, and

Chapter 4: Modalities of Divine Appearance

the roof move, as though in a bacchic frenzy. Dionysos was one of the characters in *Edonoi*, in disguise, as in Euripides' *Bacchai*. We do not know whether he also appeared in his own persona in *Edonoi*, as a divinity. It is more likely than not that he did, and he perhaps instructed the chorus to take Lykourgos to Mount Pangaion just before the exodos.[20] Even if this is right, we do not know whether he appeared among men, now revealed in his true identity, or "in epiphany" at a higher level. On my hypothesis it would be the former, but it is precisely this hypothesis that is being investigated here. On West's reconstruction of the second tragedy of the *Lykourgeia*, *Bassarai*, Dionysos conducted a dialogue with the chorus in the first epeisodion.[21] If this is right the interaction between mortals and immortals would also be of the same direct type as in the *Oresteia*, especially since, on that reconstruction, Apollo also appeared on stage, and disputed with Dionysos, in the same epeisodion.[22] The hypothesis that the Muses appeared in the exodos as a second chorus[23] would fit this modality of direct mingling between mortals and immortals. Absence of evidence does not allow any discussion of the gods in *Neaniskoi*.[24]

Similarly, we cannot be certain about anything concerning Aeschylus' *Psychostasia*. But what evidence there is tells us that *Psychostasia* showed Zeus weighing the *psychai* of Memnon and Achilles, with their mother, Eos and Thetis, on either side supplicating for their sons' lives.[25] Taplin[26] dismisses the value of the Homeric scholia[27] for the reconstruction of this tragedy and also rejects the validity of the statement in Plutarch *Moralia* 16F-17A that Zeus was one of the dramatis personae holding the scales on stage, because, he says, Zeus did not take part as a character in any other Greek tragedy, and he believes that "this suggests that there was some sort of inhibition against impersonating Zeus himself on the tragic stage."[28] This argument is not convincing. First, because the fact that different testimonia make this claim about this tragedy should not be so easily dismissed. Second, because Taplin's argument is somewhat circular, since one of the problems that need to be investigated is precisely whether there had been such an inhibition, and if there had, when it had first appeared; for it may have emerged after the production of this tragedy. Finally, because this position sits a little uncomfortably with his subsequent argument concerning Pollux 4.130: he argues, no doubt correctly, that the statement of Pollux that in Aeschylus' *Psychostasia* Zeus and those around him had appeared on the *theologeion*, and that Eos used the *geranos* to snatch Memnon's body, may be reflecting not the Aeschylean performance, but a a much later, extravagant staging.[29] It is difficult to see how this would have been the case, unless Zeus had indeed appeared on the stage in the Aeschylean production—only not on the *theologeion*, but on the low raised stage in front of the skene. For the notion that Zeus and a *psychostasia* scene absent from Aeschylus' *Psychostasia* would have been introduced in a hypothetical late extravaganza is conjuring up a state of affairs that is extrelemy unlikely in itself, even if we leave aside the other objections to Taplin's thesis set out here.

Any difficulty about Zeus' appearance in a tragedy would disappear if its apparent uniqueness—in reality its extreme rarity—in tragedy had reflected, not an inhibition against impersonating Zeus, but a tendency in earlier tragedies, a preferred choice, which then, in later tragedy, became hardened, when the notion of the ultimate unknowability of the divine will and the workings of the cosmos drifted to Zeus, whose will the other gods expressed, so that he, whose knowledge was the most complete, was not represented, but his will and plans were reported by other divinities.[30]

This hypothesis could perhaps also explain why Zeus may have appeared in this particular tragedy, Aeschylus' *Psychostasia*, in this particular scene, which at the very least evokes the notion of Zeus' will being circumscribed by certain constraints. Whatever the differences may have been[31] between on the one hand the *keres thanatoio* (of Achilles and Hector) in the Homeric weighing scene which signifies the fates of the two heroes in *Iliad* 22. 209-13, and on the other the *psychai* (of Achilles and Memnon), which is what Zeus placed in the scales in Aeschylus' tragedy, the notion of the two men's fate clearly came into play in this tragedy, since the two mothers were supplicating for their sons' life. Though the latter fact suggests that Zeus' will was relevant here, the weighing action expresses the perception that this was not the only thing that had come into play. There is ambivalence and ambiguity as between what is fated and what Zeus can do; this perception is articulated, for example, in *Iliad* 16.433-52, where Sarpedon is fated to die at that moment at the hands of Patroklos, but Zeus can save him if he so wants; however, as Hera tells him, if he did that, any other god would want to do the same, and this would create ill will and anger—and so, to put it in different terms, cosmic disorder would follow.[32] There are many ambivalences and ambiguities in Greek polytheism, such as those implicated in the notion that the world is both ruled by Zeus as sovereign, and also by all the gods, whose different spheres of competence articulate, and make up, this cosmos.[33] The type of ambivalence and ambiguity that is directly relevant here is that implicated in the relationship between on the one hand the notion of the great power of the gods, especially of Zeus, the ruler of the cosmos, and on the other the notion of some sort of constraints on this power, the notion of fate.[34] A context that stresses the

Chapter 4: Modalities of Divine Appearance 465

notion of fate places Zeus at one end of this spectrum of ambiguity, the other end of which stresses Zeus' persona as ruler of the cosmos, whose ultimate designs are complex and unknowable. It is to the latter end of the spectrum that belongs the Zeus who does not appear in person in Euripidean tragedy—except perhaps extremely rarely.[35]

In *Phryges* or *Hektoros Lytra*[36] the prologue included a brief dialogue between Hermes and Achilles.[37] So in this tragedy,[38] it seems, we have an interaction between god and man, similar to that of Athena, Apollo, and the Erinyes/Eumenides with mortals in *Eumenides*. In *Xantriai* Lyssa appeared.[39] She spoke the lines (*TrGF* iii F 169) *ek podon d' ano hyperchetai sparagmos eis akron kara, kentema glosses, skorpiou belos lego*. The fact that we are told[40] that Lyssa spoke these lines *epitheiazousa tais Bacchais* suggests that this tragedy had presented her on stage, directly interacting with the Bacchai, whom she was sending into a frenzy. It seems reasonable to believe that in *Phineus*[41] the Harpies, who were divine beings, would have been characters on stage, interacting directly with Phineus, and chased off by the Boreads who were the mortal sons of a god.[42]

Gods in disguise among mortals appear also in other Aeschylean tragedies besides *Edonoi*. In *Semele* or *Hydrophoroi*[43] Hera appeared disguised as a priestess.[44] In *Pentheus*,[45] presumably, Dionysos appeared in disguise,[46] though we cannot know whether he also appeared in his undisguised divine persona. The fact that some Aeschylean choruses consist of minor deities is another manifestation of the model of direct interaction in Aeschylean tragedies. The Erinyes in *Eumenides*, and, among the fragmentary tragedies about which we have, or can legitimately deduce, sufficient information to be able to judge, in *Kabeiroi*[47] a chorus of Kabeiroi, in *Nereides* a chorus of Nereides, in *Toxotides* a chorus of Nymphs companions of Artemis; in *Trophoi* the chorus consisted of Nysaean Nymphs, who were Dionysos' Nurses. *Prometheus Lyomenos* had a chorus of Titans,[48] and all characters except Heracles were divine, but it is probably not Aeschylean.[49] *Toxotides*,[50] which dealt with the story of Actaeon and his punishment, had a chorus of Nymphs companions of Artemis. Consequently, and since it is difficult to imagine, given the subject, that the tragedy had a chorus consisting of the companions of Artemis without having Artemis as a dramatic character, it is legitimate to believe that Artemis was a character in this tragedy, and that, since she would have interacted directly with the chorus of her companions, she appeared on the stage in the modality of direct interaction that we see in *Eumenides*.[51] The fact that in *Trophoi*[52] the chorus consisted of Nysaean Nymphs, who were Dionysos' Nurses, means that these divine beings[53] interacted with the characters, which had included at least one mortal, Medea.

Some other fragmentary tragedies had probably also involved direct interaction between deities and mortals. We know that Boreas was a character in *Oreithyia*.[54] Since it seems that he had asked for her hand in marriage and been rejected, and then eventually abducted her, he would have interacted with the human characters directly, not in the distanced interaction mode. The fragment from *Hoplon krisis*[55] F 174 is cited as being addressed to Thetis, by someone who calls upon the Nereids to come out and decide on the award of Achilles' armor. Presumably it is addressed to Thetis as part of an invocation addressed to her, and through her to all the Nereids. Thus, there is not sufficient evidence for us to be certain that Thetis was a character in this tragedy, or to know whether the Nereids appeared in it.

If *Ixion*[56] was not a satyr play, and I believe that there is no valid reason to think that it was,[57] given the story, it probably would also have involved direct interaction between gods and mortals, especially if it is right that the tragedy dealt with the purification of Ixion by Zeus after the murder of his father-in-law.[58] If so, it is not impossible that Zeus may have been a character in the tragedy. The notion that Aeschylus' *Ixion* involved direct interaction between mortals and immortals may gain a little tentative support from the consideration of the iconographical evidence. The image on side A of the kantharos London BM E 155,[59] painted in the 450s B.C., shows Ixion about to be punished; side B very probably shows an earlier episode from his impious past.[60] This representation of Ixion's punishment is very different from the few earlier representations of this subject, which show Ixion on the wheel.[61] On the London kantharos Ixion is not yet on the wheel; he is being held in front of a seated Hera by Hermes and Ares, while Athena has brought in the winged wheel. This is a purely mythological scene, with no theatrical echo; but sometimes the version of a myth represented on vases was influenced by the presentation of that myth in a tragic performance.[62] It is therefore far from implausible that the change in the iconographical articulation on the subject may have been inspired by Aeschylus' *Ixion*. Even Shapiro, who is keen to connect this vase with Pindar's *Pythian* 2, admits that this image cannot be explained as a reflection of that poem; he says that either the vase painter knew other sources as well as Pindar, "or else he had an extraordinarily vivid imagination."[63] I have always argued in favor of the autonomy of the vase painters' myth creation, and so I do not have the expectation that images are reflections of literary works; but we know that sometimes they were influenced by them. I suggest that the fact that this iconographical articulation of Ixion's

Chapter 4: Modalities of Divine Appearance

punishment, which is very different from those that (as far as we can tell, given the small numbers) had prevailed earlier, and mostly also later, in a descriptive narrative mode, may have been inspired by a tragedy in which Ixion had been shown interacting with the gods, and in which his punishment was pronounced, and perhaps the wheel shown. The fact that the hypothesis concerning this Aeschylean tragedy coincides with an iconographical schema that appears at the relevant time[64] adds a little support to the view that in this tragedy, as elsewhere in Aeschylus, men mingled with gods.

Aeschylus' *Niobe* includes a fragment[65] derived from a quotation in Aristophanes, *Birds* 1246-8. Peisetairos is speaking to Iris: "Do you know that if Zeus annoys me any further, I will incinerate his palace and the house of Amphion with fire-bearing eagles" (*melathra kai domous Amphionos kataithalos[o] pyrphoroisin aietois*). The scholia[66] tell us that this comes from Aeschylus' *Niobe*, which fits *domous Amphionos*. Dunbar notes[67] that Zeus would be the natural subject of *kataithaloun*, but adds that Zeus had not taken a direct part in the destruction of Amphion's family, and is unlikely to have said that he would. She therefore suggests various other possibilities, that it may have been said as a warning to Niobe, that, given the anger of a male god, almost certainly Zeus, referred to in F 154a.12, the multiple deaths may have been initially wrongly attributed to Zeus, or perhaps, she suggests, the sentence was hypothetical, "e.g. (Greater destruction there could not have been) if Zeus had incinerated Amph.'s halls with flaming bolts."

The most clearly identifiable modality that would make this threat comic is a paratragic inversion,[68] in which Zeus is threatened, in the ways in which he himself had threatened.[69] I hope to have shown that the notion that Zeus could not be shown on stage in Aeschylean tragedies is mistaken. Let us, then, attempt to consider the possibility that Zeus may have been involved in this tragedy. Zeus' involvement would be creating very significant meanings, which would be reflecting an important aspect of the perceptions articulated in, and articulating, this myth. Zeus' involvement would be bringing out, and stressing, the cosmic dimension of Niobe's offense. Leto was a goddess and Niobe was a mortal; a mortal boasting that he or she surpasses a deity in something is *hybris*, a serious offense against the order of the world, a transgression of the proper human limits, and of the proper distance that exists, and should be acknowledged by mortals to exist, between mortals and immortals. This is the reason why such boasters are punished very severely; it is not only because the personal *time* of a deity has been offended. Thus, in any articulation of the myth, in tragedy or in images, Apollo, Artemis, and Leto would have the effect of emphasizing the personal dimension of the offense, while Zeus' involvement would be stressing the cosmic.

There is one image which represents Zeus, Hermes, Leto, Apollo, and Artemis in connection with the Niobe myth. On the upper register of the Apulian loutrophoros Naples 3246,[70] which, it has been suggested, for good reasons, reflects Aeschylus' *Niobe*,[71] several gods are represented, Zeus and Hermes on one side, Leto, Apollo, and Artemis on the other. The fact that these gods are depicted there does not mean, of course, that they were characters in the play; the vase painter was creating his own version of the myth, and making his own selections.[72] But the choice to represent Zeus and Hermes, as well as Leto, Apollo, and Artemis, suggests that, in the parameters of selection that determined his choices Zeus and Hermes also had some role or significance in the tragedy. I submit that this offers support for the view that Zeus, as well as Hermes, were indeed involved in the action. The strength of this argument may be weakened by the possibility that deities unrelated to the plot may be represented on these vases. In my view, this notion is highly debatable; for associations that are very complex, and pertain to complex ancient perceptions, may elude the modern observer, unless an in-depth analysis to determine relationships is undertaken for every image. In any case, in this particular image the notion that Zeus and Hermes had been significant in the action of the tragedy that had partly inspired this image is strengthened by the fact that the group of Zeus and Hermes is equivalent to, and balances, the group of Leto, Apollo, and Artemis, whose role was crucial in the myth.

If this is right, Hermes' depiction would suggest that he had been Zeus' messenger in the tragedy. The exact reversal of the parody in *Birds* would entail Zeus telling Hermes to bring his threat to whomever he was threatening. Of course, it is possible that in the Aeschylean tragedy the audience heard the threat only from Hermes' report, but, since, in my view, there is no problem, about Zeus appearing in Aeschylean tragedy, it could equally well, if this view is right, have been shown on stage. We do not know how much of the Aristophanic passage is an actual quotation, so little can be based on it to attempt to reconstruct the exact formulation of the threat and the person threatened. Amphion is the most likely culprit, and thus addressee. The reason for this threat is likely to be *hybris*, not in this case, Niobe's *hybris*, which had led to the death of her children at an earlier point—unless she had subsequently compounded this with hybristic comments towards the gods—but probably, as in some versions of the myth, Amphion's *hybris*;[73] Tantalos, the hybristic cosmic sinner, cannot be wholly excluded, but Amphion is the most likely. The comic passage, then, would also have involved another reversal: Peisetairos

Chapter 4: Modalities of Divine Appearance

is committing *hybris* by threatening Zeus—though the potentially "hybristic" dimension of comedy in general and *Birds* in particular is too complex to summarize here. There is no evidence to suggest in what modality, if any, gods had appeared in *Niobe*. But if more than one deity had been involved in the action, and if Hermes had functioned as a messenger, the direct interaction mode is by far the most likely.

There are also several other tragedies the plot of which suggests that deities had appeared as characters, and probably related to mortals in the direct interaction mode, but about which we know even less than about the fragmentary tragedies just discussed, so I have not listed them.[74] Among the fragments from unidentified tragedies, Thetis was a character in the tragedy to which belongs F 350;[75] and the goddess Dike was a character in the tragedy to which belongs F 281a;[76] it is "likely, though not certain" that she is conversing with the chorus.[77]

In these circumstances, we conclude, first, that there are lots of deities in Aeschylean tragedies, where they appear as characters, and they also form choruses. In those Aeschylean tragedies for which we know, or can reconstruct with some plausibility, the modalities of interaction between deities and mortals, this interaction was of the "direct interaction" type. We do not know of any Aeschylean tragedies where deities interacted with mortals in the "distanced interaction" mode. That this is significant is also suggested by the fact that Aeschylus deploys choruses of divine beings.

III.4.iii. *Euripides*

The direct interaction between deities and mortals in Aeschylean tragedies contrasts with the modalities of interaction in Euripidean tragedies, in which there was a much greater distance between deities and mortals on the stage; closer, and sometimes intimate, contacts are mentioned, indeed some of the characters are the result of one particular type of such intimate contact, but such direct interaction is not shown on the stage. As far as I know, deities did not interact directly with mortals in any Euripidean tragedy, and there were no Euripidean choruses consisting of deities; deities only appeared at a distance, in a spatially distanced epiphany on high, or on an empty stage unseen by the tragic characters.

In four of the seventeen extant Euripidean tragedies[78] no divinity appears on the stage at all: in *Phoinissai, Herakleidai, Hecabe* (though a ghost speaks the prologue which is sometimes spoken by divinities on an empty stage), and *Medea*—though Medea's own supernatural hue is activated at the end, and she appears almost in the role of a deity in epiphany.[79] It is possible, but not certain, that there had been an epiphany of Artemis in *Iphigeneia at Aulis*.[80] Three tragedies have both a prologue spoken by divinities on an empty stage and a divinity in epiphany at the end: *Ion, Hippolytos,* and *Bacchae,* the latter involving Dionysos in the prologue, in epiphany above the house,[81] and also in disguise, as one of characters. *Troades* and *Alcestis* have a prologue spoken by divinities on an empty stage and no epiphany at the end. In *Troades* the prologue involves deities, Poseidon, subsequently joined by Athena, in the presence of Hecabe, who is sleeping and unaware of their presence. This in a way is a transformation, almost a reversal, of the real-life religious situation "epiphany in a dream," which it mimics superficially but does not bring about, frustrating any possible audience expectation of it: instead of Hecabe seeing the gods in epiphany in her dream, the gods are present, but she is not aware of them. This stresses their separateness. In *Alcestis*, in addition to Apollo and Thanatos in the prologue, there is also Heracles' reported fight with Death which involves him in direct interaction with gods; but that is not shown on the stage. *Orestes, Iphigeneia in Tauris, Helen, Electra, Suppliants, Andromache* have an epiphany and no prologue spoken by a deity.

The epiphany of Iris and Lyssa in *Heracles* does not follow the pattern of the other Euripidean epiphanies; it takes place in the middle of the play; Iris and Lyssa appear above the palace, converse, and are seen and heard by the chorus, comparably to gods in epiphany in the concluding part of other tragedies. Lyssa will interact directly with Heracles, but we do not see this. At 1003-6 the messenger reports that Athena, seen by the observers, interacted physically with Heracles, hurled a rock at him and threw him to the ground to stop his murdering frenzy; but, again, we do not see this. Lyssa had been one of the characters in Aeschylus' *Xantriai*, where she had inspired the Bacchai. It is not impossible that Euripides' deployment of Lyssa in *Heracles* may have been inspired by the deployment of the Aeschylean Lyssa, but, if so, the modality of interaction is different, since there was every reason to think that in Aeschylus' *Xantriai* it happened in the direct interaction mode on the stage. The double epiphany in *Heracles*, then, is the same as divine appearances in other Euripidean tragedies insofar as it takes place in the distanced interaction mode, but it differs from them in that it takes place in the middle of the play, and the role of the deities in epiphany is different. In *Heracles* the deities do not give answers or instructions—though they give information, and this does involve a kind of answer, for they explain what happened to Heracles. Most importantly, they, especially Lyssa, are implicated in the action. But Lyssa's action on Heracles is not shown, unlike Lyssa's ac-

Chapter 4: Modalities of Divine Appearance

tion in Aeschylus' *Xantriai*. It is like a Euripidean "translation," into the distanced interaction mode, of the operation of Lyssa in *Xantriai*.

The pattern of appearance of deities in the extant tragedies is clearly not uncharacteristic of Euripidean tragedy in general, for the fragmentary tragedies seem to show a similar pattern. As we saw in chapter I.2, Athena appeared in epiphany in *Erechtheus*. In Euripides' *Antiope* Hermes as a *deus ex machina* stops Amphion from killing Lykos; he provides resolutions to the plot, and to the question at the center of the *agon* between Amphion and Zethos, and a divine perspective on the events of the drama that turns counter to that achieved by the human characters.[82] Dionysos appeared in epiphany in *Hypsipyle*;[83] a deity, probably Athena, in *Bellerophon*,[84] probably Poseidon at the end of *Melanippe Desmotis*,[85] and *Phaethon* had probably also included an epiphany of a deity, which one we cannot be certain.[86] If *Kretes* had included a divine epiphany at the end,[87] and if its date is indeed somewhere near 438,[88] this would give us an instance of this deployment in the 430s, and confirm what appears plausible, that *Medea* refracted, and was not the inspiration for, the "epiphany on a higher level" schema. The first *Hippolytos*, the date of which is not known, also appears to have involved a deity *ex machina*.[89] There are significant uncertainties concerning Euripides' *Antigone*.[90] But it seems that Dionysos appeared in epiphany at the end.[91] It has been suggested that divinities appeared in several other tragedies, such as, for example, Heracles in *Kresphontes*,[92] but there is uncertainty.[93] The modalities of divine intervention in the two *Phrixos* tragedies are unclear.[94] In *Phrixos* B at least there was divine action, but it is unclear what was enacted, and what was part of the messenger speech.[95] It is likely that the only divine appearance on stage was that of a deity *ex machina* who told the story of the flight to Kolchis.

S. West has argued that Zeus appeared as a character in Euripides' *Alkmene*.[96] This view coincides with that reached by other scholars on the basis of certain images, which in some way or other appear to be reflecting this tragedy.[97] The case based on the images is not unproblematic, in that the modalities in which vases reflect tragedies are complex and varied, and the argument runs the danger of becoming circular.[98] West's case for the view that Zeus had appeared as a character in Euripides' *Alkmene* is based on Plautus' *Amphitruo*. It is a significant case, though, inevitably, the paucity of the evidence prevents it from being compelling. If this hypothesis is right, it strengthens my argument. First, because West suggested that Zeus appeared as a god *ex machina*.[99] This view would be further supported by the fact that, of the images thought to be reflecting this tragedy, the one thought to provide the strongest argument in favor of Zeus' being a character, which is nearest the narrative end of the narrative-emblematic spectrum,[100] stresses the distance between Alkmene on the pyre and Zeus in the sky, and is thought to be reflecting the position of the gods at a higher level.[101] This point is not neutralized by the fact that it is almost certainly the case that this image represents a scene narrated in a speech, not shown on stage;[102] for it is likely that, if Zeus had appeared on the stage at a later moment, that appearance would have helped shape the iconographical articulation of the dramatic events not shown on stage. Second, because if it is correct that Zeus had appeared in Euripides' *Alkmene*, his exceptional appearance in it would have been correlative with the fact that it would be primarily in his persona as Alkmene's lover that he would be appearing, not primarily in his persona as the sovereign god, in charge of the cosmos.[103]

Phaethon is set in Aethiopia, which is presented as a fairy tale world half beyond human experience.[104] Phaethon is supposed to marry a goddess,[105] but the marriage does not take place, and it does not look as though this goddess had been a character in the tragedy, interacting on the stage with the other characters;[106] these other characters, even when they had divine aspects, such as Phaethon, the son of Helios (who was a neighbor of the king of Aethiopia), were distanced from the "proper gods" in what was enacted on the stage. Phaethon went off to visit his father, and he died driving Helios' chariot. But the audience does not see these events. The setting of *Aiolos* was probably also a kind of fairy tale world, but Aiolos and his children were mortal. Aiolos was not a deity in Homer, in *Odyssey* 10.1-73; he was *philos athanatoisi theoisin* (2) and Zeus had made him *tamien anemon* (21). That Euripides' *Aiolos* had presented a very similar situation is suggested by the fact that the hypothesis to the play[107] begins *Aiolos para theon echon ten ton anemon d[espotei]an*; and, of course, we know that Kanake dies.

Euripides, like Aeschylus,[108] had produced a tragedy entitled *Ixion*. We do not know the date of Euripides' *Ixion*, except insofar as we can use the evidence of Philochoros, who said that the death of Protagoras was hinted at in Euripides' *Ixion*.[109] All this suggests is that, in Philochoros' knowledge, *Ixion* was produced after the death of Protagoras. As the date of this death is not certain, this is of less help than one might have hoped, though a date after 420, probably not long after 420, appears to be indicated by Philochoros' statement.[110] When mentioning Aeschylus' *Ixion* I suggested that the subject was such that it probably would have involved direct interaction between gods and mortals, especially if it is right that that tragedy had dealt with the purification of Ixion by Zeus after the murder of his father-in-law. Does the fact that Euripides also wrote an *Ixion*, then, not invalidate

Chapter 4: Modalities of Divine Appearance 473

my notion that direct interaction does not occur in Euripidean tragedies, at least not in the period covered by the extant tragedies? It may well do, and it may indeed be the case that the pattern I have proposed is only one of preferred choices. But it is also possible that because the tragedians' assumptions, perceptions of appropriateness, "aims" and so on, shaped the parameters determining selections, the selections made by Euripides on how to deal with this subject may have been different from those of Aeschylus; and that, if it is right that Euripides only deployed the distanced interaction model, what may appear to us obvious choices were excluded.

It is also possible that in this version, as is the case in some versions,[111] Ixion had been made immortal, in which case no mixing between mortals and immortals would have been involved, but I believe that this is less likely, for Ixion was perceived to have been presented as an impious and polluted man. For one thing we know about the tragedy is that, according to Plutarch,[112] when Euripides was abused because he had shown Ixion *hos asebe kai miaron*, impious and polluted, he had replied that he had not brought him off the stage (*exegagon*) until he had nailed him to the wheel. One does not have to accept the historicity of the story to believe that the knowledge it contains and presupposes is that Ixion, first, was presented in this tragedy as impious and polluted, and second, that he was shown on the stage on the wheel.[113] This suggests that the story presented by Euripides culminated in the punishment of Ixion, which was shown actually taking place. It is generally thought that this would have happened on stage through the use of the *ekkyklema*.[114] This may be right. However, since Ixion's wheel flew through the air, I suggest that it is more likely that Ixion on the wheel had appeared *apo mechanes*—with Hephaistos, who had nailed him on it, telling what has, and what will, happen. In the early versions of the myth the wheel is shown winged, and was perceived to be flying in the air; the notion that the punishment took place in the Underworld is later.[115] Consequently, I consider an appearance of Ixion *apo mechanes* nailed to the wheel, following an earlier exit at the human level on stage, to be the most effective, and, if I may make a subjective judgment, the most Euripidean of closures, especially since the Plutarch story suggests that that closure involved strong retribution. The way I envisage the *apo mechanes* appearance of Ixion on the wheel with Hephaistos is comparable to the appearance of Iris and Lyssa in *Heracles*:[116] they are brought in together on the *mechane*, then Hephaistos alights on the roof, from where he speaks, while Ixion on the wheel flies away on the *mechane*.

Some scholars have taken the passage in Plutarch to mean that the nailing on the wheel had taken place on the stage. In fact, the expression in Plutarch need not imply this, so it is not legitimate to privilege this reconstruction. On the contrary, I submit that the notion of a nailing on the stage at the closure of a Euripidean tragedy would go against the grain of what we know of the parameters shaping Euripides' preferred closure choices. It has been suggested that one image can be connected with Euripides' *Ixion*, and it provides evidence in support of the notion that in Euripides' *Ixion* Ixion had been nailed to the wheel on the stage. I will argue that this view is wrong.

In the publication of a very fragmentary skyphos in Basel, Collection of Herbert Cahn 541, in the manner of the Meidias Painter,[117] Simon has argued[118] that the (fragmentary) image that decorates it had been inspired by the production of Euripides' *Ixion*.[119] The image shows a group consisting of Hephaistos finishing off the winged wheel, extremely small fragments of two characters, who are named Kratos and Bia, about the representation of whom in this vase absolutely nothing can be reconstructed, and a fragment of a frontal Ixion below the wheel to the left. As for the rest of the scene, to the left are shown Apollo and Artemis, near the center in the upper part of the scene, to Hephaistos' left, a group consisting of a seated Zeus and a standing goddess, undoubtedly Hera, and also a male head, probably that of Hermes. It is not unlikely that the image was inspired by this tragedy. But, I would argue, inspiration in the widest possible sense, pertaining above all to the choice of subject, is all that would be involved, not a direct reflection of the tragedy. Firstly, because such inspiration is the usual modality of interaction between tragedy and Athenian vase painting. Indeed, to my knowledge, the Meidias Painter and his circle never reflected tragic performances closely.[120] Secondly, because it is not legitimate to use Plutarch to support the view that Ixion was nailed on the wheel on the stage, since, we saw, his formulation need not entail that this is what had happened. Thirdly, the articulation of the scene with the several deities seems to be reflecting late fifth-century fashion in vase decoration, rather than a tragedy, which would have had no place for all these deities. Finally, the notion that the representation of Kratos and Bia could not have been invented by the vase painter because they are personifications different in nature from the frequent personifications found in Meidian vases, such as Eukleia and Eudaimonia, is imposing an inappropriate, culturally determined classification, and underrating the vase painter's creativity. In my view, representing Kratos and Bia as Hephaistos' helpers in the nailing of Ixion would have had the effect of comparing Ixion to Prometheus in the pseudo-Aeschylean *Prometheus*; and vase painting, especially Meidian vase painting,[121] was a much more appropriate, and thus likely, *locus* for the construction of this

Chapter 4: Modalities of Divine Appearance

comparison, which carried connotations of a tyrannical Zeus, and an ambivalence as to the justice of the punishment, than a tragedy which dealt with an unambiguously negative Ixion, and concerning which, moreover, the perception was, as testified by the Plutarch story, that it showed a very impious man get just retribution.

In these circumstances, I suggest that this fragmentary skyphos does not provide evidence in support of the notion that Ixion had been nailed to the wheel on the stage in Euripides' *Ixion*; and that the available evidence indicates that in that tragedy Ixion had not been nailed to the wheel on the stage. I will now offer another argument against the view that he was, and in favor of the view that he had appeared *apo mechanes*.

If Ixion had been nailed to the wheel on the stage it is impossible to imagine how he would have exited, how Euripides would have *exegagen* him in a way that would not have turned a retributive tragic ending into a burlesque farce. There remains the theoretical possibility that Ixion had been nailed to the wheel on the stage and then he had been flown off on the *mechane*. I suggest that this dramatically implausible reconstruction would have been made impossible by the technical problems that would have been involved. I know of no actual or potential instance of such an action. The nearest example known to me, Bellerophon on Pegasos flying off on the *mechane* to scale the heavens in *Bellerophon*, would not have involved the assembling of the flight vehicle on stage; moreover, as the parody of this flight in *Bellerophon* in Aristophanes' *Peace*[122] appears to indicate, Bellerophon's flight had begun behind the *skene*, rather than on the stage proper. Of the other instances that would be in one way or another comparable to this hypothetical situation, in that they involve a mortal on the *mechane*, in *Medea*, and in *Stheneboia*, produced before 429,[123] a mortal (Medea in the first, Bellerophon on Pegasos in the second) appears *apo mechanes* at the end, "acting half like a 'god from the machine'."[124] Thus, in these two tragedies, mortals appear not simply through the same spatial, and generally physical, modality as the gods in epiphany, but also in a comparable role—comparable, but significantly different in that, unlike the deities who appear in epiphany, the mortals involved had been central characters in the action. In *Bellerophon*, produced before 425 and considered to be probably later than *Stheneboia*,[125] the situation is almost reversed, in that at some stage within the play Bellerophon takes off on Pegasos to scale the heavens to reach the gods; at the end, after he was thrown off as punishment for his *hybris*, he reappears crippled and in rags. Perseus in *Andromeda* arrived on the *mechane* flying though the air, an arrival parodied in Aristophanes' *Thesmophoriazousai*;[126] but though he intervened and saved Andromeda, this does not happen at the completion of the tragedy, and therefore his role is less comparable to *dei ex machina* than those of Medea and of Bellerophon in *Stheneboia*.

The arrival or departure *apo mechanes* on the stage seems to characterize mortals who have been given divine help so that they can fly. This is the opposite of Ixion's situation at the end of the play, when he is totally powerless and passive, subjected to eternal punishment. Like Medea, and Bellerophon in *Stheneboia*, he has undergone a transformation of status, but while they become partly comparable to *dei*, Ixion has become the opposite. Ixion starting his eternal punishment on the wheel brought in on the *mechane* accompanied by Hephaistos is also a negative mirror image of a schema we encountered in *Orestes*—but which may have been first deployed before that: Apollo in epiphany on the *mechane*, accompanied by Helen, whose deification he announces.

If the limitations of the evidence have not led us to construct a deceptive picture, the comparisons between on the one hand the extant and other, better understood, fragmentary Euripidean tragedies and on the other the different possible modalities of appearance of Ixion involving the *mechane* suggest, first, that Ixion on the wheel was not lifted on the *mechane* from the stage, but had appeared *apo mechanes* at a higher level. Since that position was one of power and positive action, while Ixion was powerless and passive, it is likely that he had not appeared in this power position alone, but had been accompanied by a *deus*. A *deus* who speaks, having arrived on the *mechane* with Ixion on the wheel, would also fit the parameters of Euripidean closure as they are known to us. In any case, even if this argument is not accepted, if it is acknowledged that only the *mechane* could have allowed Ixion on the wheel to exit, it seems perverse to imagine, without the support of any evidence, that the *mechane* would have been used differently here from the ways in which it was normally used, especially since this would also have entailed the independent difficulty of the dramatic implausibility of the nailing scene at the closure of a Euripidean tragedy.

Let us now consider the iconographical evidence further. Until recently, it was two Campanian images which were thought likely to be reflecting Euripides' *Ixion*.[127] This situation has changed, not in the sense that this connection is now rejected,[128] but in the sense that the notion that it is the Basel fragmentary skyphos that provides evidence for the tragedy has been privileged, and this has affected the reading of these two, and of some other, images. Before I discuss the two Campanian images I will show how the scene on the Meidian vase has affected the reading of Ixion images by considering the Ixion scene

Chapter 4: Modalities of Divine Appearance 477

on the Apulian volute krater Leningrad 1717 (St 424),[129] in which Hephaistos is nailing Ixion on the wheel and there are some other figures, the identity of which needs discussion. There is a winged female figure, which is almost certainly Iris.[130] There is a seated, bearded male figure with a scepter crowned by a bird, who is undoubtedly Zeus.[131] Finally, there is a female figure represented though the iconographical schema through which South Italian vases represent the figure of the Erinys, a very common figure on South Italian images, also depicted on two other representations of Ixion's punishment, in which she is especially apposite. And yet, Simon identifies her as Bia,[132] and following that, Lochin[133] is uncertain as between Bia and Erinys. The suggestion that this figure could be Bia is based entirely on the fact that Bia had been shown on the Basle skyphos, and the assumption that, therefore, we may expect her to be shown here also; this expectation is dependent on the notion that the Basle image is based on Euripides' *Ixion*. Further, this identification relies on the assumption that Bia would have been assimilated to the iconographical type of the Erinys. However, first, we know nothing about the iconography of Bia on the fragmentary skyphos, and it is no more than an unfounded assumption to assume that she may have been winged; second, on that skyphos Bia was not on her own, but with Kratos, and again it is no more than an assumption that she could have been shown on her own. Finally, and most importantly, this hypothesis cannot work when the focus switches to the creation of meaning by the viewer. For how would a South Italian viewer, who saw what to him would have been a familiar figure of Erinys, in a scene in which an Erinys is most appropriate, how could [s]he have guessed that this figure was not in fact "meant to be" an Erinys, that it was "meant to be" the *recherché* figure of Bia? Even if Bia and Kratos had been characters in Euripides' *Ixion*, and even if the viewer of the image had seen the play (which piles up assumptions on circularities), since (on that hypothesis) Bia and Kratos would have been represented together there, and here only one figure is shown, who looks like an Erinys, is not differentiated from an Erinys in anyway, and is in a context most appropriate for an Erinys, that viewer would have identified her as an Erinys.

On the Campanian neck-amphora Berlin Staat. Mus. F3023[134] Ixion on the wheel is at a higher level, while the wheel is touched by female figures, probably the Aurai, who will support it in his flight. Hermes and Hephaistos look up, Hephaistos making the gesture of *aposkopein*, and an Erinys is shown underneath the wheel. On the Campanian neck-amphora Capua Mus. Camp. 7336[135] Ixion on the wheel is presented at a higher level, there is a seated winged female figure on the right, who is probably an Aura, and a wingless standing figure on the left who appears to be giving orders.[136] She is probably the one woman of authority involved in the story, the goddess Hera. At a lower level two mortal men look up, making the gesture of *aposkopein*.

In both vases there is a distinction between the lower and the higher level, though on the Capua vase the lower level belongs to this world, and the upper to the other, while on the Berlin vase both belong to the other world, no human level is involved. In both there is interaction between the lower and the higher level, a viewing upwards, stressed through the gesture of *aposkopein*. On the Berlin vase, as on the numerous South Italian images in which one or two Erinyes appear, the Erinys is an emblematic, rather than a descriptive-narrative, figure; the Aurai are both emblematic and narrative; narrative because they suggest that this is how the wheel turned, emblematic because the whole group of Ixion on the wheel and the Aurai can be seen as an emblematic image of "Ixion's punishment." The fact that Hephaistos is looking up, making the gesture of *aposkopein*, and Hermes is also looking up, would, I suggest, locate the scene, in the eyes of the ancient viewers, at the beginning of the punishment. The Capua image would have been perceived as being even more closely anchored at the beginning of the punishment. Since mortals would not normally have been believed to be able to see Ixion on the wheel, the fact that the men make the gesture of *aposkopein*, which shows that they are looking at Ixion, means that the image would have been perceived as representing the beginning of the punishment. Another element that would point in the same direction is Hera giving orders (if that is what it is), which would also fit the beginning of the punishment.

The articulation of this image on the Capua vase, including the interaction between the two levels, is most closely comparable to two Early Lucanian images of Medea, on the bell krater in the Cleveland Museum of Art[137] and on a hydria at Policoro, Museo Nazionale della Siritide,[138] and also to an Apulian, and especially a Paestan, Alkmene.[139] In the case of Medea we know that the vertically bipartite articulation of the images corresponds to the *apo mechanes* appearance in the tragedy of the figure shown at the higher level in the images inspired by that tragedy. In the case of the Alkmene images, what is represented was almost certainly not shown on stage, but had been narrated in a speech[140]—though, we saw, it is thought that the deity represented at the higher level may have appeared *apo mechanes*. But as this is not certain, let us leave aside these *Alkmene*-related images, to avoid any dangers of circularity. In favor of the view that the Ixion image reflects something that was shown on stage, and not narrated, is, perhaps, the closer similarity with the Medea images,

Chapter 4: Modalities of Divine Appearance 479

the fact that both the Medea images and the Ixion one encapsulate the relevant tragedy's closure; and the fact that the expression *ou(k) . . . exegagon* suggests that the audience saw Ixion on the wheel.

In these circumstances, though we cannot assume that this iconographical schema reflects the closing segment of Euripides' *Ixion*, we are entitled to consider this likely. The fact that the Berlin vase has a comparable articulation, but with the human level excluded, would, I suggest, add some support to this view. Both images are iconographical creations, constructing particular meanings;[141] they deploy various elements inspired from the tragedy in the service of those constructions. No "faithfulness" to the tragic performance should be expected, hence the Aurai, for example, the Erinys, and Hera, if that is who she is. I suggested that the schema articulating the Capua image may have reflected the *apo mechanes* Ixion on the wheel flying off—with mortals looking up at stage level at the play's closure. My reconstruction of this closure would also account for both the similarities to, and the differences from, the Berlin vase. If it is right that Hephaistos had alighted on the roof, and Ixion on the wheel flew off in the *mechane*, this image would be reflecting that spatial relationship, with Hephaistos looking up as Ixion on the wheel flew off. The presence of Hermes is part of the vase painter's creativity; it may, but need not, suggest that Hermes had spoken the prologue. Of the two extant tragedies in which a different deity speaks the prologue from the one who appears in epiphany at the end, *Ion* and *Hippolytos*, Hermes speaks the prologue in one, *Ion*. This would be a comparable situation. If it is right that there was no direct interaction between deities and mortals on the stage, Hermes the crosser of frontiers would have played a role offstage in the communication between the two worlds which he might have been reporting in the prologue, as he, among other things, does of his role in the life of Ion in the prologue of *Ion*.

If this iconographical analysis is right, it would follow, first, that while the Meidian image may have been inspired by Euripides' *Ixion* in very general terms, above all in the choice of subject, the two Campanian vases would be reflecting that tragedy more closely, as is often the case with South Italian vases; for while a few Attic vases have some echoes of tragic productions, South Italian vases often reflect them more closely, along a spectrum that in the case of the Capodarso Painter goes as close to the tragic production as to represent a raised stage.[142] Consequently, if this iconographical analysis is right, the images offer some support for the view that at the closure of Euripides' *Ixion* Ixion on the wheel appeared *apo mechanes* with Hephaistos, and then flew away. This would add some support to the view that the world of this tragedy was a human world. For the *apo mechanes* appearance, deployed to show deities in epiphany, belongs to the distanced interaction modality, to a tragic world in which deities and mortals do not interact on stage. Thus, if "Ixion on the wheel," which is at the same time "Ixion mixing with gods," only appeared at a distance, on high, whether or not accompanied by a deity, this would suggest that this Euripidean tragedy had deployed the "distanced interaction" modality; that it had not involved direct interaction between mortals and immortals on the stage, but had presented the story at the human level, from the human perspective. For example, one not wholly inconceivable possibility would be that Ixion may have discovered that Zeus had slept with his own wife, and that Peirithous was Zeus' son, as happened in one variant of the myth; he may have then decided to take his revenge and assuage his lust for Hera; and/or after he had mated with the cloud which he thought was Hera he boasted that he had slept with Hera.

I am not claiming that my reconstruction of the pattern of divine appearances is right, and that therefore some other solution must be found, that excludes direct interaction in Euripides' *Ixion*. What I am claiming is that there are good reasons that do not depend on the validity of this pattern that suggest that there was no direct interaction between mortals and immortals in this tragedy.

The plot of *Protesilaos*, the date of which we do not know (though it is probably one of Euripides' early plays),[143] can be reconstructed only in its most basic lines.[144] It is therefore impossible to speculate as to the modalities of interaction between deities and mortals, and dead people and people who are alive, and belong to this world. The subject of the tragedy certainly offered scope for enacted direct interaction, especially between Laodameia and the dead Protesilaos—which, of course, is not quite the same as interaction between live mortals and immortals on the stage. But this, as we have seen, does not necessarily mean that such enactments on stage would have been the choices made by Euripides. It would be especially interesting to know what these choices had been, and also its date, for it would have been fascinating if it had been a very early play, and it had involved direct interaction on stage, which, as far as it is possible to tell, does not appear in the mature and later Euripidean tragedies.

I do not consider *Peirithous* to be by Euripides.[145] But in any case, it does not seem to be different from Euripidean tragedies in its modalities of interaction between gods and mortals; though it seems to be set in Hades, it is a Hades which, like Hades in *Odyssey* 11, is not populated by gods, but is the Land of the Dead equivalent to the normal world of humanity.[146]

Chapter 4: Modalities of Divine Appearance 481

The fact that in Euripides we do not see the Erinyes, as we do in Aeschylus, is correlative with this difference in distancing between the two tragedians. The world of the play in Euripides is much nearer the world of the audience than in the Aeschylean tragedies in which gods were present.

I am not arguing that the distances between mortals and divinities, this world and the transcendental world, and so also between the world of the tragedy and the world of the audience, are the same in all Euripidean tragedies. What I am arguing is, first, that these distances shift in the course of each tragedy; and each tragedy has its own patterns of shifting. Second, that the shiftings in each tragedy take place within certain parameters, which are different in the different tragedies. At one end of the spectrum, there is greater closeness to the divine world, and therefore greater distance from the world of the audience. For example, in *Phaethon* the setting is a fairy tale world; Phaethon is supposed to marry a goddess, he goes off to visit his father, the god Helios, nearby; he dies driving Helios' chariot. At the same end of the spectrum the deities in *Herakles* appear in the middle of the play and they, especially Lyssa, are implicated in, and seriously affect, the action. The fact that in this tragedy deities are at the less distanced from mortals end of the spectrum, is correlative with the fact that, as we saw in chapter III.3, the tragedy stresses Heracles', and thus to some extent also his world's, distance from the audience's humanity—though these distaces shifted throughout the play. At the other end of the spectrum, in, for example, *Phoinissai*, the world of the tragedy is much more distanced from the world beyond human experience, and thus far less distanced from the world of the audience; and there is no divine appearance. Finally, I am arguing that, though there are these significant differences between the different tragedies, these differences in the Euripidean tragedies we know about, as far as it is possible to determine, are also within certain parameters; in all the tragedies we know about there is a greater distance between mortals and deities than in Aeschylean tragedies; no direct interaction is enacted.

Of the nine divinities in epiphany in the extant Euripidean tragedies, Athena appears three times, and she also appears in *Erechtheus*. It seems that when the locale is Athens, or when the deity says something pertaining to Athenian institutions, especially cult, that deity is Athena. In other places it is one of the relevant deities who appears, Thetis in *Andromache*, Artemis in *Hippolytos*, the Dioskouroi in *Electra* and *Helen*, Apollo in *Orestes*, Dionysos in *Bacchae*. As we saw when discussing *Electra* and *Orestes*, different deities have different authority and persona, and the selection of the deity's identity is also correlative with this. And, we saw, Zeus never appeared in the extant tragedies. If he ever did appear in a Euripidean tragedy it seems that it would have been more in his persona as a character involved in the action than as a sovereign god.

In Euripidean tragedies, then, there are a lot of epiphanies of deities that give answers, very complex answers, which nevertheless offer much greater guidance to the tragic characters than the audience received in real life, answers that are also pertinent to the world of the audience. These answers are given by deities who are much more distanced from the mortals of the heroic age than the gods had been in earlier tragedy.

The non-Euripidean, fourth-century *Rhesos*[147] does not concern me. It deploys a conflation of different modes of divine interaction: Athena appears in the middle of the tragedy (595) and interacts intensively with mortals, an interaction that includes her deceiving Paris that she is Aphrodite; then, at 885, the Muse appears with Rhesos' corpse, only partly behaving like a *dea ex machina* of the type known to us: she also performs actions that in Euripidean tragedies only human characters do: she laments and curses.[148] This deployment of composite and varied divine appearances corresponds to the character of *Rhesos* in general: as Knox puts it, after mentioning various traits characterizing this tragedy, "all this, and more besides, seems to bear witness to a post-classical phase of tragedy, one which has abandoned fifth-century ideals of artistic economy for a lavish, varied display of individually exciting scenes."[149] The basic parameters shaping fifth-century tragedy construction have clearly changed. There is also another difference from fifth-century tragedy. In *Rhesos* there is hardly any religious problematization;[150] what there is is very thin and simple, potential material for problematization, more than anything else: the notion of *pepromenon* is mentioned in various forms by Athena (600-7, 634) and the Muse (935, 975-9), but it is not explored, or indeed problematized. Even if Athena's deception of Paris had been perceived as problematic, which I doubt, again the notion of deception by a deity is very lightly touched upon, and then abandoned; it is not explored. There is also a rather thin density of ritual and other religious references—at least compared to fifth-century tragedies.

III.4.iv. *Sophocles*

I will now consider how Sophoclean tragedies relate to this apparent pattern of a progressively greater distancing between mortals and gods.

Gods appear in only two of Sophocles' extant tragedies. In *Philoctetes*, which is late, produced at 409, Heracles appears as a god in

Chapter 4: Modalities of Divine Appearance

epiphany at the end, at 1409, playing a role similar to that of Euripidean gods in epiphany. Here the mode of interaction between mortals and gods is the same as in Euripidean tragedies, the distanced interaction.

In *Ajax*, which is early,[151] the interaction between gods and mortals is neither of the Euripidean distanced interaction type, nor of the "direct interaction" type; it is something between the two. Athena appears in the prologue, but she is not on an empty stage; she converses with Odysseus,[152] who, however, cannot see her,[153] and later with Ajax, who apparently can see her, as a result of his altered state.[154] Athena is almost certainly on a higher level and visible to the audience.[155] She leaves at the end of the prologue and does not return. This is clearly a more distanced mode of interaction than that in Aeschylean tragedies. If we compare Athena in *Ajax* with the Euripidean divine appearances, deities in epiphany and prologues on an empty stage, we find a complex set of relationships. First, Athena's appearance in *Ajax* is less distanced than divine appearances in prologues on an empty stage; she interacts with mortals; most strongly, Athena controls what Ajax sees, and though we do not see the slaughter of the sheep, we do see her controlling his sight in the sense that, as she promised Odysseus (69-70, 83-5), Ajax cannot see Odysseus; also, we see and hear Ajax, encouraged by Athena, expressing his delusion that he has killed his Greek enemies; we see on stage the results of Athena's intervention, which was crucial for the play's action. Athena in *Ajax* is also less distanced from the mortal characters than the deities in epiphany at the end of Euripidean tragedies; we see the workings of her actions taking place on the stage; she does not sudddenly appear at the end to bring solutions and issue instructions, and her close intertwining with the action on the stage does not evoke the "real-life" situation of epiphany.

In one respect she seems more distanced than the deities in epiphany: Odysseus cannot see her, while all can see deities in epiphany in Euripidean tragedies. I suggest that this was a modality differentiating this situation in the heroic age from epiphanies, as part of an idiom denoting the special relationship between certain tragic heroes and the deity. The similarities to, and differences from, *Hippolytos* may be informative in this respect. The similarity is obvious: like Odysseus with Athena, Hippolytos can hear Artemis' voice, but he cannot see her. The difference is also important: in *Hippolytos* it is the *philia* between mortal and goddess, which involves associating with each other offstage, that is presented as involving this "hearing but not seeing the goddess." So in the Euripidean tragedy "hearing but not seeing the deity" is a mark of the special relationship between deity and mortal which involves the mortal in regular contact with the deity. But that *philia* is not shown on stage. In her epiphany at the end Hippolytos senses Artemis' presence without seeing her (1391-3); this is taken to mean that she is outside his field of vision.[156] But it is possible, indeed likely, that this was so only at the beginning, and that when he heard her voice Hippolytos would have adjusted his position, so that he could see her, as the others did, a situation perhaps marked by his *horas me despoina* (as I now see you); this may make better sense of Artemis' reply, *horo; kat' osson d' ou themis balein dakry*, which can then be seen as an explanation of her imperturbable demeanor, which is now visible to Hippolytos. The parallel with Sophocles, *Ajax* must not be allowed to affect the understanding of this scene; first, because it would prejudge an issue that needs investigating, which is methodologically fallacious; and then, because the parallel is not exact; in *Hippolytos* there are other characters present who see the goddess, while in *Ajax* Ajax sees Athena only because he is in an abnormal state. The fact that Hippolytos senses Artemis before he sees her evokes their familiarity and *philia*; he senses her presence, as he had done in the past. But this is an epiphany, in which mortals can see deities, so he sees her. In Sophocles' *Ajax* we see on stage the situation which in *Hippolytos* took place offstage. Everyone sees deities when they appear in epiphany. Mortals who have a special relationship with a deity may see them in non-epiphany contexts, in which they interact with them. But there are limits to that association, and this is expressed through the "hearing but not seeing" modality, deployed in *Ajax* and, in a different way, in *Hippolytos*.

Let us compare Athena in *Ajax* with Lyssa and Iris in *Heracles*, who belong to the least distanced end of the spectrum of Euripidean divine appearances. In the interaction with the human characters, above all in the fact that Lyssa's effect on Heracles is not shown on stage, but happens inside, Lyssa and Iris are much more distanced from the human characters than Athena in *Ajax*. They are something in between a Euripidean epiphany and Athena in *Ajax* in terms of distance. Athena in *Ajax*, then, is less distanced from the mortal characters than deities are in the Euripidean tragedies we know about. This mode of interaction is more distanced than the direct interaction in Aeschylean tragedies, but less distanced than the distanced interaction in Euripidean tragedies and in Sophocles' *Philoctetes*.

Let us now consider divine appearances in the Sophoclean plays of which only fragments have survived.[157] In *Ajax Lokros*,[158] in fragment 10c, Athena seems to have just discovered the upsetting of her statue by Ajax when he violated Kassandra, and she may be imagined as having just emerged from her temple. This, if right, would suggest not a dis-

Chapter 4: Modalities of Divine Appearance 485

tanced epiphany, but same level interaction. She is rebuking the Greeks, in a way that also suggests direct interaction. The fragment does not belong to a prologue, for the papyrus has remains of a choral ode before it;[159] nor does it fit an *ex machina* context. All this suggests that Athena is interacting with the characters in the Aeschylean fashion, not in distanced epiphany.[160]

There are reasons for thinking that *Ajax Lokros* is an early play.[161] Until about 450 representations of the rape of Kassandra by Ajax that had depicted Kassandra, Ajax, and Athena, showed either the goddess herself or her statue. At about 450 a new schema appears in Attic vase painting, which involves a doubling of the presence of Athena; she is there in person, but her statue is also represented.[162] After its mid-fifth-century appearance, this schema reappears on fourth-century South Italian vases, Apulian and Campanian.[163] This pattern suggests that these representations may have been inspired by a tragedy in which the goddess and her statue were both, but separately, involved in the action, as was the case in *Ajax Lokros*, in which the goddess discovers the desecration of her statue. If so, this tragedy would have to have been produced just before 450. Also at about 450 the oinochoe Oslo OK 10.155 represents an iconographical version of this myth, the originality of which, according to Touchefeu,[164] is that it is located in a temple; Kassandra is rushing into the temple and has just reached the statue; Ajax is still outside. At least two Apulian scenes with a double Athena also show the statue in a naiskos. If it is right that in *Ajax Lokros* Athena had come out of her temple where she had discovered her statue violated, this, and the tragic differentiation of the unseen inside from the seen outside, may have inspired the stress on the inner space of the temple produced by this image. The fact that two different iconographical elements, both of which first appear at c. 450 and then reappear on South Italian vases may be connected with, can be seen as having been inspired by, *Ajax Lokros* makes this iconographical argument less negligible than it may superficially appear to be.[165] If this argument is right, *Ajax Lokros* was produced not long before 450, and would therefore have been an early Sophoclean tragedy. If this is right, it would be an instance of an early Sophoclean tragedy deploying direct, "Aeschylean" interaction.

In *Niobe*[166] Apollo and Artemis were shown interacting with mortals.[167] In the surviving fragments they are killing the daughters of Niobe, and one of the girls is pleading with Artemis to spare her. I suggest that this situation does not fit the distanced interaction model, the epiphany. It was either of the "Aeschylean" type, or of the "in-between type" that we saw in *Ajax*. It is different from that in Euripides'

Heracles, where we see Lyssa in distanced epiphany, but we only hear about the fact that she will attack and madden Heracles; it does not happen on stage.[168] Furthermore, the way in which Amphion's confrontation with Apollo is described in the hypothesis indicates at the very least that Amphion had expected a face to face contact between god and mortal.[169] We do not know the date of *Niobe*.[170]

The story about Sophocles himself playing the harp in *Thamyras* may well have been derived from comedy,[171] but whether or not this is so, the assumption behind the story must be that *Thamyras* was an early play.[172] The story of the musical contest between Thamyras and the Muses demands the direct interaction of the Muses with the other characters.[173] *Thamyras* may have been the same tragedy as *Mousai*.[174] Whether *Mousai* was a separate tragedy, or the same as *Thamyras*, its title indicates that these deities formed the chorus, and this in its turn belongs to the direct, "Aeschylean" type of interaction. If it was the same as *Thamyras*, which we found reason to date early, this would confirm that in an early Sophoclean tragedy deities were less distanced from mortals than in the later ones.

Let us now consider *Triptolemos*.[175] According to the date given by Pliny,[176] *Triptolemos* is one of Sophocles' earliest plays, produced at c. 468 B.C. It is not certain what the plot involves, though it included Triptolemos' mission to spread agriculture. Since Triptolemos, and other Eleusinian figures, were in personal contact with Demeter, according to all versions of the myth, and since in F 597 and F 598 Demeter instructs Triptolemos concerning his mission, I suggest that what we have here is same level interaction of the "Aeschylean model," especially since a geographical catalogue is much more appropriate in a direct interaction context than in an *ex machina* speech. If this is right, it fits the pattern of early Sophoclean tragedies involving direct, "Aeschylean" interaction.[177]

Tereus[178] was produced before 414, since it was parodied in Aristophanes' *Birds*.[179] It is unlikely to have been earlier than the 420s,[180] and may have been produced not long before *Birds*. Divine intervention is necessary for the denouement in which Tereus, Prokne, and Philomela turned into birds. I agree with those scholars[181] who suggest that F 589 looks like the comment of a god from the machine.[182] So it is extremely likely that there was a deity *ex machina* in this play. This would fit the pattern of deities *ex machina* appearing in later Sophoclean tragedies.

Sophocles had written two tragedies entitled *Athamas*, *Athamas* A and B,[183] of which one, the one that concerns us, involved the preparation for the sacrifice of Athamas, as punishment for the death of his son Phrixos, who was saved by Heracles, who revealed that Phrixos was still alive. Radt has compared this *Athamas* to *Philoctetes*, in that it involved an unexpected turn of events at the end, Athamas being saved at the last minute by Heracles, adding "(here also as *deus ex machina*?)."[184] In my view, the answer to this question is negative. It is true that one variant of the story in the testimonia speaks of Heracles as *epiphaneis*,[185] which could, though it need not, imply divine epiphany. However, this is the variant in the less reliable Byzantine scholia, in one case as part of a demonstrably confused account of the plot. The scholia vetera,[186] on the other hand, include the formulation *paraginomenon/paragenomenon Heraklea*, which, I submit, indicates that Heracles turned up when he was still alive, which in its turn would fit better the fact that many testimonia stress that Heracles stopped Athamas' sacrifice by revealing that Phrixos was alive. If he had appeared in epiphany he would surely have stopped the sacrifice *and* revealed that Phrixos was alive. So I suggest that in the assumptions shaping the parameters of selections that determined these formulations, Heracles had appeared while still alive, and not as a god in epiphany. This would fit also with the basic framework of heroic chronology. For the notion that Heracles, who had taken part in the Argonaut expedition, was already a god soon after Phrixos' alleged sacrifice would not fit the basic lines of established heroic age chronology; of course, the chronology of the heroic age is notoriously elastic, but what would be involved here would be a clash with the basic lines of that chronology, that functioned as parameters of determination shaping the audience's conceptual map. If this is right, this play is not relevant to divine appearances in Sophocles. If it is wrong, and there was a Heracles epiphany, it would not add any helpful information; all we can deduce about its date is that it had been produced before 423, since the play is clearly evoked in Aristophanes' *Clouds* 257—assuming that this was part of the original version of the comedy, and not an addition to the second version.

If, as it seems not unlikely, the hypothesis of *Peleus* has been correctly reconstructed, and Thetis correctly identified as a *dea ex machina* in it,[187] it becomes clear that Sophocles had already used the Euripidean schema of epiphany at least as early as the 420s. For *Peleus* was produced before c. 424, probably not long before.[188] Many years ago and in another context I had suggested[189] that a series of images on vases, the sudden boom in popularity of a previously virtually unknown Theseus subject in the 460s, depicting Theseus attacking Medea, may have been inspired by the production of Sophocles' *Aigeus*, which therefore, I suggested, was one of Sophocles' early plays. For reasons that are not relevant here, I had proposed that at the end of that tragedy Athena had appeared *ex machina*, what I now prefer to refer to as "in epiphany," intervened in the action, and foretold certain things. However, if the thesis set out here is right, that suggestion would have to be wrong. If this reconstruction is right, Athena could not have appeared as a *dea ex machina*—unless her epiphany was an early experiment that did not catch on, but was later redeployed, and eventually became the preferred choice of modality of interaction between deities and mortals. Neither alternative entails that the ending I had proposed, in which Athena intervened and foretold certain things, is not likely. On the contrary, there is an image, on side B of the cup Metropolitan Museum New York 53.11.4,[190] which shows a direct interaction between Athena and Theseus, and which, I argued,[191] following an initial suggestion by Bérard,[192] is one vase painter's version, one iconographical articulation, of the myth presented, on my hypothesis, at the conclusion of Sophocles' *Aigeus*. But if Athena had indeed played the role I had proposed at the conclusion of Sophocles' *Aigeus*, if the thesis developed here is right, she would not have done so *ex machina*. Even if we could be certain that the image on the New York cup did refract iconographically the conclusion of Sophocles' *Aigeus*, it cannot help us reconstruct the modality of the interaction between Athena and Theseus in the play. It represents a direct interaction, between them; but this image represents the myth, not its dramatic articulation; therefore, whether Athena had appeared at a higher level, or had been involved in "Aeschylean" type interaction, Attic vase painting of this time would have shown the two in "Aeschylean" interaction anyway.

Thetis appeared in *Syndeipnoi* or *Syndeipnon*,[193] which may have been the same play as *Achaion Syllogos*, and may conceivably have been a satyr play.[194] We do not know in what modality Thetis had appeared, though F 562, and the likely development of the plot, may suggest that she appeared in the *ex machina*, distanced epiphany modality.[195] But not only is this uncertain, but also the fact that we do not know the play's date means that it cannot provide evidence for our investigation.

To sum up the situation concerning the interaction between deities and mortals in the fragmentary Sophoclean tragedies. Lack of evidence makes it impossible to reach anything approaching certainty. However, I submit that it is not without significance that in those Sophoclean plays which are known, or believed on other grounds, to be early, the interaction between deities and mortals is, or seems to be, of the direct, "Aeschylean" type; while in those that are known, or believed on other grounds, to be later, the interaction is of the distanced epiphany type. *Ajax*, which is in-between in date, deploys an in-between type of interaction. This would suggest that there was a progres-

Chapter 4: Modalities of Divine Appearance 489

sive, albeit not linearly so, distancing between deities and mortals in Sophoclean tragedies. Given the scarcity of our evidence, this can only be a tentative conclusion.

III.4.v. *Modalities of Divine Appearance: Shifts, Constants, and Meanings*

In these circumstances, we may conclude that not only was there a greater distance between deities and mortals in Euripidean tragedies than in Aeschylean ones, but also that the same pattern of progressively greater distancing also appears in Sophocles, with early Sophoclean tragedies showing deities according to the "Aeschylean" model, and later ones in the "Euripidean" epiphany model, while one that is in-between in date shows an in-between modality of divine appearance. Thus, insofar as it is possible to judge, there seems to have been, in the course of the fifth century, at least as far as the three major tragedians are concerned, a shift within the tragic discourse, a development in the parameters of selections of (at the very least) the preferred choices: from the representation (in some tragedies, at one end of the spectrum) of a heroic age which stresses the mortals' intercourse with the gods, to a heroic world nearer the audience's lived reality.

All three major tragedians had produced tragedies from which the gods are absent; what changed between Aeschylus and later Euripides is the situation at the other end of the spectrum. Aeschylus produced tragedies from which the gods are absent and tragedies in which gods and mortals mingle directly, but none, as far as it is possible to tell, involving the Euripidean type "distanced interaction" or anything similar. Sophocles produced tragedies along the whole spectrum; tragedies from which the gods are absent, tragedies in which gods and mortals mingle directly (in his early tragedies), tragedies, or at the very least one tragedy, *Ajax*, involving a partly distanced interaction, and tragedies with the Euripidean type of distanced interaction. As far as we can tell, and we can tell nothing about his early tragedies, Euripides produced tragedies with no gods and tragedies with distanced interaction in various variants. He did not produce any that we know of involving direct interaction, mortals and deities intermingling, or any involving the partly distanced interaction type. Thus, distanced interaction is not found in Aeschylus or early Sophocles, while it is common in Euripides, and is also found in later Sophocles. In other words, tragedies from which the gods are absent represent the minimum contact end of the spectrum throughout; while the maximum contact between mortals and gods shown on the tragic stage becomes less close than it had been in Aeschylus and early Sophocles.

The fact that Sophocles' tragedies also show a shift towards greater distancing between deities and mortals suggests that something more than one individual's compositional whim was involved. It could be claimed that Sophocles simply followed a successful fashion in new theatrical devices. However, first, since he did not take this device over exclusively and wholesale—for his own preferred choice seems to have been tragedies from which gods are absent—simple fashion would not explain the fact that he never once (that we know of) used the earlier modality of divine appearance in his mature and late tragedies. The force of this argument is weakened by the fact that it partly relies on an *argumentum ex silentio* and partly on interpretations of scarce evidence as far as the fragmentary tragedies are concerned. But the fact that the distance between deities and mortals in *Ajax* is neither as great as in Euripidean tragedies, nor as small as in Aeschylean, but something in-between, suggests that it was not a case of adopting a successful device, but of a gradual shift towards greater distance, which eventually crystallized in the "Euripidean epiphany" mode.[196]

Consequently, the fact that this shift in choices was not limited to Euripides makes it something other than one person's idiosyncratic choice; it clearly struck a chord. So, if this pattern, this shift, is not deceptive, if it did indeed happen, is it significant? And if so, in what way?

Let us consider what was involved in the different types of tragedies. The presence or absence of deities in tragedies, like the modalities of their appearance, are correlative with the distances between the world of the tragedy and the world of the audience. The tragedies in which no deities appear are nearer the world of audience. Of course, in the world of the tragedy there is better communication with the gods, because in that world prophecies will come true. However, this is a fact known to the audience, not to the dramatic characters; the audience knows that the characters perceive their access to the will of the gods to be no better than the audience's actual access to that will is. But the audience has a broader perspective on the world of the tragedy, because of their superior knowledge—which included knowledge concerning some of the characters who were "players," gods or heroes, in the audience's religious realities. Thus, they can understand more, and can learn from the events in the world of the tragedy, which they, unlike the dramatic characters, can put in a wider perspective.

At the other end of the spectrum of distances between the world of the tragedy and the world of the audience, there was, obviously, no

Chapter 4: Modalities of Divine Appearance

real-life experience equivalent to mingling with gods in the Aeschylean *Eumenides* mode; for the audience divine appearances of this type were comparable to divine appearances in sacred drama, in which cult personnel impersonated deities; so this mingling helped make the world of the tragedy distanced and other, when compared to that of the audience.

The two modalities of divine appearances which characterize Euripidean tragedies are closer to the tragedies without gods, for they are directly comparable to reality. Thus, the earlier modality, which resembled that in sacred drama, changed, and produced two modalities; that of epiphany, and the "empty stage" modality, which is also like real life, in the sense that the audience knew that (like the gods in the Homeric poems) real deities planned and plotted things about mortals which mortals do not know, just like the deities in the prologues. Both modalities involve a greater distance between the mortal characters and the gods in the world of the tragedy, which helped bring the world of the tragedy nearer to that of the audience.

Many of the people of the heroic age were important in the (fifth-century) present because they received cult in the present, and/or were founders of cults, cities, institutions. Though many of the characters in Euripidean and later Sophoclean tragedies were such people, and they had close connection with gods, and the transcendental world (such as going to Hades alive), these connections are offstage, they are not shown, they are referred to, so that they function, we saw in chapter III.3, as distancing devices, distancing the world of the play from the world of the audience's everyday realities. Their role in the (fifth-century) present is activated mostly (though not exclusively) at the very end, as part of the answers and the closure, through a strong zooming connecting the world of the tragedy strongly with the world of the audience, above all (albeit not only), through the discourse of deities who, for example, foretell the future or order them to found a cult. Until then, the role of these dramatic characters in the present was elided, and thus the distance of these dramatic characters from the world of the audience was closed. With the activation of that role the distance between the world of the audience and the world of the tragedy increased. This distance, we saw, is correlative with the distance between mortals and deities in the tragedy. The greater the distance between mortals and deities in the world of the tragedy the smaller the distance between the world of the tragedy and that of the audience.

To sum up one aspect of the shift. While tragedies portraying a world nearest that of the audience, those without gods, continued to be produced throughout, the world in the tragedies that did involve gods changed, from something shaped on the model of sacred drama to something that deployed the present-day religious experience of epiphany, the experience that brought the world of everyday reality nearest to the gods, so the world of the tragedy appeared like an intensified version of the audience's world at its nearest to the gods. It brought the world of the tragedy nearer the human perspective of today, but in the most favorable possible version, as far as access to the world of the gods is concerned, much more so than in the tragedies from which the gods are absent. For, unlike in the latter, Euripidean tragedies with epiphanies offer authoritative, if complex, answers.

Euripidean epiphanies resembled, and so evoked, real-life epiphany, a religious experience in the audience's reality; not that in real life epiphanies occurred regularly, but they did, exceptionally, take place. From the perspective of the world of the audience, such epiphanies would have partly evoked the impersonation of deities by cult personnel. Thus, the tragic schema "divine appearance on high at the end of Euripidean tragedies" was a construct, a transformation of the tragic schema "impersonation of deities," which had been derived from the religious schema "impersonation of deities by cult personnel" in interaction, with the religious schema "real-life epiphany."[197] It would follow, then, that, far from diluting or subverting, the religious content of tragedy, Euripidean tragedies with a deity *ex machina* gave it a new and powerful injection of religious significance and resonance. For these real-life religious schemata, above all that of epiphany, would have helped shape the audience's perception of those divine appearances.

Therefore, the notion that the creation, and crystallization into the preferred choice, of the schema "deity in epiphany on high" could have been a purely "artistic" choice, with no religious resonances, simply the invention of a new theatrical device, is meaningless. For the audience, for whom the Euripidean divine appearances corresponded to a religious experience in their own life, would have in any case made sense of those divine appearances through their own assumptions about epiphanies.

Intertextuality does not alter this. For when this schema "deity on high acting in ways comparable to deities in epiphany" was first deployed, at the beginning of the establishment of this intertextual tradition, in the assumptions that both determined the tragedian's parameters of selection, and shaped the filters through which the audience made sense of the schema, the schema was inevitably made sense of through the real-life schema, the "common frame"[198] "real-life divine epiphany." Of course such schemata can be subverted, and their meanings changed; but, we saw, nothing in the extant tragedies

Chapter 4: Modalities of Divine Appearance

suggests that this was the case.[199] It may be argued that the connection with religious epiphany may have been subverted when mortals appeared in that position, on high, especially in the *mechane*, at the conclusion of a tragedy. Medea in Euripides' *Medea*, and Bellerophon in Euripides' *Stheneboia* appear *apo mechanes* at the conclusion; Bellerophon appears on Pegasos, like Medea, "acting half like a 'god from the machine'."[200] They have, in other words, through vehicles given them by divine help, become partly comparable to a *deus*. Bellerophon on Pegasos *apo mechanes* also appeared in *Bellerophon*. But in *Bellerophon* it is at some stage within the play that he takes off on Pegasos to scale the heavens, while at the end, after he was thrown off in punishment for his *hybris*, he reappears crippled and in rags. The arrival or departure *apo mechanes* on the stage seems to characterize mortals, besides Bellerophon in *Bellerophon* also Perseus in *Andromeda*; that is, mortals who have been given divine help so that they can fly. It would appear, then, that the position of on high, especially on the *mechane*, denoting epiphany, had not been subverted; on the contrary, it would seem that it had connotations of divine authority, so that a mortal only seems to appear in that position at the conclusion of the play if [s]he plays a role in some way comparable to that of a deity in epiphany. For Medea's wickedness or otherwise does not alter the fact that what she does is play a role partly comparable to that of a *deus*; that her wickedness does not subvert that role is shown by the fact that the epilogue (as well as the whole play) articulates ideas that are in harmony with those expressed by Medea's escape with divine connivance, and with the fact that she performs a role comparable to that of a *deus*, not subversive of that role.[201] Because the evidence is scarce, it is only very tentatively that I suggest the possibility that the position on high at the conclusion of a tragedy may not have been used for a mortal acting as in some way comparable to a *deus ex machina* after *Stheneboia*, which was produced before 429.[202] If this hypothesis is right, it would suggest a movement in the opposite direction from subversion, a firmer crystallization of the schema "position on high at the conclusion of a tragedy, performing certain actions," limiting its use to deities. In addition, there is a test case that shows that in the very late 420s, or soon after, the *apo mechanes* deity had serious religious significance, and had certainly not been subverted. As we saw, it is very difficult to doubt that in *Erechtheus* the cults mentioned by Athena had zoomed the world of tragedy to that of the audience, that those cults were perceived by the audience to be their own cults, and that here the world of the tragedy penetrated the world of the audience.

The fact that the audience made sense of divine appearances in tragedy through (transformed and interacting) schemata pertaining to their lived religion confirms further that they saw these divine appearances as religiously significant in the world of the tragedy. In addition, the fact that not only was Sophocles generally perceived as an exceptionally pious man, but also he was specifically connected in the tradition with a serious (dream) epiphany that led to the foundation of a cult,[203] scarcely suggests that he had been perceived to have deployed epiphanies frivolously.[204] Whoever invented this schema, and it is likely to have been Euripides, Euripides' preferred choice was, or became, to have deities in his tragedies, and that his preferred choice of divine appearance was a deity in epiphany at the end. For, we saw, the schema "divine epiphany at the end of the tragedy" is deployed in either nine or ten of the seventeen extant Euripidean tragedies, and of the tragedies that do not include an epiphany two are the earliest surviving Euripidean tragedies. As far as we can judge, the pattern of divine appearances in the fragmentary tragedies is no different.

As we saw, though there are variations pertaining to distances in the various Euripidean tragedies, they are within certain parameters. There is more variation in the distances between the world of the audience and the world of the tragedy; the variation in the distancing between deities and mortals in the tragedies is within relatively narrow parameters. This offers some further support to the view that in Euripides' parameters of selection the gods had not been theatrical devices; if they had there would have been more variation. The narrow variation suggests that in the assumptions which shaped Euripides' parameters of selection "greater distancing" was an important and significant element.

To make sense of this, and of the shift in general, and at the same time test the validity of the above conclusions, especially of the argument that, for the audience, deities in epiphany were charged with religious significance, we need to ask what, if any, are the effects of this distancing, how do the meanings these distanced divine appearances produce differ, if at all, from those produced by the nondistanced modalities? And is it possible to make sense of these differences in terms of the other facets of Euripidean tragedies?

As we saw, the distanced "Euripidean" interaction stresses the distance between mortals and gods and (the other side of this) brings the world on the tragic stage nearer to the world of the audience. Let us consider further this notion of distance. First there is now distance in the sense of separateness between deities and mortals. The two do not physically mix, either in the epiphany modality or in the empty stage modality. The fact that in Euripidean (and later Sophoclean)

Chapter 4: Modalities of Divine Appearance

tragedies, there is no representation on stage of deities mingling, physically mixing, with mortals emphasized the separateness of the two. This separateness between deities and mortals corresponds to the perception of the "real" distance, the gulf, between deities and mortals in the Greek conceptual universe, which was emphasized in some religious representations. In Greek religion there was always perceived to be distance between the two, but the relationships between deities and mortals were complex, and some myths and representations underplay the distance, others stress it. Thus, the separateness in these tragedies can be seen as articulating visibly, and being articulated by, these representations that emphasize the distance. One facet of this distance is the divinities' "otherness" to men. In Euripidean tragedies deities can mix with mortals only in disguise, when, in other words, they have concealed their otherness through taking human form. When they are undisguised they do not mix, and, when both mortals and immortals are on stage at the same time, they stand at a higher level; in other words, undisguised otherness goes together with separateness and the deities' differential location; the fact that between deities and mortals there was complete spatial separateness or differential location expressed, and thus stressed, the deities' otherness.

Consequently, in Euripidean and later Sophoclean tragedies there is an emphasis on the otherness of the gods, and on the gulf between gods and mortals. This stressing of the distance between mortals and gods and the gods' otherness is not limited to tragedy at this time. At very roughly the time in which the shift in the tragic modalities of divine appearances was probably beginning, a comparable strong stressing of the distance between mortals and gods is manifested in an important facet of Athenian cult: Pheidias' Athena Parthenos, the colossal chryselephantine cult statue for the Parthenon, which was begun in 447, and was installed in 438,[205] also stressed the goddess' otherness, the distance between human bodies and the superficially similar divine bodies and the deity's otherness, through its colossal size and its materials and techniques; besides being colossal and made of gold and ivory, it was also very highly ornate, decorated with precious materials which produced a scintillating effect, and very elaborate, with elaborate additional elements, the Nike, a highly decorated shield and helmet, a highly decorated base. All this, which to us appears excessively garish, contributed further to the goddess' distancing from the human world. There had been large size cult statues before, and there had also been chryselephantine statues in the sixth century—though it is not certain that there were any chryselephantine cult statues. But this colossal chryselephantine cult image, and the one of Zeus Pheidias made for the temple of Zeus at Olympia, created for the ancient viewers (at least so we can gather from the evidence of authors in later antiquity)[206] the feelings of awe associated with the divine. Awe was produced by the fact that these colossal cult statues articulated iconographically the gods' power and the distance between them and mortals, the human bodies that are but pale perishable reflections of the gods' perfect and imperishable bodies, of which these statues are trying to give some idea.

For our purposes it does not matter to what extent, if at all, Pheidias' Athena had reflected collective religious representations involving a greater emphasis on the distance, and to what extent the statue had shaped such perceptions, helping emphasize the distance between deities and mortals; nor does it matter to what extent the Euripidean modalities of divine appearance were influenced by the statue and its effect on collective representations, and to what extent the shift was a manifestation of the same preexisting perceptions. What is important is that the shift in the tragic modalities of divine appearances reconstructed here corresponds to the articulation of a comparable religious perception in a cult statue of central importance in Athenian religion. For this suggests that the reconstruction offered here is not a culturally determined construct, and that the shift in the tragic modalities of divine appearances was correlative with contemporary religious perceptions. This, in its turn, would support the view that this shift was significant, not a mere theatrical device.

Another effect of the Euripidean "distanced" modalities of divine appearance is the provision of information, and above all of authoritative insight, given by those distanced deities, in the epiphany modalities to the characters, in the prologue modality only to the audience. Thus, the audience, partly because of this, and partly because some of the dramatic characters are "players" in the audience's religious world, knows and understands much more than the dramatic characters. The dramatic characters, then, resemble the audience, in that the latter in their real life also inevitably had a limited perspective; but as tragic spectators they see the wider picture, part of the divine perspective, and this helps them "learn." Through the empty stage modality of divine appearance the audience gains a greater understanding of, and broader perspective into, the action enacted on stage, a greater understanding of problems; they are guided to think in a broader perspective, shown how, almost trained to learn to think in that perspective. This can be seen as one of the ways in which the tragedian was a teacher to the polis. When the epiphany mode is deployed, the audience share insights with the dramatic characters at the conclusion of the drama. This too "teaches" the audience about the wider, the divine, perspective. For these deities in

Chapter 4: Modalities of Divine Appearance

epiphany give answers, very complex answers of the type recostructed in chapter III.3, but clearer and more focussed ones than those articulated in tragedies without epiphany. These answers offered much greater guidance to the mortals in the world of the tragedy than the audience received in real life, and they were (in complex ways) also pertinent to the world of the audience.

Deities in epiphany, then, and to a lesser extent the explanations of prologue deities (and of Lyssa and Iris in *Heracles*), which framed the action and the tragic characters' problematization, offered, to a varying degree, answers or, at the very least, at the minimum end of the spectrum, a "learning" process, in a context in which the lesser distance between the world of the tragedy and the world of the audience and the greater distance of the tragedy's mortal characters from the gods brought the explorations and problematizations in the tragedy very much closer to the audience's realities. In the tragedy's world the gods are distanced, as they are "today," in the world of the audience. But, unlike what happens in the world of the audience, in the tragedies deities do eventually appear sometimes and give answers; not always, but quite often; and these answers may be complex, but they are authoritative.

Because they are distanced, because their otherness and great superiority is stressed, the Euripidean gods' pronouncements are especially authoritative. The exact degree of their authority, like their distance from mortals, differs in the different Euripidean tragedies. *Heracles* is situated at one end of the spectrum; most tragedies belong, or are nearer, to the more distanced and authoritative end.[207] At the lesser end of the spectrum of authoritativeness is Kastor in *Electra*,[208] a lesser deity who had been mortal, and who does not understand the full picture, and so does not fully understand his master's, Apollo's, actions. At the other end it would have been Zeus *ex machina* in his persona as sovereign of the world, but this never happens. This distance is too great, and thus it is represented through absence. The will of Zeus is reported by others. In a context in which distance is stressed, but authoritative answers are also given, the notion of the ultimate unknowability of the divine will does not disappear; it has drifted to Zeus the sovereign god, at a distance so great, that he cannot be represented. Zeus' "almost absence," incidentally, provides a further argument against the view that Euripidean gods were mere theatrical devices; for this "almost absence" cannot be explained if that is what they had been, but makes perfect sense as part of Euripides' religious discourse.

The fact that for the audience the Euripidean epiphany schema evoked, and so was made sense of with the help of, the "real-life epiphany" schema, gave greater religious charge to the divine pronouncements. The gods' roles in the distanced interaction modalities of divine appearance added to that authority. In *Eumenides* the gods themselves were implicated in the action, they had a stake in the development of events, and they had to try to achieve certain goals. The same seems true in at least some of the other fragmentary Aeschylean and Sophoclean tragedies involving the direct interaction model.[209] Hence also some of the tragedies of this type had choruses of deities, while, as far as I am aware, there are no choruses consisting of deities in later tragedy.[210] This involvement of the deities in the action is comparable to that in sacred drama, in which the actions and events involving deities were central. Gods in Euripidean tragedies are not implicated in the action in this way; they are at a distance, and they appear as figures of authority to instruct, reveal, foretell, explain. They may favor certain people and persecute others, but they are not implicated in the action on stage, except when they intervene as deities *apo mechanes*, with distanced authority at the end, as real gods did in epiphany. Even in Sophocles' *Ajax*, Athena, who is much less distanced than the Euripidean deities, exercises her power as a distanced deity, though we see some of its operation on stage. She is not directly implicated as she is in *Eumenides*.

The fact that in *Eumenides* deities are implicated in the action is correlative with the fact that in that tragedy the audience does not see one divine perspective, but several. Though Athena is dominant, and she speaks the will of Zeus, the other perspectives are also enacted. In some Euripidean tragedies we only see one divine perspective, expressing the will of Zeus. In some, as in *Hippolytos*, we see more than one divine perspective, Aphrodite in the prologue and Artemis in epiphany; but, we saw, the audience made sense of those perspectives through assumptions in which Aphrodite was right to be offended, and Artemis' words stress that there is a divine system guaranteed and policed by Zeus. There is no systemic or ideological conflict. The nearest we come to the latter in Euripidean tragedies is Kastor's pronouncements in *Electra* and Lyssa's dissent in *Heracles*. However, Kastor's expression of unease is articulated around his acknowledgment that Apollo is his master, and the very minor, negatively colored, Lyssa has to obey Hera's orders. This (less common) "maximum diversity" end of the spectrum in Euripides, with its ultimate order and hierarchy, is much less disturbing than the presentation of two powerful perspectives in conflict, even if the conflict is eventually resolved.

Euripidean deities are distanced, like real gods in the audience's world, and appear through a modality associated with real-life dei-

Chapter 4: Modalities of Divine Appearance 499

ties. The audience, watching a performance taking place in a sanctuary, in the presence of Dionysos (in the shape of his statue), in the course of a festival, in which a deity, whom the tragedy had zoomed to the audience's religious realities, appeared in epiphany, impersonated by an actor (which would have been perceived as a transformation of the "priestly personnel impersonating deities" schema), but doing the things that deities "normally" did in real-life epiphanies, would have perceived these deities in epiphany as representations of their deities, giving "answers" in the world of the tragedy that were relevant to their own world—especially if it is right that, as I argued in chapter I.2, there was permeability between the world of tragedy and that of the audience, and the identity of the chorus as a chorus of Dionysos in the present was drastically marginalized, but not wholly elided.

This, I suggest, confirms the conclusion that, far from diluting or subverting the religious content of tragedy, Euripidean tragedies with a deity *ex machina* gave it a new and powerful injection of religious significance and resonance.

For whatever reason these distanced modalities came into being, they clearly struck a chord, and so crystallized into the preferred choices to the extent that, as far as we can tell, they eventually eliminated the direct interaction type, so that this "greater distance and otherness" of the divinities was a constant in the parameters of selection shaping Euripidean and later Sophoclean tragedies. I suggest that there were circumstances at the relevant time that appear in some way correlative with the effects of the new modalities of divine appearances as they have been reconstructed here, in that they indicate the existence of "needs" which these modalities appear to fulfil best.

As we saw in chapter III.3, the cultural context in which the surviving Euripidean tragedies were generated involved some religious "turbulence" and anxiety. I suggested there that this helped shape Euripides' religious discourse, which developed in certain ways in response to this situation, especially the version articulated in tragedies with deep, and sometimes bleak, religious problematization. Now that we have considered the effects created by the Euripidean modalities of divine appearance it becomes clear that these effects correspond in a multifaceted way to the "needs" of those turbulent times. For these tragedies present a world from which the gods are either absent or distanced, a world which for the characters is comparable to that of the world of the audience, with often bleak and dark problematization, and very limited access to the deities—at least until the very end; but then, in the tragedies, deities often do appear, to give authoritative answers, reveal the divine will (at least partly) and (at least part of) the wider picture, involving problematizations of direct and urgent relevance to the audience. The correspondence between the perceived needs and the reconstructed effects of these modalities of divine appearance suggests that those contemporary circumstances, this climate of religious anxiety, may have helped generate, or at the very least crystallize and privilege, these modalities of divine appearance which best fulfil the needs of a turbulent world. This may explain the fact that the greater distance and otherness of the divinities was a constant in the parameters of selection shaping Euripidean and later Sophoclean tragedies.

In any case, whether or not this hypothesis is right, I suggest that the study of the modalities of divine appearances in the three tragedians has shown that a very interesting shift had taken place in these modalities, and provided further, independent, arguments in favor of the view that, far from being simple theatrical devices, divine appearances in Euripidean tragedies were charged with religious significance; and that they were part of the discourse of religious exploration woven by Euripides, which, I argued, was part of the discourse of Athenian polis religion.

Notes

1. Mastronarde remarked on this (Mastronarde 1990, 274) that the separation of gods and men is a tragic theme, and is normally expressed visually in tragedy by their not appearing together or by their occupying distinct spaces when they do share the stage; he adds (n. 81) that "it may be necessary to add the qualification 'after Aeschylus' as is often done." He says that we cannot be sure how often in Aeschylus undisguised divinities shared the stage with mortals and that (n. 83) in one type of play a god may regularly have appeared outside the prologue and the epilogue: the theomachos play such as the Dionysos plays of Aeschylus' or Sophocles' *Thamyras*. I am arguing here that there were distinct differences between the modalities of divine apppearances in the different tragedians, and that this pattern of differences is significant.

2. Which of the two is not important here—except in some cases that will be discussed below. On this question cf. Mastronarde 1990. I sometimes here use the term *ex machina* or *apo mechanes* conventionally for this type of epiphany—without implication as to whether they appeared on the crane.

3. In *Tro.* I shall be referring to this as the empty stage modality.

4. Intertextual knowledge, such as, for example, divine apprearances in the Homeric poems, must not be privileged, as it sometimes is by modern scholars, explicitly or implicitly (through the focus on the tragedian rather than the audience). First, the fifth-century audience's perception of the Homeric divine appearances was itself shaped by their lived religion experiences, through which, therefore, the intertextual input was channelled;

Chapter 4: Modalities of Divine Appearance

and second, the different media and performance contexts, recitation on the one hand, enactment of divine appearances in a course of a festival in which divine appearance is a crucial concept (cf. above part II and below) on the other, constructed different parameters for the perception of the two, and, therefore helped activate the assumptions based on lived religion most strongly, pushed them to the forefront.

5. Burkert calls this a variant of epiphany (Burkert 1997, 24).

6. I only consider these because epiphanies in poetry, whether descriptions of mythical epiphanies or (metaphorical or nonmetaphorical or partly metaphorical) claims of an actual encounter with a deity, though they are shaped by religious assumptions, involve further factors and thus complexities, while it is the commonly shared assumptions we need to consider here. On epiphanies cf. Pfister 1924, 277-323; Nilsson 1974, 225-7; Versnel 1990, 190-3; Burkert 1985, 186-8; Graf 1997, 1154-6 with bibl.; Henrichs 1996a, 546 with bibl.; Hornblower 1996, 356 bibl.

7. On two instances of "real-life" epiphanies: cf. Hdt 6.105-6; *IG* IV² 128; cf. Parker 1996, 163-5; Garland 1992, 16; 47-63.

8. For the persistence of this important aspect of epiphanies cf. Jacoby comment. to Ister 334 FF 50-3 (*FGrH* IIIb I p.652).

9. Cf. e.g. Hdt. 6.61.

10. Cf. e.g. Hdt. 6.69, where a hero slept with a woman and she (believed she may have) conceived a child (if the child had not been her husband's).

11. Cf. e.g. Burkert 1985, 186; Mylonas 1961, 261-4; Clinton 1992, 84-95.

12. On this notion cf. Hägg 1986, 46-7, 60-2; Kiechle 1970, 259-71; Burkert 1997, 27-8. Phye's impersonation of Athena to facilitate Peisistratos' return (Hdt. 1.60) has been connected with such rituals (cf. e.g. Kiechle 1970, op. cit.; Burkert 1985, 186).

13. On which cf. Burkert 1988, 81-7; cf. also Burkert 1985, 134-5; Burkert 1997, 24.

14. Hdt. 1.51 and cf. Nilsson 1906, 159; 472.

15. Burkert 1988, 84-5.

16. Cf. e.g. on the Eleusinian sacred drama Mylonas 1961, 261-4.

17. I will discuss the more complex case of *Heracles* below.

18. I am, of course, accepting the view that in *Eumenides* Apollo was not on the roof but on the platform of the *ekkyklema* (cf. ch. III.1 and n. 133).

19. *TrGF* iii pp. 159-60 F 44.

20. Cf. West 1990, 31.

21. West 1990, 42-3.

22. West 1990, 43.

23. Cf. West 1990, 45 and n. 46.

24. On which cf. *TrGF* iii pp. 259-61; West 1983, 70.

25. On Aeschylus' *Psychostasia* cf. *TrGF* iii pp. 374-77; Taplin 1977, 431-33.

26. Taplin 1977, 431-2.

27. Cf. the texts in *TrGF* iii p. 375.

28. Taplin 1977, 432.

29. Taplin 1977, 432-3.

30. Cf. below for other Aeschylean tragedies. S. West 1984, 294-5 considered this question of the alleged inhibition against representing Zeus on the tragic stage. She suggested that there is no reason why if there had been such an inhibition it should not have applied to satyr-plays and that "the undeniable rarity" of Zeus' appearance on the tragic stage may be explained primarily with reference to certain mythological preconditions. Zeus keeps his distance, and so there were relatively few circumstances in which the tragedians might be tempted to bring him on stage, chief among which were his erotic encounters, or at least those which did not present difficulties of staging, as, for example, the abduction of Europa did. She further argues that Zeus appeared as a character in Euripides' *Alkmene*. In my view the situation concerning satyr-plays is different from that concerning tragedies, because the distances between the world of the play and the world of the audience, which is of crucial importance for divine appearances, is entirely different from those in tragedy. (Cf. also n. 157 below). With regard to tragedy, since the choices made by tragedians as to subjects and handling of subjects were not divorced from assumptions of what was perceived to be appropriate to represent, it was those assumptions that shaped the parameters determining selections. So the fact that certain choices were made and certain others were not is correlative with what was felt to be appropriate. Thus, for example, the perception that it was appropriate to represent direct interaction between gods and mortals "enabled" the presentation of a story such as that shown in Aeschylus' *Toxotides*, while the perception that direct interaction was not appropriate would be conducive to a treatment of a story involving the erotic encounter of a deity and a mortal of the type seen in Euripides' *Ion*. I discuss below the view that Zeus had appeared as a character in Euripides' *Alkmene*. Here I will only say that if it is right my argument is strengthened; for if Zeus had appeared in Euripides' *Alkmene*, this exceptional appearance would be clearly correlative with the fact that he would not be appearing primarily in his persona as the sovereign god in charge of the cosmos, but as Alkmene's lover.

31. Differences commented upon by the Homeric scholia (cf. *TrGF* ad loc.).

32. Cf. also *Iliad* 22.179-81.

33. Expressed in myths such as that in Hesiod's *Theogony*, where on the one hand Zeus is the undisputed sovereign who apportioned their spheres of influence to the other gods, and on the other, the other gods had invited him to assume sovereignty (881-5), a combination of sovereignty won by the victory that was above all Zeus', brought about by his cunning and his might, and also through the consensus of the other gods. There are also other myths pertaining to Zeus' sovereignty and power in relation to other gods which may seem to raise problems about his supremacy, but which in fact express this ambiguity of Greek polytheism; cf. e.g. Hom. *Il.* 15. 187-218.

34. That is, for example, expressed in the notion in Hesiod *Th.* 464 that Kronos was fated to be overcome by his son.

35. Cf. above n. 30.

36. Cf. on this tragedy *TrGF* iii pp. 364-70; Taplin 1977, 242; 430.

37. *Vita Aesch.* (*TrGF* iii T 1) 6.

Chapter 4: Modalities of Divine Appearance 503

38. Which was probably early, if it is right that some elements on some early fifth-century vases reflect the influence of this trilogy. On the relationship between the trilogy *Myrmidones, Nereides,* and *Phryges* or *Hektoros Lytra* cf. Boardman 1976, 13-4 (with earlier bibl.), whose (rather tentative) doubts about the similarities being due to Aeschylean influence on vases do not seem to me justified in this case. It is, of course, only reflection, partial inspiration that is at issue here.

39. As we saw (above n. 22) *TrGF* iii F 168 is more likely to be part of *Semele* or *Hydrophoroi* than of *Xantriai*.

40. Cf. *TrGF* iii p. 286 ad F 169.

41. On which cf. *TrGF* iii pp. 359-61.

42. If the restorations in a passage of Philodemos are right (cf. *TrGF* iii p. 361 ad F 260), he would be saying that in Aeschylus' *Phineus* the Harpies, though they were goddesses, died at the hands of the Boreads.

43. On Aeschylus' *Semele* or *Hydrophoroi*: *TrGF* iii pp. 335-6; Lloyd-Jones 1957, 566-71; Taplin 1977, 427-8.

44. *TrGF* iii pp. 281-5 takes F 168, the fragment involving Hera in disguise collecting offerings for the Nymphs to be part of *Xantriai*. Lloyd-Jones 1957, 567-8 argues convincingly in favor of it being part of *Semele* or *Hydrophoroi*. Taplin 1977, 428 thinks it possible that Semele was in labor during the play, but the birth was finally precipitated by the thunderbolt. But if she had been in labor why should Zeus have needed to complete the pregnancy by inserting Dionysos in his thigh? And this is too important a part of the theological myth to think of a different variant here. On *Hydrophoroi* cf. also Faraone 1997, 42-3.

45. On *Pentheus* cf. *TrGF* iii pp. 298-9.

46. And perhaps also in *Bacchai*, if it is indeed a distinct play (cf. *TrGF* iii p. 137).

47. The hypothesis that this play is satyric depends on a culturally determined perception of tragedy and on ignoring Athenaeus' statement (Athenaeus 10.428F) that *Kabeiroi* (on which cf. *TrGF* iii pp. 214-6) was a tragedy.

48. Cf. *TrGF* iii p. 307.

49. West 1979, 130-48 considers the whole trilogy non-Aeschylean; West 1990, 51-72 argues that the author of the trilogy was probably Aeschylus' son Euphorion.

50. On which cf. *TrGF* iii pp. 346-9.

51. Lyssa is shown in a representation of the death of Aktaion on the bell krater Boston 00.346 (ARV 1045.7; Add 320), but this does not necessarily entail that she had been a character in Aesch. *Toxotides* (a hypothesis presented as a possibility by Trendall and Webster 1971, 62). The echoes and reflections of theatrical performances on Attic images are too indirect and complex for such a conclusion. On Lyssa cf. also Padel 1992, 163.

52. On which cf. *TrGF* iii pp. 349-51.

53. Nymphs are divine, but not necessarily immortal, though some clearly were. The category "Nymph" is very elastic.

54. On which cf. *TrGF* iii pp. 377-9; cf. F 281.

55. Cf. on this tragedy *TrGF* iii pp. 288-91.

56. Cf. *TrGF* iii pp. 210-2.

57. It seems to me that there is no positive evidence in favor of this hypothesis (I would hardly consider F 91 an argument in favor, except if one makes culturally determined judgments. Cf. the evidence and bibl. on this hypothesis *TrGF* iii p. 210).

58. Cf. Gantz 1993, 719.

59. ARV 832.37; Add 295; LIMC (=Lochin 1990) no 1; Shapiro 1994, 86-7 figs. 58-9.

60. Cf. Shapiro 1994, 86-7.

61. On images of Ixion cf. Burn 1987, 52-4 with bibl.; Lochin 1990, 859-62; Gantz 1993, 720-1; Shapiro 1994, 85-9.

62. Cf. e.g. the hydria Cracow National Museum 1225 (ARV 1121.17; Add 331) which depicts a version of the Lykourgos myth inspired by Aeschylus' *Edonoi* (cf. Trendall and Webster 1971, 49).

63. Shapiro 1994, 86.

64. Broadly speaking, since we do not know the date of this tragedy.

65. *TrGF* iv F 160.

66. Schol. Ar. *Birds* ad loc.

67. Dunbar 1995, 627-8.

68. It is not usually easy, we saw, to reconstruct the assumptions that make a joke comic. But we can reconstruct some of the parameters for the modalities for the reconstruction of paratragic constructions.

69. That a recent production of a *Niobe*, that may have been Aeschylus' *Niobe*, had taken place is surely suggested by Aristophanes *Wasps* 579-80 (cf. MacDowell 1971, 210 ad 579).

70. Cf. Sechan 1925, 83 fig. 24; Keuls 1984, 37 fig. 3; LIMC no 12.

71. Sechan 1925, 83-4; Trendall and Webster 1971, 58. Trendall 1991, 178 evokes the culturally determined concept of "likelihood" when he states that these images may look back to Aeschylus' *Niobe*, "but are more likely to reflect some later play on the same theme." In favor of the vase reflecting the Aeschylean tragedy: cf. also Keuls 1984, 37-8.

72. I have discussed the ways in which South Italian vase painters created their own versions of myths under the (partial) inspiration of tragic theatrical performances in connection with Euripides' *Medea* in Sourvinou-Inwood 1997c, 269-75, 292-6.

73. Cf. the hypothesis to Soph. *Niobe P.Oxy.* 3653 fr.2.

74. Such as, for example, *Kallisto* (on which cf. *TrGF* iii p. 216), in the story of which the direct interaction between mortals and immortals is crucial. The shade of Teiresias, which appeared in *Psychagogoi* (cf. *TrGF* iii pp. 370-4), does not belong in the category under consideration here; like Dareios' ghost in *Persai*, it is otherwordly, but not divine.

75. On which cf. *TrGF* iii pp. 416-8.

76. On which cf. *TrGF* iii pp. 380-3; Lloyd-Jones 1957, 576.

77. Cf. Lloyd-Jones 1957, 576.

78. I am not, of course, including *Rhesos*.

79. Cf. Knox 1983, 280-1; cf. also Sourvinou-Inwood 1997c, 259-60.

Chapter 4: Modalities of Divine Appearance

80. Mastronarde 1990, 284 includes it in the list of plays in which gods appear at roof level. But Diggle 1994, 422 classifies Aelian *nat. an.* 7. 39 (Eur. fr. 857 N), on which this reconstruction is based, s.v. 'Fragmenta et testimonia dubia'.

81. Cf. Seaford 1996b, 252 ad 1329-30.

82. Lines 64-97 Page (1941); cf. Nightingale 1992, 123, 130.

83. Cf. Page 1941, 83.

84. Cf. Collard, Cropp, and Lee 1995, 120 ad F 312.

85. Cf. Collard, Cropp, and Lee 1995, 244. It has also been suggested (cf. e.g. Webster 1967, 149-50) that Hippo appeared *ex machina* in the form of a horse at the end of *Melanippe sophe*; cf. the brief discussion in Collard, Cropp, and Lee 1995, 241.

86. Collard, Cropp, and Lee 1995, 197, 202, cf. fr. 782. According to its hypothesis (Austin 1968, 92.14), *Rhadamanthys* involved an epiphany of Artemis.

87. Cf. Collard, Cropp, and Lee 1995, 54-5.

88. Cf. Collard, Cropp, and Lee 1995, 58.

89. Cf. Barrett 1964, 44-5; Webster 1967, 70-1.

90. Cf. Sechan 1925, 274-90; Xanthakis-Karamanos 1986, 107-11; cf. also *P.Oxy.* 47 (1980) 6-10 no 3317; Scodel 1982, 37-42. Sechan 1925, 274-90 sets out the case for dissociating Euripides' *Antigone* from both Hyginus *Fab.* 72 and from some images on vases which had been thought to reflect it. Xanthakis-Karamanos 1986, 107-11 sets out the case for dissociating *P.Oxy.* 3317, as well as Hyginus *Fab.* 72 and the images, from Euripides' *Antigone*.

91. Cf. Webster 1967, 182; Xanthakis-Karamanos 1986, 109; cf. also Sechan 1925, 274-90 passim. Whether Heracles' intervention belongs to the Euripidean *Antigone*, or, as is much more likely, to another tragedy, it seems clear that it was as a mortal that he had interceded on behalf of Haimon and Antigone, in his lifetime, not as a god. First, the word used by Hyginus, *deprecaretur*, suggests a plea from one man to another; second, and most importantly, his plea was unsuccessful. In Greek tragedies deities do not plead with mortals, and when they intervene, their interventions are not rejected.

92. Cf. Collard, Cropp, and Lee 1995, 123, 125.

93. Some other tragedies which may have involved a divine appearance are listed by Mastronarde 1990, 289. Cf. also on other tragedies for which Webster postulates a *deus ex machina*, e.g.: Webster 1967, 95; 166, 198, 199.

94. The Hypothesis to *Phrixos* A (*P.Oxy.* 2455, Austin 1968, 101 no 31, together with *P.Oxy.* 3652 (*P.Oxy.* 52 [1984] ed. by H. M. Cockle, pp. 22-3) shows that *Phrixos* A and *Phrixos* B had the same theme; they did not deal with different parts of the Phrixos story. For the *Phrixos* B hypothesis see *P.Oxy.* 1455, fr. 17; Austin 1968, 102-3 no 32.

95. Cf. also Webster 1967, 132-6.

96. S. West 1984, 294-5.

97. Cf. Sechan 1925, with bibl. and a critical discussion of the earlier debate; Trendall and Webster 1971, 76; Webster 1967, 93.

98. I discussed these modalities with regard to vases reflecting Euripides' *Medea* in Sourvinou-Inwood 1997c, 269-75, 281-96.

99. S. West 1984, 294.

100. The Paestan bell-krater London British Museum F 149 by Python (Trendall and Webster 1971, 76-7 III.3.8).

101. Cf. Sechan 1925, 248 with bibl.; cf. also Trendall 1989, 202.

102. Cf. Faraone 1997, 41 with bibl.

103. It has been suggested (Trendall and Webster 1971, 76) on the basis of iconographical evidence, that the prologue (a fragment of which has survived [Austin 1968, fr. 151, pp. 84-5 col. III]) was spoken by Hermes.

104. Cf. Collard, Cropp, and Lee 1995, 200.

105. Lines 241-4. On the identity of this goddess cf. the critical discussion with bibl. in Collard, Cropp, and Lee 1995, 198 cf. 235 ad 236-9.

106. Even in the unlikely possibility that Aphrodite was the intended bride, and that she spoke the prologue (cf. Collard, Cropp, and Lee 1995, 201), this would have been no different from other deities speaking a prologue on an empty stage.

107. *P.Oxy.* 2457, Austin 1968, 88-9.

108. On the notion that Sophocles had also written a tragedy called *Ixion* cf. *TrGF* iv p. 267; Lloyd-Jones 1996, 134-5.

109. Philochoros *FGrH* 328 F 217.

110. Jacoby (commentary to Philochoros *FGrH* 328 F 217) connects the death with the notion of Protagoras' alleged conviction; but the historicity of Protagoras' alleged trial has now been seriously challenged (cf. Parker 1996, 208 with bibl.).

111. Gantz 1993, 719.

112. Plutarch *Moralia* 19E.

113. Webster 1967, 160 and Trendall and Webster 1971, 95 do not exclude the possibility that this was narrated in a messenger speech, but I believe that the words *ou exegagon* are more likely to suggest that the audience had seen Ixion on the wheel.

114. Webster 1967, 160; Trendall and Webster 1971, 95.

115. Cf. Gantz 1993, 718-21; cf. also Trendall and Webster 1971, 95.

116. On which cf. Mastronarde 1990, 268-9, 270; cf. also 260.

117. Simon 1976, 177-86; cf. also Burn 1987, 52-4 and pl. 34; Shapiro 1994, 88 and fig. 60; LIMC no 2.

118. Simon 1976, 177-86. Cf. also Burn 1987, 52-4.

119. Burn, in her study of the Meidias Painter, has taken a favorable view of this hypothesis (Burn 1987, 52-4); specifically, she thinks it "quite probable" that the vase is connected with the tragedy (p. 54). Cf. also Shapiro 1994, 88-9.

120. As Burn says of another scene which she connects with a Euripidean play (Burn 1987, 62). "Euripides' influence on the Meidias Painter is unlikely to have been direct. . . . It may, however, have been the production of Euripides' *Iphigeneia* which inspired the selection of this unusual subject, and Euripides' characterization of the wavering Agamemnon might have influenced the artistic representation of the figure."

121. For the Meidias Painter himself certainly constructed subtle iconographical links by such means: cf. e.g. Sourvinou-Inwood 1997c, 275-8 on the London hydria E 224.

Chapter 4: Modalities of Divine Appearance 507

122. Cf. esp. 76ff.

123. Cf. Collard, Cropp, and Lee 1995, 83, cf. 101.

124. Collard, Cropp, and Lee 1995, 82. Cf. op.cit. for the argument in favor of the view that this is the first time in the play when Bellerophon on Pegasos appears from the machine.

125. Cf. Collard, Cropp, and Lee 1995, 101.

126. Arist. *Thesm.* 1098ff.; cf. Sommerstein 1994, 229 ad 1098.

127. Webster 1967, 160; 303; Trendall and Webster 1971, 95.

128. Cf. e.g. Lochin 1990, 861.

129. LIMC Ixion (= Lochin 1990) no 3; LIMC Bia et Kratos no 2 (= Simon 1986) no 2; Pensa 1977, 26, 36.

130. Cf. Lochin 1990, op. cit.

131. He is correctly identified by Pensa (Pensa 1977, 26). The identification as Hades (cf. Sechan 1925, 394-5) is the result of the assumption that the wheel is located in the Underworld, but in fact Ixion's punishment does not take place in the Underworld until later; Pensa (Pensa 1977, 36) correctly notes that the location of this scene is not Hades. If it were Hades, Iris would be out of place. She flies through the air, and is therefore an appropiate choice for an Ixion scene in which the punishment is located in the air, but she would not be present in Hades; it is Hermes who is the messenger of the gods who crosses from the upper to the nether world.

132. Simon 1986 (=LIMC Bia et Kratos) on no 2.

133. Lochin 1990 (= LIMC Ixion) on no 3.

134. LIMC no 15.

135. LIMC no 14.

136. This is not my own loaded description, but that of *CVA* ad loc. (Capua 1 on pl. 18).

137. Cf. LIMC (M. Schmidt 1992) no 36; Taplin 1993, 116 no 1.101; Sourvinou-Inwood 1997c, 270 fig. 3.

138. Cf. LIMC (M. Schmidt 1992) no 35; Taplin 1993, 117 no 2.103.

139. Cf. above n. 101.

140. Cf. above n. 102.

141. In complex ways, comparable to those I tried to reconstruct for the South Italian images inspired, to a greater or lesser extent, by Euripides' *Medea* (Sourvinou-Inwood 1997c, 269-96).

142. Cf. e.g. Taplin 1993, 6.111; 6.112.

143. Cf. Webster 1967, 97-8.

144. Cf. Haslam 1977, 21; Oranje 1980, 169-72.

145. Cf. *TrGF* i pp. 171-78, Critias 43 FF 1-14.

146. Cf. on this Sourvinou-Inwood 1995, 71-3.

147. Cf. e.g. Knox 1985, 90-1.

148. Ritchie 1964, 132-5 stresses similarities, and marginalizes entirely the important differences, in order to argue that the appearance of the Muse in *Rhesos* is Euripidean in character.

149. Knox 1985, 91.

150. Or indeed any serious problematization.

151. Cf. e.g. Easterling 1982, 23. Lloyd-Jones 1994, 8-9 takes the view that *Ajax* is not, as usually thought, early, but a mature masterpiece, probably not much earlier than *OT*, produced in the 30s or 20s.

152. Cf. Easterling 1993b, 81-82 on this encounter.

153. Cf. e.g. Pucci 1994, 19-20.

154. Cf. Mastronarde 1990, 275. Mastronarde says that Ajax can see Athena as a mark of his altered state, while Odysseus' inability to see her is a mark of his normal mortal status.

155. Cf. Mastronarde 1990, 278; Seale 1982, 176 n. 3; Easterling 1993b, 81.

156. Barrett 1964, 409 ad 1391-3 cf. also 395-6 ad 1283.

157. I am not considering plays like *Inachos*, which are clearly satyr plays. (Like most scholars, I consider Sophocles' *Inachos* to be a satyr play [cf. Lloyd-Jones 1996, 113, 115].) The modalities of interaction between mortals and immortals in satyr plays are by definition different, since their chorus is formed of satyrs, and the distances between the world of the play and the world of the audience is also different.

158. *TrGF* iv, pp. 102-23 FF 10a-18.

159. Haslam 1976, 2.

160. Mastronarde 1990, 289 classifies *Ajax Lokros* as one of the cases in which there is insufficient evidence as to where the gods stood. The categories I am trying to define are somewhat more complex; the place where the god stood was only one of the elements defining the categories of direct interaction between deities and mortals and more distanced, epiphany type interaction. The level at which the gods stood, on the stage or on the roof or *mechane*, is one of the elements that make up these two different types. As far as *Ajax Lokros* is concerned, it is the type of interaction involved in Athena's words, as well as the possibility that she may be coming out of her temple, that leads me to classify this as direct interaction.

161. Cf. also, for this view, Haslam 1976, 2.

162. Cf. Touchefeu 1981 (=LIMC s.v. Aias II) 350; 342-4 nos 54-59 (55-9 South Italian); Matheson 1986, 101-7; cf. also Connelly 1993, 115-6. This schema is seen on two mid-fifth-cent. Attic vases, an amphora at Cambridge, Corpus Christi College 43, of c. 450, attributed to the group of Polygnotos (LIMC no 54) and the volute krater Malibu, J. Paul Getty Museum 79.AE.198 (Matheson 1986, 102 fig. 1a) of c.440.

163. LIMC (Touchefeu 1981) nos 55-9.

164. LIMC (Touchefeu 1981) 344 no 65.

165. I am grateful to Dr. Stephanie West who encouraged me to reconsider the iconography of this subject in connection with *Ajax Lokros*.

166. *TrGF* iv pp. 363-73 FF 441a-451; Barrett 1974, 171-235; *P.Oxy.* 3653 fr.2 (*P.Oxy.* 52 [1984] ed. by H. M. Cockle, pp. 32-9); Lloyd-Jones 1996, 226-35.

167. Mastronarde 1990, 289, who classifies *Niobe* as one of the cases in which there is insufficient evidence as to where the gods stood, describes the situation as follows: "[on stage, shooting into palace door?]."

Chapter 4: Modalities of Divine Appearance 509

168. Cf. also Barrett 1974, 184-5 on this divine intervention in *Niobe* and the comparison with Lyssa in Euripides' *Heracles*.

169. *P.Oxy.* 3653 fr.2. I am using the text of Lloyd-Jones 1996, 230: *Amphion on(e)idi[se ton theon prokal]on kata prosopon eis machen katan[tesai parage]nethentos de tou theou kathoplisame[nos ton bion tox]eutheis metellaxen*.

170. Not even in terms of a *terminus ante quem*, since we do not know which *Niobe*, Aeschylus' or Sophocles', was involved in the reference in Aristophanes *Wasps* 579-80 (cf. MacDowell 1971, 210 ad 579; Sommerstein 1983, 192 ad 579).

171. Cf. Lloyd-Jones 1996, 103; Lefkowitz 1981, 77-9.

172. Cf. also *DFA* 130 n. 4.

173. Cf. Mastronarde 1990, 274 n. 83; cf. also Trendall and Webster 1971, 69 ad III.2.9.

174. Cf. *TrGF* iv p. 348.

175. *TrGF* iv pp. 445-53.

176. Pliny *NH* 18, 65; *TrGF* iv pp. 446, 448 ad 600; Lloyd-Jones 1996, 300.

177. There are, of course, several cases in which we cannot even speculate about the modalities of such interaction, if any. Thus, for example, we know very little about *Phineus* A and B (cf. *TrGF* iv pp. 484-9; Lloyd-Jones 1996, 334-6), and whether or not direct interaction was involved in either the punishment or the healing.

178. Cf. *TrGF* iv pp. 435-45.

179. Aristophanes *Birds* 100-1; cf. Dunbar 1995, 164 ad loc; cf. also 139-41 ad 15.

180. On conjectures about the date cf. *TrGF* iv pp. 436. Cf. also Robertson 1975, 286-7; Stewart 1990, 164 on the statue of Prokne and Itys by Alkamenes on the Acropolis.

181. Lloyd-Jones 1996, 297 ad F 589; cf. bibl. in *TrGF* iv pp. 441 ad F 589.

182. Cf. also Dunbar 1995, 165 ad 101 on F 581.

183. On which *TrGF* iv pp. 99-102.

184. Radt 1982, 211.

185. Scholia ad Ar. *Nub.* 255f in various MS, Suda; Tzetzes; collected in *TrGF* iv pp. 99-100.

186. Cf. Starkie 1911, lxi on the distribution of the scholia in the different manuscripts.

187. Cf. Lloyd-Jones 1996, 252-3; *TrGF* iv pp. 390-4.

188. *TrGF* iv p. 392 ad F 487.

189. Sourvinou-Inwood 1979, 55-7.

190. ARV 406.7; Add 232; Sourvinou-Inwood 1990d, 407 pl.8; Shapiro 1994, 121 fig. 84 who, incidentally, dates this cup far too early. This is not the place to point out the methodological flaws of his discussion, and indeed of the whole book. But I must mention that Shapiro dismisses any arguments that do not fit his views with vague and generic statements about the uncertainty of gestures, seemingly unable to distinguish between uncertainty, ambivalence, and polysemy (which can be partly resolved in context), and ignoring the fact that the meaning of the worship gesture made by Theseus is securely demonstrated through the iconography of, among others, votive reliefs, and that that must be the starting point in reconstructing the meanings of Theseus' interaction with the goddess. But then he brushes aside the fundamental fact that Theseus is holding his

sword in his left hand (Shapiro 1994, 119), and calls it Theseus with a drawn sword! Perhaps he imagines that it does not matter; that it was a case of a politically correct vase painter wishing to offer positive role models to Athenian left-handers.

191. In Sourvinou-Inwood 1990d, 416-23.

192. Bérard 1980, 620.

193. On which cf. *TrGF* iv pp. 425-30.

194. Cf. Lloyd-Jones 1996, 280-1; *TrGF* iv pp. 425-6.

195. Cf. also Lloyd-Jones 1996, 281.

196. The fact that I call it "Euripidean epiphany" does not mean that I am assuming that it was invented by Euripides, whose tragedies it characterizes, though this is very likely; but it may well have been Sophocles who had first deployed it.

197. With the possibility that a schema "enacted epiphany," if it had existed (cf. above), may also have had a (minimum) input.

198. On common and intertextual frames cf. Eco 1981, 20-2, 32; cf. also Sourvinou-Inwood 1995, 3.

199. Only, we saw in chapter III.3, in the culturally determined readings of some modern scholars.

200. Collard, Cropp, and Lee 1995, 82. Cf. op. cit. for the argument in favor of the view that this is the first time in the play when Bellerophon on Pegasos appears from the machine.

201. Cf. above chapter III.3; and Sourvinou-Inwood 1997c, 260-2.

202. Cf. Collard, Cropp, and Lee 1995, 83, cf. 101.

203. *Vita Sophocl.* 12.

204. There may be a further argument in favour of the serious epiphany, but it is not based on solid evidence. Clinton suggested (Clinton 1992, 89-90) that at some point during the Eleusinian Mysteries the statues of the goddesses had appeared on top of the internal structure inside the Telesterion diffused with light. Because (we saw in chapter III.1 n. 222) Clinton wrongly identified the Anaktoron with the Telesterion, he thought that the internal structure may have been a structure which served to display these images, illuminated from within or close up. But since, we saw, there is every reason to think that the generally accepted view that that structure was the Anaktoron is right, there would be no objection to imagining the images being displayed on the roof of the Anaktoron; on the contrary, this would explain how they would have gotten there without being seen, and how they would be illuminated from within. If this theory is right, and it is attractive, though the evidence is inconclusive, it would have interesting implications. In III.1.vii I put forward the hypothesis that the complex use of the *skene* which we first see in the *Oresteia* may have been at least partly modelled on that Eleusinian Anaktoron. Whether or not that is right, if it is true that images of the Eleusinian deities appeared on the roof of the Anaktoron in the course of the Mysteries, I suggest that, first, in the assumptions that shaped the selections that first placed the gods on the roof of the *skene*, the perception of those gods must have been at least very partially comparable to the Eleusinian deities. Second, in the eyes of that part of the audience, the initiates (which, in my view, was the

Chapter 4: Modalities of Divine Appearance

great majority of the Athenians), who were familiar with it, the schema "Eleusinian deities on the roof of the Anaktoron" would have come into play and helped the audience see them as comparable, though, of course, not the same, and so would have further reinforced the authority of these figures. But the evidence for this rite is not solid, and it is not necessary for this hypothesis to be right for the audience to have deployed epiphany schemata to make sense of epiphanies on high.

205. On this statue cf. e.g. Stewart 1990, 157-9; 257-9, 261-2.

206. Cf. e.g. Strabo 8. 353-4; Pausanias 5.11.9; Philostratos *Vita Apollon.* 6.19.

207. *Heracles* is the only known example in the less distanced category, which would suggest very low frequency.

208. The Dioskouroi, but especially the speaking Kastor.

209. For example, in Aeschylus' *Psychostasia, Toxotides, Ixion*; in Sophocles' *Thamyras, Niobe, Aias Lokros*.

210. Though such a chorus is used to great effect in comedy, in Aristophanes' *Clouds*. But comedy, I have been arguing in this book, is an entirely different matter.

IV. A Summary of the Central Conclusion

This book has offered very many conclusions, not even a fraction of which can be summarized in this closure chapter, in which I will only give a brief summary of my central conclusion and the main arguments on which it is based.

The fifth-century audiences[1] did not perceive tragedy only as a purely "theatrical" experience, a discrete dramatic unit, simply framed by ritual, but also as part of a ritual performance. Aetiologies, deities, and other religious elements in the tragedies were not, for them, simply theatrical devices, insulated from their religious realities; they were charged with religious meanings; they were, in varying degrees and ways, part of those realities. Fifth-century tragedy was, among other things, a discourse of religious exploration, part of the religious discourse of the Athenian polis. This central conclusion is based on two separate arguments, conducted wholly independently, each consisting of many sets of investigations, also conducted independently from each other. The conclusions of the two main arguments converge—as do those of the various sets of analysis within each argument. This convergence, I submit, confirms their validity.

The first argument consists of a series of readings of the tragedies: I tried to reconstruct, as much as possible, the ways in which the ancient audiences had made sense of those tragedies in performance, and also to determine patterns of similarities and differences between the different tragedies, above all patterns in the parameters of their variability. The attempt to reconstruct the meanings constructed by the fifth-century audiences in performance, through the deployment of perceptual filters shaped by cultural assumptions which they had shared with the tragedians, showed that for those audiences the tragedies were religiously significant, and articulated, among other things, a discourse of religious exploration.

In the eyes of the ancient audience there was permeability between the world of the tragedy and their world. First, the chorus never entirely lost its identity as a chorus of Athenian citizens singing in honor of Dionysos in the present, despite its strongly dominant identity as a chorus in the world of the tragedy; awareness of the non-dominant "ritual performers in the present" identity was activated in certain places through choral self-referentiality. Thus, the ritual performance facet of the tragedy was activated, in significant places, and helped stress the tragedy's religious dimension, through stressing the fact that the tragedy was part of a religious occasion.

The world of the tragedy also penetrated the world of the audience through a type of strong zooming that brought the former very close to, and ultimately into, the latter. In all nontransgressive tragic settings the relationships between the world of the audience and the world of the tragedy were governed by a double perspective, on the one hand the world of the tragedy was distanced and other, on the other it was also part of the audience's own world; mostly, it was the audience's past.[2] The distances between the two worlds varied in the different tragedies, with the tragic world shown sometimes nearer to, sometimes further away from, the audience's realities. These distances were not static in the course of each tragedy; they shifted, manipulated through distancing and zooming devices, textual elements that distanced the world of the tragedy from that of the audience in a variety of ways, and others that brought the two very close. This double perspective and the shifting distances allowed tragedy to explore problems at a safe symbolic distance, so that the audience did not experience unease and anxiety—as they might have done, if dark possibilities appeared too close, and so threatening—and at the same time relate these explorations directly to the audience.

The preferred tragic setting, which eventually became the exclusive tragic setting, was the heroic age, in which (according to the audience's perceptions) things had happened that importantly shaped the present. This relationship is activated when the world of the audience penetrates the world of the tragedy, above all, when a deity at a tragedy's closure institutes a cult that exists in the audience's reality—a situation which would have evoked similarly enacted cult foundations in sacred drama, which were part of the audience's religious realities. The case limit in certainty and strength of penetration is the closure of Euripides' *Erechtheus*, where there can be little doubt that what was happening in the world of the tragedy was also perceived as a representation of events that shaped the audience's religious world.

Through various zoomings throughout the tragedy, the deities who appeared in epiphany at the end had been identified by the audience as representations of the deities they worshiped. Such deities, appearing on high at the conclusion of Euripidean tragedies, resembled, and so evoked, epiphanies in the audience's lived religion, in which a deity appeared, gave instructions, and as a result very often a cult was instituted. The audience saw such deities as deities in epiphany in the world of the tragedy; in the audience's own world, an actor wearing a divine mask, acting the role of a god in a mimetic performance taking place in a sanctuary during a festival would have evoked the masked

Part IV: A Summary of the Central Conclusion

impersonations of deities by cult personnel in sacred drama. Tragedies like Aeschylus' *Eumenides*, in which mortals mingled directly with gods, had no real-life equivalent; they portrayed a world very different from the world of the audience, one which, like the performance, resembled, and so for the audience would have evoked, the world, and the performance, of sacred drama.

The fact that the audience made sense of divine appearances in tragedy through schemata pertaining to their lived religion confirms that they saw these divine appearances as religiously significant, not simply as theatrical devices. This is true also of the epiphanies on high at the conclusion of the allegedly critical and ironic Euripidean tragedies. The ancient viewers were watching a performance taking place in a sanctuary, in the presence of Dionysos (in the shape of his statue), in the course of a festival, in which a deity, whom the tragedy had zoomed to their religious realities, appeared in epiphany, impersonated by an actor, evoking the "priestly personnel impersonating deities" schema, and did things that deities "normally" did in real life epiphanies. They would therefore have perceived these deities as representations of their own divinities, giving "answers" in the world of the tragedy that were also relevant to their own world. This is part of Euripides' religious discourse. Far from ironically subverting religion, Euripidean tragedies came to include a strong religious discourse, a discourse of religious exploration, which became more, not less, important in the course of the part of Euripides' career which is visible to us.

This Euripidean religious discourse emerged in response to the religious turbulence of the time, and involved complex and deep religious problematization, interwoven with a varyingly dense ritual web; it incorporated elements from contemporary philosophical discourses that were perceived as inimical to polis religion, and challenged them, offering answers which, though very complex, were ultimately reassuring.

The second argument on which the book's central conclusion is based pertains to the origins of tragedy, and its conclusions converge with those of the first. I offered a reconstruction of the festival of the City Dionysia in its classical and postclassical form, and an attempted reconstruction of the festival's earlier history, and developments. I argued that tragedy was generated, through a very complex series of developments, out of a nexus of hymns, above all dithyrambs, sung at the sacrifice of a billy goat, a *tragos*, in the course of a rite of *xenismos* of Dionysos at the City Dionysia. Comedy had been generated in a different ritual context, in the course of the same festival, out of performances at the *komos*, during the ritual dining on *stibades* of ivy; unlike the *xenismos*, this part of the festival had belonged to the stage of ritual abnormality, before the god's advent, that is, the statue's return from the Academy.

Tragedy was generated, through a very complex process, with the help of other ritual schemata, such as "sacred drama," and of performance schemata, such as perceptions pertaining to the chorus leader-poet, and poetic models. The earliest prototragedy had consisted of a *hypokrites* speaking in propria persona and an unmasked chorus; this changed into a mimetic prototragedy with masks; eventually, tragedy as we basically know it emerged.

The choruses of male citizens who had sung at the *xenismos* at the pretragic Dionysia were, above all, Athenians of the present singing in honor of Dionysos; but they were also, at the same time, invested with the persona of the Athenians of the mythological past, who had first offended the god, and then received him with honor and established his cult, insofar as the present ritual was also a reenactment of the cult's first establishement. This double identity of the participants in the ritual, above all the chorus, set the parameters for the double perspective in tragedy, which was especially conducive to religious exploration. It had also contained the seeds that led to the development of *mimesis*. When the explorations came to be centered not on the Athenians' own past, which was being reenacted as part of the ritual occasion in the present, but on stories such as that of Pentheus, the "other" identity was no longer directly connected with that of ritual performers in the present; it was truly "other," and invited masks; thus prototragedy became mimetic and eventually developed into tragedy.

The crucial factor was the ritual context and festival myth, which had been reflected in the hymns' content. For they involved the complex paradoxes implicated in the myths of resistance to Dionysos, which were especially conducive to problematizing and, above all other myths, exemplified the wider paradoxes of Greek religion in general, and invited explorations. The complexity of the explorations generated new forms, in interaction with schemata such as those of the poet as instructor; these forms then developed further, in interaction with other schemata. It was, then, problematization that was crucial for the emergence of tragedy, though other factors conducive to such developments also played a part; besides those pertaining to the developing genres' internal dynamic, with the specific choices made by particular poets, also factors pertaining to the external (above all sociopolitical) circumstances, which affected, among other things, the contexts of performance, and promoted spectacle.

Part IV: A Summary of the Central Conclusion

The conclusions of the two independent arguments, then, converge. Above all, they converge in that, on my reconstruction, religious exploration was at the very center of the generation of tragedy, which converges with the conclusions resulting from the individual tragedies' readings, that religious exploration was of fundamental importance until the end of Euripides' career. The fact that a genre may have started in a certain way does not, of course, necessarily entail that it will continue in the same way; nor, conversely, does the fact that a genre has a particular characteristic entail that it had had that characteristic from its very beginning. However, when independent arguments show, on the one hand, that this trait had been central to that genre's beginings, and on the other, that it significantly characterized that genre, both in its earlyish, and in its fully developed form, the convergence validates the separate conclusions.

There is also a more specific convergence. On my reconstruction, earliest tragedy had been characterized by, first, density of ritual content, religious elements, language, and references; second, religious exploration and problematization; and finally, a form structured through hymns, sung by a chorus representing a collectivity, the parodos and stasima, reflecting an original schema "*prosodion* and stasima at the altar," and separating segments involving *rheseis* of the *hypokrites* and/or chorus-*hypokrites* exchanges, with the chorus having a very important role. The three earlier extant Aeschylean tragedies are very close to this ritual matrix. This convergence helps validate the reconstruction. It also confirms the importance of the religious dimension. For the filters through which at least the early fifth-century audiences had made sense of the tragedies were also shaped by the "recognition," the awareness, of this ritual-tragic matrix, which would have colored their perception of the ritual, and generally religious, elements, and of the religious problematization in the tragedies. In symbiosis with this recognition, the ritual context, and the assumptions associated with the tragic performances as a result of, among other things, their history, and the presence of the statue of Dionysos, would have made these performances, and not simply their framing, be perceived as having a significant religious dimension. If such awareness is removed from our filters, if we read these tragedies through filters that lack this religious dimension of the ancient filters, we create meanings that are radically different from those constructed by the ancient audiences. If this is right, it follows that the systematic attempt to reconstruct the religious dimension, including the origins and early developments of tragedy, is not an optional extra, a speculative enterprise that it is safer and more rigorous to do without, but a necessity for all those concerned with trying to make sense of fifth-century tragedies as near as possible through fifth-century eyes.

Religious exploration and the dense web of ritual and other religious elements are not limited to the earlier extant Aeschylean tragedies; they continue in the *Oresteia*, but the exploration of human relationships has by then developed strongly, and the tragedies' canvas has become much more complex. These trends continued and developed very much further in later tragedy, with a larger canvas of more, and more elaborate, themes, and much greater focus on, and complexities in, the exploration of human relationships in their own right.

But these later tragedies, with their dramatic sophistication, complex canvases, and emphasis on human actions and relationships, still included, to a greater or lesser extent, a ritual articulation, and involved, among other things, but very importantly, religious exploration. The underlying skeleton of something resembling the ritual matrix can still be seen in Euripidean tragedies, some of which articulate deep, and sometimes bleak, religious exploration through forms that are not unrelated to, though they are much more complex and sophisticated than, the ritual matrix that had shaped earliest tragedy.

Notes

1. I am not concerned with fourth-century tragedy and audiences; cf. the excellent discussion in Easterling 1993a, 559-69.

2. Sometimes the past of Athens, more often it was more generally the Greek past, which was mostly relevant to Athens also, and which often involved people who had a place (as gods or heroes) in the audience's religious realities, because they were worshiped in Athens, or in a Panhellenic setting. What happens to the Thebes of Pentheus, and even to the Thrace of Lykourgos, is relevant to Dionysos' Athenian divine persona. In the non-religious sphere, the Greeks' behavior at Troy is part of all the Greeks' past.

Bibliography

Abbreviations

Agora xiv: H. A. Thompson and R. E. Wycherley, *The Athenian Agora* vol. xiv. The Agora of Athens. *The history, shape and uses of an ancient city centre* (Princeton 1972).
ABV: J. D. Beazley, *Attic Black-figure Vase-Painters* (Oxford 1956).
ARV: J. D. Beazley, *Attic Red-figure Vase-Painters* 2nd ed. (Oxford 1963).
Add: *Beazley Addenda. Additional References to ABV, ARV^2 and Paralipomena*, 2nd ed., compiled by T. H. Carpenter (Oxford 1989).
CHCL: P. E. Easterling and B. M. W. Knox eds., *The Cambridge History of Classical Literature*, vol. I. Part 2. Greek Drama (Cambridge 1985).
Cité: *La cité des images. Religion et société en Grèce antique* (Mont-sur-Lausanne 1984).
Concordance: J. T. Allen and G. Italie, *A Concordance to Euripides* (Berkeley 1954).
DFA: A. Pickard-Cambridge, *The Dramatic Festivals of Athens*, 2nd ed., revised by J. Gould and D. M. Lewis (Oxford 1968).
Guide: *The Athenian Agora. A Guide to the Excavation and Museum*, 4th ed. (The American School, Athens 1990).
IC: M. Segre, *Iscrizioni di Cos* (Rome 1993).
LIMC: *Lexicon Iconographicum Mythologiae Classicae* (Zurich and Munich 1981-).
LSAM: F. Sokolowski, *Lois sacrées de l' Asie mineure* (Paris 1955).
LSCG: F. Sokolowski, *Lois sacrées des cités grecques* (Paris 1969).
LSCGS: F. Sokolowski, *Lois sacrées des cités grecques. Supplement* (Paris 1962).
TrGF i: B. Snell ed., *Tragicorum Graecorum Fragmenta* vol. 1. Didascaliae Tragicae, Catalogi Tragicorum et Tragoediarum Testimonia et Fragmenta Tragocorum Minorum (Göttingen 1971).
TrGF ii: R. D. Kannicht and B. Snell eds., *Tragicorum Graecorum Fragmenta* vol. 2. Fragmenta Adespota. Testimonia volumini 1. Addenda Indices ad volumina 1 et 2 (Göttingen 1981).
TrGF iii: S. Radt ed., *Tragicorum Graecorum Fragmenta* vol. 3. Aeschylus (Göttingen 1985).

TrGF iv: S. Radt ed., *Tragicorum Graecorum Fragmenta* vol. 4. Sophocles (Göttingen 1977).

Accame 1941. S. Accame, *La Lega Ateniese del secolo IV A.C.* (Rome 1941).
Aleshire 1989. S. B. Aleshire, *The Athenian Asklepieion: The People, Their Dedications and the Inventories* (Amsterdam 1989)
Alexiou 1974. M. Alexiou, *The Ritual Lament in Greek Tradition* (Cambridge 1974).
Alfieri 1979. N. Alfieri, *Spina. Museo archeologico nazionale di Ferrara* (Bologna 1979).
Andronikos 1984. M. Andronikos, *Vergina. Oi Vassilikoi Taphoi* (Athens 1984).
Angeli Bernardini 1991. P. Angeli Bernardini, "L'inno agli dei nella lirica corale greca e la sua destinazione sacrale," in Cassio and Cerri 1991, 85-94.
Aricescu 1963. A. Aricescu, "Nota asupra unui decret elenistic inedit din muzeul regional de arheologie Dobrogea," *Studi Clasice* 5 (1963) 314-18.
Aronen 1992. J. Aronen, "Notes on Athenian Drama as Ritual Myth-Telling within the Cult of Dionysos," *Arctos. Acta Philologica Fennica* 26 (1992) 19-37.
Austin 1967. C. Austin, "De nouveaus fragments de l'*Erechthée* d'Euripide," *Recherches de papyrologie* 4 (1967) 11-67.
Austin 1968. C. Austin, *Nova Fragmenta Euripidea in papyris reperta* (Berlin 1968).
Barber 1992. E. J. W. Barber, "The Peplos of Athena," in Neils 1992, 103-17.
Barlow 1986. S. A. Barlow, *Euripides Troades* (Warminster 1986).
Barrett 1964. W. S. Barrett, Euripides *Hippolytos* (Oxford 1964).
Barrett 1974. W. S. Barrett, in R. Carden ed., *The papyrus fragments of Sophocles* (Berlin 1974) 171-235.
Barron 1980. J. P. Barron, "Bakchylides, Theseus and a woolly cloak," *BICS* 27 (1980) 1-8.
Beazley 1955. J. D. Beazley, "Hydria fragments in Corinth," *Hesperia* 24 (1955) 305-19.
Bérard 1980. C. Bérard, Review of Sourvinou-Inwood 1979, *Gnomon* 52 (1980) 616-20.
Bérard and Durand 1984. C. Bérard and J.-L. Durand, "Entrer en imagerie," in *Cité* 19-34.
Bierl 1989. A. F. Bierl, "Was hat die Tragödie mit Dionysos zu tun?," *Würzburger Jahrbücher* 15 (1989) 43-58.
Bierl 1991. A. F. Bierl, *Dionysos und die griechische Tragödie. Politische und metatheatralische Aspekte im Text* (Tübingen 1991).
Bierl 1994. A. F. Bierl, "Apollo in Greek Tragedy: Orestes and the God of Initiation," in J. Solomon ed., *Apollo: Origins and Influences* (Tucson 1994) 81-96.
Blech 1982. M. Blech, *Studien zum Kranz bei den Griechen* (Berlin 1982).

Blok 1981. A. Blok, "Rams and billy-goats: a key to the Mediterranean code of honour," *Man* 16 (1981) 427-40.
Boardman 1976. J. Boardman, "The Kleophrades Painter at Troy," *Antike Kunst* 19 (1976) 3-18.
Boardman 1976b. J. Boardman, "A curious eye-cup," *AA* 1976, 281-90.
Boardman 1978. J. Boardman, *Greek Sculpture: The Archaic Period. A Handbook* (London 1978).
Bond 1981. G. W. Bond ed., *Euripides Heracles* (Oxford 1981).
Bonnechere 1994. P. Bonnechere, *Le sacrifice humain en Grèce ancienne* [*Kernos* Supplement 3] (Athens, Liege 1994).
Bowie 1993a, A. M. Bowie, *Aristophanes. Myth Ritual and Comedy* (Cambridge 1993)
Bowie 1993b. A.M. Bowie, "Religion and Politics in Aeschylus' *Oresteia*," *CQ* 43 (1993) 10-31.
Bowie 1997. A.M. Bowie, "Tragic Filters for History: Euripides' *Supplices* and Sophocles' *Philoctetes*," in Pelling 1997c 39-62.
Braund 1980. D. C. Braund, "Artemis Eukleia and Euripides' *Hippolytos*," *JHS* 100 (1980) 184-5.
Brelich 1959. A. Brelich, "I figli di Medeia," *SMSR* 30 (1959) 213-54.
Brelich 1969. A. Brelich, *Paides e parthenoi* (Rome 1969).
Bremer 1981. J. M. Bremer, "Greek Hymns," in H. S. Versnel ed., *Faith, Hope and Worship. Aspects of Religous Mentality in the Ancient World* (Leiden 1981) 193-215.
Bremmer and Roodenburg 1997. J. M. Bremmer and H. Roodenburg eds., *A Cultural History of Humour* (Cambridge 1997).
Broadhead 1960. H. D. Broadhead ed., *The Persae of Aeschylus* (Cambridge 1960).
Brown 1984. A. L. Brown, "Eumenides in Greek Tragedy," *CQ* 34 (1984) 260-81.
Bruit 1984. L. Bruit, "Sacrifices à Delphes," *RevHistRel* 201 (1984) 339-67.
Bruit 1990. L. Bruit, 'The Meal at the Hyakinthia: Ritual Consumption and Offering', in Murray 1990, 162-74.
Brulé 1987. P. Brulé, *La fille d' Athènes. La religion des filles à Athènes à l'époque classique. Mythes, cultes et société* (Paris 1987).
Bruneau and Ducat 1983. P. Bruneau and J. Ducat, *Guide de Délos* (Paris 1983).
Burkert 1979. W. Burkert, *Structure and History in Greek Mythology and Ritual* (Berkeley 1979).
Burkert 1983. W. Burkert, *Homo Necans: The Anthropology of Ancient Greek Sacrificial Ritual and Myth* (Berkeley 1983).
Burkert 1985. W. Burkert, *Greek Religion: Archaic and Classical*² (Oxford 1985).
Burkert 1987. W. Burkert, *Ancient Mystery Cults* (Cambridge, Mass. 1987).
Burkert 1988. W. Burkert, "*Katagogia-Anagogia* and the goddess of Knossos," in Hägg, Marinatos, and Nordquist 1988, 81-8.
Burkert 1990. W. Burkert, *Wilder Ursprung. Opferritual und Mythos bei den Griechen* (Berlin 1990).

Burkert 1996. W. Burkert, *Creation of the Sacred: Tracks of Biology in Early Religions* (Cambridge, Mass. 1996).
Burkert 1997. W. Burkert, "From epiphany to cult statue: early Greek *theos*," in A.B. Lloyd, *What is a God? Studies in the nature of Greek divinity* (London 1997) 15-34.
Burn 1987. L. Burn, *The Meidias Painter* (Oxford 1987).
Buxton 1988. R. G. A. Buxton, "Bafflement in Greek Tragedy," *Metis* 3 (1988) 41-51.
Calame 1986. C. Calame, "Facing otherness: the tragic mask in ancient Greece," *History of Religions* 26 (1986) 125-42 (=C. Calame, *Le récit en Grèce ancienne. Enonciations et représentations de poètes* [Paris 1986] [Engl. trans: Calame 1995] 85-100).
Calame 1990. C. Calame, *Thésée et l' imaginaire athénien* (Lausanne 1990).
Calame 1994/5. C. Calame, "From Choral Poetry to Tragic Stasimon: The Enactment of Women's Song," in Golder and Scully 1994/5, 136-54.
Calame 1995. C. Calame, *The Craft of Poetic Speech in Ancient Greece* (Ithaca 1995).
Carlson 1996. M. Carlson, *Performance: A Critical Introduction* (London 1996).
Carpenter 1993. T. H. Carpenter, "On the Beardless Dionysus," in Carpenter and Faraone 1993, 185-206.
Carpenter 1997. T. H. Carpenter, *Dionysian Imagery in Fifth-Century Athens* (Oxford 1997).
Carpenter and Faraone 1993. T. H. Carpenter and C.A. Faraone eds., *Masks of Dionysus* (Ithaca 1993).
Cartledge 1997. P. Cartledge, "Deep plays: Theatre as process in Greek civic life," in Easterling 1997d, 3-35.
Cassio and Cerri 1991. A. C. Cassio and G. Cerri eds., *L' inno tra rituale e letteratura nel mondo antico* (Rome 1991) [= AION sez. fil. 13].
Clay 1989. J. Strauss Clay, *The Politics of Olympus: Form and Meaning in the Major Homeric Hymns* (Princeton 1989).
Clinton 1974. K. Clinton, *The Sacred Officials of the Eleusinian Mysteries* (Philadelphia 1974).
Clinton 1988. K. Clinton, "Sacrifice at the Eleusinian Mysteries," in Hägg, Marinatos, and Nordquist 1988, 69-80.
Clinton 1992. K. Clinton, *Myth and Cult: The Iconography of the Eleusinian Mysteries* (Stockholm 1992).
Clinton 1994. K. Clinton, "The Epidauria and the Arrival of Asclepius in Athens," in Hägg 1994, 17-34.
Cole 1993. S. G. Cole, "Procession and Celebration at the Dionysia," in R. Scodel ed., *Theater and Society in the Classical World* (Ann Arbor 1993) 25-38.
Coles 1974. R. A. Coles, *A new Oxyrhynchus Papyrus: The hypothesis of Euripides' Alexandros* [BICS Supplement 32] (London 1974).
Collard 1975. C. Collard ed., *Euripides Supplices* (Groningen 1975).
Collard 1991. C. Collard ed., *Euripides Hecuba* (Warminster 1991).

Collard, Cropp, and Lee 1995. *Euripides: Selected Fragmentary Plays* vol. i, ed. C. Collard, M. J. Cropp, and K. H. Lee (Warminster 1995).
Conacher 1981. D. J. Conacher, "Rhetoric and Relevance in Euripidean Drama," *AJPh* 102 (1981) 3-25.
Conacher 1996. D. J. Conacher, *Aeschylus: The Earlier Plays and Related Studies* (Toronto 1996).
Connelly 1993. J. B. Connelly, "Narrative and Image in Attic Vase Painting," in P. J. Holliday ed., *Narrative and Event in Ancient Art* (Cambridge 1993) 88-129.
Connor 1990. W. R. Connor, "City Dionysia and Athenian Democracy," in W. R. Connor, M. H. Hansen, K. A. Raaflaub, B. S. Strauss, *Aspects of Athenian Democracy* (Copenhagen 1990) 7-32.
Cook 1900. A. B. Cook, "Iostephanos," *JHS* 20 (1900) 1-13.
Cooper and Morris 1990. F. Cooper and S. Morris, "Dining in round buildings," in Murray 1990, 66-85.
Croally 1994. N. T. Croally, *Euripidean polemic: The Trojan Women and the function of tragedy* (Cambridge 1994).
Cropp 1988. M. J. Cropp ed., *Euripides Electra* (Warminster 1988).
Csapo and Slater 1995. E. Csapo and W. J. Slater, *The Context of Ancient Drama* (1995).
Dale 1954. A. M. Dale ed., *Euripides Alcestis* (Oxford 1954).
Dale 1969. A. M. Dale, "Stasimon and hyporcheme," *Collected Papers* (Cambridge 1969) 34-40.
Davies 1971. J. K. Davies, *Athenian Propertied Families 600-300 B.C.* (Oxford 1971).
Davies 1989. M. Davies, "Sisyphus and the invention of religion ('Critias' *TrGF* 1 [43] F 19 = B 25 DK)," *BICS* 36 (1989) 16-32.
de Jong 1991. I. J. F. de Jong, *Narrative in Drama: The Art of the Euripidean Messenger-Speech* (Leiden 1991).
Des Bouvrie 1993. S. Des Bouvrie, "Creative Euphoria: Dionysos and the Theatre," *Kernos* 6 (1993) 79-112;
Des Bouvrie 1993b. S. Des Bouvrie, "Aiskhulos, *Prometheus*: An Anthropological Approach," *Metis* 8 (1993) 187-216.
Detienne 1986. M. Detienne, *Dionysos à ciel ouvert* (Paris 1986).
Detienne 1989. M. Detienne, "Les Danaides entre elles. Une violence fondatrice de mariage," in M.Detienne, *L'écriture d'Orphée* (Paris 1989) 41-57, 194-8].
Deubner 1969. L. Deubner, *Attische Feste*³ (Vienna 1969).
Diggle 1994. J. Diggle, *Euripidea: Collected Essays* (Oxford 1994).
Dontas 1983. G. Dontas, "The true Aglaurion," *Hesperia* 52 (1983) 48-63.
Dover 1993. K. J. Dover ed., *Aristophanes Frogs* (Oxford 1993).
Dunbar 1995. N. Dunbar ed., *Aristophanes Birds* (Oxford 1995).
Dunn 1996. F. M. Dunn, *Tragedy's End: Closure and Innovation in Euripidean Drama* (New York 1996).

Dunn 1997. F. M. Dunn, "End and Means in Euripides' *Heracles*," in D.H. Roberts, F. M. Dunn and D. Fowler eds., *Classical Closure: Reading the End in Greek and Latin Literature* (Princeton 1997) 83-111.
Easterling 1982. P. E. Easterling ed., *Sophocles Trachiniae* (Cambridge 1982).
Easterling 1988. P. E. Easterling, "Tragedy and Ritual: 'Cry "Woe, woe", but may the god prevail'," *Metis* 3 (1988) [1991] 87-109.
Easterling 1989. P. E. Easterling, "City settings in Greek poetry," *Proceedings of the Classical Association* 86 (1989) 5-17.
Easterling 1993a. P. E. Easterling, "The end of an era? Tragedy in the early fourth century," in Sommerstein, Halliwell, Henderson, and Zimmermann 1993, 559-69.
Easterling 1993b. P. E. Easterling, "Gods on Stage in Greek Tragedy," *Grä̈zer Beiträge Supplementband V, Festschrift für Walter Pötscher*, ed. J. Dalfen, G. Petersman, and F.F. Schwarz (Graz-Horn 1993) 77-86.
Easterling 1994. P. E. Easterling, "Euripides Outside Athens: A Speculative Note," *ICS* 19 (1994) 73-80.
Easterling 1997. P. E. Easterling, "Constructing the Heroic," in Pelling 1997c, 21-37.
Easterling 1997b. P. E. Easterling, "Form and performance," in Easterling 1997d, 151-77.
Easterling 1997c. P. E. Easterling, "A Show for Dionysus," in Easterling 1997d, 36-53.
Easterling 1997d. P. E. Easterling ed., *The Cambridge Companion to Greek Tragedy* (Cambridge 1997).
Eco 1981. U. Eco, *The Role of the Reader: Explorations in the semiotics of texts* (London 1981).
Else 1965. G. F. Else, *The Origins and Early Form of Greek Tragedy* (Cambridge, Mass. 1965).
Else 1977. G. F. Else, "Ritual and Drama in Aischyleian Tragedy," *Illinois Classical Studies* 2 (1977) 70-87.
Fantham 1986. E. Fantham, "Andromache's child in Euripides and Seneca," in M. Cropp, E. Fantham, S. E. Scully eds., *Greek tragedy and its legacy: Essays presented to D.J. Conacher* (Calgary 1986) 267-80.
Faraone 1985. C. A. Faraone, "Aeschylus' *hymnos desmios* (*Eum*. 306) and Attic judicial curse tablets," *JHS* 105 (1985) 150-54.
Faraone 1997. C. A. Faraone, "Salvation and female heroics in the parodos of Aristophanes' *Lysistrata*," *JHS* 117 (1997) 38-59.
Farnell 1909. L. R. Farnell, *The Cults of the Greek States* vol. v (Oxford 1909).
Fehr 1971. B. Fehr, *Orientalische und griechische Gelage* (Bonn 1971).
Ferguson 1938. W. S. Ferguson, "The Salaminioi of Heptaphylai and Sounion," *Hesperia* 7 (1938) 1-74.
Flückiger-Guggenheim 1984. D. Flückiger-Guggenheim, *Göttliche Gäste. Die Einkehr von Göttern und Heroes in der griechischen Mythologie* (Bern 1984).

Bibliography

Foley 1985. H. P. Foley, *Ritual Irony: Poetry and Sacrifice in Euripides* (Ithaca 1985).
Foley 1993, H. P. Foley, "The politics of tragic lamentation," in Sommerstein, Halliwell, Henderson, and Zimmermann eds., 1993, 101-43.
Forbes Irving 1990. P. M. C. Forbes Irving, *Metamorphosis in Greek Myths* (Oxford 1990).
Fowler 1997. D. Fowler, "Second Thoughts on Closure," in D. H. Roberts, F. M. Dunn, and D. Fowler eds., *Classical Closure: Reading the End in Greek and Latin Literature* (Princeton 1997) 3-22.
Fraenkel 1950. E. Fraenkel, ed., *Aeschylus Agamemnon* (Oxford 1950).
Friedrich 1996. R. Friedrich, "Everything to Do with Dionysos? Ritualism, the Dionysiac and the Tragic," in Silk 1996, 257-83.
Froning 1971. H. Froning, *Dithyrambos und Vasenamalerei in Athen* (Wurzburg 1971).
Frontisi-Ducroux 1995. F. Frontisi-Ducroux, *Du masque au visage. Aspects de l'identité en grèce ancienne* (Paris 1995).
Furley 1995. W. D. Furley, "Praise and Persuasion in Greek Hymns," *JHS* 115 (1995) 29-46.
Gadbery 1992. L. M. Gadbery, "The Sanctuary of the Twelve Gods in the Athenian Agora: a Revised View," *Hesperia* 61 (1992) 447-89.
Gantz 1993. T. Gantz, *Early Greek Myth* (Baltimore 1993).
Garland 1992. R. Garland, *Introducing New Gods: The Politics of Athenian Religion* (London 1992).
Garvie 1969. A. F. Garvie, *Aeschylus' Supplices: Play and Trilogy* (Cambridge 1969).
Garvie 1986. A. F. Garvie, *Aeschylus Choephori* (Oxford 1986).
Gebhard 1973. E. Gebhard, *The Theater at Isthmia* (Chicago 1973).
Gebhard 1974. E. Gebhard, "The form of the orchestra in the early Greek theatre," *Hesperia* 43 (1974) 428-40.
Gentili 1984-5. B. Gentili, "Il coro tragico nella teoria degli antichi," *Dioniso* 55 (1984-5) 17-35.
Gercke 1981. P. Gercke, *Funde aus der Antike. Sammlung Paul Dierichs. Kassel* (Kassel 1981).
Ghiron-Bistagne 1976. P. Ghiron-Bistagne, *Recherches sur les Acteurs dans la Grèce antique* (Paris 1976).
Giangrande 1963. G. Giangrande, "The Origin of Attic Comedy," *Eranos* 61 (1963) 1-24.
Goff 1990. B. E. Goff, *The noose of words: Readings of desire, violence and language in Euripides' Hippolytos* (Cambridge 1990).
Golder and Scully 1994/5. H. Golder and S. Scully eds., *The Chorus in Greek Tragedy and Culture, One.* [= *Arion* 3.1 (Fall 1994/Winter 1995)].
Goldhill 1986. S. Goldhill, *Reading Greek Tragedy* (Cambridge 1986).
Goldhill 1988. S. Goldhill, "Battle Narrative and Politics in Aeschylus' *Persae*." *JHS* 108 (1988) 189-93.

Goldhill 1990. S. Goldhill, "The Great Dionysia and Civic Ideology," in Winkler and Zeitlin 1990, 97-129.
Goldhill 1991. S. Goldhill. *The Poet's Voice: Essays on Poetics and Greek Literature* (Cambridge 1991).
Goldhill 1994. S. Goldhill, "Representing Democracy: Women at the Great Dionysia," in Osborne and Hornblower 1994, 347-69.
Goldhill 1996. S. Goldhill, "Collectivity and Otherness—The Authority of the Tragic Chorus: Response to Gould," in Silk 1996, 244-56.
Gondikas 1990. D. Gondikas, "Ikarios," LIMC v (1990) 645-7.
Gould 1973. J. Gould, "Hiketeia," *JHS* 93 (1973) 74-103.
Gould 1996. J. Gould, "Tragedy and Collective Experience," in Silk 1996, 217-43.
Gow 1912. A. S. F. Gow, "On the meaning of the word *thymele*," *JHS* 32 (1912) 213-38.
Graf 1979. F. Graf, "Das Gotterbild aus dem Taurerland," *Antike Welt* 4 (1979) 33-41.
Graf 1985. F. Graf, *Nordionische Kulte* (Rome 1985).
Graf 1997. F. Graf, "Epiphanie," *Der Neue Pauly* (Stuttgart 1997) 1154-6.
Grandolini 1991. S. Grandolini, "Canto processionale e culto nell' antica Grecia," in Cassio and Cerri 1991, 125-40.
Green 1989. J. R. Green, "Theatre Production: 1971-1986," *Lustrum* 31 (1989) 7-95.
Green 1994. J. R. Green, *Theatre in Ancient Greek Society* (London 1994).
Griffith 1977. M. Griffith, *The authenticity of Prometheus Bound* (Cambridge 1977).
Griffith 1995. M. Griffith, "Brilliant Dynasts: Power and Politics in the *Oresteia*," *ClassAnt* 14 (1995) 62-129.
Habicht 1970. C. Habicht, *Gottmenschtum und griechische Städte* [*Zetemata* 14], 2nd ed. (Munich 1970).
Hägg 1986. R. Hägg, "Die göttliche Epiphanie im minoischen Ritual," *AthMit* 101 (1986) 41-62.
Hägg 1992. R. Hägg ed., *The Iconography of Greek Cult in the Archaic and Classical Periods* [=*Kernos* Supplement 1] (Athens 1992).
Hägg 1994. R. Hägg ed., *Ancient Greek Cult Practice from the Epigraphical Evidence* (Stockholm 1994).
Hägg, Marinatos, and Nordquist 1988. R. Hägg, N. Marinatos, and G. C. Nordquist eds., *Early Greek Cult Practice* (Stockholm 1988).
Hall 1989. E. Hall, *Inventing the Barbarian: Greek Self-Definition through Tragedy* (Oxford 1989).
Hall 1996a. E. Hall, "Is There a *Polis* in Aristotle's *Poetics*?," in Silk 1996, 295-309.
Hall 1996b. E. Hall, *Aeschylus Persians* (Warminster 1996).
Hallager, Vlasakis, and Hallager 1992. E. Hallager, M. Vlasakis and B. P. Hallager, "New Linear B Tablets from Khania," *Kadmos* 31 (1992) 61-87.
Halliwell 1988. S. Halliwell ed., *Plato: Republic 10* (Warminster 1988).

Hamdorf 1990. F. W. Hamdorf, "Tiere um Dionysos," in K. Vierneisel and B. Kaeser eds., *Kunst der Schale, Kultur des Trinkens* (Munich 1990) 401-5.

Hamilton 1990. R. Hamilton, "The Pindaric Dithyramb," *HSCP* 93 (1990) 211-22.

Hamilton 1992. R. Hamilton, *Choes and Anthesteria: Athenian Iconography and Ritual* (Ann Arbor 1992).

Harder 1985. M. A. Harder, *Euripides' Kresphontes and Archelaos* (Leiden 1985).

Haslam 1976. M. W. Haslam, "Sophocles, *Aias Lokros* (and other plays?)," in A. K. Bowman, M. W. Haslam, J. C. Shelton, and J. D. Thomas, eds., *The Oxyrhynchus Papyri* vol. xliv (1976) 1-26.

Haslam 1977. M. W. Haslam in A. K. Bowman, M. W. Haslam, S. A. Stephens, and M. L. West, eds., *The Oxyrhynchus Papyri* vol. xlv (London 1977).

Headlam 1906. W. Headlam, "The last scene of the *Eumenides*," *JHS* 26 (1906) 268-77.

Heath 1987. M. Heath, *The Poetics of Greek Tragedy* (London 1987).

Henderson 1990. J. Henderson, "The *Demos* and the Comic Competition," in Winkler and Zeitlin 1990, 271-313.

Henderson 1991a. J. Henderson, "Women and the Athenian Dramatic Festivals," *TAPA* 121 (1991) 133-47.

Henderson 1991b J. Henderson *The Maculate Muse: Obscene Language in Attic Comedy*, 2nd ed. (New York 1991).

Henrichs 1981. A. Henrichs, "Human sacrifice in Greek religion: three case studies," in *Fondation Hardt pour l'étude de l'antiquité classique. Entretiens xxvii. Le sacrifice dans l'antiquité* (1981) 195-235.

Henrichs 1982. A. Henrichs, "Changing Dionysiac Identities," in B. F. Meyer and E. P. Sanders eds., *Jewish and Christian Self-Definition*, vol. 3, *Self-Definition in the Graeco-Roman World* (London 1982) 137-60, 213-36.

Henrichs 1984. A. Henrichs, "Loss of Self, Suffering, Violence: The Modern View of Dionysus from Nietzsche to Girard," *HSCP* 88 (1984) 205-40.

Henrichs 1987. A. Henrichs, "Myth Visualized: Dionysos and His Circle in Sixth-Century Attic Vase-Painting," in *Papers on the Amasis Painter and His World* (Malibu 1987) 92-124.

Henrichs 1990. A. Henrichs, "Between Country and City: Cultic Dimensions of Dionysus in Athens and Attica," in M. Griffith and D.J. Mastronarde eds., *Cabinet of the Muses: Essays in Classical and Comparative Literature in honor of Thomas G. Rosenmeyer* (Atlanta 1990) 257-77.

Henrichs 1991. A. Henrichs, "Namenlosigkeit und Euphemismus: zur Ambivalenz der chthonischen Mächte in attischen Drama," in H. Hoffmann ed., *Fragmenta Dramatica. Beiträge zur Interpretation der griechischen Tragikerfragmente und ihrer Wirkungsgeschichte* (Göttingen 1991) 161-201.

Henrichs 1993. A. Henrichs, "'He has a God in Him': Human and Divine in the Modern Perception of Dionysus," in Carpenter and Faraone 1993, 13-43.

Henrichs 1994. A. Henrichs, "Anonymity and Polarity: Unknown Gods and Nameless Altars at the Areopagos," *Illinois Classical Studies* 19 (1994) 27-58.

Henrichs 1994b. A. Henrichs, "Der rasende Gott: Zur Psychologie des Dionysos und des Dionysischen in Mythos und Literatur," *Antike und Abendland* 40 (1994) 31-58.

Henrichs 1994/5. A. Henrichs, "'Why should I dance?': Choral Self-Referentiality in Greek Tragedy," in H. Golder and S. Scully eds., *The Chorus in Greek Tragedy and Culture, One* [=*Arion* 3.1(Fall 1994/Winter 1995)] 56-111.

Henrichs 1996a, A. Henrichs, "Epiphany," *OCD* 3rd ed. (1996) 546.

Henrichs 1996b, A. Henrichs, "Hecate," *OCD* 3rd ed. (1996) 671-3.

Herington 1970. J. Herington, *The Author of Prometheus Bound* (Austin 1970).

Herington 1985. J. Herington, *Poetry into Drama: Early Tragedy and the Greek Poetic Tradition* (Berkeley 1985).

Hester 1995. D. Hester, "Ironic Interaction in Aeschylus and Sophocles," *Prudentia* 27 (1995) 14-43.

Hoffmann 1997. H. Hoffmann, *Sotades: Symbols of Immortality on Greek Vases* (Oxford 1997).

Hollis 1990, A. S. Hollis ed., *Callimachus Hecale* (Oxford 1990).

Hornblower 1991. S. Hornblower, *A Commentary on Thucydides*. Volume I: Books I-III (Oxford 1991).

Hornblower 1996. S. Hornblower, *A Commentary on Thucydides*. Volume II: Books IV-V.24 (Oxford 1996).

Hughes 1991. D. D. Hughes. *Human Sacrifice in Ancient Greece* (London 1991).

Humphreys 1990. S. C. Humphreys, "Phrateres in Alopeke, and the Salaminioi," *ZPE* 83 (1990) 243-8.

Hutchinson 1985. G. O. Hutchinson ed., *Aeschylus: Septem contra Thebas* (Oxford 1985).

Jameson 1991. M. H. Jameson, "Sacrifice before battle," in V. D. Hanson ed., *Hoplites: The Classical Greek Battle Experience* (London 1991) 197-227.

Jameson 1994. M. H. Jameson, "Theoxenia," in Hägg 1994, 35-57.

Jameson, Jordan, Kotansky 1993. M. H. Jameson, D. R, Jordan, R. D. Kotansky, *A lex sacra from Selinous* (Durham, NC 1993) [Greek, Roman, and Byzantine Monographs 11].

Jeanmaire 1939. H. Jeanmaire, *Couroi et Couretes* (Lille 1939).

Jouanna 1992. J. Jouanna, "Libations et sacrifices dans la tragédie grecque," *REG* 105 (1992), 406-34.

Kahil 1977. L. Kahil, "L'Artémis de Brauron: rites et mystère," *AntK* 20 (1977) 86-98.

Kahil 1979. L. Kahil, "La déesse Artémis: mythologie et iconographie," in J.N. Coldstream and M.A.R. Colledge eds., *Greece and Italy in the Classical*

World. Acta of the XI International Congress of Classical Archaeology, London, 3-9 September 1978 (London 1979) 73-87.
Kahil 1983. L. Kahil, "Mythological Repertoire of Brauron," in W.G. Moon ed., *Ancient Greek Art and Iconography* (Madison Wisconsin 1983) 231-44.
Kannicht 1969. R. Kannicht ed., *Euripides Helena* (Heidelberg 1969).
Käppel 1992. L. Käppel, *Paian: Studien zur Geschichthe einer Gattung* (Berlin 1992).
Kavoulaki forthcoming. A. Kavoulaki, *Pompai: Processions in Athenian Tragedy* (Oxford, forthcoming).
Kearns 1989. E. Kearns, *The Heroes of Attica* (London 1989).
Kearns 1990. E. Kearns, "Saving the City," in O. Murray and S. Price, eds., *The Greek City from Homer to Alexander* (Oxford 1990) 323-44.
Keuls 1984. E. C. Keuls, "The Reconstruction of a Lost Greek Tragedy by Means of Literary and Archaeological Detective Work," *Liberal and Fine Arts Review* 4 (1984) 26-49.
Kiechle 1970. F. K. Kiechle, "Götterdarstellung durch Menschen in der altmediterranen Religionen," *Historia* 19 (1970) 259-71.
Knox 1979. B. M. W. Knox, *Word and Action: Essays on the Ancient Theater* (Baltimore 1979).
Knox 1983. B. M. W. Knox, "The *Medea* of Euripides," in E. Segal ed., *Oxford Readings in Greek Tragedy* (Oxford 1983) 272-93.
Knox 1985. B. M. W. Knox, "Euripides," in *CHCL* 64-87.
Koch-Harnack 1989. G. Koch-Harnack, *Erotische Symbole. Lotosblüte und gemeinsamer Mantel auf antiken Vasen* (Berlin 1989).
Kolb 1981. F. Kolb, *Agora und Theater, Volks- und Festversammlung* (Berlin 1981).
Koniaris 1973. G. L. Koniaris, "Alexander, Palamedes, Troades, Sisyphus—A Connected Tetralogy? A Connected Trilogy?," *HSCP* 77 (1973) 85-124.
Kontis 1967: I. Kontis, "Artemis Brauronia," *ADelt* 22 (1967) A, 156-206.
Kovacs 1987. D. Kovacs, *The Heroic Muse: Studies in the Hippolytus and Hecuba of Euripides* (Baltimore 1987).
Kovacs 1993. D. Kovacs, "Zeus in Euripides' *Medea*," *AJPh* 114 (1993) 45-70.
Kron 1976. U. Kron, *Die zehn attischen Phylenheroen. Geschichte, Mythos, Kult und Darstellungen* (Berlin 1976).
Kron 1988. U. Kron, "Kultmahle im Heraion von Samos archaischer Zeit. Versuch einer Rekonstruktion," in Hägg, Marinatos, and Nordquist 1988, 135-48.
Krummen 1990. E. Krummen, *Pyrsos Hymnon : festliche Gegenwart und mythischrituelle Tradition als Voraussetzung einer Pindarinterpretation* (Berlin 1990).
Kyle 1992. D. G. Kyle, "The Panathenaic Games: Sacred and Civic Athletics," in Neils 1992, 77-101.
Larson 1995. J. Larson, *Greek Heroine Cults* (Madison 1995).
Lee 1976. K. H. Lee, ed., *Euripides Troades* (London 1976).
Lefkowitz 1981. M. R. Lefkowitz, *The Lives of the Greek Poets* (London 1981).

Lefkowitz 1987. M. R. Lefkowitz, "Was Euripides an Atheist?," *Studi italiani di filologia classica* 5 (1987) 149-66.
Lefkowitz 1989. M. R. Lefkowitz, "'Impiety' and 'atheism' in Euripides' dramas," *CQ* 39 (1989) 70-82.
Lefkowitz 1991. M. R. Lefkowitz, *First-Person Fictions: Pindar's Poetic 'I'* (Oxford 1991).
Lissarague 1987. F. Lissarague, *Un Flot d' images. Une esthétique du banquet grec* (Paris 1987).
Lissarague 1990. F. Lissarague, "Why Satyrs Are Good to Represent," in Winkler and Zeitlin 1990, 228-36.
Lissarague 1995. F. Lissarague, "Identity and Otherness: The Case of Attic Head Vases and Plastic Vases," *Source* 15 (1995) 4-9.
Lloyd 1992. M. Lloyd, *The Agon in Euripides* (Oxford 1992).
Lloyd-Jones 1957. H. Lloyd-Jones ed., Appendix, in Loeb Classical Library, *Aeschylus*, vol. ii (Cambridge, Mass. 1957) 525-603.
Lloyd-Jones 1971. H. Lloyd-Jones, *The Justice of Zeus* (Berkeley 1971).
Lloyd-Jones 1983. H. Lloyd-Jones, "Artemis and Iphigeneia," *JHS* 103 (1983) 87-102.
Lloyd-Jones 1990. H. Lloyd-Jones, "Problems in Early Greek Tragedy. Pratinas and Phrynichos," in *Greek Epic, Lyric and Tragedy: The Academic Papers of Sir Hugh Lloyd-Jones* (Oxford 1990).
Lloyd-Jones 1994. H. Lloyd-Jones ed., Loeb Classical Library, *Sophocles*, vols i-ii (Cambridge, Mass. 1994).
Lloyd-Jones 1996. Loeb Classical Library, *Sophocles*, vol. iii, Fragments (Cambridge, Mass. 1996).
Lochin 1990. C. Lochin, "Ixion," *LIMC* v (1990) 859-62.
Lonsdale 1993. S. H. Lonsdale, *Dance and Ritual Play in Greek Religion* (Baltimore 1993).
Loraux 1985. N. Loraux, *Facons tragiques de tuer une femme* (Paris 1985).
Loraux 1990. N. Loraux, *Les meres en deuil* (Paris 1990).
Loraux 1990b. N. Loraux, "Heracles: the super-male and the feminine," in D. M. Halperin, J. I. Winkler, and F. I. Zeitlin eds., *Before Sexuality* (1990) 21-52.
MacDowell 1971, D. M. MacDowell ed., *Aristophanes Wasps* (Oxford 1971).
MacDowell 1989. D. M. MacDowell, "Athenian laws about choruses," in F. J. Fernandez Nieto ed., *Symposion 1982. Vorträge zur griechischen und hellenistischen Rechtsgeschichte* (Cologne 1989) 65-77.
Macleod 1982. C. W. Macleod, "Politics and the *Oresteia*," *JHS* 102 (1982) 124-44.
Malkin 1987. I. Malkin, *Religion and colonization in ancient Greece* (Leiden 1987).
Mastronarde 1990. D. J. Mastronarde, "Actors on High: The Skene Roof, the Crane, and the Gods in Attic Drama," *Classical Antiquity* 9 (1990) 247-94.
Mastronarde 1994. D. J. Mastronarde ed., *Euripides Phoenissai* (Cambridge 1994).

Matheson 1986. S. B. Matheson, "Polygnotos: An Ilioupersis Scene in the Getty Museum," *Occasional Papers on Antiquities 2, Greek Vases in the J. Paul Getty Museum* 3 (1986) 101-14.
McDermott 1989. E. A. McDermott 1989, *Euripides' Medea: The Incarnation of Disorder* (Pennsylvania State University 1989).
Meier 1993. C. Meier, *The Political Art of Greek Tragedy* (Cambridge 1993, first publ. in German 1988).
Meiggs and Lewis 1988. R. Meiggs and D. Lewis, *A Selection of Greek Historical Inscriptions*, revised edition (Oxford 1988).
Meyer 1987. M. W. Meyer, *The Ancient Mysteries: A Sourcebook* (San Francisco 1987).
Merkelbach 1980. R. Merkelbach. "Der Kult der Hestia im Prytaneion der griechischen Städte," *ZPE* 37 (1980) 77-92.
Mikalson 1991. J. D. Mikalson, *Honor thy Gods: Popular Religion in Greek Tragedy* (Chapel Hill 1991).
Miller 1978. S. G. Miller, *The Prytaneion: Its Function and Architectural Form* (Berkeley 1978).
Mills 1997. S. Mills, *Theseus, Tragedy, and the Athenian Empire* (Oxford 1997).
Miralles 1989. C. Miralles, "La creazione di uno spazio: la parola nell' ambito del dio dell' alterità," *Dioniso* 59 (1989) 23-41.
Mitchell-Boyask 1993. R. N. Mitchell-Boyask, "Sacrifice and Revenge in Euripides' Hecuba," *Ramus* 22 (1993) 116-34.
Mommsen 1975. H. Mommsen, *Der Affekter* (Mainz 1975).
Mossman 1995. J. Mossman, *Wild Justice: A Study of Euripides' Hecuba* (Oxford 1995).
Murray 1990. O. Murray ed., *Sympotica: A Symposium on the Symposion* (Oxford 1990).
Mylonas 1961. G. E. Mylonas, *Eleusis and the Eleusinian Mysteries* (Princeton 1961).
Nagy 1979. G. Nagy, *The Best of the Achaeans: Concepts of the Hero in Archaic Greek Poetry* (Baltimore 1979).
Nagy 1986. G. Nagy, "Pindar's Olympian 1 and the Aetiology of the Olympic Games," *TAPA* 116 (1986) 71-88.
Nagy 1990. G. Nagy, *Pindar's Homer: The Lyric Possession of an Epic Past* (Baltimore 1990).
Neils 1992. J. Neils ed., *Goddess and Polis: The Panathenaic Festival in Ancient Athens* (Princeton 1992).
Nightingale 1992. A. W. Nightingale, "Plato's Gorgias and Euripides' Antiope: A Study in Generic Transformation," *Classical Antiquity* 11 (1992) 121-41.
Nilsson 1906. M. P. Nilsson, *Griechische Feste von religiöser Bedeutung mit Ausschluss der attischen* (Leipzig 1906).
Nilsson 1951. M. P. Nilsson, *Opuscula Selecta*, vol. 1 (Lund 1951).

Nilsson 1957. M. P. Nilsson, *The Dionysiac Mysteries of the Hellenistic and Roman Age* (Lund 1957).

Nilsson 1967. M. P. Nilsson, *Geschichte der Griechischen Religion*, vol. I, 3rd ed. (Munich 1967).

Nilsson 1974. M. P. Nilsson, *Geschichte der Griechischen Religion*, vol. II, 3rd ed. (Munich 1974).

Nixon 1995. L. Nixon, "The cults of Demeter and Kore," in R. Hawley and B. Levick eds. *Women in Antiquity: New Assessments* (London 1995) 75-96.

Nock 1972. A. D. Nock, *Essays on Religion and the Ancient World* (Cambridge, Mass. 1972).

Nordquist 1992. G. C. Nordquist, "Instrumental Music in Representations of Greek Cult," in Hägg 1992, 143-68.

Nussbaum 1986. M. C. Nussbaum, *The fragility of goodness: Luck and ethics in Greek tragedy and philosophy* (Cambridge 1986).

Oakley and Sinos 1993. J. H. Oakley and R. H. Sinos, *The Wedding in Ancient Athens* (Madison 1993).

Oranje 1980. H. Oranje, "Euripides' Protesilaus: P.Oxy. 3214.10-14," *ZPE* 37 (1980) 169-72.

Osborne 1993. R. Osborne, "Competitive festivals and the polis: a context for dramatic festivals at Athens," in Sommerstein, Halliwell, Henderson and Zimmermann 1993, 21-38.

Osborne and Hornblower 1994. R. Osborne and S. Hornblower eds., *Ritual, Finance, Politics: Athenian Democratic Accounts presented to David Lewis* (Oxford 1994).

Padel 1990. R. Padel, "Making space speak," in Winkler and Zeitlin 1990, 336-65.

Padel 1992. R. Padel, *In and Out of the Mind: Greek Images of the Tragic Self* (Princeton 1992).

Page 1938. D. L. Page ed., *Euripides Medea* (Oxford 1938).

Page 1941. D. L. Page, Loeb Classical Library, *Select Papyri*, vol. III. *Literary Papyri: Poetry* (Cambridge Mass. 1941).

Page 1962. D. L. Page, "An early tragedy on the fall of Croesus?," *PCPS* 188 (1962) 47-9.

Palaiokrassa 1991. L. Palaiokrassa, *To hiero tes Artemidos Mounichias* (Athens 1991).

Parke 1977. H. W. Parke, *Festivals of the Athenians* (London 1977).

Parke and Wormell 1956. H. W. Parke and D. E. W. Wormell, *The Delphic Oracle* (Oxford 1956).

Parker 1983. R. Parker, *Miasma: Pollution and Purification in Early Greek Religion* (Oxford 1983).

Bibliography

Parker 1987. R. Parker, "Festivals of the Attic Demes," in T. Linders and G. Nordquist eds., *Gifts to the Gods* (Proceedings of the Upssala Symposium 1985; Upssala, 1987) 137-47.
Parker 1996. R. Parker, *Athenian Religion: A History* (Oxford 1996).
Parker 1997. R. Parker, "Gods Cruel and Kind: Tragic and Civic Theology," in Pelling 1997c, 143-60.
Pelling 1997a. C. Pelling, "Aeschylus' *Persae* and History," in Pelling 1997c, 1-19.
Pelling 1997b. C. Pelling, "Conclusion," in Pelling 1997c, 213-35.
Pelling 1997c. C. Pelling ed., *Tragedy and the Historian* (Oxford 1997).
Pembroke 1965. S. Pembroke, "The last of the matriarchs: a study in the inscriptions of Lycia," *JESHO* 8 (1965) 217-47.
Pembroke 1967. S. Pembroke, "Women in charge: the function of alternatives in early Greek tradition and the ancient ideas of matriarchy," *JWI* 30 (1967) 1-35.
Pensa 1977. M. Pensa, *Rappresentazioni dell' oltretomba nella ceramica Apula* (Rome 1977).
Pfister 1924. F. Pfister, "Epiphanie," in *RE* Suppl. IV, 277-323 (1924).
Pipili 1987. M. Pipili, *Laconian Iconography of the Sixth Century B.C.* [Oxford University Committee for Archaeology Monograph 12] (Oxford 1987).
Pippidi 1975. D.M. Pippidi, *Scythica Minora. Recherches sur les colonies grecques du littoral roumain de la mer Noire* (Bucharest 1975).
Pippin Burnett 1965. A. Pippin Burnett, "The Virtues of Admetos," *Classical Philology* 60 (1965) 240-55.
Pirenne-Delforge 1994. V. Pirenne-Delforge, *L'Aphrodite grecque* (Athens-Liege 1994) [*Kernos* Supplement 4].
Platnauer 1938. M. Platnauer, *Euripides' Iphigeneia in Tauris* (Oxford 1938).
Pöhlmann 1981. E. Pöhlmann, "Die Prohedrie des Dionysostheaters im 5. Jahrhundert und das Bühnenspiel der Klassik," *MusHelv* 38 (1981) 129-46.
Polacco 1990. L. Polacco, *Il teatro di Dioniso Eleuterio ad Atene* (Rome 1990).
Porter 1994. J. R. Porter, *Studies in Euripides' Orestes* (Leiden 1994).
Powell 1990. A. Powell ed., *Euripides, women and sexuality* (London 1990).
Privitera 1965. G. A. Privitera, *Laso di Ermione nella cultura ateniese e nella tradizione storiografica* (Rome 1965).
Privitera 1972, G. A. Privitera, "Saffo, Anacreonte, Pindaro," *QUUC* 13 (1972) 131-40.
Privitera 1991. G. A. Privitera, "Aspetti musicali nella storia del ditirambo arcaico e tardo-arcaico," in Cassio and Cerri 1991, 141-153.
Pucci 1994. P. Pucci, "Gods' Intervention and Epiphany in Sophocles," *AJPh* 115 (1994) 15-46.
Pulleyn 1997. S. Pulleyn, *Prayer in Greek Religion* (Oxford 1997).
Radt 1982. S. Radt, "Sophokles in seinen Fragmenten," in *Fondation Hardt pour l'étude de l'antiquité classique. Entretiens xxix. Sophocle.* (Geneva 1982) 185-231.

Rau 1967. P. Rau, *Paratragodia* (Munich 1967).
Raubitschek 1969. I. K. Raubitschek, *The Hearst Hillsborough Vases* (Mainz 1969).
Rehm 1994. R. Rehm, *Marriage to Death: The Conflation of Wedding and Funerary Rituals in Greek Tragedy* (Princeton 1994).
Reinhardt 1960. K. R. Reinhardt, "Die Sinneskrise bei Euripides," in K. R. Reinhardt, *Tradition und Geist* (Göttingen 1960) 227-56.
Rhodes 1981. P. J. Rhodes, *A Commentary on the Aristotelian Athenaion Politeia* (Oxford 1981).
Ridgway 1992. B. S. Ridgway, "Images of Athena on the Akropolis," in Neils 1992, 119-42.
Ritchie 1964. W. Ritchie, *The Authenticity of the Rhesus of Euripides* (Cambridge 1964).
Roberts 1984. D. H. Roberts, *Apollo and His Oracle in the Oresteia* (Göttingen 1984) [*Hypomnemata* 78].
Roberts 1987. D. H. Roberts, "Parting Words: Final Lines in Sophocles and Euripides," *CQ* 37 (1987) 51-64.
Roberts, Dunn and Fowler 1997. D. H. Roberts, F. M. Dunn and D. Fowler eds., *Classical Closure: Reading the End in Greek and Latin Literature* (Princeton 1997).
Robertson 1975. M. Robertson, *A History of Greek Art* (Cambridge 1975).
Robertson 1986. M. Robertson, "Two Pelikai by The Pan Painter," *Occasional Papers on Antiquities 2, Greek Vases in the J. Paul Getty Museum* 3 (1986) 71-90.
Robertson 1996. N. Robertson, "Athena's Shrines and Festivals," in J. Neils ed., *Worshipping Athena: Panathenaia and Parthenon* (Madison, Wisc. 1996) 27-77.
Rosenbloom 1993. D. Rosenbloom, "Shouting 'fire' in a crowded theatre: Phrynichos' *Capture of Miletos* and the politics of fear in early Attic tragedy," *Philologus* 137 (1993) 159-96.
Russo, Fernandez-Galiano and Heubeck 1992. J. Russo, M. Fernandez-Galiano, and A. Heubeck, *A Commentary on Homer's Odyssey* vol. 3, books xvii-xxiv (Oxford 1992).
Rutherford 1994/5. I. Rutherford, "Apollo in Ivy: The Tragic Paean," in Golder and Scully 1994/5, 112-35.
Rutherford 1997. I. Rutherford, "For the Aeginetans to Aiakos a Prosodion: an unnoticed title at Pindar, Paean 6, 123, and its significance for the poem," *ZPE* 118 (1997) 1-21.
Rutherford forthcoming a. I. Rutherford, *Pindar's Paeans*, Oxford, forthcoming.
Rutherford forthcoming b. I. Rutherford, "Theoria as Theatre: Pilgrimage in Greek Drama," forthcoming in *PLLS* 11 (1998).
Sarian 1990. H. Sarian, "Hestia," LIMC 5 (1990) 407-12.
Schachter 1981. A. Schachter, *Cults of Boiotia* vol. 1 (London 1981).

Bibliography

Schmid 1929. W. Schmid, *Untersuchungen zum Gefesselten Prometheus* (Stuttgart 1929).
Schmidt 1964. W. Schmidt, *Der Deus ex machina bei Euripides* (Diss. Tübingen 1964).
Schnurr 1995a. C. Schnurr, "Die alte Agora Athens," *ZPE* 105 (1995) 131-8.
Schnurr 1995b. C. Schnurr, "Zur Topographie der Theaterstätten und der Tripodenstrasse in Athen," *ZPE* 105 (1995) 139-53.
Scodel 1980. R. Scodel, *The Trojan Trilogy of Euripides* (Göttingen 1980) [*Hypomnemata* 60].
Scodel 1982. R. Scodel, "P.Oxy. 3317: Euripides' *Antigone*," *ZPE* 46 (1982) 37-42.
Scott 1984. W. C. Scott, *Musical Design in Aeschylean Theater* (Hanover, NH 1984).
Seaford 1976. R. Seaford, "On the Origins of Satyric Drama," *Maia* 28 (1976) 209-21.
Seaford 1987. R. Seaford ed., *Euripides Cyclops* (Oxford 1984).
Seaford 1987. R. Seaford, "The Tragic Wedding," *JHS* 107 (1987) 106-30.
Seaford 1990. R. Seaford, "The structural problems of marriage in Euripides," in Powell 1990, 151-76.
Seaford 1993. R. Seaford, "Dionysus as Destroyer of the Household: Homer, Tragedy, and the Polis," in Carpenter and Faraone 1993, 115-46.
Seaford 1994. R. Seaford, *Reciprocity and Ritual: Homer and Tragedy in the Developing City-State* (Oxford 1994).
Seaford 1996. R. Seaford, "Something to Do with Dionysos—Tragedy and the Dionysiac: Response to Friedrich," in Silk 1996, 284-94.
Seaford 1996b. R. Seaford ed., *Euripides Bacchae* (Warminster 1996).
Seale 1982. D. Seale, *Vision and Stagecraft in Sophocles* (London 1982).
Sechan 1926. L. Sechan, *Etudes sur la tragédie grecque* (Paris 1926).
Segal 1988a. C. Segal, "Theatre, Ritual and Commemoration in Euripides' *Hippolytus*," *Ramus* 17 (1988a) 52-74.
Segal 1988b. C. Segal, "Confusion and concealment in Euripides' *Hippolytus*: Vision, hope and tragic knowledge," *Metis* 3 *Théâtre grec et tragique* (1988b) 263-82.
Segal 1992. C. Segal, "Tragic beginnings: narration, voice and authority in the prologues of Greek drama," *YCS* 29 (1992): Beginnings in Classical Literature, 85-112.
Segal 1993. C. Segal, *Euripides and the Poetics of Sorrow* (Durham 1993).
Shapiro 1981. H. A. Shapiro, "Exekias, Ajax and Salamis: a further note," *AJA* 85, 1981, 173-5.
Shapiro 1989. H. A. Shapiro, *Art and cult under the Tyrants in Athens* (Mainz 1989).
Shapiro 1992. H. A. Shapiro, "Mousikoi Agones: Music and Poetry at the Panathenaia," in Neils 1992, 53-75.
Shapiro 1994. H. A. Shapiro, *Myth into Art: Poet and Painter in Classical Greece* (London 1994).

Shear 1993. T. Leslie Shear Jr., "The Persian Destruction of Athens: Evidence from Agora Deposits," *Hesperia* 62 (1993) 383-482.
Sherwin-White 1978. S. M. Sherwin-White, *Ancient Cos* (Göttingen 1978).
Sifakis 1971. G. M. Sifakis, *Parabasis and Animal Choruses* (London 1971).
Silk 1985. M. S. Silk, "Heracles and Greek Tragedy," *Greece and Rome* 32 (1985) 1-22.
Silk 1996. M. S. Silk ed., *Tragedy and the Tragic. Greek Theatre and Beyond* (Oxford 1996).
Simon 1976. 177-86. E. Simon, "Kratos und Bia," *WürzJhb* 1 (1976) 177-86.
Simon 1983. E. Simon, *Festivals of Attica: An Archaeological Commentary* (Madison, Wisconsin 1983).
Simon 1986. E. Simon, "Bia et Kratos," LIMC 3 (1986) 114-5.
Slater 1986. N. W. Slater, "The Lenaean Theatre," *ZPE* 88 (1986) 255-64.
Sommerstein 1983. A. H. Sommerstein, *The Comedies of Aristophanes: vol. 4. Wasps* (Warminster 1983).
Sommerstein 1989. A. H. Sommerstein ed., *Aeschylus Eumenides* (Cambridge 1989).
Sommerstein 1990. A. H. Sommerstein, *The Comedies of Aristophanes: vol. 7. Lysistrata* (Warminster 1990).
Sommerstein 1994. A. H. Sommerstein, *The Comedies of Aristophanes: vol. 8. Thesmophoriazusae* (Warminster 1994).
Sommerstein, Halliwell, Henderson, and Zimmermann 1993. A. H. Sommerstein, S. Halliwell, J. Henderson, and B. Zimmermann eds., *Tragedy, Comedy and the Polis* (Bari 1993).
Sourvinou-Inwood 1971. C. Sourvinou-Inwood, "Aristophanes, Lysistrata 641-647," *CQ* 21 (1971) 339-42.
Sourvinou-Inwood 1974. C. Sourvinou-Inwood, "Movements of populations in Attica at the end of the Mycenaean period," in R. A. Crossland and A. Birchall eds., *Bronze Age Migrations in the Aegean* (London 1974) 215-25.
Sourvinou-Inwood 1979. C. Sourvinou-Inwood, *Theseus as son and stepson: A tentative illustration of the Greek mythological mentality* (London 1979) [Institute of Classical Studies, University of London, Bulletin Supplement no. 40].
Sourvinou-Inwood 1983. C. Sourvinou-Inwood, "A Trauma in Flux: Death in the 8th Century and After," in R. Hägg ed., *The Greek Renaissance of the Eighth Century B.C.: Tradition and Innovation* (Stockholm 1983) (=Proceedings of the 2nd International Symposium at the Swedish Institute in Athens, 1-5 June 1981) 33-48.
Sourvinou-Inwood 1986. C. Sourvinou-Inwood, "Crime and punishment: Tityos, Tantalos and Sisyphos in Odyssey 11," *BICS* 33 (1986) 37-58.
Sourvinou-Inwood 1987-1988. C. Sourvinou-Inwood, "Antigone 904-20: a reading," *Annali. Istituto Universitario Orientale. Napoli*. Dipartmento del

mondo classico e del mediterraneo antico. Sezione filologica ix-x (1987-1988) 19-35.
Sourvinou-Inwood 1988. C. Sourvinou-Inwood, *Studies in girls' transitions. Aspects of the arkteia and age representation in Attic iconography* (Athens 1988).
Sourvinou-Inwood 1988b. C. Sourvinou-Inwood, "Further aspects of polis religion," in *Archeologia e storia antica Annali. Istituto Universitario Orientale. Napoli.* Dipartmento del mondo classico e del mediterraneo antico x (1988) [1990] 259-74.
Sourvinou-Inwood 1989a. C. Sourvinou-Inwood, "Assumptions and the creation of meaning: reading Sophocles' *Antigone*," *JHS* 109 (1989) 134-48.
Sourvinou-Inwood 1989b. C. Sourvinou-Inwood, "The fourth stasimon of Sophocles' *Antigone*," *BICS* 36 (1989) 141-65.
Sourvinou-Inwood 1990a. "What is polis religion?," in O. Murray and S. Price eds., *The Greek City from Homer to Alexander* (Oxford 1990) 295-322.
Sourvinou-Inwood 1990b. C. Sourvinou-Inwood, "Lire l'arkteia—lire les images, les textes, l'animalité," *Dialogues d'histoire ancienne* 16 (1990) 45-60.
Sourvinou-Inwood 1990c. C. Sourvinou-Inwood, "Sophocles' Antigone as a 'bad woman'," in F. Dieteren and E. Kloek eds., *Writing women into history* (Amsterdam 1990) 11-38.
Sourvinou-Inwood 1990d, C. Sourvinou-Inwood, "Myths in images: Theseus and Medea as a case study," in L. Edmunds ed., *Approaches to Greek Myth* (Baltimore 1990) 395-445.
Sourvinou-Inwood 1991. C. Sourvinou-Inwood, *'Reading' Greek culture: texts and images, rituals and myths* (Oxford1991).
Sourvinou-Inwood 1994. C. Sourvinou-Inwood, "Something to do with Athens: Tragedy and Ritual," in Osborne and Hornblower 1994, 269-90.
Sourvinou-Inwood 1995. C. Sourvinou-Inwood, *'Reading' Greek death* (Oxford 1995).
Sourvinou-Inwood 1995b. C. Sourvinou-Inwood, "Male and female, public and private, ancient and modern," in E. Reeder ed., *Pandora* (1995) 111-20.
Sourvinou-Inwood 1997a. C. Sourvinou-Inwood, "Tragedy and religion: constructs and readings," in Pelling 1997c, 161-86.
Sourvinou-Inwood 1997b. C. Sourvinou-Inwood, "Reconstructing change: ideology and ritual at Eleusis," in M. Golden and P. Toohey, eds., *Inventing Ancient Culture? Historicism, Periodization and the Ancient World* (London 1996) 132-64.
Sourvinou-Inwood 1997c. C. Sourvinou-Inwood, "Medea at a shifting distance: images and Euripidean Tragedy," in J.J. Clauss and S.I. Johnston eds., *Medea. Essays on Medea in Myth, Literature, Philosophy and Art* (Princeton 1997) 253-96.
Sourvinou-Inwood 1997d. C. Sourvinou-Inwood, "The Hesiodic myth of the Five Races and the tolerance of plurality in Greek Mythology," in O.

Palagia ed., *Greek Offerings. Essays on Greek Art in Honour of John Boardman* (Oxford 1997) 1-21.
Starkie 1911. W. J. M. Starkie ed., *The Clouds of Aristophanes* (London 1911).
Stevens 1956. P. T. Stevens, "Euripides and the Athenians," *JHS* 76 (1956) 87-94.
Stevens 1971. P. T. Stevens ed., *Euripides Andromache* (Oxford 1971).
Stewart 1990. A. Stewart, *Greek Sculpture. An Exploration* (New Haven 1990).
Stinton 1965. T. C. W. Stinton, *Euripides and the Judgement of Paris* [*JHS* Suppl. paper 11] (London 1965).
Stinton 1976. T. C. W. Stinton, "'Si credere dignum est': some expressions of disbelief in Euripides and others," *PCPS* 22 (1976) 60-89.
Stoessl 1987. F. Stoessl, *Die Vorgeschichte des griechischen Theaters* (Darmstadt 1987).
Stoian 1970. I. Stoian, "Une nouvelle inscription agonistique d'Histria," *Dacia* 14 (1970) 397-404.
Stroud 1993. R. S. Stroud, "Abstract: The Sanctuary of Aiakos in the Athenian Agora," *AJA* 97 (1993) 308-9.
Stroud 1994. R. S. Stroud, "The Aiakeion and Tholos of Athens in P.Oxy. 2087," *ZPE* 103 (1994) 1-9.
Sutton 1985. D. F. Sutton, "The satyr play," in *CHCL* 94-102.
Taplin 1975. O. Taplin, "The title of Prometheus Desmotes," *JHS* 95 (1975) 184-6.
Taplin 1977. O. Taplin, *The Stagecraft of Aeschylus: The Dramatic Use of Exits and Entrances in Greek Tragedy* (Oxford 1977).
Taplin 1993. O. Taplin, *Comic Angels and Other Approaches to Greek Drama through Vase-Painting* (Oxford 1993).
Taplin 1995. O. Taplin, "Opening Performance: Closing Texts?," *Essays in Criticism* 45 (1995) 93-120.
Themelis 1971. P. G. Themelis, *Brauron: Guide to the Site and Museum* (Athens 1971).
Thompson 1953. H. A. Thompson, "Excavations in the Athenian Agora: 1952," *Hesperia* 22 (1953) 25-56.
Touchefeu 1981. O. Touchefeu, "Aias II," *LIMC* 1 (1981) 336-51.
Travlos 1971. J. Travlos, *Pictorial Dictionary of Ancient Athens* (London 1971).
Travlos 1988. J. Travlos, *Bildlexikon zur Topographie des antiken Attika* (Tübingen 1988).
Trendall 1989. A. D. Trendall, *Red Figure Vases of South Italy and Sicily* (London 1989).
Trendall 1991. A. D. Trendall, "Farce and tragedy in South Italian vase-painting," in T. Rasmussen and N. Spivey eds., *Looking at Greek Vases* (Cambridge 1991) 151-82.
Trendall and Webster 1971. A. D. Trendall and T.B.L. Webster, *Illustrations of Greek Drama* (London 1971).
van Straten 1995. F. T. van Straten, *Hiera Kala: Images of Animal Sacrifice in Archaic and Classical Greece* (Leiden 1995).

van der Weiden 1991. M. J. H. van der Weiden, *The Dithyrambs of Pindar: Introduction, text and commentary* (Amsterdam 1991).

Verbanck-Pierard 1992. A. Verbanck-Pierard, "Herakles at Feast in Attic Art: a Mythical or Cultic Iconography?," in Hägg 1992, 85-106.

Vernant 1965. J.-P. Vernant, *Mythe et pensée chez les Grecs* (Paris 1965).

Vernant 1972. "Tensions et ambiguités," in Vernant and Vidal-Naquet 1972, 21-40.

Vernant 1986. J.-P. Vernant, "Le dieu de la fiction tragique," in Vernant and Vidal-Naquet 1986, 17-24.

Vernant and Vidal-Naquet 1972. J.-P. Vernant and P. Vidal-Naquet, *Mythe et tragédie en Grèce ancienne* (Paris 1972).

Vernant and Vidal-Naquet 1986. J.-P. Vernant and P. Vidal-Naquet, *Mythe et Tragédie* II (Paris 1986).

Verpoorten 1945. J.-M. Verpoorten, "La stibas ou l'image de la brousse," *HRH* 162 (1945) 147-60.

Versnel 1990. H. S. Versnel, *Ter Unus. Isis, Dionysos, Hermes. Three Studies in Henotheism* (Leiden 1990).

Versnel 1993. H. S. Versnel, *Inconsistencies in Greek and Roman Religion 2. Transition and Reversal in Myth and Ritual* (Leiden 1993).

Vickers 1981. M. Vickers, "Recent Acquisitions of Greek Antiquities by the Ashmolean Museum," *AA* (1981) 541-61.

Vidal-Naquet 1972: P. Vidal-Naquet, "Chasse et sacrifice dans l'Orestie d'Eschyle," in Vernant and Vidal-Naquet 1972, 133-58.

Vidal-Naquet 1983. P. Vidal-Naquet, *Le chasseur noir. Formes de pensée et formes de société dans le monde grec*^{2} (Paris 1983).

Vidal-Naquet 1986a. P. Vidal-Naquet, "Les boucliers des héros. Essai sur la scène centrale des *Sept contre Thebes*," in Vernant and Vidal-Naquet 1986, 115-147.

Vidal-Naquet 1986b. P. Vidal-Naquet, "Oedipe à Athènes," in Vernant and Vidal-Naquet 1986, 149-73.

Vierneisel and Kaeser 1990. K. Vierneisel and B. Kaeser eds., *Kunst der Schale, Kultur des Trinkens* (Munich 1990).

Webster 1967. T. B. L. Webster, *The Tragedies of Euripides* (London 1967).

West 1966. M. L. West, *Hesiod Theogony* (Oxford 1966).

West 1974. M. L. West, *Studies in Greek Elegy and Iambus* (Berlin 1974).

West 1978. M. L. West, *Hesiod Works and Days* (Oxford 1978).

West 1979. M. L. West, "The Prometheus Trilogy," *JHS* 99 (1979) 130-48.

West 1983. M. L. West, "Tragica VI," *BICS* 30 (1983) 63-82.

West 1987. M. L. West, *Euripides Orestes* (Warminster 1987)

West 1989. M. L. West, "The Early Chronology of Attic Tragedy," *CQ* 39 (1989) 251-4.

West 1990. M. L. West, *Studies in Aeschylus* (Stuttgart 1990).

West 1984. S. West, "Io and the dark stranger (Sophocles, *Inachus* F 269a)," *CQ* 34 (1984) 292-302.
Wilamowitz 1959. U. von Wilamowitz-Moellendorf, *Euripides, Herakles*, vol. 3 (Darmstadt 1959; 1st publ. Berlin 1889; 2nd ed. Berlin 1895).
Wiles 1997. D. Wiles, *Tragedy in Athens: Performance space and theatrical meaning* (Cambridge 1997).
Wilkins 1990. J. Wilkins, "The State and the Individual: Euripides' Plays of Voluntary Self Sacrifice," in Powell 1990, 177-94.
Wilkins 1993. J. Wilkins, *Euripides Heraclidai* (Oxford 1993).
Willink 1983. C. W. Willink, "Prodikos, 'Meteorosophists' and the 'Tantalos' Paradigm," *CQ* 33 (1983) 25-33.
Willink 1986. C. W. Willink, *Euripides Orestes* (Oxford 1986).
Willink 1990. C. W. Willink, "The goddess Eulabeia and pseudo-Euripides in Euripides' *Phoenissai*," *PCPS* 36 (1990) 182-201.
Wilson and Taplin 1993. P. Wilson and O. Taplin, "The 'Aetiology' of Tragedy in the *Oresteia*," *PCPS* 39 (1993) 169-80.
Winkler 1990. J. J. Winkler, "The Ephebes' Song: *Tragoidia and Polis*," in Winkler and Zeitlin 1990, 20-62.
Winkler and Zeitlin 1990. J. J. Winkler and F. Zeitlin eds., *Nothing to Do with Dionysos?* (Princeton 1990).
Winnington-Ingram 1961. R. P. Winnington-Ingram, "The Danaid Trilogy of Aeschylus," *JHS* 81 (1961) 141-52=Winnington-Ingram 1983, 55-72.
Winnington-Ingram 1983. R. P. Winnington-Ingram, *Studies in Aeschylus* (Cambridge 1983).
Winnington-Ingram 1985. R. P. Winnington-Ingram, "The origins of tragedy," in *CHCL* 1-6.
Wolff 1968. C. Wolff, "Orestes," in E. Segal ed., *Euripides: A Collection of Critical Essays* (Englewood Cliffs 1968).
Wolff 1992. C. Wolff, "Euripides' *Iphigenia among the Taurians*: Aetiology, Ritual and Myth," *Classical Antiquity* 11 (1992) 308-34.
Wolters 1889. P. Wolters, "Inschrift aus dem Dionysostheater," *AthMit* 14 (1889) 321-2.
Xanthakis-Karamanos 1986. G. Xanthakis-Karamanos, "P.Oxy.3317: Euripides' *Antigone*?," *BICS* 33 (1986) 107-11.
Yoshitake 1994. S. Yoshitake, "Disgrace, grief and other ills: Herakles' rejection of suicide," *JHS* 114 (1994) 135-53.
Yunis 1988. H. Yunis, *A New Creed: Fundamental Religious beliefs in the Athenian Polis and Euripidean Drama* (Göttingen 1988) [=*Hypomnemata* 91].
Zeitlin 1965. F. I. Zeitlin, "The motif of the corrupted sacrifice in Aeschylus' Oresteia," *TAPA* 96 (1965) 463-508.
Zeitlin 1970. F. I. Zeitlin, "The Argive festival of Hera and Euripides' *Electra*," *TAPA* 101 (1970) 645-69.

Zeitlin 1978. F. I. Zeitlin, "The dynamics of misogyny: myth and mythmaking in the Oresteia," *Arethusa* 11 (1978) 149-84 [=Zeitlin 1996, 87-119].
Zeitlin 1980. F. I. Zeitlin, "The closet of masks: role playing and myth-making in the *Orestes* of Euripides," *Ramus* 9 (1980) 51-77.
Zeitlin 1985. F. I. Zeitlin, "The Power of Aphrodite: Eros and the Boundaries of the Self in the *Hippolytus*," in P. Burian ed., *Directions in Euripidean Criticism* (Durham NC 1985) 52-110; 189-208=Zeitlin 1996, 219-84.
Zeitlin 1986. F. I. Zeitlin, "Thebes: Theater of Self and Society in Athenian Drama," in P. Euben ed., *Greek Tragedy and Political Theory* (Berkeley 1986) 101-41=Zeitlin 1990a.
Zeitlin 1990a. F. I. Zeitlin, "Thebes: Theater of Self and Society in Athenian Drama," in Winkler and Zeitlin 1990, 130-67.
Zeitlin 1990b. F. I. Zeitlin, "Patterns of Gender in Aeschylean Drama: *Seven against Thebes* and the Danaid Trilogy," in M. Griffith and D. J. Mastronarde eds., *Cabinet of the Muses* (1990) 103-15.
Zeitlin 1992. F. I. Zeitlin, "The Politics of Eros in the Danaid Trilogy of Aeschylus," in R.Hexter and D. Selden eds., *Innovations of Antiquity* (New York 1992) 203-52=Zeitlin 1996, 123-71.
Zeitlin 1993. F. I. Zeitlin, "Staging Dionysus between Thebes and Athens," in Carpenter and Faraone 1993, 147-82.
Zeitlin 1996. F. I. Zeitlin, *Playing the Other: Gender and Society in Classical Greek Literature* (Chicago 1996).
Zimmermann 1992. B. Zimmermann, *Dithyrambos: Geschichte einer Gattung* (Göttingen 1992).

Index Locorum

Aeschines
  2.151   79

Aeschylus
  Agamemnon   23, 57 n. 64, 231-2, 240-4, 247, 278
  Aegyptioi   207, 216, 23 n. 23
  Aitnaiai   40-1
  Amymone   207
  Bassarai   278, 463
  Cho.   23, 233-4, 240-4, 247, 270, 278
  Danaides   207, 255 n. 54, 462
  Edonoi   24, 462-3
  Eleusinioi   277-8
  Eumenides   23, 234-47, 278, 498, 515
  Hektoros Lytra   465
  Hoplon Krisis   466
  Hydrophoroi   465
  Ixion   466, 472
  Kabeiroi   465
  Kallisto   504 n. 74
  Laios   227
  Myrmonides   278
  Nereides   465
  Niobe   467-9
  Oidipous   227
  Oreithyia   466
  Pentheus   465
  Persai   16-7, 19, 24, 220-7, 265-7, 270, 274
  Phryges   465
  Prometheus Lyomenos   279, 465
  Prometheus Vinc.   252 n. 6
  Psychagogoi   504 n. 74
  Psychostasia   463-4
  Semele   465
  Septem   227-31, 274, 278
  Suppliants   203-20, 270, 274, 278
  Toxotides   465
  Trophoi   279, 465-6
  Xantriai   465, 470-1

Agathon
  Anthos/-eus   18

Alkiphron
  iv.18.16   98

Antiphanes
  189.13-17   6

Apollodoros
  iii.14.7   74

Aristophanes
  Birds
    1246-8   467-9
  Clouds
    1491-9   408
  Frogs
    886-7   295-6
    888-94   249
    1052-6   295
    1418-21   296
  Peace
    962-67   296
  Thesm.
    450-1   184
                         53
                         294

Index Locorum

Aristotle
  Poetics
    1449a10-19   162
    1449a11   184 n. 46
    1449a19-21   190 n. 93
    1451b19-26   18
    1454a39-b8   7-8

Athenaeus
  Deipn.
    1.21D   249
    10.428E   99

Demetrius of Phaleron
  FGrH 228 F 5   178

Demosthenes
  19.287   70, 79
  21.10   69, 78

Douris of Samos
  FGrH 76 F 13   76

Eratosthenes
  Erigone
    Fr. 22 Powell   110

Euripides
  Alcestis   317-22, 404, 415-6, 470
  Alexandros   360-1
  Alkmene   471-2, 502 n. 30
  Andromache   332-8. 404-6, 415-6, 470, 481
    1240   418
  Antigone   471, 505 n. 91
  Antiope   453 n. 540, 471
  Archelaos   41-5
  Bacchae   24, 271, 281, 402-3, 415-6, 470, 481
  Bellerephon   471, 475, 493
  Electra   345-50, 400, 404-6, 412, 418, 470, 481, 497-8
  Erechtheus   25-30, 39, 55 n. 41, 273, 277, 279, 405, 471, 481
  Hecabe   271-2, 339-45, 405-6, 469
  Helen   402-3, 415-6, 470, 481
    1469   79
  Heracles   322-6, 361-77, 405, 421-2, 470-1, 481, 484, 497-8
  Herakleidai   322-6, 404-6, 469
  Hippolytos   326-32, 470, 481, 483-4, 498
  Hippolytos Kalyp.   471
  Hypsipyle   471
  Ion   402-3, 470, 479
    805-6   189 n. 82
  Iph. Aul.   402-3, 470
  Iph. Taur.   31-40, 99, 301-8, 405-6, 412, 417, 420-1, 456 n. 540, 470 472-80
  Ixion   471
  Kresphontes   266, 403-4, 471
  Kretes
  Medea   282, 308-10, 403-5, 415-6, 469-70, 493

Index Locorum

Melanippe Desmotis	471	Menodotos of Samos	
Orestes	386-402,	*FGrH* 541 F 1	80
	410-14,		
	417-8, 470,	Pausanias	
	481	1.2.5	74, 90
Phaethon	471-2, 481		
Phoinissai	272-4, 377-	Philochoros	
	86, 417,	*FGrH* 328 F 5	151
	469, 481	*FGrH* 328 F 217	472
Phrixos A and B	471		
Protesilaos	480	Philodamos of Scarphaea	
Rhesos	482	*ap.* Athenaeus 372a	96
Stheneboia	475, 493		
Suppliants	271, 310-6,	Philomnestos	
	404-5, 427	*FGrH* 527 F 2	174
	n. 65, 470		
Troades	271, 350-	Phrynichos	
	61, 405-7,	*Capture of Miletus*	16, 19
	470	*Phoinissai*	17, 24
		Pleuroniai	270
Herodotos			
6.21	16	Pindar	
8.137-9	44	Fr. 75 Snell	96-8, 122,
			156
Hesiod		*Nemean* 11.1-4	114
Catalogue of Women		*Paean* 6	142, 145-
Fr. 7 M-W	60 n. 98		56
Theogony			
464	502 n. 34	Plato	
881-5	244, 502 n.	*Cratylos*	
	33	425d	6
		Gorgias	
Homer		502d	182-83
Iliad		*Ion*	
16.433-52	462	534c	146
22.209-13	462	*Laws*	
Odyssey		800c-801a	51
10.1-73	472	817c	183
IG II² 2318	69, 78-9,	Plutarch	
	99, 123	*Demetrios* 12	73
Lysias		*Moralia*	
Against Nikomachos		16F-17A	463
18	21	19E	473
		293C-E	166
Menander		418A	166
Fr. 558 K	178	527D	70, 115

557F	142
Numa	179

Proklos (ap. Photius)
320a2	145

Semos of Delos
FGrH 396 F 24	78, 174-76

Sophocles
Aigeus	487-8
Ajax	277-8, 483-4, 489-90
Ajax Lokros	484-5, 508 n. 160
Antigone	22-3, 25, 51
Athamas A and *B*	486-7
Inachos	508 n. 157
Manteis	265
Mousai	279, 486
Niobe	485-6
OT	
883-910	281-2
Peleus	487
Philoctetes	278, 482-3
409	293
Syndeipnon/-oi	488
Tereus	486
Thamyras	486
Trachiniai	23, 267, 270-1, 278
Triptolemos	486

Xenophon
Hipparch.
3.2	122

About the Author

Christiane Sourvinou-Inwood has written extensively on Greek religion, archaeology, literature, iconography, and mythology. Her books include *Theseus as Son and Stepson: A Tentative Illustration of Greek Mythological Mentality* (1979), *Studies in Girls' Transitions: Aspects of the Arkteia and Age Representation in Attic Iconography* (1988), *'Reading' Greek Culture: Texts and Images, Rituals and Myths* (1991), and *'Reading' Greek Death: To the End of the Classical Period* (1995). She has been a Senior Research Fellow at University College, Oxford and a reader at the University of Reading. The present volume is based upon the lectures she was invited to deliver in the Jackson Lecture series at Harvard University in 1994.